Children's Thinking

Fourth Edition

Robert S. Siegler

Carnegie Mellon University

Martha Wagner Alibali

University of Wisconsin-Madison

PEARSON

Prentice
Hall

Pearson Education International

Executive Editor: *Jennifer Gilliland*
VP/Editor in Chief: *Leah Jewell*
Photo Researcher (Interior): *Gladys Soto*
Composition/Full-Service Project Management:
10/12/Palatino/Interactive Composition Corporation
Production Liaison: *Maureen Richardson*
Copyeditor: *Chris Sabooni*
Cover Illustration/Photo: *(TL) Ariel Skelley / Masterfile; (TR) BananaStock/ BananaStock, Ltd./ PictureQuest;*
(BL) Laurence Mouton/ PhotoAlto/ PictureQuest; (BR) Scott Barrow, Inc. / SuperStock

Illustrator (Interior): *Asterisk Group*
Marketing Manager: *Mike Alread*
Production Editor: *Brittney Corrigan-McElroy*
Buyer: *Tricia Kenny*
Cover Design: *Bruce Kenselaar*

Pearson Education, Ltd.
Pearson Education Australia PTY, Limited
Pearson Education Singapore, Pte., Ltd.
Pearson Education North Asia Ltd.
Pearson Education, Canada, Ltd.
Pearson Educación de Mexico, S.A. de C.V.
Pearson Education–Japan
Pearson Education Malaysia, Pte., Ltd.
Pearson Education, Upper Saddle River, New Jersey

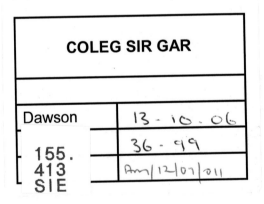

10 9 8 7 6 5 4 3 2

ISBN 0-13-129333-8

To Alexis and Mariana

Contents

Preface

Children's thinking is inherently fascinating. All of us were children once; many of us have, or expect to have, our own children someday. The ways in which children think are both familiar and foreign. We remember some of the ways in which we thought at younger ages and have impressions of the thinking of many other children as well. As adults, we observe that children's thinking seems generally reasonable, and at times surprisingly insightful. At other times, though, children's reasoning leaves us flabbergasted. Why, for example, would an otherwise reasonable 5-year-old insist that pouring water into a differently shaped container changes the amount of water, even after an adult has just told the child that the amount of water is the same as before?

Until recently, many of the most intriguing aspects of children's thinking were inaccessible to our understanding. Philosophers have argued for hundreds of years whether infants see the world as a "blooming, buzzing confusion" or in much the same way that older children and adults do. Only in the past few years, with the development of revealing experimental methods, has the answer become clear. Even newborns see certain aspects of the world quite clearly, and by 6 months of age, infants' perception resembles that of adults. These and other discoveries about children's thinking are the subject matter of this book.

Who would be interested in such a book? Anyone who is curious about children should find interesting observations and ideas in it. Anyone sufficiently motivated to take an undergraduate or graduate course in this area should find a great deal to intrigue the imagination and stimulate further interest in children's thinking and development.

This new edition incorporates many changes. The most obvious is the addition of two new chapters, one on sociocultural approaches to cognitive development and one on the development of social cognition. These new chapters reflect the enormous growth in these areas in recent years. Some material addressing these topics was present in previous editions; in this new edition, this material has been consolidated and a great deal of new material has been added.

The new chapter on sociocultural approaches begins with Lev Semenovich Vygotsky's sociocultural theory, which focuses on the influence of social interaction in cognitive development and on the importance of cultural tools, such as language and number systems, in thinking and learning. The chapter also addresses modern developments in sociocultural theory that build on Vygotsky's insights, and contemporary empirical research in the sociocultural tradition, including research about learning in interaction with adults and peers, guided participation in cultural activities, and the use of language as a tool for thinking. Educational implications of sociocultural theories also are emphasized.

The new chapter on social cognition focuses on children's understanding of social information. This is a broad area that includes knowledge about self and others; knowledge about the mind and the mental states that give rise to behavior, such as desire, intention, and belief; and knowledge about the social world, including understanding of social rules and social categories.

All of the remaining chapters have also been revised and updated. Some of the many additions are increased coverage of interrelations between perception and action, an expanded discussion of children's biological concepts, and additional information about the development of language comprehension.

As in previous editions, we have continued to emphasize the practical contributions of research on children's thinking. Some examples that are discussed are techniques for eliciting accurate recollections of events from children who need to testify in court cases, techniques for assessing children's knowledge, and instructional methods for improving reading, writing, and mathematical skills.

Each of us is fortunate to have had a rich and stimulating intellectual environment in which to work during the writing of the book. Many of our colleagues have given generously of their time to help us improve the book. Some read drafts of chapters or parts of chapters and offered feedback, including Jim Dannemiller, Chuck Kalish, Ken Koedinger, Brian MacWhinney, and Jenny Saffran. We are grateful for the opportunities to discuss children's thinking with these individuals and many others, including Karen Adolph, Zhe Chen, Judy DeLoache, Julia Evans, Susan Goldin-Meadow, David Klahr, Eric Knuth, Patrick Lemaire, Colleen Moore, Nicole McNeil, Mitchell Nathan, John Opfer, Seth Pollak, David Rakison, and Bethany Rittle-Johnson. We would also like to thank the anonymous reviewers who provided comments on the previous edition, and Maureen Kaschak and Karin Ockuly, who spent many hours tracking down references. Finally, we would like to thank Theresa Treasure, who in this edition as in the previous one, did whatever it took to get the work done in a timely fashion.

A different kind of thanks is due our friends and families, who have provided support as well as inspiration during the time we worked on this book. Robert Siegler would like to thank his children, Todd, Beth, and Aaron Siegler, who have progressed over the four editions of this book from unwittingly providing interesting examples of children's thinking to thoughtfully advancing interesting ideas about it. Martha Alibali would like to thank her husband, Peter, who offered unwavering support in myriad ways, and would also like to thank her many nieces and nephews, who provided compelling examples of children's thinking at various stages of development. These individuals make the research come alive for us, and they make our endeavors worthwhile.

We would like to dedicate this book to the new children who came into our lives during the writing of it, Robert Siegler's granddaughter Alexis, and Martha and Peter Alibali's daughter, Mariana. The opportunity to observe their thinking and to take part in their development has provided us with great joy, and we hope to learn from them for many years to come.

Robert S. Siegler
Martha Wagner Alibali

1

An Introduction to Children's Thinking

When did the sun begin? When people began living. *Who made it?* God. *How did God do this?* He put a real lot of lightbulbs in it. *Are these lightbulbs still in the sun?* No. *What happened to them?* They burnt out. No, they stay good a long time. *So are the lightbulbs still in it?* No. I think he made it out of gold. And he lit it with fire. *(Siegler, conversation with son, 1985)*

The child in the vignette above answered these questions one week before his fifth birthday. What do his answers tell us about how he viewed the world at that time? Do they reflect a simple lack of knowledge about astronomy and physics? Or do they indicate a fundamental difference between young children's reasoning and that of older children and adults? An adult who did not know the origins of the sun would never ascribe its origins to God putting lightbulbs in it. Nor would an adult link the origins of the sun to the fact that people began to be alive. Do these differences mean that children generally reason in more literal and self-centered ways than adults? Or do they just reflect a child's grasping at straws when faced with a question for which he cannot even generate a plausible answer?

For hundreds of years, people have wondered about these and related questions. Do infants see the world in the same way as adults? Why do societies throughout the world first send children to school between ages 5 and 7? Why are

TABLE 1.1 *Chapter Outline*

I.   What Is Children's Thinking?

II. Key Questions about Children's Thinking
     A.   Are Some Capabilities Innate?
     B.   Does Development Progress through Stages?
     C.   How Does Change Occur?
     D.   How Do Individuals Differ?
     E.   How Do Changes in the Brain Contribute to Cognitive Development?
     F.   How Does the Social World Contribute to Cognitive Development?

III. The Book's Organization
     A.   The Chapter-by-Chapter Organization
     B.   The Central Themes

IV. Summary

adolescents so much more likely than 10-year-olds to fervently believe in causes such as vegetarianism or environmentalism? A century ago, people could only speculate about these issues. Now, however, we have concepts and methods that magnify our ability to observe, describe, and explain the process of development. As a result, our understanding of children's thinking is growing rapidly.

The goal of this chapter is to introduce some basic issues and ideas regarding children's thinking. The first section focuses on what children's thinking involves. The next section introduces some of the enduring questions that motivate people to study cognitive development. Finally, the last section provides an overview of the book's organization. An outline of the chapter is provided in Table 1.1.

What Is Children's Thinking?

Children's thinking refers to the thinking that takes place from the moment of birth through the end of adolescence. Defining what thinking is turns out to be quite difficult, because no sharp boundary divides activities that involve thinking from ones that do not. Thinking obviously involves the higher mental processes: problem solving, reasoning, creating, conceptualizing, remembering, classifying, symbolizing, planning, and so on. Other examples of thinking involve more basic processes, processes at which even young children are skilled: using language, and perceiving objects and events in the external environment, to name two. Still other activities might or might not be viewed as types of thinking. These include being socially skillful, having a keen moral sense, feeling appropriate emotions, and so on. The capabilities in this last group involve thought processes, but they also involve many other, nonintellectual qualities. In this book, we give these boundary areas some attention, but the spotlight is on problem solving, conceptual understanding, reasoning, remembering, producing and comprehending language, and the other, more purely intellectual activities.

A particularly important characteristic of children's thinking is that it is constantly changing. How children think at particular points in development is interesting in and of itself, but even more central for understanding cognitive development are the questions of what changes occur and how the changes occur. Comparing an infant, a 2-year-old, a 6-year-old, and an adolescent, it is easy to appreciate the magnitude of these changes. But what processes could transform the mind of a newborn baby into the mind of an adolescent? This is the central mystery of cognitive development.

Consider an example of the dramatic changes that occur with development. DeVries (1969) was interested in 3- to 6-year-olds' understanding of the difference between appearance and reality. She presented children of these ages with an unusually sweet-tempered cat named Maynard and allowed them to pet him. When the experimenter asked what Maynard was, all of the children knew that he was a cat. Then, as the children watched, the experimenter put a mask of a fierce dog on Maynard's face. The experimenter asked, "Look, it has a face like a dog. What is this animal now?"

Many of the 3-year-olds thought that Maynard had become a dog. They refused to pet him and said that under his skin he had a dog's bones and a dog's stomach. In contrast, most 6-year-olds knew that a cat could not turn into a dog, and that the mask did not change the animal's identity.

How can a human being, even a very young one, believe that a cat can turn into a dog? And how does the 3-year-old who has this belief turn into the 6-year-old who scoffs at such a silly notion? We know that the change happens, the issue is how it happens.

Key Questions about Children's Thinking

What are the most important questions in the study of children's thinking? Many answers are possible, but there is widespread agreement that the following six questions are among the most important:

> Are some capabilities innate?
> Does children's thinking progress through qualitatively different stages?
> How do changes in children's thinking occur?
> Why do individual children differ so much from each other in their thinking?
> How does development of the brain contribute to cognitive development?
> How does the social world contribute to cognitive development?

Of course, these questions are interrelated in many ways. For example, understanding the roles of the brain and the social world in cognitive development is crucial to understanding how change occurs. Likewise, understanding mechanisms of change may shed light on why individual children differ from one another.

Researchers from different theoretical perspectives and different content areas have focused on different questions to varying degrees. For example, as described later, researchers who take an information-processing perspective on cognitive development tend to emphasize the issue of how change occurs, whereas researchers who take a sociocultural perspective focus on how the social world contributes to cognitive development. However, despite these differences in emphasis, each of the major theories of cognitive development has something to say about each of these main questions.

These key questions are introduced in the following sections. The emphases in this chapter are on fundamental concepts relevant to each question and on major themes that will recur repeatedly throughout the book.

ARE SOME CAPABILITIES INNATE?

When infants are born, how do they experience the world? When they see a chair, or people talking to each other, or a dog barking, what exactly do they see? What do they know, what don't they know, and what learning capabilities do they possess? If we assume that infants come into the world poorly endowed with knowledge and learning capabilities, the question becomes, "How can they develop as rapidly as they do?" If we assume that infants come into the world richly endowed, the question becomes, "Why does development take so long?"

The question of infants' initial endowment has elicited many speculations. Three of the most prominent come from the *associationist perspective*, the *constructivist perspective*, and the *competent-infant perspective.*

The associationist perspective was developed by English philosophers of the 1700s and 1800s, including John Locke, David Hume, and John Stuart Mill. They suggested that infants come into the world with only minimal capabilities, primarily the ability to associate experiences with each other. Therefore, infants must acquire virtually all capacities and concepts through learning.

The constructivist perspective, developed by Jean Piaget between the 1920s and the 1970s, suggests that infants are born possessing not only these associative capabilities but also several important perceptual and motor capabilities. Although few in number and limited in scope, these capabilities allow infants to explore their environment and to construct increasingly sophisticated concepts and understandings. For example, infants in their first 6 months are said not to be able to form mental representations of objects and events, but through actively manipulating and investigating objects, they are said to become capable of forming such representations later in their first year.

The competent-infant perspective, based on more recent research (e.g., Spelke & Newport, 1998), suggests that both of the other approaches seriously underestimate infants' capabilities. Within this view, even young infants have a much wider range of perceptual skills and conceptual understandings than had previously been suspected. These capacities allow infants, in a rudimentary way, to perceive the world and to classify their experiences along many of the same dimensions that older children and adults use.

The impressive capabilities that recent investigations have uncovered can be illustrated in the context of infants' perception of distance. Philosophers have long speculated about how people can judge the distances of objects from themselves. Some, such as George Berkeley, an associationist philosopher of the eighteenth century, concluded that the only way in which infants could come to accurately perceive distance was by moving around the world and associating how objects looked with how much movement was required to reach them. Yet, the day after infants are born, they can already perceive which objects are closer and which are farther away (Granrud, 1987; Slater, Mattock, & Brown, 1990). Clearly, some degree of distance perception is present even before infants have experience crawling and walking around the environment.

Infants also possess surprising knowledge of the properties of objects. For example, by age 3 months, the earliest age at which such knowledge has been successfully measured, infants show some understanding that objects continue to exist even when they move behind other objects and cannot be seen; that without support, objects will fall; that objects move along spatially continuous paths; and that solid objects cannot move through one another (Baillargeon, 1994; Spelke, 1994, 2000). Such knowledge is not identical to the knowledge of adults; for example, 3-month-olds seem to believe that any contact between an object and a support is sufficient to hold the object up, even when, for example, only the right edge of a block on the bottom is under the left edge of a block on top of it. By 6 months, infants show the more advanced understanding that for a support to be effective, the block on the bottom must be under a substantial proportion of the block on the top (Baillargeon, 1994).

In addition to possessing primitive versions of fundamental concepts, infants also possess general learning mechanisms that help them acquire a wide range of new knowledge. One such learning mechanism is *imitation.* When 2-day-olds see an adult move his head in a certain way, they tend to move theirs in a similar fashion; when 2-week-olds see an adult stick out his tongue, they tend to stick out their tongues in response (Meltzoff, 2002; Meltzoff & Moore, 1983). Such repetitions provide a way for infants to learn new behaviors and also to strengthen their bond with those they imitate, particularly their parents.

Another such learning mechanism is *statistical learning,* which involves extracting sequential patterns from input. In their first year of life, infants are capable of detecting such patterns both in auditory input, such as sequences of tones or linguistic sounds (Saffran, 2003b; Saffran, Aslin, & Newport, 1996), and in visual input, such as sequences of colored shapes (Kirkham, Slemmer, & Johnson, 2002). Statistical learning is a powerful mechanism by which infants can detect regularities in their environment.

Findings like these have given rise to the view that infants are quite cognitively competent. But like previous perspectives, the new view raises as many questions as it answers. If infants understand fundamental concepts, why do much older children experience such difficulty with the very same concepts? For example, if infants understand that a toy continues to exist even when a cover is placed on it, why do 3-year-olds still not understand that a cat cannot be turned into a dog simply by putting a mask on it? Reconciling the strengths that are present early in development with the weaknesses that are also present then and for years thereafter is one of the greatest challenges in understanding children's thinking.

Another challenge is specifying how innate or early-developing abilities interact with experience to yield developmental change. One approach to addressing this issue is to examine the effects of variations in experience on the nature and path of development. For example, does perceptual development differ in typically developing infants and infants who are blind or deaf from birth? Does language acquisition depend on the nature of the linguistic input that children receive? The solutions to these puzzles highlight the complex interplay between biologically specified abilities and experience in the physical and social world.

DOES DEVELOPMENT PROGRESS THROUGH STAGES?

When a girl misbehaves, her parents might console each other by saying, "It's just a stage she's going through." When a boy fails utterly to learn something, his parents might lament, "I guess he just hasn't reached the stage where he can understand this." The idea that development, including cognitive development, occurs in stages is common among psychologists as well as parents. But what exactly does it mean to say that a child is in a stage, and do children in fact progress through qualitatively distinct stages of thinking? And why might development be stagelike, rather than continuous?

The view of development as stagelike was in part inspired by the ideas of Charles Darwin (1877). Darwin is not usually thought of as a developmental psychologist, but in many ways he was one. In his book *The Descent of Man*, Darwin discussed the development of reason, curiosity, imitation, attention, imagination, language, and self-consciousness. Not surprisingly, he was most interested in the evolutionary course of these competencies, that is, in how they emerged in the course of the evolution from earlier-appearing animals to humans. However, many of his ideas could be, and were, translated into concepts about the development that occurs in an individual human lifetime.

Perhaps Darwin's most influential observation was his most basic: that over the vast period of time that living things have populated the earth, they have evolved through a series of qualitatively distinct forms. This observation suggested to some that development within a given lifetime also progresses through distinct forms or stages. Unlike Darwin himself, however, developmental theorists who adopted an evolutionary perspective further hypothesized that children would make the transition from one stage to the next quite suddenly. This stage approach directly contradicted speculations by associationist philosophers,

such as John Locke, that children's thinking develops through the gradual accre-
tion of innumerable particular experiences. Associationists compared the developmental process to a building being constructed brick by brick. Stage theorists
compared it to the metamorphosis from caterpillar to butterfly.

In the early part of the twentieth century, James Mark Baldwin hypothesized a set of plausible stages of intellectual development. He suggested that
children progressed from a sensorimotor stage, in which sensory observations
and motor interactions with the physical environment were the dominant form
of thought, to a quasilogical, a logical, and finally a hyperlogical stage. The idea
that children progress through these stages receives a certain amount of support
in everyday observations of children. Infants' interactions with the world do
seem, at least at first impression, to emphasize sensory input and motor actions.
And not until adolescence do children spend much time thinking about purely
logical issues, such as whether laws that apply to them, including those regarding
driving, voting, and drinking, are logically consistent with each other. Baldwin's
stage theory was ignored by most of his contemporaries, but it exerted a strong
influence on at least one later thinker: Jean Piaget.

Piaget, without question, added more than any other individual to our understanding of children's thinking. He made a huge number of fascinating observations about the ways in which children think at different ages. For example,
the reason that Siegler asked his son about the origins of the sun (the anecdote
at the beginning of this chapter) was because he was fascinated by Piaget's
descriptions of the answers given by children in the 1920s, and Siegler was
curious whether children in the 1980s would respond similarly (they do).
Among Piaget's other contributions were developing the stage notion to a much
greater extent than Baldwin had, and popularizing the idea of viewing intellectual development in terms of stages.

What exactly *do* we mean when we say that children's thinking progresses
through certain stages? Flavell (1971) noted four key implications of the stage
concept. First, stages imply *qualitative changes.* We do not say that a boy is in
a new stage of understanding of arithmetic when he progresses from knowing
50 percent of the multiplication facts to knowing all of them. Instead, we reserve
the term for situations in which the child's thinking seems not only better but
different in kind. For example, when a girl makes up her first genuinely amusing joke after several years of telling stories that she may call jokes, but that do
not even make sense to adults, it seems like a qualitative change. Note the
ambiguity of the term *seems like,* though. Perhaps the girl's efforts had been improving slowly for a long time but had not quite reached the threshold for what
an adult recognizes as a joke. To some degree, what constitutes a qualitative
change is in the eyes of the beholder.

A second implication of stage theories, which Flavell labeled the
concurrence assumption, is that children make the transition from one stage to another on many concepts simultaneously. When they are in Stage 1, they show

Stage 1 reasoning on all of these concepts; when they are in Stage 2, they show Stage 2 reasoning on all of them. As a result of these concurrent changes, children's thinking shows abstract similarities across many domains. When the parent in the above example said, "He's just not in a stage where he can understand this," the implication was that a general deficiency would keep the child from understanding not just the particular concept but also other concepts of comparable complexity.

Viewing children's thinking as progressing through a series of stages also has two additional implications. One, which Flavell called the *abruptness assumption*, is that children move from one stage to the next suddenly rather than gradually. Children are in Stage 1 for a prolonged period of time, enter briefly into a transition period, then are in Stage 2 for a prolonged period, and so on. The fourth assumption of stage theories is *coherent organization*. The child's understanding is viewed as being organized into a sensible whole, rather than being composed of many independent pieces of knowledge.

Thus, stage theories depict development as involving qualitative change, occurring simultaneously for many concepts, occurring suddenly, and involving a transition from one coherent way of thinking to a different coherent way of thinking. Without question, this is an elegant and appealing description. But how well does it fit the realities of children's thinking? This issue will be considered in greater depth in Chapter 2.

How Does Change Occur?

To develop is to change. Several types of change that occur during the course of development are illustrated in Figure 1.1. The depiction originally was formulated to describe changes in perceptual development (Aslin & Dumais, 1980), but the categories apply to all types of changes in children's thinking.

The left side of the figure illustrates three patterns of change that can occur in the *prenatal period* (before birth): a particular capability can develop fully, partially, or not at all. The right-hand side depicts changes occurring after birth. An already-developed ability can either be maintained or decline; a partially developed ability can grow, stay the same, or decline; and an undeveloped ability can grow or stay undeveloped.

The variety of possible patterns expands further when we realize that any given ability involves many components that may follow quite different developmental courses. For example, regardless of where infants are born, they can produce all of the sounds that are used in any of the world's languages. Over the course of childhood, however, they lose the ability to produce many sounds that are not part of their native language. On the other hand, they gain increasing facility in producing at will the sounds that are part of their own language. Thus, after infancy, the ability to produce speech sounds both declines and grows, depending on which sounds we are talking about.

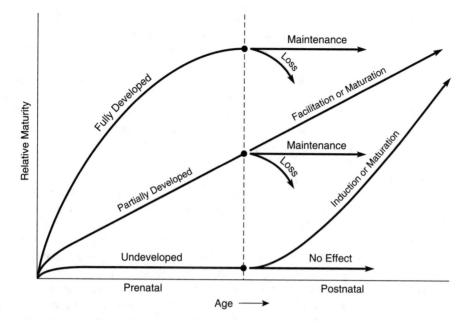

FIGURE 1.1 Illustration of several paths of developmental change (after Aslin & Dumais, 1980). Reprinted from Aslin, R.N. & Dumais, S.T., Binocular vision in human infants: A review and a theoretical framework, in L.P. Lipsitt & H.W. Reese (Eds.), Advances in Child Development and Behavior, Copyright 1980, with permission from Elsevier.

How can changes in children's thinking be explained? Two of the most influential efforts to answer this question are the Piagetian and the information-processing perspectives. Piaget suggested that the basic mechanisms that produce all cognitive changes are *assimilation* and *accommodation*. Assimilation is the process through which people represent experiences in terms of their existing understanding. A 1-year-old girl who saw a round candle might think of it as a ball if she knew about balls but not candles. Accommodation is the opposite process; in it, people's existing understanding is altered by new knowledge. The 1-year-old who saw the round candle might notice that this "ball" was different from others in having a thin object (the wick) protruding from it. This discovery might lay the groundwork for later learning that the world includes round candles.

Researchers who adopt the information-processing approach to children's thinking have been particularly interested in the process of change. They have focused on four change mechanisms that seem to play large roles in cognitive development: *automatization, encoding, generalization,* and *strategy construction*.

Automatization involves executing mental processes increasingly efficiently so that they require less and less attention. With age and experience, processing becomes increasingly automatic on a great many tasks, allowing children to see connections among ideas and events that they otherwise would miss. For example, in the first few weeks of walking home from school, a 5-year-old girl might need to completely focus her attention on the task of finding her way. Later, the activity would become automatized, and she would find her way home despite paying attention to what other people were saying and doing while she walked with them.

Encoding involves identifying the most informative features of objects and events and using those features to form internal representations of the objects and events. The importance of improved encoding in children's increasing understanding of the world is evident in the context of their learning to solve story problems in arithmetic and algebra. Often such stories include irrelevant as well as relevant information. The trick to solving the problems is to encode the relevant information and to ignore the irrelevant parts.

The third and the fourth change mechanisms are *generalization* and *strategy construction*. Generalization is the extension of knowledge acquired in one context to other contexts. Strategy construction is the generation or discovery of a new procedure for solving a problem. The workings of generalization and strategy construction can be illustrated through a single example. After repeated experience with suddenly nonfunctioning computers, lamps, toasters, and radios, a child might reach the generalization that when machines do not work, it often is due to their being unplugged. On drawing this generalization, the child might form a strategy of always checking the plug whenever pushing a machine's "on" button has no effect.

The child's construction of this strategy illustrates that change processes work together rather than in isolation. Constructing the check-the-plug strategy depended on automatizing the perception of the machines sufficiently to encode the plug as a separate part of each machine and on drawing the generalization that machines that have plugs usually do not work when the plug is disconnected. As will be evident throughout this book, these four change processes—automatization, encoding, generalization, and strategy construction—play crucial roles in improvements in children's thinking in everything from infants' statistical learning to adolescents' computer programming.

How Do Individuals Differ?

Just as children of different ages vary, so do children of any given age. Individual differences are present in all aspects of development, from height and weight to personality and creativity. However, they have received especially intense examination in the study of intelligence. This scrutiny began in earnest in the 1890s, when France initiated a program of universal public education. Recognizing that not all children would benefit from the same instruction, the French Minister of Education commissioned Alfred Binet and Theophile Simon to develop a test to identify children who would have difficulty learning from standard classroom procedures and who therefore would need special education.

The first Binet-Simon test was released in 1905. It included questions that were intuitively related to many aspects of intelligence: language, memory, reasoning, and problem solving. In 1916, Lewis Terman, a professor at Stanford University, revised the test for use in the United States and labeled it the Stanford-Binet. Updated versions remain in wide use today.

The Stanford-Binet and other intelligence tests are based on the assumption that not all children of a given age think and reason at the same level. Some 7-year-olds reason as well as the average 9-year-old; others reason no better than the average 5-year-old. To capture these individual differences among children, intelligence tests distinguish between a child's *chronological age* (CA) and the child's *mental age* (MA). Chronological age reflects the time since the child was born; if a girl was born 60 months ago, her chronological age is 5 years. Mental age is a more complex idea in that it reflects the child's performance on an intelligence test relative to that of other children. Specifically, a child's mental age is defined as the age at which 50 percent of children answer correctly as many items on the test as the particular child did. For example, if the average 5-year-old correctly answers 20 questions on a test, then a child who answered 20 items correctly would have a mental age of 5 years, regardless of whether the child is a 4-year-old, a 5-year-old, or a 6-year-old.

Terman saw that the implications of a 4-year-old, a 5-year-old, and a 6-year-old having a mental age of 5 years are quite different. For a 4-year-old, this level of performance is precocious; for a 5-year-old, it is average; for a 6-year-old, it is slow. To express these implications numerically, Terman borrowed an idea developed by Wilhelm Stern, a German psychologist, and combined the concepts of mental and chronological age to form an *Intelligence Quotient*, or IQ. A child's IQ is the ratio between the child's mental and chronological ages. This ratio is multiplied by 100, so that the IQ can be expressed as an integer, as shown below:

$$IQ = \frac{\text{Mental Age}}{\text{Chronological Age}} \times 100$$

Thus, in Terman's example, the 6-year-old who had a mental age of 5 years would have an IQ of 83 (5/6 × 100), whereas the 4-year-old who had a mental age of 5 years would have an IQ of 125 (5/4 × 100). When we consider all children of a given chronological age, their average IQ score is 100, since the average mental age for any age group is, by definition, the same as that group's chronological age. Whether the IQ score is above or below 100 (that is, whether the child's mental age exceeds or falls below his or her chronological age) indicates whether the child scored above or below average for the age group; the distance of the score from 100 indicates how far above or below average the score was.

One reason that IQ scores have been used so widely is that they predict performance in school quite well. Another reason is their stability over long periods of time. For example, a 6-year-old's IQ quite accurately predicts the child's IQ at age 16. The relation is not perfect; some children show large increases in IQ over time, and others show large decreases. There is also considerable controversy about what intelligence is and how well these or other tests measure it. Clearly, however, intelligence test scores tend to be quite stable from first grade to adulthood, and they allow quite accurate prediction of school achievement.

Until recently, no comparable predictive relation between early and later performance had been established for very young children. Scores on intelligence tests developed for children below 4 years were essentially unrelated to IQ scores of the same children when they were older. This suggested that individual differences in infant intelligence might be unrelated to individual differences in later intelligence.

Recently, however, a measure of infants' information processing has revealed some continuity between intelligence in infancy and intelligence in later childhood. The measure is surprisingly simple. When infants are repeatedly shown a stimulus, such as an object or a picture, they lose interest in it and look at it less and less. That is, they *habituate* to it. Individual infants habituate at varying rates; some reduce their looking quite quickly, whereas others take much longer to do so. The key finding is that the more rapidly that 7-month-olds habituate (stop looking), and the greater their preference for a new picture after they have habituated (often called "novelty preference"), the higher their IQ scores tend to be 4 to 10 years later (Colombo, 1993; Fagan & Singer, 1983; Rose & Feldman, 1995, 1997; Sigman, Cohen, & Beckwith, 1997). The habituation rates also are related to later achievement test scores in reading and mathematics and to general language proficiency. Further, children whose habituation rates are slowest at 7 months have higher rates of learning disabilities when they are 6-year-olds (Rose, Feldman, & Wallace, 1992).

Why should rate of habituation at 7 months predict IQ and achievement test scores years later? One explanation is that both the early and the later performance reflect the effectiveness of the child's encoding (Bornstein & Sigman, 1986; Colombo, 1993, 1995). In other words, more intelligent infants are quicker to encode everything of interest about the picture, leading them to be the first to lose interest in it. They perk up more when the new picture is shown because they more clearly encode the differences between it and the old one. Superior encoding has also been found to be related to the ability of gifted older children and adolescents to solve problems and learn quickly (Sternberg, 1999). Thus, quality of encoding may link early and later intellectual capabilities.

The large majority of research on intelligence and other areas of cognitive development focuses on individual children's behavior. However, in trying to gain additional insights, researchers have recently been extending the search both inward and outward. The inward-looking efforts examine how development of the brain is related to changes in children's thinking. The outward-looking efforts consider not only the individual child but also the formative influences of other people and of cultural institutions. Thus, the first approach builds on findings and insights from the neighboring disciplines of biology and neuroscience, and the second builds on findings and insights from sociology and anthropology. These approaches to understanding children's thinking are introduced in the next two sections.

How Do Changes in the Brain Contribute to Cognitive Development?

In general, the bigger the brain of a species, the more intelligent individuals of that species are likely to be. Without question, changes in the size, structure, and connection patterns of the brain during the course of a child's development profoundly contribute to changes in the child's thinking. These changes, which are both quantitative and qualitative, occur at three levels: (1) changes in the brain as a whole; (2) changes in particular structures within the brain; and (3) changes in the billions of cells that make up the brain (neurons).

Changes in the brain as a whole. The changes that occur in the brain as a whole are evident in large-scale increases in its weight from birth to adulthood. The brain weighs roughly 400 grams at birth; 850 grams at 11 months; 1100 grams by age 3 years; and 1450 grams by adulthood (Kolb & Whishaw, 2003). Thus, the brain of an adult weighs almost four times as much as the brain of a newborn. These changes in size make possible much more advanced thinking.

Changes in structures within the brain. The relative sizes and levels of activity of the main parts of the brain also change over the course of development. The brain can be divided into two main parts: subcortical structures and the cortex. The subcortical structures are areas atop the spinal cord, such as the thalamus, medulla, and pons (Figure 1.2). They are quite similar in the brains of humans and of other mammals, especially other primates such as apes and monkeys.

Like these subcortical areas, the cortex includes some structures that are similar in humans and other primates. Among them are the hypothalamus and the amygdala. In addition, however, the cortex includes a large structure that is far more highly developed in humans than in any other animal: the *cerebral cortex.* Sitting atop the rest of the brain, this large structure is what makes possible the high-level cognitive skills that are unique to human beings, such as language and complex problem solving.

At birth and for several years thereafter, the cerebral cortex is immature relative to other parts of the brain. This is evident both in its being a lower percentage of its adult weight and in its being less like its mature form in organization and patterns of electrical and chemical activity. The relative immaturity of the cerebral cortex has important consequences for cognitive functioning. It leads to some types of cognition being impossible early on and to others

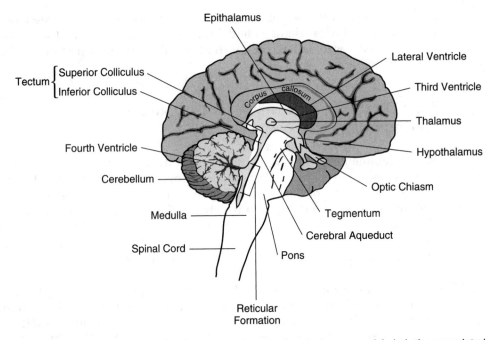

FIGURE 1.2   The structure of the brain. A number of subcortical areas are labeled; the convoluted area sitting atop them is the cortex.

being accomplished at first by more mature parts of the brain, even though the cortex will later play a dominant role in them.

As shown in Figure 1.3, the cerebral cortex includes four main lobes: the *frontal* lobe, at the front of the brain; the *parietal* lobe, at the top; the *occipital* lobe, at the back; and the *temporal* lobe, toward the bottom. Each area is particularly active in producing certain types of cognitive activity. For example, the occipital lobe is especially heavily involved in processing visual information, whereas the frontal lobe is especially involved in consciousness, planning, and the regulation of cognitive activity. As you might expect from the types of activities in which the frontal lobe is particularly active, it is especially immature at birth, relative to other parts of the brain and even other parts of the cerebral cortex. Its profound development during infancy and early childhood seems to be crucial to the rapid advances in cognitive capabilities that occur during that period. (For a good discussion of the different rates of maturation of different parts of the brain, see Chugani and Phelps, 1986.)

The cerebral cortex is divided into two halves, or *hemispheres*, connected by a dense tract of nerve fibers called the *corpus callosum*. For the most part, each hemisphere processes sensory information and motor responses from the opposite side of the body; thus, sensory inputs and motor responses on the left side of the body are processed largely by the right hemisphere, and vice versa. The two

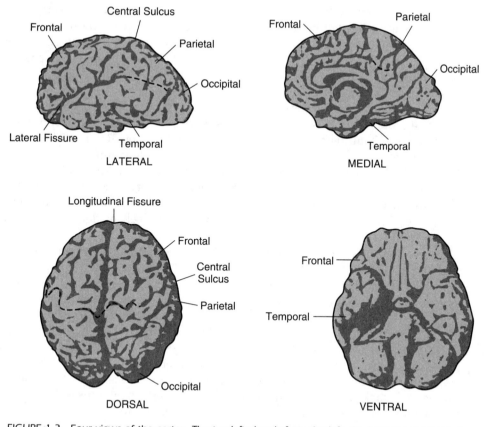

FIGURE 1.3 Four views of the cortex. The top-left view is from the left, the bottom-left view is from above, the top-right view is from the left looking at the inner surface of the right half of the brain, and the bottom-right view is from below.

hemispheres also appear to be specialized for processing information in different ways. For example, in most right-handed adults, the left hemisphere is specialized for processing information in a sequential, analytic fashion, whereas the right hemisphere is specialized for processing information in a more holistic, integrative manner. As a consequence, linguistic and logical information tends to be processed primarily in the left hemisphere, and emotional and spatial information tends to be processed primarily in the right hemisphere. Because one hemisphere plays a dominant role in carrying out these functions, they are said to be *lateralized*.

Recent studies suggest that cerebral lateralization is present even in infancy. For example, infants show hand preferences in motor tasks as early as 6 months of age, suggesting that these functions are lateralized by that time (Michel, 1998). As another example, one study compared patterns of mouth opening in 5- to 12-month-old infants as they produced babbling sounds, which are an early step in language acquisition, and non-babbling sounds. When the infants produced babbling sounds, they opened their mouths wider on the right side than on the left, suggesting left-hemisphere control, but when they produced non-babbling sounds, they opened the two sides of their mouths equally wide (Holowka & Petitto, 2002). These findings suggest that the left hemisphere is preferentially involved in language processing from early in the first year.

Changes in neurons.   A third, yet more specific, level of change that occurs in the brain involves specific *neurons* (nerve cells). Neurons are present in vast numbers in all parts of the brain—a total of between 100 and 200 billion. Over development, the neurons become increasingly interconnected.

Each neuron includes three main parts: a cell *nucleus,* which is the core of the nerve cell; a number of *dendrites,* which are fibers that bring information from other neurons to the cell nucleus; and one (or occasionally more) *axons,* which are larger fibers that transmit information from the cell nucleus to other neurons (Figure 1.4).

Neurons transmit information both electrically and chemically. Within a given neuron, the transmission is electrical. Electrical signals travel from the dendrites to the cell nucleus to the axon(s). Between neurons, the transmission is chemical. Neurons are not directly connected to each other; instead, there are tiny gaps, called *synapses,* separating the axon of one neuron from the dendrite of another. The electrical impulse traveling along the axon leads to release of chemical *neurotransmitters,* which flow across the synapse from the end of the axon to the beginnings of dendrites of adjacent neurons. When the neurotransmitters arrive at the dendrites of the receiving neurons, the information is converted back into electrical impulses, which are then transmitted within that neuron. In an adult, a single neuron often has more than 1,000 synapses with other neurons. These multiple connections allow information to be simultaneously transmitted to diverse areas of the brain (Thompson, 2000).

Synaptogenesis.   The formation of synapses between neurons (*synaptogenesis*) is far from complete at birth. Within many parts of the brain, it follows a distinctive developmental course of overproduction and pruning. Early in development, there is an explosive proliferation of synapses, causing the number of synapses in a toddler's brain to far exceed the number in an adult's. Then, over the course of childhood, the number of synapses decreases to adult levels. In one part of the frontal lobe, for example, the density of synaptic connections increases tenfold between birth and 12 months. By age 2, the density of connections there is almost twice as great as in adults. After this point, it gradually decreases, reaching adult levels by about age 7 (Huttenlocher, 1994).

In other parts of the brain, the overproduction and pruning follows the same general pattern, but with different timetables (Huttenlocher & Dabholkar, 1997). For example, in the visual cortex, the peak density of synapses is generally reached earlier than in the frontal lobe—around 1 year—and the pruning continues longer—until age 11 (Huttenlocher, 1990). However, the basic cycle of

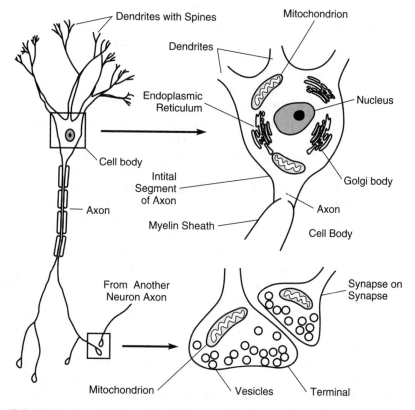

FIGURE 1.4   Structure of a typical neuron (left) including dendrites at top, cell body in the square, and axon below the square. Note that the initial segment of the axon where it leaves the cell body is uncovered; the ovals around the axon below that are myelin, an insulator that improves the rate of electrical transmission. As shown in the drawing at the bottom right, synapses are where the ends of an axon from one neuron are adjacent to the beginning of a dendrite from another neuron. Chemicals known as neurotransmitters flow across the synapse from the end of the axon to the beginning of the dendrite or to another axon, thus transmitting information from neuron to neuron.

rapid initial generation of synapses, followed by prolonged pruning of them, seems to generally hold true.

What determines the ultimate pattern of synaptic connections in the brain? The early phases of the process of synaptogenesis appear to be largely genetically controlled (Bourgeois, 2001). However, experience also plays a crucial role, especially in later phases. In particular, experience appears to be an important determinant of which synapses are maintained and which ones pruned. If experiences lead to synapses firing so that neurotransmitters are released, they tend to be maintained. If not, they tend to wither (Greenough & Black, 1992;

Greenough, Black, & Wallace, 1987). Thus, in the brain as in behavior, development involves a complex interplay of genetics and experience.

Some researchers have proposed that the early surplus of synapses is related to infants and toddlers acquiring certain kinds of capabilities more effectively than adults (e.g., Bjorklund, 1997). For example, toddlers and young children are especially good at picking up the sounds and grammar of their native languages. They are far more effective learners than those who immigrate to a new country as adults and try to learn its language then (Johnson & Newport, 1989). It is not just that the children are learning their first language and the adults their second; young children also learn phonology and syntax more effectively when they are learning it in a second language (as when a 5-year-old comes to a new country). The extra synapses in the young children's brains may be especially useful for learning the extremely complex systems of contingencies embodied in the phonology and grammar of languages such as English.

Because of the surplus of synapses available in early life, the immature brain displays an enormous capacity to adapt to variations in experience. This early *plasticity* is the reason why infants and children often show dramatic recovery from early brain damage, such as sometimes occurs as a result of injury or stroke (Stiles, Bates, Thal, Trauner, & Reilly, 2002). For example, infants or children who experience damage to portions of the brain that process language often recover fully, because other parts of the brain take over the processing of language. In effect, the brain becomes "rewired," and portions of the brain not initially specialized for language take over that function. Adults who experience damage to these same brain regions typically fare less well, because the remaining neurons in other parts of their brain are already dedicated to other functions.

Neural plasticity is not only important for recovery from injury—it also enables the brain to adapt to variations in experience due to patterns of use (Elbert, Heim, & Rockstroh, 2001). For example, compared to non-musicians, individuals who play stringed instruments display an enlarged cortical representation of the fingers of the left hand. Moreover, it appears that musical training has a greater effect on cortical organization when it begins at younger ages. Musicians who learned to play stringed instruments at an earlier age showed greater neural activation in response to stimulation of the little finger of the left hand than did musicians who learned to play at later ages (Elbert, Pantev, Wienbruch, Rockstroh, & Taub, 1995). This finding suggests that the plasticity of the human brain decreases over the life span.

HOW DOES THE SOCIAL WORLD CONTRIBUTE TO COGNITIVE DEVELOPMENT?

Understanding cognitive development requires understanding not only the brain, but also the contributions of the social world. From the day children emerge from the womb, they live in a profoundly social environment. It is social not just in including other people who interact with children—parents, siblings, other adults and other children. It also is social in including many artifacts that exist only because of people's efforts and ingenuity (such as books, television sets, computers, automobiles), many skills that reflect our cultural heritage (including reading, writing, mathematics, computer programming, video-game playing), and many values that guide strategies and problem-solving efforts in certain directions (such as speed, accuracy, neatness, truthfulness). Clearly, all of these manifestations of the social world influence what children think about and how they think about it. Developmental theories that emphasize the role of the social world in children's development are called *sociocultural* theories. Such theories are the focus of Chapter 4; however, examples that illustrate the importance of other people in children's cognitive development can be found throughout the book.

The sociocultural perspective on development was initially articulated by Lev Semenovich Vygotsky, a Russian developmental psychologist, in the early part of the 20th century. Vygotsky's theory and its modern-day counterparts ascribe a central role to the social, cultural, and historical context in explaining the process of cognitive development. The context is viewed as an integral part of children's experience, such that it is not meaningful to consider cognition or behavior as separable or distinct from the context in which it occurs (Rogoff, 1998). Moreover, developmental change is conceptualized as occurring, not only in individual children's knowledge and cognitive processes, but also in children's roles in social interactions and in their ways of participating in culturally determined forms of behavior. Thus, according to the sociocultural perspective, it is essential to investigate and analyze behavior in context if we are to understand performance at any age or developmental change in that performance.

What does it mean to investigate behavior in context? In practice, different lines of scientific inquiry have focused on different dimensions of the social and cultural context. One particularly influential approach to delineating aspects of context is Urie Bronfenbrenner's (1979) conceptualization of context as a "set of nested structures, each inside the next, like a set of Russian dolls" (p. 3). Bronfenbrenner described several concentric layers of the social and cultural context, each of which influences psychological functioning both on its own and in interaction with other layers. This framework is depicted in Figure 1.5.

As shown in the figure, the innermost layer of context consists of the *microsystems* within which development occurs. Microsystems are social relationships in which the child plays a direct part, such as the mother-child relationship, sibling relationships, and relationships with teachers and classmates. Moving outward, the next layer consists of *mesosystems,* which are made up of multiple, interrelated microsystems. For example, the microsystems of family and school interact to form a mesosystem. Families hold expectations and provide opportunities for learning that influence how children perform in school. Likewise, schools sponsor activities that influence how families interact, such as social events and parent-teacher conferences. Next are *exosystems,* which are social systems in which the child does not play a direct part, but that nevertheless

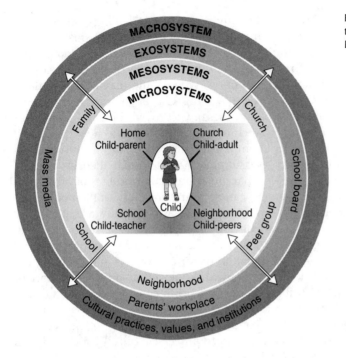

FIGURE 1.5 Schematic depiction of interacting layers of context (based on Bronfenbrenner, 1979).

influence children's development. A good example of an exosystem is the school board, which makes decisions about the organization of community schools, the length of the school year, and the nature of the required curriculum. Although children are not involved directly in this system, it clearly has an impact on their development. Finally, all of these systems are situated within the *macrosystem* of the broader cultural context. The macrosystem incorporates cultural expectations regarding how children should be cared for and what activities children should engage in at various points in development. More broadly, the macrosystem incorporates cultural practices about how families and communities are organized, cultural values about children's roles within these communities, and cultural institutions such as school and day care.

All of these systems, from the microsystems to the macrosystem, change over time. For example, children's relationships with their parents change as they grow, and societal expectations about children's behavior vary with the child's age and over the course of history. Recent formulations of Bronfenbrenner's framework have also incorporated the dimension of time at various levels of context (e.g., Bronfenbrenner, 1998).

All of these aspects of context are addressed within sociocultural theories of development. However, the bulk of research within the sociocultural tradition has focused on social interactions in which the child plays a direct role (the micro- and mesosystems), and on the opportunities for development that are afforded in various cultures and subcultures (the macrosystems).

Social interaction and cognitive development.   Vygotsky's theory focused on what he termed the "higher" psychological processes—those processes that differentiate humans from animals, such as reasoning and concept formation. Vygotsky believed that all of the "higher" psychological processes had their origins in social interactions. Children initially perform cognitive tasks with support from social partners, and over time, these social interactions are gradually internalized, until children can perform tasks on their own. Thus, according to Vygotsky, the central mechanism of developmental change is the internalization of socially shared processes.

The notion of internalization highlights the integral role of other people in guiding and supporting children's development. One type of assistance that other people provide to children is *social scaffolding,* which includes helping children think about a task appropriately, modeling ways of solving problems, and giving hints that guide the child in useful directions. The idea of social scaffolding is based on an analogy to the physical scaffolds used to construct buildings. Physical scaffolds are metal frameworks that allow construction workers to work high above the ground while putting up the basic structures of buildings. Once the basic structure is built, it can support the workers, and the scaffolding can be removed. Similarly, in social scaffolding, the activities of more competent people provide a temporary framework that allows children to think in more advanced ways than they otherwise could. After working for a while at this higher level, children can work at the level without the external support. Parents tend to teach their children in a way that fits the scaffolding model, playing active roles when children are just beginning to learn a skill, and progressively withdrawing to the background as the children show increasing mastery (Pratt, Kerig, Cowan, & Cowan, 1988; Wood, 1986).

The cultural context of cognitive development.   Vygotsky's theory also highlighted the importance of the culture in which children develop. In particular, he focused on the importance of *cultural tools* in shaping and constituting thought. Cultural tools include the entire range of culturally constructed objects and ideas that allow people to achieve their goals: machines such as calculators and computers; representational devices such as books and maps; ways of knowing about the world such as mathematics and science; notational systems such as numbers and letters; and ideas such as gravity and efficiency.

Interacting with even the most mundane cultural tools helps children better understand the social and physical world. Think about calendars and clocks, for example. Learning about them involves much more than just telling time. It also involves learning the belief of our culture that it is useful to break up time into discrete units of years, months, days, hours, minutes, and seconds. The ways in which people use these tools also is revealing. We tell children to be home by 6:00 or 6:15, and to be at school at 8:05, but never to be at home or at school by 8:07 and 30 seconds, much less at 8:07 and 30 and 7/10 seconds. We view it as useful to break up time to a certain level of precision, but not ordinarily beyond that. Countless such experiences shape the way in which children think about concepts even as basic as time.

Culture also plays a role in children's development by influencing the types of activities in which children engage. There is great variation across cultures in how children are cared for, and in the types of things that are typical for children to do. In some cultures, including the United States, children are typically segregated from adults' social and economic worlds for much of the day. In such cultures, many of children's opportunities for learning occur in the context of day care or formal schooling. In other cultures, children are routinely integrated into adult activities, including household activities such as cleaning and preparing meals, and economic activities such as farming and weaving textiles. In such cultures, most of children's opportunities for learning take place in the context of everyday situations. Such variations in children's opportunities for learning lead to variations in the nature and path of children's cognitive development. Thus, culture influences children's development by shaping how children participate in culturally valued activities.

The Book's Organization

The organization of this book can be viewed either on a chapter-by-chapter basis or in terms of the central themes that recur in many chapters. In the sections that follow, the book is described from each perspective.

THE CHAPTER-BY-CHAPTER ORGANIZATION

The book is divided into three sections. The first section, which includes Chapters 1–4, explores broad perspectives on children's thinking, including Piaget's theory, the information-processing approach to development, and the sociocultural approach to development. The second section, which includes Chapters 5–11, focuses on more specific aspects of children's thinking, such as how they perceive the world, how they use language to communicate, and how they learn reading, writing, and mathematics. The third section includes only a single chapter, Chapter 12. It is a summary of what has gone before and a look forward toward the issues that promise to be most important in the future.

The first chapter, which you are just finishing, is an attempt to define the field that is considered in this book and to introduce ideas that are important within it. Chapter 2 is devoted to the work of Piaget, whose investigations into children's thinking can fairly be said to have created the modern field of cognitive development. On topics ranging from how children infer the origins of the sun to how they order the weights of different objects, Piaget saw much that other people had missed. In addition, Piaget observed children of an extremely wide age range, stretching from the first days of infancy into late adolescence. Thus, his observations provide a feel for many aspects of development in infancy, childhood, and adolescence.

Chapter 3 examines another prominent approach to the study of children's thinking, the information-processing approach. In some ways, this approach represents a modern extension of Piaget's theory; in other ways, it represents an alternative. The basic assumptions of the information-processing approach are that children's mental activities can be characterized in terms of processes that manipulate information; that processing capacities are limited; and that the interaction between the individual's processing system and the environment leads to cognitive growth (Klahr & MacWhinney, 1998). The information-processing approach has proved especially useful for studying development, because it provides precise ideas about the mechanisms that produce cognitive change.

Chapter 4 addresses a third prominent approach to the study of children's thinking, the sociocultural approach. As discussed above, the social and cultural world has a profound effect on what children do, on what they think about, and on how they think. Research guided by sociocultural theories investigates how social and cultural factors influence cognition and development.

Chapter 5 begins the second main section of the book, which examines seven specific aspects of children's thinking: perception, language, memory, conceptual understanding, social cognition, problem solving, and academic skills. Chapter 5 focuses on perceptual development. The emphases are on the surprising number of visual and auditory skills that children possess from early in infancy, and on the relations between perception and action.

Chapter 6 examines language development. Here the discussion centers on what types of words children use first, when and how they learn grammar, how they acquire word meanings, and how they use language to communicate with others.

Chapter 7 is about the development of memory. It focuses on how the development of basic capacities, strategies, and content knowledge contribute to children's growing abilities to remember. The chapter also addresses the practical issue of whether in court cases, children's recall of what happened can be trusted, and how the accuracy of their testimony changes with age.

Chapter 8 concerns conceptual development. The early part of the chapter examines whether children internally represent concepts primarily in terms of dictionary-like definitions, in terms of loosely related characteristic features, or in terms of causally connected theories. The latter part of the chapter examines the development of several particularly important concepts: time, space, number, and living things.

Chapter 9 is about social cognition. The focus is on children's developing understanding of social information, including knowledge about the self and others, knowledge about the mind and the mental states that give rise to behavior, and knowledge about the social world.

Chapter 10 focuses on problem solving. All of us solve problems daily, but such activities play an especially large role in the lives of young children. The reason is that many tasks that older individuals find routine pose novel challenges for younger ones. Among the problem-solving processes examined in the chapter are planning, causal inference, analogy, tool use, and scientific and logical reasoning.

Chapter 11 concerns the development of reading, writing, and mathematics. Many of the skills for which development is described in the preceding chapters—perception, language, memory, conceptual understanding, and problem solving—are put to use in the classroom. Children's acquisition of academic skills illustrates how different types of thought processes work together to allow learning of complex concepts and skills.

The third main section of the book is Chapter 12. It summarizes the main conclusions that apply across the diverse areas of children's thinking and identifies key issues for future investigation.

THE CENTRAL THEMES

This chapter-by-chapter organization provides one way of thinking about the material the book covers. Another way is to consider the themes that arise in many chapters. The following are eight recurring themes.

1. The most basic issues about children's thinking are "What develops?" and "How does development occur?"
2. Four change processes that seem to be particularly large contributors to cognitive development are automatization, encoding, generalization, and strategy construction.
3. Infants and very young children are more cognitively competent than they appear. They possess a rich set of abilities that enable them to learn rapidly.
4. Differences between age groups tend to be ones of degree rather than kind. Not only are young children more cognitively competent than they appear, but older children and adults are less competent than we might think.
5. Changes in children's thinking do not occur in a vacuum. What children already know about material that they encounter influences not only how much they learn but also what they learn.
6. The development of intelligence reflects changes in brain structure and functioning as well as increasingly effective deployment of cognitive resources.
7. Children's thinking develops within a social context. Parents, peers, teachers, and the culture at large influence what children think about, as well as how and why they come to think in particular ways.
8. Increasing understanding of children's thinking is yielding practical benefits as well as theoretical insights.

A simple strategy for improving your understanding of the material in this book is to spend a few minutes now re-reading and thinking about these eight themes. Then, as you read subsequent chapters, try to notice how they unite different aspects of children's thinking.

Summary

For hundreds of years, people who have had contact with children have wondered about such questions as where the children's ideas came from and whether infants perceive the world in the same way as adults. Recent conceptual and methodological advances have greatly improved our ability to explore these and many other questions about children's thinking.

A number of the most important questions about children's thinking have long histories. Are some capabilities innate? Do children proceed through qualitatively different stages of thinking, or is development continuous? How do changes in children's thinking occur? How do individuals differ in qualities such as intelligence, and how much continuity is there between early and later abilities? How do the internal world of the maturing brain and the external world of other people shape development? These continue to be among the most basic questions about children's thinking.

A number of themes are identified that recur throughout the book. Among these are the surprising cognitive competence of infants and young children, the continuous growth of children's thinking beyond this initial competence, the challenge that children face of coping with complex tasks while having only limited processing resources, the ways in which existing knowledge influences learning, and the influence of brain development and of the social world on children's thinking.

Recommended Readings

Bronfenbrenner, U. (1979). *The ecology of human development: Experiments by nature and design.* Cambridge, MA: Harvard University Press. In this book, Bronfenbrenner presents his influential conceptualization of layers of social and cultural context.

Flavell, J.H. (1971). Stage-related properties of cognitive development. *Cognitive Psychology*, 2, 421–453. A classic analysis of stage theories of development.

Johnson, M.H., Munakata, Y., & Gilmore, R.O. (Eds.). (2002). *Brain development and cognition: A reader* (2nd edition). Oxford, UK: Blackwell. A compilation of a large number of the most important articles about the relation between development of the brain and children's thinking.

Meltzoff, A. (2002). Imitation as a mechanism of social cognition: Origins of empathy, theory of mind, and the representation of action. In U. Goswami (Ed.), *Blackwell handbook of childhood cognitive development.* Malden, MA: Blackwell. Infants in their first month out of the womb show some ability to imitate the actions of other people; this chapter summarizes some of the evidence for this surprising capability and how it develops during infancy and beyond.

2

PIAGET'S THEORY
OF DEVELOPMENT

At age 7 months, 28 days, I offer him a little bell behind a cushion. So long as he sees the little bell, however small it may be, he tries to grasp it. But if the little bell disappears completely he stops all searching.

I then resume the experiment using my hand as a screen. Laurent's arm is outstretched and about to grasp the little bell at the moment I make it disappear behind my hand which is open and at a distance of about 15 cm. from him. He immediately withdraws his arm, as though the little bell no longer existed. I then shake my hand. . . . Laurent watches attentively, greatly surprised to rediscover the sound of the little bell, but he does not try to grasp it. I turn my hand over and he sees the little bell; he then stretches out his hand toward it. I hide the little bell again by changing the position of my hand; Laurent withdraws his hand. (Piaget, 1954, p. 39)

What does this infant's odd behavior tell us? Piaget (1954) advanced one provocative interpretation: that Laurent did not search for the bell because he did not know that it still existed. In other words, his failure to search was due to his inability to mentally represent the bell's existence. It was as if the infant's thinking embodied the strongest possible version of the adage "Out of sight, out of mind."

This chapter is the only one in the book whose title includes a person's name. This is no accident. Jean Piaget's contribution to the study of cognitive development is a testimony to how much one person can do. Before Piaget began his work, no recognizable field of cognitive development existed. Yet despite thousands of studies on children's thinking having been conducted in the interim, even Piaget's earliest research is still informative. What explains the longevity of Piaget's theory?

Perhaps the most basic reason is that Piaget's theory communicates an almost tangible sense of what children's thinking is like. His descriptions feel right. Many of his individual observations are quite surprising, but the general trends he describes appeal to our intuitions and to our memories of childhood.

A second important reason is that the theory addresses topics that have been of interest to parents, teachers, scientists, and philosophers for hundreds of years. At the most general level, the theory speaks to such questions as "What is intelligence?" and "Where does knowledge come from?" At a more specific level, the theory examines development of the concepts of time, space, number, and other ideas that are among the basic intellectual acquisitions of humankind. Placing the development of such fundamental concepts into a single coherent framework has made Piaget's theory one of the significant intellectual achievements of our century.

A third reason for the theory's longevity is its exceptional breadth. It covers an unusually broad age span—the entire range from infancy through adolescence. Children's understanding of concepts such as cause and effect can be seen evolving from rudimentary forms in infancy to more complex forms in early childhood to yet more complex forms in middle childhood to even more complex forms in adolescence. The theory also encompasses an unusually broad variety of achievements at any given age. For example, it brings together 5-year-olds' scientific and mathematical reasoning, their moral judgments, their drawings, their idea of cause and effect, their use of language, and their memory for past events. One of the purposes of scientific theories is to point out the commonalities underlying seemingly unrelated facts. Piaget's theory is especially strong on this dimension.

A fourth reason for the theory's having endured is that Piaget had the equivalent of a gifted gardener's "green thumb," a knack for making interesting observations. One of these observations was quoted at the outset of this chapter: the one concerning infants' failure to search for objects if they cannot see them. Many of his other intriguing observations are described throughout this chapter.

Because of the range and complexity of Piaget's theory, it seems worthwhile to approach it first in general terms and then in greater depth. The first section of this chapter provides an overview of Piaget's theory. The second section describes children's thinking during each of his four stages of development. The third focuses on his description of the development of several especially important concepts from birth through adolescence. The fourth is an evaluation of the theory. Table 2.1 depicts this organization.

An Overview of Piaget's Theory

Piaget's theory is sufficiently broad and complex that it is easy to lose the forest for the trees. This section provides an overview of the forest.

THE THEORY AS A WHOLE

To appreciate Piaget's theory, it is essential to understand his motivation for developing it. This motivation grew out of Piaget's early interest in biology and philosophy. When he was 11 years old, he published his first article, which described an albino sparrow he had observed. Between the ages of 15 and 18, he published several more articles, most of them about mollusks. The articles must have been impressive. When Piaget was 18, the head of a natural history museum, who had never met him but who had read his articles, wrote a letter offering him the position of curator of the mollusk collection at the museum. Piaget turned down the offer so that he could finish high school.

In addition to this early interest in biology, Piaget was keenly interested in philosophy. He was especially drawn to *epistemology*, the branch of philosophy concerned with the origins of knowledge. The theory of the eighteenth-century philosopher Immanuel Kant, who, like Piaget, was most interested in the origins of knowledge, was a source of particular fascination for him.

The combination of philosophical and biological interests influenced Piaget's later theorizing in several ways. It led to the fundamental question underlying the theory: "Where does knowledge come from?" It also influenced the particular problems Piaget chose to study. He followed Kant in viewing space, time, classes, causality, and relations as basic categories of knowledge. At the same time, he opposed Kant's position that these basic categories of knowledge were innate to human beings. Instead, he believed that children came to understand the concepts increasingly deeply during infancy, childhood, and adolescence. Perhaps most important, the joint interest in philosophy and biology suggested to Piaget that long-standing philosophical controversies could be resolved by applying scientific methods. Just as Darwin attempted to answer the question "How did people evolve?" Piaget attempted to answer the question "How does knowledge evolve?"

Having this background, we can now consider the theory itself. At the most general level of analysis, Piaget was interested in intelligence. By this he meant a broader quality than what is measured on intelligence tests. He viewed intelligence as the ability to adapt to all aspects of reality. He also believed that within a person's lifetime, intelligence evolves through a series of qualitatively distinct stages. These stages, and the developmental processes that produce the transitions from one stage to the next, are described in the next two sections.

THE STAGES OF DEVELOPMENT

As noted in Chapter 1, stage theorists such as Piaget make certain characteristic assumptions. They assume that children's reasoning in earlier stages differs qualitatively from their reasoning in later ones. They also assume that at a given point in development, children reason similarly on many problems. Finally, they assume that after spending a prolonged period of time "in" a stage, children abruptly make the transition to the next stage.

Piaget postulated that all children progress through four stages and that they do so in the same order: first the *sensorimotor period,* then the *preoperational period,* then the *concrete operational period,* and finally the *formal operational period.* The sensorimotor period typically spans the period from birth to about the second birthday, the preoperational period lasts roughly from age 2 to age 6 or 7, the concrete operational period extends from about age 6 or 7 to 11 or 12, and the formal operational period includes all of adolescence and adulthood.

First consider Piaget's characterization of the sensorimotor period, which lasts from birth through age 2. Piaget believed that at birth, a child's cognitive system is limited to motor reflexes. Within a few months, however, children build on these reflexes to develop more sophisticated procedures. They begin to systematically repeat initially inadvertent behaviors, to generalize their activities to a wider range of situations, and to coordinate them into increasingly lengthy chains of behavior. Children's physical interactions with objects provide the impetus for this development.

The preoperational period encompasses the age range from 2 to 6 or 7 years. The greatest achievement of this period is the acquisition of means for representing the world symbolically: mental imagery, drawing, and especially language. Children's vocabulary increases 100-fold between 18 and 60 months (McCarthy, 1954), and their utterances progress from one- and two-word phrases to sentences of indefinite length. In Piaget's view, however, preoperational children can use these representational skills only to view the world from their own perspective. They focus their attention too narrowly, often ignoring important information. They also cannot accurately represent transformations and instead are able to represent only static situations.

The concrete operational period encompasses the age range from 6 or 7 to 11 or 12 years. Concrete operational children can take other points of view, can simultaneously take into account more than one perspective, and can accurately represent transformations as well as static situations. This allows them to solve many problems involving concrete objects and physically possible situations. However, they do not yet consider all of the logically possible outcomes and do not understand highly abstract concepts.

Formal operations, attained at roughly age 11 or 12, is the crowning achievement of the stage progression. Children who attain formal operations are said to reason in terms of theories and abstractions as well as concrete realities. This broader perspective brings with it the potential for solving many types of problems that are impossible for children in earlier stages. Although Piaget recognized that particular knowledge and beliefs continue to change, he believed that the basic mode of reasoning that characterizes the formal operational stage is sufficiently powerful to last a lifetime.

DEVELOPMENTAL PROCESSES

How do children progress from one stage to another? Piaget viewed three processes as crucial: *assimilation, accommodation,* and *equilibration.*

Assimilation.   Assimilation refers to the way in which people transform incoming information so that it fits their existing way of thinking. As an example, consider the following anecdote. When Siegler's older son was 2, he encountered a man who was bald on the top of his head and had long, frizzy hair growing out from each side. To Siegler's embarrassment, on seeing the man, his son gleefully shouted, "Clown, clown." (Actually, it sounded more like "Kown, kown.") The man apparently possessed the features that the boy believed distinguished clowns from other people, and thus became a "kown."

Assimilation is important throughout life, not just in early childhood. Consider the experience of a music critic, Bernard Levin. Levin noted that when he heard the premiere performance of Bartok's *Concerto for Violin and Orchestra,* early in Bartok's career, neither he nor other critics could make sense of it or later remember it in any detail. It was simply confusing and annoying to the ear.

However, when he next heard the piece, almost 20 years later, it seemed eminently musical. Levin's explanation was that in the ensuing period, "I had come to hear the world with different ears" (*London Daily Telegraph,* June 8, 1977). In Piaget's terms, he initially was unable to assimilate the Bartok piece to his understanding of music. Twenty years later, he was able to do so.

One interesting type of assimilation that Piaget described is *functional assimilation,* the tendency to use a mental structure as soon as it becomes available. Illustratively, when Siegler's older son was first learning to talk, he spent endless hours talking in his crib, even though no one else was present. A few years later, he would turn somersaults over and over again, despite encouragement from his parents to stop. Piaget contrasted this source of motivation with behaviorists' emphases on external reinforcers as motivators of behavior. In reinforcement, the reason for engaging in an activity is the external reward that is obtained. In functional assimilation, the reason for engaging in the activity is the sheer delight of mastering new skills.

Accommodation. Accommodation refers to the ways in which people adapt their thinking to new experiences. Returning to the "kown" incident, after biting his lip to suppress a smile, Siegler told his son that the man they had seen was not a clown; that even though his hair was like a clown's, he wasn't wearing a funny costume and wasn't trying to make people laugh. The goal was to help the child accommodate his idea of "clown" to the concept's standard meaning.

Assimilation and accommodation mutually influence each other; assimilation is never present without accommodation and vice versa. On seeing a new object, an infant might try to grasp it as he has grasped other objects (thus assimilating the new object to an existing approach). However, he also would have to adjust his grasp to conform to the shape of the new object (thus accommodating his approach as well). The extreme case of assimilation is fantasy play, in which children gloss over the physical characteristics of objects and treat them as if they were something else. The extreme case of accommodation is imitation, in which children minimize their interpretations and simply mimic what they see. Even at the extremes, elements of each process are present. Children at play do not totally ignore physical properties. (Beds almost never are assimilated as teacups, even in fantasy play.) Conversely, when we do not understand what we are doing, imitation often is imperfect. (Try to repeat verbatim a 10-word sentence from a language that you do not speak.)

Equilibration. Equilibration is the process by which children integrate their many particular pieces of knowledge of the world into a unified whole. It thus requires balancing assimilation and accommodation. It also is the keystone of developmental change within Piaget's system. Piaget saw development as the formation of ever more stable equilibria between the child's cognitive system and the external world. That is, the child's model of the world increasingly resembles reality.

Piaget also suggested that regardless of when in life it occurs, equilibration includes three phases. First, children are satisfied with their mode of thought and therefore are in a state of equilibrium. Then they become aware of shortcomings in their existing thinking and are dissatisfied. This constitutes a state of disequilibrium. Finally, they adopt a more sophisticated mode of thought that eliminates the shortcomings of the old one. That is, they reach a more stable equilibrium.

To illustrate the equilibration process, suppose a 6-year-old girl thought that animals were the only living things. (In fact, most 4- to 7-year-olds do think this; see Hatano, Siegler, Richards, Inagaki, Stavy, & Wax, 1993.) At some point, the girl might realize that plants, like animals, grow and die. This realization might create a state of disequilibrium, in which she was unsure if plants were alive and what it meant to be alive. Eventually she would learn that the critical attributes of life are growth and reproduction, that both plants and animals possess them, and that both therefore are alive. The new understanding would constitute a more stable equilibrium, since further observations would not call it into question (unless the girl later became interested in certain viruses and bacteria whose status as living things continues to be debated by biologists).

This overview of assimilation, accommodation, and equilibration might create an impression that these change processes apply solely to specific, short-term cognitive changes. In fact, Piaget was especially interested in their capacity to produce far-reaching, longer-term changes, such as the change from one developmental stage to the next. Illustratively, the particular realizations that frizzy hair that looks like a clown's does not make its bearer a clown, that plants are alive even though they don't move, and that the sun's looking like gold does not mean it is gold are part of a more general trend from preoperational to concrete operational reasoning. Piaget believed that children generalize the assimilations, accommodations, and equilibrations involved in these particular changes into a broad shift from emphasizing external appearances to emphasizing deeper, enduring qualities.

ORIENTING ASSUMPTIONS

The child as scientific problem solver.   Piaget often likened children's thinking to that of scientists solving problems about the fundamental nature of the world. He applied the metaphor even to the thinking of infants. When an infant varied the height from which she dropped food from her highchair and observed how the results varied, Piaget detected the beginnings of scientific experimentation.

At least three considerations led Piaget to concentrate on scientific reasoning and problem solving. One was his view of what development was. Piaget viewed development as a form of adaptation to reality. A problem can be viewed as a miniature reality. The way children solved problems thus could lead to insights about how they adapted to all kinds of challenges that life posed.

A second reason for Piaget's emphasis on problem solving relates to his views about how and why development occurs. Equilibration only happens when some problem arises that disturbs a child's existing equilibrium. Thus, problems, which by their very nature challenge existing understandings, have the potential for stimulating cognitive growth. If encountering problems stimulates cognitive growth, then an interest in cognitive growth would naturally lead to an interest in problem solving.

A third reason for Piaget's focus on problem solving concerns the insights that can be gained by observing children's reactions to unfamiliar situations. Piaget noted that everyday activities may be performed by rote; when this is the case, they reveal little about children's reasoning. For example, if we ask a boy to name the capital of France, and he says "Paris," we learn little about his reasoning. We just learn that he knows the particular fact. By contrast, when children are unfamiliar with problems, their solution strategies reveal their own logic.

The role of activity. Piaget emphasized cognitive activity as the means through which development occurs. Assimilation, accommodation, and equilibration are all active processes by which the mind transforms, and is transformed by, incoming information. As Gruber and Voneche (1977) noted, it was significant that Piaget titled one of his most famous books *The Construction of Reality in the Child*. Within Piaget's approach, reality is not waiting to be found; children must construct it from their own mental and physical actions.

This distinction between a found reality and a constructed reality is analogous to the distinction between a picture of a bridge and an engineer's model of the forces operating on the bridge. A picture simply reflects the bridge's superficial appearance. In contrast, the engineer's model emphasizes the relations among components and how the structure distributes stresses. Piaget believed that children's mental representations, like the engineer's model, emphasize structural relations and causes. He also believed that the only way that children can form such representations is to assimilate their experience to their existing understandings. Even when a relation is explained to them, they must actively integrate it with their own general understanding in order to remember it.

Methodological assumptions. Early in his career, Piaget perceived a trade-off between the precision and replicability that accompany standardized experimental procedures and the rich descriptions and insights that can emerge from methods that are tailored to the individual child. He also recognized the trade-off between the unexpected information that can emerge from talking with children and having them explain their reasoning and the possibility of underestimating the quality of their reasoning because of their inarticulateness.

Recognizing these trade-offs, Piaget used different methods to study different topics. His studies of infants, conducted early in his career, were based on observations of his own children, Jacqueline, Laurent, and Lucienne, in everyday situations and in simple informal experiments that he devised. His early studies of moral reasoning, causation, play, and dreams relied almost entirely on children's answers to hypothetical questions. His later studies of number, time, velocity, and proportionality relied on a combination of children's interactions with physical materials and their explanations of their reasoning.

Generally, when the choice was whether to follow standardized methods or to flexibly tailor tasks and questions to the individual child's actions and statements, Piaget opted for flexibility. This choice may have led him astray at times. Some of his conclusions may have been due to his methods' underestimating children's knowledge. However, the flexible methods also allowed him to follow up unexpected observations, resulting in remarkable discoveries and insights that might never have emerged using standardized procedures.

Possessing this overview of Piaget's theory, we now can examine the major trends that characterize his four hypothesized stages of development. To describe them as cleanly as possible, this discussion will generally avoid phrases such as "Piaget said," "Piaget believed," and "Piaget argued." These qualifying phrases should be understood to be implicit, since many of the claims are controversial. Before getting into the controversies, though, we need to understand what Piaget was saying.

The Stage Model

THE SENSORIMOTOR PERIOD (BIRTH TO ROUGHLY 2 YEARS)

Several years ago, at the first class meeting of a developmental psychology course Siegler was teaching, he asked each student to name the five most important aspects of intelligence in infancy, early childhood, later childhood, and adolescence. A number of students commented that they found it odd to describe infants as having intelligence at all. By far the most frequently named characteristics of infants' intelligence were physical coordination, alertness, and ability to recognize people and objects. Part of Piaget's genius was that he perceived much more than this. He saw the beginnings of some of humankind's most sophisticated thought processes in infants' flailings and graspings.

Piaget's account of the development of sensorimotor intelligence constitutes a theory within a theory. Infants are said to progress through six stages of intellectual development within a two-year period. (For clarity, we will refer to these as "substages" to distinguish them from the broader stages such as the sensorimotor and preoperational stages.) This might seem like too large a number of substages for such a brief time span, but when we consider that the brain of a 2-year-old weighs almost three times as much as that of a newborn, the number does not seem unreasonable. As a general rule, cognitive competence, like brain size, grows especially rapidly in the first few years.

Substage 1: Modification of reflexes (birth to roughly 1 month).   Newborn infants enter the world possessing many reflexes. They suck when objects are placed in their mouths, close their fingers around objects that come into contact with their hands, focus on the edges of objects with their eyes, turn their heads toward noises, and so on. Piaget believed that these reflexes are the building blocks of intelligence.

Even within the first month after birth, infants begin to modify the reflexes to make them more adaptive. In the first days, they suck quite similarly regardless of the type of object in their mouth. Later in the first month, however, they suck differently on a milk-bearing nipple than on a harder, drier finger, and they suck differently on both of them than on the side of their hand. Thus, accommodation can be seen even in the first month out of the womb.

Substage 2: Primary circular reactions (roughly 1 to 4 months).   By the second month, infants exhibit primary circular reactions. The term "circular" is used here in the sense of a repetitive cycle of events. The circles involve infants' actions, the effect of those actions on the environment, and the impact on the infants' subsequent actions of the effect of the earlier actions on the environment. Piaget (1954) provides the example of infants in their first few months trying to scratch and grasp all kinds of objects that they happen to touch: their mother's bare shoulder, the sheet folded over their blanket, their father's fist, and so on.

In primary circular reactions, if infants inadvertently produce some interesting effect, they attempt to duplicate it by repeating the action. If they are successful, the new instance of the interesting outcome triggers another similar cycle, which, in turn, can trigger another cycle, and so on.

These primary circular reactions are possible because Substage 2 infants begin to coordinate actions that originally were separate reflexes. In Substage 1, infants grasp objects that come into contact with their palms. They also suck on objects that come into their mouths. During Substage 2, infants put these actions together. They bring to their mouths objects that their hands grasp, and grasp objects with their hands that they are sucking on. Thus, the reflexes have already begun to serve as building blocks for more complex activities.

Primary circular reactions are more flexible than the earlier reflexes and allow infants to learn a great deal about the world. However, they also are limited in at least three ways. First, the 1- to 4-month-olds attempt to reproduce only the exact behavior that produced the original interesting event—they do not vary their behavior. Second, their actions are poorly integrated and have a large trial-and-error component. Third, they only try to repeat actions in which the outcome of the action involves their own bodies, as in sucking a finger.

Substage 3: Secondary circular reactions (roughly 4 to 8 months).   In this stage, infants become increasingly interested in outcomes occurring beyond their bodies. For example, they become interested in batting balls with their hands and watching them roll away. Piaget labeled such activities *secondary circular reactions*. Like all circular reactions, these activities are repeated over and over. Unlike the primary circular reactions, though, the interesting outcome (such as the ball rolling away) involves objects in the external world.

Between ages 4 and 8 months, infants also organize more efficiently the components of their circular reactions. Piaget described instances in which, after he started a mobile swinging, his children kicked their legs to continue the movement. As in the primary circular reactions, infants were only trying to reinstate the original interesting occurrence. However, they now could do so more efficiently. They reacted more quickly to the original event and wasted less motion.

At this point, it is tempting to conclude that infants understand the causal connection between their actions and the effects of their actions. Piaget was reluctant to credit them with this understanding, though. Rather, he thought that infants' activities were not sufficiently voluntary to say that they had independent goals. In his view, in the first month they do not form any goals, and between 1 and 8 months, they only form goals directly suggested to them by the immediate situation. Not until after 8 months do they form true goals, independent of events in the immediate environment.

Substage 4: Coordination of secondary circular reactions (roughly 8 to 12 months).   Infants approaching 1 year of age become able to coordinate two or more secondary circular reactions into an efficient routine. When Piaget (1952) put a pillow in front of a matchbox that his infant son Laurent liked, the boy pushed the pillow aside and grabbed the box. In earlier stages, the infant would not have been able to combine the two activities of pushing the barrier out of the way and getting the matchbox.

This example also illustrates another major development that occurs as children approach their first birthday. They realize that if they act in certain ways, particular effects will follow. Thus, Laurent now understood that removing the pillow would allow him to grab the matchbox.

Especially important, Substage 4 brings with it the ability to form relatively enduring internal representations of the world. Out of sight is no longer completely out of mind. Thus, when objects disappear from sight, as when they roll behind a chair, infants pursue them, rather than acting as if the objects had disappeared from the world. This ability to form mental representations is an especially important development, because it lays the foundation for all further cognitive growth.

Substage 5: Tertiary circular reactions (roughly 12 to 18 months).   With the onset of tertiary circular reactions, shortly before 1 year of age, infants transcend the remaining limits on their circular reactions. They actively search for new ways to interact with objects, and explore the potential uses to which objects can be put. As implied by the "circular reaction" label, they still repeat their actions again and again. Now, though, they deliberately vary both their own actions and the objects on which they act. Thus, the activities involve similar rather than identical behaviors. The following description of Piaget's son Laurent conveys a sense of these new competencies.

> He grasps in succession a celluloid swan, a box, etc., stretches out his arm, and lets them fall. He distinctly varies the positions of the fall. Sometimes he stretches out his arm vertically, sometimes he holds it obliquely, in front of or behind his eyes, etc. Then the object falls in a new position (for example on his pillow), he lets it fall two or three times more on the same place, as though to study the spatial relation; then he modifies the situation. (Piaget, 1951, p. 269)

These changes from primary to secondary to tertiary circular reactions show just how far infants come in the first year and a half. As shown in Figure 2.1, primary circular reactions, first seen between 1 and 4 months, involve repetitions of events whose outcomes center on the infants' own bodies, such as putting their fingers into their mouths. Secondary circular reactions, first seen between 4 and 8 months, again involve repetition of an event that by chance produced an interesting outcome, but the interesting outcome is at least slightly removed from the infants' bodies (such as the ball rolling away from them). Tertiary circular reactions, first seen between 12 and 18 months, involve the infant deliberately varying the behavior that produced the interesting outcome.

The changes embodied in these three types of circular reactions are useful for thinking about a broad range of developments in infancy. At first, infants' activities center on their own bodies; later, they increasingly center on the external world. Goals begin at a concrete level (dropping an object) and become increasingly abstract (varying the heights from which objects are dropped). Correspondence between intentions and behaviors becomes increasingly precise, and exploration of the world becomes increasingly venturesome.

Substage 6: Beginnings of representational thought (roughly 18 to 24 months). Developments in this age range are transitional between the sensorimotor and preoperational periods. In the sensorimotor period, children can only act; they cannot form internal mental representations of objects and events. In the preoperational period, children can form such internal mental operations. Substage 6 is the transition point, in which internalized representations are first produced. Consider the following scenario involving Piaget playing with his daughter Lucienne. Piaget hides a watch chain inside an otherwise empty matchbox. Previously, he had left the matchbox open far enough that Lucienne could get the chain by turning over the matchbox, but now he closes it too completely for the chain to fall out. Lucienne

> looks at the slit (in the matchbox) with great attention; then, several times in succession, she opens and shuts her mouth, at first slightly, then wider and wider! Apparently, Lucienne understands the existence of a cavity subjacent to the slit (in the matchbox) and wishes to enlarge the cavity. The attempt at representation which she thus furnishes is expressed plastically, that is to say, due to inability to think out the situation in words or clear visual images, she uses a simple motor indication (her open mouth) as "signifier" or symbol. (Piaget 1951, p. 338)

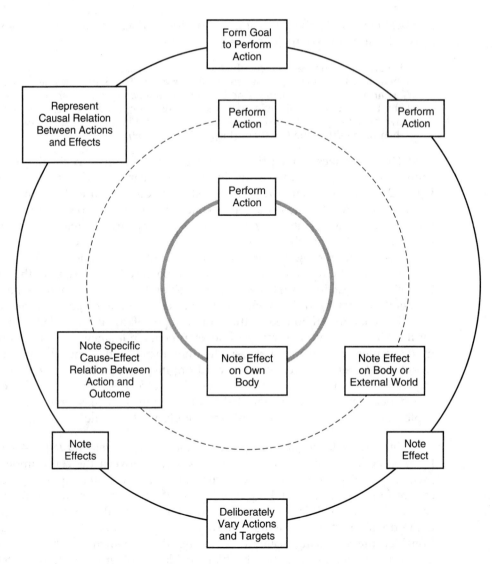

FIGURE 2.1 The child's expanding universe: primary (▬▬▬), secondary (----------), and tertiary (――――) circular reactions. Diagram best read by starting at top of each circle and proceeding clockwise.

As Lucienne opens her mouth, symbolizing her desire for the opening in the matchbox to become wider, we can almost see her internally representing the situation. That is, the representation is moving from her external actions to her mind. Such internalized representations are the hallmark of the preoperational period.

THE PREOPERATIONAL PERIOD (ROUGHLY 2 YEARS TO 6 OR 7 YEARS)

Miller (1993) nicely captured children's position as they complete the sensorimotor period by likening them to mountain climbers who, after a hard trek, discover that what they have climbed is merely a foothill to Mt. Everest. By the end of the sensorimotor stage, infants have become toddlers. They interact smoothly with objects and people in their immediate environment. Their ability to form internal representations remains severely limited, however. The growth of representational ability is the key development of the preoperational period.

Early symbolic representations. Piaget suggested that the earliest sign of internal representations is *deferred imitation,* the imitation of an activity hours or days after it occurred. For children to show such delayed imitation, they must have formed a durable representation of the original activity. How else could they imitate it so much later?

Children do not exhibit deferred imitation until late in the sensorimotor period. Consider the following description of Piaget's daughter Jacqueline kicking and screaming in her playpen.

> At 1;4(3) [*Piaget's notation for 1 year, 4 months, and 3 days*] Jacqueline had a visit from a little boy of 1;6 whom she used to see from time to time, and who, in the course of the afternoon, got into a terrible temper. He screamed as he tried to get out of a playpen and pushed it backward, stamping his feet. Jacqueline stood watching him in amazement, never having witnessed such a scene before. The next day, she herself screamed in her playpen and tried to move it, stamping her foot lightly several times in succession. (Piaget, 1951, p. 63)

Jacqueline had never before, to her father's knowledge, engaged in these behaviors. Thus, an internal representation of the playmate's tantrum must have helped her reproduce them.

Piaget distinguished between two types of internal representations: *symbols* and *signs*. The distinction is not identical to the standard English distinction between the two. Rather, it is the difference between idiosyncratic representations intended only for one's personal use (symbols) and conventional representations intended for communication (signs).

Early in their acquisition of internal representations, children frequently use symbols (the personal representations). They may choose a particular piece of cloth to represent their pillow or a popsicle stick to represent a gun. Typically, these personal symbols physically resemble the object they represent. The cloth's texture is similar to that of the pillow, and both are comforting; the popsicle stick's shape and texture are something like those of a gun barrel. Signs, by contrast, often do not resemble the objects or events they signify. The word *cow* does not look like a cow, nor does the numeral 6 have any inherent similarity to six objects.

As children develop, they make less use of the idiosyncratic symbols and more of the conventional signs. This shift is an important achievement, as it greatly expands their ability to communicate. The transition from personal to publicly accepted representations is not easy, however.

The difficulty is illustrated in Piaget's description of *egocentric communication*. Piaget applied the term "egocentric" to preschool-age children, not to castigate them for being inconsiderate, but rather in a more literal sense. Their thinking about the external world is always in terms of their own perspective. Their use of language reflects this egocentrism, particularly their use of idiosyncratic words that are meaningless to other people.

Although even very young children use signs as well as symbols, they at first do not use them consistently in a manner that other people can understand. Figure 2.2 portrays an instance of this aspect of young children's conversations. Preschoolers often speak right past each other, without appearing to pay any attention to what others are saying. Many times, even sympathetic adults cannot figure out what the children mean.

Between ages 4 and 7 years, speech becomes less egocentric. One of the earliest signs of progress can be seen in children's verbal quarrels. The fact that a child's verbal statements elicit a playmate's disagreement indicates that the playmate is at least paying attention to a perspective other than his own. Some children also are aware of the symbolization process and find it interesting in its own right. When Siegler's daughter was 4, she took great delight in saying such things as, "When I say 'chair,' I'm going to mean 'milk'; could you give me a glass of chair?"

Piaget noted that mental imagery, like language, is a way of representing objects and events. He also suggested that the development of mental imagery resembles that of language. As children become able to describe situations

FIGURE 2.2 *Two young children more or less having a conversation—an example of egocentric communication.*

verbally, they also become able to represent them as images. Further, he believed that the initial representations in both domains are limited to the child's own perspective. That is, they are egocentric.

Although language, mental imagery, and many other skills grow greatly during the preoperational period, Piaget emphasized what preoperational children cannot do. He viewed them as unable to solve many problems that are critical indicators of logical reasoning. Even the name, "*pre*operational," suggests deficiencies rather than strengths.

One of the limits on preschoolers' thinking has already been mentioned: their egocentrism. This trait is evident not only in their conversations, but also in their ability to take different spatial perspectives. Piaget had 4-year-olds sit or stand at a table in front of a model of three mountains of different sizes (Figure 2.3). The children's task was to choose which of several photographs corresponded to what children sitting at chairs at different points around the table would see. To solve the problem, children needed to recognize that their own perspective was not the only one possible and to mentally rotate the arrangement they saw to correspond to what the view would be elsewhere. This was impossible for most of the 4-year-olds; they could not imagine the view from other positions.

A second, related limit on preschoolers' thinking is that it centers on individual, perceptually striking features of objects, to the exclusion of other, less striking features. A good example of this *centration* is found in Piaget's research on children's understanding of the concept of time.

Piaget's interest in this concept has an interesting history. In 1928, Albert Einstein posed a seemingly simple question to Piaget: In what order do children acquire the concepts of time and velocity? Einstein's question was prompted by an issue within physics. In Newtonian theory, time is a basic quality and velocity is defined in terms of it (velocity = distance/time). Within relativity theory, in contrast, time and velocity are defined in terms of each other, with neither concept more basic. Einstein wanted to know whether understanding of either or both concepts was present from birth or if children understood one before the other.

FIGURE 2.3 The three-mountains problem. The child's task is to indicate how the display would look to someone viewing it from a perspective other than her own (after Piaget & Inhelder, 1969).

Almost 20 years later, Piaget (1946a, 1946b) published a two-volume, five hundred-page reply to Einstein's question. The gist of Piaget's answer was that mastery of all three concepts emerged simultaneously during the concrete operations period.

To test this view, Piaget presented a task involving two toy trains running along parallel tracks in the same direction. After the cars stopped moving, Piaget asked, "Which train traveled for the longer time (or the faster speed, or the farther distance)?" Most 4- and 5-year-olds focused entirely on a single feature, usually the stopping point. They chose the train that stopped farther down the track as having traveled faster, for the longer time, and for the greater distance. Stated differently, they ignored when the trains started, when they stopped, and the total time for which they traveled. Not until roughly age 9 did they answer correctly.

The example illustrates another of the basic qualities of children's thinking in the preoperational period. They tend to focus on static states rather than transformations. The point where each train ended constitutes a static position, readily perceivable and available for repeated inspection. The time, speed, and distance traveled are more transitory. The dimensions on which preoperational period children focus usually are static states; the dimensions they ignore usually involve transformations.

Thus, Piaget viewed 2- to 6-year-olds as having difficulty taking perspectives other than their own, as paying too much attention to perceptually salient dimensions and ignoring less salient ones, and as representing static states but not transformations. All of these descriptions suggest that such young children think about the world too simply and rigidly. They largely surmount these limitations in the next period of development.

THE CONCRETE OPERATIONS PERIOD (ROUGHLY 6 OR 7 YEARS TO 11 OR 12 YEARS)

The central development in the concrete operations period is the acquisition of *operations*. These operations are mental representations of dynamic as well as static aspects of the environment. All development up to this time has been a prelude to this achievement. In the sensorimotor period, children learned to operate physically on the environment. In the preoperational period, they learned to mentally represent static states. Finally, in the concrete operations period, they become able to represent transformations as well as static states.

The importance of operations can most easily be illustrated in the context of conservation problems. Consider children's understanding of three types of conservation: liquid quantity, solid quantity, and number. Although these conservation problems differ among themselves in certain respects, all share a basic three-phase procedure (Figure 2.4). In the first phase, children see two or more identical objects or sets of objects: two identical rows of checkers, two identical glasses of water, two identical clay cylinders, and so on. Once the children agree

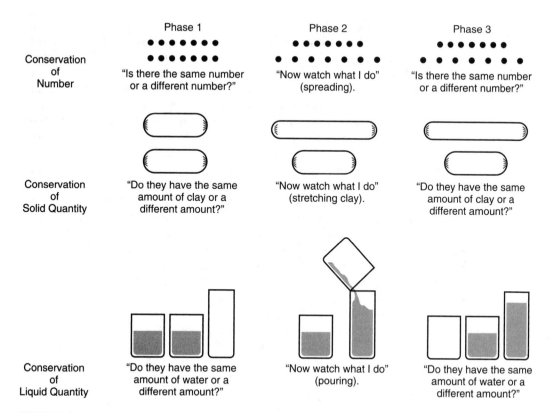

	Phase 1	Phase 2	Phase 3

Conservation of Number — "Is there the same number or a different number?" / "Now watch what I do" (spreading). / "Is there the same number or a different number?"

Conservation of Solid Quantity — "Do they have the same amount of clay or a different amount?" / "Now watch what I do" (stretching clay). / "Do they have the same amount of clay or a different amount?"

Conservation of Liquid Quantity — "Do they have the same amount of water or a different amount?" / "Now watch what I do" (pouring). / "Do they have the same amount of water or a different amount?"

FIGURE 2.4 Procedures used to test children's understanding of conservation of number, solid quantity, and liquid quantity.

that the two are equal on some dimension, such as the number of objects, the second phase begins. Here, one object or set of objects is transformed in a way that changes its appearance but does not affect the dimension of interest. Children might see the row of checkers lengthened, the water poured into a different-shaped glass, the clay cylinder remolded into a ball, and so on. Finally, in the third phase, children are asked whether the dimension of interest, which they earlier said was equal for the two choices, remains equal following the transformation of one of them. The correct answer invariably is "yes."

These problems seem trivially easy to adults and older children. However, almost all 5-year-olds answer them incorrectly. On number conservation problems, they claim that the longer row has more checkers (regardless of the actual numbers in each row). On conservation of liquid quantity problems, they claim that the glass with the taller column of liquid has more (regardless of the cross-sectional areas of the glasses). On conservation of solid quantity problems, they believe that the longer sausage has more clay (again regardless of the cross-sectional areas).

Considering what children need to do to solve conservation problems makes the 5-year-olds' difficulty understandable. They must mentally represent the spreading, pouring, or remolding transformation involved in the problem. They also must not focus all their attention on the perceptually salient dimension of height or length; they need to consider cross-sectional area and density as well. Finally, they need to realize that even though the transformed object may seem to have more of the dimension in question, it might not. That is, they need to understand that their own perspective can be misleading. Each of these is difficult for 5-year-olds to do.

In the concrete operations stage, children master all three conservation problems. They also master the train problem that was used to measure understanding of time, distance, and velocity. Piaget explained their mastery of these and many other concepts in terms of the children's now possessing mental operations. These operations allow them to represent transformations as well as static states.

Children's explanations of their reasoning on conservation problems are especially revealing. When 5-year-olds are asked to explain why the amount of water has changed, they regularly say that the water in the new glass is higher. When 8-year-olds are asked to explain why the amount of water remains the same, they point to the nature of the transformation ("You just poured it"), to changes in the less striking dimension offsetting the changes in the more striking one ("The water in this one is taller, but the water in that one is wider"), to the water looking different but really being the same, and to the reversible nature of the operation ("You could pour it back and it would be the same"). Interestingly, 5-year-olds will grant many of these points, but do not see them as implying that the two glasses have the same amount of water.

Although children in the concrete operations period become capable of solving many problems, certain types of abstract reasoning remain beyond them. Some of these problems require reasoning about propositions that are contrary to fact ("If people could know the future, would they be happier than they are now?"). Others involve treating their own thinking as something to be thought about. To quote one adolescent, "I was thinking about my future, and then I began to wonder why I was thinking about my future, and then I began to think about why I was thinking about why I was thinking about my future" (Mussen, Conger, Kagan, & Geiwitz, 1979). Still others involve thinking about abstract scientific concepts such as force, inertia, torque, and acceleration. These types of ideas become possible in the formal operations period.

THE FORMAL OPERATIONS PERIOD (ROUGHLY 11 OR 12 YEARS ONWARD)

Perhaps the most striking development during the formal operations period is that adolescents begin to see the particular reality in which they live as only one of an infinite number of imaginable realities. This leads at least some of them to think about alternative organizations of the world and about deep questions concerning meaning, truth, justice, and morality. As Inhelder and Piaget (1958) put it, "Each one has his own ideas (and usually he believes they are his own) which liberate him from childhood and allow him to place himself as the equal of adults" (pp. 340–341). From this perspective, it is no coincidence that many people first acquire a taste for science fiction during adolescence.

Many of the differences between formal and concrete operational reasoners are evident in Inhelder and Piaget's (1958) descriptions of children's and adolescents' approaches to the chemical combinations problem. The task involved four beakers, each with a particular chemical solution, and a "special" beaker with an unknown mixture of one or more of the other chemicals in it. When another chemical was added to the special beaker, the solution turned yellow. The children were asked to determine which of the four chemicals were in the solution that turned yellow and what role each played.

Concrete operational children typically generated several pairs of the chemicals, then tried all four together, and then generated a few of the possible sets of three. They often repeated combinations they already had tried and left out other combinations altogether. In contrast, formal operational children first devised a plan for systematically generating all possible combinations of the chemicals. Then they used their plan to generate each combination without redundancies or omissions.

The formal operational reasoners' more systematic approach also helped them draw a more appropriate conclusion about when and why the yellow color appeared. Concrete operations children often stopped collecting evidence after they found a single combination that turned the solution yellow. They concluded that it must have been the original solution and that all chemicals in it were necessary for the reaction to occur. In contrast, formal operations children, who tried all possible combinations, eventually learned that two different combinations produced the yellow color. What these combinations had in common was the presence of two of the chemicals and the absence of a third. (The absence of the third chemical was what distinguished the two instances that did turn yellow from two others that had both necessary chemicals in them but that did not turn yellow.) Therefore, the formal operational reasoners reached the correct conclusion that two of the chemicals were necessary to produce the change in color, that a third would prevent it from happening even if the first two were present, and that the fourth had no effect. Their focusing on the system of possible combinations allowed them to obtain the relevant data and to interpret it appropriately.

Some of the largest changes in thinking during the formal operations period involve logical and scientific reasoning (Moshman, 1998). The abstract and systematic thinking that develop especially greatly during the formal operations period are particularly crucial in such contexts. Scientific and logical reasoning problems often require applying the most abstract ways of thinking to the most challenging problems. Not surprisingly, Piaget viewed such formal operations as the culmination of the process of cognitive development, the fruition of all that had developed before.

The Development of Some Critical Concepts

The broad sweep of Piaget's descriptions of children's thinking emerges most clearly in his accounts of the development of particular concepts. Some concepts for which his descriptions are especially interesting are conservation, classes, and relations. He traced the development of each of these from their earliest origins in the sensorimotor period, through more refined versions in the preoperational and concrete operational periods, to the most sophisticated understandings in the formal operations period. People do not usually think of infants' thinking as having anything to do with that of teenagers. Part of Piaget's genius was that he saw the connection.

CONSERVATION

Conservation in the sensorimotor period. During the sensorimotor period, children acquire a simple but crucial part of the conservation concept. This might be labeled "conservation of existence," though Piaget called it *object permanence*. Adults know that objects do not just disappear from the world (although they sometimes seem to). If we want a ball and it rolls behind another object, we search for it and remove barriers if necessary to get it. Piaget observed that infants younger than 8 months do not search like this; they simply turn their attention to something else. He did not attribute this to their losing interest or being too poorly coordinated to retrieve the object. Instead, he advanced the more radical view that they did not understand that the objects still existed. He further argued that full understanding of object permanence required the entire sensorimotor period.

In Substage 1, from birth to 1 month, infants look at objects directly in front of them. However, if an object moves away, they do not follow it with their eyes. Thus, an infant will look at her mother's face when it is directly above, but will stop looking if the mother moves aside. In Substage 2, between 1 and 4 months, infants prolong their looking at the place where an object disappeared, but do not follow its movement. If they are playing with a toy and drop it, they continue looking at their hand rather than at the floor. In Substage 3, between about 4 and 8 months, they anticipate where moving objects will go, and look for them there if they are partially visible. However, if the object is completely covered, they do not attempt to retrieve it (as illustrated in the quotation at the beginning of this chapter).

In Substage 4, between 8 and 12 months, infants begin to search for objects behind or under barriers. This indicates that they realize that objects have a permanent existence. Under certain circumstances, however, 8- to 12-month-olds make an interesting mistake. If they see an object hidden twice in succession under the same container, they retrieve the object from there each time. If they then see the same object hidden under a different container, however, they look under the container where they found it before, rather than under the one where it is now. It is as if this original container had assumed an independent status as a hiding place where the object can be found. This error has been termed the "A-not-B" error.

In Substage 5, roughly between 12 and 18 months, infants stop making the A-not-B error and search wherever they last saw the object hidden. However, they remain unable to deal efficiently with transformations in which the desired object cannot be directly perceived. When a toy is first hidden under a cover, and then the toy and cover together are hidden under a pillow, and then the cover is removed so that the toy remains under the pillow, 12- to 18-month-olds do not look under the pillow. By Substage 6, however, between 18 and 24 months, babies understand even this type of complex displacement and immediately search in the right place.

At first glance, Piaget's account of object permanence may seem extremely improbable. It may seem more likely that the infants younger than 8 months fail to search for objects either because they are not sufficiently well coordinated to do so or because they quickly lose interest in the objects. An experiment by Bower and Wishart (1972), however, rendered unlikely both of these possibilities. Five-month-olds saw a toy hidden under a transparent cup. The large majority of infants retrieved it. Then the infants saw the same toy hidden under an opaque cup. Only 2 of 16 retrieved it. This experiment ruled out both motoric immaturity and lack of motivation as explanations for the infants' failure to search under the opaque cup. If they lacked sufficient interest in the toy to retrieve it, or failed because they lacked the necessary coordination, why were they interested and coordinated enough to retrieve the same object when it was hidden under the transparent cup?

Conservation in the preoperational and concrete operational periods. In the sensorimotor period, infants come to realize that the existence of objects is conserved over certain types of transformations, specifically, ones in which the object is hidden. In the preoperational and concrete operational periods, children come to realize that certain qualities of objects also are conserved even when transformations change their appearance. Spreading out objects increases the length of the row but leaves unchanged the number of objects. Pouring water from a typical glass to a taller, thinner one changes the height of the liquid column but leaves unchanged the amount of water. By the end of the concrete operational period, children realize that even when transformations alter appearances, a great many tangible dimensions are conserved: number, amount, length, weight, area, and so on.

Conservation in the formal operational period. During the formal operations period, adolescents come to understand complex forms of conservation that involve transformations of transformations. One such concept is conservation of motion. Inhelder and Piaget (1958) studied children's and adolescents' understanding of this concept by presenting them with a spring-powered plunger that shot balls of various sizes. The task was to predict where the balls would stop, to explain why some balls stop earlier than others, and to explain why balls stop at all.

Performance on this problem at various ages illustrates the types of reasoning that Piaget thought were fundamental at those ages. Preoperational children focus on only one dimension and take only one perspective. They might consistently predict that a big ball will go farther because it is stronger. Concrete operational children realize that multiple dimensions are important and take multiple perspectives. They might realize the importance of qualities of the surface on which the ball rolls, as well as of the ball itself. They also might recognize that the problem can be thought of in terms of what makes the ball stop, as well as what makes it go. Thus, they might believe that bigger balls go farther, but also that rougher surfaces lead to balls going less far.

By the formal operations period, children think of the problem in terms of sophisticated scientific concepts, such as conservation of motion. That is, they conceptualize the problem in idealized terms ("If there were no air resistance or friction . . ."). This way of thinking is a distinctive achievement of formal operations, because it involves conservation of a dimension—motion—that itself involves a transformation—movement through space. In addition, it illustrates how adolescents proceed from the actual to the possible, since no one has experienced an environment without air resistance or friction.

CLASSES AND RELATIONS

Another of Piaget's insights was seeing the connection between children's understanding of classes and relations. This connection can be illustrated with regard to numbers. What does it mean when we say that a girl understands the concept "three"? One part of the understanding is seeing what three balls, three cars, and three spoons have in common—that they are all members of the class of three-member sets. She also should understand the relation of this class to other classes—larger than sets with two members and smaller than sets with four. Piaget viewed children as originally thinking of classes and relations as separate ideas, but eventually integrating them into a unified understanding.

Understanding of classes and relations in the sensorimotor period. Piaget contended that infants classify objects according to the objects' functions. He illustrated this point by describing his daughter Lucienne's reaction to a plastic parrot that sat atop her bassinet. Lucienne liked to make the parrot move by kicking her feet while lying in the bassinet. At six months of age, she made similar kicking motions when she was out of the bassinet but still could see the parrot. Piaget interpreted this as Lucienne classifying the parrot as "something that swings when I kick my feet." Far more sophisticated categories are seen as evolving from such simple classifications.

Understanding of relations, like understanding of classes, is seen as developing out of sensorimotor actions. Piaget described his three children at 3 and 4 months as being greatly amused by the relation between the vigor of their actions and the strength of the reaction they produced. More vigorous kicking produced more vigorous swinging of objects on the bassinet; more vigorous shaking of a rattle produced louder noises; and so on. Thus, they understand the relation "the more vigorously I do something, the larger its effect."

Understanding of classes and relations in the preoperational period. Children progress considerably in classificatory ability during the preoperational period. This progress is evident when they are asked to put together a group of blocks varying in size, color, and shape. Early in the preoperational period, a boy might try to put together all of the small objects, and therefore choose a small red square, then a small blue square, then a small red triangle. However, the fact that the last object was a triangle might grab his attention, leading him to add a large red triangle and a large green triangle, thus creating a group without any unifying characteristic. Not until later in the preoperational period, around age 4 or 5 years, do children come to classify on a consistent basis. At this point, they put all small objects into one group and all big ones into another.

Although children learn to solve this type of problem during the preoperational period, other classification problems remain difficult. The limitations of their reasoning are most evident when they simultaneously need to consider competing bases of classification, as in Piaget's *class inclusion problem*. On such problems, children might be presented eight toy animals, six of them cats and two dogs. They then would be asked, "Are there more cats or more animals?" Most children below age 7 or 8 answer that there are more cats, despite the number of cats inherently being less than or equal to the number of animals.

Piaget saw this behavior as stemming from preoperational children's tendency to focus on a single dimension to the exclusion of others. To solve the problem correctly, children need to keep in mind that an object (for example, Garfield) may simultaneously belong both to a subset (cats) and to a superset (animals). They find this difficult. Therefore, they reinterpret the question in a way that allows them to solve a problem that they do understand: whether there are more cats or more animals other than cats. This leads them to compare the number of cats to the number of dogs and thus to say that there are more cats than animals.

Children's understanding of relations also grows considerably during the preoperational stage. However, their ability to focus on the relation that is relevant in the particular situation, and to screen out irrelevant ones, remains limited. To illustrate both the growth and the remaining deficiencies, Piaget (1952) presented to preoperational children the type of *seriation problem* shown in Figure 2.5. He asked them to arrange the sticks from shortest to longest in a

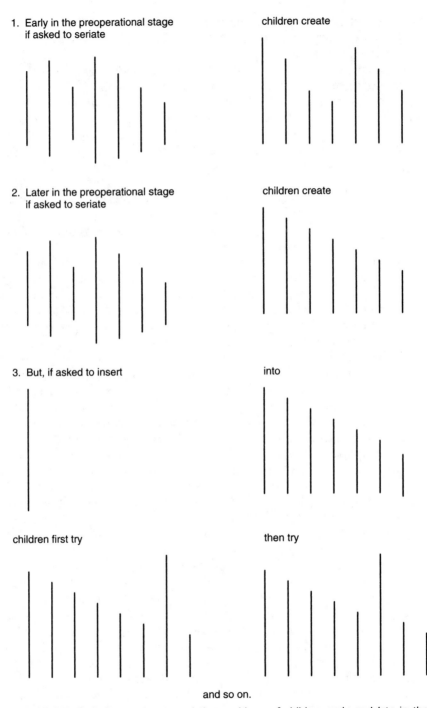

1. Early in the preoperational stage if asked to seriate

children create

2. Later in the preoperational stage if asked to seriate

children create

3. But, if asked to insert

into

children first try

then try

and so on.

FIGURE 2.5 Typical responses to seriation problems of children early and late in the preoperational stage.

single row. If they succeeded at this task, he presented them a second problem. Here they needed to insert a new stick of medium length at the appropriate point in the row they had made.

Early in the preoperational stage, between ages 2 and 4, children encounter great difficulty creating correct orderings. As in the first row of Figure 2.5, they might arrange two subsets of the sticks correctly, but not integrate the two into a single overall ordering. The shifting focus is similar to that shown when they first grouped together several small objects and then, after encountering a small triangle, started putting all triangles in the group.

Later in the preoperational stage, children can correctly order the lengths of the original set of sticks. However, they often fail to find the correct place to insert the additional stick without extensive trial and error. Piaget attributed this remaining difficulty to preoperational children's difficulty in simultaneously viewing the new stick as smaller than one stick and larger than another quite similar in size.

Understanding of classes and relations in the concrete operational period.
Piaget contended that in the concrete operational period, children come to treat classes and relations as a single, unified system. Their attempts to solve *multiple classification problems* illustrate this development. Consider the problem in Figure 2.6. Children see intersecting rows of stimuli that vary along two dimensions, in this case shape (square, circular, or oblong) and color (black, white, or gray). The task is to choose an object to put in the blank space so that all nine objects are ordered along the two dimensions. This requires identifying the two relevant classes (shape and color) and choosing an object that maintains the relations among objects already established within the rows and columns of the matrix.

Inhelder and Piaget (1964) reported that 4- to 6-year-olds selected objects that included at least one of the desired dimensions on 85 percent of problems. However, they chose the single object that included both desired dimensions on only 15 percent. By 9 or 10 years of age, the large majority of children choose the object that maintains both dimensions, revealing an ability to consider classes and relations together.

Understanding of classes and relations in the formal operational period.
Formal operational reasoning enables adolescents to think about relations among relations and about classes of classes. For example, they might first divide the students in their high school into a number of classes (nerds, jocks, skaters, preppies, druggies, etc.), and then construct higher-order classes of the groups whose members tend to be friends with each other (such as preppies and jocks).

Formal operational reasoning also leads adolescents to interpret observed outcomes within the context of logically possible outcomes. This type of reasoning was illustrated in the description of the chemical combinations problem earlier in the chapter. Formal operational reasoners not only planned a way

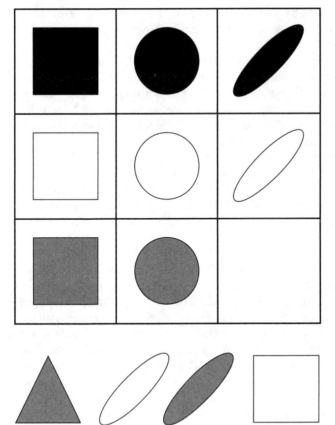

FIGURE 2.6   Type of matrix used to test children's understanding of multiple classification. The task was to decide which of the four objects at the bottom belonged in the empty square in the matrix (after Inhelder & Piaget, 1964).

to generate all possible combinations of the chemicals but also interpreted the results in terms of all of the outcomes, not just the ones where the event of interest (the yellow color) occurred. This led them to realize that although two chemicals were both present whenever the yellow color appeared, their presence was not sufficient to produce the color change, because in two other cases both were present and the solution remained clear. From this, they deduced that the color change reflected the absence of a third chemical as well as the presence of the two others.

A chronological summary.   It is easy to become confused among the numerous developmental changes Piaget described. Table 2.2 places some of the most important changes in relation to each other and may create a better feel for which types of changes occur when in development.

TABLE 2.2   Children's Thinking at Different Ages: The Piagetian Model

Stage of Development	Relevant Age Range	Typical Achievements and Limitations
Sensorimotor Period (Birth to 2 years)	Birth to 1 month	Modification of reflexes to make them more adaptive.
	1 to 4 months	Primary circular reactions and coordination of actions.
	4 to 8 months	Secondary circular reactions. No searching for hidden objects.
	8 to 12 months	Coordination of secondary circular reactions. Baby retrieves hidden objects but continues searching where objects were previously found rather than where they were last hidden.
	12 to 18 months	Tertiary circular reactions. Baby systematically varies heights from which he or she drops things.
	18 to 24 months	Beginning of true mental representations. Deferred imitation.
Preoperational Period (2 to 7 years)	2 to 4 years	Development of symbolic capacities. Growth of language and mental imagery. Egocentric communication.
	4 to 7 years	Good language and mental imagery skills. Inability to represent transformations. Child focuses on single perceptual dimension in conservation, class inclusion, time, seriation, and other problems.
Concrete Operational Period (7 to 12 years)	Whole period	Child can perform true mental operations, represent transformations as well as static states, and solve conservation, class inclusion, time, and many other problems. Child still has difficulty thinking of all possible combinations, as in the chemical problem, and of transformations of transformations.
Formal Operational Period (12 years through the rest of life)	Whole period	Adolescent can think about all possible outcomes, interpret particular events in terms of their relation to hypothetical events, and understand abstract concepts such as conservation of motion and chemical interactions.

An Evaluation of Piaget's Theory

How can we evaluate this rich and diverse theory of cognitive development? Some of the strengths of the theory were mentioned at the outset of the chapter. It provides us with a good feel for what children's thinking is like at different points in development. It addresses questions that have intrigued parents, teachers, philosophers, and scientists for hundreds of years. It surveys a remarkably broad spectrum of developments in children's thinking and covers the entire age span from infancy through adolescence. It includes countless surprising observations of how children think.

With these general virtues in mind, we can consider three more specific questions. How accurately does the theory describe the particulars of children's thinking at different ages? How useful are its stages as descriptions and explanations of children's thinking? How valid are its general characterizations of children's thinking, such as the claim that preoperational children are egocentric?

HOW ACCURATELY DOES THE THEORY DESCRIBE PARTICULAR ASPECTS OF CHILDREN'S THINKING?

Piaget's theory makes many specific claims about how children think and reason at different ages. How have these claims held up in the face of subsequent research?

The most basic issue for any scientific theory is whether other people can replicate the findings on which the theory is based. Piaget's observations were so surprising that many early experiments were conducted simply to replicate them. These replication experiments used larger, more representative samples of children and more standardized versions of Piaget's tasks, but otherwise closely resembled his approach.

In general, the attempts to replicate were successful. Larger samples of American, British, Canadian, Australian aboriginal, and Chinese children tested in the 1960s and 1970s showed the same type of reasoning that Piaget's small samples of Swiss children had shown almost half a century earlier (Corman & Escalona, 1969; Dasen, 1973; Dodwell, 1960; Elkind, 1961a, 1961b; Goodnow, 1962; Lovell, 1961; Uzgiris, 1964). Children in non-Western societies reached the stages at older ages than children in Western societies, but when they did reach the stages they showed the expected type of reasoning. This was especially true for the sensorimotor, preoperational, and concrete operational periods. Formal operational reasoning seems to be exhibited by some adolescents, but only by a minority of them, even in advanced societies, at least on the scientific reasoning problem typically used to assess formal operations (Byrnes, 1988; Kuhn, Garcia-Mila, Zohar, & Andersen 1995).

Can we accept these replications at face value? Perhaps the immature reasoning that children display in many situations is due not to their reasoning being immature, but rather to the verbal methods used both by Piaget and by the replication studies underestimating their knowledge. Critics of such methods argue that young children's inarticulateness often creates a falsely pessimistic impression of their cognitive capabilities (e.g., Brainerd, 1978). Just because children cannot explain their reasoning does not mean that the reasoning itself is deficient.

It now is apparent, however, that young children show similar reasoning when tested with nonverbal versions of Piaget's tasks. Siegler carried out one such series of experiments in which a nonverbal method was used to examine a number of Piaget's tasks, including balance scale problems; time, speed, and distance problems; and conservation of liquid quantity, solid quantity, and number problems (Siegler, 1976, 1978, 1981; Siegler & Richards, 1979). On each of these tasks, children reasoned much as would have been expected from Piaget's descriptions.

A third question is whether children possess conceptual understanding not revealed by Piaget's experiments. Here the situation is different. Throughout development, children seem to have basic understandings not evident in their performance on Piaget's problems. Many of the demonstrations of children's early understandings have been extremely clever.

Consider Baillargeon's (1987) experiment on object permanence. Piaget claimed that infants younger than 8 months do not realize that objects continue to exist when they disappear from view. Baillargeon developed a more sensitive measure that showed that even with infants as young as 4 months, out of sight does not mean totally out of mind. Her experiment involved placing a box behind a wooden board (Figure 2.7). An axle went horizontally through the middle of the board so that pushing the board made it swing. At first, the board was in a position where the box was clearly visible. Then, the experimenter set the board swinging, which hid the box from the child's line of sight. In the physically possible condition, the swinging board reached the box, which was near the apex of its swing anyway, and then swung the other way. In the physically impossible condition, the board appeared to swing right through the place where the box had been. (This effect was accomplished with trick lighting and mirrors.) Despite the box's not being visible anymore, the 4-month-olds behaved as if they were surprised when they saw the seemingly impossible event. They looked much longer than they did when the physically possible event occurred. They apparently thought the board's swinging should be impeded by the box, even when they could not see it.

The results are not unique to this particular method. Baillargeon (1993) demonstrated that 3½-month-olds showed similar surprise when the upper half of a rabbit seemed to disappear as the rabbit moved across a window where, if not for trickery, it would have been visible. In other experiments, she has shown that infants can represent as many as three hidden objects simultaneously, and that they can represent not only the fact that an object continues to exist, but also its approximate height and location. Thus, children as young as 4 months possess some understanding of object permanence.

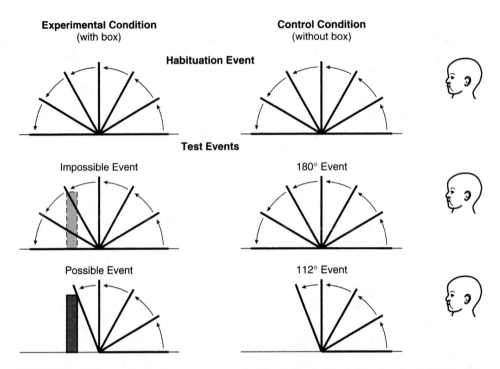

FIGURE 2.7 Baillargeon's object permanence task. After being habituated to the drawbridge swinging through 180 degrees, and seeing the barrier placed in its path, infants look longer at the impossible event, where the drawbridge seems to rotate through the space occupied by the now-hidden
barrier, than at the possible event, where it stops at the barrier's location (after Baillargeon, 1987).
Copyright © 1987 by the American Psychological Association. Reprinted with permission.

The demonstrations of earlier-than-predicted cognitive competence are
not limited to sensorimotor acquisitions. Preschoolers also show rudimentary
understanding of concepts that Piaget believed were too advanced for them.
Consider conservation of taste and of weight. Piaget believed that both of these
concepts were too difficult for preoperational stage children. However, when
3- to 5-year-olds see sugar dissolved in a cup of water, most believe that despite
the sugar not being visible, the water will taste sweet, that it will continue to
taste sweet in the future, and that it will weigh more than it did when no sugar
was in the cup (Au, Sidle, & Rollins, 1993). To explain their views, the 3- to
5-year-olds advanced explanations indicating that the sugar still exists in tiny
invisible particles that influence the taste and weight of the solution even
though it looks identical to the solution with no sugar. Thus, children in the
preoperational stage do have some understanding of conservation of taste and
of weight.

The discovery of unsuspected cognitive strengths in infants and young
children has been one of the leading stories in recent research in cognitive

development. It is interesting to consider why these competencies are being discovered now. One reason is the development of clever new methods for finding out what children understand. Another reason is that a broader range of children's thinking is being considered. The research of Gelman and her colleagues illustrates this trend (Gelman, 1990; Gelman & Gallistel, 1978; Miller & Gelman, 1983). Piaget focused on preschoolers' frequent failures on number conservation tasks and concluded that they do not grasp the concept of number. Gelman's research indicated that whether or not preschoolers grasp the concept of number, they know a great deal about numbers. They count accurately, and in a way that suggests understanding of the principles underlying counting; they know the effects that addition and subtraction have on small collections of objects; they know which numbers are bigger and which smaller; and so on.

The number of insightful demonstrations of early competence is too large to review in any detail here. Examples include work on children's understanding of causality (Ahn, Kalish, Medin, & Gelman, 1995; Oakes & Cohen, 1995), categorization (Arterberry & Bornstein, 2002; Mareschal & Quinn, 2001; Rakison & Oakes, 2003) space (Blades & Spencer, 1994; Huttenlocher, Newcombe, & Sandberg, 1994; Newcombe, Huttenlocher, & Learmonth, 1999), time (Colombo & Richman, 2002; Friedman, 2002), and properties of objects (Goubet & Clifton, 1998; Kotovsky & Baillargeon, 1994; Needham, 2001; Spelke, Breinlinger, Macomber, & Jacobson, 1992). In short, although Piaget's observations reveal a great deal about how young children think, and although they can be replicated using both verbal and nonverbal methods, they often underestimate the children's competence.

How Stagelike Is Children's Thinking?

Stage models such as Piaget's imply that children's thinking changes qualitatively from one stage to another; that within any one stage, their reasoning is similar across diverse problems; and that they are unable to learn to think in ways associated with the next higher stage until they are near that stage or in it (Brainerd, 1978; Flavell, 1971). How well do these characterizations fit what is known today about children's thinking?

Qualitative changes. Whether children's thinking undergoes qualitative change depends in large part on how closely you look at it. When viewed from afar, many changes in children's thinking appear discontinuous; when viewed from close up, the same changes often appear as part of a continuous, gradual progression. Again, the development of object permanence can be used to illustrate the general point. As noted previously, infants younger than 7 or 8 months often do not reach for objects when they see them hidden. Under the same conditions, older infants almost always do reach for the objects. Piaget interpreted these results to mean that the older infants understand that objects have a permanent existence and that the younger ones do not.

Newer evidence suggests a different interpretation—that the change is not as sudden as Piaget believed. Infants as young as 6 months succeed on the classic Piagetian object permanence task if allowed to reach immediately after the object is hidden. The longer that infants must wait before trying to get the object, the older they must be before they reach for it (Diamond, 1985). Gradual improvements in memory for the locations of hidden objects, rather than a sudden insight that objects continue to exist, seems to underlie the change.

Even if we believe that infants experience some type of insight that elevates their understanding of the continued existence of hidden objects, it is still clear that after this insight, they continue to expand their ability to locate such objects. Reaching for objects that have been placed under opaque containers is part of a more general cognitive trend—improved skill in searching the physical environment for lost or hidden objects. These search skills develop over a long period; even 4-year-olds err on some hidden object problems. Further, when older children err, their mistakes parallel those of younger children. When presented with three, rather than two, potential hiding places, infants, 1-year-olds, and 4-year-olds most often make the same type of errors. They look at locations where they have found the object previously, rather than locations where they never have found it. The frequency of errors declines, but the type of errors remains the same. (For interesting articles on young children's abilities to search physical environments and find hidden objects, see Baker-Ward & Ornstein, 1988; DeLoache, 1987, 1991, 2000; DeLoache, Miller, & Rosengren, 1997; Spencer, Smith, & Thelen, 2001.)

A branch of mathematics known as *catastrophe theory* provides justification for viewing development as both continuous and discontinuous. Catastrophe theory examines sudden changes such as the collapse of bridges. The forces that lead to bridges collapsing often build up slowly over a period of years. The visible collapse, however, can be breathtakingly sudden. Analogously, despite the seeming abruptness of cognitive progress when a boy solves a problem one day that he could not solve the day before, the progress may be based on years of gradually improving understanding. In the boy, as in the bridge, the change can be viewed as either a continuous process of small, invisible alterations or as a discontinuous shift from one state to another.

Similar reasoning on different problems. Saying that children are in a certain stage of reasoning implies that their reasoning across many tasks shares that stage's characteristics. Within Piaget's theory, an 8-year-old ideally would grasp all concrete-operations-level concepts—conservation of liquid quantity, class inclusion, seriation, and so on—and would fail to grasp all formal-operations-level concepts—thinking in terms of all possible combinations, conservation of motion, and so on.

It has become increasingly clear that this view does not accurately characterize children's thinking. Consider three concrete-operations-level concepts: conservation of number, conservation of solid quantity, and conservation of weight. Theoretically, all of these should be mastered simultaneously; a child should understand either all or none of them. Actually, however, most children master Piaget's number conservation task at around age 6, his solid quantity conservation task at around age 8, and his weight conservation task at around age 10 (Elkind, 1961a; Katz & Beilin, 1976; Miller, 1976). These data do not support the idea of concurrent development, even within the concept of conservation.

Despite the evidence against the view that children generally reason similarly across many problems, consistencies of reasoning across tasks continue to be of great interest. The motivation is rooted in everyday observations of children's reasoning. There seems to be something characteristic in 2-year-olds' reasoning that distinguishes it from 5-year-olds'; something in 5-year-olds' reasoning that distinguishes it from 10-year-olds'; and so on. That is, children of a given age do seem to reason in a characteristic way in different contexts.

In one attempt to address the issue, Flavell (1982) hypothesized that the amount of consistency of reasoning across tasks may depend on when we observe the reasoning. Children seem to reason more similarly across different concepts when they are just beginning to understand them than when they understand them better. For example, 5-year-olds solve a large variety of problems that they are just beginning to understand by identifying a single relevant dimension of the problem and focusing on it. On conservation of liquid quantity, they predict that whichever glass has the taller liquid column also has more water, regardless of the cross-sectional areas. On conservation of solid quantity, they predict that whichever clay sausage is longer also has more clay, again regardless of the cross-sectional areas. In judging which side of a balance scale will tip, they rely entirely on relative amounts of weight, ignoring distance of the weights from the fulcrum. They exhibit similar reasoning with concepts as diverse as temperature, happiness, and morality (Case, 1985, 1992a; Ferretti, Butterfield, Cahn, & Kerkman, 1985; Levin, Wilkening, & Dembo, 1984; Siegler, 1981; Strauss, 1982).

In contrast, the ages at which children solve these problems correctly varies a great deal. Even 9-year-olds generally can solve conservation of liquid and solid quantity problems; even college students often cannot solve balance scale problems. Differing amounts of experience with the problems, differences in the ease of drawing analogies to better-understood problems, and differences in the complexity of the most advanced solution strategies contribute to these differences in age of mastery.

Another potential source of consistency in children's reasoning is the level of their most advanced reasoning (Fischer, 1980; Fischer & Bidell, 1991; Halford, 1982, 1993). For example, the most advanced thinking of 9-year-olds might involve single operations. This would mean that none of their thinking involves operations on operations (as in the formal operations period). However, it would not mean that they solve correctly all problems that can be solved using single operations. Whether they solve a given problem depends on how much experience they have had with it, whether they were familiar with related problems, whether it occurred in a familiar context, and so on. In sum, unities in children's reasoning may be most apparent in their early reasoning, when they have little knowledge of the concepts involved, and in the level of the most advanced reasoning of which they are capable.

Can development be accelerated?   Piaget's views concerning the possibility of accelerating cognitive development through training are among his most controversial. Some of his comments indicate that no training could be successful. Others suggest that training might at times be effective, but only if the child already possesses some understanding of the concept and if the training procedure involves active interaction with materials.

In fact, young children can learn more than Piaget thought they could, and they can benefit from a greater variety of instructional techniques (Beilin, 1977; Field, 1987). The findings dovetail with the unsuspected early competence that children have been found to have even without training. Not only do children understand more than previously thought, they also can learn more.

However, it is important not to throw out the baby with the bathwater. Although young children can learn to solve these problems, they often find doing so exceptionally difficult. Older children who cannot yet solve the same problems typically learn them much more easily. It now is indisputable that young children can learn concepts once thought to be "too advanced" for their age group. What we still don't understand is why, when two children both don't understand a concept, the older child so often can learn it more easily.

How Well Do Piaget's General Characterizations Fit Children's Thinking?

In addition to describing children's thinking in terms of particular examples of their reasoning at particular stages (e.g., "Preoperational stage children think that the glass with the taller liquid column must have more water"), Piaget also characterized children's thinking in terms of intellectual traits. For example, he described preoperational stage children as being egocentric, precausal, semilogical, and perceptually oriented. These terms fit in some ways, but not in all. The characterization of preoperational children as egocentric illustrates many of the issues.

Recall from the discussion of egocentric communication and the cartoon of the two children talking past each other that 2- to 4-year-olds are not very skilled communicators. They often ignore what other people say to them, and they have trouble taking other people's viewpoints. These types of observations led Piaget to label their thinking "egocentric."

But in other situations, young children communicate non-egocentrically. If you ask 3-year-olds to show you their drawings, they hold the side with the artwork toward you. If they were completely egocentric, they would hold the drawing toward themselves, because they would assume that what they see is what you see. Similarly, even 2- and 3-year-olds practice deception. For example, Sullivan and Winner (1993) described a 2-year-old who feigned tears when his aunt would not play with him; when the aunt came over, the child said to his mother, "I tricked her. I made her think I was sad" (p. 160). If the 2-year-old believed that the aunt knew exactly what he knew, how could he "trick" her?

Similar demonstrations have shown that preschoolers' representations of space also are not entirely egocentric. To measure spatial egocentrism, Piaget used tasks such as the three mountains problem shown in Figure 2.3. Such problems require not only taking another perspective but also choosing between competing frames of reference: the one that children actually see and the one they are asked to imagine seeing from the other vantage point. Even adults find such choices between competing frames of reference to be difficult (Rieser, Garing, & Young, 1994). In contrast, when the competing frame of reference is eliminated (by covering the original arrangement), and children are given ways of expressing the concepts "left" and "right" (by putting a sticker on one of their hands and referring to the sticker side and the non-sticker side), even 3-year-olds can take spatial perspectives other than their own (Newcombe & Huttenlocher, 1992). This does not mean that they can take other people's perspectives as well as older children. After all, older children succeed on the three mountains task even when a competing frame of reference is present. The finding does mean, however, that under less demanding conditions, 3-year-olds can take perspectives other than their own.

Conversely, people well beyond the preoperational period continue to be "at risk" for egocentrism. A classic demonstration of this involved a situation analogous to a phone conversation. Two children were seated opposite each other at a table with a board between them; thus, they could not see each other. Each child was presented identical sets of pictures, with each picture containing an irregular design. The speaker had to describe one of the pictures so that the listener could figure out which one was being described (Krauss & Glucksberg, 1969).

Not surprisingly, older children communicate which picture they have in mind more effectively than younger ones. More surprising, even 8- and 9-year-olds often have difficulty overcoming their knowledge of what they are referring to sufficiently to generate a description that will allow the other child to understand. Further, children well beyond the preoperational period experience difficulty knowing who is to blame for the missed communication—whether the message is inadequate or whether the listener simply failed to respond properly to it. (See Beal & Belgrad, 1990; Lloyd, Mann, & Peers, 1998; Nadig & Sedivy, 2002; Robinson & Robinson, 1981; Sonnenschein, 1988; Waters & Tinsley, 1985, for discussions of egocentric communication.)

There seems little doubt that young children often behave more egocentrically than older ones. Labeling an age group "egocentric" is too strong, though. It leads us to ignore both the ways that younger children's thinking is not egocentric and the ways that older children's thinking is.

The Current Status of Piaget's Theory

If Piaget's theory underestimates young children's reasoning abilities, overestimates older children's reasoning abilities, and describes children's thinking in terms that are misleading as well as revealing, why pay so much attention to it? The simple reason is that with all of its shortcomings, the theory still gives us a good feel for how children think. It also points us in the right direction for learning more about children's thinking. Piaget recognized the intelligence in infants' early activities. In making these discoveries, he raised the issue of what additional capabilities infants might have, an issue that has led to many additional discoveries about infants' thinking. His estimate of the degree of unity in children's thinking was too high, but he discovered some important unities and pointed to the importance of searching for more of them. Finally, Piaget's basic questions are the right ones. What capabilities do infants possess at birth? What capabilities do they possess at later points in development? What processes lead to the remarkable increases in their understanding that occur with development? The remainder of this book is an attempt to answer these questions.

Summary

Piaget's theory remains a dominant force in developmental psychology, despite the fact that much of it was formulated half a century ago. Some of the reasons for its lasting appeal are the important acquisitions it describes, the large span of childhood it encompasses, and the reliability and charm of many of its observations.

At the most general level, Piaget's theory focused on the development of intelligence. The purpose of intellectual development was to allow children to adapt to the environment. This adaptation was achieved through generating progressively more accurate and encompassing representations of reality.

Piaget's general depiction included four stages of development: the *sensorimotor, preoperational, concrete operational,* and *formal operational* periods. The sensorimotor period occupies the age range between 0 and 2 years, the preoperational period between 2 and 6 or 7, the concrete operational period between 6 or 7 and 11 or 12, and the formal operational period from early adolescence to the end of life. Each period includes large changes in understanding of such important concepts as conservation, classification, and relations.

Piaget also identified three basic developmental processes: *assimilation, accommodation,* and *equilibration.* Assimilation refers to the means by which children interpret incoming information to make it understandable within their existing mental structures. Accommodation refers to the ways in which children's current understandings change in response to new experience. Equilibration is a three-step process that includes assimilation and accommodation. First, children are in a state of equilibrium. Then, failure to assimilate new information leads to their becoming aware of shortcomings in their current understanding. Finally, their mental structure accommodates to the new information in a way that creates a more advanced equilibrium.

During the sensorimotor period, infants acquire primary, secondary, and tertiary circular reactions, in which their actions become more deliberate and more systematic, and extend beyond their bodies. They also acquire a precursor of conservation—the object permanence concept—in which they realize that objects continue to exist even if they move out of sight. They also form simple understandings of classes and relations.

In the preoperational period, children become able to represent their ideas through language and mental imagery. Despite this development, Piaget primarily emphasized what preoperational children cannot do. He noted that 5-year-olds usually fail conservation, class inclusion, and seriation problems. He attributed such failures to the children's focusing on perceptual appearances rather than transformations, to their being egocentric, and to their centering on a single dimension rather than considering multiple dimensions simultaneously.

In the concrete operations period, children master these concepts and many others. They become able to represent transformations and to integrate multiple sources of information. These advances allow children to master such concepts as conservation of liquid and solid quantity, time, seriation, and class inclusion.

The formal operations period, according to Piaget, brings ability to think in terms of all possible outcomes and to view actual outcomes within this framework of logical possibilities. Children in this stage can perform systematic experiments, a skill made possible by sophisticated understanding of classes and relations. In sum, their reasoning comes to resemble that of scientists.

Piaget made a number of controversial statements about what children know at different points in development, about stages of development that they pass through, and about general characteristics of their thinking. When given either the original or nonverbal versions of Piaget's problems, children typically reason much as he described. However, they appear to have important cognitive capabilities that he did not detect.

Piaget's stage descriptions predict that children think in qualitatively different ways in different periods of development, that they reason similarly about diverse concepts, and that they cannot learn modes of thought much more advanced than those that characterize their current stage. Each of these views contains a certain amount of truth, but also has certain problems. When viewed from a distance, many developments appear to represent qualitative changes. However, when examined closely, the same changes often appear to be part of a gradual progression, with important precursors developing earlier and refinements and extensions continuing for years after. In general, the consistency of reasoning across tasks that Piaget predicted has not been found. However, considerable consistency has been apparent in children's early conceptual understanding. Young children do not learn as rapidly as older children, but it is nonetheless possible for them to acquire a great many concepts that are well beyond the understanding typical of children their age.

Piaget also described children in terms of general intellectual traits, such as egocentrism. These trait descriptions fit young children's thinking in many ways, but not in all. For example, although 5-year-olds are egocentric in some situations, they and even younger children behave nonegocentrically in other situations. Moreover, even older children and adults sometimes behave egocentrically. The trait descriptions thus seem to be in the right ballpark, but to gloss over exceptions. More generally, Piaget's theory continues to be of interest because it communicates a good feel for children's thinking and because it asks the right questions.

Recommended Readings

Brainerd, C.J. (Ed.) (1996). *PS* celebrates the centennial of Jean Piaget [special section]. *Psychological Science,* 7(4). This special issue was organized to honor Piaget on the 100th anniversary of his birth. The articles provide an overview of his life, his contributions and his legacies to the field of cognitive development.

Carey, S., & Gelman, R. (Eds.) (1991). *The epigenesis of mind: Essays on biology and cognition.* Hillsdale, NJ: Erlbaum. A group of leading researchers of cognitive development explore one of the issues that motivated Piaget's research—how biology and experience interact to produce cognitive growth—but with much more emphasis on innate and early-developing knowledge than in Piaget's theory.

Flavell, J.H. (1963). *The developmental psychology of Jean Piaget.* New York: Van Nostrand. The classic summary of Piaget's work from 1925–1960.

Moshman, D. (1998). Cognitive development beyond childhood. In D. Kuhn & R.S. Siegler (Eds.), *Handbook of child psychology: Vol. 2. Cognition, perception, & language* (5th ed.) New York: Wiley. A comprehensive review of the many changes in scientific and logical reasoning that take place during adolescence and afterward.

Piaget, J. (1952). *The child's concept of number.* New York: W. W. Norton. In this book, Piaget describes his classic experiments on class inclusion, seriation, conservation of liquid quantity, and conservation of number.

3

INFORMATION-PROCESSING THEORIES
OF DEVELOPMENT

Scene: Daughter and father in their yard. A playmate rides in on a bike.
  CHILD: *Daddy, would you unlock the basement door?*
  FATHER: *Why?*
    C: *Cause I want to ride my bike.*
    F: *Your bike is in the garage.*
    C: *But my socks are in the dryer. (Klahr, 1978, pp. 181–182)*

What thinking underlay this child's enigmatic comments? David Klahr, a prominent information-processing theorist, built the following model of the thinking that led to her initial request for him to unlock the basement door:

Top goal: I want to ride my bike.
  Constraint: I need shoes to ride comfortably.
  Fact: I'm barefoot.
    Subgoal 1: Get my sneakers.
    Fact: The sneakers are in the yard.
    Fact: They're uncomfortable on bare feet.
      Subgoal 2: Get my socks.
      Fact: The sock drawer was empty this morning.
      Inference: The socks probably are in the dryer.

> Subgoal 3: Get them from the dryer.
> Fact: The dryer is in the basement.
>   Subgoal 4: Go to the basement.
>   Fact: It's quicker to go through the yard entrance.
>   Fact: The yard entrance always is locked.
>   Subgoal 5: Unlock the door to the basement.
>   Fact: Daddies have the keys to everything.
>   Subgoal 6: Ask daddy to unlock the door.

As this example suggests, the information-processing approach to development speaks to the essential tension within children's thinking, the tension produced by children ceaselessly striving to reach their goals despite patchy knowledge, limited processing capacity, and obstacles posed by the external world. The particular strategy used in the story was means-ends analysis, which involves repeatedly comparing one's current state with one's goal and then taking steps to reduce the distance between them. In other situations, children use other strategies. To overcome their limited memory capacities, they use strategies such as rehearsal (repeating material over and over before recalling it, as when trying to remember a phone number). To overcome their limited knowledge, they use the tools provided by the culture in which they live: dictionaries, encyclopedias, calculators, the Internet, older children and adults who will answer their questions, and other devices and resources.

Information-processing theories of development vary among themselves, but they all share several basic assumptions. The most fundamental assumption is that *thinking is information processing.* Rather than focusing on stages of development, they focus on the information that children represent, the processes that they apply to the information, and the memory limits that constrain the amount of information they can represent and process. Cognitive growth is analyzed in terms of age-related and experience-related changes in these capabilities. Information-processing analyses generally are more precise than those of stage approaches; the detailed analysis of goals, subgoals, knowledge, and inferences within Klahr's model of his daughter's thinking is characteristic.

A second defining characteristic of information-processing theories of development is an emphasis on *precise analysis of change mechanisms.* Two critical goals are to identify the change mechanisms that contribute most to development and to specify exactly how these change mechanisms work together to produce cognitive growth. The flip side of this emphasis on how development occurs is an emphasis on the cognitive limits that prevent development from occurring more rapidly than it does. Thus, information-processing theories attempt to explain both how children of given ages have come as far as they have and why they have not gone further.

A third assumption of most information-processing approaches is that *change is produced by a process of continuous self-modification.* That is, the outcomes generated by the child's own activities change the way the child will think in the future. For example, in Shrager and Siegler's (1998) model of strategy choice, use of alternative strategies creates increasing knowledge concerning the effectiveness of each strategy which, in turn, changes the strategies that are used. Such self-modifying processes eliminate the need to account for special age-defined transition periods, as in Piaget's proposed transition from the concrete operations to the formal operations stage around age 12. Instead, children's thinking is viewed as continuously changing at all ages.

What is the relation of information-processing approaches to alternative views, such as the Piagetian approach? The two approaches have quite a bit in common. Both are aimed at answering the same fundamental questions: "What develops?" and "How does development occur?" Both try to identify children's cognitive capabilities and limits at various points in development. Both try to explain how later, more advanced understandings grow out of earlier, more primitive ones.

The two approaches also differ in important ways, though. Information-processing approaches place greater emphasis on the role of processing limitations, strategies for overcoming the limitations, and knowledge about specific content. There also is a greater emphasis on precise analyses of change and on the contribution of ongoing cognitive activity to that change. These differences have led to a greater use of formalisms, such as computer simulations and flow diagrams, which allow information-processing theorists to model in detail how thinking proceeds. Because of this focus on precise specification of cognitive processes, information-processing accounts of cognitive development often involve detailed, in-depth analyses of children's performance on a single task or on a narrow range of tasks. In contrast, the Piagetian approach seeks to characterize children's thinking across a broad range of tasks and content domains.

A final difference is that information-processing theories assume that our understanding of how children think can be greatly enriched by knowledge of how adults think. The underlying belief is that just as we can more deeply understand our own adult thinking when we appreciate how it developed, we also can better understand the development of children's thinking when we know where the development is going.

This chapter is divided into two main sections. In the first, we examine the basic information-processing framework. This framework provides a way of thinking about the cognitive systems of both children and adults. In the second main section, we consider five information-processing theories that focus on development. No one of these theories covers the huge expanse of topics and ages encompassed by Piaget's theory. On the other hand, each provides more precise and complete characterizations of particular aspects of development than Piaget did. The chapter's organization is outlined in Table 3.1.

TABLE 3.1   Chapter Outline

An Overview of the Information-Processing System

Any cognitive theory must come to grips with two basic characteristics of human cognition. First, our thinking is limited, both in the amount of information that we can attend to simultaneously and in the speed with which we can process the information. Second, our thinking is flexible, capable of adapting to constantly changing goals, circumstances, and task demands. Information-processing theories have attempted to come to grips with this dual nature of cognition by focusing on both *structural characteristics*, which determine the limits within which thinking occurs, and *processes*, which provide the means for flexible adaptation to a constantly changing world.

STRUCTURAL CHARACTERISTICS

Structural characteristics of the information-processing system provide its basic organization. They sometimes are referred to as the *cognitive architecture*; the analogy is to the architectural plan for a building, which specifies its main characteristics, but not the more detailed features. Structural features of the cognitive system tend to be relatively enduring; the same basic organization is believed to be maintained throughout development. Structural features are also universal; all children have the same basic cognitive organization, though the efficiency with which the different parts operate varies across individuals and age groups. This basic organization is often viewed within a three-part framework: sensory memory, working memory, and long-term memory.

Sensory memory.   People possess a special capacity for briefly retaining relatively large amounts of information that they have just encountered. This capacity is often labeled *sensory memory*. Sperling (1960) established several characteristics of sensory memory that influence processing of visual information. He presented college students a three-by-four matrix of letters for one-twentieth of a second. When asked immediately after the presentation to name the letters, the college students typically recalled four or five, about 40 percent of the list. Then Sperling changed the procedure in a small but important way. Rather than having the students recall all of the letters, he asked them to recall only the letters in one row. Since it was impossible to anticipate the identity of the row, the students needed to process all 12 letters, just as in the original task. However, requiring them to recite the contents of only one row eliminated their need to retain the information while they named the first few letters.

Sperling found that when the experimenter indicated which row to recall immediately after the display was shut off, the college students recalled 80 percent of the letters in the row. When the row's identity was indicated one-third of a second after the display was turned off, their recall declined to 55 percent. When it was indicated one second after, performance declined to the original 40 percent. Sperling's interpretation was that a one-twentieth-second exposure was sufficient for letters to create a visual *icon* (a literal copy of the original stimulus), but that the icon faded within one-third of a second and disappeared after a second. These estimates remain reasonable in light of subsequent research.

The capacity of children's sensory memory appears to increase with development. Cowan and colleagues (Cowan, Nugent, Elliott, Ponomarev, & Saults, 1999) investigated this issue in a study of sensory memory for auditory information. Participants were asked to play an attention-demanding computer game, while at the same time listening to lists of spoken digits with short intervals of silence in between the lists. Occasionally (roughly once every 13 lists), participants received a cue to report the most recent list of digits. Cowan and colleagues reasoned that, under these conditions, participants would need to recall the list from their auditory sensory memory.

Cowan and colleagues tested first-grade students, fourth-grade students, and adults using this paradigm. On average, first graders recalled about 2.5 digits, fourth graders recalled about 3 digits, and adults recalled about 3.5 digits. Thus, the capacity of children's sensory memory appears to increase with age.

Working memory.   Working memory is where active thinking occurs: constructing new strategies, computing solutions to arithmetic problems, comprehending what we read, and so on. Its operation involves combining information coming into sensory memory with information stored in long-term memory and transforming that information into new forms. For example, when we read a book, working memory combines the sensory information about the words on the page with long-term memory representations of the meanings of the words, and uses both sources of data to represent the meaning of the text as a whole.

The operation of working memory is limited in several ways. The first is its capacity, which is the number of units it can operate on at one time. This number is not large; it is usually estimated to be between three and seven units. Being more precise than this is difficult, because the exact estimates depend on the particulars of the task on which the capacity is measured. For example, estimates of capacity tend to be larger when they are based on the number of numbers that can be maintained in memory than when based on the number of letters that can be maintained (Dempster, 1981).

The limit on working-memory capacity is a limit on the number of meaningful units (chunks) that can be operated on, rather than on the number of physical units. A letter, a number, a word, or a familiar phrase can function as a single chunk, because each is a single unit of meaning. Thus, it is as easy to remember a set of three unrelated words with nine letters (*hit, red, cup*) as to remember three unrelated letters (*q, f, r*) (Miller, 1956).

The rate at which information is lost from working memory also limits cognitive functioning. Material ordinarily is lost within 15 to 30 seconds. However, at least with verbally encoded information such as words or numbers, rehearsal can maintain the information in working memory for a longer time.

Older children can maintain considerably more information in working memory than can younger ones. A large part of the reason appears to be the older children's more rapid rate of rehearsal. In general, the faster that both adults and children can rehearse verbal material, the more material they can maintain in working memory (Baddeley, 1986; Baddeley & Hitch, 1974). Faster rehearsal means less time between repetitions of a given word, and thus less likelihood that the word will be forgotten before it is rehearsed again. As shown in Figure 3.1, rate of pronunciation of words is closely related to the number of words that can be maintained in working memory. Older children's greater speed of pronunciation appears to be a large part of the reason why they can maintain more material in working memory (Hitch & Towse, 1995).

Working memory appears to include separate storage capacities for verbal and spatial information, together with an executive processor that controls attention to different sources of information (Baddeley, 1986). Information from the verbal and spatial subsystems is integrated and coordinated with information from long-term memory in a work space termed the "episodic buffer" (Baddeley, 2000).

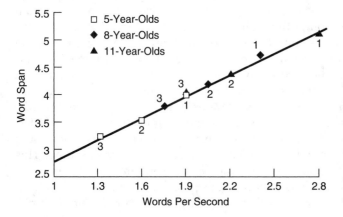

FIGURE 3.1 Memory spans of 5-, 8-, and 11-year-olds for unrelated, orally presented words as a function of articulation rate and number of syllables in words (numerals next to data points indicate number of syllables in word). For example, 11-year-olds could pronounce 2.8 single-syllable words per second, and could remember about five such words. From Hitch and Towse (1995).

The development of working memory appears to involve both changes in the amount of verbal and spatial information of each type that can be remembered, and increasingly effective separation between the two. Evidence comes from a study in which 8-year-olds, 10-year-olds and college students were presented either a series of digits, which would usually be coded verbally, or a series of locations of Xs on a tic-tac-toe grid, which usually would be coded spatially (Hale, Bronik, & Fry, 1997). The main task was to remember the digits or the locations of the Xs in the order in which they were presented. However, participants also needed to simultaneously execute a secondary task, which required either a verbal response (naming the colors of the digits or Xs) or a spatial one (pointing to the color of each digit or X within a spatial array of colors).

Not surprisingly, undergraduates recalled more information than 10-year-olds, and 10-year-olds more than 8-year-olds. More interesting, at all ages, having to perform the spatial secondary task interfered to the greatest degree with recall of the spatial information and having to perform the verbal secondary task interfered most heavily with the verbal task. This finding supported the view that spatial and verbal information are represented separately in working memory. Especially interesting, at age 8 but not thereafter, having to perform a spatial secondary task also interfered with ability to recall verbal material, and having to do a verbal secondary task interfered with ability to recall spatial material. This suggests that not until age 10 do children cleanly separate verbal from spatial information in working memory.

There are also developmental changes in the executive processes that control the content and functioning of working memory, such as the ability to inhibit attention to particular sources of information when appropriate. One compelling illustration comes from a task in which children are asked to sort cards with pictures of objects (such as red boats and blue flowers) into categories based on color or shape. Children are first asked to sort the cards along one dimension (such as color), and after several trials they are asked to "switch" and sort the cards along the other dimension (shape). Three-year-olds can easily sort the cards on the basis of either color or shape, but when asked to switch dimensions, most children fail and instead continue to sort the cards on the basis of the first dimension. By 4 years of age, however, most children can successfully perform the switch (Zelazo, Frye, & Rapus, 1996). One explanation for this developmental shift is that there are age-related improvements in executive processes that control the functioning of working memory.

Long-term memory.   Even young children are able to remember a vast assortment of experiences and facts about the world. Some of their knowledge is about specific episodes, such as their feelings when they wandered around the playground on their first day of school; this type of information is often referred to as *episodic knowledge*. Other knowledge is about enduring qualities of the world, such as that a nickel is worth five pennies; this type of information is often referred to as *semantic knowledge*. Yet other knowledge concerns procedures, such as how to ride a bicycle; this type of information is often referred to as *procedural knowledge*. These varied types of knowledge are the contents of long-term memory.

Unlike sensory and working memory, there are no limits on either how much information can be maintained in long-term memory or how long the information can stay there. Consider an experiment on recognition of faces in high school yearbooks (Bahrick, Bahrick, & Wittlinger, 1975). People were asked 35 years after graduation to recognize which yearbook pictures were of people in their high school class and which were of people from a nearby high school. In spite of all of the time that had passed, people correctly recognized 90 percent of the pictures. Thus, the name *long-term memory* is truly a fitting one.

An interesting property of the way people store information in long-term memory is that the storage is not in all-or-none form. Rather, people store information in separable units and can retrieve some units without retrieving others. This quality has been demonstrated in adults in experiments on the tip-of-the-tongue phenomenon. When adults can almost but not quite remember a word, they often can recall several of its characteristics: its first letter, its number of syllables, a word it sounds like, and so on (Brown & McNeill, 1966). This description appears to apply to children's storage of information in long-term memory as well. For example, in trying to remember the name of a friend who had moved away, Siegler's 6-year-old daughter said, "She was from South America, she had black hair, she was just as silly as I am, why can't I remember her name?" A few minutes later, she succeeded in recalling the friend's name, Gabriella.

PROCESSES

Processes are used to actively manipulate information in sensory, working, and long-term memory. Two processes that play particularly important roles in cognitive development are automatization and encoding.

The role of automatization.   Processes vary considerably in how much attention they require. Those that require a great deal of attention are often labeled *controlled*, whereas those that require little if any attention are labeled *automatic*. The amount of attention required is influenced both by the type of information being processed and by the amount of experience the child has had processing that type of material. Some types of information inherently require less attention than others. However, even with processes that at first require a great deal of attention, practice reduces the amount that is needed.

Automatic processing is important in development in that it provides an initial basis for learning about the world. One example involves frequency information, that is, data on how often various objects and events have been encountered. People retain this information even when they are not trying to do so. Thus, we have a good sense of the relative frequency with which letters of the alphabet appear (for example, if "e" or "r" is more frequent in English), although no one tries to remember such trivia. Recall of such information is influenced neither by instructions to remember nor by practice in trying to remember it. Level of recall also is equivalent over a wide age range. Children as young as 5 are as proficient as college students at retaining frequency information (Hasher & Zacks, 1984).

Children's automatic retention of information about frequencies seems to contribute to cognitive development in many ways. When children form concepts, they must learn which features go together most frequently. For example, learning the concept "bird" requires learning that the same animals tend to fly, have feathers, have beaks, and live in trees. Likewise, in learning language, infants learn which sounds tend to occur together, and they use this information to identify words within the stream of speech (Saffran et al., 1996). More subtle learning, such as learning of sex roles, also may depend on automatic processing of frequency information. When children see a large difference in the frequency with which men and women engage in an activity, they imitate same-sex models more often than ones of the opposite sex (Perry & Bussey, 1979). Children are almost never conscious of gathering information about how often men engage in an activity and how often women do. Rather, they seem to acquire the information automatically and then base their behavior on what they have observed.

Thus, processing of frequency information appears to be automatic from early in development, perhaps from birth. Other processes, however, may change from controlled to automatic as people gain experience with them. This process is known as *automatization.*

The term "automatization" is well chosen. Once skills are learned to a sufficiently high degree, they are difficult to inhibit even when it is advantageous to do so. Learning of single-digit addition provides an example of this phenomenon, as illustrated in a study by LeFevre, Bisanz, and Mrkonjic (1988). Their experiment involved presentation of a problem such as $4+5$ and then, a fraction of a second later, presentation of a single digit such as 9 slightly to the right of the first two numbers. The task was to say whether the number on the right was one of the addends in the problem. Thus, the answer for the above problem would be "No," because 9 was not one of the addends in $4+5$. However, automatized knowledge of arithmetic facts would interfere with performance on this task, leading children either to say "yes" or to take longer to say "no" when the number to the right was the answer to the addition problem than when it was neither the answer to the problem nor one of the digits.

Studies of this task indicate that the easiest single-digit addition problems are automatized quite early in learning, but that it takes several years before harder ones are (LeFevre & Kulak, 1994; LeFevre, Kulak, & Bisanz, 1991; Lemaire, Barret, Fayol, & Abdi, 1994). Second graders show the interference effects associated with automatic processing only on small number problems (both addends of five or less). Third graders show the effects on both small and medium problems (one addend of six or more), but not on large number problems (both addends of six or more). Fourth and fifth graders and adults show automatic processing on all single-digit addition problems: small, medium, and large.

As suggested by this example, automatization generally is useful, because it frees mental resources for solving other problems. For example, automatizing the addition facts would make it easier to do long multiplication problems in one's head. However, when the given problem looks like a typical problem but requires different processing, automatization can be harmful. For example, automatic activation of addition knowledge can interfere with children's performance on mathematical equivalence problems, such as $3 + 4 + 5 = 3 + \_$ (McNeil & Alibali, 2004). Such problems resemble addition problems, but differ from them in a crucial way—the position of the equal sign. Thus, depending on the circumstance, automatization can be either harmful or helpful.

The role of encoding.   People cannot represent all features of the environment; the world is simply too complex. Children often fail to encode important features of objects and events, sometimes because they do not know what the important features are and sometimes because they do not know how to encode them efficiently. This failure to encode critical elements can limit the effects of potentially useful experiences; when children do not take in relevant information, they cannot benefit from it.

Kaiser, McCloskey, and Proffitt (1986) provided a compelling demonstration of how inadequate encoding can hinder learning. They presented 4- to 11-year-olds and college students with a moving electric train carrying a ball on a flatcar. At a predesignated point, the ball dropped through a hole in the moving flatcar and fell several feet to the floor. The task was to predict the trajectory of the ball as it fell.

More than 70 percent of the children and a sizable minority of the college students predicted that the ball would fall straight down. After they advanced this hypothesis, the experimenter demonstrated what actually happened. (The ball moved in a curving path, going forward as well as down.) The children and the college students were faced with reconciling their predictions with the outcome they had seen. Their explanations revealed how expectations influence their encoding of what they saw. Some said that the ball actually had fallen straight down but that it was released from the train later than the experimenter said it was. Others said that the train gave the ball a push forward just before it was released. Interestingly, a number of the college students who encoded the ball as having gone straight down had previously passed college physics courses that included the relevant concepts. However, this experience was insufficient to change either their expectations or their encoding of what they saw.

Encoding begins to play an important role in both developmental and individual differences in the first year of life (Colombo, 1993, 1995). Evidence for its importance comes from studies of the rate at which infants take in all of the relevant information and therefore become bored with looking at an object and look elsewhere. The length of time it takes before infants stop looking at a given object drops by more than half between ages 3 and 7 months. Recall also from Chapter 1 (p. 12) that the more rapidly 7-month-olds habituate to a repeatedly displayed object, the higher their IQs as much as 7 or 8 years later. Presumably, more intelligent infants are quicker to encode everything of interest about the picture, leading them to be the first to lose interest in it. They perk up more when the new picture is shown, because they more clearly encode the differences between it and the old one.

Information-Processing Theories of Development

In the remainder of this chapter, we consider five types of theories of how information-processing capabilities develop: neo-Piagetian theories, psychometric theories, production-system theories, connectionist theories, and evolutionary theories. Each of these is best viewed as a family of theories, with the individual theories of each type sharing basic principles but also having unique features. The discussion of each family of theories includes identification of the shared general principles and description of one particular realization of those principles. The hope is that this discussion will convey the central features of the approach as well as a specific sense of how the approach is useful for understanding children's thinking.

All of these theories reflect the contributions of both Piaget's theory and adult information-processing approaches, as well as a number of other influences. Table 3.2 lists some of these. It also summarizes the goals of the theories and the mechanisms of development that they emphasize.

Neo-Piagetian Theories

The goal of neo-Piagetian theories is to maintain the strengths of Piaget's approach while adding the strengths of information-processing approaches. Typically, they incorporate stages much like Piaget's with the emphasis on goals, working memory limitations, and problem-solving strategies typical of information-processing approaches. Their greatest emphasis tends to be on how the biologically based growth of working memory and automatization of processing allow children to progressively overcome processing limits. Among the most prominent neo-Piagetian theories are those of Halford (Andrews & Halford, 2002; Halford, 1993; Halford, Wilson, & Phillips, 1998), Fischer (Fischer & Farrar, 1988; Mascolo & Fischer, 1999), and Demetriou (Demetriou, Christou, Spanoudis, & Platsidou, 2002; Demetriou, Efklides & Platsidou, 1993; Demetriou & Raftopoulos, 1999).

Probably the most prominent neo-Piagetian theory is that of Robbie Case. This theory can be divided into two main parts: the developmental stages themselves and the transition processes that produce progress between stages (Figure 3.2).

TABLE 3.2   Overview of Information-Processing Theories of Development

Type of Theory	Representative Theorist	Goal of Theory	Main Developmental Mechanisms
Neo-Piagetian	Case	To unite Piagetian and information-processing theories of development.	Automatization, biologically based increases in working memory, and strategy construction.
Psychometric	Sternberg	To provide an information-processing analysis of the development of intelligence.	Strategy construction, encoding, and automatization.
Production System	Klahr	To demonstrate via computer simulation how the cognitive system modifies its own operation.	Generalization, based on the working of regularity detection, redundancy elimination, and the time line. Also encoding and strategy construction.
Connectionist	MacWhinney	To explain how children can learn language from the data available to them.	Associative competition among simple processing units. Also generalization.
Evolutionary	Siegler	To understand how the processes of variation and selection shape cognitive development.	Associative competition among strategies. Also strategy construction and generalization.

Like Piaget, Case (1985) hypothesized that children progress through four developmental stages. He characterized these stages in terms of the types of mental representations and operations children can form while they are in them. The first stage involves *sensorimotor operations*. Children's representations in this stage are composed of sensory input, and the actions they produce in response to these representations are physical movements. In the *representational operations* stage, children's representations include concrete internal images, and their actions can produce additional internal representations. In the stage of *logical operations*, children represent stimuli abstractly; they can act on these representations with simple transformations. In the *formal operations* stage, children also represent stimuli abstractly, but they are capable of performing complex transformations of the information. In each stage, children also produce representations and actions like those they produced in earlier stages.

Examples may clarify the differences in the representations that become possible in each stage. A sensorimotor operation might involve a child's seeing a frightening face (the sensory representation) and then fleeing from the room (the motor action). A representational operation might involve the child's producing a mental image of the same frightening face (the internal representation) and using the image to draw a picture of the face (the representational action). A logical operation might involve a child's realizing that two of his friends did not like each other (the abstract representation) and telling them that they could

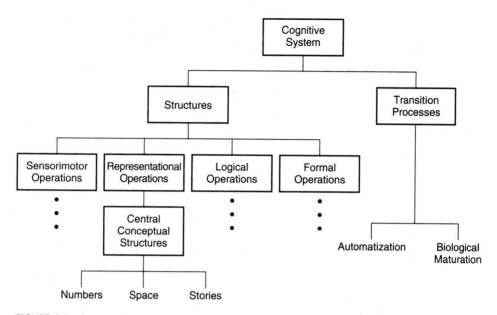

FIGURE 3.2 *An outline of the main structures and processes in Case's theory.*

have more fun if they all were friends (the simple transformation). A formal operation might involve the child's realizing that such direct attempts at producing friendships rarely succeed (the abstract representation) and therefore leading all three into a situation in which they would need to overcome some common obstacle, thus producing friendly feelings (the complex transformation). The resemblance to Piaget's stages of development seems clear.

Case's view of the developmental sequence by which children acquire understanding of particular concepts also resembles Piaget's views. Like Piaget, Case postulates broad unities in the developmental sequence across different concepts. His views are more moderate, in that the postulated similarities of reasoning are limited to particular types of knowledge. However, even across these types of knowledge, substantial commonality in the developmental sequence is evident.

In particular, Case claims that much of children's thinking is organized into *central conceptual structures*. A central conceptual structure is defined as "an internal network of concepts and conceptual relations which plays a central role in permitting children to think about a wide range of (but not all) situations at a new epistemic level" (Case & Griffin, 1990, p. 224). Case and his colleagues (Case, 1998; Case & Mueller, 2001; Case & Okamoto, 1996; Griffin, Case, & Sandieson, 1992; Marini, 1992) have focused on three main central conceptual structures, one for thinking about numbers, one for thinking about space, and one for thinking about stories. All three have a general resemblance, based on overall structural limits of the cognitive system at that age, but all also reflect the particulars of the domain to which they apply. For example, Case and Okamoto

(1996) proposed that at age 6, the central conceptual structures focus on a single dimension. In the structure dealing with numbers, this involves forming a mental number line, which allows children to perform such tasks as knowing which numbers are bigger than which other numbers. In the structure dealing with stories, the central conceptual structure at this age allows children to form mental story lines, that is, to represent the plot line of the story in terms of the sequence of events. In the structure dealing with space, 6-year-olds' thinking focuses either on the shape or location of objects, but not both. By age 8, central conceptual structures coordinating two dimensions are formed. In the domain of numbers, this allows children to coordinate two number lines, for example to understand the base 10 system dealing with numbers below 100 by coordinating understanding of 10s and 1s. In the domain of stories, it allows them to coordinate two story lines into a single plot. In the domain of space, it allows them to simultaneously represent the shapes and locations of objects.

Where Case differs most clearly from Piaget, and shows the strongest influence of the information-processing approach, is in his account of transition mechanisms. Case emphasizes working memory capacity as a determinant of cognitive growth. His claim is not that the absolute capacity of working memory increases, but rather that it functions increasingly efficiently, and that it therefore can handle more information.

How might such increases in processing efficiency occur? Case (1985) proposed that one contributor is automatization. With practice, a cognitive operation that previously required all working memory resources could be accomplished more efficiently. This would free up part of the working memory capacity for other processing. It may be useful to think of this view of working memory in terms of an analogy to a car's trunk. The capacity of a car's trunk does not change as the owner acquires experience in packing luggage into it. Nonetheless, the amount of luggage that can be packed into the trunk does change. Whereas the trunk at first might hold three suitcases, it eventually comes to hold four or five. With more efficient packing, trunk space is freed for additional cargo. Like knowledge of how to pack one's trunk, the central conceptual structures provide efficient ways of organizing goals and procedures for accomplishing the goals. Thus, they allow children to circumvent working memory limits.

Biological maturation was also assigned a role in explaining the increasing efficiency of working memory. Case (1992b) proposed that stage transitions arise from pervasive changes in electrical activity in the frontal lobes, a part of the brain particularly active in problem solving and reasoning. The specific proposal was that at the beginning of each stage, new short-distance connections develop between the frontal lobe on the left side of the brain and parts of the brain that previously had not been connected to them. During a second substage, longer-distance connections are formed within both left and right hemispheres of the brain. During a third substage, short distance connections are formed within the right hemisphere. Then the brain is ready for a new stage to begin. Patterns of electrical activity in the brain at different ages lent some support to this proposal (Thatcher, 1992).

Case and his colleagues have applied this theory to an exceptional variety of tasks. They range from scientific reasoning (Marini, 1992) to musical sight reading (Capodilupo, 1992), solving arithmetic word problems (Okamoto & Case, 1996), telling time (Case, Okamoto, Henderson, McKeough, & Bleiker, 1996; Case, Sandieson, & Dennis, 1987), handling money (Case, Okamoto, et al., 1996), drawing (Case, Stephenson, Bleiker, & Henderson, 1996; Dennis, 1992), and understanding social and emotional phenomena such as feelings, motives, and interpersonal conflict (Bruchkowsky, 1992; Case, Okamoto, et al., 1996).

Another strength of Case's theory is its usefulness for designing effective instructional techniques. Case and his colleagues have developed instructional techniques and curricula that are based on two important components of his theory: analyses of the working-memory demands of various approaches to solving problems, and analyses of the central conceptual structures that under-lie core domains.

Consider Case's analysis of missing addend problems of the form $4 + ? = 7$ (Case, 1985). Although the task appears simple, first graders who are taught it in school find it a major obstacle. After analyzing several correct and several commonly used incorrect strategies for solving missing addend problems, Case noted that most correct strategies required more working memory capacity than 6- and 7-year-olds usually possess. However, he also noted that the simplest correct strategy and the most demanding incorrect strategy made the same memory demands. The least demanding correct strategy, according to his analysis, was to count on from the one addend given in the problem and to note the number of counts required to reach the sum. On the problem $4 + ? = 7$, this simplest correct strategy would involve starting at 4 and keeping track of the number of counts needed to get from there to 7. The most demanding (and the most common) incorrect strategy was to count up first to the addend that was given and then to count on from there the number of times indicated by the sum. Illustratively, on the problem $4 + ? = 7$, children would first count to 4, then count up 7 more times to 11, and finally answer that the missing addend was 11. Case reasoned that if 6-year-olds could learn the incorrect strategy, they also could learn the correct one, because the two strategies made similar demands on working memory.

The instructional strategy that Case used was straightforward. As shown in Figure 3.3, the first step was to illustrate that the equal sign (=) meant that entities on each side of the sign were equivalent. The next step (third pair of faces) was to illustrate that the plus sign (+) meant that the child should sum the entities adjacent to the sign. After the child finished working with the faces, the focus of the instruction shifted to direct consideration of problems involving numbers. In one part of this instruction, the experimenter demonstrated the incorrectness of children's existing strategy for solving missing addend problems involving numbers by having them compare the numbers on the two sides of

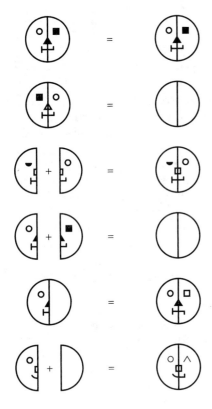

FIGURE 3.3 Faces used by Case (1978) to teach missing addend problems. The first pair of faces was used to demonstrate the meaning of the equal sign. The second pair was used to test whether the child could make the right-hand face equal to the left-hand face. The third pair was used to demonstrate that the whole on the right could be created from the parts on the left. The fourth pair was used to test whether the child could create a whole out of the parts. The fifth pair, like the missing addend problem, showed one part of the whole on the left and the whole on the right; the task was to fill in the other part of the whole on the left. The sixth pair included the plus sign, to make problem even more like standard missing addend problems with numbers.

the equal sign that their strategy yielded. This would allow them to see that on $4 + ? = 7$, the 11 that their strategy yielded does not make the entities on the two sides of the equal sign equivalent. Following this, the simplest correct procedure for solving missing addend problems (the count-on strategy described in the previous paragraph) was introduced, one step at a time.

Case (1978) reported that his teaching strategy allowed 80 percent of kindergarten children to learn to correctly solve missing addend problems. This percentage represented a considerable improvement over the 10 percent of children who were able to learn such problems from the standard State of California arithmetic workbook.

More recently, Case has applied the notion of central conceptual structures to the design of curricula for a range of mathematical concepts, including rational numbers and functions (Kalchman, Moss, & Case, 2000; Moss & Case, 1999). For each domain, Case and his colleagues began by outlining the content of the central conceptual structure that underlies skilled, fluent performance within the domain, and then designed instruction that would foster the development of that central conceptual structure. For example, the central conceptual structure for rational numbers was hypothesized to incorporate children's intuitive understanding about proportions (e.g., their understanding of "half full" and "a quarter full" as applied to beakers of water) and their numerical understanding of halving and doubling numbers (Moss & Case, 1999).

In Case's view, instruction should foster and extend the naturally occurring processes by which components of the central conceptual structures are coordinated and integrated. Based on this idea, Moss and Case (1999) developed an experimental curriculum about rational numbers that focused on aspects of the hypothesized central conceptual structure. For example, at the outset of the series of lessons, students were asked to use percentages to describe the fullness of various beakers of water. Eventually, percentages were linked to decimal fractions. This was achieved using large, laminated number lines with each number 1 meter apart, which were set up on the classroom floor. Students were asked to walk some percentage of the distance between two numbers (such as 75 percent), and it was explained that this value could be represented with a two-place decimal fraction (0.75 meters). Eventually, common fraction notation (1/2, 1/4, 1/8) was introduced by linking it to proportions and decimal fractions. The classroom activities were designed with the goal of strengthening and integrating aspects of the central conceptual structure for rational numbers.

Moss and Case implemented their experimental curriculum in a classroom of fourth-grade students, and they compared students' learning about decimals, fractions, and percentages with that of students in a control classroom from a demographically similar, nearby school that used a traditional curriculum. On a posttest that followed the rational number unit, students who received the experimental curriculum performed far better than students who received the control curriculum (69 percent vs. 39 percent correct), and their performance demonstrated a deeper understanding of rational numbers. The errors of students in the control group often reflected confusions of rational numbers and whole numbers; such errors were much less common in the experimental group. Students in the experimental group frequently referred to proportion concepts in justifying their solutions to problems involving decimals, fractions, and percents, and they were able to successfully solve problems that required overcoming misleading cues or generating new procedures. The experimental curriculum thus appeared to foster a generalized, flexible understanding of rational numbers.

These examples illustrate that Case's approach and, in particular, his analyses of working-memory demands and central conceptual structures are useful for applied as well as theoretical purposes. Moreover, these examples highlight the value and effectiveness of instructional techniques that are grounded in psychological theory.

Several criticisms of Case's theory have been voiced. Flavell (1984) noted that Case has not explicated the principles by which he determines how much working-memory capacity a procedure requires. As a result, it is often difficult to evaluate whether the estimates are comparable from one task to the next. Further, his ideas about the role of biological changes in producing stage changes are quite speculative; as yet, there is little relevant evidence available. On the other hand, Case's theory is exceptional among information-processing approaches to development in its attempt to relate basic capacities, strategies, and learning. It has yielded compelling analyses of development on many tasks and has proved practically useful as well. Also, there is a strong intuition among many researchers that improved ability to surmount memory limits does underlie much of cognitive development, though it is difficult to provide evidence that unambiguously supports the position. Thus, it seems that Case and his colleagues have taken a difficult but potentially rewarding path. To the extent that the effort succeeds, it will be a grand achievement.

PSYCHOMETRIC THEORIES

Psychometric theories are aimed at clarifying the processes measured on tests of mental abilities, such as intelligence tests. Since the beginning of the twentieth century, intelligence has been characterized by a single number, the IQ score. This practice has several drawbacks: A single number is inherently inadequate to capture a quality as rich and complex as intelligence, IQ tests may be culturally biased, and such tests do not directly measure the ability to learn and create, or the ability to apply intelligence in practical situations. IQ tests also have unique virtues, however: Scores on them are closely related to school performance at the time they are given; they predict later school performance quite accurately; and they provide a solid base from which to examine individual differences in cognitive functioning.

A number of investigators have tried to preserve these virtues while reducing or eliminating the negative qualities (Anderson, 1992; Ceci, 1990; Gardner, 1993). Probably the most prominent such theory is Robert Sternberg's *triarchic theory of intelligence.* He has applied the analysis to diverse tasks and diverse groups of children and has related his results to those yielded by traditional intelligence tests.

According to the triarchic theory (Sternberg, 1985, 1997, 1999), there are three primary aspects to human intelligence: analytical, creative, and practical. Analytical intelligence is the type of intelligence that is evaluated in most traditional tests of intelligence. It involves abilities such as analyzing, evaluating, comparing, contrasting, and critiquing. Creative intelligence comprises the abilities needed to cope with novel situations. It involves abilities such as creating, discovering, imagining, and inventing. Practical intelligence is utilized in addressing the problems that arise in everyday life, and in adapting to, shaping, and selecting environments. It involves abilities such as using and applying information.

Sternberg has argued that a common set of processes underlie analytical, creative, and practical intelligence. These processes include performance components, knowledge acquisition components, and metacomponents (Figure 3.4).

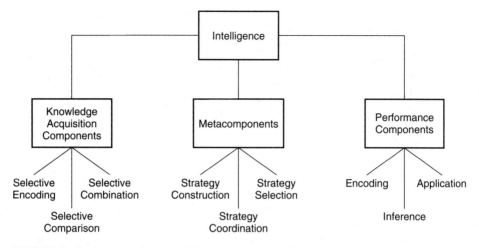

FIGURE 3.4 A schematic diagram of Sternberg's theory of intelligence.

Performance components are the processes involved in actually solving a given problem. Sternberg identified four performance components that people use to solve a great many problems: encoding, inference, mapping, and application. The way in which these performance components work can be illustrated by thinking about analogy problems. Consider the problem:

Turkey : Cranberry sauce :: Eggs: (1) Corn (2) Ham

The task is to decide whether corn or ham has the same relation to eggs that cranberry sauce has to turkey.

Sternberg suggested that the first step in solving this problem is to encode the terms. This step involves identifying each term's attributes—for example, noting that turkey is a kind of food, that it is a meat, that it is a bird, that it is eaten on Thanksgiving, and so on. Next, inference is used to specify the relation between the first and second term, in this case that turkey is often eaten with cranberry sauce. Then, mapping is used to establish the relation between the first and third terms, that turkey and eggs are both foods. Finally, application involves inducing a relation between the third term and one of the possible answers that parallels the relation between the first and second terms. Here, eggs go with ham in much the same way that cranberry sauce goes with turkey.

Knowledge acquisition components are processes involved in learning to solve problems and acquiring relevant knowledge in the first place. Sternberg has focused in particular on three knowledge acquisition processes: selective encoding, selective combination, and selective comparison. Selective encoding involves distinguishing relevant from irrelevant information. Selective combination involves integrating information in a meaningful way. Selective comparison involves relating newly encoded or combined information to previously stored information.

The importance of knowledge acquisition components in solving problems can be illustrated with respect to insight problems, such as the following one: "If you have black socks and brown socks in your drawer, mixed in the ratio of 4 to 5, how many socks will you have to take out to be sure of having a pair of socks of the same color?" For this problem, skill in selective encoding is necessary to ignore the irrelevant information about the 4:5 ratio of the two colors. (If you had socks of two colors, how many socks would you need to look at to be sure that two would match?) When this information is present, one needs to ignore it and selectively encode only the essentials of the problem. When the irrelevant information is absent, skill in selective encoding is less important, because there is less distracting information. Not surprisingly, children are more successful on such problems when the irrelevant information is omitted, and selective encoding is not required.

Some evidence suggests that children with high IQs execute knowledge acquisition processes more effectively than other children. Consistent with this view, children with high IQs benefit less than children with average IQs from instruction that focuses on such processes. The likely reason is that children with high IQs have strong knowledge acquisition skills in the first place, so instruction has little added benefit (Davidson & Sternberg, 1984).

Metacomponents are executive processes that govern the use of the other components. The metacomponents plan how to solve problems, construct problem-solving strategies, monitor progress, and evaluate performance. They also are responsible for most aspects of developmental change. As Sternberg (1984) commented, "There can be no doubt that in the present conceptual scheme, the metacomponents form the major basis for the development of intelligence" (p. 172).

The importance of metacomponents is evident in people's transfer of knowledge from one context to another. Older children and people with greater expertise are generally better able to apply their knowledge to new problems than are younger people and people with less expertise (Campione & Brown, 1984; Gentner, Ratterman, Markman, & Kotovsky, 1995; Staszewski, 1988). Knowledge is especially important; 10-year-olds who are expert at chess more successfully solve novel chess problems than adults with little knowledge of chess but whose general memory capacities are higher (Chi, 1978). However, within a given level of knowledge, people with higher IQs generally can apply existing knowledge to acquire new knowledge more rapidly (e.g., Johnson & Mervis, 1994).

The three types of basic processes—metacomponents, performance components, and knowledge acquisition components—work together in solving problems. The metacomponents serve as a strategy construction mechanism, orchestrating the other two types of components into goal-oriented procedures. When the child already possesses sufficient understanding to solve a problem, only the metacomponents and the performance components are needed to construct a problem-solving strategy. The metacomponents select which performance components to use and the order in which to use them. The performance components do the work of actually solving the problem. If the child does not yet possess sufficient understanding to solve the problem, the knowledge acquisition components also come into play. That is, the knowledge acquisition components obtain new information relevant to solving the problem and communicate this information to the metacomponents. The metacomponents then combine the new and previous understanding to construct a problem-solving strategy.

According to Sternberg (1999), these same basic processes underlie analytical, creative, and practical intelligence; the specific processes that are applied depend on the nature of the task and the situation and on the type of thinking that is required. However, despite this fundamental similarity in terms of basic processes, traditional intelligence tests and traditional methods of classroom instruction have focused primarily on analytical intelligence, to the exclusion of creative or practical intelligence. In recent work, Sternberg has focused on designing knowledge assessments and instructional methods that address practical and creative intelligence, as well as analytical intelligence.

Tests that assess all three types of thinking have proven to be more effective at predicting intellectual outcomes than traditional IQ tests, which focus on analytical abilities alone. One study of this issue involved gifted high school students who were selected for a college-level, summer psychology course. Students completed tests of analytical, creative, and practical intelligence, and their scores on these tests were used to predict their grades in the course. Grades were better predicted based on the combination of abilities than based on analytical ability alone (Sternberg, Ferrari, Clinkenbeard, & Grigorenko, 1996).

This study also involved an instructional component. All of the students used the same psychology textbook and listened to the same lectures. However, students were assigned to discussion sections that differed in their focus on analytical, creative, practical, or memory activities. Sternberg and colleagues found that students who were placed in discussion sections that matched their strengths (e.g., students with creative strengths in the section that focused on creative activities) performed better in the course than students who were placed in discussion sections that did not match their strengths. Thus, students perform better when the instructional conditions match the way they think best.

Other studies have shown that instruction that emphasizes all three types of intelligence is more beneficial for students than either conventional instruction or instruction that focuses on critical-thinking skills. This pattern has been documented in several different participant populations and with different types of course content, including third-grade students learning a social studies unit; eighth-grade students learning a psychology unit; inner-city fifth-grade students learning reading skills; low-SES middle school students in a summer reading enrichment program; and high school students in multiple subject areas (Grigorenko, Jarvin, & Sternberg, 2002; Sternberg, Torff, & Grigorenko, 1998). It seems clear that instruction that encourages creative and practical thinking as well as analytical thinking can be beneficial for many students.

How should Sternberg's theory be evaluated? Three important weaknesses can be noted. One is that the theory summarizes more than it predicts. It is not clear what types of evidence would be inconsistent with the approach. A second weakness has to do with the specification of basic processes. The functioning of these processes has been spelled out primarily for tasks that involve analytical thinking; it is less clear how they function in tasks that require creative and practical thinking. A third weakness involves the role of metacomponents in the organization of the system. The metacomponents are crucial parts of the overall theory, but their workings remain somewhat mysterious.

On the other hand, the theory is exceptional in the breadth of phenomena and of populations to which it has proven applicable. It encompasses a large number of intuitively important aspects of development and organizes them in an easy-to-grasp way. It provides a plausible outline of how a strategy-construction mechanism would operate. It has yielded important practical applications both for the assessment of intelligence and for instruction. In short, it constitutes a useful framework within which to view development, and it also has yielded substantial practical benefits.

PRODUCTION SYSTEM THEORIES

Perhaps the most difficult challenge for theories of cognitive development has been to explain how development occurs. Piaget and many others have tried to generate such explanations, but they have not been entirely successful. Consider the following evaluation:

> For 40 years now we have had assimilation and accommodation, the mysterious and shadowy forces of equilibration, the Batman and Robin of the developmental processes. What are they? How do they do their thing? Why is it after all this time, we know no more about them than when they first sprang on the scene? What we need is a way to get beyond vague verbal statements of the nature of the developmental process. (Klahr, 1982, p. 80)

One promising effort to provide more precise and satisfying explanations of change has been to model development through production systems (Klahr & MacWhinney, 1998). These are a class of computer-simulation languages that have proved useful for modeling cognitive development. Each production is a kind of if–then rule that indicates what the system would do in a particular situation. Together, the productions indicate what the system would do under a wide range of circumstances. The key properties of production systems are the following:

1. The basic organization consists of two interacting structures: a *production memory*, which is the system's enduring knowledge, and a *working memory*, which is the system's representation of the current situation.

2. The production memory includes a large number of specific productions, each of which includes a condition side and an action side.
3. The condition side of each production specifies the circumstances under which the production is applicable. The action side specifies the actions that are taken when these conditions are met. Such actions include both activities in the external world and manipulations of symbols in working memory.
4. The contents of working memory are constantly changing, because they reflect constantly changing situations. Information enters working memory both through perception of events in the external world and through taking the actions indicated by the action side of productions.
5. Thinking occurs through a cycle of a) information being present in working memory, b) the information matching the conditions of one or more productions, c) this match resulting in the actions on the action side of those productions being taken, d) the actions placing new information in working memory, thus starting the cycle anew.
6. Learning occurs through a process of self-modification, in which new productions are created and existing productions modified as a result of previous experience.

The basic organization of production systems is diagrammed in Figure 3.5.

An example of a simple production system that generates correct performance on Piaget's number conservation problem is shown in Table 3.3. The

FIGURE 3.5   The hierarchical organization of production systems.

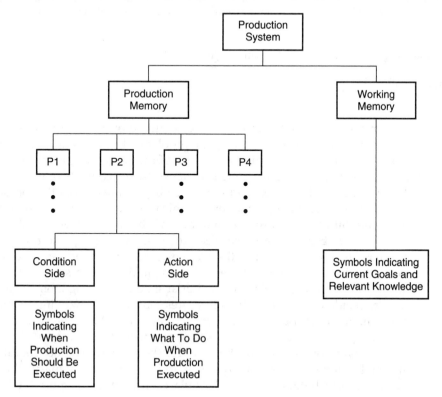

TABLE 3.3   A Simple Production System for Number Conservation*

P1: **If** you are asked about the numerical relation between two collections **and** you do not have a goal of stating the relation, **then** set a goal of stating the relation.

P2: **If** you have a goal of stating the numerical relation between two collections **and** you know the relation, **then** state the relation.

P3: **If** you have a goal of stating the numerical relation between two collections, **and** the collections had the same number of objects before a transformation **and** the transformation did not involve adding or subtracting objects, **then** the collections still have the same number of objects.

————

Initial Working Memory (WM1): Rows had same number of objects before, one row then was spread, nothing added or subtracted, question is whether rows have same number of objects now.

P1 fires.

WM2: Goal is to state whether rows have same number of objects now, rows had same number of objects before, one row then was spread, nothing added or subtracted, question is whether rows have same number of objects now.

P3 fires.

WM3: Goal is to state whether rows have same number of objects now, rows have the same number of objects, rows had same number of objects before, one row then was spread, nothing added or subtracted, question is whether rows have same number of objects now.

P2 fires.

System answers: "The rows have the same number of objects."

Source: *Adapted from Klahr & Wallace, 1976.

bottom part of the Table indicates the sequence of working-memory states that the system produces while solving the problem. The particular production system always searches downward from the top of the list of productions until it finds a production whose condition side is matched by the contents of working memory. That production then fires, and the search begins anew from the top of the list.

In the experimental situation to which the Table 3.3 production system applies, the child has been shown two rows of objects, has been told that they have the same number of objects, has seen the objects in one of the rows spread out, and has been asked whether the two rows now have the same number of objects. This information is represented in the initial contents of working memory in the bottom part of Table 3.3. The initial state of working memory matches the condition side of P1, which therefore fires, putting into working memory a goal of stating the numerical relation between the rows. When the system starts from the top again, the contents of working memory do not match P1 (because its second condition is not matched) or P2 (because its second condition is not matched.) However, the contents of working memory do match the condition side of P3, which therefore fires. This places in working memory the information

TABLE 3.4   A Portion of a Child's Time Line

(Previous Processing Episodes)	
_____	_____
_____	_____
_____	_____
87456.	Cookies on table.
87457.	I subitized.
87458.	There were three.
87459.	I heard a bird.
87460.	I picked up the cookies.
87461.	I subitized the cookies.
87462.	There were three again.
_____	_____
_____	_____
_____	_____

that the rows have the same number of objects. With this information, P2 can fire and the system states the correct answer.

Many researchers have utilized production system models as a tool for studying development (e.g., Jones, Ritter, & Wood, 2000; Klahr, Langley, & Neches, 1987; Young & O'Shea, 1981). One especially prominent advocate of production systems as a tool for explaining development is David Klahr. The key developmental mechanism in Klahr's production system theory is generalization. Number conservation provides a convenient context for explaining how his theory works.

Klahr and Wallace (1976) divided the process of generalization into three components: the time line, regularity detection, and redundancy elimination. The time line contains the data on which generalizations are based. It is a record of all the situations the system has ever encountered, the responses produced in those situations, the outcomes of the actions, and the new situations that arose. Table 3.4 illustrates the type of information that might be included in the time line's record of a single event. A child saw a group of cookies and noticed that there were three. This realization was made possible by subitizing (a process by which both children and adults can rapidly perceive the number of objects in sets ranging from one to four objects). Next, the child transformed the spatial position of the cookies by picking up in his hand. Finally, the child again subitized the collection of cookies and found that there still were three.

Such detailed records of situations, responses, and outcomes might at first seem unnecessary. Why remember so much about each experience? In fact, the information could be invaluable. In many situations, children cannot know beforehand what will turn out to be relevant. If they retain detailed information that may or may not be relevant, they later may be able to draw unanticipated generalizations. If they retain only what they already know to be relevant, however, they will miss much relevant information.

Is it realistic to think that children have a memory record similar to a time line? Observing the level of detail with which they remember certain information suggests that it is. Almost all parents have anecdotes to this effect. One of Siegler's concerns a vacation on which he and his wife and their almost-2-year-old son were staying in a motel. They wanted to go to dinner but could not find the room key. After 10 minutes of searching, the father finally listened to his son long enough to understand that he was saying: "Under phone." The father knew immediately that his son was right. He had put the key there (for reasons he no longer remembers). It seems likely that if the child remembered this relatively inconsequential detail, he probably was remembering many other details as well. Hasher and Zacks's (1984) ideas about automatic processing of frequency information and of several other aspects of experience, such as spatial locations and time of occurrence, suggest the types of content that might be entered into the time line. Thus, Klahr and Wallace's contention that children retain a detailed ledger of their experiences seems quite plausible.

The second key process, regularity detection, operates on the contents of the time line to produce generalizations about experience. This is accomplished by the system's noting places in the time line where many features are similar and where the same outcome occurs despite variations in one or more features. In number conservation, regularity detection could produce at least three types of generalizations. One would involve generalizing over different objects. Regardless of whether two checkers, two coins, two dolls, or two cookies were spread, there still would be two objects. Children also could generalize over equivalent transformations. Spreading, compressing, piling up, and putting in a circle all preserve the initial number of objects.

The third process in Klahr and Wallace's model, redundancy elimination, accomplishes a different type of generalization. It improves efficiency by identifying processing steps that are unnecessary, thus reaching the generalization that a less complex sequence can achieve the same goal. In the number conservation example, children eventually would note that it is unnecessary to subitize again after picking up the cookies. Since there were three cookies before, and since picking up objects never affects how many there are, the number still must be the same. Klahr and Wallace hypothesized that the information-processing system eliminates redundancy by examining procedures within the time line and checking if the same outcome always occurs even if one or more steps are deleted. If so, the simpler procedure is substituted for the more complex one.

When does the information-processing system have time to detect regularities and to eliminate redundancies? Klahr and Wallace (1976) advanced one intriguing possibility: Perhaps children do it in their sleep. Other possibilities are that moments of quiet play, relaxation, or daydreaming are when children accomplish these functions.

Klahr and Wallace's approach, unlike stage theories, implies that different children develop skills in different orders. In the cognitive system's attempts at self-modification, there is no reason why one type of regularity always should be detected before another type. Children learning about number conservation either could first detect that it does not matter if the rows of objects contain cookies or checkers or could first detect that it does not matter if the row of cookies is shortened or lengthened. Thus, there is less of a lock-step feel to the model than there is to stage approaches.

Another implication of Klahr and Wallace's theory relates to the idea of encoding. The way in which information is encoded in the time line shapes the learning that can later occur. Suppose, for example, that in a conservation of liquid quantity experiment, a child encodes only the heights of the water in the glasses. Such a child would not be able to detect the regular relation between increments in the height of water and decrements in its cross-sectional area. The information about cross-sectional area simply would not be available in the time line.

Klahr has been in the forefront of investigators arguing for greater use of computer simulation as a tool for modeling development. He has noted that such simulations allow more explicit and precise models of how development occurs than would otherwise be possible (Klahr, 1989, 1992; Klahr & MacWhinney, 1998). Consistent with this stance, Simon and Klahr (1995) formulated a self-modifying production system that illustrated how children could come to understand conservation. At the outset, the model could not solve the number conservation problems it was presented, but through experience trying to solve them, it figured out how to do so. Of special interest, Simon and Klahr generated two versions of the model, one corresponding to 3-year-olds and one to 4-year-olds. Both models were able to learn when given relatively extensive experience with the problems, but only the model of 4-year-olds learned from limited experience with them. These data corresponded to the results obtained with real 3- and 4-year-olds who had been presented with these experiences by Gelman (1982).

The models of the younger and older children suggested hypotheses concerning why 3- and 4-year-olds showed the patterns of learning that they did. Both models contained learning mechanisms that allowed them to learn from the more extensive experience. However, two differences between them resulted in the model of 4-year-olds, but not the model of 3-year-olds, learning from the limited experience. The model of 4-year-olds more clearly remembered the relation between the sets before the transformation, and it was more likely to check whether the differences between the lengths of the rows after the transformation corresponded to a difference in numbers of objects. These differences in the models were consistent with what is known generally about 3- and 4-year-olds. The 4-year-olds are more likely to use counting to check whether their perceptions regarding numbers of objects are correct (Sophian, 1987), and they also usually remember more about past states (Schneider & Bjorklund, 1998). Thus, the differences between the models of 3- and 4-year-olds were both consistent with past observations of these age groups and suggested hypotheses regarding why the two age groups might learn as they did in this particular context.

Not everyone shares Klahr's enthusiasm for computer-simulation models, though. Critics note that people are not computers and that unlike computers, people develop. This leads them to the conclusion that development cannot be modeled appropriately on a computer (Beilin, 1983; Liben, 1987).

As Klahr (1989) pointed out, however, ideas about development are embodied in the computer *program*, not the computer on which the program runs. The computer is simply the device used to test whether these ideas account for the known phenomena. To illustrate the point, Klahr noted that computer simulations of cognitive development do not imply that children are computers any more than computer simulations of hurricanes imply that the atmosphere is a computer.

Several limitations of Klahr's theory should be mentioned. Although he has often proclaimed the virtues of self-modifying production systems, neither he nor other investigators interested in children's thinking have yet written many of them. In addition, such self-modifying production systems thus far have been more useful for explaining previous findings than for generating new ones. On the other hand, these shortcomings do not detract from the potential of self-modifying production systems as models of development. In addition, Klahr's explanation of generalization in terms of the time line, regularity detection, and redundancy elimination is more precise and explicit than almost all other mechanisms of cognitive development that have been proposed. These are important virtues and may foreshadow additional breakthroughs.

CONNECTIONIST THEORIES

One especially "hot" approach to thinking about cognitive development (and to thinking about cognition in general) is connectionism. Like production systems, connectionist theories are computer simulations of how thinking occurs. Much of the reason for the popularity of connectionist models is their general resemblance to the workings of the brain. This makes the approach a promising candidate for modeling how thinking is achieved within the brain. The models have several key characteristics (Plunkett, 1996):

1. They are made up of large numbers of simple processing units, akin to neurons in the brain.
2. The processing units are organized into two or more hierarchically-organized layers (Figure 3.6). Typically, these include an *input layer*, whose processing units encode the initial representation of the situation; one or more *hidden layers*, whose units combine information from the input units; and an *output layer*, whose units generate the system's response to the situation.
3. The individual processing units are connected to other processing units in different layers (and sometimes within the same layer as well). The strength of each connection varies with the system's experience and is crucial in determining the processing that is done.
4. As in the brain, a given processing unit fires when the amount of activation it is receiving from all of the other processing units that are connected to it exceeds a threshold. The amount of activation that a unit receives from each unit connected to it is determined by the degree of activation of the processing unit that is sending the activation and the strength of the connection between the units.

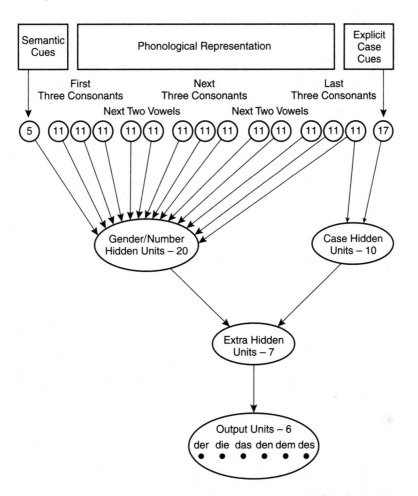

FIGURE 3.6 The connectionist model of MacWhinney et al. (1989) of how children learn the German system of articles. Note that at the top (input) level, the
model encodes five semantic features of the noun (corresponding to the "5" at
the level just below the top on the extreme left), presence or absence of 11
phonological features at as many as 13 locations in the word (also represented
at the level just below the top), and 17 explicit case cues, which indicate the
function of the noun within the sentence. These input-level units transfer activation to hidden units at the next two levels below, and eventually to the six
output units, which correspond to the six articles that accompany nouns in
German. The article that goes with the most activated output unit is advanced as
the response. Reprinted from MacWhinney, B., Leinbach, J., Taraban, R., & Mc-
Donald, J., Language learning: Cues or rules? Journal of Memory and Language,
28, 255–277, Copyright © 1989, with permission from Elsevier.

5. As in the brain, the activity of the many simple processing units occurs *in parallel* (simultaneously).
6. Knowledge is represented through the strengths of connections among all of the units in the system. There is no single location that corresponds to a particular piece of knowledge; rather the knowledge is distributed over all of the units and their inter-connections. Because of this, and because processing occurs over many units in paral-lel, these systems are often known as *parallel distributed processing* (PDP) systems.
7. Learning occurs through the system receiving input, generating a response, observing the discrepancy between it and the correct answer, and adjusting the strengths of connections among the processing units in ways that would have led to a better answer. The adjustments include strengthening some connections and weakening others. Through this process, the system implicitly learns the rules underlying correct responses to the problem, although there is no single place in which the rule is represented.
8. Generalization of the system's knowledge is based on similarity of new situations to ones the system has encountered previously. When the same types of implicit rules apply to new problems, connectionist systems are very effective in generalizing previous experience to them.

A number of researchers have advocated the use of connectionist models as a tool for understanding development: McClelland (1995), Shultz (2003), Plunkett (1996), and Marchman (1992) among them. One particularly impressive connec-tionist model, and one that illustrates the strength of the approach for modeling development, is that of MacWhinney, Leinbach, Taraban, and McDonald (1989).

MacWhinney et al.'s model depicted German children's learning of their language's system of definite articles. These definite articles are the multiple terms that in German serve the function that the single word *the* serves in Eng-lish. The task was of interest precisely because the German article system is so difficult. Which article should be used to modify a given noun depends on the gender of the noun being modified (masculine, feminine, or neuter), its number (singular or plural), and its role within the sentence (subject, possessor, direct object, prepositional object, or indirect object). To make matters worse, assign-ment of nouns to gender categories is often nonintuitive. For example, the word for *fork* is feminine, the word for *spoon* is masculine, and the word for *knife* is neuter. The relations are so complex that they seem almost impossible to learn. However, MacWhinney et al. built a connectionist model that showed how chil-dren could learn them.

The MacWhinney et al. model, like most connectionist models, involves an *input layer*, several *hidden layers*, and an *output layer* (Figure 3.6). Each of these layers contains a number of discrete units. For example, in the MacWhinney et al. model, the 35 units within the input layer represent features of the particu-lar noun that the article modifies, specifically aspects of the noun's sound, mean-ing, and context. Each of the hidden layers includes units that represent combinations of these input-level features. The six output units represent the six articles in German that correspond to *the* in English (*der, die, das, dem, den,* and *des*).

As just noted, a central feature of such connectionist models is the very large number of connections among processing units. In the MacWhinney et al. model, each input-layer unit is connected to first-level hidden units; each first-level hidden unit is connected to second-level hidden units; and each second-level hidden unit is connected to each of the six output units. Learning occurs through a cycle of the system (1) receiving initial input (in this case, a noun in a certain context); (2) projecting on the basis of the strengths of its various connections (which reflect past experience) what output to produce; (3) advancing that response; and (4) adjusting the strengths of connections between units so that connections that suggested the correct answer are strengthened and connections that suggested the wrong answer are weakened.

MacWhinney et al. tested this system's ability to master the German article system by repeatedly presenting the system 102 common German nouns. The model needed to choose which article to use with each noun in the particular context—that is, in the context of wanting to express a particular meaning with particular words. After it did this, the correct answer was presented, and the model adjusted connection strengths so as to optimize its accuracy in the future.

Following experience with this training set, the MacWhinney et al. model chose the correct article for more than 90 percent of the nouns in the original set. This could not be attributed simply to rote learning of which article accompanied each noun. When the model was presented with a previously encountered noun in a novel context, it chose the correct article on more than 90 percent of trials, despite the noun's often taking a different article in the new context than it had in the previous ones. The model also proved able to generalize to novel nouns; even when it had never encountered the particular term, it could use the term's sound and meaning to make educated guesses as to what article would accompany it.

The model's learning paralleled children's learning in a number of ways. Early in the learning process, the model, like children whose first language is German, tended to overuse the articles that accompany feminine nouns. The reason appeared to be that this form of the article is used most often within the language. Further, the same article-noun combinations that are the most difficult for German children to learn were the most difficult for the model to learn as well. The particular errors made by the model also resembled those of children.

How was it possible for the model to produce systematic behavior without learning explicit "rules" (such as "masculine nouns in dative case take the article *dem*")? The answer is that systematic behavior *emerged* from the operation of a simple mechanism (MacWhinney, 1998). Namely, the strengths of the connections between input, hidden, and output units were adjusted repeatedly to reflect the frequency with which particular combinations of noun features were associated with each article. Eventually, the pattern of connection strengths captured complex patterns of multiple, interacting cues, without the need for formal rules to specify those combinations of cues. The fact that the model could learn to apply articles correctly without learning explicit "rules" suggests that children acquiring German may also learn the system of definite articles without acquiring rules.

In constructing their model, MacWhinney and colleagues specified the number of units in each layer. The number of units in the input layer was chosen on the basis of the number of features of the input nouns that they wished to represent, and the number of units in the output layer was chosen on the basis of the number of different articles that exist in the German language. The number of hidden units was also set in advance by the researchers. As the model learns, the hidden units come to represent systematic patterns that occur among the input units, such as combinations of input features. The number of hidden units was selected by estimating how many such patterns might be important in learning the input-output relations in the domain. Models that contain different numbers of hidden units may display different patterns of learning (Quinn & Johnson, 1997).

Some recent connectionist models utilize a learning mechanism that allows the models to recruit new hidden units into the network when they are needed. In the course of learning, when the model reaches a plateau where its performance is no longer improving, it recruits a new hidden unit, and this enables new gains in learning. The recruitment of new hidden units is thought to be analogous to forming new synapses in the brain as a result of learning. A recent model of children's acquisition of conservation of number provides a good illustration of this type of model (Shultz, 1998).

Shultz's model incorporates 13 input units that code several types of information: (1) information about the length and density of each row, (2) information about which row is transformed, and (3) information about the nature of the transformation (addition of an item, subtraction of an item, compression of the row, or elongation of the row). The model also incorporates two output units. When the two output units have the same level of activation, the model "judges" that the rows are equal in number. When one of the output units has a greater level of activation than the other, the model "judges" that the row corresponding to that output unit has the greater number.

The model was trained on a set of 420 different conservation problems, which varied in terms of the length, density, and number of objects in the rows prior to the transformation, and the nature of the transformation (addition, subtraction, compression, or elongation). During training, the model was presented with conservation problems, and after each problem, the network connection strengths were adjusted using a mathematical algorithm to reduce errors in the output. When these connection strength adjustments failed to improve performance, the model recruited a new hidden unit. In general, the model displayed large improvements in performance immediately after new hidden units were recruited.

After the model successfully learned to solve the conservation problems in the training set, Shultz presented it with a set of 100 items that were not part of the training set. The model successfully generalized its learning, succeeding on 95 percent of the new items. The model's learning also paralleled children's learning in some important ways. In longitudinal studies, children tend to show sudden jumps in conservation performance; the model displayed similar sudden improvements. Children tend to succeed on conservation problems that involve small numbers before they succeed on conservation problems that involve large numbers. The model showed this exact pattern. Children also tend to choose the longer of the two rows as having more items than the shorter row (regardless of density); the model did so as well.

Connectionist models have successfully depicted a number of other developmental acquisitions as well. These include object permanence (Munakata, 1998; Munakata, McClelland, Johnson, & Siegler, 1997), understanding of time-speed-distance problems (Buckingham & Shultz, 2000; Shultz, Schmidt, Buckingham, & Mareschal, 1995), early reading acquisition (Plaut, McClelland, Seidenberg, & Patterson, 1995), second language learning (MacWhinney, 1996), category learning (Mareschal, French, & Quinn, 2000; Quinn & Johnson, 2000), and acquisition of word meanings and grammatical understanding (Elman, 1993; MacWhinney & Chang, 1995; Marchman, 1992; Plunkett & Sinha, 1992; Shultz & Bale, 2001).

As with all theories, connectionist approaches are open to criticism. One frequent criticism is that their claim to be "brain style cognition" is overstated. Nothing within them corresponds to the chemical activity that is crucial to brain functioning, and the functioning of their simple processing units bears only an abstract similarity to the functioning of neurons. Another limitation is that connectionist networks learn extremely slowly, and they require many more exposures to learn than human beings do. Although models that recruit new hidden units sometimes show sudden gains in performance, they do not show the kind of sudden insight that people fairly often do (Raijmakers, van Koten, & Molenaar, 1996). A third limitation, related to the second one, is that they do not learn the symbolic rules, such as mathematical formulas, that people do, and they may not be able to learn certain aspects of grammar (Pinker & Prince, 1988).

On the other hand, connectionist models have proven useful for modeling the many developments that do not depend on acquisition of explicit rules. Although the operation of such systems clearly differs from that of the brain, it more closely resembles it than do other computer simulation approaches. Connectionist models have proven especially useful for modeling domains such as perception and language, in which numerous, partially valid sources of information must be integrated to produce successful performance. Given these advantages, it is not surprising that the popularity of connectionist modeling of development is growing rapidly.

THEORIES OF COGNITIVE EVOLUTION

One of the most profound intellectual contributions of all time is Darwin's theory of evolution. Within evolutionary theory, competition among species is a basic aspect of existence. Species originate and change through two main processes: *variation* and *selection*. Genetic combination and mutation produce variation; survival of offspring is the basis of selection. Together, these processes have produced our planet's ever-changing mosaic of living things.

As in the biological context, competition seems to be a basic feature of cognition. Rather than species competing, however, the competitions are among ideas. The main challenges for evolutionary theories of cognitive development are to describe the competing entities within the human cognitive system, to describe how the competition among these entities leads to adaptive outcomes, and to identify the mechanisms that produce cognitive variation and selection.

A number of current models of cognitive development are based on analogies between the functions that must be accomplished to produce evolutionary and developmental change (Changeux & Dehaene, 1989; Edelman, 1987; Geary & Bjorklund, 2000; Johnson & Gilmore, 1996). Here we use Siegler's (1996, 2000) *overlapping waves approach* to illustrate the way in which the analogy to biological evolution can contribute to understanding of development.

The basic assumptions of this approach are that at any one time, children have a variety of ways of thinking about most topics; that these varied ways of thinking compete with each other for use; and that the more advanced ways of thinking gradually become increasingly prevalent. These assumptions are illustrated in Figure 3.7. At any given time, several ways of thinking (the strategies in the figure) are present in a child's thinking. (Strategies are procedures aimed at meeting particular goals.) These strategies compete with each other, and with experience, some become more frequent, some become less frequent, and some first become more frequent and later less frequent. Further, new strategies are introduced and old strategies stop being used. This overlapping waves model seems more in accord with what is known about cognitive development than do depictions that show children suddenly moving from one approach to another.

Siegler and colleagues have pursued this evolutionary model within a variety of areas: arithmetic, time telling, reading, spelling, tool use, problem

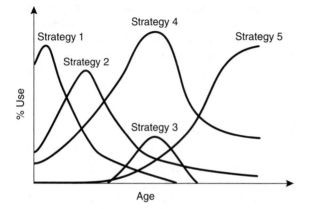

FIGURE 3.7 Siegler's overlapping waves model of cognitive development.

solving, and memory tasks, among them (Chen & Siegler, 2000; Jansen & van der Maas, 2002; Rittle-Johnson & Siegler, 1999; Siegler, 1996; Siegler & Stern, 1998; Siegler & Svetina, 2002). In each of these areas, the findings indicate that competition leads to adaptive consequences, and that basic strategy choice and discovery mechanisms produce the adaptation. The findings can be illustrated in the context of young children's learning of simple addition.

First consider the competing entities. Even 5-year-olds use a variety of strategies to solve basic addition problems such as $3 + 5$. Sometimes they *count from one*; this typically involves putting up fingers on one hand to represent the first addend, putting up fingers on the other hand to represent the second addend, and then counting the raised fingers on both hands. Other times, they put up fingers but recognize the number of fingers that are up without counting. Yet other times, they retrieve an answer from memory. Some children also know another strategy, the *count-on* strategy. Children using this strategy choose the larger of the two addends and count on from that point the number of times indicated by the smaller addend. For example, on $3 + 9$, children might think to themselves, "9, 10, 11, 12."

It is not the case that some 5-year-olds use one of these strategies and some use another. Rather, almost all children use several different strategies. In addition, on arithmetic, spelling, time telling, memory recall, analogical reasoning, tool use, and many other tasks, the majority of children have been found to use multiple strategies. Even on individual problems, the outcomes of the competition vary, so that the same child will choose one strategy one day and a different one the next (Siegler, 1987a).

Children's choices among these strategies are adaptive in several different ways. One sense in which their choices are adaptive is that they use retrieval, the fastest strategy, predominantly on simple problems where it can yield accurate performance, and they use more time-consuming and effortful strategies on more difficult problems, where such strategies are necessary for accurate performance (Siegler, 1986).

Children also choose adaptively among strategies other than retrieval. In particular, they tend to use each strategy most often on problems where it works especially well compared to alternative approaches. In evolutionary terms, strategies find their niches. For example, the count-on strategy is used most often on problems such as $2 + 9$, where the smaller addend is quite small and the difference between addends is large. On such problems, counting on is both easy to do and effective relative to alternative procedures such as counting from one (Siegler, 1987b).

Changes over time in strategy use also are adaptive. For example, in simple addition, children increasingly use the most efficient strategies, such as retrieval and counting on, and decrease their use of less efficient strategies, such as guessing and counting from one. They also acquire new strategies, such as decomposition (such as solving $3 + 9$ by thinking "$3 + 10 = 13$, 9 is 1 less than 10, so $3 + 9 = 12$").

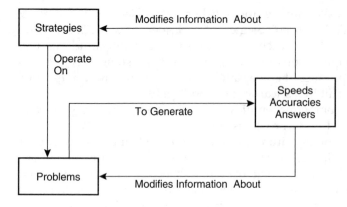

FIGURE 3.8 Overview of Siegler and Shipley's (1995) strategy choice model. Diagram best read by starting at top left.

What type of selection mechanisms could produce such adaptive strategy choices? Siegler's model (e.g., Shrager & Siegler, 1998) divides the information-processing system into representations and processes. The representations include factual information and data; the processes operate on the representations to produce behavior. For example, in the context of arithmetic, the representation includes associations between problems and various possible answers to the problems. The processes are strategies such as counting from one, counting on, and retrieval that solve problems by operating on the data in the representation.

Figure 3.8 illustrates how this type of organization could yield effective choices among strategies at any one time and adaptive changes in strategy use over time. Within the model, the use of strategies to solve problems generates answers to the problems and also generates information about the speed and accuracy with which the problem was solved. This information feeds back to provide increasingly detailed knowledge about both the strategies and the problems. Subsequent choices among strategies are made on the basis of their past effectiveness in solving problems in general, in solving particular kinds of problems, and in solving specific problems. The more effective a strategy has been in solving problems in the past, the more often it will be chosen in the future. Further, the choices among strategies become increasingly refined as children learn that a strategy that in general is the most effective is not necessarily the most effective for a particular type of problem.

This view of development has provided the basis for computer simulations of the development of arithmetic (Shrager & Siegler, 1998; Siegler & Shipley, 1995; Siegler & Shrager, 1984). To illustrate how the general theoretical assumptions are realized within a specific simulation, we describe a model of the development of single-digit addition developed by Siegler and Shipley (1995), and extended by Shrager and Siegler (1998). The simulation models how children learn to choose among three approaches: counting from one, counting on from the larger addend, and retrieval. Its working can be illustrated by considering its strategy choices on $9 + 1$. The simulation gradually learns that it is easier to solve this problem by counting on from the larger addend than by counting from one. It requires far fewer counts to say "9, 10" than "1, 2, 3, 4, 5, 6, 7, 8, 9, 10." This lesser amount of counting results in fewer errors and shorter solution times, which in turn leads to more frequent future choices of the counting-on strategy. The simulation uses this experience and similar experience with other problems to draw the generalization that counting on works better than counting from one on related problems, such as $9 + 2$ and $8 + 1$, and it uses the knowledge to generalize appropriately to unfamiliar problems.

As children increasingly choose strategies that correctly solve problems, they also increasingly associate the correct answers with the problems. For example, $9 + 1$ becomes strongly associated with 10. This association allows them to retrieve 10 as the answer to the problem. Retrieving an answer is even faster than counting "9, 10" and is just as accurate. Thus, the very success of the count-on strategy in producing correct answers leads to its own obsolescence, because it makes accurate retrieval possible.

The evolutionary perspective raises the further issue of the source of strategic variation. In particular, how are new strategies acquired? Sometimes children are taught a new strategy or imitate another person who is using it. However, the most interesting case is *strategy discovery*, in which children invent a strategy for themselves.

How do children discover new strategies? To find out, Siegler and Jenkins (1989) examined 4- and 5-year-olds' discovery of the counting-on strategy. Recall that this strategy involves solving problems such as $2 + 9$ by thinking, "9, 10, 11." Children in the Siegler and Jenkins experiment knew how to add by counting from one but did not yet know how to do so by counting on from the larger addend. The children practiced solving addition problems three times per week for 11 weeks. Because even young children can accurately report immediately after an addition problem how they solved the problem (Siegler, 1987b), it was possible to identify the exact trial on which each child first used the new strategy. This allowed Siegler and Jenkins to examine what led up to the discovery, and what the experience of discovering a new strategy was like for a child.

Almost all of the children discovered the new strategy during the course of the experiment. The time that they took to make the discovery varied widely; the first discovery came in the second session, whereas the last one did not come until the thirtieth session. The quality of the discoveries also varied widely. Some discoveries showed a great deal of insight, as exemplified by "Lauren's" protocol:

E: How much is $6 + 3$?

L: *(Long pause)* Nine.

E: OK, how did you know that?

L: I think I said . . . I think I said . . . oops, um . . . I think he said . . . 8 was 1 and . . . um . . . I mean 7 was 1, 8 was 2, 9 was 3.

E: How did you know to do that? Why didn't you count 1, 2, 3, 4, 5, 6, 7, 8, 9?

L: Cause then you have to count all those numbers.

E: OK, well how did you know you didn't have to count all of those numbers?

L: Why didn't . . . well I don't have to if I don't want to. (Siegler & Jenkins, 1989, p. 66)

What led up to the discoveries? The expectation had been that difficult problems, or situations in which children failed to solve previous problems, would elicit them. This proved not to be the case, however. The problems on which discoveries were made, and the accuracy of performance just prior to discovery, did not differ from performance in the rest of the experiment. The only distinguishing characteristic of performance immediately before the discovery was solution times that greatly exceeded the usual amount. For example, Lauren, the child quoted above, took 67 seconds to generate the answer on the trial just before her discovery and 35 seconds on the trial where she first used the new strategy. Both trials were much longer than her average time of 11 seconds. These long times were accompanied by numerous false starts, pauses, odd statements (as in Lauren's comment referring to her own counting "I think *he* said"), and other indicators of cognitive ferment.

Like Lauren, Shrager and Siegler's (1998) model of the development of single-digit addition also succeeded in discovering new strategies. In the model, the discovery process works by analyzing the sequence of operations involved in executing strategies, identifying potential improvements, and generating candidate new strategies by recombining parts of existing approaches. The model includes two general heuristics for identifying improvements and generating new strategies: (1) if a redundant sequence of behavior is detected, then delete one of the two sequences, and (2) if a strategy is more successful when the operations are executed in a particular order, then create a version of the strategy that always uses that order. When new strategies are created, and before they are used, they are passed through a "filter" that helps to eliminate flawed strategies. The filter incorporates information about the conceptual structure of the problems, such as "both addends must be represented." Candidate strategies that do not meet this criterion are rejected by the model.

Equipped with this discovery process, Shrager and Siegler's (1998) model succeeded in discovering the counting-on strategy. Further, the model's behavior was similar to that of the children in several key ways. Like the children, the model sometimes discovered the strategy following incorrect performance, and sometimes discovered it following correct performance. Also like the children, the model never executed illegal strategies. Finally, the model generalized new strategies to novel problems in a manner similar to the children. The close correspondence between the model's and the children's behavior suggests that children's strategy discovery process may work in the same way as the discovery process implemented in the model.

In some cases, children discover new strategies without being consciously aware of their discoveries. Siegler and Stern (1998) investigated this issue using inversion problems, which are arithmetic problems of the form $a + b - b = \underline{\quad}$ (such as $18 + 5 - 5 = \underline{\quad}$). Children sometimes use a *shortcut strategy* to solve these problems: they recognize that since the same number is added and then subtracted, that number can be ignored, and the other number is the solution. At other times, children use a more labor-intensive *computation* strategy; they compute the solution in two steps ($18 + 5 = 23$; $23 - 5 = 18$). Not surprisingly, the computation strategy takes much longer to execute than does the shortcut strategy. In Siegler and Stern's study of second grade students, when children used computation, they solved the problems in an average of 16 seconds, and when they used the shortcut strategy, they solved the problems in an average of 2.5 seconds.

Most interesting, children sometimes solved a problem very quickly (in fewer then 4 seconds), suggesting that they used the shortcut strategy, but claimed to have used computation when asked how they solved the problem. They appeared to use the shortcut strategy unconsciously before they could report that they had used it! Siegler and Stern termed this phenomenon the *unconscious shortcut strategy,* and they found that it was especially prevalent among children who were given problem sets that consisted solely of inversion problems, rather than sets with problems of the form $a + b - c = \underline{\quad}$ mixed in. In the group that received solely inversion problems, 14 of the 16 children (88 percent) used the unconscious shortcut strategy before they used the (conscious) shortcut strategy. It was not the case that verbal skills prevented children from expressing the shortcut strategy—almost all of the children explicitly stated the shortcut strategy on a later trial. Instead, the findings suggest that children used the shortcut strategy without being aware of it, before they could consciously recognize that they had used it.

These findings may shed some light on Lauren's difficulties in articulating her discovery of the counting-on strategy in the protocol presented above. At least in some cases, the process of strategy discovery appears to involve cognitive processes that are not easily verbalized. Other researchers have also reported evidence consistent with this view. For example, Goldin-Meadow and colleagues have demonstrated that children often express new problem-solving strategies in gestures before they express them in speech (Alibali & Goldin-Meadow, 1993; Church & Goldin-Meadow, 1986; Goldin-Meadow, 2001; Perry, Church, & Goldin-Meadow, 1988). These researchers have argued that, at least in some cases, children's emerging knowledge is implicit and not accessible to verbal report. Eventually, this knowledge is re-represented in a more explicit format, which is accessible to verbalization. Along similar lines, Dixon and Moore (1996) have argued that solvers must have intuitive understanding of a problem domain before they can generate problem-solving strategies within that domain.

What are the main limitations of Siegler's theory? One problem is that the theory seems most applicable to domains in which children use clearly defined strategies; its applicability to areas in which strategies are less well defined remains to be demonstrated. Another is that it has little to say about how the social world influences cognitive development. Still, it would be disingenuous to be pessimistic about it. The basic observation that cognitive development resembles biological evolution is beginning to emerge in many areas: perceptual development (Johnson & Karmiloff-Smith, 1992), language development (MacWhinney & Chang, 1995), motor development (Thelen, 2001), and analogical reasoning (Gentner, 1989) among them. If the approach proves half as useful in understanding cognitive development as it has in understanding biological evolution, the effort to apply the idea will be well worthwhile.

Summary

Information-processing theories of development have several distinguishing characteristics. Their basic assumption is that thinking is information processing. They emphasize precise analysis of change mechanisms. They focus on the strategies that children devise to surmount the challenges posed by the environment and by their own limited processing capacity and knowledge.

Within information-processing approaches, cognition is viewed as reflecting both structure and process. Structure refers to relatively fixed aspects of the information-processing system, process to relatively variable and changeable ones. Among the most critical structures are sensory, working, and long-term memory. Sensory memory is devoted to holding a relatively large amount of unanalyzed information for about a second after the information is encountered. Working memory involves the information in the current situation and in long-term memory that is receiving attention at any given time. Without continuing attention, information is lost from working memory within 15 to 30 seconds. Long-term memory involves our enduring knowledge of procedures, facts, and specific events. It appears to be of unlimited capacity, and information remains in it indefinitely.

In contrast to this relatively small number of structures, each of which influences thinking in almost all situations, a much larger group of processes contributes in more delimited situations. These processes vary greatly with the particular circumstances, thus giving human cognition much of its flexibility. The same situation also elicits different processes in different people, depending on their past experience and abilities. Rules, concepts, and strategies are among the types of processes that people most often use.

Several information-processing theories of development have been formulated to make understandable how creatures as helpless and ignorant as infants eventually attain the power and flexibility of the adult information-processing system. Neo-Piagetian theories are aimed at uniting Piagetian and information-processing theories. Case's approach is a particularly influential example. It posits a series of stages much like Piaget's and a set of central conceptual structures that organize thinking in domains such as number, space, and stories. It also suggests that limited working memory capacity is a major obstacle to cognitive growth. By automatizing their processing, through biological maturation, and through acquisition of more advanced central conceptual structures, children become able to perform increasingly difficult cognitive feats.

Psychometric theories are intended to reveal the processes underlying the individual differences that appear on intelligence tests. Sternberg's triarchic theory of intelligence illustrates how information-processing ideas can be used to pursue this goal. The theory holds that there are three primary aspects to human intelligence: analytical, creative, and practical. Analytical intelligence involves abilities tested on traditional IQ tests, such as analyzing, evaluating, and critiquing. Creative intelligence comprises the abilities needed to cope with novel situations, such as creating, discovering, and inventing. Practical intelligence involves abilities needed to solve everyday problems, such as using and applying information. Sternberg has argued that a common set of processes underlie all of these aspects of intelligent behavior: metacomponents, performance components, and knowledge acquisition components. Metacomponents function as a strategy-construction mechanism, arranging the other two types of components into goal-oriented procedures. Knowledge acquisition components are used to obtain new information when no solution to a problem is immediately possible. Performance components do the work of solving the problem. The theory has been applied to diverse cognitive skills and to many different populations.

Production system theories are intended to explain how changes in problem solving occur. Klahr's theory explains particularly clearly how self-modifying production systems can advance understanding of development. It focuses on the developing system's capacity for generalization. In this analysis, generalization includes three components: the time line, regularity detection, and redundancy elimination. The time line is a record of all the situations the system has encountered, its responses to the situations, and the outcomes. Regularity detection operates on the data in the time line to detect repeated patterns. Redundancy elimination looks for parts of procedures that could be eliminated without changing the outcome of processing. Together, these mechanisms allow children to generalize their knowledge to new situations.

Connectionist theories are a class of computer simulation models based on an analogy to the workings of the brain. In them, numerous simple processing units, analogous to neurons, are connected to one another with varying strengths. When presented input, the processing units receive activation from one another, with the processing activity leading to a response. The response is compared to the correct answer, and the strengths of connections are adjusted in ways that would have led to more accurate responding. MacWhinney demonstrated how such a model could learn the German language's complex system for determining which article should be attached to a given noun, and Shultz demonstrated how such a model could learn conservation of number. In both cases, the systems' learning resembled that of children, both in the types of problems that were easy or difficult to learn, and in the types of errors that were made.

Evolutionary theories are based on an analogy between biological and cognitive evolution. As emphasized in Siegler's approach, the critical contributors to change in both cases are sources of variation and sources of selection. In children's thinking, strategy discovery provides one source of variation; strategy choice procedures provide a means of selection. The two types of processes work together to change not only how often children use different strategies, but also when they use each approach. The theory has stimulated observations of how children construct new strategies and of how their use of existing strategies changes over time.

Recommended Readings

Case, R., & Okamoto, Y. (1996). The role of central conceptual structures in the development of children's thought. *Monographs of the Society for Research in Child Development, 61* (1–2, Serial No. 246). The most up-to-date presentation of Case's theory. Presents extensive evidence for Case's idea of central conceptual structures, together with a general model of how they develop.

Klahr, D., & MacWhinney, B. (1998). Information processing. In D. Kuhn & R.S. Siegler (Eds.), *Handbook of child psychology: Vol. 2. Cognition, perception, & language* (5th ed.). New York: Wiley. This chapter provides a historical account of the use of computational models to study cognitive development, as well as a detailed description of both production system and connectionist models.

O'Reilly, R.C., & Munakata, Y. (2000). *Computational explorations in cognitive neuroscience: Understanding the mind by simulating the brain.* Cambridge, MA: MIT Press. An introduction to connectionist modeling, with an emphasis on how such models implement properties of the human brain. Software and sample models are available for those who wish to work with the models directly.

Siegler, R.S. (1996). *Emerging minds: The process of change in children's thinking.* New York: Oxford University Press. A comprehensive statement of Siegler's theory, emphasizing how variability, choice, and a variety of change processes together shape cognitive development.

Sternberg, R.J. (1999). The theory of successful intelligence. *Review of General Psychology, 3,* 292–316. This article reviews some of the issues associated with conventional conceptions of intelligence, and presents Sternberg's influential theory of successful intelligence.

4

SOCIOCULTURAL THEORIES
OF DEVELOPMENT

Scene: A mother is assisting her son as he attempts to construct a puzzle depicting a truck. They are using an identical, completed puzzle as a model, and their goal is to make the child's puzzle correspond to the model. The child repeatedly attempts to place green, triangular pieces in the cargo section of the truck, even though no such pieces were used in the corresponding part of the model.

> CHILD: *(picks up two green triangles from the pieces pile without looking at the model)* Another green one. Where's the green?

> MOTHER: *Did we find any green up here? (points to the model)*

> C: *(looks at model)* This one. *(points to an incorrect place in the model)*

> M: *I think maybe that's a leftover. Do you think so?*

> C: *(nods)*

> M: *Maybe we don't need the green one, cause there isn't any green one up there, is there. Remember?*

> C: *(looks at pieces pile, puts green pieces back in it, and chooses two appropriate pieces) (Wertsch & Hickmann, 1987)*

The boy in the vignette above eventually managed to complete the puzzle correctly. However, he did not do so on his own. His mother asked helpful questions, provided guidance, and directed his behavior in ways that made it possible for him to complete the puzzle successfully. She directed his attention to the appropriate places in the model puzzle and helped him to make effective choices about what piece to place next. The social support provided by the mother extended her son's abilities beyond the scope of what he could do independently.

As this example suggests, the social world has a profound effect on what children do, on what they think about, and on how they think. Interactions with other individuals provide children with opportunities for learning and help children to perform tasks that they are not able to perform on their own. The cultural context influences children's typical activities and opportunities for social interaction and provides important tools that children can use for action and for thinking, including toys such as the puzzle in the vignette above, traditional tools such as hammers and silverware, and symbolic systems such as language and mathematics.

Developmental theories that emphasize the roles of the social and cultural world in children's development are called *sociocultural theories*. Research guided by sociocultural theories investigates how social factors influence cognition and development, and how social and cultural practices shape and define thought. This chapter examines such theories and research.

Just as Piaget was the founding father of stage theories of development, the Russian psychologist Lev Semenovich Vygotsky (1896–1934) was the founding father of sociocultural theories. Although Piaget and Vygotsky were contemporaries, their theories pointed in different directions. Whereas Piaget depicted children as little scientists, trying to understand the world largely on their own, Vygotsky portrayed them as living in the midst of other people eager to help them acquire the skills needed to live in their culture. Whereas Piaget was largely concerned with the aspects of development present among all children in all societies in all historical periods, Vygotsky emphasized factors that differ among children growing up at different times in different circumstances. The approaches are complementary, in the sense that understanding cognitive development requires understanding both the universal aspects of development and the variable ones.

Vygotsky believed that humans share some elementary psychological processes with animals, including basic attentional, perceptual, and memory processes. His theory sought to explain the processes that he viewed as differentiating humans from other animals—what he referred to as the "higher psychological processes," such as reasoning and concept formation. Vygotsky believed that the key difference in psychological functioning between humans and animals had to do with the social and cultural basis of human thought. In his view, all of the higher psychological processes had their origins in social interaction.

Organization of the chapter.   The chapter is divided into three major sections. The first section introduces the central themes of sociocultural approaches to cognitive development, beginning with central themes of Vygotsky's theory,

TABLE 4.1 Chapter Outline

I.   Central Themes of Sociocultural Approaches to Cognitive Development
    A.   Cognitive Development Occurs in Social Interaction
    B.   Psychological Functioning Is Mediated by Language and Other Cultural Tools
    C.   Cultural Norms and Other People Influence Children's Opportunities for Learning
    D.   Social and Cultural Learning Require Particular Cognitive Abilities
    E.   Summary

II. Modern Empirical Research in the Sociocultural Tradition
    A.   Learning in Interaction with Adults
    B.   Learning in Interaction with Peers
    C.   Guided Participation in Cultural Activities
    D.   Language as a Psychological Tool

III. Educational Implications of Sociocultural Theories
    A.   Sociocultural Approaches to Assessing Children's Knowledge
    B.   Educational Interventions Based on Sociocultural Principles
    C.   Learning to Use Psychological Tools
    D.   Sociocultural Interpretations of Classroom Processes

IV. Summary

and then addressing modern developments in sociocultural theory. The second major section describes several strands of contemporary empirical research in the sociocultural tradition, including research about learning in interaction with adults and peers, guided participation in cultural activities, and the use of language as a tool for thinking. The final section addresses educational implications of sociocultural theories. The chapter outline is presented in Table 4.1.

Central Themes of Sociocultural Approaches to Cognitive Development

Sociocultural approaches to cognitive development share several common themes. This section begins with two of the central themes of Vygotsky's sociocultural theory, which continue to be central within current sociocultural theories: (1) cognitive development occurs in social interaction, and (2) psychological functioning is mediated by cultural tools, including language. (Note that, although Vygotsky's works were not translated into English until the latter part of the twentieth century, these works were written in the 1920s and 1930s. The publication dates for Vygotsky's writings are sometimes misleading because they indicate the translation date, rather than the date when the original work was written.) The latter part of the section introduces two additional themes that have been emphasized primarily in sociocultural theories of the last two to three decades: (1) cultural norms and other people influence children's opportunities for learning, and (2) social and cultural learning require particular cognitive abilities on the parts of learners and teachers.

COGNITIVE DEVELOPMENT OCCURS
IN SOCIAL INTERACTION

One of Vygotsky's central claims, and a theme of sociocultural theories more generally, is that development occurs in social interaction. Children engage in direct social interactions with many different individuals on a day-to-day basis, including caregivers, siblings, extended family members, neighbors, teachers, and peers. Sociocultural theories hold that these interactions with other people have a profound influence on the course of children's development.

It is worth noting, however, that this emphasis on the social world is not unique to Vygotsky's theory, or even to sociocultural theories more generally. As described in Chapter 2, Piaget also acknowledged that other people play an important role in children's development. In particular, Piaget believed that social partners could provide children with information that might provoke states of disequilibrium, and thereby elicit cognitive change. Piaget believed that interactions with same-age peers were more likely to promote disequilibrium than interactions with older children or adults. His reasoning was that children are likely to unquestioningly accept the ideas espoused by older children and adults, but they are more likely to critically analyze and think deeply about the views held by their peers, especially when those views differ from their own.

Note that Piagetian theory conceptualizes the social environment as an outside force that influences individual children's learning and cognition. The environment provides information to the developing child, but developmental change occurs within the individual child. Thus, the basic unit of analysis in Piagetian theory is the *individual child.* The external environment is important only as an influence that can elicit particular thoughts and new equilibria in the child. In contrast, sociocultural theories view the social environment as an integral part of children's thinking and behavior, such that the child's cognition and behavior cannot be separated from the social context in which they take place. Thus, in sociocultural theories, the emphasis is on the *child in context* as the unit of analysis. Social interaction is not simply an external source of information that plays a role in individual development, but is instead an integral part of development, as well as a source of developmental change (Gauvain, 2001).

Vygotsky proposed a mechanism for developmental change that is inherently social. Specifically, he argued that developmental change occurs via the *internalization of socially shared processes.* He argued that in the course of development, every psychological function occurs twice—first at the "intermental" level (between people who are involved in social interaction), and later at the "intramental" level (within the individual). Children initially perform cognitive tasks with support from social partners, and over time, these social interactions are gradually internalized, until children can perform the tasks on their own. Thus, individual psychological processes originate in, and derive from, social interactions. From this perspective, social interaction is not merely an outside force that influences the path of development; it is instead a causal mechanism for development itself.

One example that Vygotsky used to illustrate the process of internalization is the development of pointing during infancy (Vygotsky, 1978). According to his account, the development of pointing begins with an infant's unsuccessful attempt to reach a desired object. When an adult construes the infant's actions as an attempt to draw attention to the object, the meaning of the infant's action is fundamentally changed, from an instrumental attempt to obtain the object to an attempt to communicate with the adult. However, this meaning initially exists only in the social interaction between the infant and the adult, not in the infant's mind. Eventually, the infant links the reaching action to the social situation, and begins to understand the movement as aimed, not at an object, but at another person. When the social meaning of the action is internalized by the infant, the action is fundamentally changed, becoming a "true gesture" (Vygotsky, 1978, p. 56). Thus, the meaning of the pointing action is first socially constructed in interaction between the adult and the infant, and then gradually internalized by the infant.

As a second example of internalization, consider a child learning to tie her shoes. At first, an adult assists the child, providing verbal guidance to the child about what to do next (as in "Now make a loop, and bring the other lace around it . . ."). With time, the child internalizes the sequence of steps, so that she can control her own actions without adult assistance. She may "hear" the adult's instructions in her "mind's ear," but she no longer needs the adult to provide external support for her performance.

Note that this framework emphasizes the transfer of responsibility for cognition from more skilled individuals to less skilled ones. To characterize this process, Vygotsky introduced the concept of the *zone of proximal development*. The zone of proximal development is defined as the distance between what a child can do independently, and what the child can do in interaction with an adult or a more advanced peer (Vygotsky, 1978, see Figure 4.1). This concept was based on the observation that children can often reason in more complex ways or perform more complex behaviors when they receive assistance than they can on their own. For example, the preschooler in the vignette at the outset of this chapter was able to complete a complex puzzle with assistance from his mother, but he might not have been able to complete it had he worked on his own. Similarly, a middle school student might be able to solve a complex, multi-operation algebra equation with guidance from her teacher, but she might be able to solve only much simpler equations when working alone. Solving the complex problem with the teacher's help would provide an opportunity for the student to internalize the solution procedure, and perhaps eventually to solve it on her own.

Vygotsky believed that, to accurately characterize a child's knowledge at a given point in time, it is essential to consider the child's potential competence, as manifested in the zone of proximal development, as well as the child's actual competence in independent performance. The two children depicted in

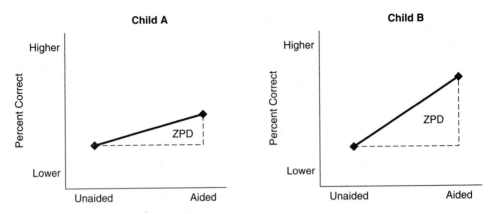

FIGURE 4.1 Two children's zones of proximal development (ZPD). The children's unaided performance is similar, but child B benefits more from another person's help.

Figure 4.1 display comparable levels of independent performance, but dramatically different levels of potential competence. Thus, an accurate characterization of each child's knowledge requires assessments of both levels. As discussed later in the chapter, Vygotsky's views have had an important impact on knowledge assessment in educational settings.

PSYCHOLOGICAL FUNCTIONING IS MEDIATED BY LANGUAGE AND OTHER CULTURAL TOOLS

Vygotsky believed that human behavior is shaped not only by direct social interactions but also by the range of *cultural tools* that are available in the time and place that development occurs. Cultural tools include both *technical tools*, which are tools for acting on the environment (such as plows, hammers, and silverware), and *psychological tools*, which are tools for thinking. Language is the prime example of a psychological tool, in that it is used as a means for regulating behavior, planning, remembering, and solving problems. However, people have invented many other psychological tools besides language, including maps, diagrams, number systems (Arabic numerals, Roman numerals), algebraic symbols, programming languages, tools for solving mathematical problems (protractors, slide rules, calculators, computer software), systems for conceptualizing dates and time (calendars, clocks), systems for filing and organizing information (the Dewey Decimal system, the Linnaen classification system for living organisms), and so forth.

Psychological tools influence the way we organize and remember information. Think for a moment about reciting the alphabet. Chances are, the "alphabet song" just popped into your mind. Research has shown that people use the alphabet song to organize their knowledge of the alphabet, so that when

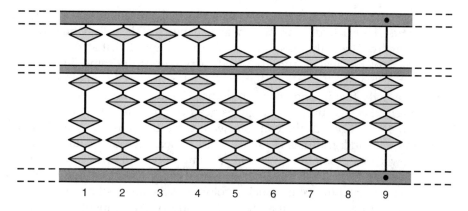

FIGURE 4.2 The number 123,456,789 as represented on an abacus. The number 1 is represented on the leftmost bar and the number 9 on the rightmost one (from Stigler, 1984).

asked, for example, "What letter comes before K?" people typically enter the alphabet at the letter H, imagining the "chunk" of the alphabet song that consists of "H I J K" (Klahr, Chase, & Lovelace, 1983).

Material artifacts can also serve as psychological tools. Some good examples are appointment books, abacuses, and rosary beads. These tools sometimes become internalized and influence thought, even in situations in which the material artifacts are absent. One compelling example of this phenomenon comes from individuals who are skilled at using the abacus.

Abacuses are commonly used in East Asian countries to solve arithmetic problems. Figure 4.2 illustrates the type of abacus that is most commonly used. Its columns represent a base-10 notation, like that used in standard computation. The column at one end (it can be either end) is the 1s column, the next column inward is the 10s column, the next column inward is the 100s column, and so on. Each column is divided into the single bead above the divider and the four beads below. The bead above the divider represents a value of 5; each of the four beads below it represents a value of 1. When the value of a column is zero, the 5s bead is at the top of the abacus and the four 1s beads are at the bottom. To represent numbers greater than zero, the operator moves beads toward the divider in the middle. Thus, if a girl wanted to add 4 + 3, she would first push four 1s beads from below the divider up toward the middle with an upward finger motion (to represent the 4). When her finger reached the top of the column, she would make a downward motion, pushing the 5s bead down toward the middle and returning two of the 1s beads that had been pushed up near the divider to their original position (to represent the 3, as 5 minus 2). This would leave the 5s bead and two 1s beads in the middle, indicating the answer, 7.

Following a hypothesis advanced by Hatano, Miyake, and Binks (1977), Stigler (1984) investigated whether individuals who are skilled at using the abacus use a "mental abacus" when they solve problems in their heads. He pre-sented 11-year-old Taiwanese abacus experts with arithmetic problems to solve mentally. The children's pattern of errors suggested that they formed a mental image of the abacus and imagined carrying out the same finger movements on it that they would on a real abacus. First, many of the children's errors were off by exactly five in one of the columns. This type of error is easy to make on the abacus, because only the single 5s bead discriminates between 2 and 7, 3 and 8, and so on. Second, the children were three times as likely as American under-graduate and graduate students to err by leaving out a column altogether. If an answer to a problem was 43,296, a common type of error for the Taiwanese chil-dren was 4,396. This type of error would occur if the children read their answers from a mental image in which a column of the abacus had faded. Thus, the chil-dren's errors suggest that they did indeed use a mental abacus when they needed to perform mental arithmetic. For these abacus experts, the abacus had become internalized, and it influenced their performance even when the physi-cal abacus was not present.

Children growing up in East Asian countries are much more likely to learn to use the abacus than their peers who are growing up in North America. Thus, this example also highlights that different cultural tools are available in differ-ent cultural settings. Such tools are an important means through which culture shapes and defines human behavior. Over the course of history, as new cultural tools become available, human behavior changes. For example, the ready avail-ability of calculators has led to a decreased emphasis on computation in math-ematics instruction in many American schools. People's behavior is shaped in large part by the cultural tools that are available to them.

Because of humans' abilities to learn from social interactions, they are able to pool their cognitive resources and build on past achievements in ways that members of other animal species cannot. Thus, cultural tools can be passed on to younger members of the cultural group, and they can also be refined further. As a result, cultural tools increase, in effectiveness as well as in number, over historical time. As an example, consider the wide variety of writing instruments that are available to the modern student (wooden pencils, mechanical pencils, ballpoint pens, markers, fountain pens, and so forth). Now think about the types of writing instruments that were available 300 years ago, or 3000 years ago. The same pattern of change over time also applies to psychological tools. For exam-ple, many of the mathematical symbols that are widely used today ($+$, $-$, $=$) were first developed in the fifteenth and sixteenth centuries. Such innovations are preserved and shared, not only across individuals, but also across genera-tions. This evolutionary process that applies to cultural tools has been termed the "ratchet effect" (Tomasello, Kruger, & Ratner, 1993).

Among cultural tools, Vygotsky accorded language special significance in psychological development. Indeed, he claimed that the moment when language becomes integrated with action is "the most significant moment in the course of intellectual development" (Vygotsky, 1978, p. 24). After this point, language is not simply a means for communication but also a means by which children can control and regulate their own actions. Language is a tool that children can use to plan their actions, remember information, solve problems, and organize their behavior. In these respects, it can be said that children's behavior is mediated by language. Some of the ways in which this mediation occurs will be discussed in more detail later in the chapter.

CULTURAL NORMS AND OTHER PEOPLE INFLUENCE CHILDREN'S OPPORTUNITIES FOR LEARNING

Modern sociocultural theorists have focused not only on the tools that culture provides, but also on how cultural norms and social practices influence the activities in which children engage, and the opportunities that children have for learning. For example, the society as a whole dictates whether or not formal schooling is available and if so, whether it is compulsory. Cultural norms influence many aspects of children's day-to-day activities, including infant care practices, child care arrangements, and expectations about work, study, and play.

Cross-cultural comparisons and in-depth studies of different ethnic groups have documented that children in different cultural communities spend their time in different ways (Gaskins, 1999; Stevenson & Stigler, 1992). Even among societies that are similar in important ways (such as industrialized societies in which all children receive formal schooling), there are wide variations in children's typical activities. One study compared the daily activities of children from Greensboro, North Carolina (United States), Suwon (Korea), Obninsk (Russia), and Tartu (Estonia). There were differences across cities in the amount of time spent in each of the activity categories examined, including play, lessons (including both formal and informal instruction), work, and conversation (Tudge et al., 1999). Play was the most common activity in all four cities, but the amount of time spent at play varied, with the Korean children spending the greatest amount of time, and the Russian children the least. Russian and Estonian children spent more time in lessons and work than did Korean and American children, and Korean children spent less time in conversation than did children in the other three sites. Thus, children's typical activities varied across cultures.

Across all four cities, there were also systematic differences between middle-class and working-class children in all of the activity categories except work. On the whole, children from middle-class families spent more time in lessons and conversation, and children from working-class families spent more time at play. Thus, different cultural communities, defined both in terms of different societies and different social classes, provide children with varying types of opportunities for learning.

Within the framework provided by the culture as a whole, parents, teachers, and other caregivers select and organize activities and social interactions that they deem appropriate for children. At times, these choices are made with explicit instructional goals in mind. For example, many North American parents arrange for their children to participate in music lessons or to visit children's museums and libraries. However, choices about activities and social partners are often made without explicit intentions to foster children's learning.

A good example of this latter type of activity is Girl Scout cookie drives. Their main goal is to raise money for the troop. However, in participating in them, the scouts learn a variety of values and skills (Rogoff, 1995; Rogoff, Topping, Baker-Sennett, & Lacasa, 2002). The learning occurs through direct interaction with troop leaders, parents, customers, and other children; through the use of tools developed by other people, such as the color-coded order forms that are provided to indicate how much of each kind of cookie is being ordered and how much money is owed; through planning routes to deliver the cookies; through figuring out how much change is needed when customers pay for their orders; through trying various sales strategies; and so on. While engaging in these activities, children acquire not only skills but also values: responsibility, courtesy, efficiency, precision, and promptness, among others. As with the skills, these values are not explicit goals of the cookie drives. Rather, they are useful byproducts, acquired in the course of pursuing the main goal of making money. Different cultures provide different learning activities, but in all cultures, children learn a wide range of values and skills through participation in activities that reflect the values of their society.

SOCIAL AND CULTURAL LEARNING REQUIRE PARTICULAR COGNITIVE ABILITIES

A major focus of modern sociocultural theories has been to specify the mechanisms involved in social and cultural learning. One approach to this issue is to delineate the cognitive abilities required for social and cultural learning, both on the part of learners and on the part of teachers.

Perhaps the most basic cognitive ability needed for social and cultural learning is the ability to establish *intersubjectivity*, which is the shared understanding between people that emerges through processes of mutual attention and communication. Not surprisingly, social interactions that involve a high degree of intersubjectivity lead to greater learning than interactions characterized by less intersubjectivity (e.g., Tudge, 1992).

The capacity for intersubjectivity emerges at an early age. Starting when infants are about 2 months old, they and their caregivers begin to display *contingent interaction*—reciprocal actions and reactions that resemble the mutual give-and-take of conversation (e.g., Bateson, 1979; Trevarthen, 1979). By about 9 months, infants can readily follow adults' gaze and pointing gestures (Butterworth, 2001; Morissette, Ricard, & Gouin-Decarie, 1995; Murphy & Messer, 1977). Through these behaviors, infants contribute to establishing *joint attention*, a state in which they and their caregivers share a common focus on particular objects or events, and a key component of intersubjectivity. Children's ability to achieve and maintain intersubjectivity continues to develop through the early childhood years, as they become increasingly able to take the perspectives of other people (e.g., Göncü, 1993).

Further insights into the cognitive abilities required for learning from social interaction have been gained from comparative studies of human children and non-human primates. Like humans, members of many other primate species can learn simply by observing the actions of other individuals (e.g., Custance, Whiten, & Fredman, 1999; Hirata & Morimura, 2000). However, according to Michael Tomasello and his collaborators, only humans are capable of certain, more advanced forms of social learning that require understanding of others as individuals with intentions and goals (Tomasello, 1998, 1999; Tomasello et al., 1993). According to this view, what is crucial in learning from social interaction is humans' ability to understand other people as being like themselves, and in particular, as having intentions and mental states like their own. Tomasello and his collaborators have identified three forms of cultural learning that rely on this understanding: imitative learning, instructed learning, and collaborative learning (Tomasello et al., 1993).

Imitative learning, according to Tomasello's definition, is learning that involves reproducing another individual's behavior *in order to achieve the same goal.* Thus, imitative learning involves understanding the relation between the other individual's behavior and his or her goal. This form of learning can be distinguished from *emulation,* which is learning that involves focusing on the end result of the other individual's behavior, without an appreciation of the relation between the specific behavior and the intended goal. Thus, emulation involves learning something about the task, whereas true imitative learning involves learning about the other individual's behavior in the task (Nagell, Olguin, & Tomasello, 1993). Tomasello has argued that most studies that purport to show imitative learning in non-human primates (e.g., Boesch, Marchesi, Marchesi, Fruth, & Joulian, 1994; Whiten, Custance, Gomez, Teixidor, & Bard, 1996) can be explained in terms of emulation, rather than true imitative learning (Nagell et al., 1993; Tomasello, 2001).

Instructed learning is learning that involves direct, intentional transmission of information from one individual to another, with the learner attempting to understand the task or material from the teacher's point of view. In instructed learning, learners internalize their teachers' instructions, and later use them to regulate their own behavior. Instructed learning takes place both in formal settings (in lessons at school) and in informal settings (a father teaching his daughter how to cast a fishing line). Human adults in all cultures regularly instruct their children, but non-human primates do not (see Boesch, 1991, for a different perspective). Both the propensity to teach and the ability to learn via instruction require at least some ability to understand other individuals' states of mind.

This ability is also required for the third type of cultural learning, *collaborative learning,* which is learning that occurs when multiple individuals engage in cooperative, goal-directed problem solving. As an example of such learning, consider two children working together to set up a track for a toy train. The track the children make together is likely to be more complex than the one either child could make independently, and each child is likely to learn something in the course of working together. Whereas imitative and instructed learning involve a process of transmission from one individual to another, collaborative learning involves a process of joint construction of the new knowledge. This process involves establishing a common goal, sharing responsibility for goal-directed actions, and cooperatively carrying out those actions—all activities that require an ability to take the perspective of the other participants in the interaction.

All three forms of cultural learning require the ability to take the perspective of another individual. According to Tomasello, this is the key ability that differentiates humans from other primates, and enables humans to learn from social interactions.

SUMMARY

In his writings in the early part of the twentieth century, Vygotsky set forth two major themes that form the foundation of sociocultural theories of development. First, cognitive development takes place in social interaction. Vygotsky conceptualized social interaction not as an external force that provokes change within the individual but as integral to the mechanism of developmental change itself. Second, human behavior is mediated by cultural tools, including both technical tools, which are tools for acting on the environment, and psychological tools, which are tools for thinking. Vygotsky viewed language as the most important psychological tool.

Modern sociocultural theories have built on these themes in a number of ways. One important focus of modern theories is on the opportunities children have for learning and for participating in activities. These opportunities depend on both cultural norms and social practices. A second major focus is on the nature of the cognitive abilities that are required for social and cultural learning. These include the ability to establish intersubjectivity and the ability to understand others as being like oneself in terms of having goals, intentions, and mental states.

Modern Empirical Research in the Sociocultural Tradition

Many active lines of inquiry in modern developmental psychology have been inspired by sociocultural theories. This section reviews central findings in several important avenues of recent research, including children's learning in interaction with adults and peers, children's guided participation in cultural activities, and the use of language as a psychological tool.

LEARNING IN INTERACTION WITH ADULTS

When adults interact with children, they often structure their interactions in ways intended to foster children's learning (Rogoff, Ellis, & Gardner, 1984; Wang, Bernas, & Eberhard, 2001; Wood & Middleton, 1975). Adults' role in such interactions is sometimes characterized using the metaphor of a *scaffold* (Stone, 1998; Wood, Bruner, & Ross, 1976). A construction scaffold is a temporary structure that is used to support workers and materials high above the ground as a building is being constructed. As Greenfield (1984) noted, construction scaffolds provide support for construction workers, extend their range of activities, and allow them to perform tasks that would otherwise be impossible. Once the structure of the building is complete, the scaffold is no longer needed. Like a physical scaffold, adults provide social scaffolding to support children's task performance. Such scaffolding allows children to extend the range of their activities and to perform tasks that would be impossible for them to perform alone. Once children can perform the tasks unaided, the social scaffold is no longer necessary.

The vignette at the outset of this chapter provides a concrete illustration of social scaffolding. The child in the vignette initially does not attend to the model that he is attempting to reproduce. His mother guides his attention to the model and gently corrects his inappropriate selection of a puzzle piece. With his mother's assistance, the child selects the appropriate pieces, and uses them to construct the puzzle correctly. The mother's behaviors extend the range of the child's performance and make it possible for him to succeed at the puzzle.

Sensitivity of adult support. In scaffolding children's performance, adults tend to tailor their support to children's level of skill development (Greenfield, 1984; Kermani & Brenner, 2001). They sometimes provide children with simpler tasks, and they sometimes simplify tasks by reducing the number of steps required or by highlighting crucial elements of the task. Depending on children's performance, adults adjust the directness and specificity of their instruction. For example, Mayan women offer more direct assistance to girls who are inexperienced at weaving than to girls who have already acquired some weaving skill, and they offer more assistance in the early, relatively difficult cycles of the weaving process than in later cycles, which tend to be easier (Greenfield, 1984). Such contingent interaction appears to help children advance their skills, especially when instruction is focused at a level just one step beyond the child's current skill level. In a study in which mothers helped their 3- and 4-year-old children learn to construct complex block pyramids, children performed best on an independent posttest if their mother's instruction had been sensitive to the child's skill level (Wood & Middleton, 1975).

Sensitive adult-child interaction also plays an important role in children's language acquisition (Hampson & Nelson, 1993; Murray, Johnson, & Peters, 1990; Nicely, Tamis-LaMonda, & Bornstein, 1999; Tamis-LaMonda, Bornstein, & Baumwell, 2001). When infants point to objects without producing words, their mothers sometimes spontaneously provide labels for the indicated objects. Infants whose mothers do so most often tend to have larger vocabularies than infants whose mothers provide labels less often (Masur, 1982). Similarly, mothers sometimes label objects that are the focus of their children's attention, even when children do not point to those objects. Toddlers whose mothers often "follow" their attentional focus in this way also tend to have larger vocabularies (Tomasello & Farrar, 1986). Relations between mothers' talk to children and children's language development also have also been documented for other, later-developing aspects of language skill, such as the ability to tell coherent, well-structured stories (Haden, Haine, & Fivush, 1997).

Although it is important that adult support is sensitive to the child's skill level, appropriately sensitive support can take many forms. One recent study (Göncü & Rogoff, 1998) contrasted several types of structured interactions in which adults helped children group photos of items into categories (baking items, eating implements, and so forth). Adults provided support to the children in one of three ways: by articulating the category rationales themselves, by inducing the children to articulate the category rationales using leading questions, or by a combination of the two (that is, first articulating the rationales themselves, and then prompting the children to articulate the rationales). Children in all three adult-support conditions performed better on an independent posttest than did children in a control condition in which the adult provided little assistance. However, as seen in Figure 4.3, children's performance was comparable in the three adult support conditions. Thus, various types of adult support are effective at fostering children's learning.

Not surprisingly, adults do a better job of scaffolding children's thinking than do the children's peers. Direct comparisons of situations in which an adult or a peer attempts to teach a child a new skill typically show that children learn more when they work with adults (Radziszewska & Rogoff, 1988, 1991). The adults' superiority as teachers is not just due to their knowing more about the problems that are being solved. Even when child and adult teachers understand a task equally well, the adults still teach more effectively (Ellis & Rogoff, 1986). This superiority appears due in large part to their style of interaction. Adults are more likely to outline the goals of the task, discuss strategies for meeting the goals, and involve learners in making decisions. In contrast, when children teach, they often just tell learners what to do without explaining the reasons, and they also frequently rely on nonverbal demonstrations (Ellis & Rogoff, 1982). Consistent with this interpretation of why adults are more effective, adults who share responsibility with learners to a greater extent promote more effective learning than adults who do not involve the children as much (Gauvain & Rogoff, 1989).

Adults' interactions with children also vary as a function of the children's characteristics. Kevin Crowley, Maureen Callanan and their collaborators documented this fact in a compelling program of research on children's interactions with parents in science museums. When parents and children visit such museums together, parents support children's exploration of the museum exhibits in several

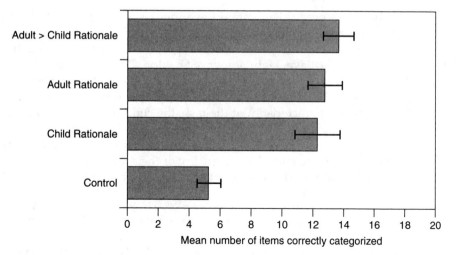

FIGURE 4.3 The mean number of items accurately categorized by children in the study by Göncü & Rogoff (1998) described in the text. In the Adult Rationale condition, adults provided the category rationales (things to eat with, things to clean the house with, etc.). In the Child Rationale condition, adults prompted children to articulate the category rationales. In the Adult > Child Rationale condition, adults first provided the category rationales and then prompted children to articulate the category rationales. In the Control condition, adults provided little assistance. Children performed well under conditions of adult support, regardless of the nature of that support. The error bars indicate standard errors.

ways (Crowley, Callanan, Jipson, et al., 2001). First, parents help children to select and encode evidence, for example, by pointing out important features of the exhibits. Second, they aid children in generating evidence, for example, by helping the children to interact with the exhibit in ways that will yield evidence that they can observe. Third, they sometimes provide explanations about how the exhibit works or about the principles that underlie the exhibit. However, the way in which parents interact with their children varies depending on the children's gender. Parents provide explanations that involve causal mechanisms much more often to boys than to girls (Crowley, Callanan, Tenenbaum, & Allen, 2001).

LEARNING IN INTERACTION WITH PEERS

Many of children's social interactions involve peers rather than adults. Peer collaborations can be beneficial for children's learning in a variety of ways: they can motivate children to try difficult tasks, provide opportunities to imitate and learn each other's skills, enable children to fine tune their understanding by explaining what they know, and allow children to participate in discussions that increase their understanding (Azmitia, 1996). These potential advantages have led to collaborative learning being widely used in many school systems.

But does peer collaboration have the desired effects on learning? The answer seems to be "sometimes yes, sometimes no." Some studies have found that solving problems with other children produces greater learning than solving problems alone (Blaye, Light, Joiner, & Sheldon, 1991; Fleming & Alexander, 2001; Perret-Clermont & Schubauer-Leoni, 1981). Others studies have not (Russell, 1982; Tudge, 1992). Still other studies have found that either outcome can occur, depending on characteristics of the task, the children, and the children's interaction (Glachan & Light, 1982; Levin & Druyan, 1993; Pine & Messer, 1998). In the following subsections, we discuss how the effectiveness of collaborations varies with the ages of the children, the quality of their interaction, their relative expertise, the difficulty of the task, and their cultural background.

Age. The ability to collaborate effectively with peers is a relatively late achievement. Even 5-year-olds, who are competent problem solvers in many circumstances, have difficulty working together to solve any but the simplest and most familiar problems (Tomasello et al., 1993). The difficulty stems from many sources, including limited ability to ignore distractions, to coordinate attention so that both partners are thinking about the same aspect of the problem, to use language sufficiently precisely to communicate ideas, and to cooperate.

Cooperation is often especially difficult for young children. Consider the following episode involving two preschoolers, one of whom had been taught how to build a copy of a Lego house and therefore was an "expert" at it. The children had been told to build a new copy of the Lego house together, but the expert was less than eager to let the novice help.

NOVICE: You gotta let me help. You said you would.
EXPERT: I will, after I finish this (the door).
   N: (Sighs, sits back, crosses arms around chest and frowns. Twenty-two seconds later, takes some blocks and begins building a section of the model—correctly. After the section is completed, he hands it to the expert.) I built this for our house.
   E: I'm the builder, you find Legos when I tell you, OK? Give me a yellow two-dot.
   N: I wanna be a builder too. She (the experimenter) said work together. My window is good . . .
   E: Well, it's not going on my house (moves copy of house out of reach of novice).
   N: (Starts shaking the table, making it impossible for the expert to continue building.)
   E: Stop it! If you don't quit it we won't get finished. I'm almost done with the door.
   N: (Stops shaking the table, observes the expert until he finishes the door.) My turn! My turn! (Azmitia, 1996, p. 142)

The novice eventually avenged the indignities done to him. When the expert continued to resist his requests for a larger role, he started pelting him with Legos. When the expert lifted his hands to protect himself, the novice smashed the copy of the Lego house. This ended the collaboration.

Quality of interaction. Even after children are able to cooperate well enough to not attack each other during collaborations, the quality of their interaction varies considerably. The nature of the interaction is an important factor in whether or not children benefit from working with a peer (Dimant & Bearison, 1991; Glachan & Light, 1982; Tudge, 1992). Children who share responsibility for the task and who become engaged in each other's thinking are more likely to benefit from collaboration than those who pay each other's reasoning less heed (Azmitia & Montgomery, 1993; Kruger, 1992; Tolmie, Howe, Mackenzie, & Greer, 1993). For example, Gauvain and Rogoff (1989) examined the efficiency of route planning among 5-year-olds who were asked to shop for specific sets of items in a toy grocery store. Children whose pairs shared responsibility for planning the route performed better than children whose pairs simply took turns performing the task.

Differences in the quality of interaction may underlie the fact that children learn more from interacting with older siblings than from interacting with other children whom they know and who are the same age as their older siblings (Azmitia & Hesser, 1993). In teaching younger children how to perform a building task, older siblings offered more explanations and more positive feedback than did the other older children. Younger children were also more likely to request explanations from their siblings than from the other older children. Thus, pairs of siblings displayed more shared involvement in the task than pairs of unrelated children.

Why does shared involvement in a task foster performance? Children who simultaneously focus on the same issues are more likely to combine each others' ideas into new theories or rules, to identify the strengths and weaknesses in each approach, and to use the other person's ideas to identify weaknesses in their own. Just talking does not improve problem solving by itself; when children solve problems alone, talking aloud about what they are doing is not beneficial (Teasley, 1995). Instead, the key seems to be the extent to which the participants actively think about each other's ideas.

Schwartz (1995) has argued that individuals working in pairs often construct more sophisticated and more abstract representations of problems than do individuals working alone. He found that across several types of problem-solving tasks, students working in pairs often developed a common representation of the problem that they could use to coordinate their different perspectives on the problem. Because these jointly developed representations bridged different perspectives, they tended to be abstract. Abstract representations often facilitate task performance, and because children working in pairs more often generate such representations, they tend to perform better than children who work alone.

Relative expertise.   Another influence on the effectiveness of peer collaborations is the relative expertise of the collaborators. Children usually benefit from interactions in which they work with a more skilled or more knowledgeable peer (Fleming & Alexander, 2001; Golbeck, 1998; Manion & Alexander, 1997; Murray, 1972; Tudge & Winterhoff, 1993). For example, in one study, novice 5-year-old Lego builders who were paired with a more expert peer improved more in their ability to copy Lego constructions than did novices who worked alone or novices who worked with other novices (Azmitia, 1988). Such interactions are also often beneficial for the more skilled peer (Mugny & Doise, 1978; Weinstein & Bearison, 1985).

Children's initial knowledge state also plays a role in whether collaboration with a more skilled peer is beneficial. At some points in development, children's knowledge is highly resistant to change, so social interaction may not lead to learning. For example, Pine and Messer (1998) examined the effects of peer collaboration on children's ability to balance objects on a fulcrum. Most children profited from the opportunity to work with a more skilled peer. However, children who began the study with a "things balance in the center" theory tended not to learn from peer collaboration. This initial theory was highly resistant to change, even in the face of disconfirming evidence that was provided by the children's social partners.

Although children tend to benefit from working with a more skilled peer, it is not essential for children who are collaborating to have different skill levels in order for progress to occur. Children also learn when they work with others who have similar skills. Several studies have shown that pairs of children who both hold incorrect views about a task or problem often benefit from working together—thus, two "wrongs" can indeed make a "right." Most of these studies have examined pairs of children who hold *different* incorrect views of a problem (Ames & Murray, 1982; Emler & Valiant, 1982). The findings suggest that conflicting views of a problem may be a trigger for knowledge change in social interaction, even if both views are incorrect.

However, at least one experiment has demonstrated that conflicting views are not essential for change to occur. Ellis, Klahr and Siegler (1993) asked pairs of fifth-grade students to collaborate in comparing the magnitudes of pairs of fractions. They found comparable patterns of success following social interaction for children in pairs in which both children used the same incorrect strategy at pretest and pairs in which children used different incorrect strategies at pretest.

One variable that may be important in integrating these findings is whether or not children receive feedback about the accuracy of their task solutions. When children receive such feedback, they often make progress, regardless of whether their knowledge is similar to or different from that of their collaborator (Ellis et al., 1993). When feedback is not provided, as in the studies by Ames and Murray (1982) and Emler and Valiant (1982), conflicting views may be essential if peer collaborations are to foster change. Indeed, one experiment showed that peer collaboration was beneficial only when children did *not* receive feedback about whether their task solutions were correct (Tudge & Winterhoff, 1993).

Task difficulty.   The difficulty of the task also influences the effects of collaboration. On tasks that are either already understood by one of the collaborators or that they would be expected to master relatively soon, collaboration tends to promote successful problem solving and learning (Ames & Murray, 1982; Perret-Clermont & Schubauer-Leoni, 1981). On tasks that neither child understands and that are well beyond either of their existing knowledge, collaboration often produces regression or no improvement in understanding (Levin & Druyan, 1993; Tudge, 1992).

The partners' relative confidence in their reasoning seems to be related to this effect. On the simpler tasks, children who answer correctly tend to be more confident than ones who answer incorrectly. This may encourage the partners who are answering incorrectly to follow their lead. In contrast, on hard problems, children whose reasoning is less advanced tend to be more confident, because they fail to realize the plausibility of alternative perspectives (Levin & Druyan, 1993). This sometimes has the unfortunate effect of leading children whose reasoning is more advanced, but who are unsure of their understanding, to shift toward the less advanced reasoning of their confident collaborators.

Cultural norms.   Cultural norms also influence children's collaborative styles and outcomes. One study that documented this phenomenon contrasted the collaborative problem solving of Navajo and Euro-American children (Ellis & Schneiders, 1989). The task involved a board game maze. Because the maze included many dead ends, it was useful to plan a route before trying to move through it. Children who had been taught part of the problem (the "teachers") worked with younger children who had not received any instruction in it (the "learners"). Since Navajo culture does not value speed as highly as mainstream American culture, and because Navajo culture values both individual autonomy and cooperation, it was expected that the Navajo teachers and learners would interact in a way that led to the learners spending more time planning without the teachers pushing them to make moves. These predictions proved accurate. Particularly on the most difficult problems, which required the most planning, the Navajo children planned for a longer time than their Euro-American counterparts. They also made fewer errors in solving the maze problems. Thus cultural values, as well as age, expertise, quality of interaction, and task difficulty, influence collaborative problem solving.

GUIDED PARTICIPATION IN CULTURAL ACTIVITIES

To characterize children's interactions in social and cultural context, Barbara Rogoff and her collaborators have introduced the concept of *guided participation* in culturally valued activities (Chavajay & Rogoff, 1999; Rogoff, 1990; Rogoff, Mistry, Göncü, & Mosier, 1993). This concept incorporates two ideas: first, the notion that children's behavior is guided by other people, and second, the notion that children participate in activities that are routinely practiced and valued in their cultural communities. Guided participation refers not only to interactions in which adults explicitly attempt to instruct children, but also to interactions in which children observe and participate in routine, everyday activities under the guidance of adults or other more skilled members of their communities, such as older siblings and peers. Such activities include dressing, doing household chores, preparing meals, and attending religious services. Children's guided participation in such activities is an important means by which children are socialized into the practices of the culture in which they develop.

According to Rogoff (1990), adults in all cultures guide children's participation in culturally valued activities. However, the particular activities in which children participate vary depending on the cultural setting. In some cultures, including the United States, children tend to be segregated from adults' social and economic worlds, and many of their opportunities for learning take place in the context of formal schooling. In other cultures, children are routinely integrated into adult activities, and many of their opportunities for learning take place in the context of everyday situations.

Cross-cultural research on patterns of guided participation. Rogoff, Mistry, Göncü, and Mosier (1993) studied children's activities and social interactions in two communities in which children are typically segregated from adults' activities (urban, middle-class communities in Salt Lake City, Utah, and Keçiören, Turkey) and two communities in which children are typically integrated into adults' activities (the indigenous Mayan town of San Pedro, Guatemala, and the tribal village of Dhol-Ki-Patti, India). Toddlers and caregivers in all four communities were observed performing routine activities (such as feeding and dressing), playing social games (such as peek-a-boo and finger games), and playing with novel objects (toys that the researchers provided, such as a puppet and a pencil case).

Rogoff et al. found that some aspects of guided participation appear to be universal across cultures. In social interactions in all four of the communities they studied, children and adults regularly attempted to bridge their individual understandings of situations, and to seek shared meaning or intersubjectivity. In all four communities, children and adults also adjusted their level of involvement with one another as their interactions progressed. This adjustment was achieved using both verbal and nonverbal forms of communication, as well as by adult structuring of children's activities.

However, there were also important differences in guided participation across the communities. In the two communities in which children are segregated from ongoing activities in the adult community (Salt Lake City and Keçiören), social interactions between adults and children tended to be structured by adults, who provided explicit verbal instruction and helped manage children's motivation using praise and other incentives. In the two communities in which children are integrated into adults' ongoing activities (San Pedro and Dhol-Ki-Patti), children took greater responsibility for social interactions, observing adults' ongoing activities and attempting to join in. Caregivers in these communities supported children's attempts to participate and often provided nonverbal demonstrations.

Implications for attention management. Rogoff et al. found that these differences in the nature of guided participation across the two pairs of communities were associated with differences in patterns of attention management. Children and caregivers in San Pedro and Dhol-Ki-Patti were more likely to attend to multiple events simultaneously than were children and caregivers in Salt Lake City and Keçiöran, who tended to focus on one event at a time (see also Chavajay & Rogoff, 1999). Rogoff et al. hypothesized that observing multiple ongoing events may help children in San Pedro and Dhol-Ki-Patti to hone their attention management skills.

These cross-cultural differences in attention management underscore the potential implications of guided participation for the organization of behavior in a wide variety of settings. Indeed, some evidence suggests that there are long-term implications to experiencing different patterns of guided participation. A recent study showed that Mayan mothers who had received extensive formal schooling tended to organize problem-solving interactions with children differently than did mothers who had received little formal schooling (Chavajay & Rogoff, 2002). Groups of three children and their mothers worked together to construct a three-dimensional jigsaw puzzle of a totem pole. Mothers who had received extensive formal schooling were more likely to suggest a "division of labor" approach, such that different members of the group worked on different aspects of the puzzle, and they were also more likely to direct the children in what to do. In these groups, most of the proposals about what to do next were initiated by mothers. In contrast, mothers who had received little formal schooling tended to work together with the children, such that all members of the group were focused on the same aspect of the construction (such as the same row of the puzzle). In these groups, proposals about what to do next were as likely to come from the oldest child in the group as from the mother. Thus, experience with the hierarchical social structures characteristic of formal schooling appears to influence the nature of mothers' interactions with their children.

Development as transformation of participation. The central construct in Rogoff's framework is *participation* in cultural activities. From this perspective, developmental change involves transformations in the nature of children's participation. In many cases, children progress over developmental time from being observers or peripheral participants in activities to being more central participants. In some cases, children eventually take on major responsibility or leadership roles. For example, a toddler might simply observe meal preparation as it takes place in her home, a preschool child might assist by setting the table, an older child might actually prepare some of the dishes, and a still older child might make decisions about what dishes to serve.

In addition to changes in the roles children play in activities, several other aspects of children's participation in activities may also change with development. These include their reasons for being involved in the activity (to obey a parent versus to accomplish a task that needs to be done), their attitudes toward taking on new roles and responsibilities, and their understanding of how different activities contribute to the larger whole (Rogoff, 1997, 1998). A complete understanding of developmental change will require understanding these dimensions of change in children's participation in sociocultural activities.

Language as a Psychological Tool

In every culture, language is a pervasive feature of social interaction, and it is also pervasive as a tool for thinking and for organizing behavior. Indeed, language is generally viewed as the most important psychological tool. There are several reasons why this is the case. First, language is an integral component of most forms of social interaction, including guided participation, instructed learning and collaborative learning. As such, language is one channel through which social interaction results in learning. Second, people use language as a means of regulating their own behavior, making plans, and solving problems, as is evident in the phenomenon of private speech. And third, the structures of language appear to influence habitual patterns of thought, even in tasks and situations that do not overtly involve language.

The linguistic regulation of behavior.   One source of evidence for the linguistic regulation of behavior is the phenomenon of *private speech.* Children frequently talk aloud to themselves as they play, explore, and solve problems. For example, a child presented with a two-digit addition problem that involves carrying (such as $17 + 28$) might use private speech as she works out the problem: "7 plus 8 is 15, carry the 1, (pause) 2, 3, 4, so its 45." Vygotsky viewed such private speech as a manifestation of children's use of language to regulate their behavior.

From this perspective, it is not surprising that children produce more private speech on more challenging tasks, for which self-regulation is more difficult (Berk, 1994). Furthermore, children's private speech declines or "goes underground" over developmental time (Bivens & Berk, 1990; Winsler, Carlton, & Barry, 2000; Winsler, Diaz, Atencio, McCarthy, & Chabay, 2000; Winsler & Naglieri, 2003). According to Vygotsky, private speech ultimately becomes *inner speech,* a silent, internalized dialogue with the self. One implication of this view is that much of thought is actually internalized language.

Relations between language and thought.   If thought consists, at least in part, of internalized language, it seems possible that characteristics of the particular language an individual speaks may influence how that individual thinks. This view, known as the *linguistic relativity hypothesis,* holds that differences in how languages encode reality are reflected in parallel differences in how speakers of the languages think. As one of the leading proponents of this view, Benjamin Lee Whorf, put it: "We cut nature up, organize it into concepts, and ascribe significances as we do largely because we are parties to an agreement to organize it in this way—an agreement that holds throughout our speech community and is codified in the patterns of our language" (Whorf, 1940).

Does language really shape thought? There is growing evidence that variations in language-specific word meanings and grammatical patterns are indeed associated with variations in performance on cognitive tasks that involve thinking, but that do not directly involve language. One explanation for these associations is that structural patterns in the language give rise to habitual patterns of thought (Lucy, 1992).

A good illustration of this idea comes from Levinson's (1997) research among Australian aboriginal speakers of the Guugu Yimithirr language. In Guugu Yimithirr, spatial information is not linguistically encoded using words that mark position relative to the body, such as "left" and "right," as is typical in Indo-European languages such as English. Instead, terms that mark absolute orientation, such as "north" and "east" are used. Levinson investigated whether the linguistic system for marking spatial relations carried over into non-linguistic cognitive tasks. In one of many such tasks, participants viewed an arrangement of toy figures of a man, a pig, and a cow on a table. Participants were then taken to a second room and seated at a table facing in the opposite direction as they had faced in the original room. They were presented with an identical set of figures, and asked to arrange them just as they had been arranged in the first room (see Figure 4.4). Most Guugu Yimithirr speakers arranged the animals so as to preserve their positions in absolute terms (for example, a cow that was facing East in the first room was positioned facing East in the test room). In contrast, speakers of Dutch, a language that, like English, encodes spatial position relative to the speaker or listener, tended to arrange the animals relative to their own bodies (a cow that was facing to the speaker's right [and East] in the first room was positioned facing to the speakers' right [and West] in the test room). Thus, language-specific patterns for coding spatial relations in either absolute or relative terms carried over into the nonlinguistic task of arranging the toy figures.

Another compelling illustration of the influence of language on thought comes from research with child and adult speakers of Yucatec Maya and English. In English, the meanings of concrete nouns often incorporate information about object shape (for example, the word *candle* suggests something long and thin). In contrast, in Yucatec, information about material is incorporated in the noun, and information about shape must often be provided as a separate term (following the pattern of the English *a cube of sugar*). For example, the Yucatec expression for *one candle* can be translated as *one long thin wax.* Thus, it can be

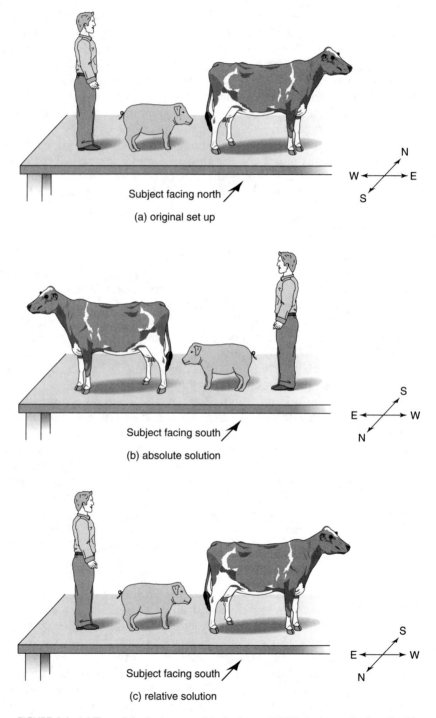

FIGURE 4.4 (a) The original set up used by Levinson (1997), in the study described in the text, (b) the absolute solution, such as that provided by most Guguu Yimithirr speakers, and (c) the relative solution, such as that provided by most Dutch speakers (based on Levinson, 1997 Figure 4).

said that the structure of English "invites" attention to object shape, whereas the structure of Yucatec "invites" attention to object material.

To test the impact of these linguistic differences on object categorization, Lucy (1992) presented adult speakers of Yucatec and English with triads of objects in which one object was designated the "pivot" (e.g., a small cardboard box), one object was of the same shape as the pivot but of a different material (e.g., a small plastic box), and one object was of the same material as the pivot but of a different shape (e.g., a small, flat piece of cardboard). Participants were asked to judge which of the other two objects was most similar to the pivot object. Almost all of the English speakers chose based on shape, whereas almost all of the Yucatec speakers chose based on material. Thus, language-specific patterns for encoding noun meanings in words appeared to influence performance on the nonlinguistic task of judging object similarity. Lucy and Gaskins (2001) used a similar task with English- and Yucatec-speaking children, and found that language-specific categorization biases emerged between ages 7 and 9 years.

In other tasks, language structure appears to influence task performance considerably before 7 years of age. One such task is spatial categorization. Choi, McDonough, Bowerman, and Mandler (1999) investigated this issue in toddlers ages 18 to 23 months who were learning either Korean or English. The two languages differ in terms of how they categorize spatial relationships. English prepositions distinguish between actions that result in containment (e.g., put *in*) and actions that result in support or attachment (e.g., put *on*). In contrast, Korean distinguishes between relations that involve tight fits (*kkita*) and relations that involve loose fits or other kinds of contact. The experiment assessed toddlers' comprehension of *in* (for English learners) and *kkita* (for Korean learners).

Children were presented with pairs of scenes as they heard sentences that included the target word. Some of the pairs of scenes contrasted in/on relations with tight/loose fit relations (such as putting rings loosely into a basket versus putting rings tightly on a post). For these pairs, English learners tended to look at the "putting rings into a basket" event while hearing sentences that included the word *in*, suggesting that the word *in* drew their attention to containment. In contrast, Korean learners tended to look at the "putting rings on a post" event while hearing sentences that included the word *kkita*, suggesting that the word *kkita* drew their attention to a tight-fit event. On control trials on which no target words were presented, the looking patterns of English learners and Korean learners did not differ. These findings indicate that, by 18 to 23 months, children are sensitive to language-specific ways of categorizing spatial relations. Thus, early spatial concepts appear not to be universal, as would be the case if they derived solely from characteristics of the human perceptual system. Instead, language plays a role in spatial categorization from an early age.

The development of language as a mediating system. The findings described above suggest that the relation between language and thought may itself undergo developmental change. As children become more fluent, and as they become socialized into the conventions of their native language, they become better able to use language as a tool for thinking.

How do children acquire the ability to use language as a tool for mediating thought? One theorist who has addressed this question is Katherine Nelson. She proposed that during the toddler and preschool years, children progress through four levels of ability to use language as a representational system (Nelson, 1996). At the first level, young children's world knowledge consists of mental models of events that are based in experience. At this level, linguistic forms (such as words) can be part of an experience, but they are not yet used to *represent* experiences (Nelson, 1999). For example, a child might associate the word "balloon" with an event in which she received a balloon from her father, but in this initial stage, she cannot yet produce the word, nor can she use the word to mentally invoke the event.

At the second level, children become capable of transforming some aspects of their mental models into linguistic form, so that they can communicate their mental models to others. However, at this level, children's mental models are still based in direct experience, and children are not yet able to alter them in response to information acquired via language. For example, a child might remember receiving a balloon from her father, and express this event by saying the word "balloon." But if her father responds by saying, "Yes, the balloon man at the fair had lots of pretty balloons," she is not able to alter her mental model of the event based on this information.

At the third level, children become capable of interpreting other people's linguistic expressions, and they can use such information to alter their own mental models. To operate at this level, children must have acquired the grammatical forms and lexical items that make it possible to interpret and participate in conversations with others. In response to the father's statement, a child at this level might call to mind the balloon man and imagine the colored balloons.

Finally, at the fourth level, children become capable of constructing entirely new mental models based on other people's statements. At this final level, language is a means for representing events. Thus, a child who hears her brother say, "At Charlie's birthday party, we each got three balloons," can use this statement to construct a mental model of the event, even though she did not witness it or participate in it.

Note that, according to Nelson, the functions served by language as a psychological tool change over development. At the early stages, words are used simply to mark aspects of mental models that have been derived from experience. At later stages, linguistic forms can be used to construct novel mental models, and these models may incorporate linguistic representations as an essential component. It is also noteworthy that, according to Nelson, children learn to use language as a psychological tool by participating in ever more complex interactions with other people. Thus, by interacting with other people, children learn to use language to mediate thought.

Educational Implications of Sociocultural Theories

Sociocultural theories have many potential implications for educational practice. One is that children's knowledge can be conceptualized in terms of their ability to perform tasks with supportive social interaction. This view of knowledge implies that children's knowledge should be assessed in terms of their ability to learn from social interaction, rather than in terms of their unaided level of performance. A second implication of sociocultural theories is that certain types of social interactions, such as guided participation or scaffolding within the zone of proximal development, should be especially beneficial for students' learning. Therefore, it may be valuable to design classroom lessons and other types of educational activities to facilitate these types of social interactions. Sociocultural theories also have focused attention on how people use cultural tools, such as mathematical notation and writing. Much of formal education involves teaching children to use cultural tools, and different approaches to teaching children how to use such tools may have different consequences for their thinking. Finally, the sociocultural perspective provides a lens through which to observe and understand social interactions. This perspective may be useful for interpreting social interactions that take place in educational settings, and for explaining how such interactions produce knowledge change.

SOCIOCULTURAL APPROACHES TO ASSESSING CHILDREN'S KNOWLEDGE

Vygotsky believed that the diagnostic tests commonly used in educational settings are oriented toward processes and skills that are already fully developed—"yesterday's development"—which he argued should not be the focus of educational practice. Instead, he argued, educators should focus on the child's dynamic developmental state—that is, processes and skills that are just beginning to develop, and that are therefore in the child's current zone of proximal development. In his view, "the only 'good learning' is that which is in advance of development" (Vygotsky, 1978, p. 89), because such learning creates new zones of proximal development. Thus, to gain information that is useful for educational purposes, one must assess children's knowledge under conditions of supportive social interaction.

Vygotsky observed that children who appear to have comparable levels of knowledge when assessed independently might actually be revealed to have very different levels of knowledge when assessed in interaction with a more skilled partner. This implies that, if children's knowledge or skill level is assessed through independent performance, as is traditional in educational settings, important information about children's abilities may be concealed. The practice of assessing children's potential for learning with assistance, rather than their independent performance, has been termed *dynamic assessment*. A recent meta-analysis of 30 studies documented that students do indeed display more knowledge when tested using dynamic assessment, as compared to more traditional measures (Swanson & Lussier, 2001).

Dynamic assessment measures yield information about children's abilities that is not identical to that provided by more static measures, such as IQ tests. In one study of this phenomenon, Ferrara, Brown, and Campione (1986) determined the number of hints from the experimenter that children needed in order to learn how to solve letter series completion problems (for example, what comes next in the following series: N G O H P I Q J ?). After all of the children had learned to solve simple letter series problems correctly, they were given more challenging problems that involved relations that had not been used in the simple problems (such as sequences that included patterns with backwards alphabetical order, such as U C T D S E R F). Children who had needed few hints to learn the simple problems performed better on the more challenging problems than children who had needed many hints. Importantly, however, this pattern was not due to children who needed fewer hints having higher IQs than children who needed many hints—the pattern held even when children's IQ was controlled statistically. Thus, a measure of children's ability to learn from social interaction (in this case, number of hints) provided information about the children's abilities that was not redundant with the information that was provided by a more static measure (in this case, IQ).

Vygotsky's emphasis on dynamic measures of children's knowledge has had an important legacy in modern educational practice. Dynamic assessment provides valuable information about children's potential for learning (Day & Cordon, 1993; Day, Engelhardt, Maxwell, & Bolig, 1997). As such, it may allow more accurate identification and assessment of children with language impairments or learning disabilities than do standard methods (Peña, Iglesias, & Lidz, 2001; Swanson, 1995). Teachers can use dynamic assessment to enhance children's performance and to tap abilities that might otherwise go unnoticed.

EDUCATIONAL INTERVENTIONS BASED ON SOCIOCULTURAL PRINCIPLES

Many educational interventions have been designed to incorporate insights about learning and development drawn from sociocultural theories. Some incorporate opportunities for particular types of social interactions that are intended to foster students' learning. One good example is the *fostering communities of learners* (FCL) approach, developed by Ann Brown and Joseph Campione (Brown, 1997; Brown & Campione, 1994, 1996).

Students in FCL classrooms engage in research on different aspects of a larger topic of inquiry, so that expertise is deliberately distributed across members of the class. For example, students in one FCL classroom investigated the "big idea" of animal-habitat interdependence. Various small groups of students researched the subtopics of defense mechanisms, predator-prey relations, protection from the elements, reproductive strategies, communication, and food getting (Brown & Campione, 1994). Individual students in the FCL classroom are then required to share their expertise in small group interactions with their classmates, so that all students have access to all of the research findings. This sharing is done in "jigsaw" groups that are composed of one student "expert" on each of the major subtopics. Finally, all students are required to perform a complex task that requires mastery of the broader topic, including information that they have learned from their peers. In the classroom studying animal-habitat interdependence, students were asked to design an animal of the future, and to justify their design decisions.

The types of activities used in FCL classrooms were designed based on sociocultural principles. One goal was to create variations in expertise across children, so that children would have opportunities to learn from one another. Another goal was to make social interaction among the children essential in order for the children to complete their work. Evaluations of the FCL approach have documented greater gains in knowledge acquisition, critical thinking skills, reading comprehension, and argumentation skills among children in FCL classrooms, compared to those in more traditional classrooms (Brown & Campione, 1994). Thus, classroom activities designed on the basis of sociocultural principles can lead to important benefits for learning.

LEARNING TO USE PSYCHOLOGICAL TOOLS

The sociocultural perspective has also focused attention on how children learn to use psychological tools. Such tools vary greatly in their ease of acquisition and use. A good example comes from research on cross-linguistic differences in number-naming systems and their implications for children's acquisition of counting skills (Miller & Paredes, 1996; Miller, Smith, Zhu, & Zhang, 1995). In English, the names for numbers between 10 and 20 are not as systematic as those above 20. The names for 11 and 12 are idiosyncratic, and the names for 13 through 19 are formed with the unit value before the decade value (as in *four*teen), which is opposite the pattern used in higher decades (as in twenty-*four*). In contrast, in Chinese, number names above 10 follow a consistent base-10 rule. A literal translation of the sequence 11, 12, 13 from the Chinese would be "ten-one, ten-two, ten-three."

Miller et al. (1995) hypothesized that if the complexity of the English number-naming system makes it difficult for children to grasp the underlying base-10 number system, then differences in Chinese and American children's counting performance should emerge only when children begin to learn the teens decade. As predicted, they found that American preschoolers had greater difficulties learning the teens than did Chinese preschoolers. As seen in Figure 4.5,

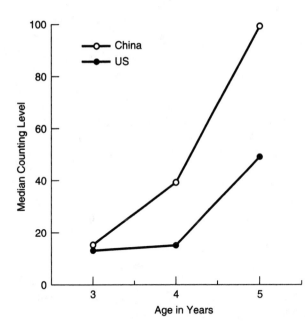

FIGURE 4.5 Counting performance of 3-, 4-, and 5-year-old children in China and the U.S. (Miller, Smith, Zhu, & Zhang, 1995). Data indicate the median of the highest number reached at each age. Counting was comparable in the two countries at age 3, when children in both countries were mastering the first 10 numbers. However, it diverged at age 4, when children needed to master numbers in the teens.

up until age 3, when most learning is focused on acquiring the arbitrary set of digits 1–10, the counting of children in the two cultures is comparable. However, after age 3, the counting of children learning the rule-governed Chinese system takes off, whereas that of children learning the arbitrary English terms for 11–20 remains gradual. The complexity of the English number system plainly is not the only reason that mathematics learning of children in the United States lags behind that of children in China and other East Asian countries. However, the characteristics of the symbolic system do appear to pose an obstacle for American children's learning.

Regardless of the particular symbol system children learn, most children learn about the number system during the preschool and early elementary years. However, individual children vary in their ability to use the number system, and these differences may depend on how well children have elaborated the "central conceptual structure" that underlies it (Griffin, Case, & Siegler, 1994). This central conceptual structure incorporates the mental number line and several related concepts, such as the idea that each successive whole number represents a set that contains more objects or that has an incrementally greater value along some dimension. To foster understanding of the number system among economically underprivileged children, Griffin, Case and Siegler developed a curriculum, entitled *Rightstart*, made up of interactive games that targeted the components of the hypothesized central conceptual structure, and in particular, the mental number line. Kindergarten children in classrooms that used the Rightstart curriculum showed substantial gains in number knowledge and in strategies for solving arithmetic problems, compared to students in control classrooms that used more traditional curricula.

In this example, an innovative, theoretically guided curriculum fostered students' understanding and use of an important psychological tool, the number system. Other ongoing programs of research are investigating effective ways to teach students how to use other psychological tools, such as the symbol system of algebra (Nathan, Stephens, Masarik, Alibali, & Koedinger, 2002) and systems for representing and interpreting data (Lehrer & Schauble, 2002). A better understanding of how psychological tools mediate thinking can help guide the design of educational opportunities that promote students' learning and use of such tools.

SOCIOCULTURAL INTERPRETATIONS
OF CLASSROOM PROCESSES

Sociocultural theories have also been applied to interpreting and explaining the social interaction processes that produce knowledge change in classroom settings. Some researchers have analyzed classroom discourse from a sociocultural perspective, examining how teachers socialize students into particular ways of speaking and thinking.

As an example, Strom, Kemeny, Lehrer and Forman (2001) analyzed a classroom discussion among second-grade students who were trying to decide whether three different rectangles (measuring 1×12, 2×6, and 3×4 square units, respectively) all had the same area. The students' teacher scaffolded the students' thinking in a variety of ways as the students attempted to reason about the mathematical properties of the rectangles. The teacher outlined and clarified the mathematical argument as the students developed it, and she supported their actions in order to highlight mathematically valuable ideas. She also linked students' everyday language for describing the area of a figure with more precise, mathematical language for describing the concept, sometimes "revoicing" students' comments in more mathematically sophisticated ways. For example, the teacher linked students' informal notion of "the amount of space taken up" with the mathematical term "area," and she introduced the idea of a square unit as a tool that could be used to quantify area. Like scaffolding in parent-child interaction, these teaching practices appear to foster students' developing understanding. Over the course of the lesson, the students' contributions to the discussion became more mathematically sophisticated, and they gradually assumed "responsibility" for articulating the mathematical argument.

As these examples indicate, sociocultural theories have much to offer educators. The sociocultural perspective provides a new way of thinking about assessment, a source of inspiration for the design of classroom interventions, a spotlight on important questions and modes of thinking, and a conceptual framework for understanding what goes on in classrooms and in small group collaborative learning sessions.

Summary

A central theme of Vygotsky's theory, and of sociocultural approaches more generally, is that cognitive development occurs in social interaction. Social interaction is conceptualized not simply as an external force that provokes change within the individual, but as part of the mechanism of developmental change itself. According to Vygotsky, developmental change occurs in the internalization of socially shared processes. Children initially perform cognitive tasks with support from social partners. Over time, these social interactions are gradually internalized, until children can perform tasks on their own. Thus, psychological functions take place first at the "intermental" level (between people in social interaction), and later at the "intramental" level (within the individual).

A second major theme of Vygotsky's theory is that human behavior is mediated by cultural tools. These include both technical tools, used to act on the environment, and psychological tools, used for thinking. Language is the prime example of a psychological tool, in that it is used as a means for planning, remembering, forming concepts, solving problems, and regulating behavior.

Modern sociocultural theories have emphasized that the opportunities children have for learning depend on both cultural norms and social practices. Characteristics of the society and the cultural context in which children develop influence the activities in which the children participate. Within the framework provided by the society and culture, caregivers select and organize activities and social interactions that they consider appropriate for children.

Modern sociocultural theories have also addressed the cognitive abilities that are required for social and cultural learning. One of these is the ability to establish intersubjectivity, the shared understanding that emerges through processes of mutual attention and communication. The foundations of intersubjectivity are evident in early infancy, and children's ability to establish and maintain intersubjectivity continues to grow throughout early childhood. Another ability that is important in learning from social interaction is the ability to understand others as being like oneself, and in particular, as having intentions and mental states like one's own. According to Michael Tomasello, three forms of cultural learning are made possible by this understanding: (1) imitative learning, which involves reproducing another individual's behavior in order to achieve the same goal, (2) instructed learning, which involves direct, intentional transmission of information from one individual to another, and (3) collaborative learning, which is learning that occurs when multiple individuals engage in cooperative, goal-directed problem solving.

Many active lines of inquiry in modern developmental psychology have been inspired or guided by sociocultural theories. Research on children's learning in interaction with adults and peers has focused on how variations in social interactions relate to learning outcomes. When adults interact with children, they often structure their interactions in ways intended to foster children's learning.

Indeed, sensitive adult-child interaction is associated with greater learning on the part of the children. However, children also learn a great deal in interaction with peers, both when they work with more skilled peers and when they work with peers of similar skill level. In general, interactions that are characterized by high levels of shared involvement lead to greater learning. In addition, age, task difficulty, and cultural norms also influence learning from peer collaborations.

One strand of research on adult-child interaction has focused on how adults guide children's participation in culturally valued activities. Cross-cultural studies have shown that the process of guided participation varies depending on how children tend to be integrated into adults' activities in the culture. In communities in which children tend to be segregated from adult activities, social interactions are typically structured by adults, and they often include explicit verbal instruction. In communities in which children tend to be integrated into adults' activities, children typically observe the activities and attempt to join in. Caregivers in these communities often support children's attempts to participate, and provide nonverbal demonstrations to help them.

Research on language as a psychological tool has focused on the linguistic regulation of behavior, the relation of language and thought, and the development of language as a mediating system. Children use language to regulate their behavior, as is evident in the phenomenon of "private speech," in which children talk aloud to themselves as they explore and solve problems. According to Vygotsky, private speech eventually becomes a silent, internalized dialogue with the self; thus, much of thought is actually internalized language. If this is the case, then characteristics of the particular language an individual speaks might influence habitual patterns of thought. Indeed, there is evidence that variations across languages in word meanings and grammatical patterns are associated with variations in performance on cognitive tasks that involve thinking but that do not directly involve language. The nature of language as a psychological tool changes over developmental time. Early on, words are used simply to label or mark aspects of mental models that have been derived from experience. Eventually, language is used to construct novel mental models of situations that have not been experienced.

Sociocultural theories have many potential implications for educational practice. First, they suggest that children's knowledge should be conceptualized in terms of their ability to perform tasks with supportive social interaction, and it should be assessed in interaction, rather than in independent performance. Second, sociocultural theories hold that certain types of social interactions (such as collaboration with more skilled peers) may be especially beneficial for students' learning. Third, the sociocultural perspective has focused attention on how children learn to use cultural tools and on how different approaches to teaching children how to use such tools have different consequences for their thinking. Finally, the sociocultural perspective provides a framework for observing and understanding the social interactions that take place in educational settings and for theorizing about how they produce knowledge change.

Recommended Readings

Brown, A.L., & Campione, J.C. (1996). Psychological learning theories and the design of innovative learning environments: On procedures, principles, and systems. In L. Schauble & R. Glaser (Eds.), *Contributions of instructional innovation to understanding learning.* Hillsdale, NJ: Erlbaum. Brown and Campione describe the theoretical principles that provide the basis for their highly successful Fostering Communities of Learning program.

Gauvain, M. (2001). *The social context of cognitive development.* New York: Guilford Press. Gauvain argues that social processes are involved in the mechanisms of learning, and she reviews evidence for this position from the domains of attention, memory, problem solving, and planning.

Rogoff, B. (1998). Cognition as a collaborative process. In D. Kuhn & R.S. Siegler (Eds.), *Handbook of child psychology: Vol. 2. Cognition, perception, & language* (5th ed.). New York: Wiley. A comprehensive review of the literature on collaboration and cognition.

Tomasello, M. (1999). *The cultural origins of human cognition.* Cambridge, MA: Harvard University Press. Tomasello argues that humans possess a unique ability for cultural learning, and that this ability allows them to pool their cognitive resources with other members of their social group.

Vygotsky, L.S. (1978). *Mind in society: The development of higher psychological processes* (M. Cole, V. John-Steiner, S. Scribner, & E. Souberman, Trans.). Cambridge, MA: Harvard University Press. A collection of essays that present central aspects of Vygotsky's theory, methods for testing the theory, and educational implications of the theory.

5

Perceptual Development

A 4-month-old girl is shown two movies with their screens side by side. In one movie, a woman is playing peekaboo. She repeatedly hides her face with her hands, uncovers it, and says, "Hello baby, peekaboo." In the other movie, a hand holds a stick and rhythmically strikes a wood block. The experimenter plays either the sound track with the woman saying "peekaboo" or the sound track with the drum beat, but not both at the same time.

Somehow, the 4-month-old knows which sound track goes with which visual sequence. She demonstrates this knowledge by looking more at the screen that displays the movie that goes with the sound track than at the screen showing the other movie.

Spelke (1976) found that almost all 4-month-olds behave as the girl in this story did. Of the 24 infants she tested, 23 looked for more time at the screen with the appropriate video accompaniment than at the alternative. Apparently, even in their first half year, infants connect sights and sounds in meaningful ways.

This example is representative of current findings about perceptual development in a number of ways. The children in the study were less than 6 months old. The investigator used a simple experimental procedure, yet asked a fundamental question about human nature: Are infants able to integrate sights with sounds from very early in life? The results of the study showed greater perceptual abilities in young infants than might have been expected.

This chapter has two central themes. First, perceptual functioning reaches adultlike or near-adultlike levels remarkably rapidly. Even newborns can see, hear, and integrate information from different sensory systems, and these abilities continue to develop rapidly during the first year. Second, perception and action are closely connected, and this connection is present from infancy. Perception provides children with information that they use to guide actions, and actions generate perceptual information for the developing child.

Perception and human nature.   The study of perceptual development raises fundamental questions about human nature. How does biological inheritance contribute to the ways in which people perceive the world? How does experience contribute? Above all, how do biological and experiential factors interact?

Empiricist philosophers such as John Locke and George Berkeley suggested that perceptual abilities are learned. Infants might at first experience the world in terms of isolated lines and angles. Gradually, they learn that these lines and angles constitute objects. Later still, they learn to infer properties of the objects, such as how far away they are, by noting the relation between how the objects look and how long it takes to crawl or walk to them. The impoverished initial endowment that these philosophers envisioned led the great early psychologist William James (1890) to hypothesize that infants experienced the world as a "great blooming, buzzing confusion."

Other theorists, such as J.J. and Eleanor Gibson (e.g., E.J. Gibson, 1969; E.J. Gibson & Pick, 2000; J.J. Gibson, 1979), hypothesized that perceptual abilities that are essential to survival are built into the infant. They noted that, like all animals, humans evolved in an environment of objects and events, and they need to perceive these objects and events accurately to survive. Further, survival requires that animals' actions be guided by their perceptions. For example, children might need to perceive whether the terrain in front of them can be walked on (solid ground) or not (water or a cliff), so that they can choose an appropriate and safe action. Therefore, the Gibsons hypothesized that perception and action are closely linked.

The Gibsons' theory did not focus solely on biological factors—they also emphasized the importance of learning in perceptual development. In their view, perceptual learning is a process of learning to detect information that is available in the environment. With experience, there are changes in infants' abilities to detect and interpret such information. At the same time, as infants develop, there are changes in the actions that they need to perform and in the movements that they can make. Thus, the Gibsons' view of perceptual development recognizes both biological and experiential factors, and emphasizes the linkage of perception and action throughout development.

Subsequent research has revealed a picture much more like that posited by the Gibsons than like that proposed by the empiricists. Even in the first months, infants seem to experience a world of objects and events that is similar in important ways to that experienced by adults (Kellman, 1988; Slater, Mattock, & Brown, 1990). All current theories recognize that people are biologically prepared to perceive the world in certain ways, and that many important perceptual capabilities are present at birth. All current theories also recognize that experience contributes to the development of perceptual abilities.

Subsequent research also has supported the view that perception and action are closely connected from the beginning of life (e.g., Bertenthal, 1996; Bertenthal & Clifton, 1998; Thelen, 1995). For example, when infants see a ball rolling in front of them, they sometimes move their hands to intercept it. Rather remarkably, they reach not where the object is when they begin the reach, but rather toward where it will be by the time their hands arrive (von Hofsten, 1993).

The linkage between perception and action is evident at the neurophysiological level as well as at the behavioral level. The visual system includes two main subsystems. One, the *ventral system*, which carries information in large part to the temporal cortex of the brain, is specialized for recognizing and representing the visual world. The other, the *dorsal system*, which carries information largely to the parietal cortex, is specialized for using perceptual information to guide action (Goodale & Milner, 1992; Milner & Goodale, 1995). Aspects of both systems are functional in the first half year of life (Johnson, Mareschal, & Csibra, 2001).

The linkage between perception and action makes complete sense if one thinks about why we perceive the environment in the first place. For any organism that moves, perception provides the information needed to act effectively in the environment. It allows us to stay in touch with a constantly changing world. There is a reason why plants don't see anything; it would do them no good because they cannot move beyond the limits of their roots anyway. In contrast, for animals that can move, sensory systems such as vision and hearing help meet the basic needs of obtaining food and avoiding predators.

The task of perception. We perceive the world through a number of sensory systems: vision, audition (hearing), gustation (taste), olfaction (smell), and a few others. Regardless of the particular sense being considered, however, the task of perception can be thought of in terms of the need to accomplish three functions: attending, identifying, and locating. *Attending* involves determining what in a situation is worthy of detailed processing. *Identifying* involves recognizing what we are perceiving. *Locating* involves specifying how far away the perceived object or event is and in what direction relative to the observer. All of these functions are performed with the goal of effectively guiding action.

An example may help to highlight the distinctions between and interrelations among the three functions. If you are in a jungle and a tiger is charging, you need to orient your attention toward the tiger, to identify it as a tiger, and to locate how far away it is. A blur of motion in the periphery of the eye might stimulate initial attention to the tiger. More careful and focused attending would

TABLE 5.1 Chapter Outline

presumably follow, leading to identification of the moving object as a tiger. Yet more careful attention would follow, specifying the location of the tiger as nearby and rapidly approaching. Information gained through attending, identifying, and locating would then be used to inform a decision about whether to climb a tree, hide, or pray. Thus, attending, identifying, and locating all serve the goal of guiding an appropriate course of action.

Although people perceive the world through a number of senses, we rely most heavily on sights and sounds. Therefore, this chapter focuses primarily on the development of vision and audition (hearing), as well as on the ways in which information from these and the other senses is integrated. The final section focuses on how perceptual information is used to guide action. The chapter focuses primarily on infants and toddlers, because many of the most important changes in perception occur very early in development. The chapter's organization is outlined in Table 5.1.

Vision

To understand the development of visual perception, it is helpful to understand a little about the mature visual system. Visual perception ordinarily originates with light being reflected from, or emitted by, an object in the environment. The light impinges on the eye and progresses through the *cornea* and *pupil* to the *lens*

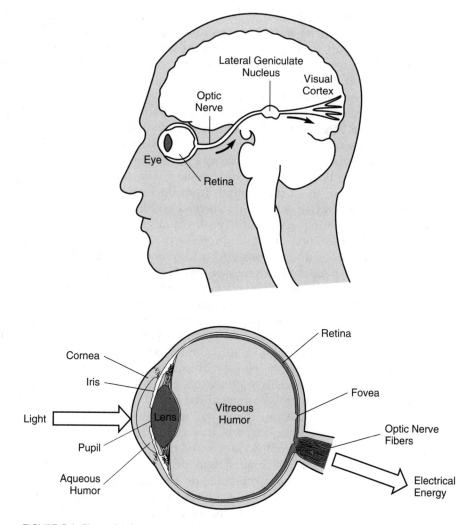

FIGURE 5.1 Flow of information within human visual system (top), and more detailed depiction of the eye (below).

(Figure 5.1). The lens bends the light rays to project a focused image on the light-sensitive *retina* behind it. Change in the shape of the lens that brings the object into focus is known as *accommodation*.

The retina includes two types of *photoreceptor* cells (receivers of light): the *rods* and the *cones*, which are so named because of their shapes. The cones are concentrated in the *fovea*, which is a small, approximately circular area near the center of the retina, where vision is the most acute. The cones respond differently to different wavelengths of light, and comparing the outputs of different types of cones enables color vision. Cones require relatively strong stimulation, so they are used primarily for day vision. In contrast, the rods are responsive even in dim light, so they are used for night vision. The rods are located in the periphery of the retina, and they are absent from the fovea.

From the retina, information is relayed to the brain by way of the optic nerve. The *visual cortex* of the brain registers the information and integrates it with previous information to form a representation of the visual scene.

This description provides the framework within which visual development occurs. But it also leaves open many questions. For example, is the development of visual perception primarily due to changes in the eye or to changes in the parts of the brain that process input from the eyes? Does the early immaturity of the brain mean that *subcortical structures* within the visual system (the retina, optic nerve, midbrain, etc.) initially play a larger role in perception than they will later? Is perception direct, in the sense of depending only on currently perceivable stimuli, or do previously formed memories also influence it?

Although people have long wondered about these questions, only recently has substantial progress been made in answering them. One important reason for this recent progress is the development of experimental methods that allow infants to demonstrate their visual competence. Infants cannot verbally describe how they see the world. They also cannot follow instructions, thus ruling out almost all conventional methods for studying perception in adults and older children. To learn about infants' perceptual capacities, then, it was essential to identify some behavior that reflected the capacities. An incredibly mundane-seeming behavior—eye movements—provided the key to revealing the perceptual world of the infant. Infants move their eyes and turn their heads to look directly at what interests them. Such actions are based on perception, because perceptual information is used to identify objects that might be worth a closer look.

Researchers have developed two primary methods for studying infant visual perception, and both capitalize on the fact that infants turn their heads toward what interests them: the *preferential-looking* paradigm and the *habituation* paradigm. In the preferential-looking paradigm, two objects or events that differ in only one way are displayed side by side, and the researcher examines whether infants consistently look more at one of them. If they do, they must perceive the difference. For example, if infants are repeatedly shown a red ball and an otherwise identical gray one, and they consistently look at the red ball, they must perceive the difference in color.

The habituation paradigm is based both on infants' propensity to look more at objects that interest them and on the fact that, like older individuals, infants grow bored with objects that are presented repeatedly. The paradigm includes two phases. First is the familiarization phase, in which an object is presented repeatedly. When infants no longer look at it much, a new object that differs in some specific way is introduced. If infants show renewed interest in the new object, they must perceive a difference between the two. These simple

methods have allowed researchers to make great progress in answering fundamental questions about how infants perceive the world.

ATTENDING TO VISUAL PATTERNS

From birth, infants look at some objects and events more than others. These preferences may be crucial to development. Cognitive growth will presumably be
more rapid if infants orient to informative parts of the environment rather than
to uninformative ones. But how informative should informative be? Objects and
events that are too far beyond infants' current knowledge of the world may be
impossible for them to understand.

Cohen (1972) made an important distinction between *attention-getting* and
attention-holding properties of stimuli. The idea is that gross physical characteristics of objects attract initial attention, but the objects' meaningfulness determines
whether attention persists. Cohen suggested that the same attention-getting
properties continue to influence perception throughout life, but that attention-
holding properties change with age and experience. Movement grabs the attention of adults as well as infants, but infants and adults differ considerably in
what they find interesting enough to be worth sustained attention. In the next
sections, we first consider attention-getting properties, and then attention-
holding ones.

The orienting reflex.   When people see a bright flash of light or hear a sudden loud noise, they orient their attention to it even before they identify what it
is. This orienting reflex seems to be present from birth. It is adaptive in helping
people react quickly to events that call for immediate action.

The orienting reflex can be controlled by the cortex, but more typically it
is controlled by subcortical brain regions. This conclusion emerged from a study
of an *anencephalic* infant (an infant born without a cortex) (Graham, Leavitt,
Strock, & Brown, 1978). The anencephalic infant showed an orienting response
when novel stimuli were presented. The infant also habituated to familiar stimuli. That is, as shown in Figure 5.2, the infant's heart rate, which initially showed
a large decrement five to seven seconds after a speech sound (a typical orienting response), stopped showing this response after six exposures to the sound.
Since this infant did not have a cortex, its abilities to orient and habituate prove
that cortical activity is not needed for these processes to occur. Subcortical mechanisms must be sufficient for both.

Especially intriguing, the pattern of orienting and habituating in Graham
et al.'s 1-month-old anencephalic infant actually was precocious. It was typical
of a 2-month-old normal infant. Graham et al. concluded that very early in development, cortical activity may hinder rather than facilitate orienting, and that
this was why the performance of the newborn anencephalic infant was unusually advanced.

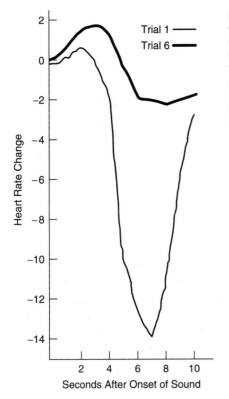

FIGURE 5.2 Orienting response of an infant born without a cortex. The curves indicate changes in the infant's heartbeat rate after he heard someone talk. On the first trial, there was a large decrease in the infant's heartbeat rate 5 to 7 seconds after the word was pronounced. This is a typical orienting-response pattern. By the sixth trial, there was little change in heartbeat rate. Thus, the infant habituated to the sound despite not having a cortex. (Adapted from Graham, Leavitt, Strock, & Brown, 1978).

Overt and covert deployment of attention. Quite often, when someone's attention is attracted by an object or event, they turn to look at it. In these cases, attention is reflected in overt behavior. Other times, however, people look at one thing but their minds are on something else entirely. In these cases, attention is being deployed covertly.

Determining whether infants can attend to something different from what they are looking at has taken considerable ingenuity. However, Johnson, Posner, and Rothbart (1994) devised a way to do so. They exposed 4-month-olds to a training procedure in which the appearance of a diamond in the periphery of one side of their field of vision usually meant that an interesting beeping, rotating, multicolored wheel would appear a half second later on the other side. The diamond was on the screen too briefly for the infants to make an eye movement to look directly at it, and infants rarely looked at the side with the diamond before the wheel appeared. However, on some trials, the colorful wheel appeared just after the diamond had appeared on the opposite side. If infants were attending to the side with the diamond, but not looking there, they presumably would be especially quick to move their eyes to the opposite side where the wheel would appear. This is exactly what happened. Thus, even though the

4-month-olds were not looking directly at the diamond, they were attending to it, demonstrating that they were capable of covert as well as overt attention.

Rules for scanning the environment. Even in their first days of life, infants do not just orient to attention-grabbing objects that appear in their visual fields; they actively seek out interesting stimulation. Haith (1980) suggested that newborns act as if they know the following five rules for finding the interesting parts of their environments:

1. If you are awake and alert, and the light is not too bright, open your eyes.
2. If opening your eyes reveals darkness, scan the environment intensively.
3. If opening your eyes reveals light, scan the environment broadly.
4. If you find an edge, stop scanning broadly and continue scanning around the edge. Cross the edge and look at the other side if you can.
5. When you are scanning near an edge, reduce the range of fixations perpendicular to the edge if there are a lot of contours in the area.

Acting in accord with these rules helps infants find some interesting aspects of their environments, but may result in their missing others. In particular, it may lead to infants scanning the edges of objects to the exclusion of their interiors. For example, as shown in Figure 5.3, 1-month-olds scan the external

FIGURE 5.3 *Visual scanning of a person's face by 1- and 2-month-olds (after Salapatek, 1975). The concentration of horizontal lines on the chin and hairline of the face on the left indicated that the 1-month-old focused on the external contours. The concentration of horizontal lines on the mouth and eye of the face on the right indicated that the 2-month-old focused on internal features as well.*

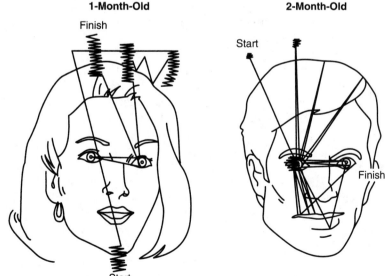

1-Month-Old   **2-Month-Old**

contours of faces and the eyes, but not until 2 months do infants examine other internal features (Haith, Bergman, & Moore, 1977; Salapatek, 1975).

These age-related changes in scanning patterns, as well as other changes in infants' attention, appear to be due in large part to the relative rate of maturation of the visual cortex and the subcortical visual structures (Bronson, 1974). Scanning can be controlled either by the visual cortex or by subcortical structures, such as the superior colliculus. The subcortical structures are more mature at birth and therefore seem to play a larger role in directing attention in the first months than they do later. This leads to the infants' attending more to the outlines of objects, such as faces, and high-contrast areas such as the eyes, because subcortical mechanisms are especially sensitive to the visual information in these areas.

Several types of evidence support the view that subcortical mechanisms play an especially large role in directing attention in the first month or two. One is the anatomical immaturity of the visual cortex at birth. It is unclear that this part of a newborn's brain is sufficiently developed to direct choices of where to look. A second source of evidence is that in newborns, subcortical areas, in particular the midbrain, are known to be strongly involved in deploying attention so as to avoid returning to locations that were focused on immediately before (Valenza, Simon, & Umilta, 1994). Third, as the cortex matures during the first year, success on a variety of attentional tasks that would seem to require cortical involvement becomes possible, and analyses of brain activity during these tasks show increasing metabolic activity in cortical areas such as the parietal lobe (Chugani, Phelps, & Mazziotta, 1987; Posner, Rothbart, Thomas-Thrapp, & Gerardi, 1998). Thus, many sources of evidence converge to suggest that there is a shift from initial subcortical dominance to later increasing cortical involvement in the deployment of visual attention. Note that this does not imply that there is no cortical involvement in visual attention in early infancy, but only that subcortical mechanisms are dominant.

Stimulus complexity. What qualities of objects and events hold an infant's attention beyond the initial attention-drawing occurrence? One attention-holding property appears to be moderate stimulation. Given a choice between a moderately bright object, a very dim object, and a very bright object, even 1- and 2-*day*-olds prefer the moderately bright one (Lewkowicz & Turkewitz, 1981). Even more striking, when the infants are stimulated by a loud noise just before such objects are presented, their preference shifts to the dim object. Maurer and Maurer (1988) suggested that this was due to the infants' trying to modulate the total amount of incoming stimulation; the loud noise and the dim light together provided a moderate level of stimulation. In keeping with this interpretation, Maurer and Maurer found that simultaneously increasing the amount of stimulation in each of three sensory modalities (sight, sound, and touch) by a small amount had the same effect on infants' attention as increasing one of them (sound) by a large amount.

In addition to preferring moderate stimulation, infants also prefer to look at moderately complex objects, rather than at ones that are extremely simple or extremely complicated. Of course, the meaning of moderate complexity changes as the infant develops. Situations that seem moderately complex to a 2-month-old often seem simple to a 6-month-old. These observations have led to the formulation of the *moderate-discrepancy hypothesis:* Infants are most interested in looking at objects that are moderately discrepant from their existing capabilities and knowledge (Greenberg & O'Donnell, 1972; McCall, Kennedy, & Applebaum, 1977).

Several findings seem consistent with the moderate-discrepancy hypothesis. As infants grow older, they increasingly look at more complex stimuli. For example, in studies in which infants are shown checkerboards, 3-week-olds spend more time looking at 2-by-2 than at 8-by-8 boards; in contrast, 14-week-olds prefer the more complex 8-by-8 boards (Brennan, Ames, & Moore, 1966). The familiarity of the specific pattern also influences preferences. When initially shown 2-by-2 and 24-by-24 checkerboards, 4-month-olds preferred the simple 2-by-2 boards. After repeated exposure to both boards, however, the infants preferred the more complex 24-by-24 patterns (DeLoache, Rissman, & Cohen, 1978). Again, as the children's ability to deal with complexity increased, they preferred more complexity.

Part of the appeal of the moderate-discrepancy hypothesis is that it suggests a mechanism of great potential importance for all aspects of cognitive development. If people are programmed to orient toward material that is just beyond their current understanding, they continually will be pulled toward more sophisticated attainments. If there were 10 possible levels of understanding in an area, they would first attend to the material that could be grasped with the simplest level of understanding, then to the material that could be grasped with the next more complex understanding, and so on. They spontaneously would choose the optimal sequence of experiences for learning, and thus would effectively regulate their own development. Because it is difficult to measure infants' knowledge, however, it also is difficult to know what is moderately discrepant from it. Thus, at present, the moderate-discrepancy hypothesis has more the status of an intriguing possibility than of a scientifically validated law.

Expectations.   Infants are oriented toward the future, as well as the present, from the first days outside the womb. For example, expectations about the future state of the world are what allow them to reach for moving objects where the objects will be, rather than where the objects are when they begin reaching (von Hofsten, 1993).

At least by the time infants are 3 months old, they also form expectations about where interesting events will occur, and they use these expectations to guide their looking. This was learned in a series of studies in which the location at which an interesting picture would appear varied either in a regular alternating sequence (left-right-left-right . . .) or in an unpredictable sequence (Canfield & Haith, 1991; Haith, 1993; Haith, Hazan, & Goodman, 1988). After less than a minute of exposure to a regular alternating pattern, 3-month-olds detected the pattern and used it to anticipate where the pictures would appear next. That is, they were more likely than infants who saw the irregular sequence of locations to look left after the picture appeared on the right, and vice versa.

Three-month-olds also form expectations about more complex patterns of events. For example, they were shown sequences in which the interesting picture's location varied in a 2/1 pattern (LLRLLR...) or in a 3/1 pattern (LLLRLLLR...). The 3-month-olds detected these patterns and used them to guide their looking, just as they had with the alternating sequence. In contrast, 2-month-olds gave no evidence of forming expectancies about these patterns. Thus, the expectations that infants form change with development.

Summary. What, then, can we conclude about development of visual attention during infancy? Certain events, such as loud noises, bright lights, and changes in the environment, attract the attention of newborns, just as they do with adults. Even in the absence of such events, newborns scan the environment in ways that lead them to attend to the most important information. For example, their eyes focus on the contours of objects rather than on internal details. They can attend to locations covertly, even when their eyes are focused elsewhere. Infants' attention also is guided from early in life by a preference for moderate degrees of stimulation and by the expectations they form.

IDENTIFYING OBJECTS AND EVENTS

How do infants identify the objects and events that they see? Infants' visual acuity and the movement and color of objects all contribute. Further, people seem to be equipped especially well to identify evolutionarily important stimuli, such as faces and human motion. This section focuses on how each of these factors contributes to our identification of objects and events.

Visual acuity. The single capability that is most crucial for identifying objects and events is the ability to discriminate them from the ongoing flux of visual stimulation. One component of this ability is visual acuity, or vision for fine detail. Visual acuity enables people to see clearly the similarities and differences among stimuli. Typically, the Snellen chart, which hangs in every optometrist's office, is used to measure visual acuity. The letters you can read from 20 feet away are used as the reference point. If you can just read at 20 feet the letters that a person with "normal" vision can read at 150 feet, your vision is said to be 20/150.

Infants' visual acuity cannot be measured by asking them to read the letters on a chart. However, their preferences for looking at one object rather than another can yield similar information. Almost all infants would rather look at alternating black and white stripes than at undifferentiated gray fields. By showing infants a gray field on one side and a set of stripes on the other, and examining whether the infants look more toward the stripes, researchers have been able to determine how much space between stripes (*spatial frequency*) infants need to see the difference.

Results obtained via this technique indicate that newborns see objects at 20 feet as well as adults with 20/20 vision see them at about 660 feet (Courage & Adams, 1990). Their acuity therefore is about 20/660. Average acuity improves to about 20/300 for 2-month-olds, 20/160 for 4-month-olds, and 20/80 for 8-month-olds. The 20/80 acuity at 8 months is about as good as that of an adult who could see better if she wore glasses but would not usually bother to do so. To give a qualitative sense of what a young infant's vision is like, Figure 5.4 illustrates the finest level of stripes that most 1-week-olds can discriminate from a gray field at a distance of 1 foot (Maurer & Maurer, 1988). It is enough to see the outlines of objects, but not their details.

Differences between infants' and adults' pattern vision are present not just in the absolute sensitivity, but in where the greatest sensitivity is. One-month-olds' sensitivity is greatest at very low spatial frequencies (widely separated stripes). Over the next few months, sensitivity becomes best at progressively higher spatial frequencies (stripes closer together). This means that 1-month-olds

FIGURE 5.4 Finest stripes that 1-week-olds can discriminate from gray field (after Maurer & Maurer, 1988).

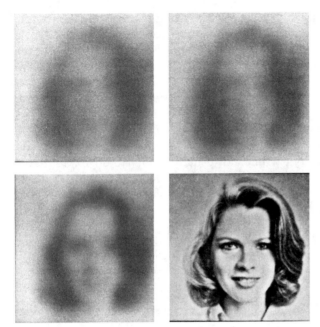

FIGURE 5.5 A woman's face, as it would appear from a distance of 5 feet to 1-, 2-, and 3-month-olds and adults (from Ginsburg, 1983). Photograph courtesy of Dr. Martin Banks.

are maximally sensitive to very coarse outlines; after this, optimal vision is found with increasingly detailed patterns. What these changes mean for infants' ability to see a woman's face is illustrated in Figure 5.5.

The development of visual acuity depends on experience with the visual world. This has been shown in infants who were born with cataracts that prevented visual input. Such cataracts are typically removed in the infants' first 6 months of life, and after the surgery the infants are fitted with contact lenses so that they can receive appropriate visual input. Immediately after the surgery, infants' acuity is no better than that of newborns. However, acuity improves rapidly, even in the first *hour* after the surgery, and this improvement continues over the following month (Maurer, Lewis, Brent, & Levin, 1999). Thus, visual experience appears to be crucial for the development of visual acuity.

Motion.   Young infants' attention is drawn to moving objects (Volkmann & Dobson, 1976), and their sensitivity to motion increases with age (Dannemiller, 2000; Roessler & Dannemiller, 1997). Even newborns have some ability to track moving objects smoothly, but this ability is initially limited to objects that are large and that move slowly (Dayton & Jones, 1964; Dayton et al., 1964). For smaller or faster-moving objects, young infants' eye movements are much less smooth. They typically fixate at the location where the object used to be for a second or two after it has moved away, and then jerk their eyes forward to a position roughly, but often not precisely, in line with the object's new location. With age, infants become better able to smoothly track moving targets using both head and eye movements (Aslin, 1981; von Hofsten & Rosander, 1996, 1997). The development of smooth visual tracking coincides with the development of sustained attention to visual stimuli (Richards & Holley, 1999).

The propensity to attend to motion exemplifies the subtle and varied ways in which our perceptual system has evolved to help us adapt to our environment. In the world in which people evolved, moving objects could represent threatening predators, enticing prey, or any number of significant events. Attending to moving objects was, and continues to be, useful for survival.

The fact that motion attracts our attention also is useful because it helps us identify objects. Intuitively, it might seem that identifying moving objects would be more difficult than identifying stationary ones. However, after analyzing the information available in the physical environment, J.J. Gibson (1966) noted that movement provides critical data about properties of objects that persist throughout the movement, such as that all parts of the object move together. Thus, infants might find it easier to perceive the unity of different parts of a single object (though not its details) if the object is moving.

Subsequent research supported this analysis. Infants' perception of objects as single entities appears to be based in large part on information provided by movement (Kellman & Short, 1987; Kellman & Spelke, 1983). For example, 3-month-olds perceive objects as separate if they move independently, but not if the same objects are stationary (Spelke & van de Walle, 1993). Thus, motion not only attracts infants' attention, it also helps them identify what they are seeing.

Color. Adults can perceive wavelengths of light ranging from roughly 400 to 700 nanometers (nm). We see particular wavelengths as particular colors. For example, we perceive wavelengths of 450–480 nm as blue, 510–540 as green, 570–590 as yellow, and 615–650 as red. Although we see some wavelengths as mixtures (for example, 500 nm is perceived as bluish-green), we see most as unambiguously one color or another.

Color is a domain in which humans demonstrate the phenomenon of "categorical perception." In categorical perception, differences between categories (such as green and yellow) seem greater than differences within a category (such as differences among various shades of yellow), even when the physical differences are identical (in this case, the differences in wavelength between the green-yellow pair and the yellow-yellow pair). Categorical perception has been demonstrated in a variety of domains, including perception of speech sounds (Eimas, Siqueland, Jusczyk, & Vigorito, 1971) and perception of facial expressions of emotion (Etcoff & Magee, 1992; Pollak & Kistler, 2002).

Because speakers of different languages label colors differently, anthropologists have speculated that the division of the wavelengths into color categories is culturally relative; that is, people in different cultures would perceive the boundaries between colors in different places. Research in infant perception and other areas, however, has indicated that this view is false. For example, Bornstein, Kessen, and Weiskopf (1976) repeatedly presented 4-month-olds with a particular wavelength until they lost interest and stopped looking at it. They then presented one of two alternative wavelengths that were equally far from the original, now "uninteresting," wavelength in physical terms. However, at least to adults, one of the new wavelengths looked like a different color than the original wavelength, whereas the other looked like a different shade of the same color.

Infants looked at the alternative that adults saw as the different color more than at the one adults saw as the different shade of the original. It has since been found that even newborns show such discriminations for some colors (Adams, 1987), and that 1-month-olds discriminate colors across the entire spectrum (Clavadetscher, Brown, Ankrum, & Teller, 1988). Thus, like adults, infants display categorical perception of color, and they place the boundaries between colors at the same places that adults do. Strikingly, this ability is in place long before infants learn the color names. These results, together with identification of cells that respond differently to different colors (DeValois & DeValois, 1975) and observations that people all over the world classify the same wavelengths as being the best examples of particular colors (Berlin & Kaye, 1969), indicate that our biological makeup plays a critical role in color perception.

Social perception. Attention to the faces of mothers, fathers, and other people has been hypothesized to play a unique role in infant development. From the first months, infants prefer looking at faces over most other objects. Until recently, however, it was unclear whether this preference was due to the infants seeing the faces as faces or to other properties of the faces that attract infants' attention. Babies like many characteristics of faces: symmetry, high contrast, movement, and sound. Thus, liking for the individual features, rather than perceiving that faces are faces, might explain the fact that infants like looking at them.

A compelling study by Dannemiller and Stephens (1988), however, established that at least by 3 months, faces as such are special for infants. Groups of 6- and 12-week-olds saw the computer-generated stimuli depicted in Figure 5.6. Although stimuli A and B differ only in having their contrast reversed, adults see Figure A as much more face-like. At 6 weeks, infants looked at the two figures equally often; by 12 weeks, however, they strongly preferred the more face-like Figure A. They do not show any change toward preferring Figure 5.6C over 5.6D, thus demonstrating that the change toward preferring the face-like Figure 5.6A is not simply due to 12-week-olds preferring pictures with thick dark edges or a dark shape in the middle. Thus, 12-week-olds seem to identify faces as faces and to look at them at least in part for that reason.

FIGURE 5.6 Stimuli presented to infants by Dannemiller and Stephens (1988). Despite A and B being identical except for the reversals of the black and white shading, A looks more facelike to adults and attracts more attention from 12-week-olds. The same infants had no preference between C and D, indicating that their preference for A was due to their perceiving its facelike quality, rather than generally preferring stimuli with thick, dark borders.

A   B

C   D

Younger infants also like looking at faces, and the faces need not have the detail of real faces to attract their attention. They just need two blobs approximately where the eyes would be and another blob where the mouth would be. Thus, newborns track the stimuli in Figure 5.7A and B more than the stimuli in Figure 5.7C and D (Johnson & Morton, 1991). Similarly, in a recent study, newborns with a mean age of 53 *minutes* old preferred looking at the face-like configuration of blobs in Figure 5.7B to its inverse, Figure 5.7C (Mondloch et al., 1999). However, the same group of newborns showed no preference between the positive-contrast and negative-contrast stimuli shown in Figure 5.6A and B.

Taken together, the findings suggest that there may be an innate mechanism that directs newborn infants' attention toward faces. The mechanism appears to operate with a fairly crude initial representation of faces, because it does not differentiate between face-like stimuli with positive and negative contrast. In the first month after birth, infants follow moving faces with their eyes more than they do most other moving objects (Johnson & Morton, 1991). This attention to faces provides infants with input for learning in detail what a face looks like.

The tendency to track moving faces declines sharply between 4 and 6 weeks after birth, a time when a number of subcortically-based reflex-like behaviors decline in frequency. By 3 months, infants track each of the four stimuli in

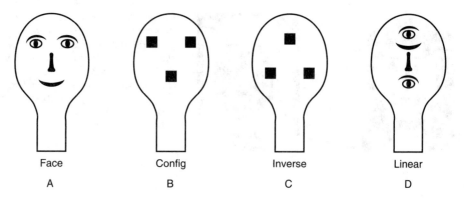

FIGURE 5.7   The four "faces" presented by Johnson and Morton (1991) to newborns.

Figure 5.7 to equal extents. This led Johnson and Morton (1991) to suggest that subcortical mechanisms are responsible for the early visual tracking of faces. After this point, the visual cortex plays a larger role in face recognition, particularly in distinguishing one face from another.

   Distinctions among faces.   In addition to liking to look at faces generally, infants prefer some faces to others. Infants as young as 12 to 36 hours old prefer their mother's face to that of female stranger (Bushnell, Sai, & Mullin, 1989; Walton, Bower, & Bower, 1992). The preference is the same regardless of whether the faces are seen in person, in a photograph, or on videotape.

   By 6 months, infants are quite good at distinguishing among human faces. Pascalis, de Haan and Nelson (2002) first presented infants with pairs of identical faces and then presented pairs that included the face from the preceding pair and a new one. Infants looked longer at the novel face in the second pair, indicating that they perceived the difference between the novel face and the original one. Remarkably, when monkey faces were used instead of human ones, 6-month-olds still preferred the novel face. Thus, at six months, infants could distinguish between different monkey faces. However, this ability declined with age: at 9 months, infants distinguished between the human faces but not the monkey ones, and this same pattern held for adults. This finding suggests that early face perception abilities are "tuned" by experience.

   Not only can infants readily tell faces apart, they also have aesthetic preferences among them. Infants look longer at faces that adults rate as attractive than faces that adults rate as unattractive (Langlois et al., 1987), and this preference has been observed in infants as young as three days old (Slater et al., 1998). The preference for attractive faces extends to the faces of women of different races, to the faces of men as well as women, and to the faces of other babies as well as adults (Langlois, Ritter, Roggman, & Vaughn, 1991). The finding also holds regardless of raters' judgments of the attractiveness of the infants' own mothers (Langlois et al., 1987).

Why might infants (and adults) prefer the particular faces they do? A large part of the explanation seems to be that faces are perceived as attractive to the degree that they fit a prototype of an average face. This prototype can be approximated by taking black and white photos of a large number of faces, averaging the shadings of each pixel within the pictures, and using the averaged values to create a composite face. Rather than generating faces that are average in attractiveness, this procedure creates faces that adults rate as being more attractive than almost any actual face, and that infants look at more than almost any actual face (Langlois, Roggman, & Musselman, 1994). These faces are average in their physical characteristics but not in their attractiveness to infants or adults.

There is evidence that infants do indeed abstract prototypes when they view human faces. After being familiarized with a set of eight faces, 6-month-old infants responded to an averaged face, which they had never seen before, as if it were familiar (Rubenstein, Kalkanis, & Langlois, 1999). Based on this finding, it seems likely that infants rapidly abstract a prototype face from their experiences with faces shortly after birth. Thus, it appears that newborns' initial representation of the human face is enriched by early experience with individual faces (Slater & Quinn, 2001).

In fact, early visual experience appears to be required in order for skill at face perception to develop normally. This issue has been investigated in infants who were born with cataracts that prevented visual input, and who had the cataracts removed in their first 6 months. Even when tested more than nine years later, children who had been deprived of visual input until 2 to 6 months of age showed subtle deficits in face perception compared to control participants (Le Grand, Mondloch, Maurer, & Brent, 2001). Thus, visual experience in the first few months appears to be essential for the normal development of face perception.

Human motion. Infants also are attracted to human motion. Even 4-month-olds look longer at displays of lights that to adults look like a cartoon of a person walking than at an equally numerous set of randomly placed lights, in which the individual lights show similar motions to those of matched lights in the "walking person" (Bertenthal, 1993). The attraction appears to be fairly specific to human motion; 4-month-olds do not show similar interest in displays that to adults look like walking four-legged spiders (Bertenthal & Pinto, 1993).

Infants' ability to discriminate varieties of human motion is surprisingly sophisticated. By 3 months of age, infants discriminate between light displays that to adults look like walking and running, and by 5 months of age, infants are sensitive to higher-order properties of human motion, such as variations in the symmetrical patterning of the limbs (Booth, Pinto, & Bertenthal, 2002). It seems likely that the perception of biological motion involves both initial representations that have been shaped by evolutionary forces, and knowledge learned from experience seeing people move (Bertenthal, 1993).

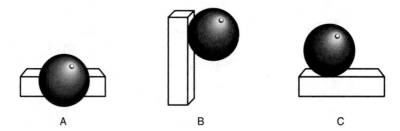

A   B   C

FIGURE 5.8 A. Configural knowledge allows us to perceive the box as a single object, rather than as two shapes alongside a ball; B. Physical knowledge indicates that if this display depicts real objects, the ball must be attached to the box, because otherwise it would fall; C. Experiential knowledge, along with configural knowledge, suggests that a ball is on top of a box, rather than the two being part of a single object. (Examples from Needham, Baillargeon, & Kaufman, 1997.)

Knowledge influences perception. Computer chess programs compete with the greatest human chess champions, but no computer vision system recognizes objects as well as a typical 1-year-old. The reason is that knowing what you are seeing, even in relatively simple situations, requires a surprising amount of knowledge.

Needham, Baillargeon, and Kaufman (1997) found that at least three types of knowledge influence infants' (and older individuals') perception of objects: configural knowledge, physical knowledge, and experiential knowledge. *Configural* knowledge is understanding of the type that enables us to know that Figure 5.8A probably depicts a single ball and box, rather than a ball and two separate shapes alongside the ball; the similar shapes on each side of the circle suggest that the circle is in front of a single object, rather than between two separate objects. *Physical* knowledge tells us that if the ball and box in Figure 5.8B depict real objects, the ball and box must be a single object; otherwise the ball could not stay suspended in midair. *Experiential* knowledge indicates that the ball and box in Figure 5.8C are probably two objects; we often encounter balls and often encounter boxes, but rarely see balls attached to boxes.

By 5 months of age, infants use both configural and experiential knowledge to determine what they are seeing, and by 8 months, they also use physical knowledge (Needham et al., 1997). For example, in one study, 4½-month-old infants viewed a stationary display that consisted of a tall, blue box and a smaller, yellow cylinder. A hand then reached into the display and moved the cylinder to the side. Infants looked longer when the blue box moved along with the cylinder than when it did not, suggesting that they viewed the display as two objects, and they were surprised when it moved as if it were a single object. In this case, the infants used configural knowledge to infer that the box was distinct from the cylinder.

A more complex version of the box-and-cylinder display was too difficult for 4½-month-old infants to interpret (Needham & Baillargeon, 1997). However, a brief experience with one of the objects enabled them to do so. After they viewed either the box alone or the cylinder alone for 5 seconds, infants correctly interpreted the box and cylinder as two objects (Needham & Baillargeon, 1998). Thus, knowledge gained through experience also plays a role in infants' perception of objects from a very early age.

Summary. Infants' visual acuity improves considerably in the first six months and beyond. Even in the first month, infants see the outlines of objects quite clearly, as well as some high-contrast interior detail. They also seem to see the same qualitatively distinct colors as adults do. Both faces and human motion attract and hold infants' attention. Surprisingly, infants prefer to look more at faces that adults consider attractive than at other faces. Thus, preferences that were once thought of as purely the product of culture-specific values turn out to emerge so early in infancy that they almost certainly reflect biological predispositions as well.

In addition to biological predispositions, knowledge is an important component of infants' abilities to identify objects and to discriminate them from one another. Infants begin to utilize configural, experiential, and physical knowledge for these purposes in their first half-year of life.

LOCATING OBJECTS

In addition to identifying objects, infants also need to locate them in space if they are to reach for them or move toward them. Perceiving an object's location requires perceiving both its direction and its distance from oneself. When the object can be seen, perceiving its direction presents no special problem; determining its distance, however, is more complex. At any one time, the display of light on the retina only specifies height and width, not distance; how can a three-dimensional world be represented in a two-dimensional retinal image? Yet, as noted in Chapter 1, even 1- and 2-day-olds solve the problem; they perceive distance with some accuracy (Slater et al., 1990). In this section, we consider some of the *monocular* cues (cues available separately to each eye) and some of the *binocular* cues (cues available only when both eyes focus on an object) that make distance perception possible.

Monocular cues to distance. The cues to distance that can be perceived through one eye working alone fall into two groups: those that rely on motion and those that are present even in stationary scenes. First consider some cues that involve motion. As objects approach us, or we approach them, they fill an increasing portion of our visual field; this is known as *visual expansion*. Similarly, when a person moves his or her head, the retinal images of closer objects move faster than those of more distant objects; this is known as *motion parallax*. A third monocular cue based on motion is *occlusion;* when one object moves in front of another, the closer object occludes the overlapping parts of the more distant one. Infants seem to use all of these monocular cues based on motion in the first months of life (Arterberry, Craton, & Yonas, 1993).

In contrast, not until 6 or 7 months do infants seem to infer distance on the basis of monocular cues that do not involve motion. These are frequently referred to as *pictorial depth cues,* since they were originally described by Leonardo da Vinci as ways of conveying relative distance within paintings. One such cue is *relative size;* other things equal, closer objects will cover more area on the retina. Another is *texture;* other things equal, closer objects will have a more differentiated surface. A third cue is *interposition,* which is like occlusion except that the objects are stationary. Five-month-olds do not appear to perceive depth from any of these pictorial cues, whereas each of them is effective in conveying information about depth to 7-month-olds (Arterberry et al., 1993). Thus, use of pictorial depth cues to infer relative distance seems to develop between 5 and 7 months.

Binocular cues to depth.   Because people's eyes are several centimeters apart, the pattern of stimulation that impinges on the two retinas almost always differs. This retinal disparity is valuable for estimating the relative distances of two objects in close proximity, or the distances of different parts of an object from one another. The value can be illustrated by going to an unfamiliar location, closing one eye, and trying to estimate which of two objects is farther away. Most people do much worse when they look with only one eye than when they use both.

Stereopsis, the ability to perceive depth solely on the basis of binocular cues, emerges suddenly at around four months. Individual infants consistently shift within a week or two from clearly not having such binocular depth perception to clearly having it (Figure 5.9). The key change seems to be segregation of neural pathways from the eye to the brain (Held, 1993). Before 4 months, information from both eyes arrives at the same cells in the visual cortex. Rather suddenly, the pathways are segregated so that information from the left eye arrives at some cells and information from the right eye at others. Additional binocular neurons receive inputs from both eyes. The brain detects disparities in the input from the two eyes and infers depth based on the degree of the disparity (the farther the object, the less the disparity).

The fact that stereopsis develops so consistently and so quickly at around 4 months might be interpreted as meaning that its development is due only to maturation. It turns out, however, that visual experience also is crucial. Administering drugs that block the neural activity that would normally occur in response to visual experience results in the segregated neuronal pathways not forming at the usual time (Stryker & Harris, 1986). As often is the case, maturation does not occur in a vacuum. Even developments that are universal and that occur at a fixed age generally require normal experience as well as maturation.

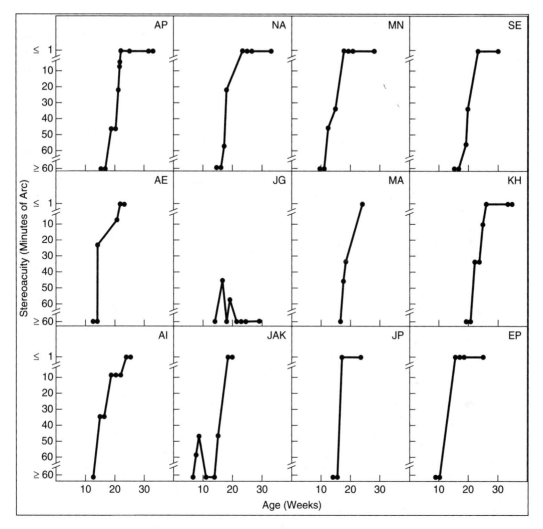

FIGURE 5.9 Changes in 12 infants' stereoacuity between 10 and 30 weeks. Note the dramatic increases that occurred for most infants between the fifteenth and twentieth weeks (after Shimojo, Bauer, O'Connell, & Held, 1986).

Summary. Infants use a variety of cues to determine the distances of objects from themselves. These include monocular cues, available to each eye individually, and binocular cues, available only when both eyes focus on the same point. Monocular cues can be divided into motion-based and pictorial cues. Even 1-month-olds seem to extract information about depth from motion-based monocular cues, but not until about 7 months are pictorial cues effective. This is one more illustration of motion aiding perception, especially young infants' perception.

The ability to perceive depth on the basis of binocular cues is called stereopsis. It arises quite suddenly at around 4 months of age, apparently based on segregation of the neural pathways connecting the eye and the brain. However, this does not imply that the development of stereopsis is entirely controlled by biological factors—normal visual experience also is crucial.

Hearing

To understand the development of auditory perception, it is helpful to understand the basics of the auditory system (see Figure 5.10). Sound waves are collected by the external part of the ear, the *pinna*. From the pinna, sound waves then pass through the *ear canal*, which leads to the *tympanic membrane*, or eardrum, which vibrates in response to sound waves. The movements of the eardrum set into motion a chain of three tiny bones called the *hammer, anvil,* and *stirrup.* The movement of these bones compresses fluid in the *cochlea,* and this in turn causes vibrations of the *basilar membrane,* which is located inside the cochlea. The part of the basilar membrane that vibrates depends on the frequency of the auditory stimulation. The actions of the basilar membrane in turn activate sensory cells, called *hair cells,* which are connected to auditory nerve fibers. Thus, sound waves enter the ear and initiate a chain of movements that culminate in neural signals in the auditory cortex.

What types of research methods are used to study infants' auditory perception? Recall that the two primary methods used to investigate infants' visual perception are preferential looking and habituation. Each of these methods has a counterpart for studying audition. In the *head-turn preference* procedure, sounds are presented from loudspeakers located to the left and right of the infant.

FIGURE 5.10 Anatomy of the ear, showing major structures of the outer, middle, and inner ear.

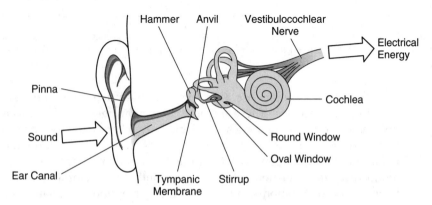

Infants' attention is drawn to one of the speakers by a blinking light, and when the infant orients to the speaker, a stimulus is presented. The stimulus continues as long as the infant orients toward the speaker. An observer who is unaware of the stimulus being presented monitors when the infant looks away. By comparing the length of time that infants orient to different sounds, one can establish what sounds infants prefer, and what perceptual distinctions they notice.

The *habituation* method is also used to study auditory perception, often using a procedure called *high amplitude sucking*. In this procedure, infants suck on a pacifier that is connected to a pressure transducer, and vigorous (high amplitude) sucking triggers the presentation of an auditory stimulus. With time, infants' interest in the stimulus declines, and their sucking rate decreases, revealing habituation. Once their sucking rate falls below a predetermined threshold, a new stimulus is presented. If infant's sucking rate increases again, then the infants must have discriminated the second stimulus from the first.

ATTENDING TO SOUNDS

Infants are responsive to sounds even before they are born. When babies in the uterus are exposed to loud sounds, they move around more and their hearts beat faster (Kisilevsky & Low, 1998). By one week after birth, infants hear and respond to a wide range of sounds. When presented with loud noises, they look startled, jerk their limbs erratically, and blink their eyes rapidly if they are open or squeeze them tightly shut if they are closed. Quieter sounds elicit less dramatic reactions. Thus, the newborn auditory system is functional from the first days.

Infants are more attentive to some sounds than others. They appear especially attentive to speech-like sounds. They react most noticeably to sounds in the frequency range (pitch) of 1,000 to 3,000 Hz, the range in which most speech occurs. They also react more to sounds that, like speech, include a range of frequencies, than to pure tones, in which all sound is at a single frequency. This is not due to their being able to hear these tones the most acutely. They detect sounds of higher frequencies at least as accurately (Schneider, Trehub, & Bull, 1979). Rather, these are the sounds that interest them enough to attract their attention. The auditory attention to frequencies in the speech range is reminiscent of the visual attention to faces and human motion—in both cases, infants are predisposed to attend to information that helps them learn about other people.

One sound that infants find especially attractive is that of their own name (Mandel, Jusczyk, & Pisoni, 1995). Already by 4 months, they attend for a greater amount of time to a loudspeaker that is saying their name than to one saying a different name with a similar stress pattern (e.g., Jojo vs Mimi).

From a very early age, infants also prefer to listen to their native language (Moon, Cooper, & Fifer, 1993). Furthermore, they are able to discriminate between snippets of different languages, even when both of the languages are unfamiliar. However, for newborns to make the discrimination, the unfamiliar languages must be from distinct language families. For example, newborn French infants can discriminate English from Japanese, but they cannot distinguish between English and German, which have similar rhythmic patterns (Nazzi, Bertoncini, & Mehler, 1998).

Identifying Sounds

Infants show an impressive ability to identify and discriminate between sounds that differ only subtly. Many of the most striking demonstrations of this ability concern speech perception. However, infants also have keen abilities for identifying and discriminating among other sounds, such as musical tones.

Speech. Two-month-olds discriminate between such similar speech sounds as *ba* and *pa, ma* and *na,* and *s* and *z.* Their perception of the differences between these sounds appears to be categorical, just as is their perception of the differences between colors. This was originally shown in experiments testing 1- and 2-month-olds' ability to discriminate *ba* from *pa* (Eimas et al., 1971). The two sounds differ only in *voice onset time* (VOT), the time when speakers begin to vibrate their vocal cords to make a sound. Despite this dimension of timing being continuous, adults hear sounds with VOTs below a certain value as *ba's* and otherwise identical sounds with VOTs above the threshold as *pa's*—we do not hear any sound as a mixture of *ba* and *pa.* Apparently 1- and 2-month-olds also perceive the speech sounds categorically. After hearing *ba* repeatedly, they dishabituate more when they hear a *pa* than when they hear a different *ba,* one whose VOT is equally far from the original *ba* but in the opposite direction. Infants have shown similar abilities to discriminate syllables that differ only in the position of the speakers' lips (*ba* versus *ga*), their tongues (*a* versus *i*), and numerous other features (Aslin, Jusczyk, & Pisoni, 1998).

Might these discriminations be due to the particular language infants hear? A study with Guatemalan infants between 4 and 6 months suggests not. The Guatemalan infants were of interest because the Spanish they hear places the VOT boundary between *ba* and *pa* at a different place than English and most other languages. In spite of this linguistic experience, the infants dishabituated in a way that indicated that they placed the boundary between *ba* and *pa* where most languages do, rather than where their native language does (Lasky, Syrdal-Lasky, & Klein, 1975). Thus, infants may enter the world with sensitivities attuned to particular boundaries.

These predispositions do not persist forever. Although infants are initially sensitive to many contrasts not used in the language they hear, they later lose sensitivity to these features. Werker, Gilbert, Humphrey, and Tees (1981) demonstrated this phenomenon with English- and Hindi-speaking adults and

7-month-olds who were brought up in Canada. The stimuli were two sounds that differed on a contrast that differentiates words in Hindi but not in English. After repeatedly presenting one sound, the experimenter abruptly switched to the other. To get a reward, subjects needed to turn their head to one side when the sound changed. Almost all of the 7-month-olds accurately perceived the change, as did all of the Hindi-speaking adults. However, only 1 of 10 English-speaking adults accurately perceived it. This decline in ability with age is reminiscent of the similar decline with age in the ability to distinguish among faces of individuals of other species (Pascalis et al., 2002).

The beginning of the decline in the ability to perceive contrasts not used in one's native language coincides in time with the beginning of infants' ability to speak their native language (Werker & Desjardins, 1995). Both occur at about age 10 months. There are declines in infants' abilities to perceive many different contrasts at about this time, including three different contrasts used in Zulu but not in English (Best, 1995), a contrast used in English but not in Japanese (Kuhl, 1998), and a contrast used in the Native American language Nthlakapmx but not in English (Werker & Tees, 1984). The decline continues for the next 8 to 10 years, at which time the ability to discriminate the sounds has diminished to adult levels.

Why does this decline in phonemic discrimination abilities occur? The reason seems to be that in the course of acquiring their native language, children learn to group together sounds that differ physically but for which these differences do not affect meaning (such as the physically different *ba* sounds studied by Eimas and his colleagues). Consistent with this interpretation, infants show considerably heightened sensitivity to the sound patterns of their native languages in the period just before they lose sensitivity to sound differences that do not matter in their language. Nine-month-olds, but not 6-month-olds (1) prefer listening to words that have sequences of phonemes that are common in their language to ones that are uncommon (Jusczyk, Luce, & Charles-Luce, 1994); (2) prefer listening to words that have stress patterns that are common in their language to ones that are uncommon (Jusczyk, Cutler, & Redanz, 1993); (3) are more likely to integrate novel two-syllable sequences into a single unit (like a word) when the two syllables conform to the stress pattern typical of their language (Morgan, 1996); and (4) are sensitive to similarities in the beginning sounds of syllables (Jusczyk, Goodman, & Baumann, 1999). Thus, increasing sensitivity to the sound patterns of their native languages precedes, and may well cause, decreasing ability to discriminate among sounds that are not meaningfully different in the infants' native language. As is often the case, developmental gains also involve losses (for a wide range of illustrations of this principle, see Baltes, 1997).

Speech perception involves much more than the ability to discriminate among sounds. Among the other skills that it requires is identifying the voices of different speakers. Infants as young as 3 days old can identify their mother's voice, and they prefer it to other voices. DeCasper and Fifer (1980) devised a procedure in which infants could trigger a recording of either their mother's voice or the voice of a female stranger by sucking on a special pacifier in different ways. The 3-day-old infants learned how to produce their mother's voice and produced it more often than the voice of the stranger.

In DeCasper and Fifer's experiment, none of the infants had spent more than 12 postnatal hours with its mother. Although this experience may explain the preference for the mother's voice, another possibility is that the preference was based on familiarity with the voice obtained before birth. Evidence supporting this possibility was found in a study in which expectant mothers were asked to read aloud Dr. Seuss' story *The Cat in the Hat* each day during the last six weeks of their pregnancy. After the babies were born, an experimenter played a tape recording of the mother reading that story or an unfamiliar one. The babies sucked at a higher rate in response to the familiar story (DeCasper & Spence, 1986).

When adults talk to infants and young children, they often speak in a style known as "motherese," or *infant-directed speech*. This style is characterized by high pitch and exaggerated intonations. In a study of German mothers, Stern, Spieker, and MacKain (1982) found that 77 percent of the mothers' utterances to infants between birth and 6 months of age fell into this category. Subsequent studies have shown that infant-directed speech is used in a wide variety of cultures and language communities (Fernald et al., 1989).

Adults have good reason to use infant-directed speech. Infants as young as 2 days old seem to prefer it. They look longer at a checkerboard pattern when the reward for looking is hearing a tape of a woman speaking simple sentences in infant-directed speech than when the reward is hearing the same woman speaking the same sentences as she would to an adult (Cooper & Aslin, 1990). The extremely early age at which this preference for infant-directed speech is shown suggests that it does not depend on associating a way of talking with other rewards that the mother provides, such as food and comfort. Instead, it seems independent of postnatal experience.

In sum, infants are able to discriminate among speech sounds, voices, and intonation patterns. They also prefer their mother's voice to that of other women, and they prefer infant-directed speech to adult-directed speech.

Music. Infants perceive the distinctions between some types of musical sounds categorically, just as they perceive colors and speech sounds categorically. In listening to the types of sounds made on a violin, adults perceive some as plucks and others as bows. The differences between plucks and bows can be reduced to a single physical dimension known as *rise time*. Two-month-olds discriminate between plucks and bows, but not between stimuli equally discrepant in rise time that adults hear as two types of plucks or two types of bows (Jusczyk, Rosner, Cutting, Foard, & Smith, 1977).

Infants also attend to the *pitch* of the sounds they hear. They can discriminate between intervals (pairs of tones) that are consonant (pleasant-sounding) and those that are dissonant (unpleasant-sounding) (Schellenberg & Trehub, 1996), and they prefer to listen to pieces that include more consonant intervals

(Trainor & Heinmiller, 1998). Thus, infants are sensitive to the relative pitches of adjacent tones.

Infants are also able to encode pitch in absolute terms. Saffran and Griepentrog (2001) presented 8-month-old infants and adults with a three-minute sequence of tones in which some pairs of tones consistently occurred together. After exposure to the tone sequence, participants were tested to determine whether they had encoded aspects of the sequence in terms of relative pitch (i.e., intervals between adjacent tones) or absolute pitch (i.e., exact tones, such as A and C). The infants' test examined whether they could discriminate between pairs of tones that had consistently occurred together in the exposure sequence and pairs of tones that had the same relative pitches, but that had not consistently occurred together. If infants encoded the exact tones that they had heard in the exposure sequence, they would show a systematic preference for one or the other of the pair types. However, if infants encoded relative pitch in the exposure sequence, they would choose randomly, since both pair types have the same relative pitches. In fact, the 8-month-olds could make the discrimination, and they preferred the novel pairs. These data indicate that the infants encoded the exact tones that they heard in the exposure sequence.

Adult participants were tested using the same items as infants, but with a forced choice task rather than a preferential listening task. On each trial, the adults were asked to choose the more familiar of the two pairs. Adults' performance was at chance, suggesting that they had encoded the intervals between adjacent notes, rather than the exact tones. Together with the infant findings, these findings suggest that there is a developmental shift from an early focus on absolute pitch, to a later focus on relative pitch. People can encode pitch in both ways at both ages, but there appears to be a developmental shift in the type of information that is most salient.

There are also other developmental changes in people's ability to discriminate contrasts in music. As with speech discrimination abilities, music perception abilities become increasingly sensitive to the types of sounds to which infants are exposed in their home environments, and infants' abilities to discriminate between unfamiliar sounds diminish with time. Lynch and Eilers (1992) presented 6- and 12-month-olds with a brief melody either in the commonly-used major scale or in the rarely-used augmented scale. The melody was presented repeatedly through a stereo speaker until infants were familiar with it. Then, the infants started hearing either the familiar melody or a version of it with one note somewhat off-key. The 6-month-olds discriminated the deviations in both cases; they turned toward the speaker more often when the off-key note was played in either the familiar or unfamiliar scale. In contrast, 12-month-olds' discrimination skills, and also those of adults, were more limited. They noticed deviations within the familiar scale but not in the rarely heard one. Similar patterns have been shown for infants' and adults' perception of mistunings of melodies in familiar Western major scales as compared to unfamiliar Javanese pelog scales. At 6 months, infants discriminated the mistunings for melodies in both scales, but musically inexperienced adults did not (Lynch, Eilers, Oller, & Urbano, 1990).

The findings raise an intriguing question: Is the similar timing of the narrowing of music and speech perception abilities a coincidence, or does it indicate a general reorganization of the auditory perception system? At present, no one knows.

AUDITORY LOCALIZATION

From birth, infants look to the source of sounds. This was first demonstrated by Wertheimer (1961), who performed a simple experiment with his daughter. Immediately after she was born, he sounded a clicker first on one side of the room and then on the other. From the first sounding of the clicker, the daughter turned her head in the direction of the sound. The same result has since been found in larger samples of newborns. The subsequent findings indicate some ability to localize the sounds within the side from which they came, as well as to locate them as being generally to the right or to the left (Morrongiello, Fenwick, Hillier, & Chance, 1994). One cue that infants rely on in localizing sound is the difference in the time it takes sounds to reach the two ears, called the *interaural time difference* (Litovsky & Ashmead, 1997).

Infants' auditory localization abilities enable them to use sound to guide their reaching behaviors. By 3 months of age, infants in totally dark rooms will reach for objects that are making sounds (Clifton, Muir, Ashmead, & Clarkson, 1993; Perris & Clifton, 1988). Infants use sound to infer not only direction, but also distance. At 6 months, infants reached for sounding objects that were 10 cm away, but they did not reach for sounding objects that were 100 cm away (Clifton, Perris, & Bullinger, 1991).

Surprisingly, newborns seem better able to localize sounds than 2- and 3-month-olds, though not better than 4-month-olds. This pattern of data, which appears in a number of contexts throughout the book, has been labeled a *U-shaped curve*. At first, performance is at a high level, then it drops, then it returns to a high level. The U-shaped pattern is of special interest, because it suggests that different mechanisms are responsible for the same behavior at different points in development. This seems to be the case in auditory localization.

Muir, Abraham, Forbes, and Harris (1979) conducted a longitudinal study in which they repeatedly examined four infants over the first four months of the infants' lives. They found that three infants showed a U-shaped pattern of auditory localization. As shown in Figure 5.11, the infants first showed high levels of head turning toward the side from which the sound came, then showed reduced levels, and then, by about four months, returned to the prior high levels. The decline in the middle was not due to lack of interest in the sounds. Even when an infant's mother or father called the child's name in the midst of a series of rattling sounds, the pattern of head turning did not change.

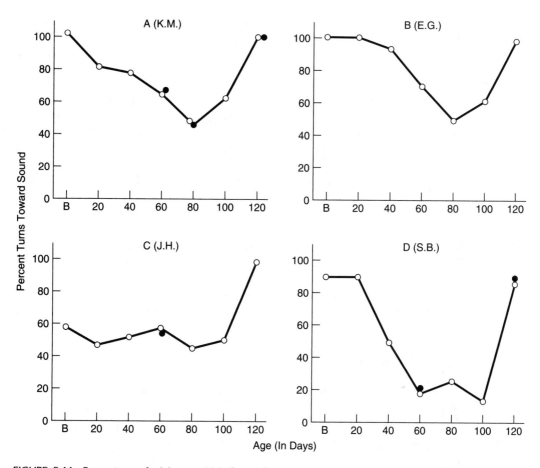

FIGURE 5.11 Percentage of trials on which four infants turned toward sounds. Infants were tested every 20 days from birth to 120 days (from Muir, Abraham, Forbes, & Harris, 1979).

Muir et al. proposed an explanation much like those proposed by Bronson (1974) and Johnson (1998) to explain U-shaped patterns in infants' visual behavior. They suggested that auditory localization in the first month after birth reflects primarily subcortical functioning. In the second and third months, cortical activity increases, and it replaces subcortical activity as the dominant influence on infants' auditory localization. However, at this point, the cortical activity is not sufficiently well developed to produce highly accurate performance, as the subcortical mechanisms had previously. Only in the fourth month does cortical activity become sufficiently mature to reinstate accurate localization.

The precision of auditory localization improves rapidly between ages 2 and 5 months, and it continues to improve more slowly until infants are roughly a year and a half old (Ashmead, Davis, Whalen, & Odom, 1991). It probably is not coincidental that the rapid improvement occurs during the time when infants' ability to control their heads is also rapidly improving. Better control allows infants to move their heads more precisely and enables them to learn how to move their heads to the optimal location for hearing (Bayley, 1969; Bertenthal & Clifton, 1998).

Summary. Infants enter the world with substantial auditory capabilities, and the capabilities develop further in the first few months. The capabilities are evident in which sounds attract infants' attention, in their ability to identify sounds, and in their ability to localize where sounds originate. Sounds with characteristics that resemble speech are especially likely to attract infants' attention. Like adults, infants appear to process both speech and music sounds categorically. Development of both speech and music perception involves losses as well as gains; toward the end of the first year, infants' perceptual abilities narrow in a way that focuses them on the types of speech and music that are part of their culture. The ability to localize sounds shows a U-shaped pattern between birth and 4 months. It is best at the two extremes, and is less good in between. A plausible explanation is that subcortical mechanisms produce the initial high level of skill, whereas cortical mechanisms produce similarly good localization beyond age 4 months.

Intersensory Integration

How do infants integrate the information they receive from different sensory systems into a single coherent experience? One plausible developmental path would be that each sensory system first develops independently and then, when all have reached a degree of maturity, they become interconnected. Piaget (1971) proposed just such a theory. Recent investigations of infants' intersensory integration suggest a quite different picture, however. It now appears that sights and sounds are integrated from birth.

Evidence for intersensory integration has already been presented under other headings throughout this chapter. Intersensory integration plays a role in all three of the major functions of perception: attending, identifying, and locating.

ATTENDING

The orienting reflex exemplifies how intersensory integration influences infants' attention. Hearing loud noises causes infants to look toward the source of the sound. That is, they use auditory information to guide visual attention.

Just as infants follow looking "rules" based on visual information, so do they follow looking "rules" based on auditory information (Mendelson & Haith, 1976). One such rule is that when you hear a sound, and you are looking somewhere else, look toward the source of the sound. Another rule concerns what to do when you already are looking at the apparent source of a sound. Under this condition, you should center attention closely on that source and shorten the length of your eye movements. The rules seem likely to promote attention to animate objects, such as people and other animals that make noise.

Consistent with these looking rules, when 5- to 7-month-olds hear a voice, they increase their scanning of a face in front of them, particularly the eyes (Haith et al., 1977). This coordination of sight and sound may help infants to associate particular faces with particular voices, a skill that is already present at 3 months of age (Brookes et al., 2001).

Bahrick (1992; Bahrick & Lickliter, 2000) has argued that infants' attention is especially attracted to information that is presented redundantly across multiple senses, and that is synchronized in time. As a result, infants learn information that is presented multi-modally before they learn information that is available in only one modality. One study of this issue explored infants' ability to learn about rhythm. Infants learned a specific rhythm (produced by a hammer tapping) more effectively when the event was presented both auditorally and visually than when it was presented in either modality alone (Bahrick & Lickliter, 2000). This bias to attend to multi-modal information may help infants link faces and voices. When people speak, their lips and faces move in a fashion that is synchronized with the sounds in both tempo and duration, and infants' attention is drawn to such multimodal displays.

IDENTIFYING OBJECTS AND EVENTS

Both sights and sounds are also used to identify objects and events. Recall Spelke's (1976) study in which 4-month-olds looked more often at the movie in which the visual images were in keeping with the sounds they were hearing (the mother playing peek-a-boo or the drum beat). If the infants were not integrating visual and auditory information in the movie, they would have had no reason to act in this way.

Four-month-olds also integrate *tactile* (touch) and visual information in identifying objects. In one experiment (Streri & Spelke, 1988), infants first explored with their hands one of two objects: either two rings connected by a rigid stick or the same rings connected by a flexible band. A thick cloth was placed so as to prevent the infants from seeing the object that their hands were exploring. After the infants habituated to handling the object, they were shown visually either the rigidly or the loosely connected rings. The 4-month-olds looked more at the object with the type of connection they had not encountered previously. The demonstration was especially interesting because during the manual-exploration phase, most infants had not touched the connection; they only played with the rings. Thus, their visual identification seemed to be based on their making an inference about the type of object that would produce the observed reactions to their pushing and pulling the rings.

One question that follows from Streri and Spelke's findings is whether visual experience promotes or hinders manual exploration abilities. To find out, Morrongiello, Humphrey, Timney, Choi, and Rocca (1994) contrasted the ability to identify objects of congenitally blind 3- to 8-year-olds with that of sighted children of the same ages who performed the task blindfolded. One possibility was that the sighted children would do better, because they had had the opportunity to learn what objects looked like when manual exploration revealed certain properties. Another line of reasoning suggested that the blind children would do better. They would have had to depend more on manual exploration, and might be more skilled at it.

In fact, blind and sighted children were equally skillful in identifying the objects through manual exploration. They were correct on an equal percentage of trials, took equally long to do the exploration, and were equally complete in their explorations. However, the older children were better on all of these measures than younger children. The findings indicate that manual exploration skills improve with age, but that the improvement is due to general cognitive and motoric improvements rather than to specifically visual experience or experience correlating manual and visual information.

LOCATING

Studies of infants' auditory localization indicate that vision and audition are coordinated from birth. In most studies of auditory localization, the primary measure of localization is head turns toward the source of the sound. Head turning would not be a useful measure if infants did not look toward the sources of sounds.

Infants' ability to control the location of their own bodies in space also requires the integration of information from multiple senses. It is obvious that vestibular (balance) information is involved in maintaining and controlling posture. Less obvious is the fact that visual information is also involved. The importance of visual information has been documented in studies that utilize a "moving room." In the moving room, the participant sits or stands on a stationary floor, and the ceiling and surrounding walls move. Infants who have just learned to stand will sway or stagger when the walls move, indicating that they adjust their posture in response to visual information (Lee & Aronson, 1974). Similarly, sitting infants sway their trunks when the see the walls move (Bertenthal & Bai, 1989; Bertenthal, Rose, & Bai, 1997). Thus, vestibular and visual information are integrated in controlling the location of the body in space.

Chronological Summary

To gain a larger, more integrated picture of perceptual development, it is valuable to consider what capacities infants possess for vision, hearing, and intersensory integration at different ages in the first year. Table 5.2 lists a number of

TABLE 5.2 Perceptual Abilities Infants Clearly Have at Different Ages

Age	Capability		
	Vision	Hearing	Intersensory Integration
Birth	Orienting reflex. Looking rules. Color vision. Size constancy. Scan external contours of objects.	Orienting reflex. Almost adultlike volume thresholds in medium- and high-frequency ranges. Prefer mother's voice.	Look toward source of sounds. Looking rules for responding to sounds. Visually guided reaching.
1 month 2 months	Motion-based monocular depth cues. Scan interiors of objects.	Categorical speech perception. Categorical perception of musical sounds.	Sounds intensify visual scanning.
3 months	Form expectations. Eyes smoothly follow moving objects. Prefer mother's face.		
4 months	Prefer organized "biological" motion patterns. Binocular depth perception (stereopsis).		Integrate sights and sounds with similar rhythms. Integrate visual and tactile information.
7 months	Pictorial depth cues are effective: interposition, relative size, etc. Use memory to infer distance.		

the capabilities that we can be confident infants have developed by the ages listed. The estimates are deliberately conservative; infants may well possess some of these abilities earlier than indicated in the table.

The table reveals an interesting pattern: Hearing seems to develop considerably more rapidly than vision or intersensory integration. All the basic developments in hearing that are listed are achieved by age 3 months. This is not the whole story, of course. Infants' hearing is still improving quantitatively beyond 3 months. For example, they are becoming able to hear softer sounds, especially in the lower frequencies. They also will later lose the ability to perceive some speech contrasts as their hearing becomes increasingly attuned to their own language. It also is possible that further research on infants' hearing will reveal some abilities they do not possess at all until after they are 3 months old, or that further research will reveal that all the visual and intersensory capabilities also develop by equally young ages. At present, however, it is striking just how advanced hearing is in early infancy. The level of development seems even more impressive when we realize that we are viewing it against the backdrop of many other extraordinarily early-developing capabilities.

Perception and Action

Why do humans perceive the world as they do? One reason is that perception provides the organism with information that is necessary for effective action in the world. Action in turn can generate perceptual information, and can improve the quality of information that is already available. Thus, perception and action form an integrated system, in the sense that each influences and contributes to the other.

PERCEPTION GUIDES ACTION

Perception is necessary to guide actions as basic as controlling posture, and as complicated as obtaining food and avoiding danger. Indeed, it can be said that the purpose of perception is to guide action. This general point is evident in many of the studies that have been discussed so far in this chapter. For example, in the moving room studies, infants used visual perception to guide their postural adjustments to the changes in the room. Similarly, in the studies of reaching in the dark for sounding objects, infants used auditory perception of sounds emanating from the objects to guide their reaching.

Studies of motor performance also highlight the crucial role of perceptual information in guiding actions such as locomotion. Infants who have perceptual impairments show delays in motor development. For example, children who are blind or who have moderate visual impairments have difficulties with balance and postural control, and they experience significant delays in achieving most motor milestones, including sitting, crawling, standing, and walking (e.g., Bouchard & Tetreault, 2000; Prechtl, Cioni, Einspieler, Bos, & Ferrari, 2001). Children who are deaf also show delays in motor development (Dummer, Haubenstricker, & Stewart, 1996) as well as slowed execution of motor movements (Wiegersma & Van der Velde, 1983). Thus, both vision and hearing appear to be involved in guiding motor actions.

ACTIONS GENERATE PERCEPTUAL INFORMATION

The relation between perception and action is a reciprocal, complementary one. Improvements in perceptual skills allow for more finely tuned actions. On the other side of the coin, action also generates perceptual information. For example, moving the head may make a sound seem louder, and this information may contribute to auditory localization. Similarly, moving in space generates patterns of visual information that may contribute to identifying objects. As J.J. Gibson (1979) put it, "We must perceive in order to move, but we must also move in order to perceive." Movements that are produced in order to generate perceptual information are often referred to as *exploratory movements.*

If the purpose of exploratory movements is to generate perceptual information, then infants should produce such movements especially often when they need perceptual information to choose a course of action. For example, when infants are presented with a situation in which they must descend a steep slope, they need to decide whether to crawl, slide, or back down. To make this decision, infants gather information using exploratory movements such as patting the slope and rocking back and forth at the brink of the slope. Infants produce more of these exploratory movements on steep slopes than shallow ones, perhaps because the consequence of making a poor decision (falling down) is more serious on steeper slopes (Adolph, 1997). In one study, infants' ability to produce exploratory movements was diminished by having them wear a heavy vest (one with pockets filled with lead). The vest made it more difficult for infants to pat the slope or to keep balance while rocking at the brink of the slope. When wearing the vest, infants made poorer decisions about whether and how to descend the slopes (Adolph & Avolio, 2000).

Because actions generate perceptual information, the development of new abilities for action has important consequences for perceptual development (Bushnell & Boudreau, 1993). Improvements in motor skills make it possible for infants to explore their environments in new ways, and consequently, to generate new sources of perceptual information.

In one study of the links between motor and perceptual development, Needham (2000) examined infants' skills at exploring objects and also examined their abilities to use object features to determine the boundaries between adjacent objects in a visual display. Infants who more actively explored one set of objects in the first part of the experiment were more likely to discriminate the boundaries between other objects in the second part of the experiment. Needham argued that infants with stronger object exploration skills are able to gather more information about objects, and this information helps them learn to interpret object features.

The onset of crawling is also linked with important changes in many other domains, including social, cognitive, and perceptual skills (Campos et al., 2000). Infants who are able to crawl display better perceptual skills in a variety of contexts than do infants of the same age who are not yet able to crawl. For example, crawlers display more postural compensations in the "moving room" than pre-crawlers, suggesting that they are more responsive to visual information (Higgins, Campos, & Kermoian, 1996). Similarly, crawlers attend more to distant objects than do pre-crawlers (Campos et al., 2000). Thus, gains in locomotor skill are linked with changes in the information to which infants attend.

One task that illustrates the links between motor skill and perception especially well is the *visual cliff* (Figure 5.12), which was first used by Gibson and Walk (1960). This task involves a clear plexiglass surface on which infants can

FIGURE 5.12 An infant approaches the visual cliff (photo provided courtesy of Dr. Joseph Campos).

crawl. One side has a tablecloth with a checkerboard pattern just below the surface; the other side has a tablecloth with the same pattern several feet below the surface. To adults, it looks like the surface falls off sharply at the boundary between the two parts. Infants able to crawl are placed on the "shallow" side, just before the boundary with the "deep" side, and their mothers beckon them to crawl across to them. Seven-month-olds who have been crawling for 6 to 8 weeks often refuse to cross, and their heart rates accelerate (a sign of fear) when they are urged to do so. In contrast, babies of the same age who are not yet crawling do not show similar signs of fear (Campos, Bertenthal, & Kermoian, 1992).

The key to this difference seems to be the experience of self-generated locomotion, rather than experience with crawling per se. In another experiment, a group of pre-crawling infants was given 40 hours of experience with a walker, which allowed them to move around independently by sitting in a seat and pushing with their feet on the floor. The infants given experience in the walker showed greater fear when beckoned to cross the visual cliff, as measured by accelerating heart rates, than infants of the same age who had not been given such experience (Bertenthal, Campos, & Kermoian, 1994). The walker provided infants with a new opportunity for action, and by performing this action, infants gained new information that led them to perceive the apparent drop-off in the visual cliff differently, and therefore to fear it. Thus, the experience of self-generated locomotion appears to be crucial for the development of wariness of heights. Consistent with this view, mammals that can locomote from birth shy away from cliffs from early in life.

Why would self-generated locomotion produce this effect? After all, the infants would often have experienced their parents carrying them from one place to another. Campos et al. (2000) have argued that the key difference between self-produced and other-produced locomotion is in the correspondences among perceptual information gleaned from different sources, including visual information, vestibular (balance) information, and somatosensory (body sensation, such as muscle and joint position) information. When infants are carried, they may not look in the direction of motion (and in fact, they often face in the opposite direction, looking over their parent's shoulder), so the visual information they receive is often inconsistent with the other information they receive from their bodies, such as vestibular and somatosensory information. Consequently, infants who are carried do not develop consistent expectations about how these different sources of information are related. In contrast, when infants move on their own, these sources of information are systematically related, so infants begin to form expectations about how these sources of information correspond. At the visual cliff, locomotor infants' expectations about the correlations between visual, vestibular, and somatosensory information are violated, and this leads them to fear making movements over the apparent edge.

Summary

We have considered infants' perceptual development from the perspectives of how each sensory system develops, and how perception is integrated with action. Perceptual functioning reaches adultlike or near-adultlike levels remarkably rapidly. Even newborns see, hear, and integrate information from different sensory systems. These abilities develop considerably further in the next six months, enabling infants to attend to, identify, and locate objects and events quite effectively. From the beginning, perception and action are closely connected, and there are complementary relationships between the two.

The properties that attract visual attention differ from those that hold it. In general, the properties that attract attention remain the same throughout life. For example, the orienting reflex leads newborns, as well as adults, to attend to loud noises and bright lights, as well as to unfamiliar objects and moving objects. Newborns as well as adults also respond to light, edges, and contours with characteristic visual scanning patterns that can be described as looking rules. Attention-holding properties, on the other hand, change greatly with age and experience. Although the visual attention of both infants and adults is held by moderate degrees of stimulation, what constitutes moderate stimulation changes with development. Similarly, although expectations seem to guide attention at all ages, the expectations that can be formed change. In the first few months, subcortical brain mechanisms appear to play an especially important role in guiding attention; after that, cortical mechanisms become increasingly important in controlling where infants attend.

A number of abilities related to visual identification of objects and events show marked growth in the first 8 months. Visual acuity improves from roughly 20/660 to 20/80. The improvement is especially marked at moderate spatial frequencies. The anatomical immaturity of the eye during the first months after birth seems responsible for many properties of vision in the first few months, such as infants preferring to scan contours rather than interiors and preferring to look at checkerboards with large checks. In addition to infants' general capabilities for identifying objects, they also have clear preferences for looking at certain objects rather than others. Among these preferred objects are human faces, particularly attractive ones, and especially one's own mother.

Locating objects demands being able to identify how far away and in what direction the objects are. Infants locate the distance of objects from themselves by using both monocular cues (cues available to each eye, even if the other is closed) and binocular cues (cues based on the difference in images on the two retinas when both eyes focus on the same location). Monocular depth cues based on motion are effective quite early, whereas pictorial monocular cues are not effective before 6 or 7 months. Binocular depth perception (stereopsis) emerges quite suddenly at about age 4 months, apparently due to a combination of maturation of the visual pathways connecting the eye and the brain and normal visual experience.

The levels of auditory perception shown by young infants are at least as impressive as their achievements in visual perception. Infants are especially attentive to speech-like sounds. This appears due to their being interested in the speech-like sounds, rather than to their being able to detect them more easily than other sounds. By 4 months, they also are interested in some particular sounds, such as their own names.

Infants' identification of both speech and some musical sounds is categorical, much like their color perception. The categorical perception is not attributable to the particular language infants hear; infants may set categorical boundaries at points different from those that appear in their native language. In addition to being able to discriminate between specific sounds, newborns also are able to identify more general speech characteristics. For example, they can discriminate their mother's voices from those of other women. They also show a preference for infant-directed speech, a form of speech characterized by high-pitched sounds and exaggerated intonations.

The development of auditory localization shows a U-shaped function. At birth and after 4 months of age, localization is quite accurate. In the interim, the ability is less acute. The pattern, like infants' pattern of visual attention, may reflect a shift from subcortical to cortical dominance.

Perception and action form an integrated system from the beginning of life, in that perceptual information guides action, and actions provide the organism with perceptual information. The role of perception in guiding action is strikingly apparent among children with perceptual deficits, such as blindness or deafness, who often show delays in motor development. People often produce exploratory actions in order to generate perceptual information, such as touching a shiny surface to determine whether it is slippery. As infants' motor skills develop, they become able to explore their environments in new ways. Thus, gains in motor skills influence infants' abilities to generate and use perceptual information.

Recommended Readings

Campos, J.J., Anderson, D.I., Barbu-Roth, M.A., Hubbard, E.M., Hertenstein, M.J., & Witherington, D. (2000). Travel broadens the mind. *Infancy, 1,* 149–219. A compelling review of the effects of learning to crawl on perceptual, cognitive, and social development.

Gibson, E.J., & Pick, A.D. (2000). *An ecological approach to perceptual learning and development.* Oxford: Oxford University Press. A comprehensive statement of the Gibsonian approach to perceptual learning and devel-opment. The core theme is that perception is a two-way relationship between the organism and the environment: the environment affords resources and opportunities for the perceiver, and the perceiver gains information from and acts on the environment.

Lynch, M.P., Eilers, R.E., Oller, D.K., & Urbano, R.C. (1990). Innateness, experience, and music perception. *Psychological Science, 1,* 272–276. Presents evidence for the role of early musical experience in music perception.

Young infants can detect an off-key note in familiar and unfamiliar scales, whereas older infants and adults can do so only in familiar scales.

Maurer, D., Lewis, T.L., Brent, H.P., & Levin, A.V. (1999). Rapid improvement in the acuity of infants after visual input. *Science, 286,* 108–110. Describes the development of visual acuity in infants who were born with cataracts that prevented visual input. After surgery to remove the cataracts, infants were fitted with contact lenses, and their visual acuity began to change within hours.

Pascalis, O., de Haan, M., & Nelson, C.A. (2002). Is face processing species specific during the first year of life? *Science, 296,* 1321–1323. Presents evidence for the role of experience in face perception. Six-month-old infants are able to distinguish among both monkey and human faces, but older infants and adults can do so only for human faces.

6

LANGUAGE DEVELOPMENT

Where you going?
I'm going.
Shoe fixed.
Talk to mommy.
Shoe fixed.
See Antho.
Anthony.
Good night.
See morrow morning. (Weir, 1962)

The preceding monologue was obtained from a tape recording of a $2\frac{1}{2}$-year-old talking in his crib before going to sleep. The child's statements exemplify several key properties of language development. First, they communicate meaning. It is easy to understand most of what is being said, even though the phrases are not the ones that older individuals would use. Second, the statements are cryptic. When children first learn to speak, they include only the essentials. They omit many of the prepositions, articles, adverbs, and adjectives that lend precision, color, and grammatical structure to the language of older individuals. Third, the language is internally motivated. No one else was in the room during Anthony's monologue. Nonetheless, he found talking sufficiently enjoyable that he spoke anyway.

Children's acquisition of language raises several fundamental questions. Perhaps the most basic parallels one alluded to in the previous chapter on perceptual development: How do children make sense of the blooming, buzzing confusion of speech sounds? Simply dividing the flow of sound into distinct words is quite demanding; no computer program yet devised can do it very well. Comprehending other people's statements requires an additional skill: understanding not only the meanings expressed directly but also unspoken implications. Speaking correctly requires yet further skills: enunciating the individual sounds, ordering words within sentences, and organizing sentences in ways that communicate coherent thoughts.

In response to these demands, children engage in a variety of mental activities that enable them to comprehend and produce speech. Their well-developed auditory perception system, described in the previous chapter, helps them to divide speech into individual words. Children's accurate perception of other people's speech and their early-developing ability to imitate help them learn to pronounce words correctly. They pay attention to and remember the order of words that they hear in particular phrases, while also searching for generally applicable grammatical rules.

Above all, children attend to meanings, both the meanings they wish to convey and the meanings other people are trying to get across. Emphasizing meaning is an intelligent approach to language acquisition. Language is a tool for adapting to the social world. Sentences that express intended meanings will further that adaptation, even given serious shortcomings in pronunciation and grammar. Sentences that do not express intended meanings will not be adaptive, even if grammar and pronunciation are perfect.

In addition to children's own efforts to learn language, parents, siblings, other adults, and other children also promote language learning. They vary their intonations in ways that attract infants' and toddlers' attention; they speak in short, simple sentences that are easy to comprehend; and they focus on objects and events that are present in the immediate environment. Cultural history is also on the language learner's side. Languages were constructed by human beings and have evolved so that children can learn them. The result is that despite the immense complexity of language, almost all children learn their native tongue quickly and painlessly.

Organization of the chapter. The chapter begins by introducing two general questions regarding language development. First, is language learning special, in the sense that it differs from other, more general forms of learning? Second, what is the biological basis for language? These general questions set the stage for the discussion of language development in the remainder of the chapter.

The remainder of the chapter is divided into four main sections, corresponding to the four main aspects of language: phonology, meaning, grammar, and communication. *Phonology* concerns the structure and sequencing of speech sounds. *Meaning* emphasizes the correspondences between particular words and phrases, on the one hand, and particular objects, properties of objects, events, and ideas on the other. *Grammar* focuses on the system of rules through which people form sentences. *Communication* involves the ways that phonology, syntax, and semantics are used to convey messages to other people and to understand what they have in mind.

Children's developing knowledge of each of these aspects of language is reflected both in their ability to comprehend language, and in their ability to produce it. In general, comprehension precedes production for all aspects of language, and often by a substantial margin. For example, infants can recognize phonological contrasts in their native language before they can produce such contrasts, and infants comprehend many words before they can produce any words.

The four aspects of language first assume prominent roles at different points in children's language learning. Knowledge of phonology begins to develop soon after birth, as infants become increasingly able to recognize and produce the sounds characteristic of their language. Meaning becomes an important issue later in the first year. Many infants demonstrate understanding of a few simple words by 6 months of age (Tincoff & Jusczyk, 1999), and they produce their first words around their first birthday. During the second year, grammar becomes an important focus. By the middle of the second year, most children demonstrate some understanding of the differences among various syntactic constructions, and soon after this age most children begin to string together phrases of two or more words. Finally, communication is complexly related to all the other aspects of language, and it could reasonably be placed at any point in the ordering. Because it can best be understood in the context of the other aspects of language, however, we examine it after them. The chapter's organization is outlined in Table 6.1.

TABLE 6.1   Chapter Outline

   I. General Issues Regarding Language Development
      A. Is Language Special?
      B. What Is the Biological Basis for Language?
  II. Phonology
      A. Development of Knowledge about the Sounds of Language
      B. Development of the Ability to Produce Sounds
 III. Meaning
      A. Early Words and Word Meanings
      B. Development Beyond the Earliest Words and Word Meanings
 IV. Grammar
      A. Early Grammatical Development
      B. Later Grammatical Development
      C. Explanations of Grammatical Development
  V. Communication
      A. Communication Through Spoken Language
      B. Communication Through Signed Language
 VI. Summary

General Issues Regarding Language Development

IS LANGUAGE SPECIAL?

There is no question that the vast majority of children learn language rapidly and well, but there is enormous disagreement about why they are able to do so. The great linguist Noam Chomsky (e.g., 1972) proposed one answer: that people possess a "language organ" that allows them to acquire language especially easily. Chomsky argued that without such a language organ, it would be impossible for children to learn a system as complex as language on the basis of the language input that they receive, because the rules of grammar are too complicated and the input too inconsistent. Furthermore, Chomsky believed that it would be impossible for general learning mechanisms (such as imitation and reinforcement) to yield knowledge about language of the sort that learners display—namely, abstract knowledge that allows them to formulate utterances that they have never encountered before. In Chomsky's view, only a special mechanism such as a language organ could account for how young children so quickly and easily learn such a complicated and abstract system on the basis of such impoverished input. Chomsky proposed that the language organ embodies innate knowledge of aspects of grammar that apply across all the world's languages, known as "universal grammar." This innate knowledge would allow children to recognize which of a few possible types of grammar their native language uses and thus to learn it quickly, despite its complexity.

Other researchers agree with the general claim that language is special, but disagree with the specific claim that the capacity to learn language is represented in a language organ that contains innate knowledge of a universal grammar. For example, MacWhinney (2002) noted that the capacity to learn language has evolved over a period of six million years. During this period, evolution has occurred, not only in the brain structures specifically relevant to language learning, but also in more general cognitive capacities and in the social structure of primate groups, which led to a need for more refined systems of communication. Thus, in MacWhinney's view, language learning is special, not because universal grammar is innate, but because language learning emerges from a unique and complex interplay of neural, cognitive, and social factors that have gradually evolved over historical time.

Several types of evidence support the general claim that language learning is special, in the sense that it differs from other, more general forms of learning. One way in which language acquisition is special is its universality. It occurs, and occurs quickly, across a wide range of environments. Children learn in cultures in which adults converse with children on topics of special interest to the children, in cultures in which adults refuse to discuss such topics, and in cultures in which they discourage young children from talking to them at all (Snow, 1986). Acquisition of most other complex cognitive skills is more dependent on favorable circumstances and direct instruction.

Another special characteristic of language acquisition is its self-motivating properties. Some children are interested in trucks, others in birds, still others in dinosaurs. In contrast, almost all children are sufficiently interested in language to master a very complex system in a relatively short time. Part of this is due to a desire to communicate. This desire is so characteristic of human beings that it is tempting to think it must apply to other animals as well. However, humans seem to be the only animals who are interested in communicating information that is of no direct importance for survival. No other animal communicates in the wild with anything like the frequency that every typically developing 3-year-old does. Even chimpanzees who have learned to communicate quite well through sign language rarely communicate just for the sake of communicating (Tomasello et al., 1993).

People's interest in language goes beyond communicating; we also try to speak grammatically, even when ungrammatical statements would communicate just as well. Beginning language users often ask questions such as Anthony's "Where you going?" Other people understand such statements, respond appropriately to them, and rarely correct them. Yet children soon abandon such immature forms in favor of grammatically correct ones. This motivation cannot be attributed to a general desire to imitate adults and older children, as young children's special tastes in clothing, music, and food indicate. Instead, the desire to learn language, like the desire to be near other people and to understand the world around us, seems to be a basic part of people's makeup.

A third way in which language is special is evident in its relation to disorders that affect thinking in general, such as Down Syndrome and Williams Syndrome (Bellugi, Lichtenberger, Jones, Lai, & St. George, 2000; Harris, Bellugi, Bates, Jones, & Rossen, 1995; Maratsos & Matheny, 1994; Vicari, Caselli, Gagliardi, Tonucci, & Volterra, 2002). Children with both syndromes tend to have IQs that are much lower than normal, usually between 50 and 70. However, the language skills of children with Williams Syndrome tend to be much better than those of children with Down Syndrome. Children with Williams Syndrome score higher than would be expected from their IQs on many tests of vocabulary and complex syntax. In fact, some adolescents and adults with Williams Syndrome speak well enough that they could be mistaken for typical adults. This almost never happens for individuals with Down Syndrome. Then again, by adolescence, children with Down Syndrome fairly often succeed on Piagetian tasks designed to measure reasoning, such as number conservation and class inclusion, that children with Williams Syndrome consistently fail. Thus, while language and thought are complexly interdependent, the patterns of performance of children with these syndromes suggest that they also are distinct.

Although many lines of evidence support Chomsky's view that language learning is special in certain ways, his specific claim that children have innate knowledge of a universal grammar has fared less well. One problem is that evidence for the existence of universal grammar is weak. Comparisons of the grammars of the world's languages reveal tremendous diversity (Slobin, 1986).

Even simple grammatical distinctions, such as that between "a" and "the," are made in remarkably varied ways. In English, "a" and "the" are separate words, though both words are placed before the noun. In Hungarian, the distinction can be signaled through the order of the verb and the direct object. In some African languages, tone patterns are used to make the distinction. In Chinese, Japanese, Polish, and Russian, the distinction is inferred purely from context. Given this diversity, it seems unlikely that language learning involves simply recognizing which of a few possible types of grammar is being heard. Instead, language learning seems to require both general learning abilities and abilities specific to language acquisition (Maratsos, 1998).

WHAT IS THE BIOLOGICAL BASIS OF LANGUAGE?

The view that language acquisition differs from other kinds of learning suggests that there is likely to be a biological basis for language. Two concepts are especially important in thinking about this issue. One is *localization*, the idea that the brain activity that underlies a specific cognitive function is concentrated in a particular part of the brain. The other is *plasticity*, the idea that brain functioning changes in response to experience.

First consider evidence regarding localization of language. Language has a distinct anatomical base. For the large majority of people, the dominant area in language processing is in the middle of the left hemisphere of the brain, in particular in Broca's Area and Wernicke's Area (Figure 6.1). Studies of patients with *brain lesions* (damaged or removed parts of the brain) indicate that damage to these areas harms language competence more than comparable amounts of damage to corresponding areas of the right hemisphere. This is true of signed languages as well as spoken languages, indicating that the critical processing in this area is not limited to speech or to the auditory modality.

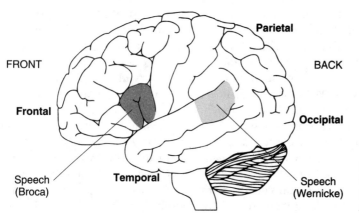

FIGURE 6.1 Side view of left hemisphere of brain, indicating locations of Broca's and Wernicke's Areas.

In addition to language processing as a whole ordinarily being concentrated in the left hemisphere, particular linguistic functions tend to be located in particular parts of the left hemisphere. For example, studies of brain-damaged patients indicate that naming of colors involves at least three areas. Lesions to an area toward the back of the brain (in the lower occipital lobe) cause loss of color vision. Lesions to Wernicke's area (Figure 6.1) cause inability to say color names. Lesions to areas in between often leave intact the ability to see colors and to list the words used to label colors (for example, by saying "red, green, blue, brown . . ."), but they interfere with patients' ability to say which name goes with which color (Damasio & Damasio, 1989, 1992).

There is also evidence that words with specifically grammatical functions are processed at different locations in the brain than other words (Neville, 1995a; Neville, Mills, & Lawson, 1992). When people read a word whose main function is grammatical (such as "the"), the brain's electrical response reaches its peak about one-quarter of a second after the word is read, and the reaction is maximal toward the front of the temporal lobe in the left hemisphere. In contrast, when people read content words (such as "dog"), the electrical response reaches its peak after about one-third of a second, and the maximal response is seen toward the rear of both hemispheres. Furthermore, the electrical activity elicited by grammatical words depends on having mastered the grammar of the language. Among 8- to 13-year-olds and among deaf adults, those with greater grammatical knowledge tend to show the distinctive response to grammatical words, whereas those with less grammatical knowledge do not (Neville, 1995a). The fact that grammatical words are processed primarily at the front of the left temporal lobe is evidence for the localization of particular linguistic functions.

Localizing linguistic functions in particular parts of the brain often proves tricky, however. Even the best accepted finding, the dominance of the left hemisphere in language use, has exceptions. For one-third of left handers, language processing occurs primarily in the right hemisphere (Kolb & Whishaw, 2003). The more specific the function, the more exceptions to the typical location in the brain.

There is evidence that the left hemisphere is already specialized for language activity in early infancy (Bertoncini, Morais, Bijeljac-Babic, & McAdams, 1989; Holowka & Petitto, 2002). However, damage to the left hemisphere early in development results in much less impairment in ability to understand and produce language than will similar damage later in development (Stiles, Bates, Thal, Trauner, & Reilly, 2002). Simply put, the brain's plasticity in the face of such damage decreases with age.

Evidence regarding this point comes from the experiences of infants born with brain abnormalities that cause life-threatening seizures. The only known way to correct these seizures is to remove the entire hemisphere that is causing the seizures, a surgical procedure known as a *hemispherectomy*. Usually, this procedure results in some degree of mental retardation (Huttenlocher, 1994), though at least one person who underwent a hemispherectomy attended and graduated from college and entered a professional career (Smith, 1984). Surprisingly, given the usual dominance of the left hemisphere in linguistic processing, people who have undergone left-side hemispherectomies before they are 1 year old develop quite normal language. The right hemisphere takes over much of the function that usually would be done by the left, and the people use language quite normally in most contexts (Stiles & Thal, 1993). One apparent cause of the recovery is that language processing takes over areas of the right hemisphere that usually support perceptual-spatial functioning. Thus, oddly enough, left hemispherectomies performed on infants sometimes result in more damage to perceptual and spatial functioning, in which right-hemisphere functioning is usually dominant, than to language functioning, in which left-hemisphere functioning is usually dominant. The pattern of results suggests that the left hemisphere may be better suited for carrying out processes involved in language processing, but these processes are shifted to the right hemisphere if the left hemisphere is unavailable. Alternatively, there may be a genetically based program that prefers to occupy tissue in the left hemisphere, but that will commandeer tissue elsewhere if the left hemisphere is unavailable (Maratsos & Matheny, 1994).

Even greater early plasticity is evident with more localized damage. If localized left-hemisphere lesions are incurred in the first year, children's prospects for close-to-normal language development are good. Their language learning in the first three years is slower (Marchman, Miller, and Bates, 1991), but by the time they are 4 or 5 years old, their language ability is generally within the normal range. In contrast, left-hemisphere damage after the first year tends to produce more lasting consequences. Thus, as is often the case, substantial plasticity in the location of processing is present early on, but the degree of plasticity decreases with development.

Phonology

DEVELOPMENT OF KNOWLEDGE ABOUT THE SOUNDS OF LANGUAGE

Infants know a great deal about the sounds of language long before they can pronounce their first word. As described in Chapter 5, from about 2 months of age, infants can distinguish among similar sounds, such as *ba* and *pa* or *a* and *i* (e.g., Eimas et al., 1971). Early on, infants are sensitive to many distinctions among sounds that are not used in their native language. However, late in the first year they begin to lose their sensitivity to distinctions that are not meaningfully different in their native language (e.g., Werker & Tees, 1984).

From a very early age, infants also recognize the sounds of their native language. Indeed, it seems likely that infants learn something about the sounds of their native language in utero, because infants as young as 2 *days* old prefer to listen to their native language rather than another language (Mehler et al., 1988; Moon, Cooper, & Fifer, 1993). Over the course of the first year, infants learn much more about the sounds of their native language (Aslin et al., 1998). For example, by 9 months infants prefer to listen to words made up of sound sequences that are used in their native language, rather than words made up of sound sequences that do not occur in their native language (Jusczyk, Friederici, Wessels, Svenkerud, & Jusczyk, 1993).

Infants use their knowledge about the sounds of their native language to help them identify individual words within the stream of fluent speech. This skill is crucial to language learning, because most utterances do not contain pauses between words. By the second half of the first year, infants can use at least three aspects of the sound patterns of their native language as clues to word boundaries, as shown in studies using the head-turn preference procedure (described in Chapter 5). One clue is the predominant stress pattern of words in their native language (Jusczyk, Cutler, & Redanz, 1993). At $7\frac{1}{2}$ months, English-learning infants successfully segment words that begin with a stressed syllable (such as *doctor* or *candle*), which is a common pattern in English, but they tend to mis-segment words that begin with an unstressed syllable (such as *guitar* and *surprise*), which is an infrequent pattern in English (Jusczyk, Houston, & Newsome, 1999).

A second clue that infants use to segment words is transitional probabilities, which are the probabilities with which sounds follow one another in the language. For example, consider the phrase "pretty baby." In English, the syllable *pre* is very likely to be followed by the syllable *ty*, because these syllables always occur together in the word *pretty*, which is a fairly common English word. However, the syllable *ty* is quite unlikely to be followed by the syllable *ba*, because the word *pretty* is often paired with other words besides *baby* (pretty dress, pretty eyes, etc.). The high probability with which *pre* is followed by *ty* suggests that *pretty* is likely to be a word, whereas the low probability with which *ty* is followed by *ba* suggests that *tyba* is unlikely to be a word. Studies using artificial language stimuli have shown that, by about 8 months, infants are capable of extracting such statistical information from a stream of fluent speech and using it to identify words (Saffran et al., 1996).

A third clue is *phonotactic* information, which involves constraints on the sequences of sounds that are allowable within individual words in the language. For example, the sequence *nt* is found in many English words (such as *ant* and *tent*), but the sequence *mt* is found in only a few. Therefore, the sound sequence *nt* signals that the sounds are probably within a single word, but the sound sequence *mt* signals that there is probably a boundary between words (as in "come to me"). Infants use such cues to segment words from fluent speech by nine months of age (Mattys & Jusczyk, 2001; Mattys, Jusczyk, Luce, & Morgan, 1999).

Taken together, these findings indicate that, even before they can produce any words, infants are surprisingly effective at tracking probabilistic features of language input. They track many features, including stress patterns, transitional probabilities, and phonotactic patterns, and they use the information they glean from such statistical learning to help them identify words in fluent speech.

DEVELOPMENT OF THE ABILITY TO PRODUCE SOUNDS

In the first year, infants not only learn to recognize and use the sound patterns of their native language, they begin to produce a wide variety of sounds as well. Before addressing how the ability to produce sounds develops, let us first consider what is involved in producing sounds in the first place.

How people speak. When people are silent, air passes freely through the windpipe, nose, and mouth in the process of breathing. We speak by impeding the airflow. The two fundamental classes of speech sounds—vowels and consonants—are produced by different types of impediments. With vowels, the only impediment to the airflow comes in the vocal cords. There is no further blocking by the tongue, teeth, or lips. Consonants, on the other hand, involve impediments by the tongue, teeth, and lips, as well as by the vocal cords. The difference can be seen in pronouncing a vowel such as the *a* in "hat" and then making a consonant sound such as the *b* in "ball." With the vowel, we do not use our lips; with the consonant, we do. All languages include both vowels and consonants.

Different vowels are distinguished primarily by the placement of the tongue. As shown in Table 6.2, the vowel sound in "meet" is produced with the tip of the tongue high and quite far forward in the mouth. In making the vowel sound in "mat," however, the tongue is much lower. (Because people usually are unaware of their tongue's location within their mouth, it may be informative to use your fingers to determine its location when you make these sounds.)

The developmental course of producing sounds. How does the ability to produce sounds develop? Infants often have difficulty producing the particular sounds they want to make. With development comes increasing ability to

TABLE 6.2 Placement of Tongue within Mouth for English Vowel Pronunciations

	Front of Mouth	Middle of Mouth	Back of Mouth
High in mouth	meet		cooed
	mitt		could
Middle of mouth	mate	glasses	code
	met		cawed
Low in mouth	mat	mutt	cod

produce the sounds at will. The following list gives a general sense of the progression (Kent & Miulo, 1995):

1. *Crying:* Infants cry from the day they are born. The crying communicates that they would like something to be different. Many parents believe that they can infer what their infant would like sheerly from the sound of the crying. Given tape recordings of their infants' cries, however, parents usually cannot tell what the infants want (Muller, Hollien, & Murray, 1974). Thus, parents must infer the cause of the crying from the context, rather than from the precise sound.
2. *Cooing:* Between 1 and 2 months, infants begin to make sounds other than cries. In particular, they coo by placing their tongue near the back of their mouth and rounding their lips. These coos resemble the *uh* sound that older individuals make in pronouncing the word "fun."
3. *Simple articulation:* At around 3 months, infants substantially increase the number of consonant sounds they make.
4. *Babbling:* By 6 months of age, infants combine consonants and vowels, and thus produce syllables. These syllables are often repeated in sequences such as *babababababa*. The intonations of the babbling increasingly resemble those of speech.
5. *Patterned speech:* Toward the end of the first year, infants increase their production of sounds that appear in their language and decrease their production of sounds that do not. Near their first birthday (give or take a few months), most say their first words.

A similar progression is observed in infants acquiring signed languages. Deaf babies cry, coo, and produce vocal babbling on about the same timetable as hearing babies. Both deaf and hearing infants who are exposed to sign languages also demonstrate *manual babble,* which consists of rhythmic, repeated motions of the hands (Petitto, Holowka, Sergio, & Ostry, 2001; Petitto & Marentette, 1991). Manual babble is thought to serve a function in the acquisition of signed languages similar to that of vocal babble in the acquisition of spoken languages.

Although parents usually view their infants' first word (or first sign) as a major milestone, the infants' achievement is quite continuous with the development of babbling before that point. For infants acquiring spoken languages, the sounds of infants' babbling and of their first words tend to be similar. Summed across a set of 15 languages, the sounds *b, p, m, d,* and *n* are the most common sounds in infants' babbling (Locke, 1983). This tendency makes understandable why in extremely diverse languages, words with these sounds, such as "papa," "mama," and "dada," are names for parents and are among the first words that children learn (Table 6.3). Babies are making the sounds anyway; languages may as well take advantage of the fact.

As seen in Table 6.3, the consonants *m* and *n* are associated with meaning "mother" but not "father." This pattern is typical; an examination of more than 1,000 terms drawn from the world's languages showed that 55 percent of the terms for "mother" included nasal sounds such as *m* and *n,* but only 15 percent of the terms for "father" did (Jakobson, 1981). Jakobson proposed an intriguing explanation for the difference. The only phonemes that can be produced when the

TABLE 6.3   Early Words for Mother and Father in 10 Languages

	Mother	Father
English	mama	dada
German	mama	papa
Hebrew	eema	aba
Hungarian	anya	apa
Navajo	ama	ataa
Northern Chinese	mama	baba
Russian	mama	papa
Spanish	mama	papa
Southern Chinese	umma	baba
Taiwanese	amma	aba

lips are pressed to the breast are nasal sounds, such as *m* and *n.* Later, infants may reproduce these sounds at the mere sight of food, to express an interest in eating, or to ask for some other change. Thus, words including *m* and *n* are especially convenient for naming the person who most often provides food and fulfills desires, the baby's mother. The use of such easy-to-make sounds to name mothers is a particularly nice example of cultures adapting to children's natures in ways gratifying to parent and child alike.

Cultures also accommodate to the phonological limitations of slightly older children by not using difficult-to-pronounce words for the objects toddlers most want to talk about (people, animals, vehicles). For example, although *str* sequences are fairly common in English (for example, "strong," "strap," "straight"), few are present in the names of objects that particularly interest young children.

Despite these accommodations of languages to infants' and toddlers' capabilities, achieving phonological competence requires a great deal of practice. The importance of such practice was illustrated in a case in which a birth defect required a cognitively typical infant to have a tube in her mouth between ages 5 and 20 months (Locke & Pearson, 1990). During this time, the infant heard a typical amount of speech, but the tube prevented her from making almost all sounds. When the tube was removed at 21 months, she immediately greatly increased the number of sounds she made, but very few were well-formed syllables. Her speech more closely resembled that of deaf children of the same age (Oller & Eilers, 1988) than that of hearing children. Only after a few months of being able to produce sounds freely did she acquire normal phonological abilities for her age.

Most children do not have full phonological proficiency until roughly school age. Some of the problems that toddlers and preschoolers experience come from their failing to produce the sound they intend. Their pronunciation is inconsistent, in the sense that they sometimes mispronounce words that at other times they pronounce correctly. Another part of the problem stems from certain sounds simply being difficult to make. Producing sounds such as *sh, th, s,* and *r* requires precise coordination of the vocal cords, tongue, teeth, and lips. Coping with other cognitive demands exacerbates the difficulty; mispronunciations increase when children try to produce grammatically complex sentences (Panagos & Prelock, 1982).

Young children cope with such challenges by choosing their words carefully. When toddlers with vocabularies as small as 25 to 75 words know more than one term for a given meaning, they tend to select the term that is easier to pronounce (Leonard, 1995; Menn & Stoel-Gammon, 1995). Conversely, once they become able to produce a sound pattern, they increase their use of terms that make use of that phonological pattern (Vihman, 1992).

Young children seem to be quite conscious of their pronunciation difficulties. For example, in one experiment, a 3-year-old was presented with a number of sentences ("I 'mell a 'kunk") and asked whether that was the way he would say it or the way his father would. On all 30 trials, the boy was correct in identifying the person who would use that pronunciation (Kuczaj, 1983). Such knowledge is an early example of metalinguistic awareness—awareness of what you know, and don't know, about language. As a concrete example of this metalinguistic awareness, consider the following conversation between a psycholinguist and his 2½-year-old son:

> FATHER: *Say "jump."*
> SON: *Dup.*
>   F: *No, "jump."*
>   S: *Dup.*
>   F: *No. "Jummmp."*
>   S: *Only Daddy can say "Dup!"* (Smith, 1973, p. 10)

Meaning

Learning the meaning of even a single word is far from simple. For example, if a parent points to a dog and says, "That's a dog," the lesson is unclear. Should the child conclude that the word "dog" means animal, collie, mammal, four-legged object, furry object, tail, ears, or any number of other possibilities? For words that are not object labels, such as verbs, the situation is even more complicated. Consider, for example, the verb "give." Whenever someone *gives* something, another person *gets* something. Consequently, whenever the word "give" is used, the word "get" could also apply to the situation. Given this inherent ambiguity in any giving event, how does a child who knows neither "give" nor "get" ever zero in on the correct meaning for each word? To make matters worse, children hear words in the context of rapidly spoken sentences addressed to other people and referring to objects and events that are not even present. Yet somehow they figure out the words' meanings. The question is how they do so. In this section, we first describe the relatively slow course of children's learning of words and word meanings up to about 18 months of age, and then the much faster acquisition that occurs thereafter.

EARLY WORDS AND WORD MEANINGS

Understanding words.   When do infants begin to link sound patterns with meanings? Some evidence suggests that, for words that are highly familiar, even 6-month-olds can do so. Tincoff and Jusczyk (1999) examined infants' comprehension of the labels "mommy" and "daddy" using a preferential-looking procedure. They videotaped each participant's parents, and then played both videos side by side, along with an audiotape of a synthesized child's voice saying either "mommy" or "daddy" (or whatever labels the participant's parents used to refer to themselves). Across trials, 6-month-old infants looked longer at the parent who was being named than at the parent who was not being named. However, they did not show this pattern when the videos presented unfamiliar men and women. Thus, by 6 months infants link the words "mommy" and "daddy" to the appropriate individuals. These findings suggest that infants may begin to form their lexicons (sets of known words) by linking names to significant individuals in their social sphere.

A few months later, infants begin to link labels more widely to objects in their environment. When 9-month-old infants hear a label paired with an object, they are more likely to attend to other objects from the same category than to other objects from a different category (Balaban & Waxman, 1997), suggesting that they understand the meanings of the object labels. At about this same age, infants also begin to respond appropriately to commands, such as "get the ball" (Benedict, 1979). Thus, word comprehension appears to be well under way by 9 months of age—considerably before most infants produce any recognizable words.

Producing first words.   The similarity between infants' babbling and their early words makes it difficult to identify just when they produce their first word. Parents often discern words months before even sympathetic friends and relatives can. It is unclear whether the discrepancy reflects parental hopes and pride or whether the parents are simply more skilled in understanding their children. In any case, most uninvolved observers place the typical age of the eagerly awaited first word between 10 and 13 months, though deviations in both directions are common.

By 18 months, a productive vocabulary of three to one hundred words is typical. These words seem to many observers to have a characteristically childlike flavor. One-year-olds use words like "ball," "doggie," and "more"; they almost never use words like "stove," "animal," and "less." In general, they refer to objects and actions that interest them, that are relatively concrete, and that they want.

Children throughout the world refer to the same types of objects with their earliest terms. They talk about people: "dada," "mama." They talk about vehicles: "car," "truck," "train." They also talk about food, clothing, and household implements, such as keys and clocks. Table 6.4 lists the 50 most common words of children in the United States. The first words spoken by children in Italy and other countries are highly similar (Caselli et al., 1995). This similarity is not limited to spoken languages; the first 50 signs produced by children acquiring American Sign Language are comparable, including such terms as "Mommy," "Daddy," "cookie," "baby," "shoes," "milk," "dog," "bye," and "ball" (Bonvillian, Orlansky, & Novack, 1983).

These examples suggest that *nouns* are prevalent in children's early lexicons. Indeed, some researchers have claimed that young children have a "noun bias," such that they learn nouns more readily than verbs (Gentner, 1982). In support of this idea, studies of children acquiring English and Italian have documented that a high proportion of children's early words are nouns (Caselli et al., 1995). However, other research suggests that the noun bias may not be universal (Bloom, Tinker, & Margulis, 1993). Verbs are as frequent as nouns in the early lexicons of children acquiring Korean (Choi & Gopnik, 1995) and verbs actually outnumber nouns in the early lexicons of children acquiring Mandarin Chinese (Tardif, 1996). It appears that differences in caregivers' speech to children may be responsible for some of these cross-language differences. Compared to English-speaking caregivers, Mandarin-speaking and Korean-speaking caregivers use more verbs in their speech to children (Choi, 2000; Choi & Gopnik, 1995; Tardif, Gelman, & Xu, 1999; Tardif, Shatz, & Naigles, 1997). Thus, the content of children's early vocabularies appears to depend in part on the language input they receive.

One-word phrases. In children's first half year of speech (roughly 12–18 months), they usually speak in single words. The demands of producing even a single word tax their cognitive resources, as evidenced by their frequently reducing multisyllabic words to a single syllable (saying "po" for "piano") and by their frequently pausing between syllables within a word (Echols, 1993; Johnson, Lewis, & Hogan, 1995). Thus, the cognitive demands of production appear to limit the meanings that toddlers can express.

Toddlers partially compensate for these limitations by choosing single words that convey larger meanings. These single words are often called *holophrases,* because they express the meaning of an entire phrase. When 1-year-olds say "ball," the word seems to imply an entire thought such as "Give me the ball," "That is a ball," or "The dog took the ball." Both context and the particular words toddlers choose make these one-word statements understandable. For example, children in the one-word stage who want a banana usually say "banana" rather than "want" (Greenfield & Smith, 1976). Because of the many things the child could want, and the relatively few aspects of bananas about which the child could be commenting, "banana" is the more informative term. However, when offered

TABLE 6.4 Words Most Commonly Appearing in the First 50 Words Children Use

Category and Word*	Frequency†	Category and Word	Frequency
FOOD AND DRINK:		VEHICLES:	
Juice	12	Car	13
Milk	10	Boat	6
Cookie	10	Truck	6
Water	8	FURNITURE AND HOUSEHOLD ITEMS:	
Toast	7	Clock	7
Apple	5	Light	6
Cake	5	Blanket	4
Banana	3	Chair	3
Drink	3	Door	3
ANIMALS:		PERSONAL ITEMS:	
Dog (variants)	16	Key	6
Cat (variants)	14	Book	5
Duck	8	Watch	3
Horse	5	EATING AND DRINKING UTENSILS:	
Bear	4	Bottle	8
Bird	4	Cup	4
Cow (variants)	4	OUTDOOR OBJECTS:	
CLOTHES:		Snow	4
Shoes	11	PLACES:	
Socks	4	Pool	3
TOYS AND PLAY EQUIPMENT:			
Ball	13		
Blocks	7		
Doll	4		

Source: Adapted from Nelson, 1973.
*Adult form of word used. Many words had several variant forms, in particular the animal words.
†Number of children (of 18) who used the word in the 50-word acquisition sequence.

a banana they do not want, 1-year-olds generally say "no" rather than "banana," presumably because saying "banana" could be misinterpreted.

Overextensions, underextensions, and overlaps. The fact that young children use a word does not guarantee that they intend the same meaning that older individuals do. Clear deviations from standard meanings are quite common up to about 2 years of age, and more subtle ones continue for years thereafter.

Children's deviations from standard meanings fall into three categories: overextensions, underextensions, and overlaps. Anglin (1986) observed each of these in the speech of his oldest daughter, Emmy. *Overextensions* involve using a word to refer not only to the standard referents but to others as well. For example, Emmy used the term "doggie" not just to refer to dogs but also to refer to lambs, cats, wolves, and cows. *Underextensions* involve limiting the use of a word to a subset of its standard referents. For example, Emmy used "bottle" to refer only to her plastic drinking bottles; she would not use it with other bottles, such as Coke bottles. *Overlaps* involve overextending a term in some ways and underextending it in others. Emmy underextended the term "brella" by refusing to apply it to a folded umbrella, but simultaneously overextended it to kites and to a leaf used to keep off rain by a monkey in her storybook.

Overextensions are the most dramatic of these errors; almost everyone notices when a child calls a cat "doggie." Underextensions are less dramatic; in everyday situations, it is often impossible to know whether a child who does not say "doggie" upon seeing a dog underextends the term or simply does not feel like talking about the dog. This created an initial impression that overextensions were more common than underextensions. Testing 1- and 2-year-olds' word meanings more directly (by showing them objects and asking "What's this?" or "Is this a _____?") has revealed a different picture, though. These studies have shown that underextensions actually are more common than overextensions (Kay & Anglin, 1982). Beginning language learners tend to be conservative in extending newly acquired words to novel referents (MacWhinney, 1989).

Form and function. What features play the largest roles in early word meanings? Two that appear to be especially important are forms and functions: the perceptual appearances of objects and the purposes that they serve. The role of form is evident in children's overextension errors (Clark, 1973). For example, children throughout the world call round things, such as walnuts, stones, and oranges, "balls." These objects share few functions with balls, but they do share a similar appearance. The importance of function in early word meanings is evident in the earliest words that children use (Nelson, 1973). These words tend to refer to things that children want (such as "more," "up," "cookie"), or objects or activities that interest them ("doggie," "car," "keys").

Form, function, and other properties can dominate early word meanings, but no single one of them always does. Bowerman (1980) illustrated this point

TABLE 6.5   *An Early Word and Its Referents*

Eve, kick.
Prototype: kicking a ball with the foot so that it is propelled forward.
Features: (a) waving limb; (b) sudden sharp contact (especially between body parts and other object); (c) an object propelled.
Selected samples. Eighteenth month: (first use) as kicks a floor fan (Features a, b); looking at picture of a kitten with ball near its paw (all features, in anticipated event?); watching moth fluttering on a table (a), watching a row of cartoon turtles on television doing can-can (a). Nineteenth month: just before throwing something (a, c); "kick bottle," after pushing bottle with her feet, making it roll (all features). Twenty-first month: as makes ball roll by bumping it with front wheel or kiddicar (b, c); pushing teddy bear's stomach against Christy's chest (b), pushing her stomach against a mirror (b); pushing her chest against a sink (b), etc.

Source: Bowerman, 1982, p. 284.

with observations of her daughters, Eve and Christy. Both overextended many of their early words. Typically, their overextensions were consistent with the particular instance from which they first learned the term. The overextensions emphasized a variety of notable features of the objects and actions they named, though form and function were the most common.

Table 6.5 presents a good example. Eve learned the term "kick" in the context of kicking a ball. She later overextended the term to describe activities with similar forms and functions, even though many of the events she referred to are not ordinarily labeled "kicks" in English. For example, she used *kick* to refer to sudden sharp contact between her arm and an object, to an object being propelled, and to the waving of a limb.

This example illustrates the demands of learning word meanings. When children hear an unfamiliar word, they cannot be sure which aspect of the situation it labels. Some words refer mainly to functions (such as "helps"), others to form (such as "big"), others to actions (such as "hits"). Interesting forms and functions increase the likelihood of children being sufficiently intrigued by an object or action to try to guess the right word for it and to use the word early on. Thus, both figure prominently in the meanings children assign to those words.

DEVELOPMENT BEYOND THE EARLIEST WORDS AND WORD MEANINGS

The course of vocabulary acquisition. Until about 18 months, word learning proceeds very slowly. At this point, however, there is a "vocabulary spurt" during which word learning accelerates. As shown in Table 6.6, average vocabulary size more than doubles between 18 and 21 months and again between 21 and 24 months. This rapid growth continues for years. Current estimates indicate that by first grade, a typical child understands at least 10,000 words,

TABLE 6.6   Size of Vocabulary at Various Ages

Age		Number of Words	Gain
Years	Months		
	8	0	
	10	1	1
1	0	3	2
1	3	19	16
1	6	22	3
1	9	118	96
2	0	272	154
2	6	446	174
3	0	896	450
4	0	1,540	318
5	0	2,072	202

Source: Adapted from M.E. Smith, 1926.

and by fifth grade 40,000 (Anglin, 1993). This means that from 1½ to 10 years, children add an average of more than 10 words per day to the set of words they understand. Increases in the number of words that children produce in their own speech occur at a similarly rapid rate (Dromi, 1986; Goldfield & Reznick, 1990).

This torrid pace suggests that children must infer the meanings of new words from only a few exposures. Studies of children's acquisition of word meanings support this conclusion. Despite the many possible meanings a word might have, 1-year-olds often can identify a new word's meaning (or at least a good approximation) from fewer than 10 exposures to it (Woodward, Markman, & Fitzsimmons, 1994). Two- and 3-year-olds often can approximate the correct meaning after a single exposure (Carey, 1978; Heibeck & Markman, 1987). But how is such "fast mapping" between a word and its meaning possible, when, as pointed out earlier, even pointing to a dog and saying "This is a dog" allows so many interpretations? The philosopher Quine (1960) labeled this question "the riddle of induction."

Different researchers have focused on different potential solutions to this riddle. Four broad classes of solutions have been proposed: (1) constraints on learning, (2) grammatical cues, (3) general cognitive processes, and (4) social cognitive skills.

Constraints on learning.   Markman (1989, 1992) proposed that children solve the riddle of induction by never considering the vast majority of logically possible hypotheses about word meanings. Instead, they focus on the meanings that adults are most likely to have in mind. This does not mean that they are mind readers. Rather, Markman suggested, their hypotheses about word meanings are constrained in ways that narrow the range of possibilities and that often lead to their first guesses being correct. She proposed that three constraints on the guesses are especially important: the *whole-object constraint*, the *taxonomic constraint* and the *mutual-exclusivity constraint.*

The *whole-object constraint* is the tendency to assume that a label for an object refers to the object as a whole, rather than to one of its parts or properties. Thus, when an adult points to a novel object and says, "This is my blicket," 2-year-olds assume that "blicket" is the name of the novel object, rather than its color or texture (Soja, Carey, & Spelke, 1991). Given the same situation, adults make the same assumption (Imai & Gentner, 1993).

When children are told, "This is an X," their guesses about what X means are particularly strongly influenced by the *shape* of the object being labeled. Both preschoolers and adults will use a newly introduced word to refer to objects that have the same shape as the original example but that differ in color, texture, material, or size (Baldwin, 1992; Landau, Smith, & Jones, 1992; Samuelson & Smith, 2000a; Smith, Jones, & Landau, 1992). They are much less likely to use the new word to refer to objects that have different shapes but that are similar in color, texture, material, or size.

The *mutual-exclusivity constraint* is the tendency to assume that, if an object has a known name, then a novel word probably refers to a different object. Thus, when children encounter a novel word in a context in which it could refer to one of two objects, and they already know a name for one of them, their first guess is usually that the word refers to the other object. For example, if 3-year-olds who already know the word "spoon" but not the word "tongs" are shown a spoon and a tongs and are told, "Show me the gug," they generally choose the tongs (Golinkoff, Hirsh-Pasek, Lavallee, & Baduini, 1985; Markman & Wachtel, 1988). This constraint does not apply only to names of objects; preschoolers also assume that novel verbs refer to actions for which they do not know a term rather than to actions for which they do know a term (Clark, 1993; Golinkoff, Hirsh-Pasek, Mervis, Frawley, & Parillo, 1995; Merriman, Marazita, & Jarvis, 1993).

The mutual exclusivity constraint appears to be in place by the time children are 1½ years old (Liitschwager & Markman, 1994). At 16 months, children more quickly learn a label for an object for which they lack an existing word than a label for an object for which they have an existing word. Over the next few years, the consistency with which children rely on the mutual-exclusivity constraint increases considerably (Merriman & Bowman, 1989).

The *taxonomic constraint* is the tendency to assume that when a new word is used to label an object, the word also can be used to refer to other objects in the same class. For example, when children as young as 18 months are shown a picture of a dog chewing a bone and told, "This is a sud," they assume that "sud" refers to dogs as a class, rather than to the dog's nose, body, or coat or to dogs chewing bones (Markman, 1989).

But how do children know whether "sud" means a general term such as "animal," a more specific term such as "dog," or a yet more specific term such as

"German shepherd"? Part of the answer is that children tend to assume, unless given evidence to the contrary, that unfamiliar words involve a *basic level* of description, that is, a level that conveys the main perceptual and functional properties of the object without being extremely specific (Golinkoff, Shuff-Bailey, Olguin, & Ruan, 1995). Children would assume that "sud" means dog, because knowing that an object is a dog tells us its main characteristics without getting into detailed distinctions among types of dogs. This assumption works out well, because language addressed to young children includes many more basic-level terms, such as "dog," than more abstract or more specific ones (Anglin, 1977; Blewitt, 1983).

In some situations, these constraints conflict with one another. For example, in one experiment, children were shown a birthday cake, told that puppets call it a "fep," and then asked whether two other objects are also feps: a pie shaped differently from the birthday cake and a hat shaped like it. When faced with such conflicts between objects' shape and their taxonomic class, 3-year-olds are more likely than 5-year-olds to choose the similarly shaped object as a fep, whereas 5-year-olds are more likely to choose the object from the same taxonomic class (Imai, Gentner, & Uchida, 1994; Merriman, Scott, & Marazita, 1993). As suggested by this example, appearance is particularly important in very young children's guesses about word meanings. With age, belonging to the same category (such as sweets) and serving the same function (such as being good to eat) become more important.

Grammatical cues.   Constraints on learning are not the only factors that help children solve the riddle of induction without much trial and error. Grammatical cues also contribute, at least by the time children are 2 or 3 years old. In the earliest study of this issue, Brown (1957) found that preschool children interpreted *"a* wug" to be an object, *"some* wug" to be an undifferentiated mass, and "wug*ing*" to be an activity. Two-year-olds also know that words introduced by saying "This is X" are usually proper names (e.g., "This is *Robert"*) (Gelman & Taylor, 1984; Macnamara, 1982), and that when a word is introduced by saying "This is an X one" (as in, "This is a tasty one") X is an adjective that indicates a property of the object (Waxman & Markow, 1998).

Grammatical cues appear to be especially important in learning the meanings of verbs. Individual verbs differ in the syntactic structures in which they can occur. Some verbs are *transitive,* which means that they require a direct object. An example is the verb "hit": "Molly hit the ball" is grammatical, but "Molly hit" is not. Other verbs are intransitive, which means that they do not take a direct object. An example is the verb "fall": "Susie falls" is grammatical, but "Susie falls the ball" is not. The syntactic structures in which a given verb occurs reveal information about the verb's meaning. For example, transitive verbs tend to involve actions that cause some effect, whereas intransitive verbs tend to involve non-causal actions. As another example, verbs that occur with prepositional phrases (for example, "Becky walked *up the hill"*) tend to convey motion. These systematic relationships between syntactic structures and verb meanings are evident in parents' speech to young children (Naigles & Hoff-Ginsberg, 1995).

From an early age, children use such information to zero in on the meanings of verbs. Naigles (1990) presented 2-year-olds with a video clip of a duck and a bunny that portrayed either a causal action (the duck pushed down on the bunny's head, causing the bunny to squat) or a non-causal action (the duck and the bunny waved their arms in circles). At the same time, children were presented with a novel verb embedded in either a transitive sentence ("The duck is gorping the bunny") or an intransitive sentence ("The duck and the bunny are gorping"). Moments later, the children were shown the two video scenes simultaneously, and they were asked, "Where's gorping?" Toddlers who had initially heard the verb in the transitive sentence looked longer at the causal action clip, but those who had initially heard the verb in the intransitive sentence looked longer at the non-causal action clip.

In a related study (Fisher, Hall, Rakowitz, & Gleitman, 1994), 3- and 4-year-old participants watched videotaped vignettes of various actions that could be construed as either transitive (the rabbit pushes the elephant) or intransitive (the elephant falls). As children watched the vignettes, a puppet described the actions in "puppet talk," using sentences such as "The rabbit is ziking the elephant" or "The elephant is ziking." The children's task was to translate the "puppet talk" into English. As would be expected if children were heeding the grammatical cues, children's interpretation of the "puppet talk" verbs depended on the sentence frames in which they were presented. When children heard the word "ziking" in a transitive sentence frame, they interpreted it to mean *pushing,* but when they heard it in an intransitive sentence frame, they interpreted it to mean *falling.*

How do young children know how syntactic structures and meanings correspond? One likely possibility is that they learn these correspondences through detecting regularities in the language input that they receive. It appears that language input provides children with a rich database over which to draw inferences about the relations between syntactic cues and word meanings. These inferences then guide the course of vocabulary acquisition.

General cognitive processes. Whereas the grammatical cues perspective emphasizes characteristics of the *language input* as a source of development of early word learning, the general cognitive processes perspective emphasizes characteristics of the *language learner.* According to this perspective, basic processes of perceiving, attending, and remembering are themselves sufficient to enable children to rapidly and effectively learn new words (Bloom, 2000; Samuelson & Smith, 1998, 2000b; Smith, Jones, Landau, & Gershkoff-Stowe, 2002). Importantly, these processes are *domain general* in the sense that they are applicable to learning many different kinds of information, and not only to language. This is a key dimension of contrast with the constraints perspective, which holds that what enables children to learn so many words so quickly are constraints that are specialized for language learning.

Markson and Bloom (1997) provided compelling evidence that general learning and memory processes can allow rapid word learning. In their experiment, 3- and 4-year-old children played a game in which they used six novel objects. During the game, children were told that one of the objects was called a "koba," and that another of the objects had been given to the experimenter by her uncle. Later, children were presented with an array of objects and asked to find both the koba and the object that the experimenter had received from her uncle. As expected, most children learned which object was the koba, and they retained this new label over a one-week and a one-month delay. More surprisingly, however, children were equally good at learning and remembering which object was given to the experimenter by her uncle. The fact that learning was comparable for the novel word and the novel fact suggests that general cognitive processes, rather than processes specialized for language, produced the learning.

General cognitive processes may also be responsible for the development of constraints on word meanings. To address this possibility, Smith et al. (2002) conducted a training study with 17-month-old children, who were young enough at the outset of the study that they did not yet generalize novel words based on object shape. In a series of seven weekly sessions, children in the trained group were taught names for objects that had one of four shapes (see Figure 6.2). Each training session involved repeatedly labeling instances of the

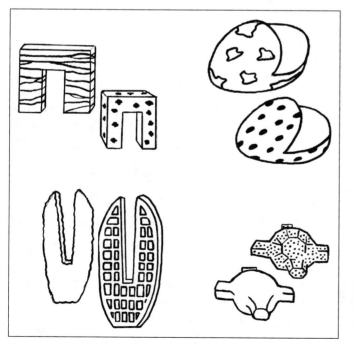

FIGURE 6.2 The four categories of objects used by Smith, Jones, Landau and Gershkoff-Stowe (2002). Instances of each category had the same shape, but differed in other attributes such as texture and color. Copyright 2002, Blackwell Publishers. Reprinted with permission.

category with a novel word ("look, a zup!"), as well as presenting a contrasting case (an object of a different shape) that was not a member of the category ("oh, that's not a zup!"). Children in the untrained group did not participate in the training sessions.

In the final week of the study, children in both groups were presented with entirely new objects and new words, and they were tested to determine whether they generalized the new words to other objects on the basis of shape. Children in the trained group did so, whereas children in the untrained group did not. Thus, children who were taught about shape-based categories during the training session used shape to infer word meaning, and they also generalized the importance of shape to novel objects and words. These data suggest that basic cognitive processes, such as attention and generalization, may be the source of patterns seen in early word learning, such as the "shape bias."

Even more striking was the effect of training on children's vocabularies, which were measured with a parent checklist at the beginning and end of the study. Children in the trained group showed a dramatic increase in the number of object names in their productive vocabularies over the course of the study, much greater than the increase shown by children in the untrained group. These data suggest that learning to attend to the shape of objects actually brought on the vocabulary spurt for these children! In more natural settings, children may initially learn a few words for shape-based categories (such as ball, cup, shoe, etc.) and then generalize over these instances to infer that shape is an important property for determining which words label which objects.

Social cues and social cognitive knowledge. Another possible source of children's ability to solve the riddle of induction lies in the social world. A great deal of language learning takes place in social interactions, including situations that involve joint attention between child and adult, scripted activities such as book reading, and routines and games such as peek-a-boo (e.g., Bruner, 1983). Both children and adults contribute to these social interactions. For example, infants attend to objects that interest them, and adults often label the objects to which children are attending (Masur, 1982). As children's language skill grows, they attempt to communicate about the things they have in mind, and most adults are highly responsive to these early efforts to communicate (Bloom, 1998; Bloom, Margulis, Tinker, & Fujita, 1996). Such social interactions provide a context in which children can learn about language and language use. Furthermore, as children's knowledge about other people grows, they can capitalize on this knowledge in language learning.

By their second year, infants realize that language generally refers to what the speaker is attending to, even if it is not what they themselves are attending to. To demonstrate that infants have this understanding, Baldwin (1991, 1993a) created a situation in which an adult was looking at one novel object and an 18-month-old at another, when the adult said, "A modi!" The children responded by shifting their attention to the object that the adult was looking at.

When later asked to get the modi, the toddlers were more likely to choose the toy that the adult had been looking at when she used the term earlier than the toy that they themselves had been looking at. Understanding of other people's intentions also aids toddlers' language learning. For example, if an adult appears to perform a novel action accidentally while saying a word, toddlers do not associate the action with the word, whereas they do associate the word with the action if the adult appears to perform the same action intentionally (Tomasello & Barton, 1994). Thus, understanding of communication, and of the social world more generally, influences children's learning of word meanings.

The social world facilitates children's word learning in other ways as well. Adults sometimes provide children with corrective feedback when they use words incorrectly (Bohannon & Stanowicz, 1988). Children also recognize that adults can serve as repositories of information about word meanings, as the following question from a 4-year-old girl attests:

> Mom, *mud* is when it rains on the dirt and it gets icky, and *dirt* is when it's dry, right? (Makris, personal communication, 2002)

Thus, through social interaction, corrective feedback, and answering questions, adults create conditions that facilitate language learning. By establishing joint attention, differentiating between intentional and unintentional actions, and asking questions, children contribute to this social learning process as well.

Beyond the riddle of induction. The preceding sections have described cues and abilities that children use to solve the "riddle of induction" as they attempt to infer the meanings of words they hear. Children appear to rely on some combination of constraints, grammatical cues, domain-general cognitive processes, and social information to zero in on the meanings of words. However, solving the riddle of induction is not the only challenge that children face in learning about word meanings. Another challenge is finding a way to express meanings for which they do not know any appropriate words.

To address this challenge, children often invent novel ways to express desired meanings. Clark (1995) cited such examples as a 24-month-old saying, "There comes the rat-man" and a 25-month-old saying, "Mommy just fixed this spear-page." The "rat-man" was a colleague of her father's who worked with rats in a psychology laboratory; the "spear-page" was a torn picture of a jungle tribe holding spears that her mother had taped together. Clark also cited the example of a 28-month-old saying, "You're the sworder and I'm the gunner." As these examples suggest, children's innovative uses of language are far from random. They reflect rules for forming new words, such as combining words or other components that are meaningful in their own right and that, when put together, have an unambiguous meaning. Such linguistic creativity allows children to express meanings that are well beyond what their limited vocabularies would otherwise allow.

What about more complex word meanings? Do children ever reorganize their initial knowledge of word meanings to reflect a more mature general level of thinking, as might be suggested by a Piagetian analysis of cognitive development? Apparently they do. Consider how 2- to 6-year-olds learn when the prefix "un" can be attached to a verb. At first glance, terms such as "uncover," "undress," "unlock," and "unstaple" would not seem to have anything in common that distinguishes them from nonwords such as "unbreak" and "unspill." Careful analysis of these words, however, suggests a pattern (Bowerman, 1982; Clark, 1995). "Un" often can be attached to verbs that involve contact between objects ("unlock," "unfasten," and "unstaple") or covering ("undress," "unveil," and "uncover"). In contrast, "un" almost never can be attached to other verbs.

Bowerman found that children's first use of these terms involved correct repetition of words that they had heard other people use, such as "unbuckled" and "untangled." Later, children began to attach the prefix in new and often incorrect ways. For example, one child said to her mother, "I hate you! And I'll never unhate you or nothing!" Such errors indicate that the child realized that "un" was a distinct part of the verbs she had heard it with, and that it could be attached to other verbs, but had not figured out when it could be used. Later errors show greater understanding that *un* usually can be attached only to verbs that involve covering or contact. For example, the same child who vowed never to unhate her mother recited a ghost story eight months later and said, "He tippytoed to the graveyard and *unburied* her." Although "unburied" does not happen to be a word in English, it does conform to the rule that "un" often can be attached to terms involving covering. The subtlety of the distinction reflects how remarkable children's learning of meaning is: How many adults could tell you the rule governing when "un" can be attached to a verb?

Grammar

All human languages have grammars, that is, rules for forming sentences. Young children are motivated to learn these grammars, even when they can communicate well without learning them, and even though they are rarely corrected for grammatical errors (Brown & Hanlon, 1970). Children's interest in learning grammar differentiates people from apes who, even when taught to express meanings through symbols, show no interest in learning the grammars of the languages they are taught.

The grammars of many of the world's languages are extremely complex. Children's ability to learn such complex systems at young ages has led some researchers to propose that there is a "critical period" in early development during which the brain is especially receptive to learning grammar. Below, we consider grammatical development in the first two years, then grammatical development at later ages, and then several explanations of how children learn grammar.

EARLY GRAMMATICAL DEVELOPMENT

Perceptual bases of grammar learning.   Even newborn infants seem to have some sensitivity to grammatical information. Shi, Werker, Morgan (1999) examined whether newborns are sensitive to the distinction between grammatical words, such as *the, in,* and *its,* and content words, such as *play, chair,* and *ball.* Words in these two categories play different roles in language: content words (such as nouns, verbs, adjectives, and adverbs) carry meaning, whereas grammatical words (such as articles, prepositions, and auxiliaries) play a structural role. Words in these two categories also differ in their perceptual characteristics. For example, grammatical words have shorter vowel durations and simpler syllable structure.

To test whether newborns could discriminate content words and grammatical words, Shi and colleagues presented 1- to 3-day-old infants with a list of either grammatical or content words. During a habituation phase, infants sucked on a special pacifier that recorded their sucking rate. When infants' interest in the word list declined sufficiently that their sucking rate reached a pre-specified criterion, a new list of words was presented. For some infants, the new list was made up of words from the same category that they had heard during habituation (either grammatical or content words); for other infants, the new list was made up of words from the other category. Infants for whom the category switched between the habituation phase and the test phase showed greater interest in the new list, as measured by greater increases in sucking rates, than did infants for whom the category stayed the same. Thus, newborns can discriminate between grammatical and content words based on perceptual characteristics of those words. A follow-up study showed that by six months, children *prefer* to listen to content words rather than grammatical ones (Shi & Werker, 2001). These findings suggest that languages mark certain grammatical distinctions in ways that are perceptually salient to young infants; such marking may facilitate learning of grammar.

Sentences.   Sentences are the basic unit of grammar. They are more than simple strings of words. Instead, they are cohesive units that express meaning and that follow conventions regarding word order, intonation, and stress. So basic are they that Anisfeld (1984) commented, "In a real sense, sounds and words exist to be used in sentences" (p. 113).

From a remarkably early age, infants are able to detect regularities across sentences in word order. To investigate this ability, Gomez and Gerken (1999) used an artificial language consisting of eight nonsense words that were presented in "sentences" that were constructed according to a set of arbitrary word-order rules. Infants were exposed to a set of sentences from this artificial language that were "grammatical" in the sense that they conformed to the word-order rules. After listening to the grammatical sentences for only two minutes, 12-month-old infants could discriminate between novel grammatical sentences (ones that had not been in the exposure set) and sentences that were "ungrammatical" in the sense that they violated the word-order rules.

Other research has shown that infants as young as 7 months can abstract patterns such as the "ABA" pattern in "sentences" like *ga ti ga* and *li na li* (Marcus, 2000; Marcus, Vijayan, Bandi Rao, & Vishton, 1999). Infants who had been habituated to an artificial language with an ABA pattern subsequently listened longer to novel sentences with an ABB pattern (such as *wo fe fe*) than to novel sentences with an ABA pattern (such as *wo fe wo*). Infants who had been habituated to a language with an ABB pattern showed the reverse preference. These findings suggest that infants readily acquire grammatical information that is abstract and rulelike.

Even before children begin to produce sentences on their own, their understanding of other people's statements in everyday contexts reflects knowledge of some of the grammatical conventions of their native language (Hirsh-Pasek & Golinkoff, 1996). For example, at ages when children are mainly producing one-word phrases, they already show some understanding of the role of word order within sentences. In one set of studies, 17-month-olds were simultaneously shown two films that differed only in who was doing what to whom. Big Bird was washing Cookie Monster in one film, and Cookie Monster was washing Big Bird in another. When asked questions such as "Where is Big Bird washing Cookie Monster?" the toddlers usually looked at the film where that action was occurring. This pattern suggests that the 17-month-olds believed that the character mentioned first in the sentence probably was doing the action, which corresponds to the usual grammatical pattern in English.

Turning to children's own speech, their earliest two-word phrases seem somewhere between pairings of individual words and true sentences. The two words in each phrase tend to express related meanings, but they are not very cohesive and often are separated by long pauses. Sometimes, they are referred to as *sequences* (of words), to distinguish them from true sentences. Thus, one 20-month-old boy produced such phrases as "train/bump," "cow/moo," and "beep/beep/trucks" (Anisfeld, 1984; the slashes indicate pauses between words). These expressions seemed to indicate meanings comparable to those of simple sentences ("The train bumped." "Cows say moo." "Trucks beep."). However, they lacked the intonational patterns and cohesion of sentences.

Along with these sequences, children begin to produce true sentences. At first, the sentences are rare, but within a few months, they become dominant. The cognitive effort needed to construct them is evident in the halting way in which young children talk. Braine (1971) estimated that 30 to 40 percent of 24- to 30-month-olds' statements are "replacement sequences," in which children build on earlier statements until they succeed in producing the desired form and meaning. Thus, Braine described a 25-month-old saying in succession, "Want more. Some more. Want some more." and a 26-month-old saying, "Stand up. Cat stand up. Cat stand up table."

Early in language learning, grammatical knowledge is often interwoven with knowledge of meanings (Corrigan, 1988; Corrigan & Odya-Weis, 1985). Children from different language backgrounds emphasize the same meaningful relations in their two-word phrases: agent-action ("Mommy hit"), possessor-possessed ("Adam checker"), attribute-object ("big car"), recurrence ("more juice"), and disappearance ("juice allgone") (Anisfeld, 1984; Bloom, 1990; Braine, 1976). Within each relation, children order words in a regular fashion. Thus, when describing an object that has disappeared, a child who said "juice allgone" would rarely if ever say "allgone juice" or "allgone milk." However, the consistency of the word ordering is specific to the meaning being expressed.

At first, children are very conservative about generalizing from the islands of grammatical competence that they have established. For example, Kuczaj (1986) observed that one of his two children initially used "are" only in declarative sentences starting with "these" or "those" ("Those are good toys."). His other child at first used "is" only at the end of sentences ("There they is."). This reluctance to extend newly acquired grammatical forms to novel contexts parallels children's conservatism about extending newly acquired word meanings to new referents and their avoidance of words that they have trouble pronouncing.

LATER GRAMMATICAL DEVELOPMENT

Once children produce true sentences, they begin to acquire many of the grammatical conventions used in adult language. For example, English-speaking children learn to indicate that an event happened in the past by appending *ed* to the verb. They learn to indicate that more than one individual was involved in an event by appending *s* or *es* to the noun. They learn to use "am," "is," and "are" in the full range of circumstances to which they apply. Acquisition of two grammatical conventions, those used to form past tenses and to ask questions, illustrate grammatical development particularly clearly.

Past tense forms. In English, the past tense forms of most verbs are produced by adding "ed" to the infinitive (such as adding "ed" to "help" to produce "helped"). However, the past tense forms of a number of particularly common verbs are exceptions to this rule, for example, "came," "went," "hit," and "ate." Indicating that events occurred in the past thus requires mastering both the rule and the exceptions.

Children appear to begin learning the past tense by treating each word as a separate case. This leads to their first past tense verbs being correct repetitions of forms they have heard, both regular (such as "jumped") and irregular (such as "ran"). However, once they have learned a fairly large number of verbs (roughly 60 to 70 in most cases), and abstracted the "ed" pattern, they impose it not only in cases where it fits but also in cases where it does not (Marchman & Bates, 1994).

This tendency helps them to infer the correct past tense form for the many regular verbs whose past tense forms they never have heard, but it also leads to *overregularized* forms such as "runned" and "eated." These overregularized forms are not the only ones that they produce at any given time. The same child who says "runned" in one sentence may say "ran" in the next, and may occasionally say "ranned" as well (Marcus et al., 1992). However, the overregularizations persist for a long time, being produced occasionally by most children from around age 2 into the school years (Marcus et al., 1992). They also cannot be dismissed as accidents. When 5- and 6-year-olds are asked to judge whether particular forms are "ok" or "silly," most indicate that both "ate" and "ated" are ok, though most judge "eated" to be silly (Kuczaj, 1978). Not until age 7 do they judge only the correct past tense form to be correct.

Questions.   Soon after children begin to use two-word phrases, they start to learn a common, but surprisingly complex, set of grammatical forms: those involved in asking questions. Quite often, the first question they ask is "What dat?" (Reich, 1986). This is soon followed by questions involving "where" ("Where Mommy boot?"), yes-no questions ("Go now?"), and questions involving doing ("What Billy doing?").

Plainly, it is a long way from these abbreviated questions to fully grammatical ones. It takes several years of experience before children consistently ask questions grammatically. For example, consider the process of learning to ask wh questions. Initially, English-learning children often maintain the basic subject-verb-object order that is typical of English and just attach a "wh" term to a sentence that they have just heard (de Villiers, 1995). A child who was told "Billy hates Mary" might ask "Why Billy hates Mary?" Later, children realize that auxiliary verbs such as "does" must be added. Sometimes they produce forms with the auxiliary verb in the wrong place ("Why Billy does hate Mary?"). Other times, they produce forms with the auxiliary verb in the right place but with the s not removed from the verb ("Why does Billy hates Mary?"). Yet other times, the same child will produce the correct form. Not until roughly age 5 do children ask such questions consistently correctly. Their persistence in learning this complicated set of forms again illustrates their high motivation to speak grammatically.

Critical periods in grammar learning.   Why are such grammatical forms learned when they are, rather than earlier or later? Lenneberg (1967) raised one intriguing possibility: that the time between 18 months and puberty is a critical period, during which the brain is especially receptive to learning grammar.

Initial explanations of grammatical acquisition seemed to contradict Lenneberg's hypothesis. For example, comparisons of adults and preschoolers who were completing their first year of living in Holland indicated that the adults' mastery of Dutch grammar was superior (Snow & Hoefnagel-Hohle, 1978).

However, studies that have focused on the end point of grammatical acquisition, rather than knowledge after one or a few years of exposure to the language, suggest that learners who start young ultimately reach higher levels of proficiency. Johnson and Newport (1989) examined knowledge of English grammar among Korean and Chinese immigrants who had come to the United States when they were between 3 and 39 years old and who had lived in the United States for between 3 and 26 years. Because age of arrival and number of years in the United States were only moderately correlated in the group they studied, the investigators could separate the influences of the age at which the immigrants began to learn English from the amount of time they had spent learning it.

Age of arrival was closely related to ultimate level of grammatical mastery. In contrast, number of years in the United States had little relation to it. Immigrants who came before age 7 knew grammar as well as native-born adults; those who came between 8 and 10 knew it slightly less well; those who came between 11 and 15 knew it somewhat less well. Most striking, very few of those who came after age 15 mastered English grammar very well at all (Figure 6.3). Only one of the 22 people who arrived that late showed as much grammatical knowledge as the least knowledgeable of the 15 people who arrived before age 11. Further, among those who arrived after age 15, neither age at arrival nor number of years in the United States correlated highly with degree of mastery. Unlike the universal mastery of the basics of English grammar seen among native speakers, some adult learners mastered English grammar to a moderate degree, and others very poorly.

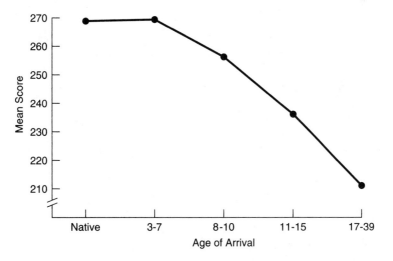

FIGURE 6.3 Performance on a test of grammatical competence as a function of age of immigration from East Asia to United States (data from Johnson & Newport, 1989).

Like Johnson and Newport's research, most studies of the critical period for grammar learning have focused on second language learning, because it would be unethical to withhold exposure to a first language from a developing child. However, there have been some rare cases of children who grew up without language input because of extreme neglect or abuse. One such child, Genie, was first discovered at age 13 years, 7 months, after having been confined to a small room from the age of 20 months. Genie made great strides in language acquisition after her discovery, but she was unable to acquire many of the more subtle aspects of grammar, such as the auxiliary verb system (for example, she consistently omitted "will" in sentences such as "I will go home") and passive constructions (she produced no sentences such as "The ball was hit by Molly") (Curtiss, 1977). These data are consistent with the idea that language input during a critical period is essential for acquiring at least some aspects of grammar. However, it is possible that Genie may have had other developmental or learning problems in addition to her lack of language exposure, so one cannot definitively conclude that her inability to acquire these grammatical structures is due to lack of input in the critical period.

One naturalistic situation in which children may grow up without language input in their early years is the case of deaf children of hearing parents. Some of these children are not exposed to fluent sign language until they enter school. Again, consistent with the critical period hypothesis, these "late learners" of sign language generally perform less well than individuals who learn sign language from birth on tests that require high grammatical competence, such as recall of complex sentences (Mayberry, 1993; Mayberry & Eichen, 1991; Newport, 1990). Late learners of American Sign Language also perform more poorly than do native signers when they later learn English in written form (Mayberry, Lock, & Kazmi, 2002).

These findings clearly support the idea that grammar learning is superior early in development. However, other studies have raised a number of questions. Some studies have shown that at least some adults who learn English as a second language do acquire grammatical proficiency comparable to that of native speakers (Bialystok & Hakuta, 1994; White & Genesee, 1992). Other studies suggest that, contrary to the critical period hypothesis, the decrease with age in the ability to learn a second language is gradual rather than sudden (Hakuta, Bialystok, & Wiley, 2003). Thus, the critical period debate is far from settled.

EXPLANATIONS OF GRAMMATICAL DEVELOPMENT

Currently, there is no generally accepted theory of grammatical development. However, several accounts seem to tell parts of the story.

Basic child grammar.   Slobin (1986) proposed that children impose a basic child grammar on whatever language input they receive. This view is a first cousin of the constraints approach to word meaning and a second cousin of Piaget's general concept of assimilation. Within Slobin's view, children expect that certain meanings are sufficiently important that they should be reflected in grammar. They also expect that particular meanings should be expressed in particular places within phrases. When meanings that children believe are important are marked by the grammar of the language where children believe they should be, children learn the grammatical conventions quickly. When the grammatical markings are in different places, or when children do not expect the meaning to be important at all, they learn more slowly.

Use of negative terms illustrates Slobin's general idea. Negatives affect the meaning of the entire phrase they modify. When we say, "He didn't run to the store," the negative in "didn't" modifies the entire verb phrase "did run to the store." Children's errors indicate that they try to keep the negative outside of the phrase, even when the language they hear places it inside the phrase. In Turkish, correct sentences specify the verb, then indicate whether the meaning is negative, and then complete the verb phrase (as in "He run didn't to the store"). Turkish children often err, however, by moving "didn't" outside the verb phrase (as in "He didn't run to the store"). Thus, children's expectations can, for a time, override the language to which they are exposed, leading to grammatical errors. More generally, the fit between children's expectations and the grammatical conventions of the language they hear influences how quickly they learn the grammar.

Semantic bootstrapping. Children's early sentences usually follow standard orders of meanings such as agent-action-recipient (e.g., "Billy hit me."). Eventually, however, children also produce sentences that deviate from such standard sequences. For example, when a child says, "Going to school sure is fun," the grammatical subject ("going to school") is not an agent, the verb ("is") is not an action, and the grammatical object ("fun") is not a recipient of any action. As children's grammatical competence grows, they also recognize that a meaningless sentence can still be grammatically correct (for example, "Frequent exercise prevents restless windows."). A full account of grammatical understanding must explain how people reach such abstract understanding of grammar and what role their initial understanding of meaning plays in the process.

Pinker (1984) proposed that early learning of grammar is based on *semantic bootstrapping*. The key idea is that children first identify the most common categories of meanings in the sentences they hear (for example, the person or thing that produces the action, the name of the action, and the person or thing affected by the action). They then use these meanings to form meaning-based categories and rules for ordering words in sentences. Finally, they use these meaning-based categories and rules to "pull themselves up" to purely grammatical categories and rules.

Such a learning process is possible because grammatical categories tend to be correlated with meanings. In English, names of persons or things usually function as nouns, actions as verbs, and attributes of persons or things as adjectives. These relations provide a basis for early analysis of sentences. For example, from frequent exposure to sentences such as "Babar jumped on the bed," children learn that in English, the agent who engaged in the action is typically named at the beginning of the sentence, that the action itself is typically in the middle, and that the recipient of the action is typically at the end. This provides a basis for the child to order words within sentences according to the agent-action-recipient framework.

These early sentence frames not only allow children to produce grammatical sentences; they also provide a basis for learning grammatical rules that are not based on meaning. Pinker hypothesized that grammatical categories such as noun, verb, subject, and predicate are innate to human beings. Children's learning task is to identify how these grammatical categories function within their particular language. They do this by establishing correspondences between the meanings they initially represent and the innately known grammatical categories. For example, they map the grammatical category "subject" onto the meaning-based concept "agent" and the grammatical category "verb" onto the meaning-based category "action." Once they code the language they hear in terms of these grammatical categories, they note regularities of ordering, phrasing, and intonation that allow them to extend the grammatical categories to cases where the grammatical subject is not an agent and the verb is not an action (such as "The house has three bedrooms" or "Going to school is fun"). In doing this, they create the purely grammatical categories that characterize mature grammatical competence.

Construction grammar.   Another approach to understanding grammatical development, the construction grammar approach, denies the existence of innate grammatical categories like those hypothesized by Pinker and Chomsky. Instead, according to this view, early grammatical development involves learning specific linguistic items, or *constructions.* A construction is defined as a "complete and coherent verbal expression associated in a relatively routinized manner with a complete and coherent communicative function" (Tomasello & Brooks, 1999, p. 162). In essence, constructions are recurrent linguistic patterns. For example, "Where's X?" is a simple construction that conveys the communicative function of seeking something. It has an abstract "slot" for a noun indicating the thing being sought ("Where's Daddy?" "Where's doggie?" "Where's bottle?").

According to the construction grammar approach, early grammatical development involves learning constructions and beginning to use them productively (Tomasello & Brooks, 1999). Beginning language learners readily substitute nouns for one another in constructions; however, verbs and other predicates must be learned one by one, each as a novel construction (Tomasello, 2000). Thus, children's early constructions often revolve around verbs or other predicate constructions, with open slots for nouns, such as "Eat X" or "See X."

The systematic two-element combinations described by Braine (1976) (such as "allgone juice," "allgone milk") are examples of such constructions.

Before 2 to 3 years of age, children tend to use only one type of construction for each verb (Lieven, Pine, & Baldwin, 1997; Tomasello, 1992). For example, a child who uses the construction "Eat X" ("Eat apple," "Eat cereal") is unlikely to also use the construction "X eats" ("Mommy eats," "Doggie eats"). Thus, learning one construction involving a particular verb does not immediately enable children to generate other constructions involving that same verb. Advocates of the construction grammar approach have taken this finding as evidence that children do not have an innate grammatical category of verb, because an innate category should allow them to quickly generalize to other new constructions (Tomasello, 2000).

With time, children extract commonalities among the individual, verb-based constructions, and in so doing they develop more abstract constructions, such as transitive sentences ("noun phrase – verb – noun phrase," as in, "Molly hit the ball," "Willie pushed the truck") and locatives ("noun phrase – verb – noun phrase – location," as in, "Amy put the cup on the table"). According to Tomasello (2000), this development occurs through processes of structure combination and analogy formation. Children begin to combine simple constructions into more complex ones; for example, the constructions "Eat X" and "X eats" may be combined into a larger construction such as "X eats X" ("Mommy eats cake"). Children also begin to notice structural similarities among various constructions and form analogies on the basis of these similarities. Eventually they extract the common structures in these analogically similar sets, and these common structures form the basis of more abstract constructions. For example, a child might notice the similarities between "X eats X," "X pushes X," and "X breaks X," and on this basis, the child might abstract the more general construction "noun phrase – verb – noun phrase." Through these mechanisms, according to construction grammar theorists, children eventually develop general syntactic structures that are no longer based on individual items.

Connectionist accounts.   As discussed in Chapter 3 (pp. 92–97), several connectionist models of development have focused on learning of grammar (e.g., Elman, 1993; MacWhinney & Chang, 1995; MacWhinney & Leinbach, 1991; Plunkett & Marchman, 1993). These models have demonstrated that computer simulations that encode features of phonology, meaning, and word order can learn complex grammatical systems such as English past tense forms and German gender and case markings.

Connectionist systems operate by detecting patterns of correlations in the language that is presented and using these correlational patterns to predict what grammatical form should be used in new situations. This type of mechanism may also be at work in children's learning of grammar. All of the connectionist models learn grammar quite slowly, as a result of exposure to thousands and thousands of instances. This fits children's learning of grammar quite well. As Maratsos (1998) has noted, grammatical systems are so complex that children's acquisition of them is by necessity more like a process of "grinding through" than like a process of testing a few hypotheses to see how the system works.

Evaluation.   How can we evaluate these alternative accounts of children's acquisition of grammar? In many ways, they resemble the proverbial story of the blind men feeling different parts of the elephant. Each explanation incorporates part of the truth, but none the totality. Slobin's and Pinker's emphasis on the role of meaning in formation of early grammatical categories seems well founded. Pinker's semantic bootstrapping idea is an attractive transition mechanism. The notion that early performance is based on learning particular constructions is also intuitively appealing. The connectionist idea that grammatical competence is based on detection of complex patterns of correlations within the language also is clearly a large part of the story. Yet the views are sufficiently different that it is unclear how they could be integrated into a single theory. In sum, the task of explaining grammatical development continues to challenge the best minds in the field.

Communication

The ultimate purpose of language is communication. Such communication can be accomplished either through spoken language or through signed language. These modes of communication are considered in the following sections.

COMMUNICATION THROUGH SPOKEN LANGUAGE

Communication to and from infants.   Rudimentary communication skills are present even in the first months after birth. Already by 3 or 4 months, infants act in ways that motivate adults to speak to them. They tend to be quiet when an adult talks to them and to vocalize more when the adult stops talking (Ginsburg & Kilbourne, 1988). In the first few months after birth, infants' and mothers' vocalizations frequently clash, in the sense of occurring simultaneously. By 3 or 4 months, however, the interactions evolve into a smooth turn-taking process, akin to that of the conversations of older children and adults. Infants of this age also tend to reproduce the general intonational pattern that their mothers just produced (Masataka, 1992). The infants' turn taking and reproduction of intonational patterns encourages adults to talk more with them than if they remained silent or behaved in ways uncorrelated with what the adult was saying (Locke, 1995).

Adults, in turn, speak to infants in ways that encourage them to listen and respond. Just as infants imitate their mothers' intonational patterns, mothers imitate the speech sounds that infants make. When mothers imitate their infants' speechlike sounds, but not other vocalizations, the infants' proportion of speech-like sounds increases (Bloom, Russell, & Wassnberg, 1987). As noted in the previous chapter, adults and older children in many cultures also use a form of speech known as infant-directed speech, or "motherese," in which they speak using high pitch, exaggerated intonations, short, simple sentences, and elongated vowels (as when saying "Wheeee"). From an early age, infants prefer infant-directed speech to adult-directed speech (Cooper & Aslin, 1990). When caregivers use infant-directed speech, infants pay increased attention to what is being said and to the caregiver's activities more generally (Fernald, 1992).

Infant-directed speech is very common among the world's cultures, but it is not universal. For example, on the island of Java, parts of Guatemala, and parts of Western Samoa, parents rarely talk to babies (Ochs & Schiefflein, 1995; Pye, 1992; Smith-Hefner, 1988). When Kaluli adults in New Guinea saw Westerners speaking infant-directed speech to babies, they wondered how the babies ever learned to speak proper language (Schiefflein, 1990). In these societies, infants and toddlers learn language primarily by observing adults speaking. These cases cannot be dismissed as minor exceptions; 100 million people live on Java. The practices may not seem very conducive to language learning, but children still master the grammars of their native language quite efficiently (Ochs & Schiefflein, 1995).

Communication to and from toddlers and older children. When babies begin to produce words, they add new strategies for communicating. Some of these strategies are unique to beginning language users. For example, some toddlers repeat entire phrases with only minimal grammatical alterations (Billman & Shatz, 1981; Keenan, 1977). When one father asked his 2-year-old son, "Are you a great big boy?" he responded, "I are a great big boy." The early responses to *wh* questions that were described previously provide another example of such imitations. The imitations often are considerably longer than the child's typical sentences at that time. Thus, they may provide a stepping stone for constructing longer and more complex sentences than the child previously generated (Schlesinger, 1982).

As children develop, they become increasingly able to take their communication partners into account when they use language (Krauss & Glucksberg, 1969; Sonnenschein, 1986, 1988). For example, children as young as 2 years of age simplify their speech when speaking to younger children (Tomasello & Mannle, 1985; Shatz & Gelman, 1973) and to dolls (Sachs & Devin, 1976). Young children also alter their communicative behavior depending on whether their listener can see them. Children as young as 3 use more verbally explicit speech when speaking to a blindfolded listener than when speaking to a listener who is not blindfolded (Maratsos, 1973), and kindergarteners use fewer gestures along with their speech when speaking to a listener who is sitting behind a curtain than when speaking to a listener face-to-face (Alibali & Don, 2001). Thus, even very young children can modify their communicative behavior to fit their listeners' needs, and this ability improves with age and experience.

Although infants and toddlers bring a great deal to the task of communication, understanding some of the finer points requires direct parental effort. Learning of politeness conventions is one prominent example, as illustrated in the following conversation (cited in Ely & Gleason, 1995, p. 252):

> CHILD: *Mommy, I want more milk.*
> MOTHER: *Is that the way to ask?*
>   C: *Please.*
>   M: *Please what?*
>   C: *Please gimme milky.*
>   M: *No.*
>   C: *Please gimme milk.*
>   M: *No.*
>   C: *Please . . .*
>   M: *Please may I have more milk?*
>   C: *Please may I have more milk?*

COMMUNICATION THROUGH SIGNED LANGUAGE

Signed languages, such as American Sign Language (ASL) and Quebec Sign Language (Langue des Signes Quebecoise, or LSQ), are true languages in every sense of the word. They have lexicons that consist of thousands of signs and grammars that are as rich and complex as the grammar of any spoken language. There are hundreds of different signed languages that are used in Deaf communities throughout the world. Like spoken languages, each one is unique—users of one sign language generally cannot understand other sign languages.

Deaf children who acquire sign languages from birth, and hearing children who acquire spoken languages from birth, show closely parallel paths of language acquisition (Petitto, 1992, 1995). Both groups babble, produce one-word phrases, and produce two-word phrases at similar ages; they produce grammatical forms such as past tenses, negatives, and questions at similar ages; and they acquire similar meanings and similar communicative competence at similar ages. Older children in both groups use considerable amounts of nonliteral language, such as metaphor, simile, and invented words (Marschark & West, 1985; Marschark, West, Nall, & Everhart, 1986).

The similarities in children's acquisition of sign and speech led Petitto (1995) to suggest that the same language acquisition mechanism leads to learning of both spoken and signed language. She hypothesized that this mechanism recognizes input that is structured in the way that both spoken and signed language is, and that once the learning system recognizes relevant input, it stimulates motor activity (speech or manual activity) that responds to that structure, regardless of whether the structured input is seen or heard.

Stokoe (1960) described three dimensions that determine meaning within individual signs. One is the location at which a sign is made. The most common locations, in order of frequency, are the area in front of the body where the hands ordinarily move, the chin, the trunk, the cheek, the elbow, and the forehead. These also are the locations at which young children find it easiest to produce signs, one more instance of languages' having evolved to facilitate learning (Bonvillian, Orlansky, & Novack, 1983). A second dimension that distinguishes signs is the shape or configuration of the hands. Several common handshapes are shown in Figure 6.4. The third dimension of variation among signs is the action or movement involved in making the sign. For example, the ASL sign for "candy" is produced by making a rotating movement with the index finger at the cheek. Of these three dimensions, location appears to be easiest for children to master, and handshape the most difficult. In a study of nine children (ages 5 to 18 months) acquiring ASL, Bonvillian and Siedlecki (2000) found that children were most accurate in producing the location of a target sign (over 80 percent correct), next most accurate at producing movement (about 60 percent correct), and least accurate at producing handshape (about 50 percent correct).

FIGURE 6.4   Some hand shapes that are commonly used in American Sign Language.

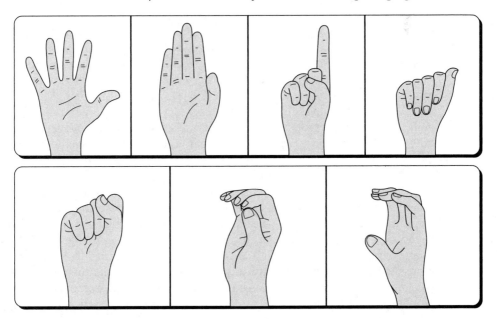

Deaf children of hearing parents who are not exposed to signed languages in early childhood often invent simple gestural languages, called *home sign systems*, for communicating with their families. These children use their home sign systems to communicate information, make requests, tell stories, and talk about objects and events, both present and absent (Goldin-Meadow, 2003; Morford & Goldin-Meadow, 1997; Phillips, Goldin-Meadow, & Miller, 2001). Such children even use home sign to talk to themselves! Thus, home sign systems serve the same functions as do conventional languages. Based on their observations of a set of ten home signers, Goldin-Meadow and Morford (1985) commented, "Communication in humans is a resilient phenomenon; when prevented from coming out of the mouth, it emanates almost irrepressibly from the fingers" (p. 146).

One of the most striking aspects of home sign systems is that they have language-like structure at a variety of levels. Each child's home sign system can be characterized by a simple grammar that specifies how individual signs are combined into sentences (Goldin-Meadow & Feldman, 1977; Goldin-Meadow & Mylander, 1984, 1998). For example, in most (but not all) children's home sign systems, when describing an action on an object, the object is named before the action ("apple eat"). Furthermore, like signs in conventional sign languages, individual signs within home sign systems are made up of components, such as handshape and motion, that combine in systematic ways to express meaning (Goldin-Meadow, Mylander, & Butcher, 1995). Thus, home sign systems are structured like conventional languages, both at the sentence level and at the level of individual signs. Moreover, it is clear that children create these language-like structures on their own, because the gestures used by the children's hearing parents do not display such structure (Goldin-Meadow & Mylander, 1983).

Despite their similarities, home sign systems also differ from true signed languages in important respects. Most important, home sign systems are less systematic and less grammatically complex than true signed languages are. Why might this be the case? Unlike signed languages, home sign systems are invented by individual children, rather than being passed down and refined from generation to generation. In addition, home sign systems tend to be shared by only a few individuals (with only one native speaker, the inventor), rather than by an entire linguistic community. These factors appear to be important in the evolution of full-fledged, conventional languages.

In Nicaragua in the late 1970s, a number of deaf home signers were brought together in the nation's first school for the deaf. As these children attempted to communicate with one another, the set of individual home sign systems that they brought to the situation began to cohere and become systematized into a new, shared language. The new sign language that emerged in this situation was far more systematic and grammatically complex than any of the individual home sign systems upon which it was based, and it became even more complex as the next generation of young deaf children learned it as a native language (Kegl,

Senghas, & Coppola, 1999; Morford & Kegl, 2000; Senghas & Coppola, 2001). This new language is called Lengua de Signos Nicaraguense (Nicaraguan Sign Language), and it is one of few instances of the birth of a new language that has been observed systematically.

Summary

The acquisition of language in the first few years of life is one of children's greatest achievements. They quickly learn phonology, meanings, and grammar, and they use this knowledge in the service of communication. Phonology refers to the production and comprehension of speech sounds. Meaning refers to relations between words and what they describe. Grammar involves the ordering of words into sentences, as well as the specification of tense and number. Communication is the way phonology, grammar, and meaning are used together to express desires and intentions, elicit reactions, and provide information.

Phonologies of all languages involve production of vowels and consonants. Impeding the usual flow of air is critical to both. However, they differ in the particular type of impediment that produces them. With vowels, the only impediments are produced by the vocal cords; with consonants, the tongue, teeth, and lips produce additional ones. Infants know a great deal about the phonology of their native language before they can produce any words. They are initially sensitive to many distinctions among sounds; however, late in the first year, they begin to lose their sensitivity to distinctions that are not meaningfully different in their language. Infants' ability to produce sounds develops in a regular sequence. First infants cry, then they coo, then they produce consonant sounds, then they babble, and then they produce words. Languages throughout the world take advantage of the types of syllables that babies babble most often by making these names of caregivers: *mama*, *dada*, and so on. The ease of understanding what beginning speakers say is improved both because they avoid words with difficult-to-make sounds and because languages tend to use relatively easy-to-pronounce words to name objects that young children wish to discuss. Later phonological development occurs in the ability to control the sounds that are made and in the clarity of pronunciation.

Throughout the world, children's first words express similar meanings. The words refer to people, animals, toys, vehicles, and other objects that interest children, that are relatively concrete, and that the children want. Even when beginning language users say the same words as adults, they may not assign the same meanings to them. At first, children underextend some meanings, overextend others, and develop some meanings that are underextended in some ways and overextended in others. The rate of acquisition of new words is at first gradual, but it speeds up greatly at about age 18 months. Some factors that may be involved in this vocabulary spurt are constraints that narrow the range of possible word meanings, grammatical cues to word meaning, general cognitive processes such as learning and memory, and social experience. Children also use a variety of clever strategies to invent words for expressing meanings when they do not know any appropriate standard word.

Grammatical development begins in infancy, when children begin to distinguish grammatical from content words, and when they become sensitive to regularities in word order in the language that they hear. When children begin to produce two-word phrases, they need to order words within their utterances. At first, children base their ordering of words on the words' meanings. The orders follow standard patterns such as agent-action and possessor-possessed object. After the two-word period, children learn to form a wide variety of grammatical constructions, many of them based on categories that have no clear correspondence to meanings. Among the factors that contribute to formation of purely grammatical categories and rules are children's expectations about the forms grammars should take, bootstrapping from early meaning-based categories to later grammar-based ones, learning of constructions, and detection of regular patterns within the language.

Children communicate both through spoken language and through signed language. Long before infants say words, they motivate older people to talk to them by moving in synchrony with speech intonations and making sounds when the other person stops talking. Adults and older children motivate young children to listen by adopting the conversational style known as infant-directed speech, involving high pitch, exaggerated intonations, and simple sentences. Both deaf and hearing children who are exposed to signed languages use those languages to communicate, and deaf children who are not exposed to signed languages invent and use informal sign systems, called home sign systems, which have a simple, language-like structure. There are notable parallels in the order and timing of linguistic development between children who are learning spoken languages and children who are learning signed ones. These parallels suggest that there may be a general motivation to communicate and to find regular structures in communicative input, regardless of whether that input arrives through the eye or the ear.

Recommended Readings

Bloom, P. (2000). *How children learn the meanings of words.* Cambridge, MA: MIT Press. In this book, Bloom argues that word learning depends on general cognitive abilities, including the ability to infer others' intentions and certain general learning and memory abilities.

Goldin-Meadow, S. (2003). *The resilience of language.* New York, NY: Psychology Press. This book summarizes Goldin-Meadow's path-breaking research about the gesture systems developed by deaf children with no language input.

Johnson, J.S., & Newport, E.L. (1989). Critical period effects in second language learning: The influence of maturational state on the acquisition of English as a second language. *Cognitive Psychology, 21,* 60–99. An unusual study that examines the relation between age at onset of immersion in a language and the degree to which people master the language's grammar. Makes a strong case for a critical period in grammatical acquisition.

Saffran, J.R., Aslin, R.N., & Newport, E.L. (1996). Statistical learning by 8-month-old infants. *Science, 274,* 1926–1928. Compelling evidence that infants are able to segment words from fluent speech based solely on the statistical relationships between neighboring speech sounds.

Senghas, A. & Coppola, M. (2001). Children creating language: How Nicaraguan Sign Language acquired a spatial grammar. *Psychological Science, 12,* 323–328. A study of language creation in a group of deaf Nicaraguans who were not exposed to conventional sign language in early childhood. When this group came together in Nicaragua's first school for the deaf, a new sign language was "born," and this sign language has become more systematic with each successive generation of learners.

7

MEMORY DEVELOPMENT

My brother Colin was trying to get Blowtorch (an action figure) from me, and I wouldn't let him take it from me, so he pushed me into the wood pile where the mouse trap was. And then my finger got caught in it. And then we went to the hospital, and my mommy, daddy, and Colin drove me there, to the hospital in our van, because it was far away. And the doctor put the bandage on this finger. (Billy, a 4-year-old) (Ceci & Bruck, 1998)

There was only one problem with Billy's detailed recollection of this slightly traumatic event—the event never happened!

The 4-year-old who delivered this utterly convincing rendition of his "memory" of catching his finger in a mousetrap was part of an experiment. The purpose of the experiment was to determine when children's testimony about abuse and injuries to themselves can be believed. The situation was somewhat unusual—once a week for 10 weeks, children in the experiment were asked leading questions about events that had never happened to them. For example, Billy had been asked such questions as "Tell me if this has ever happened to you. Do you remember going to the hospital with a mousetrap on your finger?" "Can you tell me more?" "What happened next?" The quotation above is of Billy telling a different adult about his experience.

Although the situation may seem contrived, it is not very different from that which children frequently face in child abuse cases. It has been estimated that child witnesses are interviewed an average of 10 times before their cases come to trial (Whitcomb, 1992). Nor are the questions asked of child witnesses any less leading. Consider the following sequence from a highly publicized 1989 trial in which the head of a daycare center was charged with abusing the children who attended the center. Some of the abuse was believed to involve kitchen utensils:

PROSECUTOR: *Did she touch you with a spoon?*

CHILD: *No.*

P: *No? OK. Did you like it when she touched you with a spoon?*

C: *No.*

P: *No? Why not?*

C: *I don't know.*

P: *You don't know?*

C: *No.*

P: *What did you say to Kelly when she touched you?*

C: *I don't like that.*

What makes the reliability of children's memory in such cases so critical is that mistakes in either direction are disastrous. If a jury does not believe a child who accurately reports abuse, the perpetrator may abuse other children. If the jury believes a child who falsely reports abuse, an innocent person may spend years in jail. So how can we know when children should be believed? Are younger children, who may not distinguish as clearly between fantasy and reality, more likely than older children to report events that never happened? Or are older children, who can imagine a greater range of events, more likely to do so? What kind of questioning is needed to get children to testify about events that are uncomfortable for them to discuss, without leading them to report events that never happened? With more than 100,000 children testifying in legal cases each year (Ceci & Bruck, 1993, 1998), and more than 40 percent of children who testify in sexual abuse cases being below age 5 (Gray, 1993), answering these questions about children's memory is critically important.

Psychological research is especially useful for determining the reliability of children's eyewitness testimony. In experiments, unlike in court cases, we can know for sure what really happened and can use that as a comparison point for children's reports. The answers that are starting to emerge from such experiments tell us a great deal about memory development in general and about children's eyewitness testimony in particular.

Children's Eyewitness Testimony

People often think of memory as a series of photographs, or a movie, of their experiences. If this were the case, eyewitness testimony would not be a problem; the witness would simply recount exactly what happened. However, at no age is memory nearly this complete or this accurate. Adults, like children, fail to remember what they saw, "remember" events that never happened, and combine separate experiences into a single composite. Preschoolers' memories are somewhat less accurate than those of older individuals, but the difference is one of degree rather than kind—everyone has memory lapses and confusions.

A useful way of thinking about memory is to divide it into three phases, ordered along the dimension of time: encoding, storage, and retrieval. Memory for any event requires encoding the important information when the event occurs, then storing the information in memory for later use, and finally retrieving it when it is needed. Each step offers potential pitfalls. People may not take in all of the important information at the time when the event occurs; they may take in the information but store it in a form that is vulnerable to forgetting; or they may encode and store it effectively, but be unable to retrieve it when it is needed.

ENCODING

When people encode information, they form two types of representations: verbatim and gist (Brainerd, Reyna, Howe, & Kingma, 1990). Verbatim representations include the literal details of the situation: the exact words spoken, the expressions on the people's faces, the color of the walls, and so on. Gist involves the meaning or essence of the events: Who did what to whom. People encode both types of information, but the representations of gist last much longer than the verbatim information. Everyday experience illustrates the difference; when you read a story, you remember the exact words only briefly, but you may remember the basic plot for years.

Part of the reason for young children remembering somewhat less well than older individuals is that their encoding places greater emphasis on verbatim information, relative to gist (Brainerd et al., 1990). Since everyone forgets verbatim information more quickly than the gist of what happened, the young children's emphasis on verbatim information leads to more forgetting. Like older children, younger ones encode the gist of events; however, their relative emphasis on gist is not as great. They also fail to encode some important aspects of events altogether.

A large part of the reason for younger children's less complete encoding of gist concerns their lesser knowledge. Memory for an event does not occur in a vacuum; it reflects people's prior knowledge about what is important and what is plausible in the situation. For example, in a study in which 3- to 7-year-olds were asked about a visit to a doctor, 7-year-olds very rarely said "yes" when asked such outlandish questions as "Did the nurse lick your knee?" In contrast, 3-year-olds quite often answered such questions affirmatively, especially when questioned a long time (three months) after the visit (Gordon, Ornstein, Clubb, Nida, & Baker-Ward, 1991). Older children's greater knowledge of what does and does not go on during visits to the doctor's office presumably helped them both to encode what actually occurred during the visit and to rule out the possibility that a nurse could have licked their knee there.

Prior knowledge is a two-edged sword, though. It generally leads to more accurate recall, but it can also produce distortions. Stereotypes about other people are one source of such distortions. Consider what happened when a group of preschoolers heard stories that depicted a character named Sam Stone as a clumsy oaf (Leichtman & Ceci, 1995). After four such stories, a man introduced as Sam Stone visited the classroom for two minutes; the visit was pleasant but uneventful. The following day, it was "discovered" that a teddy bear was dirty and a book was torn; the question was who was responsible.

The children's prior knowledge about Sam Stone by itself did not lead to many claims that he was responsible for the damage. However, when the stereotype was paired with leading questions that suggested that Stone was the culprit, 72 percent of 3- and 4-year-olds claimed that Stone had done it, 44 percent claimed they had seen him do it, and 21 percent maintained their claim even when asked, "You didn't really see him do it, did you?" Children who had not heard the stories before the visit were less likely to make these claims, as were older preschoolers (5- and 6-year-olds) who had heard them.

As illustrated by this example, people's memories are not limited to what actually happened. Instead, memories are a mixture of what people see, what they know, and what they infer. Children's inferences are frequently correct, but sometimes they are mistaken. Thus, in the Sam Stone experiment, some children reported seeing him soak the teddy bear with water and smear crayon on it (which could have explained the condition they found it in the next day). These plausible inferences are much of what make it so difficult even for experts to discern when children's testimony is accurate and when it is not. When more than 100 clinicians and researchers who specialize in issues regarding children's eyewitness testimony were shown videotapes of children talking about what Sam Stone had done, they were unable to identify which children were reporting accurately and which were not (Leichtman & Ceci, 1995).

STORAGE

Better storage of information also contributes to older children's more accurate memory. One aspect of this phenomenon that is particularly relevant for eyewitness testimony involves suggestibility. Children below age 6, in particular, tend to be more suggestible than older children, in the sense that their recall of events can be greatly influenced by experiences that occur after the original event but before the time of retrieval, that is, while the information is stored (Bruck & Ceci, 1999). Thus, when asked leading questions after the relevant events occurred, preschoolers often change their recall in directions consistent with the implications of the questions they are asked (Clarke-Stewart, Thompson, & Lepore, 1989;

Goodman & Clarke-Stewart, 1991). Suggestive questions can lead children to "recall" not just unimportant events but also events affecting their bodies, such as nurses blowing in their ears (Ornstein, Gordon, & Larus, 1992), pediatricians sticking fingers or sticks into their genitals (Bruck, Ceci, Francoeur, & Renick, 1995), and strangers putting yucky things in their mouths (Poole & Lindsay, 1995). Older children and adults are also suggestible, but much less so than preschoolers.

Another technique that is commonly used in legal cases, but that can distort children's memories, is asking them to imagine events and then asking them to report whether the imagined event occurred. Such imagining often leads to children reporting the imagined event as real and continuing to do so thereafter (Foley, Harris, & Herman, 1994; Parker, 1995). The same phenomenon occurs when children are asked to draw events that did not actually occur—they often report later that such events actually happened (Bruck, Melnyk, & Ceci, 2000). Preschoolers are especially likely to show difficulties in *reality monitoring*, which is the ability to distinguish what they imagined or thought about from what really happened.

A final influence on the quality of stored information is time. As time passes, people forget. The forgetting is especially marked in young children. Even when they remember as much as older children immediately after the event, they forget the material more rapidly (Brainerd & Reyna, 1995). Much of the forgetting occurs relatively soon after the event, but forgetting continues indefinitely. Over periods of one to two years, periods that are comparable to those that often elapse between the original abuse and trial dates, the accuracy of children's recall deteriorates considerably. Relative to their recollections immediately after the event, children become more likely to omit important information and to include information that is plausible but that did not happen (Goodman, Hirschman, Hepps, & Rudy, 1991; Poole & White, 1993).

RETRIEVAL

When asked open-ended questions about events (for example, "What happened at school today?"), children tend to provide accurate and relevant information. However, they also often underreport what happened, particularly during the preschool years. Asking more specific questions leads to greater reporting of events that actually happened. For example, when 5- and 7-year-old girls were questioned following a genital examination, they did not admit any genital contact unless asked such specific questions as "Did the doctor touch you here?" (Saywitz, Goodman, Nichols, & Moan, 1991). As long as the questions do not indicate that the questioner prefers a certain answer, asking specific questions soon after an initial event seems to protect memories from decaying more than it produces false recollections (Ceci & Bruck, 1998).

The conditions under which children are asked to retrieve information greatly influence what and how much they remember. One important influence is whether they need to recall the information from memory ("Where did the doctor touch you?") or just to recognize it ("Did the doctor touch your tongue?"). People of all ages find recognition much easier than recall.

Children also remember more when they are encouraged to think deeply about the event. For example, when 5- and 6-year-olds were asked to draw as well as tell what happened when they visited a fire station, they recalled more than when they were simply asked to talk about the visit (Butler, Gross, & Hayne, 1995). Presumably, drawing the fire station caused them to think about the visit more deeply. Along the same lines, children are more accurate at reporting events that they directly participated in than events that they observed or heard about (Gobbo, Mega, & Pipe, 2002). It is likely that children think more deeply about events they actually experience than about events they simply see or hear about.

The expectations of the person asking the questions also influence children's memories of events. When the questioner believes that certain events happened, preschoolers are more likely to report those events (Ceci, Loftus, Leichtman, & Bruck, 1994; Goodman & Clarke-Stewart, 1991). Biased interviewers convey their expectations in a variety of ways, such as by setting an accusatory emotional tone for the interview, by providing misinformation, and by using highly specific, leading questions (Bruck & Ceci, 1999). In an effort to be cooperative, children sometimes tell the adult what he or she seems to want to hear.

The frequency with which questions are asked also influences children's memory performance. Children often provide different answers when asked the same question more than once. This is not entirely attributable to forgetting; not infrequently, a child will not remember an important detail at an earlier time but will remember it later. Young children may also change their answers when a question is repeated in an effort to please the interviewer. For example, Poole and White (1991) found that when 4-year-olds were asked repeated yes/no questions about an event they had witnessed, they often changed their answers, both within a single interview and across interviews.

CONCLUSIONS ABOUT CHILDREN'S EYEWITNESS TESTIMONY

Studies of children's memory for events lead to the following five conclusions about their eyewitness testimony:

1. Children's recounting of events reflects what they encoded initially, their experiences during the storage interval, and the conditions under which they retrieved the information.
2. In the absence of interviewer bias, even preschoolers accurately recall much that is relevant to legal cases. The testimony may be lacking in detail, but what they say is generally accurate.

3. Preschoolers are especially vulnerable to the effects of misleading questions and stereotypes. Everyone is vulnerable to these influences, but preschoolers are more influenced by them than older children or adults.
4. The vulnerability is present with events that involve children's own bodies and events with sexual overtones, as well as with less personal experiences.
5. To obtain the most accurate and complete recall, questions should be asked in a neutral fashion, they should be sufficiently specific to elicit memories that might otherwise not be reported, and the questioning should not be repeated more often than necessary.

WHAT DEVELOPS IN MEMORY DEVELOPMENT?

As suggested by the data concerning eyewitness testimony, older children generally remember more accurately than younger ones. But why is this the case? Four types of explanations seem most likely.

One explanation is that older children have superior basic processes and capacities. Translated into terms of a computer analogy, this view suggests that development occurs in the hardware of memory—its absolute capacity or speed of operation. A second explanation emphasizes strategies. Older children know a greater variety of memory strategies than younger children and use them more often, more efficiently, and more flexibly. A third explanation highlights metacognition—knowledge about one's own cognitive activities. Older children better understand how memory works; they may use this knowledge to choose strategies and allocate memory resources more effectively. Finally, older children have greater prior knowledge of the types of content they need to remember; this greater content knowledge may be a major source of their superior memory. Of course, these four hypotheses are not mutually exclusive; all of them, or any combination of them, could contribute to the superiority of older children's memory (Brown & DeLoache, 1978).

In the remainder of this chapter we consider the contributions to memory development of these four potential sources of change (Table 7.1). Just to preview what will emerge, it appears that some of the sources of development contribute more than others, and that some play large roles in certain periods of childhood but not others. It may be worthwhile to apply what you have learned about eyewitness testimony and about children's thinking in general to predict which of these sources of memory development will be most influential in infancy and early childhood, in middle childhood, and in late childhood and adolescence.

Basic Processes and Capacities

Basic processes are frequently used, rapidly executed memory activities such as association, generalization, recognition, and recall. They are among the building blocks of cognition, in the sense that all more complex cognitive activities are

TABLE 7.1   Chapter Outline

built by combining them in different ways. Because they are used so frequently, age-related differences in them could account for an enormous number of other differences in memory.

The role of basic processes in memory functioning is especially dominant early in life. Infants do not possess memory strategies, they are ignorant about the workings of their own memory, and they lack knowledge of the world. Still, they manage to learn and remember a great deal. Their relatively skillful execution of basic processes is what makes this possible.

EXPLICIT AND IMPLICIT MEMORY

Basic processes allow children to form both explicit memories and implicit memories. Explicit memories are ones that can be described verbally, that are conscious, or that can be visualized as a mental image (Nelson, 1995). Implicit memories are ones that are not evident in these ways but that can be detected in other, less direct ways, such as patterns of solution times or physiological responses.

A study by Newcombe and Fox (1994) illustrates the difference. They showed 9-year-olds pictures of preschool classmates from five years earlier and pictures taken at the same time of children who went to another preschool. Roughly half of the 9-year-olds showed some explicit recognition of their preschool classmates; they were more likely to say that a child who attended preschool with them was in their class than to say that a child who did not was. The other half of the 9-year-olds did not show such explicit recognition. Regardless of whether the children showed such explicit memory, however, they showed physiological reactions characteristic of memory more often when they saw pictures of children from their original class than when they saw pictures of other children. These physiological responses indicated implicit recognition, regardless of whether the children consciously recognized their former classmates.

Implicit memory is not limited to physiological responses; it is also evident in behavior. For example, when children have seen pictures previously, they can recognize blurry versions of them more often than when they have not seen the pictures, even though they have no conscious awareness of having seen the pictures previously (Drummey & Newcombe, 1995). As a second example, children are better at matching full faces with partial faces when the faces are those of children they once knew (such as former classmates) than when the faces are those of unfamiliar children (Lie & Newcombe, 1999).

Infants form implicit memories from birth onward, but they may not form explicit ones until 6 to 8 months of age (Nadel & Zola-Morgan, 1984; Nelson, 1995). The evidence for this view includes both behavioral and physiological data. The behaviors indicative of memory that infants show before this age (such as looking at novel objects more than familiar ones) elicit especially active processing in parts of the brain associated with implicit processing, such as the striatum and the cerebellum. The behaviors indicative of memory that infants show after this age but not before it (such as reproducing sequences of behaviors after an extended delay) draw heavily on brain structures associated with explicit processing, such as the prefrontal cortex and the amygdala. Some of the structures associated with explicit memory, especially the prefrontal cortex, mature very late, which may explain why young infants do not appear to form such memories. Yet other structures, in particular the hypothalamus, are sufficiently mature in the first few months after birth to support implicit processing, but seem to require further maturation to support explicit processing. Thus, substantial postnatal brain maturation may be necessary before infants can form explicit memories.

Next we consider some specific processes that produce memories: association, recognition, recall and generalization.

ASSOCIATION

Association is one of the most basic of basic processes. It is difficult to even imagine cognitive development taking place without the ability to associate stimuli with responses. Not surprisingly, given its centrality, the ability to associate stimuli and responses is present from birth. In one experiment that demonstrated this fact (Siqueland & Lipsitt, 1966), whenever a buzzer sounded, newborns received a sweet solution for turning to the right, and whenever a tone sounded, they received the solution for turning to the left. The newborns quickly learned to turn to the correct side, indicating that they associated one sound with turning left and the other with turning right.

RECOGNITION

As with association, recognition is present from birth. This is apparent in newborns' patterns of habituation and dishabituation. When newborn *preterm* infants are presented a picture repeatedly, their looking at it gradually falls off; when they are shown a different picture, their looking immediately increases (Werner & Siqueland, 1978). Thus, they implicitly recognize the old picture as familiar, and reduce the time they spend looking at it, and then recognize the new picture as unfamiliar, and look longer at it.

Infants' recognition of objects is surprisingly durable. Even two weeks after they are habituated to a particular form, 2-month-olds continue to prefer to look at other forms that they have not seen previously (Fantz, Fagan, & Miranda, 1975). Further, as noted in Chapter 1, the rate at which 7-month-olds habituate to stimuli predicts their later IQs quite accurately (Rose et al., 1992; Rose & Feldman, 1995). This may be due either to infants and children who quickly recognize objects having more time and energy to learn about other aspects of the world or to rapid habituation in infancy being indicative of generally more efficient information processing.

On what basis do infants recognize objects as familiar? To answer this question, Strauss and Cohen (1978) habituated 5-month-olds to an object with a particular size, color, form, and orientation (for example, a large, black arrow pointing down). Later, the infants were shown the original object plus another one that varied in one or more of these attributes. The alternative object might be a large, white arrow pointing down. In the example, for the infants to prefer the new object, they would need to remember the color of the original, for this is the only dimension that differentiates the new object from the old one.

Immediately after 5-month-olds were shown the original stimulus, they remembered all four attributes. Fifteen minutes later, they remembered only form and color. Twenty-four hours later, they remembered only the form. Thus, infants' recognition of the type of object they saw (for example, an arrow) is quite durable, but their memory for its properties, such as size, orientation, and color, is less enduring. This enduring importance of form in infants' memory is reminiscent of their reliance on shape in inferring early word meanings (Chapter 6).

Recognition is strikingly accurate even at young ages; 2-year-olds recognize pictures more accurately than adults recall them (Perlmutter & Lange, 1978). By 4 years, the accuracy of recognition is truly remarkable. In one study, 4-year-olds answered correctly 100 percent of questions concerning whether they had seen a picture earlier, despite their having seen as many as 25 other pictures between their two exposures to the repeated one (Brown & Scott, 1971). Even when preschoolers were asked to recognize small differences—for example, whether a dog in the picture was sitting or standing—they still recognized correctly 95 percent of the pictures (Brown & Campione, 1972). The ability to recognize subtle distinctions improves further beyond the preschool period (Sophian & Stigler, 1981), but in general, recognition is excellent from early in development.

IMITATION AND RECALL

Soon after birth, infants recall actions well enough to later imitate them. For example, when 6-week-olds see adults engage in activities that the infants sometimes do on their own, such as sticking out their tongues or opening and closing their mouths, they do that activity more often 24 hours later than do infants who did not see the adult engage in the activity (Meltzoff & Moore, 1994). The imitation is specific to the activity the infant saw. Infants who saw the adult stick out his tongue increased their frequency of tongue protrusions but not their frequency of opening and closing their mouths. Infants who saw the adult open and close his mouth showed the opposite pattern. To imitate these actions, infants must recall what they earlier saw.

The range of activities that infants imitate and the length of time over which they imitate them expand considerably over the next year. By 9 months of age, infants are capable of recalling and imitating 24 hours later not only naturally occurring actions but arbitrary ones such as pressing a button to trigger a beeping sound (Meltzoff, 1988). By the age of 14 months, infants will repeat even more unusual actions after more time has passed. For example, they will press their forehead against a panel to make a light go on four months after they saw an adult do it (Meltzoff, 1995b). The developmental changes in the activities that infants will imitate is reminiscent of Piaget's hypothesized circular reactions, in which infants first only repeat activities that involve their own bodies and later repeatedly engage in activities involving external objects. Such early imitation provides infants a way of learning from other people, as well as demonstrating that infants are capable of recalling activities months after they saw them.

INSIGHT, GENERALIZATION, AND INTEGRATION OF EXPERIENCES

Several of infants' basic capabilities have been revealed in a series of experiments involving mobiles (Rovee-Collier, 1995, 1999). In these experiments, a mobile is placed above an infant's crib, and a string is tied to the infant's ankle and to the mobile, so that the mobile moves and makes noise when the infant kicks that leg (Figure 7.1). Three-month-olds' learning on this task often comes quite abruptly. At a certain point in the session, they suddenly begin kicking much more often (Rovee & Fagen, 1976). The abruptness of the change suggests that infants, like adults, may from time to time have insights about how things work.

Three-month-olds' encoding of the relation between their kicking and the mobile's moving is often surprisingly literal, though. Even differences that seem

FIGURE 7.1 An infant making a mobile move by kicking his leg (photograph courtesy of Carolyn Rovee-Collier).

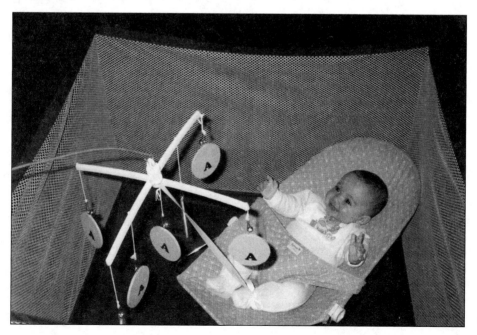

totally irrelevant to adults, such as having a different color cloth on the infants' crib on the second occasion, lead 3-month-olds not to generalize their earlier learning to a new mobile. However, given exposure to several similar mobiles, they learn to generalize to new ones (Rovee-Collier, 1989). Thus, 3-month-olds have the capacity to generalize, but they display it only under highly facilitative circumstances.

Infants also are able to integrate related experiences that occur fairly close in time. If 3-month-olds encounter the mobile a second time within three days of the initial exposure, they will better recall the relation five to seven days later than if they encountered the mobile only once or if they encountered it on two occasions separated by four days or more (Rovee-Collier, Evancio, & Earley, 1995).

To explain such integration of memories over time, Rovee-Collier (1995) proposed the construct of a *time window.* The basic idea is that there is a certain period during which children can integrate information and strengthen initial memories (the time when the window is open). Once this period ends, the window is closed, and even highly similar occurrences are stored separately and not integrated with the original one. The duration for which the time window is open is determined in large part by forgetting of the initial information; once information is forgotten, the time window is closed. Since older children generally forget more slowly, their time windows tend to be longer for any given task.

Presenting the second, similar event toward the end of the time window, when memories of the details of the original event are less strong than they were originally but not yet forgotten, is especially effective in preserving initial memories. This is true not only for infants, but also for older children and adults (Rovee-Collier, 1995; Rovee-Collier, Adler, & Borza, 1994). The finding has an interesting implication for eyewitness testimony. Asking children questions toward the end of their time window for the original event, when their memory of it is starting to weaken, may be especially effective for preserving the memory (Brainerd & Ornstein, 1990).

INHIBITION

To think well, we must prevent irrelevant ideas from intruding. Because concepts tend to be associated both with ideas that are relevant and ones that are irrelevant in the particular situation, efficient use of memory and other cognitive processes involves inhibiting ideas that are not useful in the situation. Illustratively, if you are trying to master a new physics concept, it may be helpful to inhibit thoughts of what you are planning to have for dinner.

The frontal lobe seems to play a crucial role in inhibition. It is one of the last areas of the brain to develop, showing substantial development toward the end of the first year, and also between 4 and 7 years and beyond (Luria, 1973; Thatcher, Lyon, Rumsey, & Krasnegor, 1996). The effects of this neural development during infancy can be seen on ability to perform tasks that require inhibition of response tendencies, such as Piaget's A-not-B task. On this task, infants see an object hidden and retrieve it several times at Location B; then they see it hidden at Location A. To succeed, the infants must inhibit the tendency to reach where the reward has been obtained in the past, and reach where it is now. Adult monkeys can ordinarily perform this task; however, if their frontal cortex is removed or frozen, they lose the ability and instead reach to the former hiding place (Diamond, 1985; Goldman-Rakic, 1987). Such experiments cannot be performed on human infants. However, it has been learned that between 6 and 12 months, the time when human infants become able to perform the task, they show increasing electrical activity in the frontal lobe while performing it (Bell & Fox, 1992). The improved inhibitory capabilities allow more enduring memory for the new location. Thus, Diamond (1985) found a steady increase in the delay that infants could tolerate and still search where the object was most recently hidden. At 7 months, infants would search at the correct location with delays as long as 2 seconds; at 9 months, with delays as long as 6 seconds; and at 11 months, with delays as long as 10 seconds (Figure 7.2).

Further parallel developments between ability to inhibit responses and frontal lobe functioning are present between four and seven years. An everyday example of this development is ability to play "Simon Says." When the adult has

FIGURE 7.2   Delays at which infants between 7 and 12 months can succeed on the A-not-B task (after Diamond, 1985).

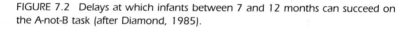
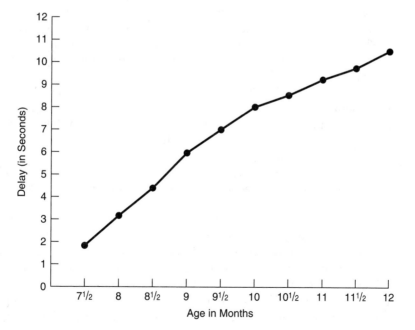

been saying "Simon Says" but then fails to say it, 4-year-olds find it difficult to inhibit executing the command. Seven-year-olds find it much easier to show the needed inhibition. Many similar changes occur between 4 and 7 years on tasks that require inhibition (Dempster, 1992). For example, to remember lists of words, children must focus on words on the most recent list and inhibit associated terms and words from other lists. Part of 4- and 5-year-olds' difficulty on such tasks is that they fail to inhibit such related terms and recall them as being on the new list (Harnishfeger & Bjorklund, 1994). Similarly, to exhibit conservation of liquid quantity, children must inhibit the perceptual information that the tall, thin glass looks like it has more water, and focus on the fact that nothing was added or subtracted (Dempster, 1992). Again, 4- and 5-year-olds have difficulty doing this. Supporting the view that young children's difficulty on the conservation task lies in ignoring interfering information, if the misleading cues are removed—for example by putting a shield in front of the glasses containing the liquid—4-year-olds consistently succeed on the task (Bruner, 1966). Thus, growing ability to inhibit inappropriate responses and to block out interfering information seem to contribute considerably to cognitive development during infancy and early childhood.

PROCESSING CAPACITY

One of the most controversial issues about children's thinking is whether the amount of information that they can actively process at one time (their working memory capacity) changes with age. There is no question about the potential importance of such changes. If young children cannot simultaneously process as much information as older ones, their ability to learn and remember should be less than that of older children. But does working memory capacity in fact expand?

This question has been addressed by examining how many randomly selected letters or single-digit numbers children of different ages can remember. Figure 7.3 illustrates that the number increases steadily with age. Most 5-year-olds can correctly recall lists of four digits, but not longer ones, whereas most adults can recall lists with seven digits. Such data have led a number of investigators, among them Pascual-Leone (1970, 1989), to propose that the absolute number of symbols that people can hold in working memory more than doubles from infancy to adulthood.

Although the data are clear, the implications for whether working memory capacity changes with age are not so obvious. The demand on cognitive resources that a task imposes reflects both the child's resources and the task. Developmental improvements in performance can be produced either by an increase in the child's resources or by a decrease in the resources the child expends in doing the task. Consider some reasons why older children might remember longer lists of numbers, even if the absolute capacity of their working memory

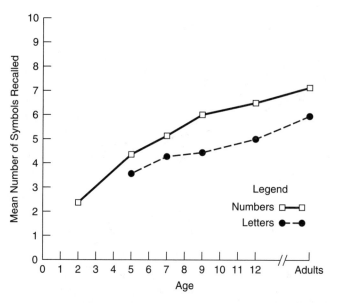

FIGURE 7.3   Improvement with age in memory span for numbers and letters (after Dempster, 1981). Copyright © 1981 by the American Psychological Association. Adapted with permission.

did not differ from that of younger children. The older children know more about numbers. This greater familiarity could help them remember the numbers more efficiently. They also know more strategies, such as rehearsal, for enhancing their recall. They also are more skillful in choosing when to use the strategies they know. Thus, it is clear that older children can store more material in working memory, but it remains unknown (and perhaps unknowable) whether this is due to change in the actual capacity of working memory or to changes in knowledge and strategies that allow more material to be stored within the same capacity (as in the car trunk analogy in Chapter 3).

PROCESSING SPEED

Speed of information processing, like the number of numbers that can be held in memory, increases greatly with age. This has been found for immediate processing (Hoving, Spencer, Robb, & Schulte, 1978; LeBlanc, Muise, & Blanchard, 1992), processing of information in working memory (Hale, 1990; Hale et al., 1997; Hitch & Towse, 1995; Miller & Vernon, 1997), and retrieval of information from long-term memory (Hale, 1990; Kail, 1986, 1988; Whitney, 1986). The general form of the improvement is not in dispute. As shown in Figure 7.4, processing speed increases most rapidly at young ages, with the rate of change slowing thereafter, though speed continues to increase well into adolescence (Kail, 1991). However, considerable controversy has arisen over whether the increased speed is due to greater use of more efficient strategies, to greater familiarity with the items being processed, or to increases in speed per se.

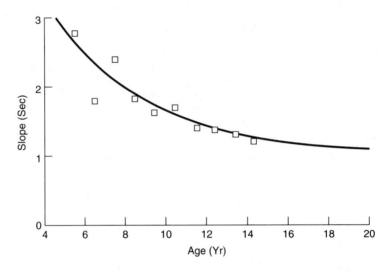

FIGURE 7.4   Change in estimated processing speed as a function of age. The values indicate times to perform basic operations; thus, 5-year-olds take roughly three seconds per operation, but 14-year-olds take only slightly more than one second per operation. The estimates are based on performance of children and college students in 72 experiments, published over a 30-year period (after Kail, 1991).

Recent evidence suggests that speed of processing per se increases with maturation. At a given age, children who are more physically mature (that is, a greater percentage of the height that would be expected from their parents' heights) process information more quickly (Eaton & Ritchot, 1995). Although practice also produces faster information processing, the relation between age and processing speed does not seem to be reducible to older children having more practice at the tasks. The mathematical function that best describes the increase in processing speed with age is different from the one that best describes the improvements that come with practice (Kail, 1991; Miller & Vernon, 1997). Further, similar increases in processing speed are present for tasks that children rarely encounter (for example, mental rotation) as for ones they encounter daily (such as reading and arithmetic). Thus, speed of processing increases with age, above and beyond increases attributable to practice and superior strategies. The faster processing leads to improved performance on many tasks.

EVALUATION

Basic processes are large and direct contributors to memory development from the first days out of the womb. Even very young infants associate, recognize, recall, generalize, and perform other basic processes. These capacities allow them to remember a tremendous amount before they possess strategies, understanding of memory, or content knowledge. Further, without basic capacities, all other memory activities would be futile. For example, rehearsing a phone number would be pointless if we could not associate the phone number with the person whose number it was. The number of associations that are made, the length of time over which experiences are recalled, the time window within which experiences are integrated, the variety of circumstances over which generalizations are drawn, and the speed with which all of these processes are executed increase substantially during and after infancy. However, basic processes allow infants to learn and remember from the earliest days of life.

BASIC PROCESSES AND THE PUZZLE OF INFANTILE AMNESIA

Given that infants can recognize, associate, and learn, why are adults almost never able to remember anything that happened to them in their early years? Think about it: What do you remember about your life before you were 3? Although some people's earliest memories date from around age 2 (Eacott & Crawley, 1998, 1999; Weigle & Bauer, 2000), most people remember very little that occurred before the of 3 (Bruce, Dolan, & Phillips-Grant, 2000; Pillemer & White, 1989; Rubin, 2000). Adults' memories of the few years after age 3 also tend to be scanty. Most people remember only a few events, usually ones that were extremely meaningful and distinctive, such as a trip to Disneyland, being in a hospital, or a sibling being born. The phenomenon is not limited to human beings; rats and many other mammals also show little recall of events that occurred early in their lives (Spear, 1984).

How might this inability to recall early experiences be explained? The sheer passage of time does not account for it; recall from Chapter 3 people's excellent recognition of pictures of people who attended high school with them 35 years earlier. Another seemingly plausible explanation, that infants do not form enduring memories at this point in development, also is incorrect. Children between $2\frac{1}{2}$ and 3 years old can remember experiences that occurred many months before, and some remember experiences that occurred during their first year of life (Myers, Clifton, & Clarkson, 1987; Peterson, 2002). Similarly, 1-year-olds who are exposed to simple sequences of actions (such as making and striking a gong) demonstrate recall of those sequences up to a year later (Bauer, Wenner, Dropik, & Wewerka, 2000), with memory becoming increasingly robust and long-lasting over the age range 13 to 20 months (see Figure 7.5). Nor does Freud's (1905/1953) hypothesis that infantile amnesia reflects repression of sexually charged episodes explain the phenomenon. While such repression may occur, people cannot remember ordinary events from the infant and toddler periods either.

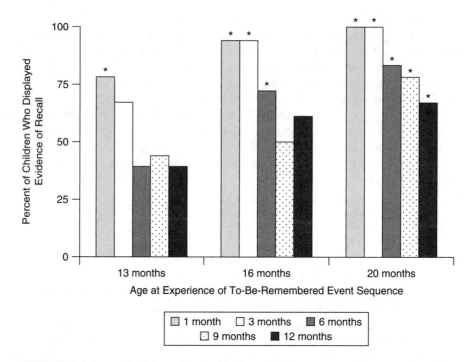

FIGURE 7.5 Percent of children who displayed recall of an event sequence at various delay intervals after initially experiencing the event at 13, 16, or 20 months. The asterisks indicate values that are significantly different from chance performance (data drawn from Bauer, Wenner, Dropik, & Wewerka, 2000).

Three other explanations seem more promising. One involves physiological changes relevant to memory. Maturation of the frontal lobes of the brain continues throughout childhood. This part of the brain, and in particular, the prefrontal cortex, may be critical for remembering particular episodes in ways that can later be retrieved (Diamond, 1990; Newcombe, Drummey, Fox, Lie, & Ottinger-Alberts, 2000; Schacter, 1987). Demonstrations of infants' and toddlers' long-term memory typically involve their repeating sequences of actions that they had earlier seen or done (e.g., Bauer, 1996; Bauer et al., 2000). The brain's level of physiological maturation may support these types of memories, but not ones requiring explicit verbal descriptions.

A second explanation involves the influence of the social world on children's talk about the past. Adults often engage young children in conversations about past events. Early on, adults provide most of the structure and content for these conversations, scaffolding children's memories of past events (for example, "Remember when Aunt Molly came to visit?"). Some mothers use a highly elaborative style, encouraging children to provide many details about past events and frequently expanding on children's contributions to the conversations. Other mothers use a less elaborative style, asking specific questions but rarely prompting for details (Fivush & Fromhoff, 1988). Numerous studies have shown that children whose mothers use a highly elaborative style remember more than children whose mothers are less elaborative (Haden, Haine, & Fivush, 1997; Harley & Reese, 1999; Leichtman, Pillemer, Wang, & Koreishi, 2000). However, regardless of parental style, over time children begin to participate more actively in conversations about the past, bringing up past events as topics and describing the events themselves (Nelson & Fivush, 2000).

Participating in adult-guided conversations about past events may help young children store information in ways that will endure into later childhood and adulthood (Fivush & Hammond, 1990; Hudson, 1990). Through hearing and telling stories with a clear beginning, middle, and ending, children may learn to extract the gist of events in ways that they will be able to describe many years later. Consistent with this view, parents and children increasingly engage in discussions of past events when children are around 3 years old. However, hearing such stories is not sufficient for younger children to form enduring memories. Telling such stories to 2-year-olds does not seem to produce long-lasting, verbalizable memories (Goleman, 1993).

A third likely explanation for infantile amnesia involves incompatibilities between the ways in which infants encode information and the ways in which older children and adults retrieve it. Whether people can remember an event depends critically on the fit between the way in which they earlier encoded the information and the way in which they later attempt to retrieve it. The better able the person is to reconstruct the perspective from which the material was encoded, the more likely that recall will be successful.

A variety of factors can create mismatches between very young children's encoding and older children's and adults' retrieval efforts. The world looks very different to a person whose head is only two or three feet above the ground than to one whose head is five or six feet above it. General knowledge of categories of events (a birthday party, visit to the doctor's office, baseball game) help older individuals encode their experiences ("I remember the baseball game I went to on my seventh birthday"), but again infants and toddlers are unlikely to encode many experiences within such knowledge structures (Nelson, 1993). Likewise, infants and toddlers do not use language to encode events, but recall in older children is often mediated by verbal cues and questions. Children have some ability to recode pre-verbal memories into verbal form, particularly if they re-experience the context in which the original event occurred (Bauer, Kroupina, Schwade, Dropik, & Wewerka, 1998). However, children who experience events before the onset of narrative skills seldom recall them in verbal form at a later time (Peterson & Rideout, 1998). This holds true even for traumatic events such as injuries that require emergency care.

These three explanations of infantile amnesia are not mutually exclusive; indeed, they support one another. Physiological immaturity may be part of why infants and toddlers do not form extremely enduring memories, even when they hear stories that promote such remembering in preschoolers. Hearing the stories may lead preschoolers to encode aspects of events that allow them to form memories they can access as adults. Conversely, improved encoding of what they hear may help them better understand and remember stories, and thus make the stories more useful for remembering future events. Thus, all three explanations—physiological maturation, hearing and producing stories about past events, and improved encoding of key aspects of events—seem likely to be involved in overcoming infantile amnesia.

Strategies

A nine-year-old boy memorized the license plate number of a getaway car following an armed robbery, a court was told Monday.... The boy and his friend ... looked in the drug store window and saw a man grab a 14-year-old cashier's neck.... After the robbery, the boys mentally repeated the license number until they gave it to police. (*Edmonton Journal,* January 13, 1981, cited in Kail, 1984)

Without using this memory strategy, known as rehearsal, the boys almost certainly would have forgotten the license number before they could tell the police. But what are memory strategies, how do children acquire them, and how do they choose when to use them?

Strategies are "cognitive or behavioral activities that are under the deliberate control of the subject and are employed so as to enhance memory performance" (Naus & Ornstein, 1983, p. 12). Children employ strategies in all phases of memorization: when they encode material, when they store it, and when they retrieve it. Many age-related improvements in memory reflect acquisition of new strategies, refinement of existing ones, and application of existing strategies to additional situations.

Although many particulars vary with the strategy, certain features characterize the development of all strategies (Waters & Andreassen, 1983). When children first acquire a memory strategy, they use it in only some of the situations where it is applicable. They limit it to materials for which the strategy is easy to use and to situations that are relatively undemanding. They also are quite rigid in applying the strategy and often fail to adapt to shifting task demands. All of this changes with development. Older children use strategies in more diverse situations, including ones that make the strategies difficult to execute; they use higher-quality versions of strategies; they tailor them to the particulars of the situation; and they derive greater benefits from using the strategies.

Another general feature of strategy use is that it varies with children's experience. For example, German second- and third-graders use certain strategies for organizing material more often than do American age peers (Kurtz, Schneider, Carr, Borkowski, & Rellinger, 1990). Why is this the case? It does not appear to be any inherent difference between German and American children. After children of both nationalities receive brief training in the organizational strategy, they use it equally often. Instead, the source seems to be differences in adults' approaches. When asked whether they teach children such strategies, German parents and teachers reported doing so considerably more often than did American parents and teachers (Kurtz et al., 1990).

We next consider some of the specific strategies that children use, how their use changes with age, and why the changes occur.

SEARCHING FOR OBJECTS

Even before their second birthday, children begin to use rudimentary strategies. Several of these strategies are evident in the way they search for hidden objects. In one study (DeLoache, Cassidy, & Brown, 1985), 18- to 24-month-olds saw a Big Bird doll hidden under various objects such as pillows. They then had to wait three or four minutes until the experimenter asked them to find the doll. The toddlers engaged in a variety of strategic activities to keep alive their memories of the doll's location. While waiting, they looked at the hiding place, pointed to it, and named the hidden object. They did not engage in these activities nearly as frequently when Big Bird was in plain sight, thus indicating that the strategies were limited to situations in which they were needed to remember Big Bird's location.

Very young children's use of such strategies is fragile; they use them only under the most favorable circumstances. Thus, when an object was hidden under one of three identical cups, rather than under a more distinctive object such as a pillow, 2-year-olds did not engage in strategic activities such as watching or touching the correct cup. In contrast, 3-year-olds extended to these confusable objects the types of strategic activities, such as naming and pointing, that younger children applied only to more distinctive objects (Wellman, Ritter, & Flavell, 1975). In general, familiarity with the task setting leads to more consistent and efficient strategy use (Schneider & Sodian, 1988).

Development of strategies for finding hidden objects continues for a number of years. For example, when asked to find an object hidden under one of six identical cups placed on a spinning turntable, 8-year-olds spontaneously used the strategy of picking up from the table a gold star or a paper clip and placing the marker on the relevant cup; 5-year-olds usually required hints from the experimenter to use this strategy; 3-year-olds either did not use the strategy at all or did so only after a great deal of prompting (Beal & Fleisig, 1987; Ritter, 1978).

REHEARSING

When verbatim recall is essential, repeating information over and over can be very helpful. School-age children often use this strategy to good advantage, as was illustrated in the license plate anecdote at the beginning of this section.

However, children younger than age 6 or 7 would have been considerably less likely to repeatedly rehearse the numbers in the license. In one study of the uses of such rehearsal, 5- and 10-year-olds were shown seven pictures and saw the experimenter point to three of them. The children knew they would need to point to the same three pictures in the same order after waiting for 15 seconds. Far more 10- than 5-year-olds moved their lips or audibly repeated the pictures' names over and over in the 15 seconds between when the pictures were presented and when the children were asked to name them. Those children who rehearsed in this way recalled more than those who did not (Flavell, Beach, & Chinsky, 1966).

Sometimes these results are interpreted to mean that 5-year-olds do not rehearse and that older children do. The reality is more complex, though. Trial-by-trial examination of children's serial recall has shown that on some trials, most 5-year-olds rehearse in the same way as older children (McGilly & Siegler, 1989, 1990). They also recall correctly more often on trials where they rehearse than on trials where they do not.

Teaching rehearsal strategies leads 5-year-olds to use them more and to recall more than they did previously. However, the levels of recall do not rise to the levels of older children, and the young children often do not continue rehearsing more often in new situations (Hagen, Hargrove, & Ross, 1973).

Organizing

When people need to recall material, but not necessarily in the original order, they often reorganize it into easier-to-remember forms. For example, when 10-year-olds are asked to remember the terms "couch, banana, dog, chair, apple, rat, table, cow, orange," they often organize the terms into three categories—furniture, fruit, and animals. Then they try to remember by thinking to themselves something like, "Furniture, let's see, was there a table, yes, 'table'; was there a lamp, no; was there a chair, yes 'chair'"; and so on.

The development of such organizational strategies largely parallels the development of rehearsal. As with rehearsal, 5- and 6-year-olds use organizational strategies less often than 9- and 10-year-olds (Carr, Kurtz, Schneider, Turner, & Borkowski, 1989). However, like older children, younger children sometimes do use organizational strategies (Bjorklund & Coyle, 1995), and children who use such strategies tend to remember more than those who do not (Schneider, 1986). The same type of trial-to-trial variability that is present in rehearsal strategies is also evident in use of organizational strategies (Coyle & Bjorklund, 1997).

Many children display a fairly abrupt transition from not using organizational strategies to using them quite consistently. This rapid "jump" in performance has been documented in research on individual children's memory performance over a series of weekly sessions (Schlagmueller & Schneider, 2002).

Children appear to recognize the benefits of organizational strategies, and once they have discovered the strategies, they use them regularly.

Children can learn organizational strategies as early as age 4 or 5 years, and learning the strategies helps them remember more (Lange & Pierce, 1992). On the other hand, they often do not transfer the learning to new situations, even to ones that resemble the original one (Williams & Goulet, 1975).

SELECTIVE ATTENTION

As noted in the Chapter 5 discussion of attention-getting properties of stimuli, much of infants' attention has an elicited, involuntary feel to it. Children soon begin to attend more selectively, though, to information important for meeting their goals. For example, 4-year-olds who are told that they later will need to remember some toys tend to name those toys more often during the waiting period (Baker-Ward, Ornstein, & Holden, 1984). This suggests that they selectively attend to the toys they need to remember.

As with rehearsal and organization, selective attention strategies become considerably more prevalent between preschool and middle childhood. The increasing selectivity is particularly tangible in the task shown in Figure 7.6. Children see two rows of boxes, with six boxes in each row. Inside each box is a toy animal or household object; the boxes with animals have a picture of a cage on top, and those with household objects have a picture of a house. Some children are told that they will need to remember where each animal is, others that they will need to remember where each household object is. Then they are

FIGURE 7.6 Apparatus used by Miller and her colleagues (e.g., DeMarie-Dreblow and Miller, 1988) in selective-attention experiments. During the study period, children could open any of the 12 boxes to see what was inside, but on the test, they would be asked only about the content of the 6 boxes with the marking they had been told was relevant (cage or house). Photo courtesy of Patricia Miller.

given a study period, during which they can open any boxes they think will help them remember the location of the relevant objects. A sensible strategy for a child who needed to remember the animals would be to open each box marked with a cage, to find out which animal was in each one.

The selectivity with which children focus their attention on the relevant category increases greatly between ages 3 and 8 (DeMarie-Dreblow & Miller, 1988; Miller & Seier, 1994). The least advanced children, who also tend to be the youngest children, look indiscriminately in both types of boxes during the study period. Somewhat more advanced children look more often in the boxes of the relevant category but still also look fairly often in the boxes in the other category. Yet more advanced children look almost exclusively in the boxes of the relevant category but do not recall more than those children who also look at some irrelevant boxes. Only the most advanced children both limit their attention completely to the relevant boxes, and remember more than children who deploy their attention less selectively.

Part of older children's superior deployment of attention involves its greater systematicity. This was demonstrated in an analysis of 4- to 8-year-olds' eye movements (Vurpillot, 1968). The children were shown pictures of houses with six windows, like those in Figure 7.7. They needed to determine whether the house on the left was identical to that on the right, and if not, where they differed. Ideally, children would scan a window in the house on the left, then the corresponding window in the house on the right, then another window in the first house, then the corresponding window in the second house, and so on until they either found a difference or had examined all of the windows. Systematically proceeding through the different windows, for example from top to bottom and left to right, also seemed a desirable way to deploy attention, because it would assure that all windows would be compared without repetition.

With age, children's scanning became increasingly systematic. Older children more often looked back and forth between corresponding windows in the two houses and more often proceeded down a column or across a row within a house. They also more often examined all windows before answering that the houses were identical. To summarize, with age, children's attention becomes more focused on relevant information and more systematic.

ALTERNATIVE EXPLANATIONS OF STRATEGIC CHANGE

These findings raise the question: Why would children not use a helpful strategy? Initial attempts to account for this phenomenon focused on two reasons why preschoolers might not use rehearsal. One was that they have a *mediational deficiency* (Reese, 1962). According to this view, young children do not use strategies such as rehearsal because the strategies do not lead to them recalling more than if they do not use them. The other proposed explanation was that young

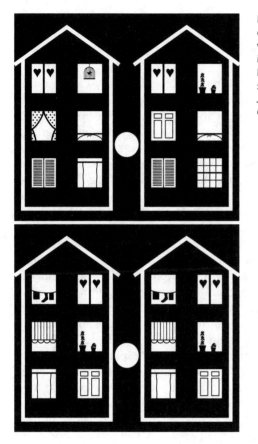

FIGURE 7.7 Stimuli used by Vurpillot (1968) to study development of visual attention. Children needed to find whether houses were different (as in the top pair) or identical (as in the bottom pair) (after Vurpillot, 1968). Reprinted from Vurpillot, E., The development of scanning strategies and their relation to visual differentiation, Journal of Experimental Child Psychology, 6, 632–650, Copyright 1968, with permission from Elsevier.

children's infrequent use of such strategies was due to a *production deficiency* (Flavell, 1970). According to this view, the problem was children not choosing to use the strategy, even though using it would have aided their memory.

Today, neither of these positions seems to provide an adequate explanation. The mediation-deficiency hypothesis fails to explain why young children's recall usually increases when they are taught strategies. The production-deficiency hypothesis does not explain why most 5-year-olds sometimes rehearse, nor why they sometimes would choose to rehearse and other times not.

What seems necessary to understand preschoolers' limited use of rehearsal and other memory strategies is a deeper appreciation of the costs as well as the benefits of using a strategy. In many cases, young children both realize fewer benefits from using strategies and incur greater costs than older children. When people first learn a strategy, the costs in mental effort required to use it are greater than they will be later on. For example, rehearsing a set of numbers while simultaneously performing another task (such as tapping one's index finger on a table as fast as possible) produces greater decrements in performance on the secondary task for younger than for older children (Guttentag, 1984, 1985; Kee & Howell, 1988). The greater decrease in young children's tapping rate seems to be due to the greater mental resources they need to expend in order to rehearse.

This analysis suggests that young children's use of a strategy can be raised either by increasing the benefits or decreasing the costs of using it. Consistent with this prediction, children more often rehearse, and rehearse in more sophisticated ways, when the benefits to them of using the strategy are increased, for example by paying them money for successful recall (Kunzinger & Wittryol, 1984). Strategy use also increases when the costs of using the strategy are decreased, for example by presenting material that is relatively easy to rehearse (Ornstein, Medlin, Stone, & Naus, 1985; Ornstein & Naus, 1985). Children's use of a strategy thus is sensitive to both its costs and its benefits. Increases with age in strategy use reflect both greater benefits and lower costs to the older children.

The concepts of mediation and production deficiencies were proposed to explain why children often do not use strategies that would improve their recall if they used them. The opposite phenomenon also occurs: fairly often, children use strategies that do not initially help them remember better (Bjorklund & Coyle, 1995; Miller, 1990; Miller & Seier, 1994). This phenomenon has been termed a *utilization deficiency*. The lack of improved recall seems to reflect the cost in mental resources of using the strategies negating the benefits that the strategies convey. Consistent with this analysis, when an experimenter reduces the mental effort needed to use a strategy by executing part of it for the child, younger children benefit from strategies that otherwise would not increase their recall (DeMarie-Dreblow & Miller, 1988; Miller, Woody-Ramsey, & Aloise, 1991).

The existence of utilization deficiencies raises the question of why children would ever use strategies that do not help their recall. A key to answering this question may lie in the fact that utilization deficiencies generally occur with newly acquired strategies. The efficiency of executing any procedure increases with practice; this finding is so consistent that it is referred to as the "law of practice" (Newell & Rosenbloom, 1981). Thus, if a newly learned strategy already yields performance as successful, or even almost as successful, as a well-practiced strategy, the odds are excellent that with practice, the new strategy will yield more successful performance. So why not use it? Utilization deficiencies thus may reflect the cognitive system acting as if it implicitly knows the law of practice.

EVALUATION

Age-related improvements in the frequency of use and quality of children's strategies play a large role in memory development between the preschool years and adolescence. During this time, frequency and quality of rehearsal, organization, and selective attention improve greatly. Development of memory strategies is not limited to changes in how often the strategies are used. Older children also use more effective versions of the strategies, use them in difficult as well as easy contexts, and generally increase their recall more substantially when they use them.

One intriguing phenomenon related to memory strategies is that training children to use such strategies is no guarantee of their continued use. This raises the question, "How do children decide which strategy to use?". One possibility is that children rely on their metacognitive knowledge (knowledge of relevant strategies, task difficulty, and their own cognitive capacities) to make such decisions.

Metacognition

Metacognition can be divided into two types of knowledge: explicit, conscious, factual knowledge and implicit, unconscious, procedural knowledge (Brown, Bransford, Ferrara, & Campione, 1983). As an example of explicit metacognitive knowledge, even preschoolers are consciously aware that it is easier to remember a few items than many. However, much metacognitive knowledge is unconscious; the knowledge influences behavior without our being aware of it. Such implicit metacognitive knowledge is apparent when good readers slow down their reading when a book becomes difficult, without even realizing they are doing so. In this section, we examine the development of both explicit and implicit metacognitive knowledge and how they affect children's ability to remember.

EXPLICIT METACOGNITIVE KNOWLEDGE

Children beyond preschool age and adults possess a large fund of explicit knowledge about thinking in general and memory in particular. This knowledge includes information about tasks ("It's easier to remember the main point of a passage than to remember the passage verbatim"), information about strategies ("Rehearsing a telephone number is useful for remembering it"), and information about people ("Older children usually remember more than younger ones"). Much of this knowledge seems to be acquired between ages 5 and 10.

Probably our most basic knowledge of memory is that it is fallible. Almost all children beyond age 6 know that they forget, but a substantial minority of 5-year-olds (30 percent) deny that they ever do (Kreutzer, Leonard, & Flavell, 1975). Young children's overoptimism about their memory capacities can be seen in other contexts as well. For example, when 4-year-olds were asked how many of 10 pictures they would remember, most thought they would remember all 10 (Flavell, Friedrichs, & Hoyt, 1970). Their estimates of what they would remember were higher than those of older children, even though they actually remembered less. The preschoolers' overoptimism may reflect wishful thinking as well as lesser abstract knowledge; when asked to predict how much other children would remember, they were less overoptimistic than in predicting their own performance (Stipek, 1984).

During elementary school and beyond, children and adolescents acquire a wide range of knowledge about how tasks, strategies, and characteristics of learners affect memory (Schneider & Bjorklund, 1998; Weinert, 1986). Approximately half of first-graders know that it is easier to remember the gist of a story than it is to remember the story verbatim; virtually all fifth graders know this (Kreutzer et al., 1975). Similarly, approximately half of first graders know that recognition is easier than recall, whereas virtually all fifth graders do (Speer & Flavell, 1979). The growth in metacognitive knowledge during this period may be stimulated by the increasing amount of remembering children need to do at school, and by the feedback they receive on whether they have remembered correctly.

Much research on this type of explicit factual knowledge of cognition has been motivated by the plausible assumption that children's increasing knowledge about memory and about the general cognitive system leads them to choose better strategies and to remember more effectively. Evidence for this intuitively reasonable position has been surprisingly hard to obtain. Early investigations revealed only weak relations (Cavanaugh & Perlmutter, 1982). More recent analyses of the results of many studies have yielded evidence of somewhat stronger relations between metamnemonic knowledge and memory performance (Schneider & Bjorklund, 1998; Schneider & Pressley, 1989). Still, the relation is not as strong as many people's intuitions would suggest.

IMPLICIT METACOGNITIVE KNOWLEDGE

In contrast to their limited explicit, factual knowledge about memory, toddlers and preschoolers show impressive implicit knowledge. This is especially evident in their monitoring of their own cognitive activities. For example, 2-year-olds show that they monitor their use of language when they spontaneously correct their mistakes in pronunciation, grammar, and naming of objects. They also show such monitoring in comments on their own and others' use of language, and in their adjusting what they say to listeners' knowledge and general cognitive level (Clark, 1978). For example, Siegler's 2½-year-old daughter once told him, "You're a 'he,' Todd's a 'he,' and girls are 'she's.'" Two weeks later, she encountered difficulty pronouncing the word "hippopotamus" and explained, "I can't say it because I can't make my mouth move the right way."

Such self-monitoring enables even young children to experience a feeling of knowing that can help them anticipate how well they will later remember. Illustratively, in one study, 4- and 5-year-olds were shown photographs of children whom they knew to varying degrees. Even when 4- and 5-year-olds did not remember the name that went with a photo, they accurately predicted whether they would be able to remember the name if given the set of names of all of the children in the photos (Cultice, Somerville, & Wellman, 1983).

Despite this early ability to monitor thought processes well enough to experience feelings of knowing, and despite the fact that such monitoring improves further during the elementary school period (Zabrucky & Ratner, 1986), the skill is far from perfectly developed even among older students (Pressley, 1995; Zabrucky & Ratner, 1986) and adults (Narens, Graf, & Nelson, 1996; Reder & Schunn, 1996). Problems are especially persistent in monitoring one's understanding well enough to detect a lack of understanding of what other people are saying. For example, even a fairly large percentage of college students failed to detect the blatant contradictions in the following paragraph:

> Some snakes have a poisonous bite, but some snakes are harmless and even help us. The garter snake, for example, helps us by keeping bad insects away from our gardens. Garter snakes eat these insects. They find the insects by listening for them. The insects make a special noise. Garter snakes do not have ears. They cannot hear the insects. They can hear the sounds of the insects. That is how they are able to find the insects. (Elliott-Faust, 1984; cited in Schneider & Pressley, 1989, p. 167)

Good readers and poor ones differ greatly in ability to monitor their comprehension. Older and better readers slow down and often return to the place in the text where comprehension difficulties began. In contrast, younger and poorer readers rarely return to problem spots (Garner & Reis, 1981; Whimbey, 1975). The situation is paradoxical; the younger and less-skilled readers have more reason to re-read (because they typically understand less well on the first reading), but they do so less often.

Self-monitoring skills are especially critical for choosing what and how much to study. Not surprisingly, older children more effectively monitor their knowledge, and more effectively adapt their study strategies to how well they know the material. The amount of time children study before saying that they know material increases steadily from age 4 at least through age 12 or 13, presumably because older children's monitoring of their knowledge reveals that they have not mastered the material until later in the studying process (Dufresne & Kobasigawa, 1989; Flavell et al., 1970). Older children also focus more of their attention on material they have not yet mastered, again presumably because their monitoring suggests that this material needs the greatest attention (Bisanz, Vesonder, & Voss, 1978).

Allocating study time is a tricky business, though. Consider just the dilemma posed in receiving the results of earlier tests and then studying for later tests on the same material. Is the best strategy to concentrate primarily on the topics that caused the most errors earlier, or is it better to devote study time to other topics as well? Focusing on the sections that you didn't remember should help performance on that material, but might lead to worse performance on the material you correctly recalled the first time. On the other hand, reviewing the better-learned portions might be a waste of time.

Not surprisingly, children who are just learning to study have difficulty making these choices. In one experiment where children were given a chance to study after performing partially correctly on an initial memory test (Masur, McIntyre, & Flavell, 1973), 7- and 9-year-olds took different paths. The 9-year-olds focused on the items they had not remembered; the 7-year-olds distributed their attention more widely. The 9-year-olds' strategy sounds more sophisticated, but it was no more helpful than that of the 7-year-olds. The two strategies led to equal improvements in recall on the second test. The items children forgot between the first and second testings canceled out the items that they previously had not remembered but later did. Some problems just do not have good solutions.

EVALUATION

Metacognition is at the same time intriguing and frustrating as an explanation of memory development. Part of the appeal resides in the plausibility of its central premise—that what children know about memory influences how they attempt to remember. Another part lies in the potential generality of the influence of metacognitive skills and knowledge. For example, knowing the relative usefulness of strategies could improve children's strategy choices in a wide range of situations. Yet another part of the appeal resides in the potential benefits of teaching metacognitive knowledge and skills. Metacognitive knowledge and skills are potentially both instructible and broadly applicable. This makes them better candidates for instruction than basic processes, which are difficult if not impossible to change. Teaching metacognitive knowledge also offers an advantage over teaching specific strategies that can only be used in narrow circumstances, such as rehearsal, which can only be used for rote memorization. Improved knowledge of metacognitive skills, such as how to monitor comprehension, can have broadly beneficial effects on children's learning (Baker, 1994; Borkowski, Johnston, & Reid, 1987; Palincsar & Brown, 1984; Pressley, 1995).

The frustrating aspect of metacognition becomes apparent when we try to determine whether children's increasing metacognitive knowledge helps them remember better. Both memory performance and knowledge about memory improve with age. However, the relation between memory performance and amount of knowledge about memory is not especially strong (Schneider & Bjorklund, 1998). This raises the question of how much impact metacognition actually has on memory development.

One useful way of thinking about the issue is summarized in the proverb, "Many a slip 'twixt the cup and the lip." Metacognitive knowledge may influence memory performance only when each of a relatively long series of conditions is met. Consider what might be involved in a girl's using metacognitive knowledge to choose a strategy for remembering verbatim a long list of numbers.

The girl would need to know that her memory was not perfect and that she might not remember all of the numbers. When she heard the particular list of numbers, she would need to monitor her own memory well enough to recognize that her storage of the numbers was insufficient to hold them in memory without using some strategy. She also would need to know a relevant strategy, such as rehearsal, and would need to choose it rather than a less effective alternative. Finally, for her to use the relevant strategy more often in the future, she would need to attribute whatever benefit she derived to using the strategy rather than to some other factor, such as trying harder.

This perspective makes understandable both the considerable success that can be gained from teaching children metacognitive skills and the frequent findings of weak relations in the everyday environment between metacognitive knowledge and memory performance. If all links in the chain are present, as would often occur in carefully planned instructional programs, metacognitive knowledge can considerably aid memory performance. If even one link is missing, however, as would often occur in the everyday environment, the relation can disappear.

Consider how this seems to operate in one area—transfer of strategies to new situations. Even if children know a strategy, use it, and witness improved memory as a result, they rarely transfer the strategy to new situations unless they also attribute the improvement in memory to use of the strategy (Borkowski, Carr, & Pressley, 1987; Fabricius & Hagen, 1984; Pressley, Levin, & Ghatala, 1984). Children and adults who have been taught to use a strategy that improves their memory often attribute the improvement to factors other than the strategy. For example, Fabricius and Hagen (1984) created a situation in which 6- and 7-year-olds sometimes used an organizational strategy and sometimes did not. The children recalled considerably more when they used the strategy. Although all children had the opportunity to make this observation, only some attributed the difference to using the strategy. Others attributed the successes to looking longer, using their brain more, or slowing down. The children's attributions concerning the cause of their success predicted whether they employed the strategy a week later in a slightly different situation. Fully 99 percent of children who earlier attributed their success to the use of the new strategy used it on the second occasion, compared with 32 percent of those who thought other factors responsible.

Whatever the theoretical status of metacognitive knowledge, its practical importance is clear. In the discussion of children's reading in Chapter 11, we will encounter a remarkably successful training program initiated by Palincsar and Brown (1984) to teach poor readers to understand better what they are reading. The program teaches them to effectively monitor their comprehension of the text they are reading and also supplies strategies for dealing with failures to comprehend. Anything that works as well as this program is well worth learning more about.

Content Knowledge

Older children know more than younger ones about almost everything. In general, the more that people know about a topic, the better they learn and remember new information about it. Therefore, greater content knowledge would lead older children to remember more, even if there were no other differences between them and younger children.

Prior knowledge of related content affects memory in several ways. It influences how much and what children recall. It influences their execution of basic processes and strategies, their metacognitive knowledge, and their acquisition of new strategies. Under some circumstances, it exerts a greater influence than all other factors combined. Evidence concerning each of these points is discussed next.

EFFECTS ON HOW MUCH CHILDREN REMEMBER

The fact that older children regularly recall more than younger ones is due in large part to the older children knowing more about the material they are trying to remember. Content knowledge exerts such a large impact that more knowledgeable children often remember more than less knowledgeable adults. For example, when shown chess positions on a board and then asked to reconstruct them from memory on an empty board, 10-year-old chess experts outperformed adults who were novices at the game (Chi, 1978). This finding was not attributable to the children being smarter or possessing better memories. When the children and adults were given a standard digit span task, the adults remembered more (Figure 7.8). Later comparisons of child chess experts with equally proficient adult experts showed that the children recalled chess configurations just as well (Schneider, Gruber, Gold, & Opwis, 1993). Children generally remember more than adults about types of content that they know better, such as titles of children's TV programs and books (Lindberg, 1980, 1991; Schneider & Bjorklund, 1998). Thus, differences in content knowledge can outweigh all of adults' other memory advantages.

Differences in content knowledge also can influence memory for that type of content more than the child's overall IQ does. Schneider, Korkel, and Weinert (1989) examined German children's memory for a story about a fictitious young soccer player and his experiences in "the big game." The children who heard the story included equal numbers of children with high soccer knowledge and above-average IQs, high soccer knowledge and below-average IQs, low soccer knowledge and above-average IQs, and low soccer knowledge and below-average IQs.

As might be expected, children with high soccer knowledge remembered more about the stories, drew a greater number of correct inferences, and noticed more inconsistencies within the story than those with lower knowledge.

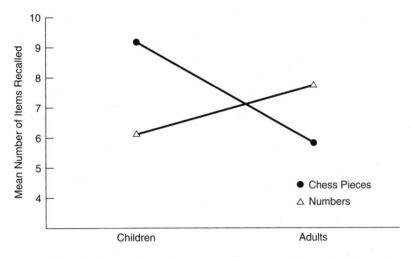

FIGURE 7.8 Number of chess pieces and numbers recalled by 8- to 10-year-old chess experts and adult chess novices immediately after presentation (after Chi, 1978). The child chess experts recalled the positions of more chess pieces, but did not recall more numbers than the adults.

Surprisingly, though, at each level of expertise, higher-IQ children did not remember any more about the soccer game than did lower-IQ children. High-IQ children acquire expertise faster (Johnson & Mervis, 1994), and this may lead to their becoming expert on a greater range of topics. When knowledge is equivalent, however, memory for new information also tends to be equal.

EFFECTS ON WHAT CHILDREN REMEMBER

As noted in the discussion of children's eyewitness testimony, what children know before an experience greatly influences what they remember about it. Thus, preschoolers who already knew that Sam Stone was a clumsy oaf "remembered" that he was the one who had soiled the teddy bear during his visit to the classroom.

Knowledge that children gain *after* an experience can also influence what they remember. Greenhoot (2000) presented kindergarten children with stories about encounters between a target character and another child, and then assessed children's memory for events in the stories. Several days later, children were given some additional information about the story protagonist—either information that suggested that the protagonist was nice and well-liked, or information that suggested that the protagonist was mean and disliked. After receiving this information, children were interviewed again about the initial stories. Children revised their memories of the stories in ways that were consistent with the new information that they had acquired. Children who learned that the protagonist was nice and well-liked reported more positive behaviors, and children who learned that the protagonist was mean and disliked reported more negative behaviors. Thus, knowledge gained after the original experience of the stories led children to alter their memory reports.

Knowledge sometimes leads children to remember incorrectly, but it more often helps them remember correctly. Much of this benefit comes from the knowledge allowing children to draw correct inferences. Thus, young children who hear a story about a helpless creature with a broken wing remember that the story was about a bird, even when that fact is not explicitly mentioned (Paris, 1975). Similarly, knowledge helps children remember what did not happen. Recall how the 7-year-olds, but not the 3-year-olds, knew that the nurse at the doctor's office had not licked their knees. Thus, content knowledge helps people remember both what happened and what did not.

SCRIPTS

Many events recur frequently in similar forms. When children bake cookies, attend birthday parties, eat meals, or go to doctor appointments, the particulars vary from occasion to occasion, but the basic structure is the same. For example, going to a doctor's office generally involves going to the office, telling the receptionist that you are there, sitting in the waiting room, getting up when your name is called, going with the nurse to another room, and waiting for the doctor or nurse to come and do whatever they're going to do.

By the age of 3, children represent such routine activities in the form of *scripts*, which are knowledge structures that describe the way that events usually go. Even preschoolers possess scripts for eating at their daycare center and at restaurants (Nelson, 1978), attending birthday parties (Nelson & Hudson, 1988), going about their daily routine (Fivush & Hammond, 1990), and engaging in other familiar activities. The scripts are especially apparent in children's mistakes in remembering events that for the most part conform to the script but that deviate in certain particulars (Fivush & Hammond, 1990; Nelson & Hudson, 1988). For example, when preschoolers eat at a nice restaurant, they often recall paying before eating, as they would have done at a fast-food restaurant. Such confusions between the script and particular events are particularly prevalent in the preschool period. By age 7, children discriminate more clearly between what usually happens and what happened on the particular occasion (Farrar & Goodman, 1992).

Which experiences lead children to form scripts? One influence seems to be the stories that parents tell them and the questions that the parents ask about past events. For example, Hudson (1990) observed that in most families, parents' requests for young children to recall information largely center on recalling past events. Parents tend to ask the questions in an order that parallels the usual order of activities: "How did we get to the birthday party?" "What did you give

Billy when you got there?" "Did you have something to eat at the party?" The sequence of questions helps children realize both what is important and the order in which the important events usually occur (Nelson, 1993).

Children use scripts not only to recall their own experiences but also to remember stories about other people, such as fairy tales. Many stories that are told or read to children follow a standard form in which the setting is described, an event happens, characters have an internal response, they set a goal, they attempt to reach the goal, and they obtain (or fail to obtain) the goal (Trabasso, van den Broek, & Suh, 1989). Often several such sequences occur, in which earlier outcomes create new goals and attempts by the characters to meet the goals.

Typically, 3-year-olds' retellings of such stories omit the characters' main goals and internal reactions, and they include details that are unrelated to the main sequence (Trabasso & Nickels, 1992; Trabasso & Stein, 1995). The retellings of 4-year-olds focus more exclusively on relevant actions, but they still often omit the characters' goals and intentions. Not until age 5 do children's retellings consistently include all of the key parts of the story. Thus, between ages 3 and 5, children both narrow their script for fairy tales so that it focuses on the most important events and broaden it to include the psychological states that impel the characters' actions.

CONTENT KNOWLEDGE AS AN EXPLANATION FOR OTHER MEMORY CHANGES

Changes in basic capacities, strategies, and metacognition contribute to age-related improvements in children's memory for specific content. The inverse is also true, however: Increasing content knowledge improves efficiency of basic processes, acquisition and execution of strategies, and metacognitive knowledge.

First consider the effect of increasing content knowledge on efficiency of execution of basic processes. At least from age 5, children automatically encode the relative frequency of events, and do so very accurately. However, 5-year-olds' encoding of frequency information is even more accurate when the content is familiar (such as pictures of classmates) than when it is not (pictures of children who are strangers) (Harris, Durso, Mergler, & Jones, 1990). Similarly, the more that people know about the content they are trying to remember, the more material they can maintain in working memory (Huttenlocher & Burke, 1976).

Next consider how content knowledge influences the use and efficiency of memory strategies. Children use strategies such as organization more often for remembering groups of familiar items than for remembering groups of less familiar ones (Bjorklund, Muir-Broaddus, & Schneider, 1990). Moreover, the greater efficiency when strategies are executed with familiar content is sufficient so that 8-year-olds who rehearse familiar items subsequently remember as much as 11-year-olds who rehearse unfamiliar ones (Zember & Naus, 1985).

Familiar content also facilitates learning of new strategies. Chi (1981) examined a 5-year-old's learning of an alphabetic retrieval strategy for her classmates' names. (First think if any names start with A; then think if any names start with B, etc.). Although the strategy was novel, the girl learned it and applied it to recalling her classmates' names rather easily. However, the same girl could not then apply the alphabetic strategy she had already learned in the familiar context to remembering a new set of names of people she had never met.

These results may hold an important implication for how children learn new strategies. Early in the acquisition process, they may employ strategies effectively only on familiar content. Practice using the strategies with the familiar content may lead to execution of the strategies becoming automatized and making fewer demands on the children's processing resources. This automatization, in turn, allows children to apply the strategies to more demanding, unfamiliar content. Thus, the familiar content may serve as a kind of practice field upon which children exercise emerging memory strategies.

Finally, content knowledge influences metacognition. Child chess experts not only remember more than adult novices about chess positions they see, but also more accurately predict the relatively large number of viewings required before they will be able to perfectly reconstruct from memory the positions on the board. Clearly, all aspects of memory are influenced by content knowledge.

HOW DOES CONTENT KNOWLEDGE AID MEMORY?

Content knowledge aids memory through a number of mechanisms. One is encoding of distinctive features. By focusing attention on distinctive features, content knowledge helps children remember different entities. For example, part of the way that scripts aid memory is by indicating what children should encode. When they go to a birthday party, the script indicates that they should be sure to note the present they gave to the birthday child, the presents that other children gave, the games that were played, the type of cake that was served, and any favors that they brought home. Similarly, much of the benefit of expertise is in knowing which information should be encoded. Chess experts can so accurately recall board configurations primarily because they encode groups of pieces that have certain functions—protecting the king, attacking the bishop, and so on—and relate them to the overall situation. When presented with a random configuration of chess pieces, experts are no better than novices at recalling the arrangement (Chi, 1978). Thus, part of how content knowledge helps memory is by enhancing encoding.

Another key mechanism through which content knowledge exercises its effects is spreading activation. When people think about a topic, the topic becomes activated, in the sense that people can quickly retrieve information about it. The activation automatically spreads from topics that are receiving attention to others that are associated with it, thus facilitating retrieval of information about them.

For example, when children think about their summer vacation, they may remember eating lobster at the vacation site, which may remind them of eating lobster on other occasions, eating mussels and clams on other occasions, and so on. If someone asked them just after they had this thought whether mussels have shells, they probably would be able to answer "yes" more quickly than usual.

As children learn about a topic, spreading activation helps them remember increasingly effectively. Consider why children who are knowledgable about a topic might use organizational strategies more effectively and more often (Rabinowitz & Chi, 1987). Suppose two 8-year-old boys, differing in knowledge of birds, both needed to remember a set of words including "hawk," "penguin," and "chicken." The more knowledgable boy probably would know that all three are birds, whereas the less knowledgable one would probably know only that hawks are. For the more knowledgable boy, activation would spread among all three terms and the general category of birds, whereas for the less knowledgable one, activation would spread only between "bird" and "hawk." This would lead to the more knowledgable boy being more likely to use "birds" as a category for organizing his memory of the three examples, and it would help his recall to a greater extent if he did so (since the "bird" category would activate all three original terms). Thus, spreading activation may lead knowledgable children to use strategies more often and to the strategies aiding their recall to a greater extent.

EVALUATION

Any explanation of memory development must reserve a large place for increasing knowledge of specific content. Content knowledge increases steadily from infancy through adulthood. It is clearly related to how well children remember, as was evident in the studies of memory for chess positions, for soccer, and for fairy tales. It provides scripts within which children can organize new information, allows them to check on the plausibility of their memories, facilitates their drawing of inferences, and helps them encode distinctive features of objects and events. It also contributes to the development of other competencies that have been proposed as explanations of memory development, such as basic capacities, strategies, and metacognition. Without question, increasing content knowledge is a large part of the reason why older children remember more than younger ones.

What Develops When in Memory Development?

Different aspects of memory may not only contribute different amounts to memory development, but also may make their greatest contributions at different times. Table 7.2 summarizes the contributions of basic processes and capacities, strategies, metacognition, and content knowledge during several periods of life.

TABLE 7.2 Contributions of Four Aspects of Memory During Several Periods of Development

Source of Development	Age		
	0–5	5–10	10–Adulthood
Basic Capacities	Many capacities present: association, generalization, recognition, etc. By age 5, if not earlier, absolute capacity of sensory memory at adult-like levels.	Speed of processing increases.	Speed of processing continues to increase.
Strategies	A few rudimentary strategies such as naming, pointing, and selective attention.	Acquisition and increasing use of many strategies: rehearsal, organization, etc.	Continuing improvement in quality of all strategies.
Metacognition	Little factual knowledge about memory. Some monitoring of ongoing performance.	Increasing factual knowledge about memory. Improved monitoring of ongoing performance.	Continued improvements in explicit and implicit knowledge.
Content Knowledge	Steadily increasing content knowledge helps memory in areas in which the knowledge exists.	Steadily increasing content knowledge helps memory in areas in which the knowledge exists. Also helps in learning of new strategies.	Continuing improvements.

Many basic processes, such as ability to associate objects with each other and to recognize familiar objects, are present at birth. These processes are crucial in enabling children to learn and remember from the first days of life. It is unknown whether the absolute capacity of memory increases with age. However, speed of processing increases from birth through late adolescence, and this helps the functional capacity of memory to increase regardless of whether the absolute capacity increases.

Memory strategies begin to contribute to memory development somewhat later than basic capacities. The earliest known strategies appear in the second year, but many other important strategies, such as rehearsal, organization, and elaboration, become prominent between ages 5 and 7. The quality of the strategies, their frequency of use, and the flexibility with which they are tailored to the demands of specific situations continue to develop well into later childhood and adolescence.

Two types of metacognitive skills, explicit factual knowledge about memory and implicit procedural knowledge, seem to have different developmental courses. Implicit metacognitive knowledge is evident quite early. Even toddlers sometimes monitor their comprehension and develop feelings of knowing, though the range of situations in which they do so continues to grow for many years thereafter. In contrast, explicit knowledge about memory appears to develop primarily between ages 5 and 15, perhaps in response to attending school and needing to remember a great deal of arbitrary information.

Content knowledge contributes to memory development from infancy onward. It influences both how much and what children remember. It also affects the efficiency of execution of basic processes, learning of new strategies, and metacognitive knowledge about memory. Together, basic capacities, strategies, metacognition, and content knowledge account for the two essential features of memory development: first, that even newborn infants have the ability to learn and to remember what they learned, and second, that the effectiveness of memory continues to improve throughout infancy, early childhood, middle childhood, and adolescence.

Summary

Children are being called increasingly often to testify in court cases. Research on the accuracy of their testimony indicates that when they are asked open-ended and unbiased questions, even preschoolers' recall is accurate and relevant. However, asking biased questions and inducing stereotypes may lead children, especially preschoolers, to report events that never happened. To obtain accurate and complete memory reports, interviewers should ask questions in a neutral fashion, the questions should be sufficiently specific to elicit memories that children might not otherwise report, and the questioning should not be repeated more often than necessary.

Memory development has been attributed to changes in four types of causes: basic processes and capacities, strategies, metacognition, and content knowledge. Basic capacities and processes, such as the abilities to associate and recognize, are already present in newborns. By age 3 months, infants display many other basic processes. They generalize, remember the gist of events, and even show insight. Processing speed increases throughout childhood and adolescence. The number of symbols that can be held in working memory also improves gradually over this period, but it is unclear whether this is due to changes in the absolute capacity of memory or to other improvements. Despite the fact that children are capable of most basic memory processes from a very young age, most people remember almost nothing that occurred before the age of 3 years. This phenomenon is termed "infantile amnesia," and it is likely due to a combination of several factors. Possible causes of infantile amnesia include physiological changes in the brain, changes in the ways that children talk about past events with other people, and incompatibilities between the ways in which infants encode information and the ways in which older children and adults retrieve it.

The use of broadly applicable memory strategies such as rehearsal, organization, and selective attention increases rapidly between 5 years and adolescence. Children who use such strategies typically remember more than those who do not. Changes in the quality of strategies and the range of situations in which they are used continue well beyond the ages at which they are first adopted. Strategies can be taught to children earlier than the children would ordinarily use them. However, children who have received such training often fail to use the strategies in subsequent situations, and they use them less effectively than older children. This may be due to a combination of lesser benefits and greater costs to the children of using the strategies, as well as to the children's not perceiving the connection between using the strategy and remembering better. Overall, learning of these strategies seems to account for an important part of memory development, particularly in middle childhood and beyond.

Metacognition includes two distinct types of knowledge: explicit and implicit. Explicit knowledge about memory is conscious and verbalizable. It involves factual knowledge about strategies, tasks, and capacities. Implicit knowledge, in contrast, is not conscious or verbalizable; it involves such processes as monitoring one's comprehension and feelings of knowing. Implicit knowledge of memory is already evident among toddlers. Explicit knowledge is not evident as early, but between ages 5 and 10, it too becomes quite extensive. Development of both types of metacognitive knowledge continues throughout life.

Knowledge of related content greatly affects children's memory at all ages. Content knowledge allows children to remember more than they otherwise would, influences their ability to learn strategies, helps them make plausible inferences, and allows them to form scripts for remembering sequences of events. Under some circumstances, differences in content knowledge can outweigh all other changes in memory that come with age and experience. Children who are experts on topics such as chess and soccer exhibit truly impressive memory in their area of expertise, though their memory in other areas is unexceptional. Encoding of distinctive features and spreading activation appear to be two of the mechanisms that help children with high content knowledge to better remember new information.

Recommended Readings

Bruck, M., & Ceci, S.J. (1999). The suggestibility of children's memory. *Annual Review of Psychology, 50,* 419–439. A readable review of research on the accuracy of children's eyewitness testimony and conditions that make it more and less accurate.

Kail, R. (1991). Developmental changes in speed of processing during childhood and adolescence. *Psychological Bulletin, 109,* 490–501. Intriguing evidence that the basic speed of information processing increases with age over the entire period from early childhood through adolescence.

Miller, P. & Seier, W. (1994). Strategy utilization deficiencies in children: When, where, and why. In H. Reese (Ed.), *Advances in child development and behavior* (Vol. 25). New York: Academic Press. This review presents a large body of evidence documenting the sur-

prising finding that children often use strategies before their recall benefits from them, and suggests several explanations for why they do so.

Rovee-Collier, C. (1999). The development of infant memory. *Current Directions in Psychological Science, 8,* 80–85. A brief, informative summary of research demonstrating that infants' memory processes are fundamentally similar to those of older children and adults.

Schneider, W., & Bjorklund, D.F. (1998). Memory. In D. Kuhn & R.S. Siegler (Eds.), *Handbook of child psychology: Vol. 2. Cognition, perception, & language* (5th ed.). New York: Wiley. A comprehensive review of research on memory development, with a particular focus on memory strategies and on non-strategic factors in memory development.

8

Conceptual Development

EXPERIMENTER: *It's twelve o'clock in the afternoon and the sun is shining really bright. You already ate something today, but you're still very hungry, so you decide to eat pancakes with syrup, orange juice, cereal, and milk. Could that be lunch?*

KINDERGARTNER: *No . . . because lunch you have to have sandwiches and stuff like that.*

E: *Can you have cereal for lunch?*

K: *No.*

E: *Can you have pancakes for lunch?*

K: *No . . . No.*

E: *Well, how do you know if something is lunch or not?*

K: *If the time says 12:00.*

E: *This was 12:00.*

K: *Well, I don't think so.*

E: (Repeats story.) *Is that lunch?*

K: *I know . . . that one is not lunch . . . you have to eat sandwiches at lunch.*

E: *Can you have anything else?*

K: *You can have drinks, but not breakfast.* (Keil, 1989, pp. 77, 291)

This child's concept of lunch clearly differs from that of older children and adults. But what can we conclude from the difference? Is it simply an isolated confusion between typical and essential characteristics of lunch? Or is it symptomatic of a more general tendency of younger children to understand concepts superficially and not to grasp their core meaning?

Concepts involve grouping together different entities on the basis of some similarity. The similarity can either be quite concrete (a concept of dogs) or quite abstract (a concept of justice). Concepts allow us to organize our experience into coherent patterns and to draw inferences in situations in which we lack direct experience. If told that malamutes are dogs, a child immediately also knows that they have four legs, a tail, and fur; that they are animals; that they probably are friendly to people; and so on. Concepts also save us mental effort, by allowing us to apply previous knowledge to new situations. Once we have the concept "kitten," we do not need to think hard about this particular scrawny, taffy-colored kitten to guess what she would like to eat.

The tendency to form concepts is a basic characteristic of human beings. Infants form concepts even during their first months (Haith & Benson, 1998; Quinn & Eimas, 1995). Within a few years, children acquire a huge number of concepts. Consider a few that most 5-year-olds in the United States possess: tables, gold, animals, trees, Nintendo, dirt bikes, running, birthdays, winter, fairness, time, and number. Some of these concepts involve objects, others events, others ideas, others activities, and yet others dimensions of existence. Some of the objects are part of nature; others are artifacts made by people to serve a specific purpose. Some of the concepts are possessed by children throughout the world and have been throughout history. Others are specific to children living in advanced industrial societies of the late twentieth century. Some are broadly applicable; others are quite narrow.

In this chapter, we look at conceptual development from two perspectives. One focuses on conceptual representations in general; the other focuses on the development of a few particularly important concepts (Table 8.1).

TABLE 8.1   Chapter Outline

  I. Conceptual Representations in General
      A. Defining-Features Representations
      B. Probabilistic Representations
      C. Theory-Based Representations

 II. Development of Some Particularly Important Concepts
      A. Time
      B. Space
      C. Number
      D. Biological Concepts

III. Summary

TABLE 8.2   Classic Characterizations of Older and Younger Children's Concepts

Description of Younger Children's Concepts	Description of Older Children's Concepts	Theorist(s)
Concrete	Abstract	Piaget (1951)
Perceptual	Conceptual	Bruner, Goodnow, & Austin (1956)
Holistic	Analytic	Werner & Kaplan (1963)
Thematic	Taxonomic	Vygotsky (1934/1962)
Global	Specific	Inhelder & Piaget (1964)

The approach that emphasizes the development of conceptual representations in general is based on the assumption that the nature of people's minds leads them to represent most or all concepts in a particular way. The nature of this representation is of primary interest; the details of the particular concepts are secondary. This approach has been most common in studying object concepts such as tools, furniture, and vehicles, where the particulars of the concept are less important than the concept's representativeness.

If the nature of people's minds leads them to impose a certain type of representation, and if young minds differ fundamentally from older ones, then young children's concepts may also differ fundamentally. For example, their concepts may be concrete, whereas those of older children may be abstract. Many of the most prominent developmental theorists have subscribed to this *representational development hypothesis.* Table 8.2 lists some of the contrasts between younger and older children's concepts that have been proposed.

The other main approach has been to focus on the development of a few inherently important concepts. Certain concepts, such as time, space, number, and living things, are so basic to our understanding of the world that their development is important in its own right. These concepts have played central roles in the theories of philosophers such as Kant and psychologists such as Piaget. They also may develop differently than other concepts. Unlike most concepts, they are largely universal across cultures and historical periods, they are present in rudimentary form in infancy, and they are constantly used. It is hard to imagine how people could learn such concepts if there were not some relatively specific biological basis for them. For example, if people did not encode events as occurring before or after each other, what experiences could lead to their doing so? Understanding of these basic concepts often changes dramatically during development, but their core seems to be part of our inheritance as human beings (Spelke, 1994, 2000). In the sections that follow, we first consider the development of conceptual representations in general and then the development of a few particularly important concepts.

Conceptual Representations in General

How do people represent concepts? Three main possibilities have been proposed: defining-features representations, probabilistic representations, and theory-based representations. The differences among the proposed representations can be seen in the depictions of the concept "uncle" in Figure 8.1. *Defining-features representations* are like dictionary definitions. They include only the necessary and sufficient features that determine whether an example is or is not an instance of the concept. *Probabilistic representations* are more like the articles in encyclopedias. Rather than just representing a few features that must always be present, people may represent concepts in terms of a large number of properties that are somewhat, but not perfectly, correlated with the concept. Thus, uncles tend to be nice to their nieces and nephews, though they are not necessarily so. Finally, *theory-based representations* are akin to chapters in a science textbook, in that they

FIGURE 8.1 Ways in which the concept "uncle" might be represented within defining features, probabilistic, and theory-based approaches.

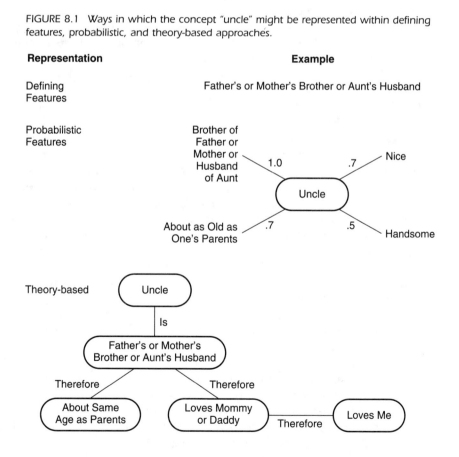

emphasize causal relations among elements of a system. Children's conceptual representations may include explanations for why their uncles tend to be nice, why they tend to be about as old as their parents, and so on.

Are young children capable of generating all of these types of representations? As previously noted, some of the most eminent developmental theorists—Piaget, Vygotsky, Werner, and Bruner, among others—thought not. Although they used different terminology, all hypothesized that young children cannot form what we are calling defining-features representations. We next consider the evidence on which they based this view and whether they were right.

DEFINING-FEATURES REPRESENTATIONS

What would it mean for people to represent concepts in terms of defining features? First, they would know the concepts' necessary and sufficient features. Second, they would use these features to determine whether particular examples were instances of the concept.

Piaget, Bruner, and others based their view that young children could not form defining-features representations largely on observations of children playing with objects. They presented children several types of objects, such as toy animals, vehicles, and furniture, and observed which ones children put together. They found that older children typically divide the objects into categories with a defining feature: They put animals with animals, vehicles with vehicles, and so forth. In contrast, a typical preschooler might put together a dog and a car (because dogs like to ride in cars), a cat and a chair (because cats like to curl up in chairs), and a game and a shelf (because games belong on shelves). Such groupings led Inhelder and Piaget (1964) to conclude that preoperational stage children's concepts were *thematic* (organized in terms of a common activity or theme), whereas concrete operations stage children's concepts were *taxonomic* (organized in terms of hierarchically organized categories, like those used to classify plants and animals in biology).

Vygotsky (1934/1962) used a similar task to study conceptual development. He presented children a number of blocks that differed in size, color, and shape, and asked them to group together those that went together. Children ages 6 years and older who were given this sorting task typically chose a single quality as the defining feature. For example, they might choose color as necessary and sufficient for membership in a group, and put all the red blocks together, all the green blocks together, and so on. Preschoolers, however, seemed to form what Vygotsky called *chain concepts*. These were concepts in which the basis of classification changed from example to example. They might put together a few red blocks; then put a few triangular blocks, green as well as red, together; and then put a few green blocks together.

These types of observations led Vygotsky to hypothesize that children pass through three stages of conceptual development. Very early, they form thematic concepts, stressing relations between particular pairs of objects. Later, they form chain concepts by momentarily classifying on the basis of abstract dimensions such as color or shape, but often forgetting what they were doing and switching the basis of their categorization. Still later, during the elementary school period, they form true concepts, based on stable, necessary, and sufficient features.

Evaluation. The defining-features view of concepts has led to a number of discoveries about preschoolers' conceptual understanding: that they often do not sort objects along a single consistent dimension; that they tend to arrange objects according to how the objects interact, rather than according to their categorical relations; and that they find different relations of interest than do adults.

But should we believe the broader theoretical claim that young children's concepts differ fundamentally from those of older children and adults? Probably not. Research conducted to test whether young children can form types of concepts typical of older children has consistently shown that they can. For example, Bauer and Mandler (1989a) found that even 1-year-olds form taxonomic concepts. They presented children of this age with sets of three objects. The target object was placed in the middle, and children were asked, "See this one? Can you find another object just like this one?" Of the remaining two objects, one was related to the target object thematically and the other taxonomically. For example, in one problem, the object in the middle was a monkey, the object related to it taxonomically was a bear, and the object related to it thematically was a banana. The 1-year-olds chose the taxonomically related objects (the monkey and the bear) as being the similar ones on more than 85 percent of trials.

If even 1-year-olds understand taxonomic relations, why would the impression have arisen that 4- and 5-year-olds cannot understand them? Confusing children's interests with their capabilities may be the reason. Young children may put dogs and frisbees together, rather than dogs and bears, because they find the relation between dogs and frisbees more interesting. Supporting this interpretation, Smiley and Brown (1979) found that preschoolers who sorted objects thematically could, when asked, explain perfectly the taxonomic relations as well. Other studies have documented flexible use of both thematic and taxonomic categories in preschoolers. These studies suggest that children's tendency to use one type of concept or the other depends on the context in which the task is presented (Blaye & Bonthoux, 2001) or on the nature of the task instructions (Waxman & Namy, 1997). Cole and Scribner (1974) reported similar findings with tribespeople in Africa. Experimenters could elicit the ostensibly more-sophisticated taxonomic sortings from the tribespeople only by asking, "How would a stupid man do it?" Both the children and the tribespeople possessed the relevant concepts, but they chose not to apply them in the particular situation.

Another contributor to the misimpression has been underestimating the role of specific content knowledge in conceptual understanding. Although young children represent some concepts in terms of defining features, they do not know what the defining features are for many other concepts. Consider an experiment

TABLE 8.3   *Stories from Keil and Batterman (1984)*

Characteristic Features But Not Defining Features

There is this place that sticks out of the land like a finger. Coconut trees and palm trees grow there, and the girls sometimes wear flowers in their hair because it's so warm all the time. There is water on all sides except one. Could that be an island?

Defining Features But Not Characteristic Features

On this piece of land, there are apartment houses, snow, and no green things growing. This piece of land is surrounded by water on all sides. Could that be an island?

in which 5- and 9-year-olds heard two stories describing a particular object and then were asked whether that object could be an example of a particular concept (Keil & Batterman, 1984). As shown in Table 8.3, one story indicated that the object included many features people associate with the concept, but also indicated that it lacked the defining feature. The other story indicated that the object included the defining feature, but lacked many associated features.

The 9-year-olds generally emphasized the defining features; they usually said that the story at the top of Table 8.3 did not describe an island but that the story at the bottom did. The performance of the 5-year-olds was in some ways different and in other ways similar. The 5-year-olds did not rely on the defining feature on as many concepts as the 9-year-olds. However, on familiar concepts, such as "robbers," the 5-year-olds did rely on defining features, and on relatively unfamiliar concepts, such as "taxis," the 9-year-olds did not consistently do so. (The fact that the study was conducted in a small town probably had a lot to do with the concept of *taxi* being unfamiliar.) Thus, both younger and older children can form defining-features representations, but knowledge about the defining features of particular concepts increases with age.

Probabilistic Representations

From the time of Aristotle until relatively recently, most concepts have been viewed as having defining features. Children and adults might or might not know the defining features, but they were there to be known. Today, however, the prevailing view among philosophers is that most concepts do not have defining features. Consider the term "chair." At first glance, a chair would seem to have the defining attributes, "an object with four legs, intended to be used for sitting." But what about beanbag chairs, which have no legs? What about chairs in modern art museums, which never were intended for sitting? The situation is more extreme for complex terms, such as "game" and "mercy." It is difficult to even imagine what the defining attributes might be for such concepts.

These difficulties with identifying defining features open the possibility that all of us, adults as well as children, represent most concepts in terms of probabilistic relations between the concept and various features, rather than in terms of a few defining features. Eleanor Rosch, Carolyn Mervis, and their colleagues have developed an appealing theory based on this view of concepts. The central theme is that instances of most concepts are united by family resemblances rather than by defining features. The instances resemble each other to varying degrees and in varying ways, much like different family members do, but there is no set of features that all of them possess. Rosch and Mervis' theory is built around four powerful ideas: cue validities, basic-level categories, correlations among features, and prototypes.

Cue validities.   How might children decide whether objects are examples of one concept or another? Rosch and Mervis (1975) suggested that they do so by comparing *cue validities*. The basic idea is that the degree to which the presence of a feature makes it likely that an object is an example of a concept depends on the frequency with which the feature accompanies that concept and on the infrequency with which the feature accompanies other concepts. For example, the feature "capable of flight" makes it likely that an object is a bird in proportion to the frequency with which birds can fly and in proportion to the infrequency with which other things can. Because most (though not all) birds can fly, and because most (though not all) other things cannot fly, flight is a highly valid cue for an object's being a bird.

The idea of cue validities helps the probabilistic approach explain a phenomenon that proved troublesome for the defining-features approach: that some instances of a concept seem like better examples of it than others. Within the defining-features approach, if a robin and an ostrich both have the necessary and sufficient features for birds, why would robins seem like better examples of birds than ostriches? The probabilistic approach suggests that objects perceived as better examples are ones whose features have higher cue validities for that concept. Thus, people view robins as better examples of birds than ostriches, because the robins' color, size, and ability to fly are more valid cues to their being birds.

The cues that people consider in forming concepts change considerably over the course of development. Infants in the first few months are already sensitive to cue validities, but the types of cues on which they focus change with age and experience. Infants initially pay greatest attention to visible and audible features, but with experience, they pay increasing attention to more abstract ones (e.g., Eimas & Quinn, 1994; Madole & Cohen, 1995). There is a reason why infants form categories such as dogs and running but not ones such as tools or fairness.

Despite this early emphasis on perceptual cues, infants' categories are not limited to ones based solely on perceptual features. Even in the first year of life, infants have knowledge about causal and functional attributes of objects that they can use to guide their categorization (Mandler, 2000; Mandler & McDonough, 1993). For example, infants who have been familiarized to a set of artificial-looking

TABLE 8.4   Examples of Superordinate, Basic, and
Subordinate Category Members

Superordinate Level	Basic Level	Subordinate Level
Furniture	Table	End table
Animal	Bird	Canary
Food	Vegetable	Asparagus
Tool	Hammer	Tack hammer
Vehicle	Car	Miata

toy animals show renewed interest in a toy chair, even if that chair has been painted to be perceptually similar to the animals (Pauen, 2002). Thus, infants appear to use their emerging conceptual knowledge, such as knowledge of the animate-inanimate distinction, in forming categories from an early age.

Basic-level categories.   Rosch, Mervis, Gray, Johnson, and Boyes-Braem (1976) noted that many categories are hierarchical, in the sense that all instances of one category are necessarily instances of another. They proposed that these hierarchies typically include at least three levels (Table 8.4): a general one (the *superordinate* level), a specific one (the *subordinate* level), and one of middling generality (the *basic* level). The basic level is the level at which cue validities are maximized. For example, "chair" is a basic-level category because it has parts with very high cue validities, among them legs, a back, and a seat. Superordinate categories, such as "furniture," do not have features with comparably high cue validities. Some pieces of furniture have legs and others do not; some are for sitting and others are not. Conversely, subordinate categories, such as "kitchen chairs," share all features of the basic-level category, but lack features that clearly discriminate them from other instances of the basic-level category. What features cleanly discriminate kitchen chairs from dining room chairs? Rosch et al. concluded that basic-level categories are more fundamental classifications than either superordinate or subordinate categories.

If basic-level categories are indeed basic, children should learn them before they learn superordinate or subordinate categories. This implication has been tested by presenting infants with a habituation procedure. First, the infants are repeatedly shown members of a basic-level category until they reduce their looking at the objects. Then they are presented either a novel member of the same basic-level category or a member of a different basic-level category within the same superordinate category. For example, they might repeatedly be shown horses, and then be shown either a giraffe or another horse.

Research with 3- to 9-month-olds has consistently shown that infants dishabituate when shown members of a different basic-level category (Colombo, O'Brien, Mitchell, Roberts, & Horowitz, 1987; Quinn, Eimas, & Rosenkrantz,

1993; Roberts, 1988). For example, after repeatedly being presented pictures of horses, infants dishabituated when shown similar size pictures of giraffes, zebras, or cats (Eimas & Quinn, 1994). However, using the same methods, infants have been shown to form more general categories as well (Behl-Chadha, 1996). For example, when shown several different mammals, 3- and 4-month-olds dishabituated when shown birds, fish, or furniture, but not when shown other mammals. Thus, infants are able to form basic-level categories but also more general, superordinate ones.

Although basic-level categories play prominent roles in early conceptual understanding, some of the particular categories differ considerably from those that adults consider basic. Illustratively, the objects that 1-year-olds label "balls" often include such objects as round candles, round coin banks, and multisided beads. Their "ball" category seems to correspond to the adult category "things that can roll." Mervis (1987) labeled such notions *child-basic categories*. The particulars of "child-basic" and standard-basic categories often differ, but Mervis argued that the principles by which they are formed are the same. Both young children and adults include in their basic categories objects that can be used to achieve similar functions and that have similar appearances. Differing perspectives on what constitutes an interesting function lead to the differences in the categories that are possessed at different ages.

How do children move from child-basic to standard-basic categories? Grasping the role of perceptually insignificant but functionally important attributes may be critical for making the transition (Tversky, 1989; Tversky & Hemenway, 1984). For example, young children initially ignore the slots in round coin banks and the wicks on round candles and focus on the more perceptually striking round shape. Once the child understands the purpose of the slots and wicks, the conceptual distinctions become easier to understand. In keeping with this interpretation, 2-year-olds can move from child-basic to standard-basic categories if an experimenter identifies perceptually subtle attributes that are critical to category membership and explains the importance of those attributes (Banigan & Mervis, 1988).

Correlations among features. Conceptual understanding involves more than knowing the cue validities of individual features. Correlations among features are at least as essential. Features of objects in the world are not randomly distributed but rather tend to cluster together. Things that slither along the ground also tend to have scales, to be long and thin, to be difficult to see in their natural environments, and so on. Fortunately, even 10-month-olds are adept at noting correlations among features and at using the correlations to form new concepts (Younger, 1990, 1993).

Prototypes. A fourth concept emphasized by Rosch and her colleagues was that of prototypes. Prototypes are the most representative instances of concepts—that is, the examples that have the highest cue validities. Lassie was

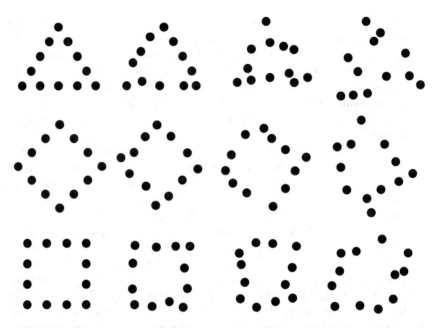

FIGURE 8.2 On the extreme left, from top to bottom, the prototypic triangle, diamond, and square are displayed. In each row, increasingly distorted versions of the prototypes are displayed from left to right (after Bomba & Siqueland, 1983). Copyright © 1983 by Academic Press, Inc. Reprinted from Bomba, P. C., & Siqueland, E. R., The nature and structure of infant form categories, Journal of Experimental Child Psychology, 35, 294–328, Copyright 1983, with permission from Elsevier.

a prototypical dog because she had qualities (such as size, shape, bark) representative of dogs in general.

Infants as young as 3 months abstract prototypical forms. Bomba and Siqueland (1983) showed 3- and 4-month-olds a variety of dot patterns generated by randomly transforming an original "prototype" shape, such as an equilateral triangle (Figure 8.2). During this initial phase of the experiment, infants never saw the prototype. However, exposure to examples derived from the prototype (such as the shapes in the rightmost three columns of Figure 8.2) led infants later to act as if they had seen the prototype as well. When they were shown the prototype along with an unfamiliar pattern, they preferred looking at the other pattern; they acted as if they had seen the prototype often and were bored with it. Over time, as memory for the particular dot patterns decreased but the general concept remained, the 3- and 4-month-olds actually showed more interest in shapes they had seen, but apparently did not remember, than in the prototype, which they had not seen but did "remember." Older children and adults show similar patterns of being more confident that they have seen prototypes, which actually have never been shown, than forms derived from the prototypes, which they have seen (Bransford, 1979).

Evaluation.   Viewing conceptual representations in terms of probabilistically related features has much to recommend it. Even in the first year, infants abstract prototypical patterns, form basic-level categories, and notice cue validities and correlations among features. With development, they form increasing numbers of superordinate and subordinate level categories, move from child-basic to standard-basic categories for those concepts on which they started with child-basic categories, and become sensitive to more complex and subtle correlational patterns.

The probabilistic-features approach also has some weaknesses, though. One that it shares with the defining-features approach is vagueness about what constitutes a feature. For example, what features make up the concept "a beautiful face"? The features clearly are more complex than hair of a certain color, eyes of a certain shape, lips curved at a certain angle, a nose of a certain form, and so on. Much more important than these tangible attributes are relations among the features, how they fit together. Yet it is unclear whether relations such as "fitting together" can usefully be viewed as features; given that many of the most beautiful faces strike us as unique, it also is unclear whether they are based on probabilistic relations at all.

Another weakness, related to the previous one, is that the approach does not specify how children determine which features of unfamiliar objects and events they should encode and which they should ignore. As discussed in Chapter 3, determining which features to encode is often quite difficult. Yet, unless children encode the important features and relations, they cannot learn their cue validities.

Some researchers have proposed that infants and children are guided toward encoding relevant features through implicit theories of what is important (R. Gelman & Williams, 1998; Wellman & S. Gelman, 1992, 1998) The role of such theories is considered in the next section.

THEORY-BASED REPRESENTATIONS

What concept has the following members: children, portable TVs, jewelry, and photo albums? The question seems bizarre until we hear the answer: things we would take out of the house first in case of a fire. Suddenly, the strangeness of the concept disappears (Barsalou, 1985).

As this example suggests, there is more to concepts than correlations among features or defining features. Concepts also embody theoretical beliefs about the world and the relations of entities to each other. These theoretical beliefs influence our reactions to new information. To understand this influence, contrast your reaction to the statement "Today I saw a car with orange wheels" with that to the statement "Today I saw a car with square wheels." Both situations are novel; people would not have had an opportunity to calculate cue validities or feature correlations for either the orange wheels or the square ones.

Neither is in the least prototypical. Yet our theoretical beliefs lead us to react differently to the two statements. When we hear that a car has orange wheels, we infer that the owner may be a prankster or a hippie, that the rest of the car may also be brightly painted, and that the car probably functions normally. When we hear that a car has square wheels, we infer that it cannot move, that it was not intended to function normally, and that it may be a sculpture intended to elicit surprise. Such inferences reflect our informal theories about how cars work and why people do strange things.

Keil (1989, 1994) proposed an insightful theory regarding the role that such informal theories play in conceptual development. The following are among the main principles he suggested:

1. Most concepts are partial theories, in that they include explanations of relations among their parts and of their relations to other concepts.
2. Theories are complexly tied to people's associative knowledge; they do not stand apart from it.
3. Causal relations are basic within these theories; they are more useful than other types of relations.
4. Hierarchical relations also are especially informative.

The import of these assumptions can be illustrated with regard to a hypothetical situation. Suppose a girl was asked, "Why do yaks have four legs rather than three or five?" She might answer that four legs can be moved in pairs, which allows yaks to run relatively fast and still maintain their balance. This answer suggests that the child possesses theoretical understanding that allowed her to go beyond defining features and probabilistically related features to explain *why* the world is the way it is. The answer also illustrates the relation between associative knowledge and theoretical beliefs, in that it reflects both specific memories of the running of other four-legged animals and an informal theory of how running works. The role of causal relations is evident in the child's explaining four-leggedness in terms of what it allows yaks to do. Finally, the fact that the child knew that she could reason from her knowledge of animals in general to a particular animal, yaks, attests to the usefulness of organizing concepts into hierarchies.

Theoretical understanding is present in concepts of very young children, as well as in those of older children and adults. This is not to say that the understanding is the same at all ages. The accuracy and interconnectedness of the theoretical beliefs, as well as the frequency with which they are relied on, increase with development. Keil (1989) hypothesized that at all ages, concepts include both theoretical connections and isolated factual information. However, as theories become increasingly sophisticated, they explain an increasingly broad range of the factual knowledge.

Although people generate many informal theories, a few "core theories" may be especially important (Wellman & S. Gelman, 1992, 1998). In particular, Wellman and Gelman hypothesized that children are predisposed to develop three core theories: one concerning inanimate objects (*naive physics*), one concerning living things (*naive biology*), and one concerning the human mind (*naive psychology*). These core theories are said to organize a great deal of their knowledge about the world and help them in acquiring additional knowledge. As Wellman and Gelman (1998) noted, these three domains are central to basic survival as well as to everyday interactions with others and with the physical world:

> Knowledge about other humans enables negotiating social interactions and managing important tasks of mating and childrearing; knowledge about plants and animals fosters food-gathering, avoiding predators, and maintaining health; knowledge about physical objects allows prediction of the effects of one's own and others' physical actions, the creation and use of tools, and so on. (Wellman & Gelman, 1998, p. 524)

One of the distinctive characteristics of these core theories is that they differ in the types of causal relations that operate. Consider how we would answer a single question, "Why did X move?," depending on whether we were talking about a pebble, a fish, or a person. With the pebble or any other inanimate object, we would explain the movement by citing physical contact with another moving object, as in "The pebble shot across the road because a truck ran over it." With a fish or other biological entity, we would usually explain movement with regard to the function it serves for the species, as in "Birds fly south to stay warm in winter." With a person, we would explain the movement in terms of the individual's goals, such as "The boy went to the store to buy a CD."

When do children first possess core theories? Spelke (1994) speculated that infants begin life with a primitive theory of inanimate objects, which she labeled a theory of physics. This theory includes the knowledge that the world is composed of physical objects that are cohesive, have boundaries, have substance, move only when touched by another object, and move in continuous ways through space and time. As one source of evidence, she cited Baillargeon's (1987, 1994) finding that 4-months-olds show surprise when a drawbridge appears to move through another solid object (Chapter 2). She also cited her own findings (Spelke et al., 1992) that 4-month-olds show surprise when objects seem to jump from one point to another without passing through intermediate positions or when seemingly independent objects start moving and stop moving in tandem.

Wellman and Gelman (1998) suggested that the first theory of psychology may emerge at around 18 months, and the first theory of biology at around 2 or 3 years. Even infants, however, have some sense of the differences among inanimate objects, people, and other living things. For example, infants as young as 5 to 8 weeks old imitate mouth movements (such as sticking out the tongue or opening the mouth wide) that are produced by another person; however, they do not imitate similar movements produced by inanimate objects, such as a tube with a "tongue" that can protrude, or a box with a "mouth" that can open on one side (Legerstee, 1991). Infants also show surprise if inanimate objects begin moving without any force being applied to them, but not if people do so (Spelke, Phillips, & Woodward, 1995).

At what point does such knowledge constitute a "theory"? We address this issue below in the section on children's biological concepts.

Evaluation.   The theory-oriented approach to conceptual development is bold and promising. Concepts are at their heart relational; causal relations are often especially critical. Children seem to focus on these causal relations from early in life. Knowing the causal relations helps children encode the most relevant information in a situation. The causal knowledge also helps them to draw inferences, to generalize, and to understand their experience.

The approach raises at least as many questions as it answers, however. One of its limitations is vague definition of what qualifies as a theory. A physicist's theory of matter differs profoundly from that of a typical adult, much less from that of an infant. Within scientific theories, internal consistency, parsimony, and formalization are important qualities. None of these qualities is shared by the concepts of infants and young children. Similar problems arise in trying to distinguish core theories from non-core ones.

This vagueness about what qualifies as a theory, and what qualifies as a core theory, has led to different researchers using the term *theory* in very different ways. Carey (1985) proposed that very young children possess only two theories: a theory of physics and a theory of psychology. She suggested that they eventually differentiate these two into roughly a dozen theories, corresponding to major disciplines taught at universities: physics, chemistry, biology, psychology, economics, and so on. In contrast, Keil (1989) argued that concepts in general are theoretical and that young children may have innumerable theories. Without clearer specification of when understanding counts as a theory, and when it counts as a "core" theory, such disagreements are inevitable.

Despite these difficulties, viewing concepts in terms of theory-based representations is a promising approach to conceptual development. Many issues remain to be resolved, but the approach's emphasis on the role of causal relations within conceptual understanding seems an especially important insight. The propensity to explain our experiences is a basic property of human beings; it plays a central role in many of the concepts we form, both large and small.

Summary.   What can we conclude about children's conceptual representations? From very young ages, children seem to be capable of representing concepts in all three ways that have been discussed: defining features, probabilistically related features, and informal theories. The prominence of these different types of representations within children's conceptual understanding may change, however. In particular, when children are just beginning to form a concept, probabilistic relations between features and the concept may play an especially large role. Early on for some concepts and later on for others, children form simple theories that involve causal relations, both among different aspects of the concept and between the concept and related ideas. Eventually, for concepts that fit the defining features model, children distinguish between those features that are definitional and those that are only characteristic.

Development of Some Particularly Important Concepts

Some concepts are so important, and so pervasive, that they merit special attention. These concepts develop among children in all cultures, and probably at all times in history. All have their origins early in development. All also develop in ways that reflect the influence of the surrounding culture. Among these especially important concepts are time, space, number, and certain fundamental biological concepts, such as living things.

TIME

The concept of time includes both experiential and logical aspects. *Experiential time* refers to our subjective experience of the order and duration of events. *Logical time* involves properties that can be deduced through reasoning. An event that starts later and ends earlier than another must have taken a shorter time.

Experiential time. Without a sense of the order in which events occur, the world would be an extremely difficult place to understand. It should not be surprising, therefore, that infants in their first year already notice such order. For example, when interesting photos are repeatedly shown in the order "photo on right; photo on right; photo on left," 3-month-olds detect the pattern and begin to look to the appropriate side even before the photo appears (Haith, Wentworth, & Canfield, 1993). They would not know where to look if they did not encode the order of events.

Similarly, children as young as 4 months of age discriminate between movies run forward and backward that show the effects of gravity on liquids and solid objects (Friedman, 2002; Friedman, Gardner, & Zubin, 1995). Since the events in the movies are identical except for the order in which they occur, the infants must be encoding that liquids and solids are typically higher at the earlier time and lower at the later time, rather than vice versa. Four-month-olds discriminate between movies run forward and backward that show liquid being poured into a glass (Friedman, 2002), and 8-month-olds (though not 4-month-olds) discriminate between movies run forward and backward that show a block being dropped and falling to the floor (Friedman et al., 1995).

Further evidence that infants understand order comes from studies in which infants view sets of actions and have the opportunity to imitate them. By the time infants are 12 months old, they are able to imitate sequences of two actions in the correct order (Bauer, 1995). Thus, understanding of temporal order seems well established in the first year of life.

There is also some evidence that infants are able to estimate the durations of events. Colombo and Richman (2002) exposed infants to a sequence in which a light was presented for two seconds, followed by a dark period of either three or five seconds. This pattern was repeated eight times, and on the ninth repetition the light was omitted. Infants showed a deceleration in their heart rate that was closely synchronized with the time when they expected the light to recur. Thus, it appears that infants can accurately estimate lengths of time a few seconds in duration.

Of course, it is not until much later that children can explicitly estimate the durations of events. By five years, children can estimate durations up to 30 seconds quite accurately, especially if given feedback about the true durations (Fraisse, 1982). Older children become increasingly adept at using counting to help them estimate the intervals. However, counting only produces accurate estimates if the units of time being counted are equal; counting quickly to 10 does not take the same amount of time as counting slowly to 10. Many 5- to 7-year-olds count with units of varying duration, which results in their inaccurately estimating the passage of time when they use counting strategies (Levin, 1989).

Still later developing is a sense of durations stretching over weeks or months. By age 4 years, children begin to gain such competence; they consistently judge an event that happened one week ago to have occurred more recently than one that happened seven weeks ago (Friedman, 1991). Children of this age also accurately judge whether their birthday or Christmas was more recent if one occurred in the recent past (the last 60 days) and the other did not (Friedman et al., 1995). However, not until age 9 do children judge accurately which event was more recent when both occurred more than 60 days earlier.

Understanding of durations that stretch into the future presents an even greater challenge for children. Four-year-olds are generally unable to distinguish the distances of events that will occur in the near future and events that will occur in the distant future. For example, 4-year-olds who were tested one week before Valentine's Day did not consistently judge that Valentine's Day would occur sooner than Christmas. The ability to distinguish the distances of future events emerges around age 5, and becomes more differentiated in the ensuing years (Friedman, 2000). Why might understanding of the past develop before understanding of the future? One probable reason is that the quality of children's memories may provide them with cues about the past (for example, more recent events are remembered more vividly). Such experiential cues are not available for reasoning about the future.

In the early elementary school years, children learn about conventional ways of representing time, such as weeks, months, and years, and these representations begin to play a role in their judgments of future events. Between 8 and 10 years, children begin to accurately judge the distances of future events, such as holidays, by relying on their mental representation of the year (Friedman, 2000).

Logical time. To measure logical understanding of time, Piaget (1969) presented children with two trains that ran in the same direction along parallel tracks; the question was which train traveled for the longer time. Although the two trains started and stopped at the same times, children below 6 or 7 years generally said that the train that stopped farther down the track traveled the longer time, as well as the longer distance and the faster speed. Piaget concluded that preoperational children lacked a logical understanding of time, speed, and distance.

Subsequent studies have replicated Piaget's observations but cast doubt on his interpretation. For example, when 5-year-olds observe cars moving in circular paths, rather than along straight lines, they have little difficulty deducing from the starting and ending times which car traveled for the greater total time (Levin, 1977). They also show understanding of these logical properties in comparing the sleeping times of two dolls that were said to fall asleep and wake up at the same or different times (Levin, 1982). In these cases, there were no strongly interfering cues, such as unequal stopping points, on which children could base incorrect judgments. It thus appears that 5-year-olds understand the logical relations among beginning, ending, and total time, but that their grasp is sufficiently fragile that interfering cues can lead to their not relying on it.

Young children are not the only ones who do not always use the logical understanding of time, speed, and distance that they possess. Older children and adults have the same problem. Think about this situation: When a race car travels around an oval track, do both its doors move at the same speed? Most adults believe that they do, but in fact they do not. The door toward the outside of the track is covering a greater distance in the same time, and therefore is moving faster.

The reason that the problem is so difficult is that it flies in the face of what Levin, Siegler, and Druyan (1990) labeled the *single-object/single-motion intuition.* This is the belief that all parts of a single object must move at the same speed. Young children, older children, and college students share this intuition. They all consistently say that all parts of a single object travel at the same speed.

Despite the single-object/single-motion intuition ordinarily persisting at least from third grade through college, it can be overcome through physical experiences that dramatically contradict it. Levin et al. presented sixth graders with a 6-foot-long rod, one end of which was attached to a pivot. The child and the experimenter both held the rod while walking around the pivot on four trials. On two of the trials, the child held the rod near the pivot, and the experimenter held it at the far end; on the other two trials, their positions were reversed. The difference in the speed at which children needed to walk while holding the inner and outer parts of the rod was sufficiently dramatic for them not only to learn that the outer part moved faster, but also to generalize the insight to other problems in which different parts of a single object moved at different speeds. The physical experience accomplished what years of informal experience and formal science instruction usually fail to do. As one boy said, "Before, I hadn't experienced it. I didn't think about it. Now that I have had that experience, I know that when I was on the outer circle, I had to walk faster to be at the same place as you" (Levin et al., 1990). Such physical experiences may help children understand concepts at a deeper level than classroom instruction usually does.

SPACE

From early in life, people, like other animals, encode not just *when* events occur but also *where* they occur. Under ideal circumstances, these encodings are very accurate from early in life. For example, as shown in Figure 8.3, when 1-year-olds see a Sesame Street toy buried in a long, thin, sandbox directly in front of them, and then wait while the experimenter smoothes the sand, they are very accurate in choosing where to dig for the toy (Huttenlocher, et al., 1994).

This basic ability to code space gets us started, but it does not overcome the many complex problems posed by the need to locate ourselves and objects in space. We can represent spatial locations and distances in at least three ways: in relation to our own position, in relation to landmarks, or in relation to an

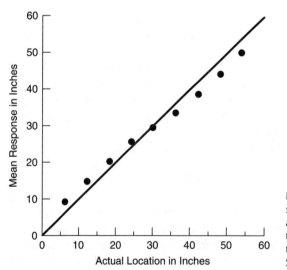

FIGURE 8.3 Mean location at which 1-year-olds searched, for objects that had been buried within a sandbox, graphed against the objects' true locations. Note how close the searches were to the true locations (after Huttenlocher, Newcombe, & Sandberg, 1994).

abstract framework (Huttenlocher & Newcombe, 1984). *Egocentric representations* involve locating objects in relation to ourselves. Thus, a target's position can be represented as "10 paces to my left." *Landmark-based representations* locate targets relative to other objects in the environment. Thus, we could represent a location by thinking, "I parked the car on the yellow level near the Section B sign." *Allocentric representations* locate targets relative to an abstract frame of reference, such as that provided by a map or coordinate system. The name allocentric reflects the fact that within such representations, any position can serve as the center or reference point for thinking about the surrounding space.

Egocentric representations. Piaget (1971) suggested that infants in their first year exhibit a kind of sensorimotor egocentrism. Recall from Chapter 2 that egocentrism refers to young children's tendency to view the world solely from their own perspective. Piaget claimed that in infancy, the egocentrism is quite literal, and that infants represent locations of objects only in relation to themselves. For example, they might continue to represent an object as being a right turn away from themselves even after they moved to the opposite side of the object, resulting in its now being on their left.

Piaget's hypothesis was supported by subsequent findings that 6- and 11-month-olds frequently fail to compensate for changes in their own spatial position relative to a toy (Acredolo, 1978). In these experiments, a child is placed in a T-shaped maze and repeatedly finds a toy by crawling straight and then turning in a particular direction (such as to the left) at the intersection. Then the child is moved to the other end of the T-shaped maze and turned back toward the middle, thus requiring a turn in the opposite direction (to the right) to find the toy. Most 6- to 11-month-olds continue to turn in the direction that previously led to the toy. Not until 16 months do children compensate for the change in their position.

However, this sensorimotor egocentrism is not absolute, even at such young ages. Infants' difficulty in adjusting to changes in spatial position can be mitigated if distinctive landmarks provide cues to the object's location (Rieser, 1979). Under such conditions, 6-month-olds usually turn in the appropriate direction, even when it differs from the direction that previously led to the toy.

How do infants learn to represent space in a way not tied to their own position within it? Just as experience with self-produced motion helps infants perceive depth well enough to avoid going over the visual cliff (Chapter 5, pp. 178–179), so it appears crucial for learning about space more generally (Campos et al., 2000). Eight-month-olds who crawl or who have had extensive experience in a walker succeed considerably more often in locating objects' spatial positions than infants of the same age who neither crawl well nor have experience with walkers (Bai & Bertenthal, 1992; Bertenthal et al., 1994). The longer children have been locomoting, the greater their advantage (Kermoian & Campos, 1988).

What is it about self-produced locomotion that leads to this ability to overcome the egocentric perspective? Bertenthal et al. (1994) suggested that when infants crawl, they must continuously update their representation of where
they are relative to the surrounding environment. Consistent with this view,
when 12-month-olds walk to the other side of a layout and have the opportunity to look at all times at the point where a prize is hidden, they both look at
it more then children who are carried and subsequently do better in turning toward the object from the new position (Acredolo, Adams, & Goodwyn, 1984).

Self-produced movement can enhance children's representation of space
even when the space they are representing is not the one through which they
are walking. This was learned in a clever experiment on the spatial imagery of
5-year-olds (Rieser et al., 1994). The children were students in the same kindergarten class, but were studied while they were at their homes. Some children
were asked to imagine being in their classroom, walking to the teacher's chair,
and turning around to face the class. Then they were asked to point to where various objects in the room would be from that vantage point. Few could do so accurately. However, when children from the same class were asked to imagine the
same actions while they actually walked and turned around in their own kitchen
or bedroom, their pointing was very accurate. The fact that the walking was in a
location far removed from the place they were imagining did not prevent the
walking from aiding their imagery. Similar findings were obtained with 4-year-
olds and 9-year-olds, and in a location other than the children's home (a research
laboratory). The findings indicate that self-produced movement activates people's
representation of space, even if they are not in the particular space being imagined. More generally, it suggests that the systems that produce motor activity and
spatial representations are closely linked (Rieser et al., 1994).

Landmarks. We often give directions in terms of landmarks, as in "You
go through the Fort Pitt Tunnel, turn off at the Banksville Road exit, and go
south until you hit MacFarlane Road." We do this because landmarks provide a
way of dividing the environment into manageable segments. In a sense, they
allow people to apply a divide-and-conquer strategy to solving the perennial
problem of how to get from here to there.

Representation of spatial locations in terms of landmarks begins in the first
year. As noted previously, 6-month-olds' representations of an object's position
survive a change in perspective if a distinctive landmark is near the object
(Rieser, 1979). People as well as objects can provide such landmarks; 9-month-
olds at times use their mothers' location as a landmark for locating interesting
objects near her (Presson & Ihrig, 1982).

The use of landmarks undergoes considerable refinement beyond this initial period (Huttenlocher & Newcombe, 1984; Newcombe, 1989). Before children's first birthday, only landmarks immediately adjacent to the target lead to
accurate location of targets. By about 2 years, landmarks that are more distant
from the target also help. By age 5, children can represent an object's position

relative to multiple landmarks, a much more powerful procedure for establishing exact locations. For example, they can represent an object as being midway between two other objects.

Although landmarks help young children locate objects in space, they can also distort their representations of the distances separating objects. Piaget, Inhelder, and Szeminska (1960) reported that preoperational stage children estimate the distance separating objects as smaller when a landmark (another object) is between them than when no such landmark is present. Subsequent studies have confirmed that most 4-year-olds, and about half of 5- and 6-year-olds, show this pattern (Fabricius & Wellman, 1993; Miller & Baillargeon, 1990). Their main difficulty, as Piaget suggested, is that they focus on only one of the segments and mistake the distance within it for the entire distance.

Allocentric representations.   Frequently, barriers or sheer distance prevent us from seeing our intended destination. Such situations demand integration of spatial information from multiple perspectives into a common abstract representation. Such representations are perhaps the most purely spatial of the three types. Egocentric and landmark-based representations can be easily reduced to a verbal form (as in, Wrigley Field is to my left; the restaurant is near DuPont Circle). In contrast, allocentric representations, which include all relations among the entities within the space, are very difficult to describe verbally.

Although intuition suggests that forming such allocentric representations is more challenging than relying on landmarks, 1-year-olds rely on allocentric representations in some situations in which they do not use landmarks. This was demonstrated in a study by Hermer and Spelke (1994), using a room like the one diagrammed in Figure 8.4. Participants were tested in a rectangular room, with a red barrier in front of each corner. They saw a toy hidden in one corner of the room, were blindfolded and turned around 10 times, and then needed to locate

FIGURE 8.4 Diagram of room used to study infants' searching in Hermer and Spelke (1994). The "X" marks the spot at which the object was hidden; the only difference between the conditions was that in the room diagrammed on the right, one wall adjoining the hiding location was blue, thus providing a landmark for locating the hidden object.

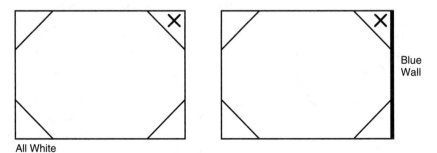

All White

the hidden object. Sometimes all four walls of the room were white; in this condition, participants needed to rely on allocentric representations, since no landmarks were present, and twirling blindfolded and stopping at an unknown point would have disrupted their initial egocentric orientation. Under these conditions, the best performance possible was to form a representation based on geometric properties of the space, equivalent to "the toy is in a corner with a long wall on the left and a short wall on the right." Use of such a representation would lead to equal numbers of searches at the two corners that fit the description (Figure 8.4). This is what both 1-year-olds and adults do.

In another condition, a landmark was established, either by putting a blue cloth on one of the walls next to where the object was hidden or by putting a teddy bear there. Adults used these landmarks to guide their search consistently to the corner where the object was hidden. In contrast, the 1-year-olds were oblivious to the landmark. As previously, they searched predominantly in one of the two corners with the long and short wall in the proper positions, but they searched equally often in the two corners that fit that description. The finding suggests that from early in development, children have a basic allocentric sense of space and use it to orient themselves, even in situations in which they cannot use landmarks to supplement it.

However, a follow-up study by a different team of researchers indicated that 1-year-olds can use landmarks to supplement geometric information. Learmonth, Newcombe, and Huttenlocher (2001) tested children in an all-white room with various types of landmarks (a bookcase, a door, and a colored wall). Contrary to Hermer and Spelke (1994, 1996), they found that the children could combine geometric information and landmark information. Children went to the correct corner both when it was marked by a landmark (such as the door) and when it was unmarked (opposite the door).

What caused children of the same age to rely on allocentric representations in one study, and landmark-based representations in the other? The key to this puzzle turns out to be the size of the rooms. The studies showing that children did not rely on landmarks were conducted in very small rooms (4 × 6 feet), whereas the studies showing that children combined geometric and landmark information were conducted in much larger rooms (8 × 12 feet). In a direct comparison of children's performance in rooms of different sizes, Learmonth, Nadel, and Newcombe (2002) found that, indeed, young children do not use landmarks in small rooms, but they do use them in larger rooms. One possible explanation for this finding is that rooms of different sizes demand different sorts of spatial thinking because they allow for different sets of possible actions. Unlike the smaller room, the larger room allowed plenty of space to move about, so it may have been more likely to engage thinking in service of locomotion.

More generally, this set of studies highlights that the type of spatial thinking people engage in depends crucially on the nature of the task and on features of the environment. Understanding how knowledge about space develops will require further research about how children at various points in development weigh different potential sources of spatial information in different settings (Newcombe & Huttenlocher, 2000).

How is spatial knowledge acquired?   One obvious source of spatial information is action within the environment. Developmental changes in infants' capabilities for action, such as the onset of crawling, allow them to obtain new information about the environment, and this information informs their spatial representations. As noted above, self-produced locomotion seems especially important in enabling children to override egocentric representations of space.

Other forms of perceptual experience also play a crucial role in refining spatial representations, as studies of visually impaired people have shown (Rieser, Hill, Talor, Bradfield, & Rosen, 1992). Rieser et al. contrasted the spatial representations of adults who developed severe visual impairments either early in life (almost always before birth) or later in life (usually after age 10). The task was to imagine standing at a particular landmark facing in a particular direction in a familiar part of one's neighborhood and to point toward where other imagined landmarks would be. Those whose visual impairments began early in life and whose peripheral vision was impaired represented the spatial layout much less accurately than those whose impairments started later or whose peripheral vision was intact. The finding suggested that early perceptual learning is critical for the development of accurate spatial representations.

The centrality of spatial knowledge within one's culture also influences the degree to which children develop spatial skills. Evidence for this came from a unique study of aborigines living in the western desert of Australia (Kearins, 1981). These aborigines have followed a nomadic hunting and gathering lifestyle for thousands of years. Their children do not attend formal schools. On most tests of cognitive functioning, the children do far less well than children of the same ages in Europe and North America.

Kearins reasoned, though, that a different picture might emerge if the focus was on types of thinking that were important in the aboriginal culture. Spatial thinking fit this criterion. Much of aboriginal life is spent trekking between widely spaced wells and creeks. Whether a particular location has water depends on capricious rainfall patterns. Few obvious landmarks exist in the stony desert to indicate the wells' and creeks' locations; thus, high-quality spatial thinking is important for survival.

This reasoning led Kearins to contrast the spatial memory of aboriginal children raised in the desert with those of Australian children raised in the city. An experimenter presented 20 objects arranged in a 5 × 4 rectangle. After 30 seconds, she picked up the objects and then asked children to rearrange them as they were before.

The aboriginal children's memory for the spatial locations proved superior. They also differed from the urban children in their strategies for remembering. The aboriginal children studied in silence. When subsequently asked how they remembered where objects had been, they often said they remembered "the look of it." In contrast, the city-dwelling children used verbal rehearsal; they could be heard whispering and saying aloud the names of the objects while they studied them. The urban children's strategy is effective for remembering verbal material of the types needed to do well in school, but the aboriginal children's strategy is more useful for remembering spatial information. Thus, each group relied on strategies that were useful for the tasks of greatest importance in their everyday lives.

NUMBER

Understanding of numbers involves two basic types of knowledge: understanding of cardinality and understanding of ordinality. *Cardinality* refers to absolute numerical size. A common property of people's arms, legs, eyes, and feet is that there are two of them. The cardinal property of "two-ness" is what these sets share. *Ordinality* refers to relational properties of numbers. That someone is the third-tallest girl in the class and that five is the fifth number of the counting string are ordinal properties.

Understanding of cardinal properties. Understanding of cardinality begins early in infancy. In their first half year, infants can discriminate one object from two and two objects from three (Antell & Keating, 1983; Starkey, Spelke & Gelman, 1990; van Loosbroek & Smitsman, 1990). This was learned through the use of the habituation paradigm. Infants were shown a sequence of pictures, each of which contained a small set of objects, such as three circles. The sets differed from trial to trial in size of the objects, brightness, distance apart, and other properties, but they always had the same number of objects. Once the infants habituated to displays with this number of objects, they were shown a set that was comparable in other ways to the displays they had seen but that had a different number of objects. Infants increased their looking time to the set with the novel numerosity, suggesting that they had abstracted the number of objects in the previous sets.

But do these findings indicate a true understanding of number, or might they be due to some other variable that is confounded with number, such as the length of the contour of the objects, or the visible surface area of the objects? In studies designed to tease apart these factors, it appears that infants do indeed respond based on contour length (Clearfield & Mix, 1999) or visible surface area (Feigenson, Carey, & Spelke, 2002), rather than on number per se. However, several other studies with strict control conditions have shown that infants can discriminate quantities based on number alone (Wynn, Bloom, & Chiang, 2002; Xu & Spelke, 2000). Furthermore, infants' ability to discriminate among small quantities extends to sequences of events as well as static arrays of objects (Canfield & Smith, 1996; Starkey et al., 1990). For example, when 6-month-olds see a puppet repeatedly jump twice until they grow bored, and then see the puppet jump three times or one time, they show renewed interest, indicating that they discriminated among the number of jumps (Wynn, 1995). Thus, it appears that infants are capable of discriminating quantities based on number, as well as on continuous dimensions such as surface area and contour length. However, when continuous dimensions as well as number vary, infants often rely on the continuous dimensions.

Most studies of infants' discrimination of number have utilized numbers smaller than three. Infants are not able to discriminate among sets of objects with larger numerosities, unless the sets differ by a large ratio (such as 8 versus 16; Xu & Spelke, 2000). Not until 3 or 4 years of age are children able to discriminate four objects from 5 or 6 (Starkey & Cooper, 1980; Strauss & Curtis, 1984). These findings suggest that infants identify small cardinalities through *subitizing*, a quick and effortless perceptual process that people can apply only to sets of one to three or four objects. When we see a row of between one and four objects, we feel like we immediately know how many there are; in contrast, with larger numbers of objects, we rarely know the exact number. Adults and 5-year-olds are similar to infants in being able to very rapidly identify the cardinal value of one to three or four objects, but not larger sets, through subitizing (Chi & Klahr, 1975).

Infants' nascent understandings of cardinality also make it possible for them to recognize the consequences of adding and subtracting small numbers of objects. Wynn (1992a) found evidence for this ability in 5-month-olds. As seen in Figure 8.5, infants saw a toy mouse on a stage, then saw a screen come up in front of them, then saw a hand place another toy mouse behind the screen, and then saw the screen drop. Sometimes the result was what would be expected by adding the one new object to the one that was already behind the screen; other times (through trickery) it was not. The infants looked for a longer time at unexpected outcomes (either one mouse or three mice) than at the expected outcome (two mice), suggesting that they expected that $1 + 1 = 2$. Other infants saw a subtraction event, in which two mice were placed on stage and hidden by the screen, and then one mouse was removed from behind the screen. Again, infants looked longer at the unexpected outcome (two mice) than at the expected one (one mouse), suggesting that they expected that $2 - 1 = 1$.

Based on these findings, Wynn (1992a) has argued that "infants are able to calculate the precise results of simple arithmetical operations" (p. 750). Can infants really perform arithmetic? Wynn's basic finding has been replicated several times (Simon, Hespos, & Rochat, 1995; Uller, Huntley-Fenner, Carey, & Klatt, 1999); however, some attempts to replicate it have not succeeded (Wakeley, Rivera, & Langer, 2000), suggesting that infants' calculation abilities are not very robust. Another caveat is that, as for cardinality, infants demonstrate understanding only when the "problems" involve very small numbers (three or fewer). Children do not understand the consequences of adding even slightly larger numbers, such as $2 + 2$, until they are 4 or 5 *years* old (Huttenlocher, Jordan, & Levine, 1994; Starkey, 1992).

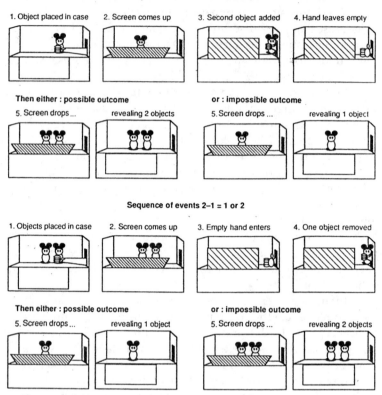

Sequence of events 1+1 = 1 or 2

1. Object placed in case   2. Screen comes up   3. Second object added   4. Hand leaves empty

Then either : possible outcome   or : impossible outcome

5. Screen drops...   revealing 2 objects   5. Screen drops ...   revealing 1 object

Sequence of events 2–1 = 1 or 2

1. Objects placed in case   2. Screen comes up   3. Empty hand enters   4. One object removed

Then either : possible outcome   or : impossible outcome

5. Screen drops...   revealing 1 object   5. Screen drops ...   revealing 2 objects

FIGURE 8.5 *Sequence of events used by Wynn (1992a) to test infants' under-standing of addition and subtraction. Copyright 1992 by Nature Publishing Group. Reprinted with permission.*

Why might infants demonstrate arithmetic competence only with small numbers? As noted above, one possible explanation is that infants determine the number of objects by subitizing (Haith & Benson, 1998). This process is effective with very small sets, but not for sets of four or more objects. The case illustrates an important general lesson. Understanding children's thinking requires understanding the processes they are using to solve the problems. The findings with infants might lead to the conclusion that infants "understand" addition. This is true in a sense, but it leaves totally unclear why they can apply it only to sets of one to three objects. The idea that infants solve the small number problems with a process that cannot be applied to larger sets, and that the process that can be applied to larger sets (counting) develops considerably later, makes understandable both their competence and their incompetence.

Counting. At 3 or 4 years of age, children become proficient in another means of establishing the cardinal value of a set—counting. This allows them to assign numbers to larger sets than can be subitized. Gelman and Gallistel (1978) noted the rapidity with which children learn to count and hypothesized that the rapid learning was possible because it was guided by knowledge of *counting principles.* In particular, they hypothesized that young children know:

1. The *one-one principle:* Assign one and only one number word to each object.
2. The *stable order principle:* Always assign the numbers in the same order.
3. The *cardinal principle:* The last count indicates the number of objects in the set.
4. The *order irrelevance principle:* The order in which objects are counted is irrelevant.
5. The *abstraction principle:* The other principles apply to any set of objects.

Several types of evidence indicate that children understand all of these principles by age 5, and some of them by age 3 (Gelman & Gallistel, 1978). Even when children err in their counting, they show knowledge of the one-one principle, since they assign exactly one number word to most of the objects. For instance, they might count all but one object once, either skipping or counting twice the single miscounted object. These errors seem to be ones of execution rather than of misguided intent. Children demonstrate knowledge of the stable order principle by almost always saying the number words in a constant order. Usually this is the conventional order, but occasionally it is an idiosyncratic order such as "1, 3, 6" that a particular child uses consistently. The important phenomenon is that even when children use an idiosyncratic order, they use the same idiosyncratic order on each count. Preschoolers demonstrate knowledge of the cardinal principle by saying the last number with special emphasis and by responding with that number when asked how many objects there are in a set that they have counted. They show understanding of the abstraction principle by not hesitating to count sets that include different types of objects. Finally, the order irrelevance principle seems to be the most difficult, but even here, 5-year-olds demonstrate understanding. Many of them recognize that counting can start in the middle of a row of objects, as long as each object is eventually counted. Although few children can state the principles, their counting performance suggests that they know them.

Gelman and Gallistel (1978) argued that one reason the principles are important is that understanding of them guides children's acquisition of counting skill. This argument rests on the assumption that children understand the principles before they count accurately. However, a variety of subsequent findings have indicated that children actually count skillfully *before* they understand the principles that underlie counting (Bermejo, 1996; Briars & Siegler, 1984; Frye, Braisby, Lowe, Maroudas, & Nicholls, 1989; Wynn, 1992b). Experience with counting may provide a database from which children can distinguish essential features of the usual counting procedure (such as counting each object once and only once) from incidental ones (such as starting at the leftmost or rightmost end of a row).

Ordinal properties of numbers. Ordinality refers to the relative positions or magnitudes of numbers. A number may be first or second in an order, or it may be greater or less than another number. Mastery of ordinal properties of numbers, like mastery of cardinal properties, begins in infancy. However, it seems to begin later, at around 10 months.

The most basic ordinal concepts are *more* and *less.* To test whether infants understand these concepts as they apply to numbers, Feigenson, Carey, and Hauser (2002) had 10- and 12-month-olds watch an experimenter place different numbers of crackers sequentially into two different containers. The infants were then allowed to crawl to get the crackers from the container of their choice. In comparisons of one versus two and two versus three crackers, both 10- and 12-month-olds consistently chose the container with the greater number of crackers. However, both groups of infants chose randomly in comparisons that involved numbers greater than three, such as three versus four and two versus four. Thus, as for cardinality, infants' knowledge of ordinality appears to be limited to very small numbers.

However, one recent study suggested that infants may understand ordinal relations that involve fairly large values, if the ratio between the values is high. Brannon (2002) used a habituation paradigm to examine infants' ability to discriminate between increasing and decreasing sequences. In order to make this discrimination, infants must recognize that one sequence changes so that each successive set has *more* than the previous set, and the other sequence changes so that each successive set has *less.* Infants were habituated to either increasing sequences (such as 2, 4, 8 and 4, 8, 16) or decreasing sequences (such as 8, 4, 2 and 16, 8, 4) until they lost interest. In both types of sets, the ratio between adjacent numerosities was always 1:2. Infants were then tested with a novel sequence that was either the same direction or the opposite direction as the sequences to which they had been habituated (for infants in the increasing group, either 3, 6, 12 or 12, 6, 3). Eleven-month-old infants, but not 9-month olds, showed renewed interest in the test set with the novel direction, indicating that they distinguished the increasing from the decreasing sequence.

As for cardinality, extending these early understandings of ordinality to larger sets and to values that are close together takes a substantial amount of time. By age 2, children perform better than chance at making ordinal judgments with pairs of values up to six, even on difficult pairs such as 4 versus 5 and 4 versus 6 (Brannon & Van de Walle, 2001). However, children do not display full-fledged competence with larger numbers until several years later.

The task most often used to examine understanding of ordinality in early childhood involves asking questions such as "Which is more, 6 oranges or 4 oranges?" Not until age 4 or 5 can children solve such problems consistently correctly for the numbers from one to nine (Siegler & Robinson, 1982). Their difficulty in determining the larger number is greatest with numbers that are relatively large and close together (such as 7 versus 8). Counting skills may be important in the development of this ordinal knowledge; the number that occurs later in the counting string is always the larger number, and it is easier to remember which number comes later when the numbers are farther apart.

In sum, it appears that infants have a rudimentary understanding of ordinality by the end of their first year. However, this understanding is fragile, and it is displayed only with small numbers, or in situations in which the ratio between values is large. An important task for future research in this area is to map out the developmental course of this knowledge, and to investigate how it relates to later understanding of ordinality that relies on knowledge of counting.

BIOLOGICAL CONCEPTS

Like time, space, and number, biology has been considered a "foundational" domain in human cognition, because knowledge about biological phenomena is important for basic survival, as well as for getting along in everyday life (Wellman & Gelman, 1998). From this perspective, it is not surprising that human children seem to be fascinated with living things.

Biological knowledge involves several interrelated concepts. These include fundamental biological categories, such as living things, animals, and plants, and basic biological processes, such as growth, inheritance, and illness. Research on children's biological understanding has focused on when children demonstrate understanding of biological categories and processes, on how children acquire such knowledge, and on the extent to which children's knowledge about biology forms a coherent "theory" of the domain of biology.

Biological categories. When do children begin to distinguish between biological entities and other sorts of entities? The most basic biological distinction, and the earliest acquired, is the distinction between animate and inanimate objects (Gelman & Opfer, 2002; Rakison & Poulin-Dubois, 2001). Even before their first birthday, infants categorize birds as different from airplanes and animals as different from vehicles (Mandler & McDonough, 1993, 1998a). They also recognize that animals differ from other types of objects in being able to drink and to sleep (Mandler & McDonough, 1996, 1998b).

On what basis do infants begin to discriminate animate and inanimate objects? One possibility is the presence of certain features, such as having a face. As described in Chapter 5, faces are particularly compelling for human infants (Dannemiller & Stephens, 1988; M. H. Johnson & Morton, 1991). Within the face, the eyes may be especially important (S. C. Johnson, Slaughter, & Carey, 1998). An early bias to attend to eyes or faces could provide a basis for distinguishing animate from inanimate objects.

Another source of information that infants may use to discriminate animate and inanimate objects is motion. Early in their first year, infants discriminate between biological and nonbiological motion (e.g., Bertenthal, 1993), and they begin to associate different types of motion with animate and inanimate objects. For example, by 9 months, infants seem to expect that humans are capable of self-initiated motion, but inanimate objects are not. They demonstrate increased negative affect when they see a robot move independently (via a remote-controlled device), but not when they see a human being do so (Poulin-Dubois, Lepage, & Ferland, 1996). Infants also seem to expect goal-directed movement from humans but not from inanimate objects. By 6 months, infants display different patterns of looking to events that involve a human arm reaching out to touch an object and events that involve a mechanical "arm" reaching out to touch the object (Woodward, 1998).

The distinction between *living* and *nonliving* things is much more difficult for children than the distinction between animate and inanimate objects, and it is acquired much later. Even elementary school children often make errors when asked which things are alive (Carey, 1985; Richards & Siegler, 1984). One especially difficult category for children is that of plants. Between the ages of 3 and 5, children demonstrate knowledge that, like animals, plants take in food and water (Inagaki & Hatano, 1996), grow (Hatano et al., 1993; Hickling & Gelman, 1995), heal after injuries (Backscheider, Shatz, & Gelman, 1993), and die (Nguyen & Gelman, 2002). Further, children recognize that, like animals, plants die due to illness or old age (Nguyen & Gelman, 2002), they decompose after death (Springer, Ngyuen, & Samaniego, 1996), and they cannot return to life after they die (Nguyen & Gelman, 2002). However, for several years beyond preschool, children remain unsure whether plants should be grouped with animals as living things (Hatano et al., 1993; Richards & Siegler, 1984). Not until late elementary school do most children possess an integrated concept of living things that includes both animals and plants.

Biological processes.   To be a uniquely *biological* process, a process must be viewed as depending not on psychological mechanisms (such as desire) or physical mechanisms (such as physical force), but on specifically biological mechanisms. For many uniquely biological processes, this understanding emerges in the early preschool years.

One of the most fundamental biological processes is self-generated *movement*. The work reviewed above indicates that children have a rudimentary understanding of biological motion in infancy. By the preschool years, children's knowledge about biological and nonbiological movement is well differentiated. Preschoolers make accurate predictions about what types of objects are capable of movement (Massey & Gelman, 1988), and they offer different sorts of explanations for biological and nonbiological movement. For example, preschoolers report that a hopping chinchilla moves "by itself," whereas a hopping wind-up toy moves because of human intervention (Gelman & Gottfried, 1996). Thus, children recognize that biological mechanisms that produce movement are distinct from physical ones.

Preschoolers also understand *growth* as a fundamental biological process. By age 3 or 4, children know that only living things grow; inanimate objects such as toys and furniture do not (Carey, 1985; Rosengren, Gelman, Kalish, & McCormick, 1991). Preschoolers also understand that biological growth is essentially unidirectional, with organisms growing from smaller to bigger but not the reverse. Similarly, they know that growth proceeds from simpler to more complex forms (from caterpillar to butterfly, or tadpole to frog) rather than the reverse (Rosengren et al. 1991). Preschoolers also realize that people cannot prevent a baby animal from growing, even if they "want to keep it forever in the same size because it's so small and cute" (Inagaki & Hatano, 1987). Thus, they recognize that growth depends on biological mechanisms and not on psychological processes such as desire.

Inheritance is another fundamental biological process for which understanding emerges in the preschool years. Of course, preschool children do not have knowledge about genetic transmission or DNA, but nevertheless they display a rudimentary understanding of inheritance. They know that baby animals grow into beings that resemble adults of their species, even if they do not look like them at birth, whereas the same will not happen with dolls or other inanimate objects (Gelman & Wellman, 1991). Children also realize that a baby animal will grow up to become an adult of its own kind, even if it is raised by parents of another species (Johnson & Solomon, 1996). Likewise, if an animal is raised in an environment that is more appropriate to another type of animal, children understand that the animal will still have characteristics appropriate to its own kind. For example, a cow raised among pigs will moo (not oink) and have a straight tail (not a curly one). Children also apply this understanding to seeds planted in a setting more appropriate for another type of plant, such as an apple seed planted in a pot of flowers (Gelman & Wellman, 1991; Peterson & Siegal, 1997).

Children's early conception of inheritance appears to involve specifically biological mechanisms. Springer and Keil (1991) asked children to rank-order a number of different possible mechanisms for how a flower, a dog, and a metal can acquired their colors. For the flower and the dog, children preferred natural mechanisms, including both natural internal mechanisms (such as "the baby flower turned pink because its mom gave it something while it was growing inside the seed that made it pink") and natural external mechanisms (such as "the sun and rain fell on it while it was growing inside the seed and made it pink"). In contrast, for the can, children preferred a mechanical explanation that involved a human agent (such as "the worker who made the can did something that made it turn green").

However, despite this evidence for early understanding, preschoolers' conception of inheritance remains limited for several years. For example, preschoolers believe that mothers' desires may play a role in their children's inheritance of physical traits (Weissman & Kalish, 1999). Thus, it appears that preschoolers believe that there are psychological as well as biological mechanisms that underlie inheritance. It is not until about age 7 that children understand the importance of biological parenthood and birth in accounting for physical resemblance between parents and offspring (Solomon, Johnson, Zaitchik, & Carey, 1996).

Preschool children also understand *illness* as a fundamental biological process. Four- and 5-year-olds realize that illness can be caused by an invisible mechanism, namely, the action of germs (Kalish, 1996). Based on knowledge of germs, preschoolers predict that risky actions, such as eating food from the garbage, will not cause illness if germs are not present, and innocuous actions, such as eating food that had fallen in water, will cause illness if germs are present. Furthermore, preschoolers distinguish the causes of illness from the causes of psychological reactions, such as sadness (Kalish, 1997). They realize that physical contact with a contaminant will lead to illness, even if the affected individual has no knowledge of the contaminant. However, emotional reactions to a contaminant (such as beliefs that something is disgusting or "yucky") depend on knowledge of the contaminant. Thus, they differentiate a biological reaction to a contaminant (illness) from an emotional reaction to the same contaminant (disgust).

Despite their early understanding of the mechanisms that cause illness, preschoolers' knowledge about illness remains limited. Most preschoolers do not understand that illness takes time to develop; instead, they tend to predict an instantaneous response to contamination (Kalish, 1997). Further, they tend to view the outcomes of causes of illness in an all-or-none fashion (Kalish, 1998b). For example, if all of the children in a particular classroom played with a sick child, preschoolers tend to predict that either all or none of the children would get sick. Thus, children fail to recognize that causes of illness operate in a probabilistic fashion.

In sum, although their knowledge is limited in important ways, preschool children do understand basic aspects of several fundamental biological processes, including movement, growth, inheritance, and illness. Furthermore, in most cases, preschoolers distinguish biological mechanisms from psychological and physical ones. Thus, by preschool, children have knowledge about causal mechanisms that are uniquely biological.

How do children acquire knowledge of biology?   From a developmental perspective, it is important to understand not only the nature of children's biological knowledge, but also how such knowledge is acquired. A number of alternative accounts of how children acquire biological concepts have been proposed. Some researchers have claimed that humans have innately specified brain structures or processes that foster their learning of biological concepts. For example, Atran (1994) has argued that humans are born with a "biology module," which developed over evolutionary time, that fosters early and rapid learning about living things. One key source of evidence for this view is cross-cultural similarities in the nature and content of children's biological knowledge (Lopez, Atran, Coley, Medin, & Smith, 1997).

Other researchers have focused on the roles of experience and environmental input in children's acquisition of biological knowledge (e.g., Callanan, 1990; Springer, 1995, 1999). For example, Inagaki (1990) found that 5-year-old children who had raised goldfish as pets at home were better able than children who had not raised goldfish to make predictions about the behavior of an unfamiliar animal (a frog). Thus, the experience of caring for a pet helped children to acquire biological knowledge that they could generalize to another species. Children also acquire biological knowledge in everyday interactions with parents and other caregivers. Gelman and colleagues (Gelman, Coley, Rosengren, Hartman, & Pappas, 1998) observed mothers as they read picture books about animals with their 1- and 2-year-old children. They found that mothers' statements and gestures often emphasized the taxonomic relations among different types of animals and sometimes described or pointed out characteristics of different categories of animals or of animals in general. Such implicit teaching may contribute to children's developing biological knowledge.

Explicit teaching also contributes to the development of children's biological knowledge. Solomon and Johnson (2000) investigated the role of explicit instruction in 5- and 6-year-olds' understanding of biological inheritance. They taught children a key fact ("babies come from their mothers' bellies) and they also provided them with some rudimentary information about genes ("tiny things called genes inside of us make us what we are," "rabbits with brown fur have brown fur genes and rabbits with white fur have white fur genes"). Children who received instruction not only learned the taught concepts, but they also reorganized their knowledge about inheritance to highlight the importance of birth in mediating physical resemblance, but not similarities in beliefs, between parents and offspring. Thus, instruction provoked substantial change in children's conceptions of inheritance.

Of course, both nature and nurture play important roles in children's acquisition of biological concepts. Young children all over the world are fascinated with animals and plants, and they are highly motivated to learn about them. The social and cultural context in which children develop provides them with many opportunities for learning about living things. In some cultures, at least part of this learning takes place within formal instruction. However, children also learn about biology through their own direct experiences of nature, through interacting with pets, farm animals, and houseplants, and through conversations, stories, and television programs.

Does children's knowledge form a coherent "theory" of biology? Based on the compelling evidence for knowledge of biological categories and processes in preschool, some researchers have argued that children possess a naïve "theory" of biology even before they receive formal schooling (Hatano & Inagaki, 1994; Inagaki & Hatano, 2002; Keil, 1992). What characteristics must children's knowledge have in order to be considered a "theory"?

Wellman and Gelman (1992, 1998) proposed four criteria that characterize theoretical understandings: fundamental categories unique to the domain, causal explanations unique to the domain, unobservable explanatory constructs, and coherent organization. As described above, from a very early age, children's biological knowledge incorporates knowledge about fundamental categories such as animate objects, living things, animals, and plants. By preschool, children understand that the actions of biological entities reflect causal processes that are unique to the domain of biology, such as growth, inheritance, and illness. They also understand that some of these processes are mediated by unobservable explanatory constructs that are unique to the domain of biology, such as germs. Finally, learning new information sometimes leads children to reorganize their biological knowledge; thus, it appears that this knowledge has a coherent structure. Taken together, these findings suggest that preschoolers' understanding of biology constitutes a true theory, at least according to these criteria.

Summary

Conceptual development can be approached either by considering conceptual representations in general or by focusing on particular concepts of special importance. Conceptual representations in general can assume at least three forms. Defining-features representations depict concepts in terms of a few necessary and sufficient features. Probabilistic representations include many features that are associated with the concept to varying degrees, but no feature that is necessary and sufficient for category membership. Theory-based representations focus on causal relations among different aspects of conceptual understanding.

A number of prominent developmental theorists, including Piaget, Vygotsky, Werner, and Bruner, have formulated versions of the representational development hypothesis. According to this hypothesis, young children cannot form representations based on defining features. However, even 1-year-olds have proved capable of relying on such features with familiar concepts. Young children do appear to rely on defining-features representations less often than do older individuals, but they clearly can form them.

Both children's and adults' representations often emphasize probabilistic relations rather than defining features. Beginning in infancy, children abstract prototypical forms, detect cue validities, note correlations among features, and generate basic-level categories. Within a relatively short time, children also begin to form subordinate and superordinate concepts, move from child-basic to standard-basic concepts, and abstract increasingly complex correlational patterns.

Theory-based representations emphasize the role of causal and hierarchical relations. Many of children's concepts seem to have theoretical aspects that facilitate inferences, explanations, and generalizations, and that help children overcome the influence of superficial perceptual similarity. There may also be certain core theories, such as theories of biology and of the mind, that have different qualities than concepts in general; the ways in which such theories differ from others, however, are not yet clear. Some concepts have theoretical aspects from early in life, but the depth and scope of theory-based concepts clearly increase greatly with development.

Another perspective on conceptual development is provided by focusing on the particulars of the development of concepts of special importance. Among these central concepts are time, space, number, and living things. These concepts are worthy of unusual attention because they are used to represent a vast range of experiences, because they are present in some form from infancy to old age in all of the world's cultures, and because understanding the world would be impossible without them.

Time has both experiential and logical aspects. Infants as young as 3 months encode the order in which events occur, thus showing a sense of experiential time. By age 5 years, they also can estimate reasonably well the durations of relatively brief events. By the same age, children have some knowledge of the logical relations among beginning, ending, and total time, though their grasp is tenuous and can easily be disrupted by misleading cues.

Locations and distances within space can be represented in terms of relations to oneself, in terms of relations to landmarks, or in terms of an abstract system. Egocentric representations lead infants younger than 1 year to continue turning in the direction that previously led to a goal, even when their position relative to the goal changes. Self-produced locomotion, in particular crawling and walking, appears critical to infants overcoming the tendency to represent space egocentrically. Landmarks close to objects help infants locate objects in space even during their first year. Similarly, even in the first year, infants can form allocentric representations, in which they represent space in terms of the entire spatial layout. Early experience correlating the flow of visual information with one's own movements may be critical for forming such allocentric representations of space.

Understanding of numbers involves understanding both cardinal and ordinal concepts. Children understand certain cardinal and ordinal properties of numbers in infancy. This is evident in their habituating to sets with a given number of objects and in their ability to choose the set with the larger number of objects. By the end of the preschool period, children supplement their early understanding of cardinality with understanding of counting and number conservation. They also supplement their understanding of ordinality with knowledge of numerical magnitudes.

Children's biological knowledge involves both fundamental biological categories, such as plants, animals, and living things, and uniquely biological processes, such as growth, inheritance, and illness. The earliest acquired biological distinction is that between animate and inanimate objects. Over time, children's knowledge about biological categories becomes richer and more differentiated, with understanding of plants as living things being a relatively late achievement. For many uniquely biological processes, understanding emerges in the early preschool years. However, preschoolers' knowledge of biological processes is relatively limited, and it continues to be enriched throughout childhood. Nevertheless, preschoolers' knowledge of biology has several hallmarks of theoretical understanding, including fundamental categories unique to the domain, causal explanations unique to the domain, unobservable explanatory constructs, and coherent organization. Thus, children appear to have a theory of biology starting in the preschool years.

Recommended Readings

Inagaki, K., & Hatano, G. (2002). *Young children's naïve thinking about the biological world*. New York: Psychology Press. A comprehensive review of children's understanding of biological concepts. The authors make the case that children's knowledge about biology constitutes a naïve theory well before the onset of formal schooling.

Kearins, J.M. (1981). Visual-spatial memory in Australian aboriginal children of desert regions. *Cognitive Psychology, 13,* 434–460. An unusual study documenting the superior spatial skills that Australian aboriginal children develop in the course of their long treks through the desert.

Newcombe, N.S. & Huttenlocher, J. (2000). *Making space: The development of spatial representation and reasoning*. Cambridge, MA: MIT Press. An integrative account of the development of spatial thinking and reasoning, with a focus on the importance of inter-actions between biological preparedness and experience in the physical world.

Rieser, J.J., Garing, A.E., & Young, M.F. (1994). Imagery, action, and young children's spatial orientation: It's not being there that counts, it's what one has in mind. *Child Development, 65,* 1262–1278. Action, perception, and imagery are linked in complex and surprising ways. This study demonstrates that walking through one space improves children's representations of other spaces, if children are thinking about those other spaces while they are walking.

Wellman, H.M., & Gelman, S.A. (1998). Knowledge acquisition in foundational domains. In D. Kuhn & R.S. Siegler (Eds.), *Handbook of child psychology: Vol. 2. Cognition, perception, and language* (5th ed.). New York: Wiley. This chapter argues articulately for the existence of "love domains" in which children possess theory-based knowledge.

9

The Development of
Social Cognition

JEREMY (AGE THREE): *Mommy, go out of the kitchen.*
　　MOTHER: *Why, Jeremy?*
　　JEREMY: *Because I want to take a cookie.* (from Peskin, 1992)

The child in the vignette above wanted to deceive his mother but was not quite able to pull it off. He seemed not to realize that *telling* his mother about his planned misbehavior would probably have the same outcome as her *seeing* it. Conversations such as this one reveal that young children's understanding of other people is profoundly different from that of adults. This chapter focuses on children's cognition about the social world—their understanding of themselves and other people, of how the human mind works, and of social rules and social categories.

Children develop in a world filled with other people. As emphasized by sociocultural theories (Chapter 4), social relationships have a profound effect on what children do, on what they think about, and on how they think. Furthermore, social relationships are essential for healthy development and for optimal functioning throughout life. Given these facts, the importance of understanding children's thinking about other people and about the social world seems clear.

From an evolutionary perspective, there is obvious survival value in understanding human behavior and social relationships. Individuals who are better able to negotiate social relationships are likely to survive longer and reproduce more. This line of thinking implies that certain aspects of social cognition may have a biological basis that was laid down through natural selection over evolutionary time. If this is the case, it seems likely that even young infants should display some rudiments of social cognition. However, it is also readily apparent that experiences with other people provide children with many opportunities for learning about the social world.

One of Jean Piaget's deep insights about development as a general process provides a particularly useful way of thinking about the development of social cognition. Piaget (1952) suggested that during infancy, reality exists primarily at the interface of the child's actions and the external environment. From this starting point, development proceeds both inward, allowing children to gain a better understanding of themselves, and outward, allowing them to gain a better understanding of the broader world.

In addition to being a useful way of thinking about the development of social cognition, Piaget's insight provides the basis for our organization of this chapter. The first section focuses on foundations of social understanding, including initial understanding of other people and oneself. The second section examines how children extend this initial social understanding inward, to grasp the nature of their own and other people's mental lives, including the roles of intentions, desires, and beliefs in producing behavior. The third and final section describes how children extend their early understanding outward to the broader social world, thus learning about socially defined rules of appropriate behavior and about social categories such as those based on gender, race, and ethnicity. The chapter's organization is outlined in Table 9.1.

TABLE 9.1   *Chapter Outline*

I.   Foundations of Social Cognition
    A.   Understanding of Others
    B.   Understanding of the Self

II.   Knowledge about Mental States and Activities
    A.   Understanding of Intention
    B.   Understanding of Desires
    C.   Understanding of Beliefs
    D.   Understanding of Thinking
    E.   Understanding of Knowing
    F.   Understanding of Pretending
    G.   Understanding of Fantasy
    H.   Sources of Development of Understanding of Mind

III.   Understanding of the Social World
    A.   Understanding of Social Rules
    B.   Understanding Social Categories and Groups

IV.   Summary

Foundations of Social Cognition

To learn about the social world, infants and children need to pay attention to social stimuli. Of course, people are more interesting than many of the other objects in infants' perceptual worlds—much more so than ceilings, stoves, or strollers, for example. Furthermore, as noted above, there is likely to be an adaptive value in attending to social information. Thus, it is not surprising that an interest in attending to and interacting with other people is one of the earliest manifestations of social cognition.

One of the most basic tasks that infants and children face in learning about the social world is acquiring an understanding of self and others. Infants need to learn that they are individuals who exist apart from other objects and people. Later in development, children need to develop a self-concept that incorporates information about their physical characteristics, their likes and dislikes, and their dispositions. They also need to form concepts of other people that incorporate similar types of information. The foundations for these concepts are laid down in early infancy, and these concepts undergo continued change throughout childhood and adolescence.

UNDERSTANDING OF OTHERS

Infants' social worlds are filled with other people, including parents, siblings, other family members, and other care providers. Developing an understanding of these other people is one of the most fundamental tasks that infants and children face in learning about the social world.

Attention to social stimuli. As discussed in Chapter 4, infants are highly attentive to human faces and voices. Even newborns prefer facelike to non-facelike stimuli (Mondloch et al., 1999). Infants are especially attentive to complex sounds such as human speech, and they are capable of making fine discriminations among the sounds used in human langauges (Eimas et al., 1971). Infants also show a special preference for infant-directed speech, or "motherese" (Cooper & Aslin, 1990).

From a very young age, infants also seem to expect people to behave differently from objects, and they react differently to people and objects. As noted in the previous chapter, Legerstee (1991) found that 5- to 8-week-old infants imitated mouth movements (such as sticking out the tongue or opening the mouth wide) that were produced by another person (see also Meltzoff & Moore, 1977). However, the infants did not imitate similar movements that were produced by inanimate objects, such as a tube with a "tongue" that could protrude, or a box with a "mouth" that could open on one side. Infants also smile more at people than at objects (Ellsworth, Muir, & Hains, 1993), and they appear surprised when an inanimate object moves on its own, but not when a person does so (Spelke et al., 1995).

Young infants are also able to distinguish among particular other people. At birth, infants can discriminate their own mother's voices from the voices of other women (DeCasper & Fifer, 1980). Early in the first year, infants begin to recognize their caregivers, and they begin to develop emotional attachments to them. The emergence of "stranger anxiety" late in the first year indicates that, by this time, infants strongly distinguish familiar from unfamiliar people in their social worlds.

Early social interactions.   As noted in Chapter 4, starting when infants are about 2 months of age, they and their caregivers begin to display *contingent interaction*—reciprocal actions and reactions that resemble the mutual give-and-take of conversation (e.g., Bateson, 1979; Trevarthen, 1979). Such reciprocal interaction implies that from an early age, infants anticipate certain types of behavior on the part of their interaction partners.

By about 3 months, infants expect that other people will interact with them. When caregivers display a "still face" and do not move or speak, infants smile less and avert their gaze, their heart rates change in ways that indicate arousal, and some infants fuss or cry (Kisilevsky et al., 1998; Toda & Fogel, 1993; Tronick, Als, Adamson, Wise, & Brazelton, 1978). These responses suggest that the "still face" violates infants' expectations about caregivers' interactive behavior.

Infants' expectations about the nature of social interactions appear to be fairly specific. In one study, an adult engaged with infants in either a "normal" peek-a-boo game or a "scrambled" peek-a-boo game, in which the components of the game (hiding the eyes, revealing the eyes, saying "peek-a-boo") were performed in a random order. Four- and 6-month-old infants in the scrambled-game condition smiled less and looked to the experimenter more than did infants of the same ages in the normal-game condition (Rochat, Querido, & Striano, 1999). These findings suggest that the infants had expectations about how the adult would interact with them, and these expectations were violated in the scrambled-game condition.

Infants begin to follow adults' gaze at about 3 months of age. This skill gradually becomes more robust, and it is well established by 9 months (Butterworth, 2001). At about this same time, infants also begin to follow adults' pointing gestures (Morissette et al., 1995; Murphy & Messer, 1977). By following their caregivers' gaze and gestures, infants contribute to establishing *joint attention,* a state in which they and their caregivers share a common focus on particular objects or events, as described in Chapter 4. Joint attention is thought to be an important prerequisite for the development of communicative skills. By monitoring the focus of adults' attention, infants are able to link adults' utterances with the correct referents (Baldwin, 1991, 1993b).

Early understanding of emotional expressions.   From early in the first year, infants are able to discriminate among different emotional expressions. In one study of this ability, Walker (1982) presented 5-month-old infants with two films of an unfamiliar adult. In one of the films, the adult was speaking angrily and making angry facial expressions and gestures, and in the other film, the adult was speaking happily and making happy facial expressions and gestures. The sound-track to one or the other film was played through a loudspeaker. Infants looked longer at the film that matched the soundtrack, regardless of whether it was happy or angry, suggesting that by 5 months of age they had some knowledge about different emotions and how they are expressed facially and vocally.

In the second half of the first year, infants begin to gauge the emotional reactions of other people in order to evaluate situations or objects as safe or risky. This phenomenon, termed *social referencing*, has been demonstrated in infants as young as 6 months of age (e.g., Walden & Ogan, 1988). One classic study of this issue investigated 12-month-old infants' willingness to cross the deep side of the visual cliff (described in Chapter 5). When their caregivers posed a frightened or angry expression, none of the infants crossed over the deep side, but when their caregivers posed a joyful expression, most of the infants did so (Sorce, Emde, Campos, & Klinnert, 1985). Thus, infants are able to use information gained from the social world to guide their behavior. In this sense, infants recognize other people and their emotional expressions as a potential source of information.

Concepts of other people. Infants' behavior in social interactions and their responses to others' emotional expressions indicate that they have an emerging concept of other people. As children's language and cognitive skills grow, their concepts of others become more explicit and more accessible to verbal expression. Studies of young children's concepts of other people indicate that these concepts undergo substantial change over development (Livesley & Bromley, 1973; Ruble & Dweck, 1995; Shantz, 1983). The general progression is from a focus on concrete, external, observable characteristics to more abstract, internal, nonobservable ones.

When asked to describe particular others, children younger than about 5 years tend to focus on external, observable qualities such as physical appearance, possessions, and typical activities. They also focus on how others' behavior relates to themselves. The following example is a representative description of a friend provided by a child younger than five:

> John is my best friend. We play in the street. He has a big sister. I like him because I play with his toys. (Livesley & Bromley, 1973, p. 265)

Starting in preschool, children also sometimes explain others' behaviors in psychological terms (such as "He's scared," "Mommy is sad") (Lillard & Flavell, 1990). However, preschoolers' psychological attributions are generally situation specific, and they do not refer to enduring dispositions or traits.

With time, children's knowledge about the psychological causes of behavior becomes more abstract and more complex. By middle childhood, they begin to describe others and explain their behavior in terms of dispositions or traits (Alvarez, Ruble, & Bolger, 2001; Eder, 1989; Kalish, 2002; Rholes & Ruble, 1984). In one study of this issue, Rholes and Ruble (1984) presented children with vignettes that were designed to reveal personality traits of the actors in the vignettes. Children were then asked to predict the actors' behavior in other, similar situations. Children who were 9 years and older perceived the behaviors in the initial vignettes to be caused by the actors' dispositions, and they predicted consistent behavior in the new situations. Younger children, in contrast, did not predict consistent behavior in the new situations. Based on these findings, Rholes and Ruble inferred that an appreciation of dispositions as stable, enduring characteristics of other people emerges in middle childhood.

However, other research suggests that young children do appreciate dispositional information, at least in some situations. In a study described by Feldman and Ruble (1981), children were presented with brief videotapes of people and then were asked to describe those people. Some of the participants simply described the actors, whereas other participants described the actors after being led to believe that they would soon meet and interact with them. When future interaction was expected, even 5- and 6-year-olds included some dispositional information in their descriptions. For example, compare these descriptions provided by children in the 5-to-6-year-old age group:

> No future interaction expected:
>   She was throwing balls into the bucket. She was throwing Frisbees at the target. She has dark hair. She went into another room.

> Future interaction expected:
>   She is good at games and she's probably nice. She tries very hard. I think she likes to play games. (Feldman & Ruble, 1981, p. 202)

The expectation of future interaction with the target person led children to focus on psychological attributes, rather than observable characteristics, such as external appearance and activities, in their descriptions.

By adolescence, children's descriptions of others routinely incorporate information about nonobservable characteristics, such as traits and consistent patterns of behavior, and they also include information about the importance of social context in shaping individuals' behavior. The following is an excerpt of a description provided by a 15-year-old boy.

> Phil is very modest. He is even shyer than I am with strangers and yet is very talkative with people he knows and likes. He always seems good-tempered, and I have never seen him in a bad temper. He tends to degrade other people's achievements and yet never praises his own. He does not seem to voice his own opinions to anyone. He easily gets nervous. (Livesley & Bromley, 1973, p. 199)

Like this example, adolescents' descriptions of other people reveal an appreciation of the psychological complexity and situational variability of others' behavior.

UNDERSTANDING OF THE SELF

The self is perhaps the most important individual in any person's social world. Infants become aware of themselves at a surprisingly early age. Over time, infants and children develop a full-fledged concept of themselves, which includes knowledge about perceptual, physical, social, and psychological aspects of the self.

Awareness and recognition of self. When do babies first become aware of themselves? That is, when do they understand that they are individuals who exist apart from other objects and people? One approach to investigating this issue is to study infants' attention to images of themselves and others. When shown a videotape of themselves and one of a peer, even 3-month-old infants prefer to look at the peer (Bahrick, Moss, & Fadil, 1996), suggesting that by this early age, infants can discriminate themselves from others.

Another approach to investigating this issue is to examine when infants begin to recognize themselves in a mirror. In the "rouge test," depicted in Figure 9.1, a red mark is surreptitiously placed on the infant's nose as the mother wipes the infant's face (Amsterdam, 1972; Bullock & Luetkenhaus, 1990; Lewis & Brooks-Gunn, 1979). The infant is then placed in front of a mirror. Most 12-month-olds touch the mark on the nose of the mirror image. However, by about 15 months, most infants touch their *own* noses, thus indicating that they recognize the infants in the mirror as themselves.

Might this developmental trend be due to infants' growing experience with mirrors? To find out, Priel and deSchonen (1986) carried out the rouge test with infants from an Israeli desert community who had never seen mirrors or other reflective surfaces. They found that these infants showed the same developmental pattern as comparison infants from a nearby city, all of whom had had experience with mirrors. In both groups, no children between 6 and 12 months old touched their own noses, some children between 13 and 19 months did so, and almost all children between 20 and 26 months did so.

Other aspects of children's behavior also demonstrate that self-recognition is well established by age 2. Most 2-year-olds will look and smile more at photographs of themselves than at photographs of peers. In addition, most children of this age refer to themselves using their name or a personal pronoun, and some children know their age or their gender (Lewis & Brooks-Gunn, 1979).

Concepts of the self. Rochat (2001) has argued that beginning at birth, and accelerating at about 2 months of age, infants develop an implicit, preverbal concept of the self that includes both perceptual and social components. Infants' perceptual self-knowledge consists of knowledge about their own bodies and their own competencies for action, which they acquire through self-exploration and through experiencing the effects of their own actions in the world. Their social self-knowledge consists of knowledge about their own

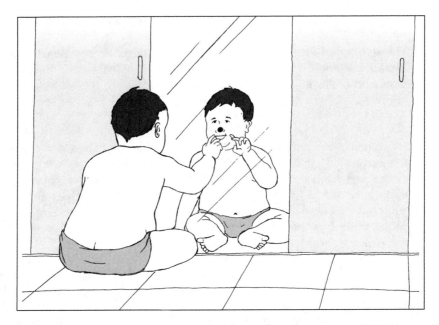

FIGURE 9.1 The "rouge test." A red mark was surreptitiously placed on this 12-month-old infant's nose by his mother as she wiped his face. Note that the infant reaches out to touch the nose of the infant in the mirror, rather than his own nose. By about 15 months, most infants touch their own noses in this situation.

patterns of behavior, which they acquire through interacting with others and seeing how they and others differ. According to Rochat, this early perceptual and social self-knowledge forms the basis for more explicit, reflective knowledge about the self, such as the self-knowledge that children begin to express in language in the toddler years and beyond.

As children's language and cognitive skills grow, the nature of their self-concepts also changes. In the toddler years, children begin to classify themselves in terms of age, sex, physical characteristics (such as "I'm big"), and evaluative qualities, such as goodness or naughtiness (such as "I'm a good girl") (Stipek, Gralinski, & Kopp, 1990). By the early preschool years, most children can readily describe themselves in language. Preschoolers typically describe themselves in terms of concrete, observable characteristics, such as their physical characteristics, possessions, and typical activities (Keller, Ford, & Meacham, 1978). For example, the following self-description was provided by the niece of one of the authors, a 5-year-old girl:

> I have friends. My eyes are hazel. I have a mom and a dad and a big brother and a little sister. I used to have a dog, but it died. I go to school. I do ballet. (Makris, personal communication, 2002)

Like this child, most preschoolers seldom mention psychological characteristics in their self-descriptions. Nevertheless, preschoolers do have a basic understanding of their own dispositions. In one study, children were presented with pairs of statements (such as "when I get angry, I feel like hitting someone" or "when I get angry, I feel like being quiet") and asked to select the statement from each pair that better described them (Eder, 1990). This task makes fewer demands on language skills than does the task of describing oneself in words. For children as young as $3\frac{1}{2}$ years old, Eder found that children's statement selections were consistent across related pairs, and the selections cohered into psychologically meaningful dimensions, such as self-control, self-acceptance, and extraversion. Thus, children as young as $3\frac{1}{2}$ appear to have conceptions of themselves that incorporate psychological dimensions.

Children's self-concepts change in important ways as they develop (Harter, 1998). Their representations of self become better organized as various aspects of self-understanding (including perceptual, physical, social, and psychological understandings) are coordinated and integrated. With time, children's self-concepts also become more abstract and more psychological (Mohr, 1978). In middle childhood, children often describe themselves in relation to others, rather than in absolute terms (such as "I'm smarter than my sister"), and by late childhood, most children describe themselves in terms of general dispositions or traits (such as "I'm friendly and outgoing"). As children approach adolescence, their self-descriptions begin to reflect their expanding set of social roles and relationships (such as student, daughter, friend, girlfriend), and the importance of social context (such as "I'm usually pretty serious, but when I'm with my friends, I can be very silly") (Harter, 1999).

Thus, children's descriptions of themselves become more abstract, more comparative, and more differentiated over developmental time. Along with this shift, their concepts begin to incorporate information about variability in behavior and about the importance of the social context. Thus, children's concepts of themselves, like their concepts of other people, reveal a general progression from an early focus on stable, external, observable characteristics to a later focus on more variable, internal, and nonobservable ones.

Knowledge about Mental States and Activities

Building on this foundation of understanding self and others, one particularly important task is for children to extend their social understanding inward, to grasp the nature of their own and other people's mental lives. Children need to learn that people have goals, intentions, and expectations; that people know some things and not others; and that the fact that they themselves believe something does not mean that other people do. Briefly stated, children need to acquire an understanding of the workings of the human mind.

One way in which people gain an understanding of the mind may be through consciousness of the self. We are aware of some of the workings of our own minds, and this may provide a basis for generalizing to the minds of others (Harris, 1992; Johnson, 1988; Smiley & Huttenlocher, 1989). How is it, though, that we come to understand that we have purposes, beliefs, knowledge, intentions, and desires? After all, no one has ever seen a purpose or a belief, and we do not attribute purposes or beliefs to cars, trees, or most other animals. Yet even toddlers are aware of such mental processes, as indicated by their everyday language (Bartsch & Wellman, 1995):

> ROSS (2 YEARS, 10 MONTHS): *Mommy can't sing it. She doesn't know it. She doesn't understand. (p. 41)*
>
> NAOMI (2 YEARS, 11 MONTHS): *I'm dreaming flowers and doggies. (p. 41)*
>
> ADAM (2 YEARS, 11 MONTHS): *I think it's gum drops . . . Nope. (p. 46)*

As these snippets of toddlers' conversations reveal, by their third birthday children already are thinking about what they and other people think, know, dream, and understand. How do children develop such knowledge so quickly, especially when the mind's contents are so elusive?

Some investigators have argued that psychology is a "core" domain, and that children enter the world predisposed to form reasonable theories about how the mind works (Gelman, 2003; Gopnik & Meltzoff, 1994; Leslie, 1994; Wellman & Gelman, 1998). Wellman and his collaborators have formulated a particularly influential version of this idea. They proposed that from roughly three years onward, children have a naive theory of how the mind works. The purpose of the theory is to explain human actions, and in particular, intentional actions, which are voluntary actions that the actors undertake for some reason (such as because they want something). Wellman and colleagues labeled this theory a *belief-desire theory of mind* because its central tenet is that internal beliefs and desires lead to actions. The theory's basic organization is outlined in Figure 9.2.

According to Wellman and colleagues, a full-fledged theory of mind requires understanding that mental states, such as beliefs, desires, and fantasies, are internal entities, distinct from reality, and that such mental states relate to the world in particular ways. Stated more generally, it requires understanding that the contents of the mind *represent* those in the world. Understanding mental states as representations of reality enables individuals to predict and explain others' actions. For example, if a girl knows that her brother *believes* that there are cookies in the cookie jar, she can expect that her brother will look in the cookie jar when he wants to have a cookie. Furthermore, she can expect her brother to look in the cookie jar, even if she knows that their mother has removed the cookies and placed them in the freezer. It is her brother's representation of the world, and not the true state of the world, that dictates his actions. A true *representational* theory of mind involves understanding that the mind represents the world, and that such representations are related in systematic ways to actions.

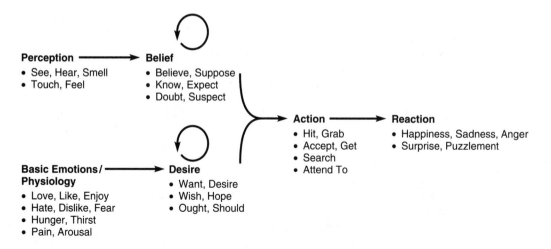

FIGURE 9.2   Wellman's (1990) depiction of children's belief-desire theory of mind.

As seen in Figure 9.2, the "core" of children's theory of mind is their understanding of intentions, desires, and beliefs, and how these relate to action. However, children must also come to understand many other mental activities. Recent research has addressed how children understand two major classes of mental activities: those that are primarily concerned with representations of the "real" world, such as thinking, knowing, and guessing, and those that are primarily concerned with representations of fictional worlds, such as pretending, fantasizing, imagining and dreaming. In the following sections, we first review recent research addressing the development of understanding of intention, desire and belief. We then consider children's understanding of thinking, knowing, pretending, and fantasizing.

UNDERSTANDING OF INTENTION

A rudimentary understanding of intention emerges in infancy. By 6 months of age, infants seem to grasp that people tend to perform particular sorts of actions in particular sorts of situations. For example, in one study, 6-month-old infants saw an actor repeatedly either speak to or reach for something hidden behind a barrier. After the infants were habituated to either the speaking event or the reaching event, the hidden "something" was revealed to be either a person or an object. Infants who had seen the speaking event looked longer at the object than at the person, indicating surprise that the actor would be speaking to an object. However, infants who had seen the reaching event looked longer at the person than at the object, suggesting that they expected the actor to reach toward an object, but speak to a person (Legerstee, Barna, & DiAdamo, 2000).

Thus, by age 6 months, infants recognize that people have different intentions toward people and objects.

These findings suggest that young infants understand some important regularities about intentional action. However, for a full-fledged understanding of intention, it is not enough to recognize that people act in generally predictable ways—one must also appreciate that people's actions are driven by mental states such as desire and belief. Thus, a true concept of intention requires understanding that *mental states* guide people's actions. One way to test for this understanding is to examine whether infants respond differently to the same action when the action is performed intentionally and when it is performed accidentally. In one study of this issue, adults demonstrated actions and then immediately produced a verbal cue indicating that the action was either accidental ("Whoops!") or intentional ("There!"). Infants as young as 14 months were more likely to imitate the adult's action if the action was marked as intentional than if it was marked as accidental (Carpenter, Akhtar, & Tomasello, 1998). Similarly, 2-year-olds are more likely to learn a new word for an action if the action appears intentional than if it appears accidental (Tomasello & Barton, 1994).

Infants' understanding of intention can also be tested more directly. Meltzoff (1995a) showed 18-month-old infants an adult trying to produce a target action (such as pushing a button with a stick) but failing to succeed. When the infants were then given a chance to play with the objects, they tended to produce the action the adult had tried to achieve, even though they had never seen that action performed. However, when children saw a toy robot perform as the adult had (that is, try but fail to push the button with the stick), the infants did not produce the target action. Thus, by 18 months, infants seem to recognize what a person is trying to do, even if the person does not succeed. Moreover, they apply this understanding to other people but not to inanimate objects, such as toy robots.

It is clear that infants distinguish between intentional and unintentional actions at an early age. However, this does not imply that understanding of intention is fully developed in infancy. Indeed, early understanding of intention appears not to involve understanding that intention is independent of the outcome of the ensuing behavior. As a consequence of this limited understanding, young children often confuse mistakes, accidents, and reflexes with intentional behavior (e.g., Astington, 1991; Shultz, 1980). For example, Shultz (1980) elicited reflexive knee-jerk movements from young children using a reflex hammer and then asked children whether they meant to perform the movements. Most 3-year-olds claimed that they meant to move their leg, whereas most 5-year-olds realized that the movement was beyond their control and correctly denied that they meant to do so. In general, if the outcome of an action is positive, 3-year-olds assume that the action was intentional. Four- and 5-year-olds are much better at distinguishing intentions from fortunate accidents.

UNDERSTANDING OF DESIRES

Desires are mental states that can be motivated by physiological states (such as hunger, thirst, and pain) or by emotions (such as love, anger, and fear). Children as young as 12 months appear to have a rudimentary understanding of desire and how it motivates action. For example, Phillips, Wellman, and Spelke (2002) demonstrated that 12-month-olds can connect information about others' direction of gaze and emotional expressions to their actions. Infants viewed an actor who looked at one of two stuffed kitties (one orange, the other gray) with an expression of interest and joy, and said, "Oooh, look at the kitty," in a pleasant voice. A screen was then drawn over the scene, and reopened two seconds later. When the screen reopened, the actor was holding either the kitty she had been regarding or the other kitty. Infants looked at this scene for longer times when the actor was shown holding the kitty that she had *not* looked at when she made the earlier positive comment, suggesting that they found this outcome surprising. Thus, at 12 months, infants appear to recognize the connection between an actor's looking and expression of positive emotion, which often indicate desire, and her subsequent action.

By about 18 to 24 months, many children also begin to use mental state terms to describe their desires (such as, "Want juice") and associated emotional states (such as, "I'm scared") (Bartsch & Wellman, 1995). By this age, infants also seem to understand that others may have desires that differ from their own. Repacholi and Gopnik (1997) offered infants a choice between a Goldfish cracker and a piece of broccoli. Not surprisingly, most infants chose the cracker. They then observed the experimenter profess a preference for the broccoli, using both facial expressions and words ("Mmm, this broccoli is yummy"). The experimenter then asked the infants to give her something to eat. Most 14-month-olds gave her their own preferred food (the cracker), but most 18-month-olds gave the experimenter her preferred food (the broccoli). Thus, by 18 months, infants can reason about others' desires.

Wellman and colleagues (Bartsch & Wellman, 1995; Wellman, 1990) have argued that children's early understanding of desire is nonrepresentational. That is, young children understand that people relate to objects in the sense that they desire those objects; however, they do not yet understand that people *mentally represent* the objects that they desire, whether accurately or inaccurately, in particular ways. Because a rudimentary understanding of desire does not require understanding of mental representations, understanding of desire emerges before understanding of other mental states that do require such understanding, such as belief (Astington, 1993; Bartsch & Wellman, 1995; Gopnik & Slaughter, 1991; Lillard & Flavell, 1992). For example, 2-year-olds consistently predict that characters in stories will act in accord with their desires, even when the children themselves would make a different choice. However, 2-year-olds are considerably less likely to predict that characters will act in accord with their beliefs, for example, beliefs about where a hidden object is located, when those beliefs differ from the children's own (Wellman & Woolley, 1990).

UNDERSTANDING OF BELIEFS

Wellman and his collaborators credit children with a full-fledged, representational theory of mind when they achieve an understanding of beliefs and of the role of beliefs in motivating action. Children achieve this understanding sometime between the ages of 3 and 4 (Wellman, Cross, & Watson, 2001).

Of course, some rudimentary elements of belief understanding are in place before age 3. One of these involves understanding the relation between perceptions and mental states. Between about 18 months and 3 years, children begin to understand visual perspective taking. They realize that others may see something that they do not, and they eventually realize that the same object may look different to two people who view it from different perspectives (Lempers, Flavell, & Flavell, 1977). By 18 months to 2 years, most children also correctly use the word "see" to describe visual perception (Flavell & Miller, 1998).

Not only must children learn the relations between perceptions and mental states, but they must also learn how perceptions and mental states relate to reality. One important achievement in this domain is understanding the *appearance-reality distinction,* which is the knowledge that looks can be deceiving. To examine children's understanding of this distinction, Flavell, Flavell, and Green (1983) presented 3-, 4-, and 5-year-olds with deceptive objects, such as sponges that had been painted to look like rocks. The children were encouraged to play with the objects so that they could learn that the objects were not what they appeared to be. They were then asked questions about what the objects looked like and what they "really, really were." Children also examined objects through a magnifying glass, and they were then asked about how big the objects looked and how big they "really, really were."

Most 4- and 5-year-olds could answer these questions correctly. However, most three-year-olds claimed not only that the sponge looked like a rock but also that it *was* a rock. When they looked at an object through a magnifying glass, the 4- and 5-year-olds again differentiated appearance from reality, but the 3-year-olds thought both that the object looked big when viewed through the magnifying glass and that it really *was* big. These findings are not unique to children growing up in Western societies; children growing up in China perform these tasks in the same ways (Flavell, Zhang, Zou, Dong, & Qi, 1983).

Understanding others' visual perspectives and understanding the distinction between appearance and reality are both important achievements in children's developing understanding of belief. However, the "gold standard" that researchers use to demonstrate understanding of belief is success on tasks that require understanding of one's own or another person's *false belief.* One such task is a "misleading appearance" task. In the typical version of this task, a child is shown a box of Smarties (a type of candy) with pictures of the Smarties on the outside of it. When asked what the box contains, both 3-year-olds and older children say "candy." Then the box is opened, and to the children's surprise the box contains something else, such as pencils. Most 5-year-olds find this amusing, admit that they were surprised, and predict that other children who had not looked into the box would also expect it to contain candies. In contrast, most 3-year-olds miss the humor, claim that they always knew that the box contained pencils, and predict that other children also would know from the beginning that pencils were in the box (Gopnik & Astington, 1988). The following illustrates the response of a typical 3-year-old:

> ADULT: *Look, here's a box . . . What's inside it?*
> 3-YEAR-OLD: *Smarties!*
> A: *Let's look inside . . .*
> 3: *Oh . . . holey moley . . . pencils.*
> A: *. . . When you first saw the box . . . what did you think was inside it?*
> 3: *Pencils.*
> A: *Nicky (child's friend) hasn't seen inside this box . . . When Nicky sees the box, what will he think is inside it?*
> 3: *Pencils.* (Astington & Gopnik, 1988, p. 195)

Another popular test of children's understanding of false belief is a "location change" task, which involves a story in which the location of an object is changed (see Figure 9.3): "Maxi puts his chocolate into the cupboard. He goes out to play. While he is outside, he can't see that his mother comes and transfers the chocolate from the cupboard into the table drawer. She then leaves to visit a friend. When Maxi comes home to get his chocolate, where will he look for it?" (Wimmer & Perner, 1983). Most children younger than 3 years of age respond that Maxi will look in the drawer, where the chocolate actually is. However, by age 4 years, most children respond that Maxi will look in the cupboard, where he originally put the chocolate. This developmental pattern is again not limited to Western children. For example, children of the Baka, a hunter-gatherer tribe that lives in the African rainforest, answer false belief questions much like children in the United States and Europe do (Avis & Harris, 1991).

Many factors affect children's performance on false belief tasks, and there have been a huge number of studies that involve variations of the "standard" tasks. A recent meta-analysis of 178 separate studies revealed five main factors that affect children's performance and the age at which most children succeed (Wellman et al., 2001). First, children tend to perform better, and to succeed at younger ages, if the story involves deception as the motive for the change (such as if the chocolate was moved in order to trick the protagonist). Second, children perform better and succeed earlier if they carry out the transformation themselves (such as if the children move the chocolate themselves, rather than watching the experimenter move it). Third, children perform better and succeed earlier if the target object is not present when the false belief question is asked (such as

Maxi puts chocolate in cupboard.

Maxi goes outside to play.

Mother moves chocolate from cupboard to drawer.

Mother leaves.

Maxi comes back to look for the chocolate.

Where will Maxi look?

FIGURE 9.3 Schematic representation of the location change task developed by Wimmer & Perner, 1983.

if the chocolate was removed from the drawer and eaten, so that it is no longer present). Fourth, children perform better and succeed earlier with stories in which the protagonist's belief is explicitly stated or pictured (such as if the story explicitly states, "Maxi thinks his chocolate is in the drawer") than with stories in which the protagonist's belief needs to be inferred. Finally, children older than about 4 years tend to perform better if the false belief question emphasizes the time frame involved (such as, "*When Maxi comes back,* where will he look *first* for his chocolate?"). However, all of these performance-enhancing factors do not alter the general developmental trend: children progress from below-chance performance to above-chance performance on false belief tasks during the preschool years.

Children's false-belief performance has given rise to vociferous controversy. The controversy does not involve the findings themselves—they are easy to replicate—but rather their proper interpretation. In many ways, the arguments are reminiscent of those surrounding Piaget's findings regarding such concepts as conservation (Chapter 2). One group of researchers argues that 3-year-olds fail the false-belief task because they lack a specific competence central to the task—in this case, a theory of mind that recognizes that other people's minds include representations that can differ from their own (e.g., Astington & Gopnik, 1991; Flavell & Miller, 1998; Perner, 1991). Another group argues that 3-year-olds possess the competence in question but fail the false-belief task because of the demands that the task places on verbal skills or understanding of conversational conventions (e.g., Lewis, Freeman, Hagestadt, & Douglas, 1994; Lewis & Osborne, 1990; Siegal & Peterson, 1994). A third group also emphasizes the general information processing demands of the task, such as the ability to reason with complex, hierarchical rules or the ability to inhibit a dominant response. Researchers in this group argue that such demands are inherent to understanding other people's minds, so children cannot pass false belief tasks until these abilities are in place (e.g., Carlson & Moses, 2001; Carlson, Moses, & Hix, 1998; Frye, 2000; Frye, Zelazo, Brooks, & Samuels, 1996; Russell, Jarrold, & Potel, 1994).

What can be concluded about 3-year-olds' understanding of belief, and in particular, their understanding that others may hold beliefs that differ from person to person, and that also may differ from reality? After reviewing the voluminous literature on this issue, Flavell and Miller (1998) reached the following, reasonable conclusion.

> Many young 3-year-olds probably do have some beginning understanding, but this understanding is severely limited in several respects. It is fragile, with its expression easily impeded by information processing and other limitations . . . It is probably rarely accessed spontaneously in the child's everyday, extralaboratory life . . . Finally, the understanding itself may be different from what the older child possesses–more implicit, more procedural, less accessible to reflection and verbal expression. (p. 874)

Understanding of belief is a crucial component of a representational theory of mind. However, belief is only one of several mental states that children need to learn about. Others include mental states that represent the "real world" and mental states that represent fictional worlds. We next consider children's understanding of some of these other representational mental states.

UNDERSTANDING OF THINKING

In general terms, thinking is simply "the mind . . . making some kind of mental contact with some content" (Flavell, Green, & Flavell, 1995, p. 3). Thinking typically involves forming a mental representation of the real world or of a possible real world.

By about age 3, children have a basic understanding of many essential aspects of thinking. They know that only people (and perhaps some other animate creatures) can think, and that inanimate objects such as vehicles and furniture do not think (Dolgin & Behrend, 1984; Lillard, Zeljo, Curenton, & Kaugars, 2000). They know that thinking is an internal, mental activity that involves the mind and brain (Johnson & Wellman, 1982; Wellman, 1990). They also know that thoughts can be about things that are not physically present, and they are able to distinguish thinking about an object from other related activities such as seeing the object, touching it, and talking about it (Flavell et al., 1995).

However, preschoolers' understanding of thinking also has distinct limitations. For one, preschoolers seem to underestimate people's amount of mental activity. For example, they often fail to attribute mental activity to a person who is sitting quietly, looking at something, listening to something, reading, or talking (Flavell, Green, & Flavell, 1993; Flavell et al., 1995). When preschoolers do recognize that someone is thinking, they often have difficulty inferring the content of the person's thinking, even if the available evidence is strong and unambiguous (Flavell et al., 1995).

Preschoolers' understanding of their own thinking is also limited. Even 5-year-olds often have difficulties reporting their own mental activities. In one experiment, children were asked to think silently about the room in their homes where they keep their toothbrushes. Moments later, many children denied that they had been thinking at all, and among those who acknowledged that they had been thinking, many were unable to report the contents of their thoughts (Flavell et al., 1995). In another study, 5- and 8-year-old children were seated in a special "Do not think" chair and asked not to think about anything at all. After 25 seconds, children moved to an ordinary chair, and they were then asked whether they had had any thoughts when they were sitting in the "do not think" chair. The large majority of 5-year-olds did not acknowledge that they had thoughts during the interval, but the large majority of 8-year-olds did (Flavell, Green, & Flavell, 2000).

UNDERSTANDING OF KNOWING

Knowing is a mental state that involves representing a true state of affairs with high certainty. Children recognize these features of knowing, and they are able to distinguish knowing from thinking and other forms of mental activity by about 4 years of age (Montgomery, 1992). Even before this age, children seem to have a rudimentary understanding of how people acquire knowledge. For example, 3-year-olds attribute knowledge of what is inside a box to a person who looks inside the box, but not to someone who touches the box (Pillow, 1989; Pratt & Bryant, 1990). However, children's understanding of the links between perceptual experience and knowledge is initially quite limited. Not until about age 5 do children have a solid understanding that different modalities of perceptual experience yield different types of knowledge, for example, that touching an object does not yield knowledge about its color (O'Neill, Astington, & Flavell, 1992; Pillow, 1993).

Children's understanding of how they themselves acquire knowledge also increases during the preschool years. Young children often have difficulty identifying *how* they learned the things they know. To investigate preschoolers' ability to monitor the sources of their own knowledge, Gopnik and Graf (1988) provided children with information about the contents of a drawer either by allowing them to look inside, by telling them what was inside, or by providing them with a clue that they could use to infer what was inside. When children were asked how they knew what was inside, 3-year-olds had great difficulty identifying the source of their knowledge. Five-year-olds, in contrast, were readily able to do so.

Young children also frequently have difficulty identifying *when* they acquired information. For example, Taylor, Esbensen, and Bennett (1994) told preschoolers a story that included a novel fact, namely, that tigers' stripes provide camouflage. When questioned immediately after the story, most 4-year-olds and many 5-year-olds claimed that they had known that fact for a long time. A follow-up study indicated that preschool children are more likely to recognize transitions in their own knowledge when they learn new *behaviors* (such as how to count in Japanese) than when they learn new *facts* (such as the meanings of the Japanese counting words) (Esbensen, Taylor, & Stoess, 1997). Thus, young children seem to view action as the best indicator of knowing (Perner, 1991).

UNDERSTANDING OF PRETENDING

Pretense is "the projecting of a supposed situation onto an actual one, in the spirit of fun" (Lillard, 1993a, p. 349). Pretense involves using objects and actions to represent other objects or actions; thus, pretense involves both mental activity and visible behavior. Children begin to engage in pretend play between 12 and 18 months of age. For example, a girl might pretend that a banana is a telephone and hold one end to her ear and talk into the other. Such pretending requires at least an implicit understanding that one object can represent another. This understanding seems likely to be a precursor to the realization that objects also can be represented by thoughts and mental images (Bretherton, 1984; Leslie, 1987). In this sense, pretense may be an early manifestation of an emerging understanding of mental representation.

But do young children really understand pretense as involving mental representations? Some evidence suggests that they think of pretense in terms of action, rather than in terms of mental states. Lillard (1993b) presented 4-year-olds with a troll doll that was hopping like a rabbit. The children were told that there were no rabbits in the land of the trolls, and that this particular troll did not know anything about rabbits. Despite this fact, the majority of children reported that the troll was *pretending* to be a rabbit. Thus, the 4-year-olds did not understand that in order to pretend to be a rabbit, one must know what a rabbit is.

Another source of evidence that young children do not understand the role of mental representation in pretense comes from their judgments about who and what can pretend. In one study of this issue (Lillard et al., 2000), many 3- and 4-year-olds claimed that inanimate objects could pretend, especially when the inanimate objects were costumed to look like animate ones (such as a truck costumed like a cat) or when the objects moved like animate ones (such as a train that moved like a worm).

It seems clear that external features of pretense, such as appearance and action, are highly salient to young children. However, a focus on external features does not imply that children have no knowledge about the mental states involved in pretense. To the contrary, several recent studies suggest that preschool children do have some knowledge about the mental underpinnings of pretense. For example, Custer (1996) presented 3-year-olds with scenarios in which a story character held a mental representation that differed from reality. In one story, the child was told that the character was pretending that there was a fish on his fishing line when there was actually a boot on the line. The child was then asked to choose which of two pictures showed what was in the character's mind—a fish or a boot. The 3-year-old participants often chose the correct picture, suggesting that they understood that pretense involves mental representations.

In a related study, Davis, Woolley, and Bruell (2002) presented children with a sequence of pictures illustrating a story about a girl, a bird, and a butterfly. The final picture depicted the girl with the bird nearby. The girl was waving her arms as if to fly, and a "thought bubble" above the girl's head indicated that she was thinking about the butterfly. Children were asked which of the two animals the girl was pretending to be. The girl's flying actions were consistent with both the bird and the butterfly, so if the children did not understand that pretending involves thinking about something, they should have chosen randomly between the two animals. However, even 3-year-olds were quite successful at this task, and 4- and 5-year-olds performed perfectly. Taken together, these studies suggest that by age 3, children have begun to understand that pretense involves mental representation. This understanding improves with age, and seems to be relatively well established by about age 5.

UNDERSTANDING OF FANTASY

Fantastical thinking can be defined as "ways of reasoning about the physical world that violate known physical principles" (Woolley, 1997). Such thinking is pervasive in many children's lives. Examples include beliefs in magic, in imaginary companions, and in fantasy figures such as witches, fairies, and Santa Claus. Research on children's understanding of fantasy has focused on the extent to which children engage in fantastical thinking and on children's understanding of the distinction between fantasy and reality.

One common form of fantastical thinking is belief in magical events and processes. Many children seem to believe that people can control real-world objects and events either through special thoughts, such as wishes, or through special actions, such as casting a spell, saying magic words, or stepping on a crack. But do children truly "believe" in magic, or do they recognize that such beliefs belong to the realm of fantasy?

Children often deny that they hold magical beliefs, but their actions give them away. Subbotsky (1993) told 4- to 6-year-old children a story about a magic box that could transform drawings into the objects they represented when the magic words "alpha beta gamma" were recited above the box. After the story, children were asked whether they believed in the magic box, and most children claimed that they did not. When children returned to the lab a few days later, the researcher showed them a box and some objects that he claimed had been produced by putting drawings in the box and saying the magic words. The children were also given some drawings of desirable items (such as a ring) and some drawings of frightening items (such as a wasp). The researcher then left the children alone in the room with the box. Nearly all of the children (about 90 percent at each age level) attempted to use the box to transform some of the pictures. Furthermore, they chose the desirable drawings, and avoided the frightening ones. Many children tried repeatedly to transform various drawings, and when the researcher returned, they expressed disappointment that the magic box "didn't work." These findings suggest that up to age 6, most children actually do believe in magic, even though they may deny this belief when asked directly.

Children's understanding of magic appears to shift during the early elementary years. Phelps and Woolley (1994) investigated children's reliance on magic as a way to explain surprising physical events (such as one magnet making another magnet move without touching it). They found that the tendency to invoke magic as an explanation decreased between the ages of 4 and 8. Moreover, children tended to invoke magical processes as an explanation primarily when they were unable to provide an adequate physical explanation for the observed event.

Another common form of fantastical thinking is belief in imaginary companions (Gleason, Sebanc, & Hartup, 2000; Taylor, 1999). In an interview study with 152 3- and 4-year-olds and their parents, Taylor and Carlson (1997) found that 28 percent of children had imaginary companions, and some children had more than one. A subset of the children was interviewed again when they were 6 or 7 years old. By this age, fully 63 percent of the children either currently had or previously had had some form of imaginary companion (Taylor, 1999).

Children's imaginary companions take a variety of forms (see Table 9.2). Some children invent invisible people or animals whom they treat as if they are

TABLE 9.2   *Examples of Children's Imaginary Companions*

Name	Description	Source
Margarine	A very kind girl who attended the child's playgroup. She had long, yellow braids that dragged behind her on the floor.	Taylor, 1999
Fake Rachel	A pretend version of a real friend named Rachel. Fake Rachel was available to play with when "real" Rachel was not around.	Taylor, 1999
Star Friends and Heart Fan Club	Groups of preschool-aged children with whom the child celebrated birthdays, went to the fair, and spoke a language called Hobotchi.	Gleason, Sebanc, & Hartup, 2000
Nutsy and Nutsy	Two birds (a male and a female) who lived in a tree outside the child's bedroom window, had brightly colored feathers and talked incessantly. They joined family outings by riding on top of the car, and they had places set at the family dinner table.	Taylor, 1999
Dipper	A dolphin the size of a door who had sparkles and stripes and who lived far away on a star.	Taylor, 1999
Herd of cows	A group of cows of varying sizes and colors that were often fed or diapered like infants. They were discovered when the child's father accidentally stepped on one.	Gleason, Sebanc, & Hartup, 2000
Barnaby	A "bad guy" with a black mustache who liked to scare people and who lived in the bedroom closet.	Taylor, 1999

Sources:

Taylor, M. (1999). *Imaginary companions and the children who create them.* New York: Oxford University Press.

Gleason, T.R., Sebanc, A.M., & Hartup, W.W. (2000). Imaginary companions of preschool children. *Developmental Psychology, 36,* 419–428.

real companions. These invisible companions often serve as playmates for the children who create them. Some children also treat stuffed animals as real companions and endow them with personalities and other behaviors that remain consistent over time (for example, the comic strip character Calvin's stuffed tiger, Hobbes). For these children, these stuffed animals are more than simple toys or security objects—they are part of an extended fantasy, much the same as invisible imaginary companions might be. Some children do not create companions, but instead create imaginary characters whom they act out themselves on a regular, consistent basis—a sort of "imaginary identity" that they frequently take on. And some children create imaginary companions that are negative or frightening—more like "imaginary enemies" than "imaginary friends." Thus, fantasy adds richness and drama to many children's social worlds.

Do children who have imaginary companions realize that these companions are not "real"? That is, do they understand that their imaginary companions are mental representations of a fictional world? The available data suggest that they do. Taylor (1999) describes her experience conducting a study in which she interviewed children about their "pretend friends."

> We have the distinct impression that after children spend a period of time answering detailed questions about a pretend friend for a researcher who listens carefully and even takes notes, they begin to wonder if the adult might be confused. So at some point during the interview, children are apt to help the interviewer by saying, "It's just pretend, you know" or "She isn't real." (Taylor, 1999, p. 112)

Another form of fantastical thinking that is pervasive in childhood is belief in fantasy figures, including both supernatural figures such as monsters, ghosts, and fairies, and conventional, event-related figures such as Santa Claus and the Tooth Fairy. In a survey of parents of 4- to 6-year-olds, approximately 40 percent of parents reported that their children believed in monsters and fairies, and more than 80 percent reported that their children believed in Santa Claus (Rosengren, Kalish, Hickling, & Gelman, 1994). Parents also reported that they encouraged children's beliefs in event-related figures more than they encouraged children's beliefs in supernatural figures. For example, many families reported leaving milk and cookies for Santa or carrots for his reindeer next to the chimney on Christmas Eve. There is also a great deal of general cultural support for children's beliefs in these conventional, event-related figures, as is evident in the fact that Santa can be seen at almost every American shopping mall during the Christmas season. Thus, it is not surprising that most children who celebrate Christmas also believe in Santa Claus.

Does believing in Santa Claus imply that children have a poor grasp of the distinction between fantasy and reality? Taylor (1999) argues that it does not. Given the extent of parental and community support for believing in Santa Claus, it is not surprising that most children believe the Santa Claus story. But such beliefs do not imply that children have general difficulty understanding that fantasy figures are not real. In fact, this understanding has been demonstrated in children as young as 3. When asked to categorize a number of different objects and figures as either "make-believe" or "real," most 3-year-olds were quite successful (Harris, Brown, Marriot, Whittall, & Harmer, 1991). They put monsters, ghosts, and witches in the "make-believe" box, and dogs, houses, and bears in the "real" box.

Thus, preschoolers do appear to understand the distinction between fantasy and reality. However, the age at which children make this distinction in any particular case depends on several factors, including the availability of alternative explanations for fantastical occurrences (such as physical as opposed to magical causation), the amount of social support for the fantasy, and the origin of the fantasy. Children appear to grasp the distinction better for fantasies they create themselves, such as imaginary companions, than for fantasies that are provided to them ready-made and with extensive social support, such as Santa Claus.

SOURCES OF DEVELOPMENT
OF UNDERSTANDING OF MIND

What factors contribute to children's developing understanding of mind and mental activities? There is a great deal of disagreement about the sources of development of this understanding. The bulk of the research on this issue has focused on children's understanding of belief. However, some studies have addressed understanding of other mental states and activities, such as pretense and fantasy.

Some researchers have emphasized *maturation* of processes specifically useful for understanding social information as the main source of development (e.g., Baron-Cohen, 1991; Fodor, 1992; Leslie, 1994). Researchers in this group have emphasized consistency in the timing of development of understanding of mind. In particular, there is strong consistency across studies in the timing of the development of false belief understanding: the large majority of 5-year-olds have no trouble with false belief tasks, whereas equally large majorities of 3-year-olds do (Wellman et al., 2001).

Researchers in this camp have also emphasized findings regarding the especially great difficulty shown by children with autism in tasks that measure understanding of how people's minds work. Autism is a rare developmental disability (affecting roughly 1 in 1,000 children) characterized by qualitative impairments in social interaction and communication and by repetitive, stereotyped patterns of behavior, interests, or activities (APA, 1994). Children with autism often score poorly on IQ tests, but their performance on tasks requiring understanding of other people's minds, including the false belief task, is worse than would be expected on the basis of their general intelligence (Baron-Cohen, 2001; Baron-Cohen, Leslie, & Frith, 1985).

Children with autism also use mental verbs such as "think" and "know" less often than do other children of similar degrees of retardation (Tager-Flusberg, 1992). Further, they are impaired in their ability to engage in pretend and fantasy play (Baron-Cohen, 1987). On the basis of such findings, some researchers have argued that the mechanisms that allow understanding of the mind are partially independent from those used to understand other phenomena, and that children with autism suffer from a specific impairment to the mechanisms that allow understanding of their own and other people's minds (Frith, 1989; Leslie, 1991).

Other researchers have emphasized the *growth of general abilities*, such as information-processing capacities, as the primary source of development of understanding of mind (e.g., Carlson & Moses, 2001; Carlson et al., 1998; Halford, 1993; Rice, Koinis, Sullivan, Tager-Flusberg, & Winner, 1997). Tasks that tap understanding of mind pose a considerable information-processing load. For example, the false belief task requires children not only to remember what the other person saw, but also to inhibit saying what they themselves know to be true. Consistent with the interpretation that inhibiting vivid impressions is part of the problem, 3-year-olds do better on the false-belief task when they are only told what the true situation is, rather than seeing it with their own eyes (Zaitchik, 1991). Similarly, 3-year-olds do better on the false-belief task when the information-processing requirements are reduced, for example by having the child thoroughly learn the premises of the original problem (Lewis et al., 1994) or by actively engaging the child in deceiving the target person (Hala & Chandler, 1996; Sullivan & Winner, 1993; Wellman et al., 2001). Thus, the development of general information-processing capacities may underlie improvements between 3 and 5 years on the false belief task and related tasks.

A third approach has emphasized *experience with other people* as a source of development of understanding of mind (e.g., Dunn, 1988; Hughes & Dunn, 1998; Perner, Ruffman, & Leekam, 1994; Ruffman, Slade, & Crowe, 2002). One way in which this issue has been addressed is by examining associations between variations in family structure and performance on tasks that tap understanding of mind. This research has shown that preschoolers with greater numbers of brothers and sisters perform better on the false belief task than children with fewer siblings, presumably because they have more chances to learn about other people's thinking (Jenkins & Astington, 1996). Having an older sibling appears to be particularly beneficial (Ruffman, Perner, Naito, Parkin, & Clements, 1998).

Why might sibling status be associated with understanding of mind? One likely possibility is that children with siblings are especially likely to engage in activities that promote the development of understanding of mind. For example, having an older sibling is an important support for pretend play (Youngblade & Dunn, 1995), and children who engage in more social pretend play in general demonstrate a more advanced theory of mind (Harris, 2000; Schwebel, Rosen, & Singer, 1999). Likewise, children with siblings have many opportunities for

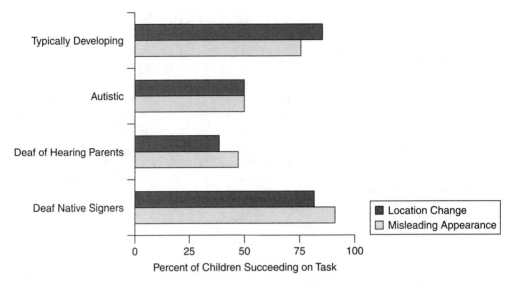

FIGURE 9.4 Performance of deaf native signing children, signing deaf children of hearing parents, autistic children, and typical preschoolers on two theory of mind tasks, a location change task (analogous to the "Maxi" task depicted on page 320) and a misleading appearance task (analogous to the "Smarties" task described on pages 318–319). (Based on Table 1, Peterson & Siegal, 1999).

communicating about mental processes, and such communication appears to be an important factor in the development of understanding of mind. Children who as 2-year-olds talked about their feelings relatively often with their parents do better as 3-year-olds on theory of mind tasks, even when general verbal ability is controlled for statistically (Cutting & Dunn, 1999; Dunn, Brown, Slomkowski, Tesla, & Youngblade, 1991).

Additional evidence for the importance of communication comes from studies of deaf children, who often show delays in developing understanding of mind (Figueras-Costa & Harris, 2001; Lundy, 2002; Peterson & Siegal, 2000; Woolfe, Want, & Siegal, 2002). As seen in Figure 9.4, these delays are especially likely to be seen in deaf children who are being raised by hearing parents, and less likely to be seen in deaf children who are being raised by deaf parents and who are native speakers of sign language (Courtin, 2000; Peterson & Siegal, 1999). One likely explanation for this pattern is that hearing parents of deaf children are often unable to converse fluently in sign language, and they are consequently less likely to communicate with their children about mental processes than are deaf parents of deaf children, who are usually fluent in sign language.

A fourth, somewhat related, approach has focused on *language development* as a potential source of development of understanding of mind (e.g., Astington, 2000; Olson, 1988). Several recent studies have demonstrated correlations between language abilities and the development of theory of mind. These include studies of normally developing children (Astington & Jenkins, 1999), children with autism (Happe, 1995; Tager-Flusberg, 2000), and deaf children of hearing parents (Jackson, 2001).

There are a number of different ways in which language might be involved in theory of mind development. One possibility is that general language abilities are involved in theory of mind. For example, children may use language to mentally represent the past situation in the face of conflicting information from the visual display (the chocolate had been in the drawer but now it is in the cupboard) (Astington, 2000). Another possibility is that the development of theory of mind depends on the acquisition of words for mental states, such as *think, know,* and *wonder* (Olson, 1988).

A third possibility is that language is involved in understanding of mind in a more fundamental way. De Villiers and de Villiers (2000) have argued that language provides children with representational structures called *complement structures* that enable them to embed one idea in another (such as *"he said that he drank the milk," "he thought that* the chocolate was in the drawer"). They hypothesized that the ability to embed ideas in this way is crucial for the development of false belief understanding. Consistent with this hypothesis, de Villiers and de Villiers found that understanding and use of complement structures was an excellent predictor of both simultaneous and subsequent performance on theory of mind tasks. Thus, language development, and in particular, development of the ability to use complement structures, may underpin children's ability to reason about beliefs and other representational mental states.

Fortunately, there is no need to choose among maturation, general cognitive capacities, experience with others, and language development as potential sources of children's developing understanding of mind. These four classes of explanations are not mutually exclusive, and it is likely that each is involved in some way in developing understanding of one's own and other people's minds. The challenge is to understand how cognitive mechanisms and relevant experiences together produce the pattern of conceptual development that emerges so consistently in the preschool period.

Understanding of the Social World

Thus far, this chapter has focused on children's understanding of individuals, including oneself and other people, and of individual minds. Understanding of individuals is clearly important for adaptive functioning and social interaction, but it is not all there is to social cognition. Another important task for children is to learn about the broader social world. This section describes how children extend their early understanding of individuals outward to the broader social world. We focus on how children learn about socially defined rules of appropriate behavior and about social categories such as those based on gender, race, ethnicity, and social class.

UNDERSTANDING OF SOCIAL RULES

Social rules are conventions that are accepted within a social or cultural group. Some examples include clothing styles (such as "boys do not wear dresses"), mealtime customs (such as "set places at the table with the fork on the left and the knife and spoon on the right"), and rituals for social interaction (such as "address unfamiliar adults with their titles rather than their first names"). Some social rules are framed as general rules for appropriate behavior, such as "don't talk with food in your mouth" or "say thank you after receiving a compliment." Other social rules apply only in more limited situations, such as "do not share your food," which is a common rule in many school cafeterias, but in few other settings.

Social rules differ from moral rules (such as "do not steal") in terms of their arbitrariness (Turiel, 1983, 1994). In contrast to social rules, moral rules protect others' rights and welfare, and as such, they are not arbitrary. Children appreciate the difference between social and moral rules as early as 3 years of age. In one study, 3-year-olds judged violations of moral rules, such as stealing a playmate's apple, to be wrong across a wider range of settings than violations of social rules, such as eating ice cream with one's fingers (Smetana & Braeges, 1990). Moreover, by 3½, children believe that violations of moral rules would still be wrong even if an adult did not see them, but violations of social rules would not be wrong in this situation (Smetana & Braeges, 1990).

Additional evidence about children's understanding of the distinction between social and moral rules comes from children's responses to transgressions of those rules. Nucci and Turiel (1978) observed preschoolers' responses to naturally occurring transgressions of social and moral rules and found that children were much more likely to respond to moral transgressions than they were to social transgressions. Children's responses to moral transgressions included emotional reactions and verbal statements about the transgressions, about others' feelings, and about the rules. These types of responses were much less frequent in response to transgressions of social rules. Thus, children distinguish social from moral rules from an early age.

Preschool children sometimes believe that people "cannot" violate social rules, just as they cannot violate physical laws (Levy, Taylor, & Gelman, 1995). However, when asked to explain why the two types of violations cannot occur, children give different sorts of reasons (Kalish, 1998a). Children as young as 3 years old often claim that violations of physical laws (for example, turning a ball into a bird) are impossible. However, when confronted with violations of social rules (for example, bathing with clothes on), they do not claim that such violations are impossible but rather that such actions are not permitted or could lead to adverse consequences. Thus, 3-year-olds distinguish social rules from physical laws, as well as from moral rules.

At around 4 years of age, children begin to understand that following social rules depends both on knowledge of the rules and on intentions to follow them. Kalish (1998a) asked 3- and 4-year-old children to predict the behaviors of other children who either *did not know* or *intended to violate* various physical laws and social rules. The 4-year-olds predicted that other children would violate social rules if they did not know the rules or if they intended to violate them. However, they did not predict that other children would violate physical laws, even if they did not know the laws or intended to violate them. In contrast, 3-year-old participants did not reliably differentiate between physical laws and social rules depending on the intentions or knowledge of the actors. Thus, 4-year-olds, but not 3-year-olds, understand when mental states such as knowledge and intentions matter for following rules and when they do not.

UNDERSTANDING SOCIAL CATEGORIES AND GROUPS

Another aspect of knowledge of the broader social world is knowledge about the social categories and groups that are meaningful in society. Of course, there are many different ways of classifying individuals into social categories. Some of the social categories that children learn about in childhood are those based on gender, race, ethnicity, and social class.

Children's knowledge about gender. Children are aware of gender and gender stereotypes from a remarkably early age. At 18 months, infants can match male faces to male voices and female faces to female voices (Poulin-Dubois, Serbin, & Derbyshire, 1998). At the same age, in a visual preference task, boys looked longer than girls at vehicles, and girls looked longer than boys at dolls. These preferences became even more pronounced by 23 months of age (Serbin, Poulin-Dubois, Colburne, Sen, & Eichstedt, 2001). These findings suggest that children possess gender categories from a very early age.

One important achievement in the development of understanding of gender is *gender constancy*, which is the understanding that sex is biologically based and that changes in external features, behaviors, or desires do not alter an individual's sex. Lawrence Kohlberg (1966) proposed that children acquire an understanding of gender constancy in a predictable sequence of three stages. The first stage, *gender labeling*, is reached by most children between the ages of 2 and 3. In this stage, children can accurately label their own and others' sex. However, they also believe that changes in superficial, external features such as clothing and hairstyle can cause changes in sex. They do not yet realize that sex is permanent, and they believe that individuals can change their sex if they wish to do so. The second stage, *gender stability*, is reached by most children in the early preschool years. In this stage, children understand that sex is stable over time—therefore, male babies will grow up to be boys and eventually men, and female babies will grow up to be girls and eventually women. However, they continue to believe that changes in superficial attributes and activities can cause changes in sex. The third stage, *gender consistency,* is reached by most children between the ages of 4 and 8. In this stage, children recognize that sex remains constant despite changes in external features, behaviors, or desires. They recognize that sex depends on internal, nonobservable, and situationally consistent characteristics.

There is substantial evidence, both from the United States and from other countries, that children's understanding of gender constancy emerges in the sequence outlined by Kohlberg (De Lisi & Gallagher, 1991; Munroe, Shimmin, & Munroe, 1984). However, there is also evidence that knowledge of specific facts can influence the time course of the developmental sequence. In particular, children who know that boys and girls have different genitals are more likely to demonstrate gender constancy than children of the same age who do not have this knowledge (Bem, 1989).

Although the evidence is strong that children's knowledge of gender constancy emerges in a predictable sequence, there has been considerable controversy about the implications of this knowledge. In particular, there is little empirical support for an association between measures of gender constancy and behavior based on understanding of gender. For example, long before children attain gender constancy, they prefer to play with gender-typical toys (Lobel & Menashri, 1993), and they are more likely to model their behavior after same-sex models than opposite-sex models (Bussey & Bandura, 1984). Furthermore, increases in gender constancy are not linked to increases in preferences for gender-specific roles and activities (Martin & Little, 1990; Smetana & Letourneau, 1984). Children behave in gender-typed ways even if they do not understand that gender is constant over the lifetime.

Kohlberg's theory of the development of gender constancy specifies the sequence in which children learn important concepts about gender, but it does not specify *how* they learn these concepts. To account for how children learn about gender, Martin and Halverson (1981) proposed an information-processing theory, called gender schema theory. They argued that children first acquire gender identity, and then construct *gender schemas,* which are knowledge structures that organize information about gender. Gender schemas incorporate knowledge about gender stereotypes and about behaviors and activities typical for each sex. According to the theory, children use their gender schemas to guide their behavior. As seen in Figure 9.5, when children encounter an object, behavior, or activity, they first decide whether it is for males or for females. Based on this initial classification, they decide whether or not to learn more about the object, activity or behavior. Children approach and learn more about things that they classify as relevant to their own gender, and they avoid or ignore things that they classify as not relevant to their own gender. Thus, children's schema about their own gender becomes richer and more entrenched over time.

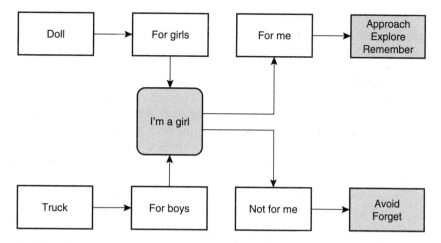

FIGURE 9.5 Operation of the gender schema. Based on Martin & Halverson, 1981.

As predicted by gender schema theory, children prefer novel objects that are labeled as intended for their sex, and they remember more details about such objects than about objects labeled as intended for the opposite sex (Martin, Eisenbud, & Rose, 1995). Furthermore, children who have stronger gender schemas display more gender-typed behavior than do children who have weaker gender schemas, and they are more likely to process information along gender lines (Welch-Ross & Schmidt, 1996). Thus, children's gender schemas influence both their cognitions and their behaviors.

Other researchers have focused on the role of the social world in children's learning about gender. For example, Bussey and Bandura (1999) have argued that children learn about gender through three major modes of influence, each of which involves other people. First, children learn about gender through *observational learning*. Children attend to models in their own environment and in the mass media, and they extract information about gender roles by drawing inferences from the models' behaviors. Second, children learn about gender-appropriate conduct through *enactive experience*, or learning based on the outcomes of one's own actions. For example, fathers often react negatively to feminine toy play on the part of their sons. By noting others' reactions to their behaviors, children learn what types of behaviors are gender-appropriate. Third, children learn about gender through *direct teaching*. Parents and other individuals sometimes directly instruct children about gender-appropriate behavior, such as by saying "Big boys don't cry."

Children are exposed to many sources of information about gender, and both cognitive and social factors appear to contribute to the development of their gender schemas. However, specifying how various sources of information are integrated over the course of development remains an important challenge for research in this area. Understanding the sources of children's knowledge about gender may lead to a better understanding of variations in gender-specific behavior, and may also help shed light on how gender bias develops.

Children's knowledge about race, ethnicity, and social class.   As described above, children's developing understanding of gender has been conceptualized in terms of a sequence of discrete stages. A similar approach has been applied to children's developing understanding of race and ethnicity (e.g., Aboud, 1988).

One recent stage model of children's understanding of race and ethnicity is that of Quintana (1994, 1998), which incorporates a sequence of four ordered stages. This model provides a useful framework for organizing findings about the development of understanding of race and ethnicity.

The first stage, which characterizes children between approximately ages 3 and 6, focuses on the *integration of affective and perceptual understandings* of ethnicity and race. In this stage, children become aware of the existence of different racial and ethnic groups, and they begin to develop attitudes toward racial and ethnic groups that mirror the attitudes prevalent in the broader society. When their attitudes are probed, children in this stage often express negative reactions toward members of particular ethnic groups and in some cases toward members of their own ethnic group (Aboud, 1988). Surprisingly, children's racial attitudes during this period are not systematically related to their parents' attitudes (Branch & Newcombe, 1986), and they appear to be based instead on broader societal views. However, at this stage, children's attitudes tend not to be reflected in their choice of playmates or their behaviors during play (Doyle, 1983).

During this first stage, children also learn to perceptually differentiate among different racial and ethnic groups. By about age 4, most children can accurately apply the labels "black" and "white" to people, dolls, and pictures, and with time, they become better able to distinguish individuals of other racial and ethnic groups (Aboud, 1988; Barrett & Short, 1992). At this stage, young children's verbal descriptions of racial and ethnic groups tend to focus on external, physical manifestations of race and ethnicity, such as skin color or clothing (such as traditional Native American dress) (Aboud, 1988).

Children at this stage also display a rudimentary understanding of social class. They are able to distinguish rich from poor on the basis of external features, such as clothing, residence, and possessions (Ramsey, 1991). However, they do not yet grasp the importance of more abstract factors such as level of educational attainment and occupational prestige in determining social class.

In the second stage, which characterizes children between approximately ages 6 and 10, children display a *literal understanding* of ethnicity and race. By this time, children's ability to categorize other people in terms of race and ethnicity is highly accurate. Their verbal descriptions of other racial and ethnic groups shift from emphasizing external characteristics to including more nonobservable characteristics, such as language spoken, food preferences, and celebration of ethnic holidays (Quintana, 1994). The same shift from external to nonobservable features also applies to children's understanding of social class. In middle childhood, children often invoke psychological qualities in distinguishing rich from poor (such as rich people "earn their money and save it," poor people "are lazy") (Leahy, 1983).

During this second stage, children's negative attitudes toward other racial and ethnic groups tend to decrease (Doyle, Beaudet, & Aboud, 1988; Kowalski & Lo, 2001; Powlishta, Serbin, Doyle, & White, 1994). Their understanding of individuals becomes richer and more differentiated, and they come to recognize that people of different races are similar in important ways, and that people of the same race are often very different from one another. Thus, they begin to appreciate both between-group similarities and within-group differences. These understandings are associated with decreases in prejudice (Doyle & Aboud, 1995). Of course, individual children vary in whether and how strongly they hold biases based on race, ethnicity and social class. One factor that seems to play a role in the development of such biases is the extent to which adults highlight distinctions among groups of people. The more that adults highlight group distinctions, the more likely children are to display own-group preferences and out-group discrimination (Bigler, Spears-Brown, & Markell, 2001).

In the third stage, which characterizes children between approximately ages 10 and 14, children develop a *social understanding* of race and ethnicity. During this stage, children become aware of more subtle characteristics of race and ethnicity, such as differences among ethnic groups in social class. They also begin to recognize that ethnicity may play a role in social interactions, such as in friendship formation, and in the dynamics of group interaction. Finally, they also recognize that ethnicity and race may influence how individuals perceive and respond to other people (Quintana, 1994).

In the fourth stage, adolescents begin to develop *ethnic identity* and *ethnic-group consciousness*. At this stage, adolescents conceive of ethnicity as a subjective dimension of identity that individuals may or may not choose to actively express. They become aware of perspectives, attitudes, and experiences that are shared within an ethnic group, and in this sense, they tend to take a group perspective on ethnicity, sometimes even conceiving of individuals as "representatives" of their ethnic group (Quintana, 1994). As a consequence, stereotyping and ethnocentric attitudes often increase in adolescence (Black-Gutman & Hickson, 1996).

This sequence of stages specifies *what* children of various ages understand about race and ethnicity, but it does not specify *how* this understanding develops. As with gender, understanding *how* knowledge about race and ethnicity develops remains an important challenge for research in this area. A better understanding of the forces that drive change may help guide the design of programs to reduce or, ideally, eliminate prejudice.

General patterns in children's understanding of social categories. A general trend is apparent in children's developing understanding of social categories such as gender, ethnicity, race, and social class. Early on, children tend to focus on external, physical manifestations of group membership. For example, they rely on skin color to differentiate racial groups, dress and typical activities to differentiate gender groups, and possessions to differentiate social class groups. Over development, children's understanding of social categories becomes more abstract, and children begin to incorporate nonobservable, inferred characteristics into their conceptions of social groups. For example, their conceptions of ethnic groups begin to incorporate information about language, food preferences, and ethnic holidays, and their conceptions of social class groups begin to incorporate information about occupational prestige and educational attainment. Eventually, children's understanding of social categories becomes more differentiated, as they begin to consider the broader social implications and the social context of group membership.

This same general trend from a focus on concrete, observable characteristics to a focus on more abstract, nonobservable attributes is also apparent in children's developing understanding of themselves and other individuals. Of course, in all of these areas, such general trends are a simplification of a complex path of development that varies substantially across individuals and contexts. However, the broad strokes of development appear to fit such general trends well.

Summary

The foundations of social understanding include interest in attending to and interacting with other people and initial understanding of other people and oneself. Over developmental time, children extend this initial social understanding inward, to grasp the nature of their own and other people's mental lives, and they also extend this understanding outward, to grasp the nature of the broader social world.

An interest in other people is one of the earliest manifestations of social cognition. Even newborns are highly attentive to human faces and voices. Before they are 2 months old, infants react differently to people and objects, and they also seem to expect people to behave differently from objects. Starting at about 2 months of age, infants and their caregivers begin to display reciprocal actions and reactions, termed "contingent interaction." Early in the first year, infants are also able to discriminate among different emotional expressions. By the second half of the first year, infants are able to gauge others' emotional reactions to situations, and use this information to guide their own behavior—an ability called social referencing.

As children's language and cognitive skills grow, they begin to form explicit concepts of other people. These concepts undergo substantial change during childhood and adolescence. Preschool children tend to focus on characteristics such as physical attributes and typical activities when they describe other people. By middle childhood, they begin to describe others in terms of dispositions or enduring traits. Thus, the general progression is from a focus on concrete, external, observable characteristics to a focus on more abstract, internal, non-observable ones.

During the first year, infants also begin to understand that they are individuals who exist apart from other objects and people. At 3 months, infants can discriminate videos of themselves from videos of others, and by about 15 months, they can recognize mirror images of themselves. Like their concepts of other people, children's concepts of themselves undergo substantial change as they develop. In the toddler years, children begin to classify themselves in terms of age, sex, and physical characteristics. In the preschool years, children typically describe themselves in terms of concrete, observable characteristics, such as physical attributes, possessions, and typical activities. By middle childhood, children's self-concepts become more abstract and more psychological. Their representations of themselves become better organized as various aspects of self-understanding (including perceptual, physical, social, and psychological understandings) are coordinated and integrated.

To understand themselves and other people, children need to understand the workings of their own minds and those of other people. A true "theory of mind" requires understanding that mental states, such as beliefs, desires, and fantasies, are internal entities, distinct from reality, and that such mental states may represent the state of the world. The core of children's theory of mind is their understanding of intentions, desires, and beliefs, and how these mental states relate to action. Children demonstrate a rudimentary understanding of intention, desire, and belief in the toddler years. However, it is not until between ages 3 and 4 that children understand that such mental states represent the state of the world (either accurately or inaccurately) and that others may hold beliefs that differ from person to person, and that also may differ from reality.

In addition to intention, desire, and belief, there are many other mental activities that children must also come to understand. Recent research has focused on two major classes of mental activities: those that are primarily concerned with representations of the "real" world, such as thinking and knowing, and those that are primarily concerned with representations of fictional worlds, such as pretending and fantasizing. Understanding of thinking and knowing emerges gradually in the preschool and early elementary years. Play activities that involve pretending and fantasizing are observed much earlier in development. However, an understanding of pretense as involving mental representation, and an appreciation of the distinction between fantasy and reality, are later achievements.

Children also need to learn about the social conventions and the social structure of the broader society in which they develop. One important aspect of this knowledge is understanding of social rules. Children appreciate the difference between social and moral rules as early as age 3. At around age 4, children begin to understand that following social rules depends both on knowledge of the rules and intentions to follow them.

Another aspect of understanding the broader society is knowledge about social categories, such as those based on gender, race, ethnicity, and social class. In learning about such social categories, children initially tend to focus on external, physical manifestations of group membership, such as skin color to differentiate racial groups, and dress and typical activities to differentiate gender groups. Over development, children begin to incorporate nonobservable characteristics into their conceptions of social groups, and eventually, they begin to consider the broader social implications and the social context of group membership. Thus, with development, children's understanding of social categories becomes more differentiated and more abstract.

Recommended Readings

Bussey, K., & Bandura, A. (1999). Social cognitive theory of gender development and differentiation. *Psychological Review, 106,* 676–713. This paper reviews major theoretical approaches to the development of understanding of gender and presents a social learning theory about how such knowledge is acquired.

Flavell, J.H., & Miller, P.H. (1998). Social cognition. In D. Kuhn & R.S. Siegler (Eds.), *Handbook of child psychology: Vol. 2. Cognition, perception & language* (5th ed.). New York: Wiley. A comprehensive review of research about the development of understanding of mind.

Taylor, M. (1999). *Imaginary companions and the children who create them.* New York:

Oxford University Press. Taylor reviews her extensive research on the nature of children's imaginary companions, the characteristics of the children who create such companions, and children's understanding of the distinction between fantasy and reality. Includes many compelling examples.

Wellman, H.M., Cross, D., & Watson, J. (2001). Meta-analysis of theory-of-mind development: The truth about false belief. *Child Development, 72,* 655–684. This paper presents a meta-analysis of 178 studies of the development of false belief understanding. The authors identify several factors that influence how preschoolers perform on tasks designed to assess false belief understanding.

10

PROBLEM SOLVING

Georgie (a 2-year-old) wants to throw rocks out the kitchen window. The lawnmower is outside. Dad says that Georgie can't throw rocks out the window because he'll break the lawnmower with the rocks. Georgie says, "I got an idea." He goes outside, brings in some green peaches that he had been playing with, and says: "They won't break the lawnmower." (Waters, 1989, p. 7)

Georgie's triumph over those who would spoil his fun illustrates the essence of problem solving: a goal, an obstacle, and a strategy for circumventing the obstacle and reaching the goal. In Georgie's case, the goal was to throw things out the window; the obstacle was his father's disapproval; the solution strategy was "throw peaches, not stones." Not bad for a 2-year-old.

Problem solving is a central part of all of our lives. Deciding what courses to take next semester, what word will complete a crossword puzzle, how to find misplaced keys, and how to answer a brain teaser all demand problem solving. Probably not a day goes by without our trying to solve some problem.

Problem solving also provides much of the purpose for other cognitive processes such as perception, language, memory, and conceptual understanding. If we ask why evolution would result in people's being able to perform these processes, a large part of the answer must be that they enhance people's ability to solve problems that the environment presents. That is, they help people adapt to challenging circumstances.

As pervasive as problem solving is in adults' lives, it probably is even more pervasive in the lives of children. With age and experience, people learn ways of circumventing obstacles so that situations that once posed problems no longer do. For example, when a child first goes to a friend's house a few blocks away, figuring out the best way to walk home represents a real problem. With repeated visits, however, it poses no problem at all. Because children encounter so many situations that are new to them, they constantly need to solve problems.

How do children cope with these challenges? DeLoache, Miller, and Pierroutsakos (1998) suggested the apt metaphor of the child as *bricoleur.* "Bricoleur" is a French term for a kind of tinkerer, someone who uses any materials at hand to solve whatever problem arises. As suggested by this metaphor, children combine reasoning, conceptual understanding, strategies, content knowledge, other people, and any other available resources for reaching their goals. Their solutions may not always be elegant, but they usually find a way to get the job done.

Organization of the chapter. This chapter includes two main sections (Table 10.1). The first provides an overview of children's problem solving. The initial part of the overview describes several general themes that have emerged from research on children's problem solving. Then, a number of these themes are illustrated in the context of development of problem solving on a single task: the balance scale.

The second section of the chapter focuses on specific problem-solving processes: planning, causal inference, analogy, tool use, and scientific and logical reasoning. These processes were chosen for special attention because children frequently use them and because changes in their effectiveness have much to do with changes in the overall effectiveness of problem solving. These are not the only problem-solving processes that children use—they use far too many for all of them to be discussed in a single chapter—but they are among the most important ones.

TABLE 10.1 *Chapter Outline*

I. An Overview of Problem Solving
    A. Central Themes
    B. An Example of the Development of Problem Solving

II. Some Important Problem-Solving Processes
    A. Planning
    B. Causal Inference
    C. Analogy
    D. Tool Use
    E. Scientific and Logical Reasoning

III. Summary

Children sometimes perform the specific problem-solving processes discussed in this chapter on their own, sometimes with the assistance of more capable adults, and sometimes in collaboration with peers or other children. The focus of this chapter is on the problem solving that children do on their own; research that addresses collaborative and assisted problem solving was discussed in Chapter 4.

An Overview of Problem Solving

CENTRAL THEMES

Task analysis. Task analyses are careful examinations of problems, intended to identify the processes needed to solve them. For example, a task analysis of the standard algorithm for multidigit addition (for example, $375 + 536$) would involve such components as adding the numbers in the rightmost column, writing the ones digit of the resulting sum as part of the answer, carrying the tens digit of the initial sum (if there is one) to the tens column of the original problem, adding the carried number to the other numbers in the tens column, and so on. In situations in which people solve problems efficiently, task analyses can indicate what they are doing. In situations in which people cannot solve problems efficiently, task analyses can suggest places where they might have difficulty and what the source of difficulty might be.

Consider an example of how task analyses can lead to insights about children's problem solving. Klahr (1985) presented 5-year-olds with a puzzle in which a dog, a cat, and a mouse needed to find their way to a bone, a piece of fish, and a hunk of cheese, respectively. To solve the puzzle, children needed to move all three animals to the locations with the appropriate food. Superficially, the greater the number of moves needed to reach the goal, the harder the problem would seem.

Klahr's task analysis, however, indicated that different problems created varying degrees of conflict between the child's immediate goal of getting each animal to its desired food and the child's higher goal of getting all three animals to the right positions. Some problems required children temporarily to move an animal already at its goal away from the goal, so that another animal could reach its goal. These problems were more difficult for the preschoolers than problems that required more moves but did not entail any conflict among the different animals' goals. Other problems required children to resist the temptation to move an animal to its destination when it was one move away and instead to make a different move. These problems were even more difficult than the problems that required moving an animal away from a goal it had already reached. The detailed analysis of the task and the conflicts it created between immediate and longer-term goals enabled Klahr to identify the approach that many children used: trying on each move to increase the fit between the current and the desired arrangement of pieces. This approach, called *means-ends analysis*, is a widely used problem-solving strategy.

Encoding. As discussed in Chapter 3, encoding involves identifying the critical information in a situation and using it to build an internal representation of the situation. Children often fail to encode important features of a task because they do not know what the important features are, because they cannot comprehend them, or because they do not know how to encode them efficiently. This failure to encode critical information can prevent children from learning from potentially useful experiences. If they are not taking in the relevant information, they cannot benefit from it.

Misencoding often dooms problem-solving efforts to failure. In one such case, 4- to 11-year-olds and college students watched a moving electric train carrying a ball on a flatcar. At a predesignated point, the ball dropped through a hole in the moving flatcar and fell several feet to the floor. The child's task was to predict the trajectory of the ball as it fell (McCloskey & Kaiser, 1984).

More than 70 percent of the 4- to 11-year-olds, and a sizable minority of the college students, predicted that the ball would fall straight down. After they advanced this hypothesis, the experimenter ran the trains so that participants could see what actually happened. (The ball fell in a parabolic trajectory.) The children and the college students were faced with reconciling their predictions with the outcome they saw.

Their explanations revealed how misencoding can influence problem solving and reasoning. Some said that the ball fell straight down, just as they thought it would. Others said that the train gave the ball a push forward just before it was released. Interestingly, a number of the college students who encoded the ball as having fallen straight down had previously taken and passed college physics courses. Apparently, this experience was insufficient to change either their expectations or their encoding of what they saw. As will be demonstrated in this chapter, changes in encoding play a critical role in the development of a variety of types of problem solving.

Mental models. To solve problems, people often construct mental models of the task and what they need to do to solve it (Crowder, 1996; Gentner & Stevens, 1983; Halford, 1993; Johnson-Laird, 1983; Markovits & Barrouillet, 2002). Even young children form models of how complex systems work, as reflected in a 3-year-old's question, "Why doesn't my blood come out when I open my mouth?" (DeLoache et al., 1998, p. 801). The comment suggests a mental model of the circulatory system in which blood moves around the inside of the body, but in which it is everywhere rather than being limited to veins, arteries, and capillaries.

Halford (1993) identified several central characteristics of good mental models. The most important is that the model accurately represents the structure of the problem. That is, relations among components of the mental model should parallel the essential relations in the problem. When the model's structure parallels that of the situation depicted in the problem, people feel that they understand; otherwise, they feel they do not, even if they can generate a solution by other means, such as by remembering it. The structure depicted within a mental model includes not only static features but also dynamic ones, such as the moves and operations that are possible. The mental modeling process also involves abstraction, in which nonessential features of the problem are stripped away and not represented. This stripping away of incidental features facilitates generalization from the mental model of the original problem to related problems with different superficial characteristics but a parallel structure.

Forming mental models often requires children to reconcile what they are told by other people with their own experience. For example, children must wonder what adults mean when they say that the earth is round, when everyone can see that it is flat. In trying to solve this problem, American 6- to 11-year-olds devise at least five mental models (Vosniadou & Brewer, 1992). Some children conceive of the earth as a disk, thus reconciling the statement that it is round with the observation that it looks flat (Figure 10.1). Others hold a dual-earth model, in which there are two earths, a round one up in the sky (perhaps derived from seeing models of the solar system) and a flat one on the ground where they live. Yet others conceive of the earth as a hollow sphere, with people living on flat ground inside the sphere, and the top part, the sky, covering the ground like a dome. Still others think of the earth as a flattened sphere, with people living on the flat part. Finally, some children understand the earth as a complete sphere. Between first and fifth grade, the percentage of children thinking of the earth as a complete sphere increases, and the percentage adopting the other models decreases. Even in fifth grade, however, 40 percent of American children relied on mental models other than the completely spherical one.

Cross-cultural studies (e.g., Samarapungavan, Vosniadou, & Brewer, 1996) have shown that many of these mental models of the earth occur across cultures. For example, like American children, children growing up in India commonly hold both the disk model and the hollow sphere model. A likely explanation is that children in both cultures must reconcile their own observations that the earth is flat with information they receive from adults or in school that the earth is round. However, other models are culture-specific. Indian children commonly hold a model that was not observed among American children—namely, they often think of the earth as floating on water. Culture-specific models presumably draw on the specific "folk cosmologies," or informal theories about the universe, to which children are exposed. The idea that the earth floats on water is a common theme in Indian folk cosmologies, so this model may reflect children's attempts to integrate this folk view with their own experience. As in the American sample, the percentage of Indian children thinking of the earth as a complete sphere increases over development, and the percentage adopting other models decreases. However, even at third grade (the oldest age tested), 58 percent of the Indian children relied on mental models other than the completely spherical one.

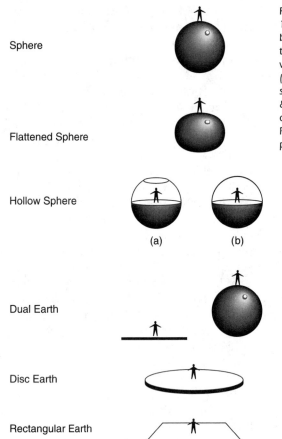

Sphere

Flattened Sphere

Hollow Sphere

      (a)   (b)

Dual Earth

Disc Earth

Rectangular Earth

FIGURE 10.1 Mental models of the earth of 6- to 11-year-olds (from Vosniadou & Brewer, 1992). All but the rectangular earth represent children's efforts to reconcile adults' claim that the earth is round with the flatness that they observe around them (especially in Champaign-Urbana, Illinois, where the study was conducted). Reprinted from Vosniadou, S., & Brewer, W., Mental models of the earth: A study of conceptual change in childhood, Cognitive Psychology, 24, 535–585, Copyright 1992, with permission from Elsevier.

Domain-general and domain-specific knowledge. Problem-solving processes vary in the range of situations to which they can be applied. As the names suggest, domain-general processes can be applied relatively broadly, whereas the range of applicability of domain-specific processes is narrower.

At first, it might sound like domain-general processes must make a larger contribution to problem-solving performance than domain-specific ones; after all, they are more broadly applicable. The issue is not so simple, however, because there is a trade-off between the breadth of applicability of a process and its efficiency in solving any particular type of problem. Processes that are broadly applicable tend not to be as efficient in solving a specific class of problems as are processes precisely tailored to fit those problems. Thus, even though adults' general problem-solving skills are greater than children's, the specific chess strategies of child chess experts studied by Chi (1978) allowed them to solve chess problems more effectively than less experienced adult players who needed to rely more on general problem-solving processes to generate their moves.

Although the relative importance of domain-specific and domain-general processes has often been debated, it almost certainly is more useful to think about how the two work together than to compare their independent contributions (Ceci, 1989; Sternberg, 1989). The reason can be understood by returning to the anecdote about Georgie and the peaches. Without the specific knowledge that peaches are softer than stones, Georgie could not have generated his solution. He also could not have done so without general problem-solving skills, such as understanding that there may be different routes to the same goal, or without knowledge of intermediate generality, such as the knowledge that any object in a particular range of sizes and shapes can be thrown. Problem solving relies on knowledge and processes of many levels of generality. The key issue is how children integrate such diverse information into efficient problem-solving procedures, rather than whether specific or general knowledge is more important.

Developmental differences. Many of the best-known claims regarding cognitive development involve problem-solving processes that young children supposedly cannot perform. For example, Piaget (1970) and Inhelder and Piaget (1964) claimed that preoperational children were incapable of scientific and deductive reasoning. In contrast, they depicted formal operational adolescents as excelling at these types of reasoning (Inhelder & Piaget, 1958).

More recent investigations, however, have not supported these categorical distinctions. Indeed, one theme of this chapter might be given the paradoxical title "young children's competence and older children's incompetence." Numerous studies have shown that young children are far more competent problem solvers than they had been given credit for being. The key to revealing these competencies has been simplifying problems by eliminating sources of difficulty extraneous to the process being examined. Complementarily, numerous other studies have shown that adolescents (and adults) are far less logical and rational than once was believed. Their planning, scientific reasoning, and powers of deduction all fall short of the ideal of the formal operational reasoner.

These findings do not imply that problem solving is similar in early childhood and adolescence. In fact, it differs profoundly. The change, however, is not typically from being absolutely unable to execute a process to being able to do so. Instead, most changes involve the range of situations in which children successfully execute the problem-solving processes. Older children can fight their way through thickets of memory demands, linguistic subtleties, and misleading cues that utterly defeat younger children. They also learn how to solve new problems much more quickly. Thus, although young children are more competent and older ones less so than was once thought, plenty of age-related improvement in problem solving still is evident.

Processes of change. Many recent studies of problem solving have sought not only to identify differences between younger and older children's problem solving, but also to shed light on *how* children's problem solving changes. One tool that has been used to investigate the nature of change is the *microgenetic method,* which involves obtaining frequent samples of children's thinking as their thinking is undergoing change (Siegler & Crowley, 1991). These frequent samples of children's thinking provide more precise data about change processes than could otherwise be obtained.

Microgenetic studies have revealed several consistent findings about the nature of change in children's problem solving. One is that change does not ordinarily involve a simple substitution of a more advanced problem-solving strategy for a less advanced one (Alibali, 1999; Kuhn, 1995; Siegler, 1995; Tunteler & Resing, 2002). Older, less adequate strategies continue to be used, often for prolonged periods of time, even after new, better strategies are generated. This holds true even in cases in which children can explain why the new approach is superior (Siegler & Jenkins, 1989). Thus, application of new ways of thinking tends to be halting and piecemeal, rather than sudden and complete.

A second consistent finding is that children generally think about problems in multiple ways at any given time. This cognitive variability is evident before periods of rapid change, during them, and after them, although it is often heightened during them (Alibali & Goldin-Meadow, 1993; Siegler & Svetina, 2002). Cognitive variability is evident in infants, children, and adults, and in a wide variety of problem-solving tasks, including motor tasks (Adolph, 1995), conservation (Church, 1999; Siegler, 1995), memory tasks (Coyle & Bjorklund, 1996), mathematical problems (Goldin-Meadow & Alibali, 2002; Siegler, 2002), problems about gear movement (Perry & Lewis, 1999), and problems that involve understanding novel technologies (Granott, 2002).

A third consistent finding is that innovations follow success as well as failure. Failure is not necessary to motivate discoveries; children generate new approaches to solving problems when older approaches have been yielding correct solutions as well as when they have not (Karmiloff-Smith, 1992; Siegler & Stern, 1998). At times, children discover new strategies on the same problem that they had shortly before solved correctly using an older approach (Siegler & Jenkins, 1989).

Are the change processes that are observed in microgenetic studies comparable to those observed in more traditional studies in which children are observed or tested less frequently? To find out, Siegler and Svetina (2002) directly compared change that occurred in a group of children who were studied on a microgenetic time scale (over the course of seven experimental sessions, all within a 10-week period) with change that occurred in another group of children who were studied on a cross-sectional time scale (in two assessments, one year apart). The study focused on 6- to 8-year-old children completing matrices, such as the one shown in Figure 2.6 (p. 52). In each 3×3 matrix, eight of the nine cells were filled in, and the entries varied in systematic ways across the rows and columns. The children's task was to select the correct answer from among six choices that varied in terms of form, size, color, and orientation.

Siegler and Svetina found that the patterns of change in the microgenetic sample were highly similar to those observed in the cross-sectional sample.

Children in both groups made the same type of error most frequently—choosing a duplicate of an object that was already present in the matrix. The absolute percentage of errors that were duplicate errors was also remarkably similar across groups—59 percent in the microgenetic sample and 57 percent in the cross-sectional sample. Both groups also showed increases over time in the percentage of choices in which orientation and size were correct, and neither group showed increases in the percentage of choices in which color and form were correct. Thus, the changes observed on a microgenetic time scale and those observed on a cross-sectional time scale were impressively similar. These data suggest that lessons learned about change from microgenetic studies can indeed be generalized to change on broader time scales.

AN EXAMPLE OF THE DEVELOPMENT OF PROBLEM SOLVING

To obtain a feel for the development of problem solving, it is helpful to consider changes from infancy to adulthood on a single task. The balance scale provides a useful context for considering these changes. Even infants in their first half-year can solve some balance-scale problems; even college-educated adults usually fail to solve others. Changes occur along a wide variety of dimensions relevant to problem solving: children's untutored rules for solving the problem, their ability to learn from experience with it, and their encoding of the problem, among them. Further, development of problem solving on this task exemplifies a number of properties of problem solving in general.

Rules for solving problems. Figure 10.2 illustrates a type of balance scale on which children's problem solving has often been examined. The scale includes a fulcrum and an arm that can rotate around it. The arm can tip left or right or remain level, depending on how weights (metal disks with holes in them) are arranged on the pegs on each side of the fulcrum. However, a lever (not shown in the figure) is typically set to hold the arm motionless. The child's task is to predict which (if either) side would go down if the lever were released.

A task analysis of this problem indicated that two variables influence this outcome—amount of weight on each side of the fulcrum and distance of the

FIGURE 10.2 The balance scale. Metal disks are placed on a peg on each side of the fulcrum. Children need to decide which side of the balance will go down, given the particular configuration of weights on pegs (from Siegler, 1976).

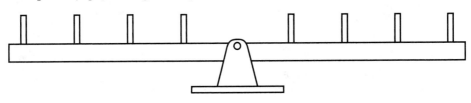

weight from the fulcrum. Thus, the keys to solving such problems are to attend to both of the relevant dimensions and to combine them appropriately. This analysis, together with the known tendency of young children to focus on a single relevant dimension, led Siegler (1976) to hypothesize that children would solve such problems by using one of the four rules depicted in Figure 10.3:

> *Rule I:* If the weight is the same on both sides, predict that the scale will balance. If the weight differs, predict that the side with more weight will go down.
> *Rule II:* If one side has more weight, predict that it will go down. If the weights on the two sides are equal, choose the side with the greater distance (i.e., the side that has the weight farther from the fulcrum).
> *Rule III:* If both weight and distance are equal, predict that the scale will balance. If one side has more weight or distance, and the two sides are equal on the other dimension, predict that the side with the greater value on the unequal dimension will go down. If one side has more weight and the other side more distance, muddle through or guess.
> *Rule IV:* Proceed as in Rule III, unless one side has more weight and the other more distance. In that case, calculate torques by multiplying weight times distance on each side. Then predict that the side with the greater torque will go down.

But how could it be determined whether children use these rules to solve balance-scale problems? Asking children how they solved the problems would be the simplest strategy, but answers to such questions could either overestimate or underestimate their knowledge. The answers would give a misleading positive impression if children simply parroted information they heard at home or in school. The answers would give a misleading negative impression if children were too inarticulate to communicate knowledge they in fact possessed.

In light of these difficulties, Siegler formulated the *rule assessment method* to determine which, if any, rule a given child used. This rule assessment method involved generating problems for which different rules yielded specific patterns of correct answers and errors. As shown in Table 10.2, the types of problems used to assess children's rules were:

1. *Balance problems:* The same configuration of weights on pegs on each side of the fulcrum.
2. *Weight problems:* Unequal amounts of weights, equidistant from the fulcrum.
3. *Distance problems:* Equal amounts of weights, different distances from the fulcrum.
4. *Conflict-weight problems:* One side with more weight, the other side with its weight farther from the fulcrum, and the side with more weight goes down.
5. *Conflict-distance problems:* One side with more weight, the other side with "more distance," and the side with more distance goes down.
6. *Conflict-balance problems:* The usual conflict between weight and distance, and the two sides balance.

Children who used different rules would produce different patterns of responses on these problems (Table 10.2). Those using Rule I would always predict correctly on balance, weight, and conflict-weight problems and would

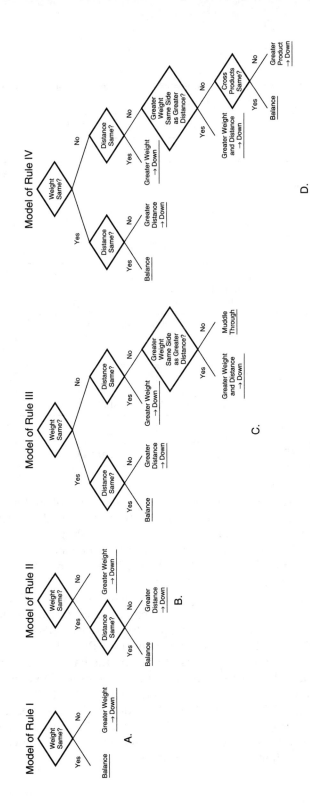

FIGURE 10.3 Rules for solving balance-scale problems (from Siegler, 1976).

TABLE 10.2 Predicted Percentage of Correct Answers on Each Problem Type for Children Using Each Rule

Problem Type	Rule			
	I	II	III	IV
Balance	100	100	100	100
Weight	100	100	100	100
Distance	0 (Should say "Balance")	100	100	100
Conflict-Weight	100	100	33 (Chance Responding)	100
Conflict-Distance	0 (Should say "Right Down")	0 (Should say "Right Down")	33 (Chance Responding)	100
Conflict-Balance	0 (Should say "Right Down")	0 (Should say "Right Down")	33 (Chance Responding)	100

always predict incorrectly on the other three problem types. Children using Rule II would behave similarly, except that they would answer correctly on distance problems. Those adopting Rule III invariably would be correct on all three types of nonconflict problems and perform at a chance level (33 percent correct) on the three types of conflict problems. Those using Rule IV would solve all problems correctly.

When presented the types of problems shown in Table 10.2, more than 80 percent of 5- to 17-year-olds consistently used one of the four rules (Siegler, 1976). Five-year-olds most often used Rule I, 9-year-olds most often used Rule II or III, and 13- and 17-year-olds usually used Rule III. Few children of any age used Rule IV. Similar sequences of rules on the balance-scale task have been observed in a number of subsequent studies (Amsel, Goodman, Savoie, & Clark, 1996; Damon & Phelps, 1988; Ferretti & Butterfield, 1986; Jansen & van der Maas, 2001, 2002; Marini, 1992; McFadden, Dufresne, & Kobasigawa, 1986; Surber & Gzesh, 1984; Zelazo & Shultz, 1989). In addition, as the rule sequence suggests, at least some of the transitions between rules have been found to be discontinuous (Jansen & van der Maas, 2001).

The expected developmental changes in performance on the six problem types also emerged. For example, consider performance on conflict-weight problems. As shown in Table 10.2, children using Rule I consistently solve such problems correctly. They predict that the side with more weight goes down, which, as previously noted, is by definition correct on conflict-weight problems. In contrast, children using Rule III, who realize that both weight and distance are important, muddle through or guess on all types of conflict problems. They therefore would not usually solve conflict-weight problems correctly. Consistent with this analysis, the 5-year-olds in Siegler (1976), most of whom used Rule I, were correct on 89 percent of conflict-weight problems, but 17-year-olds, most of whom used Rule III, were correct on only 51 percent. Adults have also been found to be slower than 6-year-olds in solving such problems (van der Maas & Jansen, 2003). Developmental decrements in performance are sufficiently rare that this data pattern is strong support for the rule analysis that predicted it would occur.

Development of the ability to solve balance-scale problems actually begins well before age 5. Some such ability emerges in infancy. Case (1985) presented infants a balance scale with a bell beneath one end. Pushing down on that end made the bell ring. By 4 to 8 *months* of age, infants who saw an experimenter produce the ringing sound by hitting that end of the arm responded by reaching to strike or touch that end themselves. By 12 to 18 months, infants imitated the experimenter's solution to a harder problem: depressing one end of the beam so that the other end would go up and ring a bell above it. By 2 to 3½ years, children could figure out the solution to this problem without seeing the experimenter solve it first. By 4 to 5 years, children could even make the bell ring when they were given a heavy and a light block and needed to put a block on each end of the scale in such a way that the bell above one end would ring.

Halford and colleagues (Halford, Andrews, Dalton, Boag, & Zielinski, 2002) used a more traditional balance scale task with children as young as 2 years of age. They modified the standard apparatus so that there were only three pegs on each side of the scale rather than four, as in the standard balance scale. They also placed a rabbit on one end of the scale and a duck on the other, so that children could easily label the sides of the scale. In their experiments, children were asked, "Tell me if the ducky will go down, or the bunny will go down, or will they both stay up?" Halford et al. found that children as young as 2 years could make accurate predictions when small numbers of weights and small distances were used, and when only one dimension varied at a time.

Turning to much older children, an anecdote may convey just how specific problem-solving skills often are. In the original (1976) study, Siegler almost decided not to include the 16- and 17-year-olds. The headmistress of the school told him that the students would perform perfectly, since they had learned about balance scales in *two* previous science courses. Both Siegler and the headmistress were surprised when fewer than 20 percent of the students used Rule IV.

A later conversation with a science teacher in the school proved revealing. The teacher pointed out that the balance scale in the experiment was an arm balance, whereas the balance scale used in the classroom was a pan balance, in which pans with varying amounts of weight could be suspended from hooks at varying distances from the fulcrum. Retesting a few students indicated that they indeed could solve comparable problems presented on a pan balance! This limited generalization is, unfortunately, the rule rather than the exception in problem solving.

Learning and encoding. One reason for identifying both the typical developmental sequence of rules and the rules used by individual children is to predict which instructional experiences will help particular children learn. To illustrate this point, Siegler (1976) identified 5- and 8-year-olds who used Rule I on the balance-scale task on a pretest. The children were then presented feedback experience. In this feedback experience, children first were given a problem and asked which side of the balance scale would go down. Then the lever that had held the arm motionless was released, and children saw whether their prediction was correct. Each child received such feedback on one of three types of problems. Some received balance and weight problems, problems that their pretest approach would solve correctly. Others received distance problems, which their existing rule would not solve correctly, but which they would be able to solve correctly when they acquired the next rule in the typical developmental sequence. Yet others received conflict problems, which they would not understand even qualitatively until they reached Rule III.

The moderate-discrepancy hypothesis (p. 151) suggested that the most effective problems for promoting learning would be somewhat, but not greatly, beyond the child's initial level. Thus, for children who used Rule I, distance problems would be most helpful, because they were solvable by Rule II, the next rule that Rule I children typically would acquire.

Consistent with this hypothesis, both 5- and 8-year-olds who were presented with distance problems usually advanced to Rule II. Also as expected, both 5- and 8-year-olds who were presented with feedback on weight problems, which their existing approach (Rule I) already solved, continued to use Rule I. Reactions to the conflict problems, however, differed somewhat from the prediction. As expected, most 5-year-olds made no progress. Unexpectedly, however, most 8-year-olds benefited greatly from experience with them. The 8-year-olds often advanced to Rule III, which entailed qualitative understanding of the roles of weight and distance on all problems.

Why might 5- and 8-year-olds, all of whom used Rule I initially, have reacted differently to experience with the conflict problems? Examination of videotapes of a few children solving conflict problems suggested that encoding of the balance-scale configuration played a critical role in determining learning. The 8-year-olds seemed to encode information about both the amount of weight on each side of the fulcrum and the distance between each pile of weights and the fulcrum. In contrast, 5-year-olds seemed to see each configuration solely in terms of two piles of weights, one on each side of the fulcrum. They did not appear to encode the distances of the weights from the fulcrum. If 5-year-olds' encoding was limited in this way, their failure to learn from the conflict problems would not be surprising. They simply would not be taking in the relevant information about distance.

To test whether improved encoding was in fact related to learning, 5- and 8-year-olds who used Rule I were presented with an encoding test. They were shown an arrangement of weights on pegs for 10 seconds. Then the arrangement was hidden behind a board, and they were asked to "make the same problem" on an identical balance scale that did not have any weights on it. Putting the right number of weights on the two sides indicated accurate encoding of weight; putting the weights on the appropriate pegs indicated accurate encoding of distance.

The 8-year-olds usually placed the correct number of weights on the correct pegs, showing that they accurately encoded both weight and distance. The 5-year-olds, in contrast, usually put the right number of weights on each side of the fulcrum, but generally put them on the wrong pegs. They showed little if any encoding of the weights' distance from the fulcrum.

To further test whether limited encoding was related to 5-year-olds' lack of benefit from experience with conflict problems, other 5-year-olds who used Rule I were taught to encode distance as well as weight. Then they were given feedback on the same conflict problems that previously had not produced learning in children of this age. The instruction in encoding made a big difference. Although none of the untrained 5-year-olds had benefited from feedback on such conflict problems, 70 percent of those who received encoding training did. Thus, encoding seems to be strongly related to learning.

Generality. Children approach a variety of problems in ways similar to those they use on the balance scale. Consider development of the ability to solve projection of shadows problems (Siegler, 1981). On this task (Figure 10.4), each of two T-shaped bars was located between a light source and a screen. The question was which object would cast the larger shadow on the screen if the light sources were turned on. Typically, 5-year-olds based their judgments on a single dimension; they judged that the larger object always cast the larger shadow. This parallels their basing all of their balance-scale judgments on the single dimension of the amount of weight on each side. Among 8- and 9-year-olds, the most common approach was Rule II, in which children relied on the dominant dimension (here the size of the objects) unless its value for the two choices was equal; if so, they considered a second dimension, the distance of the objects from the light source. Among 12- and 13-year-olds and adults, Rule III predominated; they consistently considered both dimensions, but did not know the proportionality formula for integrating them. Finally, as with the balance scale, few people of any age knew Rule IV, the proportionality rule that solves all problems

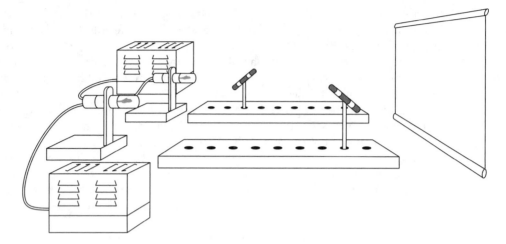

FIGURE 10.4 *Projection of shadows apparatus used by Siegler (1981). Turning on the point light sources led to different-size shadows on the screen, with the shadows' sizes depending on the length of the T-shaped bars and their distances from the light sources and the screen.*

correctly. Similar sequences of rules have been found on a wide variety of problems, among them problems involving temperature and sweetness (Strauss, 1982), happiness and fairness (Marini, 1992), personality diagnosis (Marini & Case, 1994), fullness (Bruner & Kenney, 1966), and inclined planes (Ferretti et al., 1985; Zelazo & Shultz, 1989).

One especially common finding has been that 4- to 6-year-olds base many of their problem-solving approaches on only a single dimension on problems for which two or more dimensions are relevant. This is the case not only with the problems just listed but also with liquid- and solid-quantity conservation problems; time, speed, and distance problems; probability problems; transitive inference problems; spatial reasoning problems; understanding of narratives, social dilemmas, monetary value, and emotional reactions; musical sight reading; and use of quantitative adjectives (Andrews & Halford, 1998; Bruchkowsky, 1992; Capodilupo, 1992; Case & Okamoto, 1996; Case et al., 1996; Dean, Chabaud, & Bridges, 1981; Dennis, 1992; Griffin, Case, & Sandieson, 1992; Levin, Wilkening, & Dembo, 1984; Marini & Case, 1989; Siegler, 1981; Siegler & Richards, 1979; Surber & Gzesh, 1984).

These findings do not mean that 4- to 6-year-olds cannot consider more than one dimension in solving a problem. They can and often do. Nor is it the case that young children are the only ones who rely on unidimensional rules in situations in which more than one dimension is relevant. Adults also often do this (e.g., Neisser & Weene, 1962). However, children of this age do appear to have especially strong preferences for unidimensional rules; persuading them that such rules are incorrect can be very difficult.

The finding of developmental differences in learning on the balance scale also is typical of learning in many situations. A number of the most venerable constructs regarding cognitive development have been based on observations of developmental differences in learning: stages, critical periods, and readiness, among them. For example, consider the following observation from the first decade of this century about *reading readiness:*

> Much that is now strenuously struggled for and methodized over in these early years of primary reading will come of themselves with growth, and when the child's sense organs and nervous system are stronger. . . . Reading will be learned fast when the time comes. Valuable time is wasted on it in the early years. (Huey, 1908, pp. 303, 309)

The language is quaint, but the basic observation—that older children learn faster than younger ones—remains true. How can we explain such differences in learning, which emerge even when younger and older children's initial performance is identical? We already have seen how differences in one problem-solving process, encoding, contribute to older children's greater facility in learning about balance scales. We now examine the contributions of a number of other critical processes to many other types of problem solving.

Some Important Problem-Solving Processes

This section focuses on several important problem-solving processes: planning, causal inference, analogy, tool use, and scientific and logical reasoning. Of course, these are not the only problem-solving processes that children use, but they are among the most fundamental and pervasive ones. Moreover, improvements in these processes are in large part responsible for changes in the overall effectiveness of children's problem solving as they develop.

PLANNING

Planning is future-oriented problem solving (Haith, 1994). It is used most often in complex and novel situations, in which we lack well-trodden paths to follow and are likely to make mistakes if we do not plan. Even in such novel situations, however, people often act without planning, at times to their regret (Friedman, Scholnick, & Cocking, 1987). Such failures to plan have often been lamented, but are understandable. Consider just a few of the reasons why children might not plan when doing so would help them solve problems (Ellis & Siegler, 1997):

1. Planning requires inhibiting the tendency to act immediately. Ability to inhibit actions develops slowly over the course of childhood (Dempster, 1993).
2. Children often are overoptimistic about the likelihood of succeeding without planning (Stipek, 1984).

3. Planning entails a risk of wasted effort, for example if the child fails to execute the plan correctly or the problem is beyond the child's ability to solve (Berg, 1989).
4. Planning often requires coordination with other people; this is challenging for everyone, but especially so for children, who frequently bicker, lose track of the original task, and refuse to cooperate (Baker-Sennet, Matusov, & Rogoff, 1992).
5. If children don't plan, other people, especially parents, may save them from the consequences of their failure to do so. For example, if they do not allocate sufficient time for homework, parents may help them (Ellis, Dowdy, Graham & Jones, 1992).

With all of these obstacles and reasons not to plan, it is a little surprising that children ever do so. Yet quite often they do, from infancy onward.

Means-ends analysis.   Means-ends analysis is an especially useful and widely applicable form of planning. As discussed in the dog-cat-mouse experiment earlier in the chapter, it involves comparing the goal we would like to attain with the current situation and reducing differences between the two until the goal can be met. The process demands simultaneously keeping several items in mind: subgoals, procedures for meeting the subgoals, and discrepancies between the current state and the overall goal.

Infants near the end of their first year already use means-ends analysis. Willatts (1990) presented 12-month-olds with a foam rubber barrier, behind which was a cloth with a string attached to it and a toy that sometimes was attached to the string and other times was just nearby. When the toy was attached to the string, rather than just being nearby, babies were quicker to remove the barrier, to touch the cloth, and to reel in the string. Thus, the 12-month-olds appeared to form and execute a three-step plan: move the barrier, pull the cloth, and reel in the string to get the toy.

In Willatts' study, the relation of the goal (the toy) and the means to achieve the goal (the string) was readily perceivable—the string was visibly connected to the toy. However, in many types of problems, the goal and the particular sequence of actions necessary to achieve it are not directly perceivable, and must be generated in advance by the problem solver. Bauer and colleagues (Bauer, Schwade, Wewerka, & Delaney, 1999) found that the ability to generate a path to reach a goal that is not visible emerges by 21 months of age. They presented 21- and 27-month-old children with four problems that involved assembling components to make a toy. For each problem, children were first shown the goal state (for example, a rattle made of a wooden block enclosed in a plastic barrel), and the toy was then disassembled outside of the children's view. Children were then given the components (the block and the two halves of the barrel) and encouraged to assemble the toy. Overall, children successfully solved about 40 percent of the problems; in 90 percent of these solutions, they performed the target actions in precisely the correct order, suggesting that they had planned the sequence of actions in advance. The 27-month-olds showed more evidence of planning than did the 21-month-olds, but even children in the younger group successfully planned on some of the trials. Thus, by 2 years of

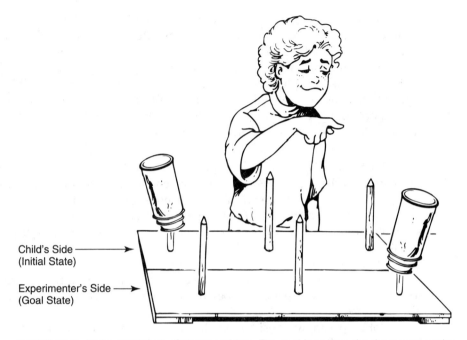

Child's Side ⟶
(Initial State)

Experimenter's Side ⟶
(Goal State)

FIGURE 10.5   Three disk Tower of Hanoi problem. The goal is to have the three cans on the child's side match the three on the experimenter's side. Only one can at a time can be moved and smaller cans cannot be placed on top of larger ones. The problem can be solved in seven moves (from Klahr, 1989).

age, children can generate a sequence of actions to achieve a goal, even when the goal and the means to achieve it are not readily perceivable.

The continuing development of means-ends analysis in subsequent years involves large changes in the number and complexity of subgoals that children can keep in mind at once and in their ability to resist the lure of short-term goals to pursue longer-term ones. These changes can be seen in 3- to 6-year-olds' approaches to the Tower of Hanoi problem (Figure 10.5). The game is to make one's own stack of cans into the same configuration as the experimenter's stack in as few moves as possible. There are only two rules: Move only one can at a time, and never place a smaller can on a larger one (because it would fall off). To appreciate the planning that is necessary to solve such problems, try to find the optimal (seven-move) solution to the problem in Figure 10.5.

Not surprisingly, older children can solve longer problems. Most 3-year-olds solve two-move problems (problems that require two moves to progress from the initial arrangement to the goal); most 4-year-olds solve four-move problems; and most 5- and 6-year-olds solve five- or six-move problems (Klahr & Robinson, 1981; Welsh, 1991). More interesting than these changes in the length of problems that children can solve are changes in the strategies they use in planning which moves to make. The 3-year-olds' strategies are limited to direct efforts to move disks to their goal. When they cannot move a can to its goal because another can is on top of the one they want to move, they often break the rules and move the can anyway. The older children react to such situations by planning subgoals that move them in promising directions for fulfilling their original goals. They also look further ahead in planning their moves. Even at age 6, however, children have difficulty solving problems that require them to make a move away from attaining a short-term goal, the same difficulty that children of this age encountered on the dog-cat-mouse problem described earlier (Klahr, 1985).

Route planning. One use of planning is to choose the most efficient route for reaching a destination. For example, when children are told to put away possessions that they have strewn about the house, they try to minimize the distance they must travel. They might pile up the clothes, games, books, and toys scattered around the first floor before hauling the heap to their bedroom on the second floor.

The ability to plan routes develops early. Children near their first birthday often journey to rooms they cannot see at the beginning of a trip in order to get toys they also cannot see at the beginning (Benson, Arehart, Jennings, Boley, & Kearns, 1989).

Not surprisingly, considerable development in route-planning skills occurs beyond this early period. Even in the short time between ages 4 and 5, children's skill at planning increases considerably. The 5-year-olds consider more alternative routes before starting, do less backtracking, and correct errors more quickly than do 4-year-olds (Fabricius, 1988).

Older children also fit strategies to circumstances more precisely. In one study of 4- to 10-year-olds (Gardner & Rogoff, 1990), some children were told that they needed to plan how to get from one point to another, and that both speed and avoiding wrong turns were important factors. Other 4- to 10-year-olds were told that the only important consideration was avoiding wrong turns. Under both conditions, 4- to 7-year-olds planned some of the route in advance and the rest as they came to choice points. The 7- to 10-year-olds did the same when both speed and avoiding wrong turns mattered. However, when only choosing the most direct route mattered, the older children often planned the entire sequence of choices before they began, which led to their reducing their number of wrong turns. The older children thus realized the benefits of planning when speed was unimportant and avoided the time cost of planning when speed was important. In contrast, the younger children's failure to plan in the condition where speed was irrelevant led to their making as many errors there as when speed did matter.

CAUSAL INFERENCE

As described in Chapter 8, those who view concepts as implicit theories emphasize knowledge of causal relations as central to conceptual understanding.

So important are causal relations for unifying our understanding that the philosopher David Hume described them as "the cement of the universe." Not surprisingly, then, problem solving is often an effort to determine the causes of events. For example, when a child takes a clock apart to see how it works, the child is trying to find out what causes each part to move. Two-year-olds' endless "Why" questions, such as "Why do dogs bark?" are also sometimes efforts to understand causes. (At other times, they are simply efforts to annoy their parents.)

Why people infer causal connections among events has long intrigued philosophers and psychologists. There is nothing in the external world that forces such inferences. It might seem obvious to us when one pool ball hits another and the second ball begins to roll that the rolling of the first ball caused that of the second. But is this inference logical? Couldn't the second ball simply have begun rolling for some other reason? Would we draw the same inference if we opened the trunk of a car and the car's radio suddenly turned on?

The Humean variables.   British philosopher David Hume (1739–1740/1911) hypothesized that three features lead people to infer that events are causally related: The events occurred close together in time and space (*contiguity*); the event labeled the "cause" preceded the event labeled the "effect" (*precedence*); and the cause and effect consistently occurred together on past occasions (*covariation*). In line with Hume's hypothesis, each of these variables influences children's (and adults') causal inferences.

Infants in their first year already use both temporal and spatial contiguity to infer causal connections. In the experiments that established this point (Leslie, 1982; Oakes, 1994; Oakes & Cohen, 1990, 1995), 6- to 10-month-olds were repeatedly shown films of a moving object colliding with a stationary one and the stationary object then starting to move. Then the infants saw sequences that either violated spatial contiguity (the second object moved despite the first not reaching it) or that violated temporal contiguity (the first object struck the second but the second did not move until 3/4 of a second after the collision). Events that violated spatial and temporal contiguity elicited longer looking than events that maintained them, suggesting that the violations surprised the infants.

By age 5, and perhaps earlier, children also use the order of events to infer that one event caused the other. When 3- and 4-year-olds are shown three events in the order A-B-C and then asked, "What made B happen?", they tend to choose Event A, which preceded Event B, rather than Event C, which followed it (Bullock & Gelman, 1979; Kun, 1978). It should be noted, however, that 3-year-olds show this understanding of precedence in fewer situations than older children. In some situations, as many 3-year-olds say that the second event caused the first as say the reverse (Corrigan, 1975; Kuhn & Phelps, 1976; Shultz, Altmann, & Asselin, 1986; Sophian & Huber, 1984). All studies, however, find that by age 5 children consistently choose the earlier event as the cause.

The importance of consistent covariation of events seems to be the last of the three Humean variables to be understood. Young children are especially likely to ignore this variable when it conflicts with contiguity. For example, 5-year-olds rarely attribute a causal connection to a sequence in which one event always follows five seconds after another event (Mendelson & Shultz, 1976). In contrast, 8-year-olds and adults do see the delayed but consistent relation as indicating that the two events are causally connected. To summarize, contiguity is influential even in infancy; precedence is sometimes considered in attributing causes by age 3 and consistently by age 5; and covariation becomes increasingly influential after age 5.

Beyond the Humean variables. Children's causal inferences extend beyond Hume's analysis in several respects. From infancy they grasp that the size of an effect is related to the size of the cause. In one experiment, 11-month-olds were habituated to a medium-size object colliding with a stationary object and causing it to move a certain distance (Kotovsky & Baillargeon, 1994). Then they either saw a larger moving object cause the stationary object to move farther or saw a smaller moving object cause the stationary object to move farther. They looked for a longer time when the smaller object caused the larger movement, suggesting that they expected the smaller object to exert the smaller effect.

From about age 3, children also distinguish between physical causality and psychological causality. In a study that demonstrated this point (Schlottman, Allen, Linderoth, & Hesketh, 2002), children ages 3 to 9 were first presented with three pictures, one depicting physical causation (a man kicking a ball, causing it to fly into the air), one depicting psychological causation (one man chasing another man, causing him to run), and one depicting an action that was non-causal, in the sense that it did not cause some other action to occur (a man walking). Children were then presented with movies of red and green shapes moving in various patterns, and after each movie, they were asked to indicate which of the pictures was like the movie. At all ages, when children saw a moving shape collide with a stationary one and the stationary object then begin to move, they almost always chose the physical causation picture. In addition, when they saw a moving shape approach a stationary one *without* touching it, and the stationary object then begin to move, they almost always chose the psychological causation picture. Thus, by 3 years of age, children interpret different kinds of schematic events (contact versus non-contact events) in terms of different causal mechanisms.

Children also understand from early in development that different types of causal explanations are appropriate for different types of entities. Even preschoolers realize that something inside of animals causes them to move when they want to do so (Gelman & Gottfried, 1996; Opfer & Gelman, 2001; Simons & Keil, 1995). They are not too clear about what that something is, but they believe it is different from the causes of motion of inanimate objects. This general distinction probably leads them to look in different directions for the specific causes of motion of animate and inanimate objects.

These examples illustrate a larger principle: From early in life, children emphasize the importance of causal *mechanisms* over all other clues to the causes of events. When they understand a causal mechanism, they expect events to be consistent with it. For example, the causal mechanism relevant to colliding objects is force. Other things being equal, a smaller moving object will exert a smaller force on a stationary object, resulting in a smaller movement. Even infants appear to see violations of this relation as surprising. Similarly, the causal mechanism relevant to non-contact events is psychological—that is, understandable in terms of the agent's intentions and beliefs. By 3 years of age, children interpret non-contact events in terms of psychological causation, even when the agents involved are shapes rather than animate beings.

Different situations present varying types of information for inferring what caused the event to occur. Sometimes these sources of information point to the same conclusion; other times they do not. Much of the challenge in deciding among alternative potential causes of events is deciding which type of information to weigh most heavily. At least from age 3 onward, children seem to use a set of strategy-choice rules for making these decisions (Shultz, Fisher, Pratt, & Rulf, 1986). When information about causal mechanisms is available, children use it. When it is not, they tend to rely on temporal and spatial contiguity and other perceptually striking events. Only when neither of these types of information is available do children consider less striking factors that are correlated with the effect's occurrence, such as delayed but regular covariation between cause and effect.

Once children understand causal relationships, they use this knowledge in other sorts of problem solving, such as forming categories and drawing inferences. Indeed, some evidence suggests that children weight causal information especially heavily in categorization (Keil, Smith, Simons, & Levin, 1998). In one study of this issue (Ahn, Gelman, Amsterlaw, Hohenstein, & Kalish, 2000), 7- to 9-year-olds learned descriptions of novel animals. Some children were told that one feature of the animal caused two additional features (such as "Promicin in their nerves makes taliboos have thick bones and large eyes"). Children were then presented with two additional animals and were asked to select which one was another member of the category (another taliboo). One of the additional animals was missing the causal feature (promicin in the nerves) and the other possessed the causal feature, but was missing an effect feature (large eyes). In both cases, the new animals possessed two of the three key features; however, children were much more likely to choose the animal that possessed the causal feature and was missing an effect feature as a category member than they were to choose the animal that was missing the causal feature but had the effect features. Thus, information about causal mechanisms appears to be particularly salient in children's thinking, not only for evaluating causation, but also for forming categories.

ANALOGY

Analogical reasoning is a pervasive and powerful process. It involves solving problems by identifying corresponding structures or functions in objects or events that are being compared (Gentner et al., 1995; Goswami, 2001; Halford, 1993). For example, understanding the metaphorical statement "a camera is like a tape recorder" requires understanding the function that each device serves— to record the present for future examination. Analogy is widely used in every-day reasoning and problem solving, as well as in more specialized settings, such as among scientists generating hypotheses at laboratory meetings, or among politicians attempting to sway voters at political rallies (Dunbar & Blanchette, 2001).

The development of analogical reasoning resembles that of causal infer-ence. The range of analogies that children understand and generate increases greatly with age. For example, when presented the camera/tape recorder anal-ogy, 6-year-olds tend to cite such superficial similarities as that both are black, whereas 9-year-olds focus on their common functions (Gentner et al., 1995). On the other hand, even infants and toddlers draw successful analogies under some circumstances, and under other circumstances, even college-educated adults fail to do so. This resemblance between causal and analogical reasoning is no coin-cidence. Drawing appropriate analogies often depends critically on understand-ing and identifying parallels in the causal relations being compared (for example, why people use tape recorders and cameras).

Developmental similarities in analogical reasoning. A nascent ability to form analogies is present by the end of the first year. Chen, Sanchez, and Campbell (1997) presented 10- and 13-month-olds a series of three problems in which appealing toys were placed behind a barrier. The problems were like those presented by Willatts (1990); infants needed to remove the barrier and pull a towel with a string attached to the toy, rather than a towel with a string that was not attached to the toy. In Chen et al.'s study, however, children first tried to solve the problem on their own, then saw their parent model how to solve the problem, and then were presented conceptually identical problems that varied in superficial features, such as the particular objects involved, their colors and sizes, and whether the child tried to obtain the toy from a sitting or standing position. After seeing their parent's solution to the first problem, 13-month-olds were able to solve subsequent problems increasingly efficiently, even when the problems did not look very similar to the original one. The 10-month-olds could also draw appropriate analogies, but only when the subsequent problems looked more similar to the one they had seen solved.

By preschool age, children form more complex analogies. In one study, 3-to 5-year-olds heard a story in which a genie needed to transport jewels across a wall and into a bottle (Brown, Kane, & Echols, 1986). The genie solved the problem by rolling up a piece of posterboard so that it formed a tube, placing the tube so that it led into the mouth of the bottle, and then rolling the jewels down through the tube and into the bottle. After hearing this story, children were presented a problem about an Easter bunny who needed to transport eggs across a river and into a basket on the other side. Children needed to show how they could use a piece of posterboard to transfer the eggs into a basket that was on the other side of a river that was drawn on the floor. Some 5-year-olds, but few 3-year-olds, solved the Easter bunny problem by using a strategy analogous to that used in the genie story. However, if asked questions about the central facts of each story (what goal the main character was trying to achieve, what obstacle made it difficult to do so, what the main character did to overcome the obstacle), both 3- and 5-year-olds consistently solved the problem. Thus 3-year-olds could draw the relevant analogy, but they needed to be reminded of the key components to draw the relevant parallels.

By age 4, children form analogies without prompting in some situations. Tunteler and Resing (2002) presented 4-year-olds with brief stories and then asked them to complete physical tasks that could be solved using approaches analogous to those described in the stories. For example, one story described an elderly lady whose bag fell into the bushes. She could not reach the bag, but she used her walking stick to retrieve it. After hearing this story, the experimenter asked children to retrieve a plastic bottle that was out of reach on a tabletop. A set of 14 tools was available to children to use in solving the problem. All of the problems could be solved in either an analogical way (using a tool with the same function as the tool described in the story) or in an unrelated, non-analogical way (using a different type of tool and a different action).

Children in an experimental condition were given two such problems to solve each week for a period of six weeks, and children in a control condition were given two problems to solve in the first and last weeks only. Children in both groups spontaneously selected the analogical tool more often than would be expected by chance alone, indicating that 4-year-olds can spontaneously form analogies. Furthermore, children in the experimental group increased their use of analogical problem solving from the first session to the final session, whereas children in the control group did not. Thus, practice in analogical reasoning improved the young children's spontaneous formation of analogies.

Although infants and young children can spontaneously form analogies in some situations, older children and adults fail to see many others. Like the 3-year-olds in Brown et al.'s (1986) study, college students often fail to recognize analogies that they readily draw when the parallel is called to their attention (Holyoak & Thagard, 1995).

The same variables generally influence the analogical reasoning of young children, older children, and adults. People of all ages are more likely to recognize analogies between situations when superficial characteristics (such as the characters' names) as well as deep characteristics (such as goals, obstacles, and potential solutions) are similar (Goswami, 1992, 1995a). They also are more likely to analogize when they have encountered several previous problems with the same solution principle, rather than just one (Chen, 1999; Crisafi & Brown 1986; Gholson, Emyard, Morgan, & Kamhi, 1987), and when the procedures used to solve the source problem and the target problem are highly similar (Chen, 1996, 2002). Complete encoding of relevant structural features is similarly important to analogical problem solving at all ages (Chen et al., 1997; Gentner et al., 1995). The likelihood of drawing analogies changes with age, but the variables that increase or decrease that likelihood tend to be the same.

Developmental differences. These similarities in the variables that influence the likelihood of generating relevant analogies should not obscure the profound changes that occur with age in analogical reasoning. Young children require explicit hints or demonstrations to draw analogies that older children draw without such assistance (Brown et al., 1986; Chen et al., 1997; Crisafi & Brown, 1986). Their analogizing is also hindered by superficial perceptual dissimilarities and associations that exert much less influence on the analogizing of older children and adults (Chen, 1996; Chen, Yanowitz, & Daehler, 1995; Goswami & Brown, 1990).

Comparable developmental trends are evident in interpretation of metaphors (Gentner, 1988; Winner, 1988). When presented with the metaphor "The prison guard was a hard rock," 6- and 7-year-olds most often produce literal or magical interpretations, such as "the guard worked in a prison that had hard rock walls" or "the guard had hard, tough muscles" (Winner, Rosenstiel, & Gardner, 1976, p. 293). In contrast, 13- and 14-year-olds consistently emphasize the relation between psychological and physical characteristics, as in the explanation "The guard was mean and did not care about the feelings of the prisoners" (Winner et al., 1976; p. 293). In general, children correctly interpret metaphors based on appearances of the objects being compared before they correctly interpret metaphors for which only relational structures are parallel. Further, with age, children become increasingly likely to interpret relationally those metaphors that can be viewed either in terms of similarities between objects or similarities between relations (Gentner, 1988).

Why does analogical reasoning improve with age? One reason is increasing content knowledge. As children acquire greater knowledge, they increasingly understand the centrality of properties that are not superficially striking. Returning to the tape recorder/camera example, children learn that the key feature of these devices is information preservation, rather than color, size, or other obvious characteristics. A second source of development of analogical reasoning is language (Gentner et al., 1995). Language provides names for abstract relations that otherwise might not be recognized as similar. Thus, referring to both cameras and tape recorders as "information-preservation devices" calls attention to a similarity they share with each other and with other superficially different objects such as books and portraits.

TOOL USE

Children do not solve problems in a vacuum. They use available tools to help them. Given the right problem, almost anything can serve as a tool: canes, rakes, spoken and written language, maps, mathematical notation, even other people. Tools vary in their breadth of applicability and in how directly they lead to solutions, but all provide ways for children to solve problems that otherwise would exceed their capabilities.

Among the first tools that children use are their mothers (Mosier & Rogoff, 1994). When attractive toys are placed out of reach, 6- to 13-month-olds use their mothers instrumentally to obtain the toys. They look back and forth beseechingly between the mother and the toy, make "gimme" gestures with their hands and fingers, lean toward the toys, and vocalize. As with any good tool, other people greatly expand the range of problems children can solve.

Children do not wait long to also begin using inanimate objects as tools. In one study, $1\frac{1}{2}$- and 2-year-olds saw an experimenter pull in an attractive toy by using a rake (Brown, 1989). Then the toddlers were asked to get the toy themselves. They were strapped into a seat so that they could not move, but had available a variety of potential tools. For example, a child who had seen the toy obtained with a long rake might have within reach a long cane, a short rake, a long straight stick that was the same color as the original rake, and a long, squiggly, flexible object. The toddlers were quick to choose, and their choices were almost always good ones. They chose tools that were rigid, that had an end that was appropriate for pulling, and that were long enough to reach the toy. They were indifferent to whether the tool was the same color as the one they had seen used originally. They also were perfectly willing to substitute canes for rakes. Thus, they understood the causal properties that led to the tools being appropriate for solving the problem.

In Brown's study, the experimenter demonstrated how to use the rake before toddlers attempted to retrieve the toy on their own. Chen and Siegler (2000) investigated whether the experimenter's demonstration was important in fostering children's tool use. In their study, 18- to 35-month-olds either saw the experimenter demonstrate how to use a tool to retrieve a toy, received a hint about using the appropriate tool ("Can you use this to get the toy?"), or received neither the demonstration nor the hint. Children in both the demonstration and the hint conditions were more likely to display tool use on later trials than were children in the control condition, suggesting that they learned from the demonstration and the hint. Furthermore, across trials in the study, children used the tool strategy more consistently, they executed the strategy more skillfully, and they made better, more refined choices among the available tools.

Symbolic representations as tools. Symbolic representations, such as maps, scale models, and pictures, also are widely useful problem-solving tools. By three years, children demonstrate considerable facility in using this type of tool. In a classic demonstration of this skill, DeLoache (1987) showed $2\frac{1}{2}$- and 3-year-olds a small toy being hidden in a scale model of a room. Then children were asked to find the toy in a room that was a life-size version of the scale model. If the toy in the scale model was hidden under a miniature chair, it could be found under the corresponding life-size chair in the room. The experimenter gave instructions such as, "Watch! I'm hiding Little Snoopy here. I'm going to hide Big Snoopy in the same place in his big room!" (DeLoache, 1995, p. 110).

Despite the small (7-month) difference in average age of children in the two groups, they differed greatly in ability to use the scale model. The 3-year-olds found the hidden object without error on more than 70 percent of trials; the 2½-year-olds found it without error on fewer than 20 percent. This was not attributable to failure to understand the situation or failure to remember the demonstration with the model. Children of both ages consistently recalled where the miniature object was hidden within the model when they were asked about it. Rather, the difference was in younger children's inability to use the scale model to infer the object's location in the larger room.

Why would 2½-year-olds encounter such difficulties in using the scale model to solve the problems? One possibility was that they did not understand how any type of representation could be used as a tool to solve such problems. To test this interpretation, DeLoache (1987) showed 2½-year-olds line drawings or photographs of the larger room and told the toddlers to use them to find the object. The same children who failed with the scale model succeeded with the line drawings and photographs. Thus, they could use some symbolic representations as tools for solving problems.

DeLoache suggested that the source of the 2-year-olds' difficulty with scale models was a conflict between viewing them as interesting objects in their own right and as representations of another object. Consistent with this interpretation, having 3-year-olds first play with a scale model—which would lead them to think of the model more as an interesting object in itself—decreased their later success in using it to find hidden objects. Conversely, eliminating any potential interaction with the model—by putting it in a glass case where it could be seen but not touched—allowed 2½-year-olds to find the hidden objects more successfully than usual (DeLoache, 1989, 2000). This interpretation also makes understandable why pictures and photographs can be used as problem-solving devices earlier in development than scale models: they are not very interesting as objects, and thus the conflict does not arise (DeLoache & Burns, 1994; Troseth & DeLoache, 1996).

Another clever experiment provided particularly compelling evidence for the interpretation that young children have difficulty viewing the scale model as both an object itself and as a representation of another object. DeLoache, Miller, and Rosengren (1997) created a version of the scale model task in which 2½-year-old children were led to believe that a "magic shrinking machine" had caused the room to *turn into* the model. Thus, in the children's view, the scale model was not a representation of the other room—it *was* the other room. To make the "shrinking machine" scenario believable, children were first shown the machine itself (an oscilloscope with flashing lights), and they placed a large troll doll in front of it. The machine was turned on, and the experimenter and child left the lab for about 10 seconds, during which time strange sounds could be heard coming from the lab. When they returned, children saw a tiny troll doll in front of the machine. Next, children were presented with a portable, tent-like room (purportedly the troll's room), and the shrinking machine was aimed at the room. Once again, the experimenter and child left the lab for a brief period, during which time more strange sounds could be heard. When they returned, children saw a scale model of the portable room in front of the shrinking machine.

For the experiment proper, the troll and the room were "enlarged" again (with the shrinking machine operating in "reverse"), and the troll was hidden in the room. The room with the hidden troll was then "shrunk" again, and children were asked to find the troll in the tiny room. The 2½-year-olds immediately searched in the correct location on almost 80 percent of the trials—much better than children of the same age had performed in the standard version of the task, which required viewing the scale model as a representation. The shrinking room task did not require children to view the model as both an object in its own right and as a representation of the larger room. Instead, children believed that the model *was* the larger room.

The work of DeLoache and colleagues highlights some of the reasons why symbolic tools are difficult for young children to understand and use. At the same time, the work demonstrates that children's ability to use symbolic representations such as tools undergoes a great deal of development in the first few years of life (DeLoache, 2002). This is fortunate, because so many of the tools that are important in modern life involve symbols: spoken and written language, counting systems, measuring instruments, and, of course, computers. However, the symbolic tools that culture provides are not the only ones that children use— they also create new ones of their own.

Self-created symbolic tools.   In one study of novel symbolic tools, Eskritt and Lee (2002) examined the symbolic notations that children in Grades 1, 3, 5, and 7 devised to help them succeed at the memory game "Concentration." The game uses a deck made up of pairs of cards with identical pictures. At the outset of the game, all of the cards are placed face down in a random array. A player turns over one card, and then turns over a second card in an effort to find the card that matches it. The player's "turn" continues as long as he or she turns up pairs; when the player turns up two cards that do not form a pair, the turn is ended. Ordinarily, the game is played with more than one player, but the children in Eskritt and Lee's study played alone. For these children, the object of the game was to match up all the pairs in as few turns as possible.

Before allowing children to begin the game, Eskritt and Lee offered them the opportunity to "write or draw anything you want to help you win the game in fewer turns." Children made a variety of different types of notations to help them remember the identities and the locations of the cards, including some notations that involved pictures, and some that involved words. As seen in Figure 10.6, First-grade students tended to produce notations that did not include information that would aid their memory; however, fifth- and seventh-grade students

FIGURE 10.6 Examples of notations produced by a younger child and an older child for the Concentration game when asked to "write or draw anything you want to help you win the game in fewer turns." Note that the notation produced by the younger child does not contain information that would aid the child's memory of the locations and identities of the cards, but the notation produced by the older child does. From Eskritt and Lee (2002), Copyright © 2002 by the American Psychological Association. Reprinted with permission.

often produced notations that incorporated information about the identities and locations of the cards, such as diagrams with sketches of various cards. Not surprisingly, the quality of the notations influenced children's success at the game—children who produced better notations won the game in fewer turns.

In a follow-up study, Eskritt and Lee asked one group of seventh-grade students to make notations at the outset of the game, and another group simply to study the cards. Children who made notations were led to believe that they would use their notations in playing the game. However, instead of playing the game, children's notations were removed, and they were presented with two "surprise" tasks. In one of the tasks, children were presented with a new deck that included the cards from the original deck as well as some new cards, and they were asked to identify the cards that had been in the original deck. In the other task, children were asked to indicate the location of each of the cards that they identified as being from the original deck. Children in the two groups performed equally well at recognizing the cards. However, the children who had made notations performed much more poorly at indicating the locations of the cards than did the children who had simply studied the cards. Thus, children's self-generated symbolic notations served to store information about the locations of specific cards. When the notations were unexpectedly removed, children's memory for locations suffered.

Another type of self-created symbolic tool is informal maps. Karmiloff-Smith (1979, 1986, 1992) investigated children's use of such maps in a study in which 7- to 11-year-olds played the part of ambulance drivers who needed to transport a sick patient to the hospital. The patient's home was represented by a picture at one end of a 40-foot roll of paper; the hospital was represented by a picture at the other end. In between were 20 choice points. Each choice point involved two choices, one of which led to a dead end. Children were told to make the trip once without the patient, so that they could find the fastest route. They were also encouraged to mark up the paper to help them remember which route to take later.

Within the one-hour session, children often changed the types of marks they made, even when the original marks were optimally informative. One

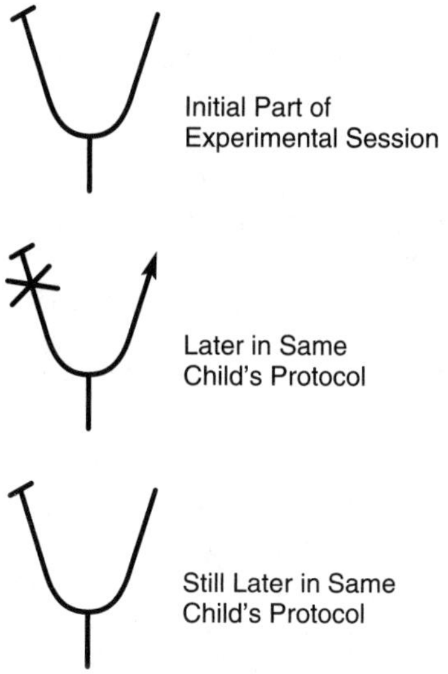

Initial Part of
Experimental Session

FIGURE 10.7 Maps drawn by a 7-year-old at three points during a session. Note how redundant features are added in the second representation but eliminated in the third (after Karmiloff-Smith, 1986). Reprinted from Karmiloff-Smith, Stage/Structure versus Phase/Process in Modeling Linguistic and Cognitive Development, in I. Levin (Ed.), Stage and structure: Reopening the debate. Copyright © 1986 by Ablex Publishing Corporation. Reproduced with the permission of Greenwood Publishing Group, Inc., Westport, CT.

Later in Same
Child's Protocol

Still Later in Same
Child's Protocol

7-year-old's marks are depicted in Figure 10.7. At first, she indicated the dead end simply by placing a bar perpendicular to the path. Then she began augmenting this representation by putting both the bar and an "X" on the wrong path and an arrow on the right one. Finally, she returned to the original, leaner notation.

Why would children abandon a correct approach that allowed them to perform effectively? The issue is not unique to map drawing; the same phenomenon is present in children's number conservation and class inclusion strategies and in their use of past tense and causal verbs (Bowerman, 1982; Markman, 1979). Karmiloff-Smith (1992) suggested that the process reflects a drive that children have to understand *why* their strategies work. Children's first goal seems to be to perform correctly. Attaining that goal does not satisfy them forever, though. If they do not understand why an approach works, or suspect that another approach might be more effective, efficient, or elegant, they may abandon the original method, at least temporarily. Understanding this type of cognitive motivation, and the way in which children decide when to experiment with alternative approaches, is one of the deeper challenges confronting current theories of cognitive development.

Tools for measuring. Measurement procedures such as counting, weighing, and using rulers are especially useful tools for solving many problems. Like all of the other problem-solving techniques, however, they are two-edged swords. Used appropriately, they enhance problem solving; used inappropriately, they lead it down erroneous paths.

Consider how inappropriate use of measurement techniques, and in particular, inappropriate use of counting, can lead children astray. Miller (1989) asked 3- to 10-year-olds to give two turtles equal amounts of food (the food was represented by pieces of clay of varying sizes). Most children used a counting strategy, in which they gave one piece to one turtle, the next piece to the other turtle and so on. This resulted in an equal division of the number of pieces of food, but not usually of the amount of food, since some pieces were bigger than others. Belief in the effectiveness of the counting procedure ran sufficiently deep that when several preschoolers found they had given one more piece of food to one of the turtles, they simply cut in half a piece that belonged to the other turtle and gave one piece to each, thus equalizing the numbers. With age, children more often attempted to create equal-size pieces, but they still counted out equal numbers for each turtle, even when the attempt to standardize their size failed. Not until age 9 did most children divide the food into equal amounts, rather than equal numbers of pieces. The difficulty is reminiscent of 5- to 9-year-olds inaccurately estimating the passage of time because they did not count in units of equal duration (Levin, 1989). Measurement tools expand children's capabilities, but they also can seduce them into making mistakes.

SCIENTIFIC AND LOGICAL REASONING

Scientific thinking. Children often have been likened to scientists. Both ask fundamental questions about the nature of the universe. Both also ask innumerable questions that seem utterly trivial to others. Both are granted by society the time to pursue their musings. This "child as scientist" metaphor has motivated a great deal of research on how children form hypotheses, generate experiments, and interpret data.

Despite some global resemblances between children's problem solving and that of scientists, there also are large differences. Some of these involve the quality of experiments. Children are less likely than adults to design unconfounded experiments, which hold constant all variables except the one whose effect is being examined; thus their experiments often have multiple interpretations (Chen & Klahr, 1999; Klahr, Fay, & Dunbar, 1993; Kuhn, Schauble, & Garcia-Mila, 1992). They also often conduct too few experiments to obtain the evidence they need to draw a well-founded conclusion (Klahr, 2000; Klahr et al., 1993; Kuhn, et al., 1995). Finally, children often fail to integrate information across multiple experiments. They sometimes interpret individual experimental outcomes "locally," instead of seeking an interpretation that holds across an entire set of experiments (Klahr, 2000).

Understanding of the logic of experimentation is not entirely lacking in childhood, though. When presented two potential experiments for deciding a simple question, and asked which is the better approach, first and second graders prefer the experiment that would yield conclusive evidence over the one that would not (Sodian, Zaitchik, & Carey, 1991). Furthermore, elementary school students can learn how to design unconfounded experiments if they are provided with instruction that focuses on why confounded comparisons are inconclusive and why unconfounded comparisons are conclusive (Chen & Klahr, 1999). Thus, with instructional support, elementary school students can learn the rationale for experimental comparisons that vary only one factor at a time. On the whole, however, children's abilities to generate experiments for testing hypotheses and to devise ways of deciding between alternative hypotheses are quite limited.

Another important weakness in children's scientific reasoning has to do with separating theory and evidence. Children often hold informal "theories" about everyday and scientific phenomena, and these theories influence their evaluation of evidence (Koslowski, 1996; Zimmerman, 2000). They sometimes fail to distinguish conclusions based on observations from conclusions based on their prior theories or beliefs (Dunbar & Klahr, 1988; Kuhn, Amsel & O'Loughlin, 1988; Kuhn et al., 1995; Metz, 1985). They have particular difficulty in interpreting experiments that yield results inconsistent with their prior beliefs. The ability to change one's views in response to unexpected observations is particularly important in scientific contexts, because new evidence frequently suggests unexpected conclusions.

Schauble (1990) performed a particularly interesting study of the interplay of prior beliefs, experimentation, and interpretation of data. Children aged 9 to 11 were presented a computer game involving toy race cars. The task was to determine the causal impact on the race cars' speed of five factors: engine size, wheel size, presence of tailfins, presence of a muffler, and color. In the game, a large engine and medium-sized wheels made the car go faster, muffler and color were irrelevant, and absence of tailfins increased the car's speed when the engine was large and had no effect when the engine was small.

The children had eight sessions in which to learn about the effects of the five features. In each session, they could equip cars with any features they chose, and then compare the speeds of cars with those features. The task was not inherently difficult. By varying one feature and holding all others constant, children could quickly establish the effect of each variable. An adult scientist who was presented the task identified the causal roles of all features in a single session.

The 9- to 11-year-olds were much slower to identify the causal relations. One reason was that more than half of their experiments were invalid. In such invalid experiments, the cars that children designed often varied in two or more ways, so that it was impossible to determine which factor caused the difference in their speeds. Even when children performed valid experiments, they often drew conclusions inconsistent with the evidence but consistent with their prior beliefs. Further, even after they first hypothesized a correct role for a variable and obtained evidence consistent with the hypothesis, they vacillated between the correct new hypothesis and the incorrect expectation produced by their prior view.

The picture of the 9- to 11-year-olds' scientific reasoning was not entirely bleak, however. The children showed substantial learning over the eight sessions. The percentage of their experiments that were valid increased, they drew appropriate conclusions increasingly often, and their predictions of the race cars' speeds became more accurate. Thus, with practice in scientific reasoning, children's experimental methods and their ability to draw appropriate conclusions both improve considerably.

Adults also often fall short of the ideals of scientific problem solving. They bias interpretations of data so that it fits their prior beliefs, they continue to rely on incorrect old hypotheses after they have generated correct new ones, and they vary more than one variable when performing experiments (Kuhn et al., 1995; Oaksford & Chater, 1994; Shaklee & Elek, 1988). They also rarely organize sets of experiments into overarching plans, which results in the experiments often not yielding a clear conclusion (Schauble, 1996). The adults' experiments are better crafted, though, and their interpretations of data are usually less biased than those of children. For example, in one study that presented tasks similar to the race car problem, adults varied one variable at a time in 56 percent of their experiments, versus 34 percent for 11-year-olds, and the adults drew valid inferences in 72 percent of cases, versus 43 percent for the 11-year-olds (Schauble, 1996). Thus, scientific reasoning improves substantially with age, but identifying causes through valid experimentation and data interpretation remains a challenge for adults as well as children.

Logical reasoning. Consider the following, impeccable, logic of a 4-year-old: "If it doesn't break when I drop it, it's a rock . . . It didn't break. It must be a rock" (Scholnick & Wing, 1995, p. 342). And consider a 3-year-old's comment to her mother upon getting an already-opened can of soda from the refrigerator, "Whose is this? It's not yours, 'cause it doesn't have lipstick" (DeLoache et al., 1998, p. 801). The 3-year-old's reasoning seems to be: "My mother always gets lipstick on cans when she drinks from them; there's no lipstick on this can; therefore she didn't drink from it."

These statements are everyday examples of *deductive reasoning,* a process that can be used to solve problems whenever the information provided in the initial statement of a problem is sufficient to ensure that a particular solution is correct. In deductive reasoning, if the premises are true, the conclusions that follow from it are logically necessary. Deduction is often contrasted with *inductive reasoning,* which involves generalizing from observations. Conclusions produced via inductive reasoning may be highly probable, but they are not certain. The following examples, devised by Galotti, Komatsu, and Voelz (1997), illustrate the difference:

Deductive Problem	**Inductive Problem**
All poggops wear blue boots.	Tombor is a poggop.
Tombor is a poggop.	Tombor wears blue boots.
Does Tombor wear blue boots?	Do all poggops wear blue boots?

In the deductive problem, we can conclude with 100 percent certainty that Tombor wears blue boots. After all, he is a poggop and all poggops wear blue boots. In the inductive problem, we cannot conclude with certainty that all poggops wear blue boots. We cannot draw this conclusion even if we have seen 1,000 poggops and all wore blue boots. There always may be a poggop somewhere whom we have not seen and who wears red boots; if so, not all poggops wear blue boots. Therefore, the best answer to the inductive problem is that we cannot tell whether all poggops wear blue boots.

Although young children use both deductive and inductive reasoning, it is unclear that they understand the difference between them (Gellatly, 1987; Markovits, 1993; Murray, 1987; Murray & Armstrong, 1976). Consider kindergartners' and fourth graders' responses to the Tombor questions and others like them. Kindergartners responded similarly to the inductive and deductive problems; they thought both types of statements were equally likely to be true. In contrast, fourth graders more often thought that the deductive conclusions were true, they were more confident that they were true, and they reached their conclusions more quickly than on the inductive problems. All of these findings suggested that the fourth graders, unlike the kindergartners, understood that deductive and inductive reasoning were different (Galotti et al., 1997).

Young children's difficulties in understanding deductive inference run deep. Some evidence suggests that 4-year-olds consider deductive inferences no more certain than pure guesses (Pillow, Hill, Boyce, & Stein, 2000). Pillow and colleagues presented children with a puppet and two toys of different colors. The toys were then hidden in separate containers, outside of the children's (and the puppet's) view. Next, the puppet either looked into one of the containers and made a claim about the color of the toy in the other container (a deductive inference), or simply made a claim about the color of one of the toys without looking into either container (a guess). Children were asked to rate how certain the puppet was about his belief. Four-year-olds' ratings of the puppet's certainty did not differ for inference trials and guess trials. However, by age 6, many children rated inferences higher than guesses, and by age 9, almost all children did so. With age, children's explanations of the puppet's reasoning also improved. Few 4-year-olds but many 9-year-olds offered explanations that invoked the premises of the deduction, such as "Because he saw the other one is yellow."

These and other examples suggest that young children view their deductive inferences as not differing from other sorts of inferences, such as lunch not including cereal and orange juice. Such failure to distinguish between logically necessary and empirically likely outcomes would explain young children's eagerness to verify by empirical means relations that older children and adults view as purely logical relations (Efklides, Demetriou, & Metallidou, 1994; Galotti & Komatsu, 1989; Kuhn, 1989; Overton, Ward, Noveck, Black, & O'Brien, 1987). For example, 7-year-olds frequently insist that the experimenter open her hand before accepting as true the statement, "Either the chip I am holding in my hand is blue or it is not blue" (Osherson & Markman, 1975).

Children's failure to distinguish between empirically likely and logically necessary outcomes also makes more understandable the seemingly opposite tendency of young children to reach conclusions when the evidence does not logically allow them to do so (Acredolo & Horobin, 1987; Byrnes & Overton, 1986). For example, in a game in which four boxes were opened in succession, and children needed to say after each box was opened whether they could tell for sure which box a red chip had come from, most 5-year-olds chose the first box they saw that contained red chips, even in the face of the question, "Could it have been one of the other (unopened) boxes" (Fay & Klahr, 1996).

Why does it take children so long to understand deductive reasoning, even though they reason deductively from quite young ages? Halford (1993) proposed that three factors are influential: understanding of the basic logic of deduction, choices among alternative strategies, and information-processing limits.

Within Halford's theory, deductive reasoning originates in understanding of concrete situations. This can be illustrated in the context of *transitive inference* (If A > B, and B > C, then A > C). Halford suggested that children might first exhibit such reasoning in the context of everyday activities, such as playing with blocks. In particular, they might notice that if Block A was bigger than Block B, and Block B bigger than Block C, then Block A invariably was also bigger than Block C. This initial understanding could serve as a mental model, useful for deciding how to represent other orderings. Consistent with this view, 4-year-olds can analogize from the story of *Goldilocks and the Three Bears*—in which Daddy Bear's possessions are always the largest, Baby Bear's the smallest, and Mommy Bear's in between—to solve transitive inference problems that they otherwise would be unlikely to solve (Goswami, 1995b).

Within Halford's model, a second source of development of logical deduction involves better choices among alternative strategies. Children typically know several strategies for solving problems, and young children may choose strategies other than deduction even when they understand the basic logic of deduction. Transitive inference again can be used as an illustration. Under some circumstances, even 5-year-olds solve these problems by logical means (Trabasso, Riley, & Wilson, 1975), but they also know and use alternative strategies for solving them. One such alternative is simply to assume that the most recently mentioned object is the largest on whichever property is being compared (Halford, 1984). This simplification strategy reduces the information-processing load, but it does so at the risk of a wrong guess about the ordering (as illustrated in Figure 10.8). Another strategy that accomplishes the same goals—but that also has drawbacks—is remembering the gist of the premises but not their details, for example by forming an impression that a given stick is usually referred to as being longer than others (Brainerd & Reyna, 1990). Because these strategies often lead to wrong answers, over time children increasingly rely on the alternative approach of deduction.

Hypothesized Representation:

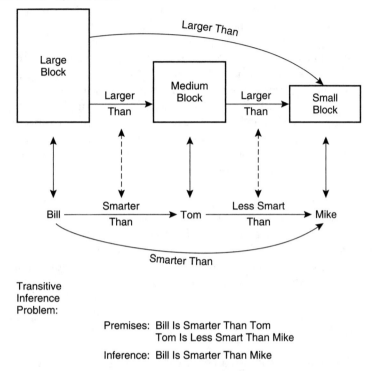

Transitive
Inference
Problem:

Premises: Bill Is Smarter Than Tom
Tom Is Less Smart Than Mike

Inference: Bill Is Smarter Than Mike

FIGURE 10.8 *Halford's (1993) analysis of how a child might err on a transitive inference problem through analogizing to prior knowledge about blocks. Bill actually might or might not be smarter than Mike.*

The final development involves increases in information-processing capacity. Such increases allow children to hold all of the relevant information in memory in more complex situations and thus allow them to reason deductively in those situations as well as in less demanding ones.

One implication of Halford's theory is that teaching children strategies that accurately represent the logical relations among the premises but that reduce the information-processing load should improve their performance on deductive problems. For syllogism problems (such as "All A's are B's, All C's are B's, Are all A's also C's?"), Venn diagrams provide one such strategy. Adults frequently use Venn diagrams spontaneously on such problems (Oakhill, 1988), but children rarely know how to do so. However, teaching sixth and eighth graders to use Venn diagrams helps them avoid such logical errors as concluding that in summer, there are more tanned women at the beach than there are women at the beach (Agnoli, 1991).

Other researchers have also focused on the importance of instruction in children's learning about deductive reasoning. For example, Morris and Sloutsky (1998) examined the effects of an experimental Russian mathematics curriculum that explicitly focuses on deductive reasoning and in particular on the distinction between conclusions that are logically necessary and conclusions that need empirical verification. Students who received the experimental curriculum showed greater gains in deductive reasoning than did other students who received more traditional instruction. Surprisingly, many students who did not receive explicit instruction did not develop a full understanding of deductive reasoning, even by age 16. Instruction may be a crucial factor in the development of deductive reasoning, and in the absence of instruction, many students may not develop full competence.

Thus, there appear to be many sources that contribute to the development of deductive reasoning. With experience and instruction, children acquire an improved understanding of the basic logic of deduction, and they learn ways to circumvent their information-processing limits, such as better ways to represent the premises within deductive problems. This new knowledge allows them to make better choices among alternative strategies for solving deductive problems and consequently leads to better reasoning.

Summary

Problem solving involves children's efforts to orchestrate a large number of processes to overcome obstacles and attain goals. It is influenced greatly by the structure of the task; this makes accurate task analyses essential for understanding both successful and unsuccessful attempts to solve problems. Encoding of the critical information in the task, forming appropriate mental models from the encoded information, integration of general and specific knowledge, and selection of appropriate problem-solving strategies are among the main determinants of success in solving problems. Recent research has indicated that younger children are more competent, and older children less competent problem solvers than was once believed. However, substantial development in the range of problems that children can solve also is present.

These general patterns are evident in performance on the balance scale. Task analyses suggested that children would use one of four solution rules to solve balance scale problems, ranging from basing all judgments on the amount of weight on each side to computing torques when necessary. Application of the rule-assessment approach indicated that children used these rules. Some of the approaches, particularly 4- to 6-year-olds' tendency to base judgments on a single, salient dimension, have proved general across many tasks. Developmental differences in learning about balance scale problems are due in large part to limitations of young children's encoding. Helping children encode relevant information helps them learn more effectively.

Among the most prominent problem-solving processes are planning, analogical reasoning, causal inference, tool use, and scientific and logical reasoning. Planning is future-oriented problem solving. It is used most often in complex and novel situations. One frequent type of planning is means-end analysis, which involves progressively reducing differences between the current state and the goal. Simple forms of means-end analysis are evident in children's first year, both in solving balance-scale problems and in obtaining distant toys. Development of planning occurs primarily in the number and complexity of subgoals children can maintain in memory, and in their ability to avoid the temptation of meeting short-term goals at the expense of longer-term ones.

Many causal inferences are based on three variables whose importance was identified by the eighteenth-century philosopher David Hume: contiguity, precedence, and covariation. Even infants are influenced by contiguity. Precedence sometimes exerts an influence by age 3 and consistently does so by age 5. Covariation in the absence of contiguity becomes increasingly important beyond age 5. However, a fourth variable is given even greater weight than these three: the presence of mechanisms that could plausibly cause the effect. Preschoolers' choices among alternative potential causes reflect primary attention to mechanisms that could produce the effects, secondary attention to perceptually striking information such as contiguity, and tertiary attention to other cues such as consistent covariation. Once children form causal inferences, they use this information in categorization and other sorts of problem solving.

Very young children can form analogies in simple situations, yet even adults often fail to recognize other, potentially useful analogies. Many of the same variables influence children's and adults' success in analogizing. These include factors such as the degree of similarity between the source and target problems, the nature of the analogical relationship, and the number of problems that have previously been solved with the same solution principle. However, older children and adults recognize many more analogies than do young children, especially when superficial features of problems obscure the relation between the old and new situations.

Use of tools to solve problems is also evident among very young children. Some of these tools, such as canes and rakes, can be used to attain goals directly. Others, such as maps and scale models, are effective in less direct ways. Tools are often advantageous for problem solving, but this is not always the case. Their availability can lure children into mistakes, as well as helping them solve otherwise difficult problems.

Scientific and logical reasoning are relatively late-developing competencies. Children find it particularly difficult to design experiments that yield clear conclusions regarding their hypotheses. They also find it difficult to separate theory from evidence; often their initial assumptions influence both the experiments they design and the conclusions they draw from the evidence. Adults also have these kinds of difficulties, but to a lesser degree. With regard to logical thinking, even young children deduce some conclusions, but the

distinction between inductive and deductive reasoning is not usually understood until late childhood or adolescence, and sometimes not even then. Much
of the difficulty is in distinguishing conclusions that are necessary, given the
premises, from ones that are simply probable. Many sources contribute to the
development of deductive reasoning, including improved understanding of
the basic logic of deduction, better choices among alternative strategies, and
learning new ways to circumvent information-processing limitations. These
improvements occur both with experience in solving deductive problems and
with direct instruction.

Recommended Readings

DeLoache, J.S. (2002). The symbol-mindedness of young children. In W.W. Hartup & R.A. Weinberg (Eds.), *Minnesota Symposium on Child Psychology: Vol. 32. Child psychology in retrospect and prospect.* Mahwah, NJ: Erlbaum. In this chapter, DeLoache summarizes her research on children's understanding of symbols and their ability to use symbolic representations to solve problems.

Halford, G.S. (1993). *Children's understanding: The development of mental models.* Hillsdale, NJ: Erlbaum. An integrative account of how changes in mental models, working memory capacity, and problem-solving experience shape cognitive development.

Klahr, D. (2000). *Exploring science: The cognition and development of discovery processes.* Cambridge, MA: MIT Press. In this book, Klahr synthesizes research on preschoolers through adults to provide a comprehensive account of the psychology of scientific discovery.

Kuhn, D., Garcia-Mila, M., Zohar, A., & Andersen, C. (1995). Strategies of knowledge acquisition. *Monographs of the Society for Research in Child Development, 60*(4, Serial No. 245.) Unusually precise descriptions of children and adults in the process of acquiring new knowledge.

Vosniadou, S., & Brewer, W. (1992). Mental models of the earth: A study of conceptual change in childhood. *Cognitive Psychology, 24,* 535–585. Interpreting what adults mean is not easy, especially when their claims contradict seemingly obvious truths. Children's mental models of the earth's shape illustrate both the children's ingenuity and the ambiguity of even simple statements that we make to them, such as "The earth is round."

11

Development of Academic Skills

I struggled through the alphabet as if it had been a bramble-bush; getting considerable worried and scratched by every letter. After that, I fell among those thieves, the nine figures, who seemed every evening to do something new to disguise themselves and baffle recognition. But, at last I began, in a purblind groping way, to read, write, and cipher, on the very smallest scale. (Pip, in Dickens's Great Expectations)

Cognitive development does not go into suspended animation while children are at school. What they learn there influences their general cognitive capabilities, as well as their specific knowledge and skills. The influence works in the other direction as well; children's general cognitive capabilities greatly influence what they learn in the classroom.

Practical decisions concerning children's educations, as well as theories of cognitive development, depend on the mutual influence of intra- and extraclassroom factors. For example, parents need to decide whether to start their children in school as soon as they are eligible or to hold them back and have them start the next year. In many communities in the United States, it has become common to hold children, especially boys, back for a year. The logic is that they will be more mature, and able to learn more, when they are older.

To test whether the year of waiting leads to children learning more in first grade, a team of investigators examined children in a locality where 95 percent of children still start school as soon as they are eligible (Bisanz, Morrison, & Dunn, 1995; Morrison, Griffith, & Alberts, 1997; Morrison, Smith, & Dow-Ehrenberger, 1995; Varnhagen, Morrison, & Everall, 1994). The studies used the cutoff design, which involves comparing the performance of children whose birth dates fell just before their district's cutoff for entrance into kindergarten with the performance of those whose birth dates fell slightly after that date and who therefore were slightly too young to be admitted that year. The groups being compared were within one month of each other in average age, but one group entered first grade a full year before the other. The question was whether attending first grade at the older age would result in more learning by the children whose birthdays were slightly after the cutoff.

The results were clear: Despite the 11-month difference in age, children who barely made the cutoff progressed just as much in reading and math during first grade as children who barely missed it and enrolled in first grade a year later. When the two groups finished first grade, their performance was indistinguishable. The pattern of results was not due to the children who just made or just missed the deadline being unusual. On tasks such as number conservation, where schooling would not be expected to be influential but where age would be, the children who were almost a year older at the end of first grade did considerably better (Bisanz et al., 1995). Further, the IQs and parental backgrounds of children in the two groups were similar. Other studies using the cutoff design in other localities have yielded similar results (Crone & Whitehurst, 1999; Naito & Miura, 2001). There may be other reasons to hold children back from starting school, such as advantages in athletics and social maturity, but for purposes of learning to read and do math there seems to be no good reason to do so (Stipek, 2002).

Organization of the chapter.   This chapter focuses on children's learning of the three R's: reading, 'riting, and 'rithmetic. The first section begins by examining the arithmetic skills that are acquired in the preschool period and early in elementary school, and then progresses to more complex arithmetic, algebra, and computer programming. The next section begins by examining reading skills that children acquire prior to formal instruction, then the process of reading individual words, and finally the comprehension of larger units, such as stories. The final section describes how children write their first drafts of essays and stories and then proceeds to how they revise (or fail to revise) what they wrote. Table 11.1 summarizes the organization.

Basic questions about academic skills.   When people think of the role of psychology in schools, the first thoughts that typically come to mind are of standardized tests. Educators use scores on IQ and achievement tests to help make a variety of important decisions, including placement in gifted programs, provision of special education, and college admissions.

Such tests are useful for predicting future school achievement and as an index of how much children know about given subjects. However, they tell us

TABLE 11.1   Chapter Outline

I.   Mathematics
    A.   Single-Digit Arithmetic
    B.   Complex Arithmetic
    C.   Algebra
    D.   Computer Programming

II. Reading
    A.   The Typical Chronological Progression
    B.   Prereading Skills
    C.   Identifying Individual Words
    D.   Comprehension
    E.   Instructional Implications

III. Writing
    A.   The Initial Drafting Process
    B.   The Process of Revision

IV. Summary

relatively little about the processes through which children learn, nor about how to teach children more effectively. Because of the great importance of these latter topics both for understanding children and for helping them, research on children's thinking has focused increasingly on the specific processes involved in learning. These learning processes are the focus of this chapter.

Regardless of whether we are talking about math, reading, or writing, several questions about specific learning processes and instructional issues are central:

1. How do children allocate attentional resources to cope with competing processing demands?
2. How do children choose which strategy to use from among the approaches that they know?
3. Should instructors directly teach the techniques used by experts in an area, or are indirect teaching approaches more effective?
4. What causes individual differences in knowledge and learning?

These questions have led to discovery of some striking unities in children's thinking in different subject areas. Consider, for instance, children's strategy choices in arithmetic, reading, and spelling. In all three areas, children need to choose whether to state answers from memory or revert to more time-consuming alternatives. To add numbers, children need to decide whether to retrieve an answer and say it or to generate an answer by counting. To read words, they need to decide whether to state a pronunciation that they retrieved from memory or to sound out the word. To spell, they need to decide whether to write a retrieved sequence of letters or to look for the word in a dictionary. Despite the differences among these subject areas, children seem to make all three decisions through the same strategy choice process. In this chapter, we consider both specific findings in mathematics, reading, and writing, and general patterns across them.

Mathematics

As discussed in Chapter 8, by the time children enter school, the majority have a basic understanding of numbers. Most 5-year-olds can count at least to 20, know that counting involves assigning one and only one number word to each object, recognize that different sets of n objects have their numerosity in common, and know the relative sizes of the numbers 1 through 10. This leaves a great deal to learn, though: arithmetic, algebra, geometry, and so on.

SINGLE-DIGIT ARITHMETIC

Single-digit arithmetic seems like the simplest of skills, calling only for retrieval of answers from memory. This impression is misleading, however. In the first few years of elementary school, children use a wide variety of strategies to solve problems such as $3 + 6$ and $8 + 5$. They not only retrieve answers from memory, but also count on their fingers from one, count from the larger of the two addends (on $3 + 6$, counting "6, 7, 8, 9"), and infer answers from knowledge of related problems ("$6 + 5$, hmm, I know, $5 + 5 = 10$, so $6 + 5$ must be 11") (Fuson & Kwon, 1992; Geary, Fan, & Bow-Thomas, 1992). Even college students use strategies other than retrieval surprisingly often—on about 30 percent of single-digit addition problems (Geary, 1996; LeFevre, Sadesky, & Bisanz, 1996). In particular, they count on from the larger addend or decompose difficult problems into two simpler ones (for example, $9 + 6$ might be decomposed into $10 + 6$ and $16 - 1$). Arithmetic also requires use of diverse parts of the brain. Magnetic resonance imaging (MRI) studies of people performing arithmetic problems indicate that the prefrontal cortex, the motor cortex, the parietal lobe, and a number of other areas in both hemispheres of the brain are involved (Rueckert et al., 1996). Thus, arithmetic is more complex than it looks.

The development of single-digit arithmetic. Most contemporary children start to learn arithmetic quite early. By the time they enter kindergarten, many can solve a number of single-digit addition and subtraction problems. Their learning of these problems may be accelerated by educational television programs such as *Sesame Street*. Studies before the television era (e.g., Ilg & Ames, 1951) did not find similar competence until children were in first grade.

Use of varied arithmetic strategies is not limited to addition. For example, to multiply, second through fourth graders sometimes repeatedly add one of the multiplicands the number of times indicated by the other (solving 6×8 by adding eight 6s or six 8s), sometimes make hatch marks and count or add them (solving 3×4 by drawing three groups of four hatch marks each and counting or adding them), sometimes retrieve answers from memory, and sometimes base answers on those of related problems (Cooney, Swanson, & Ladd, 1988; Lemaire & Siegler, 1995).

As children gain experience, their strategies change. The most striking change is toward increasing use of retrieval. After a few years of adding and subtracting, and after about a year of multiplying and dividing, most children retrieve answers to most of the basic arithmetic facts. Their use of strategies other than retrieval also changes. When children begin to add, they rely most often on putting up their fingers and counting from 1. As they gain skill and understanding, they increasingly use more sophisticated strategies, such as counting from the larger addend or decomposing a relatively hard problem into two easier ones (such as solving $9 + 7$ by thinking "$10 + 7 = 17; 17 - 1 = 16$").

During the same period, children also come to solve arithmetic problems increasingly quickly and accurately. The changes in speed and accuracy come about both because of changes in which strategies are used and because of changes in how efficiently each strategy is executed. The strategies that predominate in later use, such as retrieval and counting from the larger addend, are inherently faster than the strategies used most often initially, such as counting from one. Within any given strategy, speed and accuracy also increase.

The same developments are seen among children in Europe, North America, and East Asia, despite striking differences in their school systems (Fuson & Kwon, 1992; Geary, Bow-Thomas, Fan, & Siegler, 1993; Lemaire & Siegler, 1995; Naito & Miura, 2001). However, children in Europe and East Asia use more advanced strategies earlier than children in the United States and increase their speed and accuracy more rapidly. For example, East Asian children usually retrieve answers from memory, count from the larger addend, or rely on related arithmetic facts at ages when children in the United States still usually count from one (Geary et al., 1993).

Choices among strategies. One of the most striking characteristics of children's arithmetic is how adaptively they choose among alternative strategies. This adaptiveness is evident in children's choices of whether to state a retrieved answer or to use a *backup strategy* (a strategy other than retrieval). Even among 4- and 5-year-olds, the harder an addition problem (measured either by large numbers of errors or long solution times on the problem), the more often children solve it via a backup strategy, such as counting from one or the larger addend (Siegler & Shrager, 1984).

Using backup strategies most often on the hardest problems is adaptive because it helps children balance concerns of speed and accuracy. Consider a first grader's choice between solving an addition problem by stating a retrieved answer or by counting. Retrieval is faster, but counting tends to be more accurate on difficult problems. Young children reconcile these goals by using retrieval primarily on the easier problems, where it can yield accurate answers, and by using backup strategies primarily on the more difficult problems, where such strategies are necessary for accurate performance. In other words, children tend to choose the fastest approach that they can execute accurately. As shown in Figure 11.1, children make similarly adaptive strategy choices between backup strategies and retrieval in subtraction and multiplication (Siegler, 1986).

FIGURE 11.1 The more difficult an arithmetic problem, as measured by percentage of errors on it, the more often children use overt strategies (data from Siegler, 1987a, 1988b; Siegler & Shrager, 1984). The label "% Overt Strategy Use" in the figure is used because in these experiments, backup strategy use was assessed through videotapes of children's overt behavior while solving the problems.

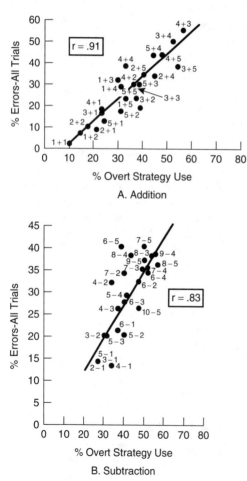

A. Addition

B. Subtraction

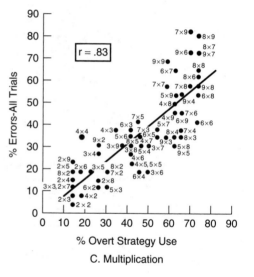

C. Multiplication

A model of strategy choice. How do children choose so adaptively among the alternative strategies that they know? The Siegler and Shipley (1995) strategy choice model that was discussed in Chapter 3 focuses on this question. Here, we examine the way that the model makes the choice that was just described: whether to state a retrieved answer or to use a backup strategy to solve an addition problem.

The mechanism by which the model makes this choice involves two interacting parts: a representation of knowledge about particular problems, and a process that operates on the representation to produce performance. The representation involves associations of varying strengths between each problem and potential answers, both correct and incorrect, to that problem. For example, in Figure 11.2, the answer 6 is connected to the problem "3 + 4" with a strength of .12, the answer 7 is connected to it with a strength of .29, and so on.[1]

Representations of different problems can be thought of as varying along a dimension of peakedness. In Figure 11.2, the representation of "2 + 1" is a *peaked* distribution, because most associative strength is concentrated in a single answer (the peak of the distribution). The representation of "3 + 4," in contrast, is a *flat* distribution because associative strength is distributed among a number of answers, with no one of them constituting a strong peak.

The process operates on this representation in the following way. First, the child sets a *confidence criterion.* This confidence criterion is a threshold that must be exceeded by the associative strength of a retrieved answer for that answer to be stated.

Once the confidence criterion is set, the child retrieves an answer. The probability of any given answer being retrieved on a particular retrieval effort is proportional to the associative strength of that answer relative to the associative strengths of all answers to the problem. Thus, because the associative strength connecting "2 + 1" and "3" is .79, and because the total associative strength connecting "2 + 1" with all answers is 1.00, the probability of retrieving "3" as the answer to "2 + 1" is .79.

If the associative strength of whatever answer is retrieved exceeds the confidence criterion, the child states that answer. Otherwise, the child may either again retrieve an answer and see if it exceeds the confidence criterion or abandon efforts to retrieve and instead use a backup strategy to solve the problem.

---

[1]These estimated associative strengths were based on children's performance in a separate experiment. Four-year-olds received simple addition problems and were asked to "just say what you think the right answer is as quick as possible without putting up your fingers or counting." The purpose of these instructions was to obtain the purest possible estimate of the strengths of associations between problems and answers. The values in Figure 11.2 indicate the proportion of trials on which children advanced a given answer to a given problem in this retrieval-only experiment. Thus, when presented the problem 3 + 4, children advanced the answer "6" on 12 percent of trials. Similar estimates for individual children emerged in a study in which individual children were presented the same problems on 10 occasions.

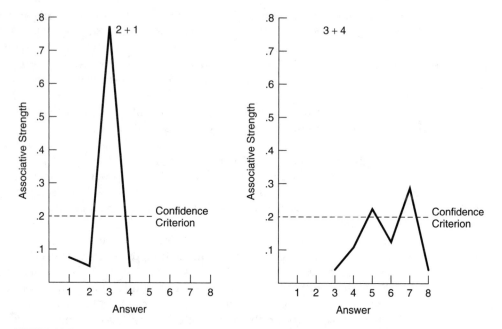

FIGURE 11.2   A peaked and a flat distribution of associations. The peaked distribution would lead to less frequent need for children to use overt strategies, fewer errors, and shorter solution times (from Siegler, 1986).

Within this model, the more peaked the distribution for a problem, the more often that retrieval, rather than a backup strategy, will be used on the problem. This is because the greater the concentration of associative strength in one answer, the higher the probability that the most strongly associated answer will be retrieved, and the higher the probability that that answer's associative strength will exceed the confidence criterion and thus allow the retrieved answer to be stated. Similarly, because the answer with the greatest associative strength ordinarily is the correct answer, the greater the concentration of associative strength in that answer, the more probable that the retrieved answer will be correct. Thus, the high correlations between percentage of errors on a problem and percentage of backup strategies on the problem (Figure 11.1) emerge because both errors and strategy choices on each problem reflect the peakedness of that problem's distribution of associations.

How do some problems come to have peaked distributions and others flat ones? A basic assumption of the strategy choice model is that children associate the answers they state with the problems on which they state them. Because children have at different times stated different answers to a problem, they will associate all of these answers to some degree with the problem. The more often an answer is stated on a problem, the more likely that the problem will elicit that answer on future presentations. Thus, a problem such as 2 + 1 comes to have a more peaked distribution of associations than $3 + 4$ because children are more likely to correctly count three fingers, and thus to associate the answer "3" with $2 + 1$, than they are to correctly count seven fingers and associate the answer "7" with $3 + 4$. Consistent with this view, children who execute backup strategies the most accurately in first grade use retrieval the most often by second grade (Kerkman & Siegler, 1993).

This last finding and the model as a whole have an interesting instructional implication: The common policy of discouraging children from using their fingers to add is misguided. Many teachers repeatedly instruct children not to use their fingers. They have a certain logic on their side. One of the goals of education is to make younger and less skillful children more like older and more skillful ones. Older and more skillful children do not use their fingers; therefore, by this logic, neither should younger and less advanced ones.

The strategy choice model, however, suggests that pushing children not to use their fingers may actually retard learning. Children with greater knowledge of arithmetic possess more peaked distributions of associations; they do not use their fingers because they can accurately retrieve answers to the problems. Younger and less knowledgeable children, however, use backup strategies precisely because they lack peaked distributions of associations. Forcing them to retrieve answers will lead to many errors, which, since each response adds to the associative strength of that answer, will strengthen wrong answers to the problem. Thus, paradoxically, pressuring children not to use their fingers may lead to them needing to use them for a longer time than if they were not pressured. As is often the case, the most direct method for pursuing an instructional goal is not necessarily the most effective one.

Individual differences.   One of the uses of this model has been in making understandable the ways in which children differ from each other. The model suggested two dimensions along which children could differ: the peakedness of their distributions of associations and the stringency of the confidence criteria that they set. The first would reflect differences in how well children know correct answers to the problems. The second would reflect differences in how sure children needed to be before they would state a retrieved answer.

Examination of first graders' addition and subtraction indicated that their performance differed along both dimensions (Kerkman & Siegler, 1993; Siegler, 1988a). The children could be classified into three groups: good students, not-so-good students, and perfectionists.

The contrast between the performance of good and not-so-good students was evident along all of the dimensions that might be expected from the names. The good students were faster and more accurate on both retrieval and backup strategy trials, and they used retrieval more often. They also scored far higher on standardized achievement tests.

The differences between the performance of good students and perfectionists were more interesting. The two groups were equally accurate and scored similarly well on achievement tests, but they differed in strategy use. Good students retrieved answers to more problems than either of the other two groups; perfectionists used retrieval less often than the other two groups, less even than the not-so-good students. When perfectionists did use retrieval, however, they were extremely accurate.

In terms of the model, good students were children who possessed peaked distributions of associations and set moderately stringent confidence criteria. Not-so-good students were children who possessed flat distributions and who set low confidence criteria. Perfectionists were children who possessed peaked distributions but who set very stringent confidence criteria.

To test this interpretation, three variants of the Siegler and Shipley (1995) model were created. The variants were identical except in the two variables hypothesized to distinguish the three groups: peakedness of distributions of associations and stringency of confidence criteria. The simulations produced the strategy choices and accuracy patterns characteristic of each group, thus indicating that the variables hypothesized to be important had the predicted effects.

The example illustrates a point made in the beginning of this chapter—a deeper understanding of thinking can be attained by examining specific cognitive processes, rather than by focusing on standardized test scores. The difference between the good students and perfectionists on one hand and the not-so-good students on the other was evident in standardized achievement test performance. This difference reflected better and worse knowledge of arithmetic. However, the difference between the good students and perfectionists was not, and could not, be detected by achievement tests. These children were comparably knowledgeable, but differed in cognitive style. Their patterns of performance represented different ways of being good at arithmetic, rather than a better way and a worse way. By predicting that children would differ along these dimensions, the model contributed to understanding of early individual differences beyond what could be learned from achievement tests.

Mathematical disabilities. Based on poor performance in class and poor standardized test scores, approximately 6 percent of children in the United States are labeled as having mathematical disabilities (Badian, 1983; Gross-Tsur, Manor, & Shalev, 1996). Like the not-so-good students described previously, these children have difficulty both in executing backup strategies and in retrieving correct answers (Geary, 1994; Geary, Hamson, & Hoard, 2000). As first graders, they frequently use immature counting procedures (such as counting from one rather than from the larger addend), they execute backup strategies slowly and inaccurately, and they use retrieval rarely and inaccurately. By second grade, they use somewhat more sophisticated counting procedures, such as counting from the larger addend, and their speed and accuracy improve. However, they continue to have difficulty retrieving correct answers, then and for years after (Geary, 1990; Geary & Brown, 1991; Goldman, Pellegrino, & Mertz, 1988; Jordan, Levine, & Huttenlocher, 1995). As they progress through school these children encounter further problems in the many skills that build on basic arithmetic such as multi-digit arithmetic and algebra (Hanich, Jordan, Kaplan, & Dick, 2001; Zawaiza & Gerber, 1993; Zentall & Ferkis, 1993).

Why do some children encounter such large problems with arithmetic? One reason is limited exposure to numbers before entering school. Many children labeled "mathematically disabled" come from impoverished families with little formal education. By the time children from such backgrounds enter school, many are already far behind other children in counting skill, knowledge of numerical magnitudes, and knowledge of arithmetic facts.

Another key difference involves working memory capacity. Learning of arithmetic requires sufficient working memory capacity to hold the original problem in memory while computing the answer so that the problem and answer can be associated. Children with mathematical disabilities cannot hold as much numerical information in memory as their age peers (Geary, Bow-Thomas, & Yao, 1992; Koontz & Berch, 1996; Passolunghi & Siegel, 2001). They also demonstrate impairments in other aspects of working memory, including visual-spatial processes and executive processes, which involve coordinating incoming information and allocating it to cognitive tasks (Bull, Johnston, & Roy, 1999; Keeler & Swanson, 2001; McLean & Hitch, 1999). Limited conceptual understanding of counting, arithmetic operations, and place value adds further obstacles to these children's learning of arithmetic (Geary, 1994; Geary et al., 2000; Hanich et al., 2001; Hitch & McAuley, 1991). Thus, mathematical disabilities reflect a combination of limited background knowledge, limited processing capacity, and limited conceptual understanding.

Understanding of principles.   As skill in arithmetic increases, so does understanding of the principles on which arithmetic is based. One such principle is the inversion principle—the idea that adding and subtracting the same number leaves the original quantity unchanged. Children display an emerging understanding of inversion as it applies to sets of objects by about 4 or 5 years of age (Klein & Bisanz, 2000; Vilette, 2002). For example, kindergarteners recognize that a set of objects remains the same number if two objects are removed and then two objects are added. However, children's understanding of inversion as it applies to problems presented in numerical form lags considerably behind. This can be seen in performance on problems of the form "$a + b - b = ?$" (such as $5 + 8 - 8 = ?$). Children who solve such problems through applying the inversion principle would answer in the same amount of time regardless of the size of b, because they would not need to add and subtract it. In contrast, children who solve the problem by adding and subtracting b would take longer when b was large than when it was small, because adding and subtracting large numbers takes longer than adding and subtracting small ones.

Between 6 and 9 years of age, performance on all $a + b - b$ problems becomes faster. However, 9-year-olds, like 6-year-olds, take longer on problems where b is large than on ones where it is small (Bisanz & LeFevre, 1990;

Stern, 1992). The improved speed on all problems appears due to improved understanding of addition and subtraction procedures. The continuing difference between times when b is large and when it is small suggests that neither 6- nor 9-year-olds have sufficient understanding of concepts, in particular, of the inversion principle, to consistently answer such problems without adding and subtracting. Not until age 11 do most children, like almost all adults, ignore the particular value of b and solve all problems equally quickly, thus demonstrating conceptual understanding of the inversion principle.

A related concept that takes surprisingly long for children to understand is that of mathematical equality. Even third and fourth graders frequently do not understand that the equal sign means that the values on each side of it represent the same quantity. Instead, they believe that the equal sign is simply a signal to execute an arithmetic operation. When asked to define the equal sign, they often state that it means to "add up all the numbers" (McNeil & Alibali, in press). On typical problems such as $3 + 4 + 5 = \_\_\_$, this misinterpretation does not cause any difficulty. However, on atypical problems, such as $3 + 4 + 5 = \_\_\_ + 5$, it leads most third and fourth graders either to just add the numbers to the left of the equal sign, and answer "12," or to add all numbers on both sides of it, and answer "17" (Perry et al., 1988; Rittle-Johnson & Alibali, 1999).

On problems such as $3 + 4 + 5 = \_\_\_ + 5$, children frequently make hand gestures that indicate knowledge that is not evident in their verbal statements. For example, some children who answer "12" and explain that they just added $3 + 4 + 5$ also motion with their hands toward the number to the right of the equal sign. Children who on a pretest frequently show such discrepancies between their speech and their gestures subsequently learn more from instruction in how to solve these problems than do children whose gestures and speech on the pretest reflect the same understanding (Alibali & Goldin-Meadow, 1993; Goldin-Meadow, Alibali, & Church, 1993; Goldin-Meadow & Singer, 2003; Perry et al., 1988). Similarly, children whose pretest verbal explanations are vague as well as incorrect subsequently learn more from instruction than those whose explanations are clear but incorrect (Graham & Perry, 1993). These findings exemplify a result that has been obtained in many contexts: heightened variability of thought and action tends to accompany readiness to learn (Goldin-Meadow et al., 1993; Siegler, 1994; Thelen, 1992).

Effects of context.   Gary Larson spoke for many when, in a "Far Side" cartoon, he depicted Hell's Library as stocked entirely with books of arithmetic and algebra word problems. The difficulty presented by such problems is often caused by their convoluted wording ("Joe has 23 marbles; he has 7 more than Bill had yesterday before he gave Joe half of his marbles; has Bill lost all of his marbles?"). Such phrasings burden working memory, and children often have difficulty interpreting them (Mayer, Lewis, & Hegarty, 1992; Stern, 1993; Verschaffel, De Corte, & Pauwels, 1992).

Recognition of the working memory burden that word problems impose has led some researchers to recommend that small numbers be used when word problems are first taught (Lesgold, Ivill-Friel, & Bonar, 1989). The logic is that simpler numbers will reduce the memory load. The flaw in this logic, however, is that people usually interpret the problem before they begin doing the arithmetic; thus the two processes operate at different times. Probably for this reason, using simpler numbers does not help children interpret the word problems (Rabinowitz & Woolley, 1995).

Even when story wordings are not convoluted, unfamiliar contexts often lead children not to apply procedures that they use successfully in other contexts. This was illustrated in a study of 9- to 15-year-old Brazilian children who were the sons and daughters of poor families in a large city (Carraher, Carraher, & Schliemann, 1985). The children contributed financially to their families by selling coconuts, popcorn, corn-on-the-cob, and other foods at street stands. Their work required them to add, subtract, multiply, and occasionally divide in their heads (one coconut costs x dollars; five coconuts cost . . .). Despite having had little formal education, the children could tell customers how much purchases cost and how much change they should get.

Carraher et al.'s study of these children involved presenting them with three types of problems. Some were problems that could arise in the context of customer-vendor transactions. ("How much do I owe for a coconut that costs 85 cruzeiros and a corn-on-the-cob that costs 63?") Other problems involved similar situations but with goods not carried by the child's stand. ("If a banana costs 85 cruzeiros and a lemon costs 63 cruzeiros, how much do the two cost together?") Yet others were numerically identical problems but presented without a sales context ("How much is 85 + 63?"). The children solved almost all of the problems involving goods sold at their stand and most of the problems that involved selling unfamiliar goods. However, they solved fewer than half of the problems without the sales context. The children clearly knew how to add, but did not always know when the skill should be used.

Context effects have also been demonstrated in American children's selection of strategies for solving arithmetic problems. For example, Bjorklund and Rosenblum (2002) found that children used more sophisticated strategies to solve arithmetic problems when the problems were presented in an academic context (an adult asking, "How much is 2 + 3?") than when they were presented in a game context (determining how many spaces to move a piece in a chutes and ladders game after throwing two dice). In the academic context, children most often retrieved number facts or counted from the larger addend. In the game context, children most often counted from one to obtain the total. Thus, children do not always use the most sophisticated strategy that they know. Features of the problem and the context influence children's strategy choices.

Context also influences the conceptual knowledge that children activate. McNeil and Alibali (in press) asked seventh-grade students to define the equal sign in three different contexts—in a typical addition problem ($4 + 8 + 5 + 4 = \_$), in a problem with addends on both sides of the equal sign ($4 + 8 + 5 = 4 + \_\_$), or by itself (=). Most seventh-grade students who saw the equal sign on its own or in a typical addition problem offered incorrect definitions ("it means add all the numbers"), but most seventh-grade students who saw the equal sign in a problem with addends on both sides offered correct definitions ("it means two things are the same"). Thus, conceptual knowledge is not all-or-none. Instead, children activate different aspects of conceptual knowledge in different contexts.

COMPLEX ARITHMETIC

Once children have mastered basic arithmetic facts, they learn algorithms for solving multidigit problems. However, many children fail to grasp the relation between the procedures for solving these problems and the concepts that underlie the procedures. The resulting memorization without understanding creates fertile ground for misconceptions to grow. These misconceptions are exemplified by the "bugs" that show up in children's learning of the multidigit subtraction algorithm.

Buggy subtraction algorithms. Brown and Burton (1978) investigated acquisition of multidigit subtraction skills. They used an error analysis method, much like the rule-assessment approach that was used to study balance-scale problems (pp. 349–350). It involved first presenting problems on which particular incorrect rules ("bugs") would lead to specific errors and then examining individual children's patterns of correct answers and errors to see if they fit the pattern that would be produced by a buggy rule.

Many of children's errors reflected such bugs. Consider the pattern in Table 11.2. At first glance, it is difficult to draw any conclusion about this boy's performance, except that he is not very good at subtraction. With closer analysis, however, his performance becomes understandable. All three of his errors arose on problems where the *minuend* (the top number) included a zero. This suggests that his difficulty was due to not understanding how to subtract from zero.

Analysis of the problems on which the boy erred (the first, third, and fourth problems from the left) and the answers he advanced suggests the existence of two bugs that would produce these particular answers. Whenever a problem required subtraction from 0, he simply flipped the two numbers in the column with the 0. For example, in the problem $307 - 182$, he treated $0 - 8$ as

TABLE 11.2   Example of a Subtraction "Bug"

307	856	606	308	835
−182	−699	−568	−287	−217
285	157	168	181	618

8 − 0, and wrote "8" as the answer. The boy's second bug involved not decrementing the number to the left of the zero (not reducing the 3 to 2 in 307 − 182). This lack of decrementing is not surprising because, as indicated in the first bug, the boy did not borrow anything from this column. Thus, the three wrong answers, as well as the two right ones, can be explained by assuming a basically correct subtraction procedure with two particular bugs.

Although such bugs are common among American children, they are far less common among Korean children (Fuson & Kwon, 1992). A major reason appears to be that Korean children have a firmer grasp of the base-10 system and its relation to borrowing. The more transparent relation within East Asian languages between the names of multidigit numbers and their place in the base-10 system, noted in Chapter 4, may make it easier to acquire the relevant understanding (Miller et al., 1995). Thus, the Korean term for 57 is "5 10s and 7 1s." This phrasing makes it easier to see why, on problems such as 57 − 29, it is reasonable to change 5 10s and 7 1s into 4 10s and 17 1s. Such understanding makes it more likely that children's borrowing will maintain the value of the original number. More broadly, children's conceptual understanding of place value guides their application of the subtraction procedure.

Fractions.   When presented the problem $1/2 + 1/3$, many children answer $2/5$. They generate such answers by adding the two numerators to form the sum's numerator and adding the two denominators to form its denominator. This misunderstanding is far from transitory. Many adults enrolled in community college math courses make the same mistake (Silver, 1983).

Much of children's difficulty in fraction arithmetic arises from their not thinking of the magnitude represented by each fraction. This is evident in children's errors in estimating the answer to $12/13 + 7/8$ (Table 11.3). On a national achievement test, fewer than one-third of U.S. 13- and 17-year-olds

TABLE 11.3   *Estimating the Sum of Two Fractions**

ESTIMATE the answer to 12/13 + 7/8. You will not have time to solve the problem using paper and pencil.

Answer	Percentage Choosing Answer	
	Age 13	Age 17
1	7	8
2	24	37
19	28	21
21	27	15
I don't know	14	16

*From National Assessment of Educational Progress (Carpenter, Corbitt, Kepner, Lindquist, & Reys, 1981).

accurately estimated the answer to this simple problem (Carpenter, Corbitt, Kepner, Lindquist, & Reys, 1981). Yet how could adding two numbers that are each close to 1 result in a sum of 1, 19, or 21?

A similar misunderstanding of the relation of symbols to magnitudes is evident in children's attempts to deal with decimal fractions. Consider how they judge the relative size of two numbers, such as 2.86 and 2.357. The most common approach of fourth and fifth graders on such problems is to say that the larger number is the one with more digits to the right of the decimal point (Ellis et al., 1993; Resnick et al., 1989). Thus, they would judge 2.357 larger than 2.86. Such choices appear to be based on an analogy between decimal fractions and whole numbers. Since a whole number with more digits is always larger than one with fewer digits, some children assume that the same is true of decimal fractions.

Another group of children made the opposite responses. They consistently judged that the larger number was the one that had fewer digits to the right of the decimal. Thus, 2.43 would be larger than 2.897. Many of these children reasoned that .897 involves thousandths, .43 involves hundredths, hundredths are bigger than thousandths, so .43 must be bigger than .897.

The difficulty in understanding decimal fractions does not disappear quickly. Zuker (1985, cited in Resnick et al., 1989) found that one-third of Israeli seventh and ninth graders continued to make one of the two errors just described. Thus, with decimal fractions as with multidigit subtraction, children's failure to understand the number system leads to systematic and persistent errors.

However, just as there are cross-cultural differences in children's understanding of multidigit subtraction, there are also cross-cultural differences in children's understanding of fractions. Once again, language differences may be part of the reason. The part-whole relationship denoted by common fractions is expressed more transparently in some East Asian languages than it is in English. For example, in Korean, the value 1/3 is spoken as *sam bun ui il*, which can be translated literally as "of three parts, one." By making the part-whole relation explicit, the Korean language may facilitate children's acquisition of fraction understanding. Consistent with this view, Korean first- and second-grade students outperform their American and Croatian peers in linking fractions with pictorial representations (Miura, Okamoto, Vlahovic-Stetic, Kim, & Han, 1999).

ALGEBRA

Learning algebra greatly increases the power of children's mathematical reasoning. A single algebraic equation can be used to represent and reason about an infinite number of situations. This power is frequently not realized, however. Students often have substantial difficulties learning algebra, in part because they cannot straightforwardly generalize their prior knowledge of arithmetic to algebra (Herscovics & Linchevski, 1994). In arithmetic, operations are carried out on numbers and yield other numbers, whereas in algebra, operations are carried out on algebraic expressions and yield other algebraic expressions. In learning algebra, students must learn to view symbolic expressions (including ones that include variables or multiple terms, such as $2x$ or $x + 3y + 5$) as mathematical entities in and of themselves.

Problem solving. In the view of many students, learning algebra boils down to learning the "rules" of algebraic manipulation. Indeed, learning algebra does involve learning a new form of symbolic notation and learning how to operate on this symbolic notation in order to solve problems. Many students have difficulty in applying the rules of algebraic manipulation correctly, and their errors reveal an incomplete grasp of the symbolic notation and a weak understanding of the conceptual basis of these rules. Students' difficulties in problem solving often arise from incorrect extensions of correct rules (Matz, 1982; Sleeman, 1985). For example, since the distributive principle indicates that

$$a \times (b + c) = (a \times b) + (a \times c),$$

some students draw superficially similar conclusions, such as

$$a + (b \times c) = (a + b) \times (a + c).$$

As another example, students sometimes inappropriately apply the rule that, in isolating the variable, one must "do the same thing to both sides of the equation." Koedinger and Nathan (2004) reported that students frequently "did the same thing" to both sides of one of the operation signs, rather than both sides of the equal sign, as seen in the sample student work in Figure 11.3.

Students use a variety of procedures to determine whether transformations of algebraic equations are appropriate. Among 11- to 14-year-olds, the most frequent strategy is to insert numbers into the original and transformed equations to see if they yield the same result (Resnick, Cauzinille-Marmeche, & Mathieu, 1987). This procedure reveals whether the transformation is allowable, though it

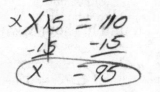

FIGURE 11.3 Student work showing an incorrect application of one of the rules of algebraic manipulation (from Koedinger and Nathan, 2004). Note that the student "did the same thing" to both sides of the plus sign, rather than both sides of the equal sign. Copyright © 2004 by Lawrence Erlbaum Associates. Reprinted with permission.

rarely indicates why. Another common approach is to justify the transformation by citing a rule. Some students cite appropriate rules, but many others cite distorted versions of rules, as in the previous examples.

As with multidigit subtraction and decimal fractions, students' difficulties in solving algebra problems often stem from not connecting procedures with underlying principles. Students' understanding of algebra often centers on the procedures themselves, rather than on what the procedures mean and why they work. Without such connections, algebra becomes a meaningless exercise in remembering which arbitrary symbol manipulations are permitted and which are not. Because many students in traditional algebra curricula fail to develop such connections, recent efforts to reform algebra curricula emphasize the conceptual underpinnings of the symbolic notation and of algebraic manipulations (National Council of Teachers of Mathematics (NCNM), 2000).

Representational fluency. In addition to solving problems, competence in algebra involves the ability to generate, reason with, and translate among different ways of representing mathematical information, including equations, graphs, tables, and words (Brenner et al., 1997; Kaput, 1989; Knuth, 2000; NCTM, 2000). This set of skills has been termed "representational fluency" (Nathan et al., 2002).

To translate mathematical information from one representation to another, students must have skills both for comprehending the given representation and for producing the target representation. For example, to successfully "translate" a story problem into an equation, students must be able to comprehend the story problem sufficiently well to understand the mathematical relations expressed in it, and they must also be able to generate an equation that represents those mathematical relations in the symbol system of algebra.

Translating among representations poses substantial difficulties for many students (Heffernan & Koedinger, 1997), and these difficulties extend well beyond high school. For example, 37 percent of freshman engineering students at a major state university could not write the correct equation to represent the simple statement, "There are six times as many students as professors at this university" (Clement, 1982). Most wrote $6s = p$. At first glance, this seems logical. The impression crumbles, however, when the realization hits that $6s = p$ means that multiplying the larger value (the number of students) by 6 yields a product equal to the smaller value (the number of professors).

The power of algebra ultimately comes from mathematical representations, such as algebraic symbols and graphs, that allow for abstraction over particular situations. To tap into the power of algebra, students need to be able to construct abstract representations that correspond to particular situations, and to reason fluently with these abstract representations. Indeed, the most recent standards for mathematics instruction developed by the National Council of Teachers of Mathematics (2000) emphasize using abstract representations to model mathematical situations, not only at the high school level, but also in middle school. Some researchers (e.g., Carpenter, Franke, & Levi, 2003) have even called for an integration of algebraic ideas, including some forms of abstract representations, into the elementary curriculum. It remains to be seen whether introducing abstract representations earlier in students' mathematical experience will lead to more fluent and appropriate use of such representations.

COMPUTER PROGRAMMING

Students currently attending school receive far more computer programming experience than those of even 10 years ago. Advocates of providing such experience have contended that it would produce not only skill at programming, but also enhanced general problem-solving ability. In one notable effort in this direction, Papert (1980) designed the LOGO language with the goal of helping children acquire such broadly useful skills as dividing problems into their main components, identifying logical flaws in one's thinking, and generating well-thought-out plans.

When learned in standard ways, LOGO proved insufficient to meet these goals. However, *mediated instruction,* in which LOGO is taught with an eye toward building transferable skills, has been quite successful in producing them (Carver & Klahr, 1987; Klahr & Carver, 1988; Lehrer & Littlefield, 1991, 1993; Littlefield, Delclos, Bransford, Clayton, & Franks, 1989). Like conventional instruction in computer programming, mediated instruction involves teachers demonstrating to students how to use commands and concepts and providing the students with feedback on their attempts to use them. However, mediated instruction also involves teachers explicitly noting when particular commands and programs illustrate general programming concepts, and drawing explicit analogies between the reasoning used to program and to solve problems in other contexts.

Such mediated instruction has produced a variety of kinds of desirable transfer. For example, Klahr and Carver (1988) demonstrated that mediated instruction in LOGO can create debugging skills that are useful outside as well as inside the LOGO context. Their instructional program was based on a task analysis of debugging. Within this analysis, the debugging process begins with the debugger determining the outcome that a procedure yields, and observing if and how its results deviate from what was planned (for example by running a computer program and examining its output). Following this, the debugger describes the discrepancy between desired and actual outcomes, and hypothesizes types of bugs that might be responsible. The next step is to identify parts of the program that could conceivably produce the observed bug. This step demands dividing the program into components so that specific parts of the program are identified with specific functions. Following this, the debugger checks the relevant parts of the program to see which, if any, fail to produce the intended results; rewrites the faulty component; and runs the debugged program to determine if it now produces the desired output.

The 8- to 11-year-olds who received this instruction took barely half as long to solve LOGO debugging problems as children who had not encountered it. They also improved their debugging of standard English instructions for accomplishing such tasks as traveling to a destination. The improvement seemed due to the children applying the skills taught in the program: analyzing the nature of the original discrepancy from the anticipated results, hypothesizing possible causes, and focusing their search on relevant parts of the instructions, rather than simply checking them line-by-line.

Younger children also can gain problem-solving skills from mediated instruction in LOGO. Presenting such instruction to second graders led to better performance on standardized tests of analogical reasoning and also enhanced ability to analyze geometric shapes in terms of their similarities and differences (Lehrer & Littlefield, 1993). These results show that when taught via mediated instruction, LOGO can produce the type of transferable problem-solving skills envisioned by its originators.

Reading

Development of reading can be viewed either chronologically (what happens at particular ages) or topically (how does competency x develop). This section first provides a brief chronological summary of reading acquisition; then it focuses at greater length on some particularly important topics in the area, such as prereading skills, word identification, and comprehension.

THE TYPICAL CHRONOLOGICAL PROGRESSION

Some researchers have characterized learning to read in terms of a series of stages. For example, Chall (1979) hypothesized that reading develops in five stages. The stages make reading acquisition seem neater and tidier than it really is, but they do convey an overview of the main achievements and the sequence in which they occur.

In Stage 0, lasting from birth to the beginning of first grade, children master several prerequisites for reading. Many learn to identify the letters of the alphabet, to write their names, and to read a few words. As with arithmetic, young children's knowledge of reading seems to be considerably greater today than it was 50 years ago. The improvement may be due to educational programs such as *Sesame Street*. and to often-repeated, attention-grabbing television commercials.

In Stage 1, which usually occupies first and second grade, children acquire *phonological recoding skill*, that is, ability to translate letters into sounds and to blend the sounds into words. Children also complete their learning of the letter names and sounds in this stage.

In Stage 2, most commonly occurring in second and third grade, children begin to read fluently. They identify individual words more quickly. However, Chall indicated that at this stage, reading is still not used for learning. The demands of word identification on children's processing resources remain sufficiently great that acquiring new information through reading is difficult.

In Stage 3, which Chall identified with fourth through eighth grade, children become capable of obtaining new information from print. To quote her, "In the primary grades, children learn to read; in the higher grades, they read to learn" (p. 24). At this point, however, most readers only can comprehend information presented from a single perspective.

In Stage 4, which occupies the high school years, children come to comprehend written information presented from multiple viewpoints. This makes possible more sophisticated understanding of history, economics, and politics than was previously possible. It also allows appreciation of the subtleties of great works of fiction, which are presented much more often in high school than earlier.

This chronology points to two major themes in children's acquisition of reading skills: the centrality of comprehension as the ultimate purpose of reading, and the need for efficient word identification so that comprehension of difficult material is possible. Before children can acquire word identification skills, though, they need certain prior capabilities. These are discussed in the next section.

PREREADING SKILLS

Children acquire some prereading skills effortlessly—for example, the knowledge that (in English) text proceeds from left to right, that it proceeds from the extreme right on one line to the extreme left on the next, and that spaces between letter sequences signal separations between words. This knowledge is evident in their imitation writing; even before they know how to write the letters, their "writing" goes across horizontal lines and is segmented into scribbles of roughly the length of a word separated by small spaces (Levin & Korat, 1993; Teale & Sulzby, 1986). Two other prerequisites for reading are considerably more challenging, though: identifying letters and distinguishing the separate sounds within words.

Letter perception. To read alphabetic languages such as English, children must learn the unique combination of horizontal segments, vertical segments, curves, and diagonals that define each letter. Even after this initial learning, children still often confuse letters that differ only in orientation—*b* and *d*, and *p* and *q*, for example (Adams, 1990). Such confusions may arise because in contexts other than reading, orientation rarely affects identity. A boy's dog is his dog regardless of the direction in which it faces. In any case, by second or third grade, the large majority of children no longer confuse letters.

Many parents and teachers, as well as researchers, have wondered whether learning letter names before beginning school helps children learn to read. The picture is complex, but at least a preliminary conclusion is possible. Kindergarteners' ability to name letters predicts their later reading achievement scores, at least as late as seventh grade (Vellutino & Scanlon, 1987). At first glance, this would seem to indicate that early learning of letter names causes children to read better. However, teaching letter names to randomly selected young children does not facilitate their reading (Adams, 1990; Venezky, 1978). Together, the two facts suggest that learning the letter names does not cause better reading. Rather, other variables, such as interest in print, general intelligence, perceptual skills, and parental interest in their children's reading, probably are responsible both for some children learning the letter names early and for those children tending to read well later.

Phonemic awareness. Another prerequisite for reading alphabetic languages such as English is realizing that words consist of separable sounds. This realization has been labeled *phonemic awareness.* Even after several years of speaking a language, most children seem unaware that they are combining separate sounds to make words. Liberman, Shankweiler, Fischer, and Carter (1974) illustrated this point with 4- and 5-year-olds. The children were told to tap once for each sound in a short word. Thus, they were supposed to tap twice for "it" and three times for "hit." Performance on this and other measures of phonemic awareness proved to be an excellent predictor of reading achievement in the early grades (Bruck, 1992; Olson, Forsberg, & Wise, 1994). Especially important, training 4- and 5-year-olds in phonemic awareness skills (for example, identifying which of three words does not contain the same sound) leads to improved reading and spelling performance as much as four years later (Bradley & Bryant, 1983; Byrne & Fielding-Barnsley, 1995; Byrne, Fielding-Barnsley, & Ashley, 2000; Vellutino & Scanlon, 1987). A recent review of 52 studies concluded that training in phonemic awareness led to benefits for word identification, spelling, and reading comprehension (Ehri et al., 2001).

Why should phonemic awareness enhance reading achievement? Thinking about the process by which children learn to read suggests an answer. When children are taught to read, they learn the sounds that typically accompany each letter. Unless they can blend these sounds into a word, however, the knowledge of sound-symbol correspondences does little good. Being able to distinguish the component sounds within words, the skill measured on phonemic awareness tasks, seems critical to being able to blend sounds together to form words, and thus to read.

Phonemic awareness may be fostered by simple activities such as reading nursery rhymes to children. How well children know nursery rhymes at age 3 predicts their later phonemic awareness and reading readiness, even when the contributions of the mother's educational level and of the child's age and IQ are statistically controlled (Maclean, Bryant, & Bradley, 1987). The minimal contrasts that often occur between words at the ends of lines within nursery rhymes (such as *horn* and *corn, muffet* and *tuffet*) may help children isolate the individual sounds that are present within each syllable and recognize that words are made up of such separable sounds. School-based reading instruction also promotes such skill; children who barely made the cutoff for entrance into school show greater phonemic awareness at the end of first grade than do children of almost identical age who just missed the cutoff and therefore spent the year in kindergarten (Bentin, Hammer, & Cahan, 1991). Thus, phonemic awareness both promotes reading and is promoted by it.

Precocious readers.   Some 2- and 3-year-olds can read. They usually have not received any special instruction; instead, they crack the alphabetic code on their own. What distinguishes these precocious readers from other children? As a group, they tend to be of above average IQs, but their scores usually are not exceptional (Jackson, 1988). Conversely, although about half of children with very high IQs start reading by age 5, the other half do not (Roedell, Jackson, & Robinson, 1980).

Precocious readers differ from most other children in several ways (Jackson, Donaldson & Cleland, 1988; Jackson, Donaldson, & Mills, 1993). Some have to do with intellectual capacities. Early readers tend to have unusually great verbal knowledge and large working memory spans. Other distinctive characteristics involve early mastery of prereading skills. Most such children can recite the alphabet and identify some capital letters before age three. Yet other unusual features involve interest in reading: such children tend to be more interested in reading than most other children.

Contrary to the fears of a number of educators, precocious reading does not adversely affect later school performance. Children who know how to read when they enter school remain superior readers through at least sixth grade (Durkin, 1966; Jackson et al., 1993). However, it cannot be concluded that the early reading causes the later superiority. Exposing randomly selected children to two years of reading instruction prior to first grade did not result in their reading better at the end of third grade (Durkin, 1974/75). At minimum, though, precocious reading does children no harm and foreshadows later good reading.

IDENTIFYING INDIVIDUAL WORDS

Rapid and effortless word identification is essential not only for good comprehension but also for making reading enjoyable. The consequences of not having these skills are evident in a remarkable statistic reported by Juel (1988): 40 percent of fourth graders who were poor at word identification said that they preferred cleaning their room to reading. One said, "I'd rather clean the mold around the bathtub than read." Such attitudes are not only disastrous for reading per se, they also pull down achievement in other subjects, since all demand skillful reading to master the material (Stanovich, 1986). Poor word identification skills also lead to children not reading more than the minimum required for class, which exacerbates the problem. As Adams (1990, p. 5) noted, "If we want to induce children to read lots, we must teach them to read well."

Children use two main word-identification procedures: *phonological recoding* (sometimes called *decoding*) and *visually based retrieval*. In both, children first look at a printed word and then locate the entry for the word in long-term memory. The difference concerns what happens in between. When children phonologically recode a word, they translate the visual form into a speech-like one, and use this speech-like representation to identify the word. When they visually retrieve a word, they do not take this intermediate step. The two approaches are not quite as distinct as the description suggests; for example, children sometimes phonologically recode the first letter or two and then retrieve the word's identity. Despite these mixed cases, the distinction still seems to correspond to a genuine difference in word-identification strategies.

The difference between the two word-identification processes is echoed in the difference between two of the major approaches to reading instruction. The *whole-word approach* emphasizes visual retrieval; the *phonics approach* emphasizes phonological recoding. Historically, educational practice has gyrated erratically between the two. At the beginning of this century, most teachers in the United States emphasized phonics. Between the 1920s and the 1950s, most emphasized visual retrieval. In recent years, most again emphasized phonics. Two likely reasons for the switches are that both methods do eventually succeed in teaching most children to read, and that neither method succeeds in teaching every child to read well. In addition, neither approach has to be pursued in pure form. Most teachers use both. The issue is not whether children need to learn letter-sound relations or whether they need to retrieve words rapidly, but how early and to what extent each skill should be emphasized.

Another reason the debate has not been resolved is that plausible arguments can be made for each position. The whole-word argument: Skilled readers rely on visually based retrieval; the goal of reading instruction is to produce skilled readers; therefore, beginning readers should be taught to read like skilled ones. The phonics argument: For children to learn to read, they must be able to identify unfamiliar words; phonological recoding skills allow them to do this; therefore, beginning readers should be taught in a way that will allow them to read independently.

Understanding the processes by which children learn to read provides an informed basis for choosing between these arguments. In the next section, we examine the two word-identification processes and how children choose which to use to identify a particular word. The analysis suggests an explanation for why one of the instructional approaches has proved more effective than the other.

Phonological recoding. Phonological recoding allows children to read words that they otherwise would not know. An analysis of a basal reader makes evident why this skill is so important for beginning readers. Firth (1972) examined almost 3,000 words that occurred in a basal reader for first and second graders.

More than 70 percent of the words were presented five or fewer times, and more than 40 percent of the words only once. Some basal readers repeat words more frequently, but more repetitive material tends to degenerate into the mind-numbing "Look, look, see Spot" style, so memorable to those who encountered it. Thus, early attainment of phonological recoding skill is essential for enabling beginning readers to identify the many words that they have rarely, if ever, encountered.

Beyond allowing children to read independently, skillful phonological recoding also contributes to efficient visually based retrieval. Jorm and Share (1983) and Share and Stanovich (1995) described how this might occur. Their basic assumption was that children learn the answers that they state; this was the same assumption made by Siegler and Shipley (1995) about arithmetic learning. If children lack good phonological recoding skills, they will be forced to rely more often on context to infer words' identities. Context is often an undependable guide, though; relying on it will lead to many errors. In contrast, accurate sounding out will increase the association between the printed and the spoken word, thus increasing the likelihood of the child's being able to retrieve the word's identity through visual retrieval.

Visually based retrieval. It is tempting to describe the development of word-identification skills by saying that at first children sound out words, and later they use visually based retrieval. In fact, the progression is more complex. Many children can retrieve the identities of a few words even before they know any sound-symbol correspondences. Gough and Hillinger (1980) provided the example of a preschooler who learned to read two words: "Budweiser" and "Stop." The boy learned the first word from beer cans, the second from road signs. Context provided clues to these words' identities. Many preschoolers, however, also can read a few words without contextual clues, for example, when they are typed on an index card. A girl might know that she knows two words and that "Budweiser" is the long one and "Stop" is the short one. Next, she might learn the word "Coke." Since "Coke" and "Stop" both have four letters, she would need some feature other than length to discriminate between them. Perhaps she would notice the difference in their first letter and conclude that if the word is short and starts with a letter that has one curve, it is "Coke," but if it is short and starts with a letter that has two curves, it is "Stop."

Although the first uses of visually based retrieval may rely on one or two features, the retrieval process eventually incorporates parallel processing of a great many sources of information (Seidenberg & McClelland, 1989). Among these sources are information from the particular letters, from the word as a whole, and from the surrounding context. Use of multiple cues, including the letters in the word and the surrounding context, begins as early as first grade. When first graders substitute one word for another, the word they choose usually has the same first letter as the word that is present and is also consistent with the surrounding context (Weber, 1970). Thus, multiple sources of information influence visually based retrieval from the beginning of reading.

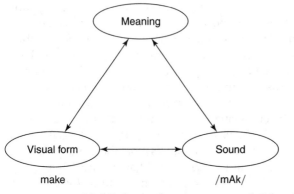

Multiple pathways to word identification. Seidenberg and colleagues (Harm & Seidenberg, 1999; Plaut et al., 1996; Rayner, Foorman, Perfetti, Pesetsky, & Seidenberg, 2001; Seidenberg & McClelland, 1989) have used connectionist models (see Chapter 3) to develop an account of how readers utilize both phonological recoding and visually based retrieval in the process of word identification. The model also specifies how the relative roles of the two pathways change as individuals acquire reading skill.

The model rests on the assumption that children eventually acquire associations among the sounds of words, the visual forms of words, and the meanings of words (see Figure 11.4). Even before they learn to read, children have strong links between sound and meaning, based on their experience with spoken language. Later, when children learn to read, they gradually acquire the associations between the visual forms of words and their sounds and meanings.

The model was trained by presenting it with opportunities to form associations between the visual forms, sounds, and meanings of words, and to receive corrective feedback. During training, the model learned the links between visual form and sound more quickly than the links between visual form and meaning. The reason for this is because spelling is systematically related to pronunciation, so visual form and sound are more closely correlated than visual form and meaning. Early in the training period, when the model was presented with the visual form of a word, it relied primarily on the pathway from visual form to sound to meaning to identify the word. Over time, as the model acquired more experience with words, the direct pathway from visual form to meaning became stronger, because the links between visual form and meaning were strengthened each time a word was successfully comprehended. As this more direct pathway became stronger, it began to "win out" in word identification over the more indirect pathway (visual form to sound to meaning). Thus, the connectionist model reveals a possible mechanism by which skillful phonological recoding could contribute to efficient visually based retrieval, as described by Jorm and Share (1983) and Share and Stanovich (1995).

The model suggests that early in the process of learning to read, children capitalize on their existing knowledge (from spoken language) of links between sound and meaning and on the systematic relationships between visual form and sound. To identify words, they initially use a phonologically mediated pathway, which relies first on the link between visual form and sound, and then on the link between sound and meaning. With reading experience, the direct pathway from visual form to meaning becomes stronger. So, as children acquire more experience with words, they begin to use direct visual retrieval.

The model also yielded an interesting implication: Learning to read may actually change the quality of children's representations of the sounds of words. Children's early representations of the sounds of words often do not incorporate information about subword units, such as individual sounds or phonemes. For example, based on their experience with spoken language, children may realize that "make" and "bake" are different words, but they may not explicitly represent the fact that the initial consonant is what differentiates the words. In the connectionist model, as the mappings between the visual forms of words and their sounds were learned, the model developed more specific representations of the sounds of words, and it began to explicitly represent subword units, such as individual phonemes and rhymes (such as the "ake" in "make" and "bake"). This suggests that, as children learn the mappings from visual form to sound, they may develop more explicit representations of subword units, such as individual phonemes and rhymes. Thus, the model implies that learning to map between the visual forms of words and their sounds promotes phonemic awareness. And indeed, learning to read does seem to improve children's phonemic awareness (Rayner et al., 2001).

Strategy choices in word identification. As in arithmetic, skilled readers choose adaptively among reading strategies. They use the fast retrieval approach when it can yield correct answers, and resort to backup strategies, such as sounding out, on the more difficult words (Figure 11.5). This observation raises the issue of how children know whether to use phonological recoding or visually based retrieval to identify a particular word, when both pathways are available.

The decision process may be the same as the one children use in arithmetic. When they encounter a word, they try to retrieve its identity based on the visual form of the word. If the alternative they retrieve has sufficient associative strength, they say it. Otherwise, they resort to a backup strategy, such as sounding out the word. Alternatively, as suggested by the connectionist model described above, children may attempt to use both visual retrieval and phonological recoding simultaneously. The route that most quickly yields an answer of sufficient strength is the route that is used to identify the word.

This perspective, combined with evidence that use of phonological recoding contributes to efficient visually based retrieval, implies that phonics-based instruction should be superior to the whole-word approach in helping children identify words quickly and accurately. The logic is that accurate use of backup strategies will build strong associations between words and their printed forms, thus making possible fast and accurate retrieval. This prediction has proven correct. In both

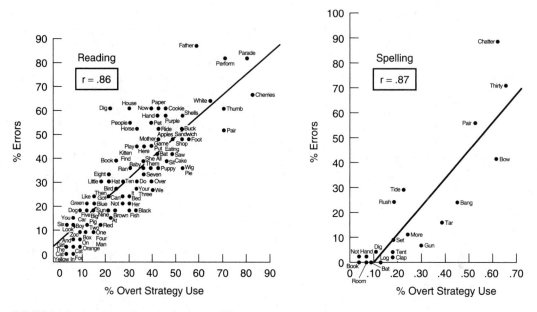

FIGURE 11.5   As with arithmetic, the more difficult the word, as measured by percentage of errors, the more likely that children will use overt strategies to read or spell it (from Siegler, 1986).

classroom and laboratory tests, phonics-based approaches have been found to be superior in promoting reading achievement (Adams, 1990; Foorman, Francis, Fletcher, Schatschneider, & Mehta, 1998; National Reading Panel, 2000).

Dyslexia. Some children, despite being of normal intelligence, have extraordinary difficulty learning to read. Two distinct problems have been identified which correspond to the two main word-identification processes described in this section. The more common problem, *phonological dyslexia,* involves particular difficulty in phonological recoding. The less common one, *surface dyslexia,* involves difficulty in visually based retrieval (Rack, Snowling, & Olson, 1992; Stanovich, Siegel, & Gottardo, 1997; Wagner & Torgeson, 1987).

These forms of dyslexia can be distinguished by asking children to read *exception words* (words with irregular symbol-sound correspondences, such as "pint" and "yacht") and *pronounceable nonwords* (strings of letters that are not words but that can be sounded out, such as "thack"). Surface dyslexics, whose main difficulty is with visually based retrieval, have greater problems with the exception words, which other people can retrieve from memory. Phonological dyslexics, whose main problem is with sounding out, have greater difficulty with the pronounceable nonwords, which, since they are novel, require phonological decoding (Castles & Coltheart, 1993; Manis, Seidenberg, Doi, McBride-Chang, & Peterson, 1996).

Most children who have problems with pronounceable nonwords also have trouble with exception words, and vice versa. Thus, the distinction between phonological and surface dyslexia is usually one of degree of impairment in the two skills. However, about 25 percent of children are within the normal range on one task but below it on the other (Manis et al., 1996).

Children diagnosed as dyslexic tend to continue to be poor readers as adults. Even in those cases where their reading reaches near-normal levels, they continue to have difficulty reading nonwords, for which they must rely on their phonological recoding skills, and their phonemic awareness continues to be poor (Bruck, 1990, 1992). Presumably, experience with reading allows them often to use retrieval, but the difficulty with sounding out unfamiliar words remains (Manis, Custodio, & Szeszulski, 1993).

Fortunately, the situation is not hopeless. Teaching poor readers strategies for circumventing phonological recoding difficulties, or intensively working to improve the phonological recoding skills themselves, can have substantial positive effects. For example, Lovett et al. (1994) examined the effects of strategy training that taught poor readers to draw analogies between new and already-known words, to try alternative vowel pronunciations when their first guess does not work, and to identify parts of words that are known and then focus attention on the rest of the word. Given 35 hours of instruction in these strategies, the children made significant improvements in standardized tests of word identification and spelling relative to other poor readers who were given similar amounts of instruction in problem solving and study skills. Thus, although dyslexia is a persistent and difficult-to-remedy problem, training that illustrates ways around it can be helpful.

COMPREHENSION

Among the many academic skills that children acquire, reading comprehension may be the most important. It allows them to learn, to pursue interests, and to escape boredom.

The reading comprehension process can be divided into four components: lexical access, proposition assembly, proposition integration, and text modeling (Perfetti, 1984). *Lexical access* involves identifying words and accessing their meanings. In reading, lexical access is the process by which children retrieve the meaning of a printed word from long-term memory. *Proposition assembly* involves relating words to one another to form meaningful units. For example, in the sentence "The sick boy went home," the reader would construct the propositions "There was a boy," "The boy was sick," and so on. *Proposition integration* involves combining individual propositions into larger units of meaning. Finally, *text modeling* refers to the processes by which children draw inferences and relate what they are reading to what they already know. For example, readers could draw on knowledge about sick children and distances between schools and homes to infer that one of the boy's parents may have picked him up and driven him home, even though the sentence did not mention this happening.

Perfetti's analysis helps to clarify the relation between reading comprehension and listening comprehension. Both require forming propositions, integrating them, and constructing a general model of the situation. However, the lexical access processes differ. In reading, lexical access requires a translation between written words and meanings; in listening, lexical access requires a translation between spoken words and meanings. Beginning readers' greater competence in translating spoken words into meanings accounts for their listening comprehension exceeding their reading comprehension. Not until seventh or eighth grade do most children eliminate this gap, so that their reading and listening comprehension are similar (Sticht & James, 1984).

What develops in reading comprehension? What we comprehend is closely related to what we remember. Thus, it is not surprising that the main influences on memory development—basic processes, strategies, metacognitive understanding, and content knowledge—also influence reading comprehension.

Two basic processes whose development contributes to improvement in reading comprehension are automatization of word identification and increasingly efficient operation of working memory. Automatizing word identification helps reading comprehension in the same way that automatizing arithmetic helps learning of more advanced mathematics: it frees cognitive resources. Consistent with this view, degree of automaticity of word identification early in first grade is predictive of reading comprehension not only at that time, but through the end of third grade (Lesgold, Resnick, & Hammond, 1985). Similarly, word identification skills are a strong predictor of reading comprehension among fourth-grade students (Zinar, 2000). The increasingly efficient operation of working memory helps comprehension for similar reasons. Children who can maintain more material in memory have a better chance to integrate previous and new ideas and to understand connections among them. Large working memory capacity seems especially helpful in coping with ambiguous wordings, for which comprehension requires maintaining more than one interpretation until the ambiguity is resolved (Daneman & Tardif, 1987).

Acquisition of strategies also influences the development of reading comprehension. Often, such strategies involve adjusting the speed and carefulness of reading to the difficulty of the material and one's goals in reading it. For example, good readers go through trash novels much faster than textbooks. However, this type of flexible strategy use develops surprisingly late. For example, 10-year-olds show little use of skimming when detailed understanding is unnecessary for answering the question; not until age 14 is such skimming common (Kobasigawa et al., 1980).

Reading comprehension is also influenced by metacognitive understanding of the reading process (e.g., Zinar, 2000). At all ages between first grade and adulthood, better readers monitor their understanding of what they are reading more accurately than do poor readers (Baker, 1994). The comprehension monitoring of both good and poor readers improves with age, but the difference between good and poor readers also remains. Such comprehension monitoring leads older and better readers to adopt a variety of strategies for dealing with comprehension difficulties: returning to the source of the confusion, slowing down until comprehension is restored, trying to visualize the scene, and reducing abstractions to concrete examples.

A final source of age-related improvements in reading comprehension is increasing content knowledge. Children who have such knowledge can check the plausibility of their interpretations of what they are reading against what they already know. They also can draw reasonable inferences about motivations, events, and consequences that are implicit rather than stated. Although any relevant prior knowledge can aid comprehension, knowledge of causal connections is especially helpful. The more that readers focus on causal relations, the higher their recall (Trabasso, Suh, Payton, & Jain, 1994). With age, children represent a wider range of causal links, which improves their comprehension. For example, 8-year-olds focus mainly on causal links within an episode, whereas 14-year-olds emphasize links across episodes as well (van den Broek, 1989). In sum, improvements in the efficiency of execution of basic processes, in strategy use, in metacognition, and in content knowledge all contribute to age-related improvements in reading comprehension.

INSTRUCTIONAL IMPLICATIONS

Importance of adequate background knowledge.   One implication of these findings for the teaching of reading is that teachers should ensure that all students have the prior knowledge needed to understand what they read. The problems that arise when children lack such content knowledge are evident in the saga of "The Raccoon and Mrs. McGinnis," a story that appeared in a second-grade textbook.

> Mrs. McGinnis, a poor but good-hearted farmer, wishes on a star for a barn in which to house her animals. Instead, bandits come and steal the animals. A raccoon, who habitually looks for food at night on Mrs. McGinnis' doorstep, follows the bandits and then climbs a tree to be safe from them. The bandits see the raccoon's masked face and mistake it for another bandit. Frightened, they release the animals and inadvertently drop a bag of money they had stolen from someone else. The raccoon picks up the bag of money, returns to Mrs. McGinnis' doorstep to continue looking for food, and drops the bag on the doorstep. The next morning, Mrs. McGinnis finds the money and attributes the good fortune to her wish of the night before.

Although most adults find this story quite charming, the charm was lost on the second graders who read it. It simply confused them. Beck and McKeown

(1984) hypothesized that the problem was that the children lacked two critical concepts needed to understand the sequence of events: coincidence and habit. Therefore, before another group of second graders read the story, an experimenter told them that coincidences involve two events just happening to occur together, with neither causing the other, and that habits often lead people and animals to engage repeatedly in the same activities. The experimenter also introduced several useful background facts: that the dark circles around raccoons' eyes look like masks, that raccoons habitually hunt for food at night, and that raccoons often pick up objects and carry them to other locations.

This background knowledge helped children understand the story. The explanation of the concept of coincidence increased the number of children who contrasted what Mrs. McGinnis thought had happened with what actually had. Moreover, children who received the background information, unlike many of their peers, did not conclude that the raccoon tried to help Mrs. McGinnis. Thus, possession of relevant background knowledge seems essential for good reading comprehension.

Importance of metacognition for comprehension. Another effective instructional approach, *reciprocal teaching,* is based on findings regarding the role of metacognition in reading comprehension. This approach, developed by Annemarie Palincsar and Ann Brown (1984), was originally designed to improve the reading of a group of seventh graders from disadvantaged backgrounds. Although these students' word-identification skills were at their grade level, their comprehension was two to three years behind. Palincsar and Brown hypothesized that the heart of the students' difficulties was inadequate comprehension monitoring. In particular, they posited that the students needed to improve their execution of four processes involved in comprehension monitoring: summarizing, clarifying, questioning, and anticipating future questions.

In reciprocal teaching, the teacher works with students in small groups, and group members take turns leading discussion of a particular text. Initially, the teacher serves as the discussion leader. After both students and teacher read a paragraph, the teacher summarizes it, points to sentences that need clarification, anticipates likely questions, and predicts what will happen next in the story. On the next paragraph, one or more students carry out these activities. Then it is the teacher's turn again. Over time, all students take a turn in the leader role. Palincsar and Brown (1984) found that this turn taking was essential, because at first, students were quite inept at the skills. In their study, at the beginning of the training, only 11 percent of students' summary statements captured the main idea of the paragraph. By the end of the more than 20 sessions, 60 percent of their statements did so.

Palincsar and Brown (1984) found that instruction had many positive effects on the seventh graders' reading comprehension. After each day's instruction, they read new paragraphs and answered from memory 10 questions about them.

On a pretest before the program began, the children averaged 20 percent correct on the test. At the end of the program, they averaged more than 80 percent correct. The improved comprehension for such paragraphs was still evident when the seventh graders were retested six months after the program ended. Even more impressive, on tests that were part of regular classwork in science and social studies, the trained children improved from the 20th percentile of their school to the 56th percentile.

Subsequent findings have also been encouraging. A review of 16 studies of reciprocal teaching revealed positive effects with students from fourth grade to adulthood, with both low-achieving and average students, with groups ranging from 2 to 23 students, and with either experimenters or classroom teachers providing the instruction (Rosenshine & Meister, 1994). The gains also have been maintained for at least six months to a year after the instruction (Palincsar, Brown, & Campione, 1993). Comparisons with other methods of promoting reading comprehension show that reciprocal teaching is at least as effective as alternative approaches (e.g., Johnson-Glenberg, 2000).

What lessons can we draw from this success story? One lesson is the value of teaching skills in contexts that match as closely as possible the contexts in which the skills will be used. In reciprocal teaching, comprehension monitoring skills are taught in the context of reading meaningful material, the same context as that in which comprehension monitoring is used in the classroom. Another lesson involves the importance of actively engaging students in learning. Recall from Chapter 4 that the effectiveness of collaboration depends on the more expert partner actively involving the less expert one in the problem-solving process. Such engagement is integral to reciprocal teaching. From the beginning, students are encouraged to attempt the relevant processes (summarizing, questioning, etc.), and their roles progressively increase as their competence grows. Thus, the effectiveness of reciprocal teaching stems at least partially from its teaching skills in a context similar to the one in which they will be used and to the instructional process actively engaging students in learning.

Writing

A venerable sorrow of teachers is how badly students write. The difficulty does not end in childhood. Computer companies produce machines capable of executing millions of instructions per second but rarely produce a manual that explains clearly how to operate them. Lack of writing skills is particularly unfortunate because of the huge role of writing in modern life. For example, business personnel spend an estimated 19 percent of their working hours writing memos, letters, and technical reports (Klemmer & Snyder, 1972).

Writing can be divided into two processes: initial drafting and revision. Both demand that writers surmount a variety of challenges: the mechanical demands imposed by punctuation, spelling, and grammar; the organizational demands needed to make the content comprehensible; and the demands of meeting the author's purpose, whether that purpose be persuading, describing, or conveying a point of view (Boscolo, 1995). Given how many goals must be considered simultaneously, it is no wonder that most people find writing difficult.

THE INITIAL DRAFTING PROCESS

Few people other than teachers have a good sense of what children's compositions are like. The following essay, a better-than-average effort for an 8-year-old, communicates the flavor:

> I have not got a bird but I know some things about them. They have tow nostrils and They clean Ther feather and They eat seeds, worms, bread, cuddle firs, and lots of other things. and they drink water. When he drinks he Puts his head up and it gose down. A budgie (birdie) cage gets very dirty and peopel clean it. (Kress, 1982, pp. 59–60)

This story reflects three sources of difficulty that children face in writing: the kinds of topics that are discussed, the need to simultaneously pursue multiple goals, and the mechanical demands of writing (Bereiter & Scardamalia, 1987).

Demands of unfamiliar topics. To write a story, children must first activate relevant information in long-term memory. In many cases this is difficult, because the topics are ones that children would never ordinarily think about (such as, "What I know about birds"). Under such conditions, they must pull together material from diverse parts of their memory and generate an organization for thinking about them. The 8-year-old's essay about birds exemplifies what often happens: a list of facts about a topic, rather than an organized discussion of it.

Demands of multiple goals. People write to pursue a variety of goals: to amuse, to intrigue, to inform, to arouse, and to generate enough material to satisfy teachers. Intonations and nonverbal gestures, which can achieve some of these purposes in speech, are unavailable in writing. Further, the feedback that writers receive during the initial drafting process is ordinarily limited to their own reactions to what they have written. This is quite different from the situation in conversations, where other people's questions and comments often suggest new goals and paths to pursue. Thus, writing demands formulating goals with little outside stimulation, keeping them in mind for long periods, and independently judging when they have been met.

How do children cope with the need to pursue multiple goals? Scardamalia and Bereiter (1984) labeled children's typical approach the *knowledge-telling strategy*. This strategy simplifies the writing task to the point where only one goal at a time needs to be considered. The strategy can be summarized in terms of two commandments: 1) Answer directly the question that was asked; 2) Write down relevant information as it is retrieved from memory. The "budgie" story exemplifies the results of using this approach. Initially, the child answered the basic question: "I do not have a bird, but I know some things about them." Then she listed several facts she remembered about birds. The simplicity of this organization accounts for one of the most striking features of children's compositions: their brevity. In the elementary school years, compositions typically are half of a typed page or less.

With experience in writing, children come to sequence goals into standard organizations that help them cope with the memory demands of writing. An unusual natural experiment reported by Waters (1980) demonstrated how skill in coordinating multiple goals develops with practice. Waters analyzed 120 essays written by a girl (herself) during second grade. All the essays were written in response to a "class news" assignment. Each day, students were to write about that day's events.

Waters intensively examined five essays she had written on consecutive days at the beginning of the year, five in the middle, and five at the end. As shown in Table 11.4, story contents at first were limited to the date, weather, and

---

TABLE 11.4   *Stories Written at Beginning, Middle, and End of Year for Class News Assignment*

SEPTEMBER 24, 1956
Today is Monday, September 24, 1956. It is a rainy day. We hope the sun will shine.
We got new spelling books. We had our pictures taken. We sang Happy Birthday to Barbara.

JANUARY 22, 1957
Today is Tuesday, January 22, 1957. It is a foggy day. We must be careful crossing the road.
This morning, we had music. We learned a new song.
Linda is absent. We hope she come back soon.
We had arithmetic. We made believe that we were buying candy. We had fun.
We work in our English books. We learned when to use **is** and **are.**

MAY 27, 1957
Today is Monday, May 27, 1957. It is a warm, cloudy day. We hope the sun comes out.
This afternoon, we had music. We enjoyed it. We went out to play.
Carole is absent. We hope she comes back soon.
We had a spelling lesson, we learned about a **dozen.**
Tomorrow we shall have show and tell.
Some of us have spelling sentences to do for homework.
Danny brought in a cocoon. It will turn into a butterfly.

Source: Waters, 1980.

class activities. Later, they also included information about peers, duties, and materials brought to school.

More generally, the later stories showed a greater number and variety of goals than the earlier ones. In many of the later essays, each time Waters recalled an event, she seemed to form the goal of noting the time at which the event occurred and then describing her reaction to the event. This prearranged sequence of goals reduced processing demands by suggesting content beyond the sheer occurrence of events. Still, even her longer essays were less than a third of a typed page long.

Helping young elementary school children to consider two or more goals simultaneously, and to relate these goals to each other, may improve their writing. Bereiter and Scardamalia (1987) found that a surprisingly simple instructional device promoted this objective. They gave children a deck of cards with common sentence openings: "Similarly," "For example," "On the other hand," and so on. Children were asked to choose one of these prompts when they could not think of what to say next. The logic was that these sentence openings would lead children to consider relations among previous sentences and to take into account the readers' perspective as well as what they, as authors, wanted to say. The prompts led to children writing essays with more content, and more richly interconnected content, even though the prompts did not specify what the content should be.

As people develop expertise in writing, they progress from the knowledge-telling strategy to the *knowledge-transforming strategy* (Bereiter & Scardamalia, 1987). This strategy is defined by the writer trying simultaneously to meet two goals: deciding what information to convey and deciding how to convey it in a way that the anticipated audience will understand. Professional writers consistently use this strategy; many other adults use it on those occasions when they are knowledgeable about the topic of their essay. The strategy begins with an analysis of the subject of the essay and adoption of a point of view. Subsequent cognitive activities include moving back and forth between knowledge of the content area being discussed and knowledge of rhetorical devices that can be used to translate content into the desired form. The approach also involves frequent comparisons between what the writer would like to say and what he or she has written on the page. A useful byproduct of the knowledge-transforming strategy is that the process of writing often increases the writers' knowledge. Trying to communicate a position to readers forces them to recognize gaps and contradictions in their own thinking. Resolving these gaps and contradictions often leads writers to deepen their understanding of the topic.

The trend toward greater use of the knowledge-transforming strategy can be seen in the amount of time spent planning before beginning to write. In general, college students take *more* time before they start writing than do fifth graders (Zbrodoff, 1984). They spend this time planning what their position will be, how they will argue for it, and what rhetorical devices they will use to do so.

The flexibility with which writers adapt to task constraints also increases with age. Fifth graders take the same, minimal amount of time to start, regardless of time and length constraints. This is what would be expected from use of the knowledge-telling strategy; writing begins as soon as a direct response to the question can be generated. In contrast, college students increase their planning time when the assignment requires a longer essay and when they have more time to complete it (Bereiter & Scardamalia, 1987).

Mechanical requirements. A third type of difficulty encountered in writing involves the mechanical requirements of forming letters, spelling words correctly, and putting capital letters and punctuation marks in the right places. These mechanical demands force many children to proceed so slowly that they forget what they are trying to say.

To test how mechanical demands and slow rate of production affect children's writing, Bereiter and Scardamalia (1982) asked fourth and sixth graders to compose essays under one of three conditions. In the typical-writing condition, children wrote as they ordinarily would, thus encountering both the mechanical demands and the slow rate of writing. In the slow-dictation condition, they dictated their essays to a scribe who had been trained to write at the child's writing speed. This released children from the mechanical requirements of writing but not from its slow pace. In the standard-dictation condition, children dictated into a tape recorder at their normal speaking rate. This released them from both the mechanical requirements and the slow pace of ordinary writing.

Children in the standard-dictation condition, burdened by neither mechanical demands nor slow rate, produced the best essays. Children in the slow-dictation condition, burdened by slow rate but not by mechanical demands, produced the next best essays. Children in the typical-writing condition, burdened by both slow rate and mechanical demands, produced the worst essays.

These findings highlight one of the reasons writing is difficult for children: it taxes their working memory capacity. When working memory demands are lessened, children's performance improves. Indeed, there is evidence to suggest that both individual and developmental differences in writing skill are related to differences in working memory capacity (Kellogg, 1996; McCutchen, 1996, 2000; Swanson & Berninger, 1996). As children become more fluent with the mechanical aspects of writing, the process of generating text requires fewer working memory resources. As a consequence, children become better able to focus their attention on other aspects of the task of writing.

These findings further suggest that teaching children to type or use word processors might improve the quality of their writing, since it would reduce working memory demands by allowing them to decrease attention allocated to handwriting and spelling. A review of 32 studies on the effects of word processing indicated that it has this desired effect. Access to word processing usually resulted in higher-quality writing (Bangert-Downs, 1993). The effects were largest with students who were not good writers under other circumstances. Positive effects continued to be found when students who previously wrote essays on the word processor returned to writing them by hand. The improvements in writing quality were not huge, but they were quite consistent. Thus, by removing the mechanical demands of writing by hand, word processors can help students improve their writing.

THE PROCESS OF REVISION

Few first drafts are well written. Unfortunately, even students whose initial drafts cry out for changes rarely revise them; they usually just hand in the first draft. Worse yet, when students make revisions, the changes do not consistently result in improved quality (Fitzgerald, 1987). This raises the question of why revisions tend to be so inadequate.

Revision can be divided into two main processes: identification of weaknesses and their correction (Baker & Brown, 1984). To identify weaknesses, people must compare a unit of text, such as a sentence or paragraph, with an internal representation of the text's intended properties. Such a comparison requires the writer to be clear about the goals that the writing was intended to serve, even when the words on the page are confusing or distracting.

Children, as well as many adults, have difficulty identifying weaknesses in texts. For example, in a study by Beal (1990), children needed to correct essays presented to them that included missing sentences, impossible-to-interpret sentences, and direct contradictions. Fourth graders detected only 25 percent of these glaring problems, sixth graders only 60 percent. In general, elementary school children tend to overestimate the clarity of texts (Beal, 1996).

In the more typical case where children need to revise their own compositions, egocentrism exacerbates the difficulty. Children have trouble separating what they themselves know from what their readers could reasonably be expected to know. To illustrate this point, Bartlett (1982) asked children to revise either their own essays or an essay written by a classmate. The focus was on how well children detected two types of errors: grammatical errors and ambiguous references (such as "The policeman and the robber fought. He was killed."). If egocentrism contributed to the problem of recognizing weaknesses, children presumably would have more difficulty correcting ambiguous references in their own stories, where they knew the intended references, than in those of other children. On the other hand, egocentrism would not lead to their having more difficulty correcting their own grammatical errors than those of other children.

As anticipated, children were quite good at noticing other children's referential ambiguities but much less good at recognizing their own. Detection of grammatical errors, where egocentrism was not as much an issue, was more similar for their own and other children's essays. A major part of the development of revision skills, then, is ability to separate one's own perspective from that of the reader.

One inference that might be drawn from this finding is that writers should wait before revising. The logic is that psychological and temporal closeness to the composition increase egocentrism in the period immediately after the piece is written, and thus interfere with efforts at revision. With time, greater objectivity might be possible.

Such advice does not get at the heart of the problem, though. The quality of fourth to twelfth graders' revisions is no better when they revise an essay a week after writing it than when they revise immediately (Bereiter & Scardamalia, 1982). It appears, therefore, that students may as well begin revising as soon after writing as is convenient. Waiting, in and of itself, does not help.

Even when children detect a problem in their writing, they still must repair it. Fortunately, children make such repairs quite effectively, at least when they recognize the problem spontaneously. For example, both fourth and sixth graders in Beal's (1990) study effectively corrected those problems that they detected themselves. The case was different, however, with weaknesses that adults pointed out after the children had missed them. The older students were fairly effective in fixing these problems, but the younger children were quite ineffective.

Even for older children, it is not always beneficial to simply point out parts of an essay that need revision. McCutchen and colleagues found that when sentences that needed revision were cued, seventh-grade students tended to focus on surface-level errors (such as spelling and punctuation) rather than more serious, meaning-based errors (such as disruptions in chronological sequence) (McCutchen, Francis, & Kerr, 1997). College students made better use of the cues and often made meaning-based revisions where appropriate.

The key to successful revision seems to be the ability to adopt multiple perspectives. This helps both in detecting and diagnosing problems with the original draft and in correcting problems that other people note. Thus, in writing, as in reading and mathematics, coordinating diverse types of knowledge, and shifting attention flexibly among them, is essential for successful performance.

Summary

When they go to school, children build on their earlier understanding of numbers to acquire many new skills and concepts: simple and complex integer arithmetic, fractions, algebra, and computer programming among them. Development of simple arithmetic involves acquisition of more advanced strategies and increased speed and accuracy. The same pattern of development is found in North America, Europe, and East Asia, though the rate of development of arithmetic is faster among East Asian children. Individual differences among children are evident both in amount of knowledge and in the types of strategies that are preferred.

Children often do not understand the underlying concepts in mathematics beyond simple arithmetic. This creates a variety of misconceptions and distortions, among them buggy subtraction rules, misunderstanding of decimal fractions and of the equal sign, and inappropriate use of algebraic manipulations. Mediated instruction, emphasizing not only computer programming concepts and commands but also their applicability to other situations, can improve general problem solving competence as well as programming skill.

Learning to read involves acquisition of prereading skills, word-identification procedures, and comprehension. Among the most important prereading skills are letter perception and phonemic awareness. Teaching phonemic awareness skills to preschoolers leads to lasting increases in reading achievement.

Children use two main word-identification methods: phonological recoding and visually based retrieval. Both methods begin with examination of the printed word and end with access to the word's meaning and pronunciation in long-term memory. Phonological recoding also involves an intermediate step in which print is translated into sounds. The two skills are related in that accurate phonological recoding may aid development of strong associations between the printed word and its long-term memory entry and thus aid visually-based retrieval.

Reading comprehension is influenced by the same factors that influence memory development: improvements in basic processes, strategies, content knowledge, and metacognitive understanding. Helping children understand critical background content and improving their metacognitive processing has resulted in substantial improvements in reading comprehension.

Writing is a challenging task for most children. They have difficulty establishing clear goals in the absence of the prompts and feedback that conversation provides. They also have difficulty reconciling the competing demands of executing the mechanics of writing, forming grammatical sentences, expressing meanings, and anticipating the reader's reaction. In response, they first adopt the knowledge-telling strategy, which involves stating a reaction to the question that was posed and then listing supporting evidence in the order in which it is retrieved from memory. The strategy produces brief, listlike compositions. A major change that occurs with age and experience in writing is improved ability to coordinate goals, which allows writers to produce more extensive and interesting essays. This eventually enables writers to progress to the knowledge-transforming strategy, a strategy that demands more planning but that pays off in higher-quality products.

Skill at revising also improves with age and experience. The largest gains come in recognizing problems in the text. Once children recognize problems, they are reasonably skillful at fixing them. Underlying the improvement in identifying problems is growing ability to separate one's own knowledge from that of readers.

Recommended Readings

Bereiter, C., & Scardamalia, M. (1987). *The psychology of written composition.* Hillsdale, NJ: Erlbaum. An excellent summary of what is known about how children write and how their writing can be improved.

Geary, D.C. (1994). *Children's mathematical development: Research and practical implications.* Washington, DC: American Psychological Association. This book integrates issues ranging from what mathematical competencies are inherent to human beings to how mathematical disabilities arise.

Goldin-Meadow, S. (2001). Giving the mind a hand: The role of gesture in cognitive change. In J.L. McClelland & R.S. Siegler (Eds.), *Mechanisms of cognitive development: Behavioral and neural perspectives.* Mahwah, NJ: Erlbaum. An intriguing description of how watching children's hand gestures, as well as listening to what they say, can help us understand not only what they know, but also how their knowledge changes.

Palincsar, A.S. & Brown, A.L. (1984). Reciprocal teaching of comprehension-monitoring activities. *Cognition and Instruction, 1,* 117–175. One of the most successful applications of psychological principles to the task of improving learning in the schools. Seventh graders with serious reading comprehension problems became able to comprehend at an above average level through participation in this program.

Rayner, K., Foorman, B.R., Perfetti, C.A., Pesetsky, D., & Seidenberg, M.S. (2001). How psychological science informs the teaching of reading. *Psychological Science in the Public Interest, 2,* 31–74. This monograph reviews research about skilled reading and learning to read, and considers the implications of the research for reading instruction.

12

CONCLUSIONS FOR THE PRESENT; CHALLENGES FOR THE FUTURE

"So how do children think?" (A seven-year-old, reacting to her father's description of what this book is about)

Previous chapters have focused on perception, language, memory, conceptual understanding, social cognition, problem solving, and academic skills separately. The division has made it easier to consider the unique properties of children's thinking in each area. However, such divisions can obscure the continuing themes that unite different aspects of cognitive development. The two main goals of this concluding chapter are to discuss these unifying themes and to identify issues that seem likely to be central in the future.

In the opening chapter of the book, we listed eight themes that apply to children's thinking in general. These themes also provide the framework for this final chapter. The chapter is divided into eight sections, with each section focusing on a particular theme. The first part of each discussion summarizes current knowledge relevant to the theme. The second part introduces issues that are just beginning to be addressed. Among these "challenges for the future" are some of the largest and most interesting issues about children's thinking, such as whether learning and development are the same or different and what mechanisms give rise to developmental change. The chapter's organization is summarized in Table 12.1.

TABLE 12.1 Chapter Outline

I.   The most basic issues about children's thinking are "What develops?" and "How does development occur?"
   A.   Current Knowledge about What Develops and How Development Occurs
   B.   Future Issues

II. Four change processes that seem to be particularly large contributors to cognitive development are automatization, encoding, generalization, and strategy construction.
   A.   Current Knowledge about Change Processes
   B.   Future Issues

III. Infants and very young children are far more cognitively competent than they appear. They possess a rich set of abilities that allow them to learn rapidly.
   A.   Current Knowledge about Early Competence
   B.   Future Issues

IV. Differences between age groups tend to be ones of degree rather than kind. Not only are young children more cognitively competent than they appear, but older children and adults are often less competent than we might think.
   A.   Current Knowledge about Differences Between Age Groups
   B.   Future Issues

V.   Changes in children's thinking do not occur in a vacuum. What children already know about material that they encounter influences not only how much they learn but also what they learn.
   A.   Current Knowledge about the Effects of Existing Knowledge
   B.   Future Issues

VI. The development of intelligence reflects changes in brain structure and functioning as well as increasingly effective deployment of cognitive resources.
   A.   Current Knowledge about the Development of Intelligence
   B.   Future Issues

VII. Children's thinking develops within a social context. Parents, peers, teachers, and the overall society influence what children think about, as well as how and why they come to think in particular ways.
   A.   Current Knowledge about Social Influences on Children's Thinking
   B.   Future Issues

VIII. Increasing understanding of children's thinking is yielding practical benefits as well as theoretical insights.
   A.   Current Practical Contributions of Research on Children's Thinking
   B.   Future Issues

IX. Summary

---

1. The most basic issues about children's thinking are "What develops?" and "How does development occur?"

When investigators of children's thinking write in journal articles, "The purpose of this investigation is ... ," they almost never complete the sentence with "to find out what develops" or "to find out how development occurs." Modesty, and the realization that no one study is likely to meet these goals, prevents researchers from mentioning them. Yet they are the deepest motivations of research on children's thinking. Always keeping them in mind is critical to understanding what the research is all about.

CURRENT KNOWLEDGE ABOUT WHAT DEVELOPS AND HOW DEVELOPMENT OCCURS

On one of the rare occasions when investigators stated their views about "what develops," Brown and DeLoache (1978) suggested that in the domain of memory development, there are four major sources of growth: basic processes, strategies, metacognition, and content knowledge. These sources of memory development provide a useful guide for thinking about what develops in other areas of cognitive development as well.

Many examples from previous chapters attest to the pervasive contribution to cognitive development of changes in these four types of capabilities. Improvements in basic processes were not only invoked to explain improved functioning of immediate, short-term, and long-term memory (Hale et al., 1997; Kail, 1991). They also were used to explain changes in the complexity of the stimuli infants prefer to look at (McCall et al., 1977), in the consistency of toddlers' reliance on the mutual exclusivity constraint in acquiring new vocabulary items (Markman, 1989), in preschoolers' success in making transitive inferences (Halford, 1993) and acquiring a theory of mind (Carlson & Moses, 2001; Russell et al., 1994), and in school-age children's reading and arithmetic (Adams, Treiman, & Pressley, 1998; Geary, 1994).

Similarly, changes in strategies were seen in contexts other than rehearsal, organization, and the other mnemonic strategies. Improved strategies also helped children to solve increasing numbers of class inclusion problems and measurement problems correctly (Miller, 1989; Trabasso et al., 1978), to solve simple addition and inversion problems (such as $3 + 4 - 4 = \_\_$) more quickly and efficiently (Siegler & Jenkins, 1989; Siegler & Stern, 1998), to use the *ed* ending to generate past-tense verbs (Marcus, 1996), to allocate attention increasingly systematically (Miller & Seier, 1994), and to write more elaborate descriptions of the day's events on "class news" assignments (Waters, 1980).

Improved metacognition not only aided memory functioning (Schneider & Pressley, 1989), it also allowed 1-year-olds to understand that their mother's words referred to what she was looking at (Baldwin, 1993a; Tomasello & Barton, 1994), 4-year-olds to understand that other people could believe something that the child knew was not true (Astington & Gopnik, 1991), school-age children to generate symbolic tools that helped them to play a memory game (Eskritt & Lee, 2002), and adults to teach route planning more effectively than fourth graders because they more deeply realized the need to engage children in the learning process (Gauvain & Rogoff, 1989).

Finally, superior content knowledge did not only lead to more accurate memory of visits to doctors' offices, fairy tales, and soccer games. It also led 4-month-olds who had played with two separate objects to be surprised when they later saw them move in tandem (Needham et al., 1997); 3- and 4-year-olds with older siblings to understand other people's thinking better than age peers without older siblings (Ruffman et al., 1998); 5-year-olds to solve transitive inference problems better when they concerned relations among the bear family in *Goldilocks and the Three Bears* (Goswami, 1995b); and 14-year-olds to comprehend stories better because they form links between episodes as well as within them (van den Broek, 1989).

Hypotheses about how development occurs, like hypotheses about what develops, reflect the interconnectedness of cognitive development. Recall some of the diverse contexts in which changes in children's thinking appeared due to improved encoding: infants' increasing tendencies to form categories based on abstract features (Eimas & Quinn, 1994; Madole & Cohen, 1995), toddlers' movement from child-basic to standard-basic categories once they begin to encode functionally important features such as the wicks on round candles (Tversky & Hemenway, 1984), preschoolers' reading of words such as "Coke" and "Budweiser" on the basis of encoding distinctive features of their lengths and initial letters (Gough & Hillinger, 1980), and school-age children's improved ability to learn about balance scales once they encode distance as well as weight (Siegler, 1976).

FUTURE ISSUES

Making substantial progress on such difficult issues as what develops and how development occurs will require advances in both theories and methods for studying development. One need is for theories that are both broadly applicable and precisely stated. Such theories could focus attention on critical issues, raise questions that have not been considered before, and serve as a point of departure from which to formulate ideas.

For many years, Piaget's theory served these integrative and agenda-setting functions. Arguments between "pro-Piagetians" and "anti-Piagetians" dominated journals, books, and conferences. But those days are past. Very few people would argue today that infants younger than 8 months have no understanding of object permanence, that 5-year-olds are completely incapable of understanding transformations, or that cognitive development can be divided into neat, orderly stages. Equally few people would argue that the difficulties that children have with the standard versions of Piagetian tasks are just due to methodological artifacts, or that there is no unity in children's thinking at given ages. Instead, most students of cognitive development would subscribe to the more moderate positions that infants and young children encounter genuine difficulty understanding the skills and concepts emphasized by Piaget, but that they have some early understanding of them, gradually acquire greater understanding, and organize their thinking in coherent, but complex, ways.

Moderation has its virtues, but also its costs. Piaget was right in some of his views and wrong in others, but right or wrong, his theory lent coherence to findings about many aspects of children's thinking. What is needed now is a successor that has the virtues of Piaget's theory while surmounting at least some of its drawbacks. In other words, a theory is needed that, like Piaget's, includes the entire age range from infancy to adolescence; addresses areas as diverse as problem solving, conceptual understanding, memory, and moral judgments; and uncovers heretofore unknown changes in children's thinking.

In previous chapters, we encountered a number of efforts at formulating such broad yet detailed theories. Each of them has added to our understanding of cognitive development, but none has captured the imagination of the field as Piaget's theory did. The question now is how can we work toward such a theory.

One way to promote such theoretical progress is to study children's thinking using methods that examine changes as they are occurring. Providing a precise and plausible account of change has been the weak point of both Piaget's theory and more recent theories of cognitive development. Explaining change is inherently difficult, but the difficulty appears to have been exacerbated by the methods traditionally used to study children's thinking. These methods contrast performance of children at relatively widely spaced ages; if differences between age groups are observed, the researcher attempts to infer what happened between the younger and older age. Unfortunately, this strategy of inferring how changes must have occurred from observations widely spaced in time leaves open many possible paths to change, especially since changes in children's thinking often do not proceed by the most direct route we can imagine.

One method that can reveal the indirect paths that change often takes is the microgenetic method. As described in Chapter 10, the microgenetic method involves obtaining frequent samples of children's thinking as their thinking is undergoing change. Studies using this approach have documented that children's thinking is characterized by variability, that change often involves regressions as well as progressions, and that not all children follow the same path of change, even when they encounter the same types of problems (e.g., Granott & Parziale, 2002; Siegler & Svetina, 2002; Tunteler & Resing, 2002).

One example of a microgenetic study is Karmiloff-Smith's (1986, 1992) study of children drawing maps for an ambulance driver to follow while delivering a patient to the hospital (p. 370–371). By examining the sequence of maps that the children drew, Karmiloff-Smith discovered that the maps often regressed from efficient and informative notations to ones with considerable redundancy, before returning to the earlier efficient and informative formats. Without examining the changes in drawing from one map to the next, Karmiloff-Smith would have been unlikely to detect these regressions. More generally, such detailed data about change indicate to theorists what exactly they need to explain. Thus, research using microgenetic methods holds promise for shedding light on the process of change.

Another approach that has promise for promoting theoretical progress is research investigating how developments in one domain affect development in others. Traditionally, researchers are trained to have expertise in a single domain, so most studies focus on developments within individual domains, such as language development, perceptual development, memory development, and so forth. However, child development is not as simple as that. Gains in one domain have the potential to influence performance and development in other domains as well. To achieve a deep understanding of developmental processes, it will be essential to understand relations among domains and how they play out over development—essentially, to reintegrate the study of child development.

Fortunately, some researchers are beginning to take a more integrative approach. For example, as described in Chapter 5, Joseph Campos and colleagues are exploring how developments in motor skills influence perceptual development. In particular, learning to crawl has important consequences for perceptual development. Infants who are able to crawl display better perceptual skills in a variety of contexts than do infants of the same age who are not yet able to crawl. For example, crawlers attend more to distant objects than do pre-crawlers of the same age, leading to more accurate perception of absolute distances (Campos et al., 2000). When placed in a "moving room," in which the floor is stationary but the walls and ceiling move, crawlers adjust their posture more than do pre-crawlers of the same age, suggesting that they are more responsive to visual information (Higgins et al., 1996). Crawlers also show more signs of wariness on the visual cliff (see pp. 179) than do pre-crawlers of the same age. These findings are not spurious correlations—pre-crawlers who receive locomotor experience in walkers, which allow them to move independently by pushing with their feet on the floor, also show enhanced wariness of the visual cliff (Campos et al., 1992).

Developments in motor skills also influence cognitive development. Crawlers perform better than precrawlers of the same age on Piaget's A-not-B task. In this task, infants must search for an object that they see hidden at a new location (B), after they have seen it hidden several times at a different location (A). Crawlers are much more likely to search at the correct location (B) on this task than are precrawlers (Horobin & Acredolo, 1986; Kermoian & Campos, 1988). Furthermore, as infants gain weeks of crawling experience, they can tolerate longer and longer delays between the hiding event and the search, and still search successfully at location B (Campos et al., 2000). Thus, learning to crawl appears to influence infants' object knowledge and their spatial search performance.

Neuropsychological studies also support the view that cognitive and motor development are closely integrated. One source of evidence comes from studies of children with neurodevelopmental disorders (Diamond, 2000). Many disorders that are primarily characterized by deficits in cognitive abilities are also accompanied by impairments in motor skill. For example, motor coordination problems and movement disturbances are common among children with Attention Deficit Hyperactivity Disorder (Kadesjo & Gillberg, 1998), Specific Language Impairment (Hill, 1998; Hill, Bishop, & Nimmo-Smith, 1998), and autism (Leary & Hill, 1996). Another source of neuropsychological evidence comes from brain imaging studies, which have shown that the brain regions that subserve cognitive and motor functions are often activated together (Diamond, 2000). In particular, the prefrontal cortex, which is crucial for complex cognitive tasks, and the cerebellum, which is important in motor skills, are often co-activated (Berman et al., 1995). Thus, many lines of evidence indicate that cognitive and motor skills are interrelated. A challenge for future research will be to specify precisely how gains in motor skill influence cognitive development, and vice versa.

Other examples of integration across domains have been presented throughout the book. For example, studies of interrelations between language and categorization were described in Chapter 4 (e.g., Lucy & Gaskins, 2001), and studies of interrelations between language and theory of mind were discussed in Chapter 9 (e.g., de Villiers & de Villiers, 2000). As these examples suggest, the "engines" that drive developmental change in one domain often come from another domain. Thus, research that integrates across domains promises to foster theoretical progress in understanding how development occurs.

2. Four change processes that seem to be particularly large contributors to cognitive development are automatization, encoding, generalization, and strategy construction.

CURRENT KNOWLEDGE ABOUT CHANGE PROCESSES

Although understanding of change processes in children's thinking is just beginning to accelerate, we do know that large contributions are made by four families of processes: automatization, encoding, generalization, and strategy construction. *Automatization* refers to a procedure coming to be executed invariably and with minimal or no expenditure of cognitive resources whenever the relevant situation appears. Related concepts include freeing cognitive resources, shifting from controlled to automatic processing, and shifting from serial to parallel processing. *Encoding* involves representing objects and events in terms of sets of features and their relations. Ideas that overlap with encoding include assimilation, discrimination, differentiation, identification of critical features, and formation of mental models. *Generalization* refers to extrapolating known relations to new cases. Similar constructs include induction, abstraction, transfer, regularity detection, and analogical reasoning. Finally, *strategy construction* involves integrating the other processes to adapt to task demands. Related mechanisms include accommodation, strategy discovery, and the operations of metacomponents and central conceptual structures.

TABLE 12.2   Some Demonstrations of the Importance of Automatization, Encoding, Generalization, and Strategy Construction

Process	Domain	Investigator
Automatization	Mechanics of writing essays	Bereiter & Scardamalia (1987)
	Basic arithmetic	Lemaire et al. (1994)
	Word identification in skilled reading	Harm & Seidenberg (1999)
	General theory of development	Case (1992a)
Encoding	Individual differences in infants' intelligence	Rose et al. (1992)
	Preschoolers' focus on gist of stories	Brainerd et al. (1990)
	Older children's equation solving	McNeil & Alibali (2004)
	General theory of development	Sternberg (1999)
Generalization	Infants' learning about mobiles	Rovee-Collier (1999)
	Toddlers' overregularization of "ed" past tense	Marcus et al. (1992)
	Preschoolers' analogical problem solving	Tunteler & Resing (2002)
	General theory of development	MacWhinney et al. (1989)
Strategy Construction	Infants' means-ends analysis	Willatts (1990)
	Toddlers' tool use	Chen & Siegler (2000)
	Older children's scientific experimentation	Kuhn et al. (1995)
	General theory of development	Siegler (1996)

Although understanding of these mechanisms is far from complete, each undoubtedly contributes to a wide range of developments. A few of these are listed in Table 12.2.

The four processes are important for their joint contribution to development, as well as for each process's individual contribution. To get a feel for how they might together produce development in a particular area, think about the counting-on strategy for adding numbers (Chapter 3). This strategy involves first identifying the larger addend and then counting up from it the number of times indicated by the smaller addend. On 2 + 5 and 5 + 2, for example, a child using the counting-on strategy would note that 5 was the larger addend, count "5, 6, 7," and answer, "7."

Now consider how the four processes might work together to generate this strategy. Constructing the strategy depends on having previously formed the generalization that adding a + b always yields the same answer as adding b + a. Otherwise, there would be no basis for always counting from the larger addend, regardless of the order of addends in the problem. This generalization, in turn, depends on appropriate encoding. To learn that addend order is irrelevant, children need to encode the features "first addend" and "second addend," as well as the particular addends within each problem. Finally, encoding not only the particular addends but also the categories "first addend" and "second addend" probably requires automatizing other processes, such as counting, so that they do not require all of the child's processing resources, allowing the child to do the thinking needed to discover the new strategy.

FUTURE ISSUES

The influence of automatization, encoding, generalization, and strategy construction is not unique to cognitive development. All are essential to learning in general, regardless of when in life the learning occurs. This leaves a major unanswered question, however: Are there change mechanisms that are uniquely developmental, that is, mechanisms that only operate during certain periods of life?

A common way of addressing this issue is to ask whether learning and development are the same or different (Feldman, 1995; Fischer & Granott, 1995; Halford, 1995; Siegler, 2000). The terms are certainly used differently. Acquisitions tend to be labeled "development" when they consistently occur at a particular age, when they are universal across cultures, and when they are universal among individuals within a culture. Acquisitions tend to be labeled "learning" when they are acquired at a variety of ages, in some cultures but not others, and by some but not other individuals within a culture. These linguistic distinctions, however, leave open the basic question of whether the same or different processes give rise to the outcomes labeled "development" and "learning."

Developmental neuroscientists have distinguished between two types of processes that give rise to changes in the brain: experience-expectant and experience-dependent (Bruer & Greenough, 2001; Greenough et al., 1987). This distinction also seems useful for thinking about the neural substrates of learning and development and about how the processes might differ.

Experience-expectant processes correspond to the "development" end of the development-learning continuum. Such processes are hypothesized to be based on the early synaptic overproduction and pruning over broad areas of the brain that was described in Chapter 1 (pp. 16–17). In experience-expectant processes, the initial overproduction of synapses is maturationally regulated, but which ones are pruned depends on experience. Normal experience at the normal time results in neural activity that maintains typical connections; lack of such experience at the usual time results in atypical connections. Thus, there is a sensitive period (Bailey & Bruer, 2001; Bornstein, 1989) in which relevant experience must occur for the experience to have the usual effect on brain development. The type of experience that is relevant to such experience-expectant processes is experience that has been widely available throughout the evolutionary history of the species.

Greenough et al. (1987) suggested that one advantage of such experience-expectant processes is that they allow both efficient acquisition in normal environments and reasonable adaptation to abnormal ones. In particular, the genes provide a rough outline of the eventual form of the process, thus facilitating acquisition under normal circumstances. Unusual environments or physical deficiencies, however, lead to different neural activity, which creates alternative organizations of brain activity that are adaptive given the atypical circumstances.

Direct support for this account comes from observations of brain activation in deaf and blind individuals (Neville, 1995b; Neville & Bavelier, 2002). Children who are completely deaf receive no auditory experience. As a result, certain areas of the brain that would be devoted to auditory processing if the brain were receiving both auditory and visual stimulation instead come to be devoted to visual processing. Conversely, blind children receive no visual experience. As a result, some areas of their brains that under ordinary circumstances would be devoted to visual processing come to be devoted to auditory or tactile processing. The brains of deaf and blind children do not show these unusual processing patterns at birth. They emerge only after the children's brains do not receive the typical input in the months after birth (the sensitive period). Thus, the brain is predisposed to devote certain areas to processing certain types of stimuli, but if the expected pattern of stimulation is not present, the brain uses the area to process signals from other senses.

The other side of Greenough et al.'s dichotomy involves *experience-dependent* processes. These are the neural substrate of what is usually thought of as learning. With experience-dependent processes, formation of synaptic connections depends on experiences that vary widely among individuals in whether and when they occur. The experience-dependent processes appear to operate through the formation of synapses in response to specific neural activity, caused by partially or totally unsuccessful attempts to process information. Such synapses can be generated as rapidly as 10–15 minutes after a new experience (Chang & Greenough, 1984). Synapse production under such circumstances appears to be localized to the site of the previous information processing. However, as with experience-expectant processes, more synapses are produced than will later be present. The synapses that are maintained are those involved in subsequent neural activity.

This analysis suggests both similarities and differences between experience-expectant and experience-dependent processes. In both cases, the change mechanism involves a cycle of synaptic overproduction and pruning. Also in both, neural activity determines which synapses are maintained. However, the events that trigger the production of synapses and its degree of localization within the brain distinguish the two types of processes. The challenge now is to provide similarly precise descriptions of change mechanisms at the cognitive level, so as to better understand the similarities and differences between learning and development.

3. Infants and very young children are far more cognitively competent than they appear. They possess a rich set of abilities that allow them to learn rapidly.

Current Knowledge about Early Competence

Literally from the day they emerge from the womb, infants possess a variety of perceptual capabilities. They see the world in color (Adams, 1987) and accurately perceive the relative distance of objects from themselves (Slater et al., 1990).

They look in the direction from which sounds come (Morrongiello, Fenwick, et al., 1994) and prefer listening to tape recordings of stories read to them before birth (DeCasper & Spence, 1986). By 4 months of age, their seeing and hearing become considerably more acute. They prefer looking at faces over other types of objects (Dannemiller & Stephens, 1988), and they prefer looking at attractive faces over unattractive ones (Langlois et al., 1994). They also prefer listening to their own name over the names of other people (Mandel et al., 1995). Integration of information from different senses also is evident from birth, and even more so by age 4 months. Infants use sounds to guide their looking (Haith, 1980), sights to guide their reaching (von Hofsten, 1993) and knowledge gained from manual exploration of objects to guide their looking (Needham et al , 1997; Streri & Spelke, 1988).

The early competence is not restricted to perception. Infants less than 1 year old possess rudimentary understanding of a variety of concepts, including time (Colombo & Richman, 2002; Friedman, 2002), space (Bai & Bertenthal, 1992), number (Wynn, 1992a), and causality (Oakes & Cohen, 1995). They can solve problems via means-ends analysis (Willatts, 1990), analogical reasoning (Chen et al., 1997), and letting their mothers know what they want (Mosier & Rogoff, 1994). They respond differently to people and to objects (Legerstee, 1991; Spelke, et al., 1995), and they have expectations about how other people will interact with them, so they react negatively when caregivers display a "still face" and do not move or speak (Tronick et al., 1978), or when adults violate the "rules" of a familiar game such as "peek-a-boo" by performing the actions in a scrambled order (Rochat et al., 1999).

One reason that infants are able to do so much so quickly is that they possess a variety of generally applicable learning processes. From the first days outside the womb, infants orient their attention toward bright lights, loud noises, moving objects, and other potentially informative stimuli (Aslin, 1993; Cohen, 1972). They form associations, recognize familiar objects, generalize what they have learned to similar objects, and imitate some actions of other people (Meltzoff & Moore, 1989; Rovee-Collier, 1995; Siqueland & Lipsitt, 1966). By 2 to 4 months, they form expectations and abstract prototypical patterns (Bomba & Siqueland, 1983; Haith et al., 1993). By 10 months, they detect correlations among features and use them to form new concepts (Younger, 1993). In their first year, they begin to detect statistical regularities in patterned input, in both auditory and visual modalities (Kirkham et al., 2002; Saffran, 2003a, 2003b; Saffran et al., 1996).

These general learning processes are not the only reason for children's early cognitive competence. Infants' and toddlers' thinking also seems to be biased in certain directions that help them learn. In particular, infants seem to form valid assumptions about a variety of aspects of the physical and social worlds that aid perceptual and conceptual development. One such assumption involves the nature of physical objects. Infants younger than 6 months old already seem to expect that all parts of a physical object will move together, that objects cannot move through spaces occupied by other objects, and that objects must move in continuous paths (Baillargeon, 2002; Kellman & Spelke, 1983; Spelke et al., 1992). By 18 months, toddlers seem to expect that new words will refer to all objects within a given class (the taxonomic constraint) and that new words will not mean the same thing as existing words (the mutual exclusivity constraint) (Markman, 1989; Merriman & Bowman, 1989). Infants and toddlers also are biased toward assigning causal relations a central position in their concepts (Leslie, 1982) and toward using causal relations to guide their memories of events (Bauer & Mandler, 1989b).

It is important to remember that these early competencies are part of the story of cognitive development, but only part. Infants' and toddlers' understandings and capacities almost always differ greatly from those of older children. Taken together, though, the early competencies, the generally applicable learning mechanisms, and the more specific biases to think of the world in certain ways promote exceptionally rapid cognitive growth in the first few years.

FUTURE ISSUES

Probably the single largest issue regarding infants' cognition concerns how to reconcile the competence they show under some circumstances with the incompetence they show under others. A model by Munakata et al. (1997) provides a start in this direction. The model concerns development of object permanence. Recall from Chapter 2 that Piaget (1954) hypothesized that infants younger than 8 months do not understand that objects continue to exist when they can no longer be seen. He supported this interpretation with evidence that 6- and 7-month-olds do not reach for toys that are taken from them and placed under an opaque container. However, subsequent experiments (e.g., Baillargeon, 1987; Hespos & Baillargeon, 2001) demonstrated nascent understanding of object permanence at three months. When 3-month-olds are shown a stationary object on a table, then have their view of it occluded, and then see a moving object appear to go through the space where the stationary object had been, they look longer than when they see the same motion but without having seen the stationary object earlier. This finding suggested that the 3-month-olds represented the unseen object and looked for a long time because they were surprised to see another object appear to go through it. The question was why it would take infants so long to show knowledge of object permanence in their reaching, when they showed such understanding so much earlier in their looking.

One possibility was that infants understand the principle of object permanence by 3 months, but that they do not know until considerably later that they can act on one object (the opaque container) to retrieve another (Baillargeon, 1994; Diamond, 1991). Arguing against this possibility, and the related possibility that the infants did not want to retrieve the toy, the same infants who do not remove an opaque container to get a toy will remove an otherwise identical transparent container to get it (Bower & Wishart, 1972; Munakata et al., 1997). They also will press a button to get a toy they can see but not to get a toy they cannot see (Munakata et al., 1997).

Munakata et al. suggested a different explanation: that infants in their first half year possess representations of the continuing existence of hidden objects that are strong enough to elicit looking but not strong enough to elicit reaching. Studies of brain-damaged adults indicate that the damage often results in visual representations that are strong enough to maintain behaviors that are not too demanding on the representations but not ones that place greater demands on them (Farah, Monheit, & Wallace, 1991). Reaching may well be more demanding than looking; not only does it require a greater expenditure of energy, but infants do not consistently reach for interesting objects until about 4 months, whereas they look at them from birth (von Hofsten, 1993). Thus, infants' representations of hidden objects, like the representations of brain-damaged people, may be strong enough to succeed in favorable situations but not in more challenging ones.

To test whether this idea could explain infants' competence on some object permanence tasks and incompetence on others, Munakata et al. (1997) formulated a connectionist model. Like the MacWhinney et al. (1989) connectionist model of the development of German grammar (p. 94), Munakata's model of object permanence included an input layer, a hidden layer, and an output layer. Also as in the other connectionist model, each layer included a number of processing units, and there were many connections between processing units in different layers.

The experience received by the Munakata et al. model involved codes corresponding to a barrier and a ball. Sometimes the barrier moved in front of the ball, thus occluding it, and then moved away to reveal it again (Figure 12.1). This corresponded to infants seeing objects disappear behind other objects and then reappear when the other objects moved.

As the network gained experience with these situations, it learned to represent the continued existence of the ball and to predict that the ball would reappear where it had been earlier when the barrier moved away. At first, the model maintained such representations only over brief periods of occlusion; it gradually learned to maintain them over longer and longer periods. This corresponded to

FIGURE 12.1 Representation of ball and barrier presented to Munakata et al. (1997) model. At first, (Time 0) the barrier is to the left of the ball. Then it moves rightward until it is in front of the ball (Times 4–6). Then it moves leftward, revealing that the ball is still present (Time 7). After encountering a number of episodes like this, the model learns that the ball continues to exist even though it cannot be seen.

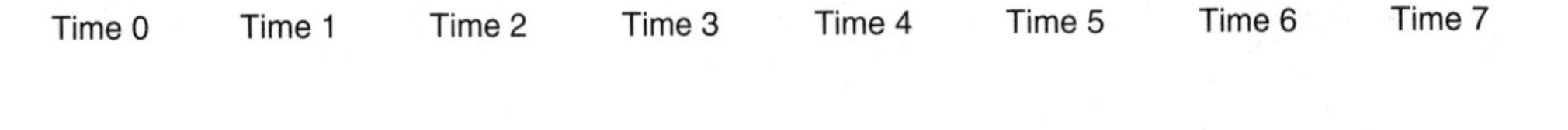

Time 0   Time 1   Time 2   Time 3   Time 4   Time 5   Time 6   Time 7

Diamond's (1985) finding that between 6 and 12 months, infants gradually extend the periods of occlusion over which they show object permanence.

Especially important in the present context, the model demonstrated how measures of reaching could reveal representations of occluded objects long before reaching measures revealed comparable knowledge. Within the model, the same representation of the object motivated looking and reaching. However, the process of strengthening connections between the representation and the reaching system was programmed to start later and to proceed more slowly than learning the connections that led to looking. Due to this slower strengthening of connections between the representation of the object and the reaching system, at any given point in development, a stronger representation of an object was needed to elicit reaching than to elicit looking.

This simulation has interesting implications for the general issue of how to reconcile infants' competence in some situations with their incompetence in others. When infants show competence in a situation, it is tempting to ascribe to them the kind of high-level understanding that would lead adults to engage in the behavior. Adults know as a general principle that objects continue to exist even when they cannot be seen. It is possible that infants' longer looking times when objects seem to disappear reflect the same type of surprise an adult would feel. However, the longer looking times may just imply a tendency to look at unusual events. After moving unusually slowly in a traffic jam, we are not surprised when we drive past the scene of an accident, but we tend to look at the cars involved anyway. The Munakata et al. model illustrates how detection of an unusual event could trigger longer looking times without surprise and without understanding of principles. It also indicates how experience seeing objects disappear behind barriers and then reappear when the barriers moved could eventually lead to competence via reaching as well as looking measures. Thus, the model provides a way of reconciling infants' competence and incompetence, as well as a perspective on what they know about object permanence and how they come to know it.

> 4. Differences between age groups tend to be ones of degree rather than kind. Not only are young children more cognitively competent than they appear, but older children and adults are often less competent than we might think.

CURRENT KNOWLEDGE ABOUT DIFFERENCES BETWEEN AGE GROUPS

As discussed in the previous section, infants and toddlers have a much richer cognitive life than was suspected until recently. The same is true of preschoolers. Consider just Piagetian tasks and concepts that were once thought impossible for children below age 7. Placing distinctive stickers on the left and right side of the three-mountains apparatus allows 3-year-olds to distinguish between their own spatial perspective and that of someone sitting on the other side of the mountains; thus, they are not always egocentric (Newcombe & Huttenlocher, 1992). When 3- to 5-year-olds see sugar dissolved in a cup of water, they believe that the water will weigh more than it did before, despite no change being visible; this indicates some understanding of conservation of weight (Au et al., 1993). Preschoolers also possess greater understanding of numbers than Piaget recognized; they can add and subtract small numbers, identify the larger of two numbers, and count in a way that reflects understanding of the structure of the number system (Geary, 1994).

At the other end of the age spectrum, adults' reasoning has turned out to be less rational than once thought. Without training, even high school and college students rarely solve Piagetian formal operations tasks, such as balance scale and shadow projection problems (Byrnes, 1988; Kuhn et al., 1995). Even after taking college physics courses, many students believe that when a car circles an oval, the door toward the outside moves at the same speed as the door toward the inside, despite the door toward the outside moving farther in the same time (Levin et al., 1990). Such difficulties are not limited to scientific reasoning. Shaklee (1979) reviewed a host of irrational aspects of adults' thinking. Adults will bet more on a cut of a deck of cards when playing against a nervous opponent than when playing against a relaxed one. They become more confident of their ability to win a game of pure chance after having time to practice it. When asked to judge which of two sequences of random events is more likely, they ignore the randomness if one sequence sounds more representative. For example, they say a couple is less likely to have six children in the order "girl, girl, girl, boy, boy, boy" than to have them in the order "girl, boy, boy, girl, boy, girl." In short, although young children act like budding scientists in some contexts, educated adults ignore the most basic logical considerations in others.

As implied by these findings of cognitive competence in early childhood and of illogical thinking in adulthood, development generally is an incremental process, occurring gradually over many years. Consider findings regarding children's understanding of the mind. Around their first birthday, infants show some understanding that other people have intentions; when an adult says, "That's a *dax*," they interpret *dax* as referring to the object at which the adult is looking, even if they themselves are looking at something else (Baldwin, 1993a). Two-year-olds understand that other people's desires influence their behavior, but not ordinarily that other people's beliefs are also influential (Wellman & Woolley, 1990). Four-year-olds understand that beliefs as well as desires influence people's behavior (Wellman et al., 2001), and they also distinguish between appearance and reality (Astington & Gopnik, 1991; Flavell, Flavell, & Green 1983). However, they believe that they can remember far more than they really can (Flavell et al., 1970) and they often do not see the necessity of using strategies to help them remember (Schneider & Pressley, 1989). Understanding of how to monitor one's reading comprehension, how to allocate study time among tasks, and how to assess other people's intentions continues to develop through adolescence and adulthood (Baker, 1994; Pressley, 1995). Lengthy and complex sequences of development, such as that involved in learning about our own and other people's minds, are the rule rather than the exception.

FUTURE ISSUES

Discoveries of young children's previously unsuspected competence, and of adults' previously unsuspected incompetence, have doomed many explanations of development. It is no longer tenable to believe that preschoolers' inherent egocentrism makes it impossible for them to take other people's perspectives. Nor is it tenable to believe that their mediation deficiencies makes it impossible for them to benefit from using memory strategies or that their wholistic thinking precludes them from forming concepts with defining features. These falling dominos, in turn, have made a more general belief about children's thinking increasingly indefensible: that it is possible to state a single age at which children acquire a particular concept.

The age at which children understand a concept often has been equated with the age at which most children succeed on a particular task that involves the concept. For example, for many years children were said to understand the concept of number when they could solve Piaget's number conservation task. As investigators devised additional tasks that measured understanding of numbers in different ways, however, it became clear that the ages at which different numerical tasks could be solved varied dramatically. At what age, then, do children understand the concept of number?

One plausible approach to answering this question is to identify understanding with the earliest form of understanding. Braine (1959) argued for this view when he wrote, "If one seeks to state an age at which a particular type of response develops, the only age that is not completely arbitrary is the earliest age at which this type of response can be elicited" (p. 16).

Braine's statement is entirely reasonable, as far as it goes. When one considers the many years that often separate initial from mature understanding, however, a paradox becomes evident. Adopting the initial-competence criterion puts us in the position of saying that many concepts are understood at young ages yet also of saying that children fail many reasonable indexes of understanding for years thereafter. Stated another way, if we adopt the initial-competence criterion, most understanding develops after the concept is understood.

Brown (1976) advocated an alternative criterion for conceptual understanding: that of *stable usage*. Children would not be viewed as understanding a concept until they could use it in most or all situations to which it applies. The problem here is evident in Braine's comment. What exactly does a child understand when he or she can use a concept in some situations but not in most? It does seem arbitrary to identify understanding with anything other than the earliest form of understanding. However, it seems misleading to identify it with the earliest understanding.

The object permanence data cited in the previous section illustrate the difficulty. Do infants understand object permanence at 3 months, when their looking times suggest such understanding? Or do they understand it at 9 months, when they begin to reach for hidden objects? Or do they not understand it until sometime later, when they know as a general principle that an object must continue to exist somewhere, even if they have no idea where it is (as when older children misplace their keys)? Given the complexity of cognitive development, it almost always will prove impossible to provide a meaningful statement about *the* age at which children acquire a cognitive capability. Models that specify how children think under various conditions, and how they come to think in those ways, are needed to deal with this complexity.

One approach that has great promise for addressing this complexity is the *dynamic systems* approach (Fischer & Bidell, 1998; Lewis, 2000; Thelen & Smith, 1994; van Geert, 2000). The central principle of dynamic systems approaches is *self-organization,* which is the principle that order can result from the interactions of various components of a complex system (Thelen, 1989). The developing child is a complex system with order (that is, organized behavioral states) resulting from the interactions of many forces at any given point in time. Some of these forces are the child's genetic and physical endowment, the child's history of relevant experiences, the particular task set for the child, and the context in which the behavior occurs. These components could combine in a potentially unlimited number of ways; however, in practice, for any complex system, only a limited number of stable states tend to occur. The components interact to "push" the system into one of these states, which are called *attractor states.* For example, in early locomotor development, although there are many possible ways of moving, only a few stable forms of crawling tend to occur with any frequency, the most common being belly crawling and hands-and-knees crawling (Adolph, Vereijken, & Denny, 1998). Thus, belly crawling and hands-and-knees crawling are attractor states.

The components of developing systems are constantly changing, so the attractor states themselves also change over time. Some behaviors become more stable over time, and others less so. For example, as an infant gains body strength and postural control, she may shift from belly crawling to hands-and-knees crawling. Her hands-and-knees crawling behavior may become more skilled and more consistent, and her belly crawling may become less so.

Within the dynamic systems approach, it does not make sense to ask about *the* age at which children acquire a particular capability. A more appropriate question is how the levels of various component systems influence whether a child is in a state in which he or she displays a particular capability. To return to the object permanence example discussed above, what are the factors that influence whether object permanence is displayed in looking responses, reaching responses, or both? The explanation that Munakata et al. put forward is that the crucial component system is the strength of the child's representation of the object. If this view is correct, then experiences that build up the strength of the object representation should push the child into the more advanced state, and experiences that decrease the strength of the representation should push the child into the less advanced state. Alternatively, it may be the case that multiple component systems matter. For example, it may be that in addition to representation strength, hand-eye coordination is also essential for progress to the more advanced state. Thus, within the dynamic systems framework, one empirical strategy is to generate and test hypotheses about which component systems are responsible for changes in the behavioral state of the organism.

One empirical prediction derived from the dynamic systems framework is that a system should display increased variability at transition points, as it moves from one stable state to another stable state. This phenomenon has been documented in a wide variety of domains, including locomotor skills (Vereijken & Thelen, 1997), conservation (Church & Goldin-Meadow, 1986), mathematical problem solving (Alibali & Goldin-Meadow, 1993), language deveopment (Evans, 2002), matrix problem solving (Siegler & Svetina, 2002), and the development of theory of mind (Amsterlaw & Wellman, 2001).

Dynamic systems approaches are provocative because they pose new questions about the nature of knowledge and about developmental processes. Such models focus attention on *how* various factors influence children's performance, rather than on the age at which a given ability is acquired. They provide a framework for conceptualizing the interactions between component systems, including subsystems that, within a more simplistic analysis, might have been called "nature" and "nurture." Further, they provide a way of thinking about the context specificity and variability of behavior, and about the roles of different component subsystems in generating new behavioral forms. As such, dynamic systems approaches promise to contribute to a deeper understanding of the complexity of children's thinking.

> 5. Changes in children's thinking do not occur in a vacuum. What children already know about material that they encounter influences not only how much they learn but also what they learn.

CURRENT KNOWLEDGE ABOUT THE EFFECTS OF EXISTING KNOWLEDGE

People almost always find it easier to understand, learn, and remember in areas in which they already have some knowledge. With experience looking at checkerboards, infants come to prefer looking at more complex arrangements (DeLoache et al., 1978). Toddlers use grammatical cues to help them learn the meanings of novel words (Naigles, 1990). Preschoolers use scripts that they have abstracted from their experiences with birthday parties and restaurants to remember new parties and restaurants (Hudson, 1990; Nelson, 1993). School-age children with some knowledge of conservation and class inclusion more easily master the concepts than do less knowledgeable children (Inhelder et al., 1974; Strauss, 1972).

Prior content knowledge influences what people learn as well as how much they learn. Such effects are especially evident in the relatively rare cases in which knowledge interferes with learning and remembering. Learning the sounds of their native language leads infants and young children to progressively lose the ability to discriminate sounds that are not differentiated within it (Werker & Desjardins, 1995) and leads children past age 7 to progressively lose the ability to fully master the grammar of another language (Johnson & Newport, 1989). Knowledge of typical eating patterns leads preschoolers to reject the possibility that lunch could consist of cereal and orange juice (Keil, 1989). Negative stereotypes, based on previous observations of a person's clumsiness, lead children to incorrectly "remember" that the person engaged in other misdeeds (Leichtman & Ceci, 1995). School-age children's well-established knowledge of addition causes them difficulties when they encounter novel problems such as $3 + 4 + 5 = 3 + \_\_$ (McNeil & Alibali, 2002, 2004).

Prior knowledge does not operate as a mechanism apart from the previously mentioned change processes. Rather, the prior knowledge, along with incoming information, provides data on which the change processes operate. Put another way, prior knowledge helps determine what the change processes do: what features children encode, what generalizations they draw, what strategies they construct, and what operations they automatize. The nature of the change processes, however, determines how they do it.

FUTURE ISSUES

Some of the most controversial issues about children's knowledge concern hypothesized high-level knowledge structures, such as "theories" that characterize core domains such as physics, biology and mind. Two sets of issues are particularly important in this area. First, do such high-level structures exist, and do they differ from other types of knowledge? Second, assuming that children do have theories of core domains, how do such theories come to be, and how do they change?

The issue of whether children have theories in core domains hinges on the definition of "theory." Wellman and Gelman (1992, 1998) proposed four criteria for theoretical understanding: fundamental categories unique to the domain, causal explanations unique to the domain, unobservable explanatory constructs, and coherent organization. There is now substantial evidence that children's knowledge in certain domains meets these criteria. For example, as discussed in Chapter 8, there is substantial evidence that children's early understanding of biology constitutes a theory.

Whether these four properties differentiate children's understanding of "core" domains from their understanding of innumerable other domains, however, is open to question. All four properties also characterize such obviously non-core domains as baseball. Knowledge of baseball includes categories unique to the domain (pitcher, catcher, home run), a specific kind of causality (centered on the goal of having scored a greater number of runs after nine innings), invisible explanatory constructs (baseball savvy, clutch hitting), and a coherent organization. Yet if knowledge of baseball qualifies as a core theory, there must be thousands of them. As Wellman and Gelman (1998) noted, "It is not yet clear how many domains children distinguish in all nor which analytic criteria identify foundational domains of thought" (p. 554).

Paradoxically, although proponents of viewing conceptual understanding in terms of theories have emphasized the domain specificity of knowledge and of learning mechanisms, their most important long-term contribution may be an insight that applies to all domains. Traditionally, almost all analyses of development have assumed that knowledge proceeds from concrete to abstract. According to this view, children first learn about aspects of the world that they can see, hear, and touch, and later learn about invisible aspects, such as causal relations, that connect these tangible objects, events, and qualities. Proponents of the core knowledge approach, however, have emphasized that in foundational domains, even infants and young children think in terms of underlying causes and invisible entities: momentum, force, intentions, deceptions, germs, inheritance, and so on. Such thinking has been viewed as distinguishing knowledge of core domains from knowledge of other areas (Wellman & Gelman, 1998).

However, the tendency to emphasize causes and other unobservable explanatory constructs from early in learning may not be limited to core domains—it may apply to all domains (Simons & Keil, 1995). Toddlers' non-stop "why" questions are not limited to a small set of core domains; they ask about the causes of all kinds of phenomena. Similarly, young children's frequent use of the term "because" extends to all kinds of topics, not just a few special ones. Perhaps in recognition of children's constant search for explanations, when adults explain a new game or concept, they usually begin by describing the basic goals and the causal structure. When they describe tic-tac-toe, for example, they usually start by saying that the idea of the game is to win and that you win by getting three Xs or three Os in a row. This understanding of causality is useful; children have been found to possess abstract understanding of the causal structure of tic-tac-toe that allows them to recognize the value of advanced strategies even before they use them (Siegler & Crowley, 1994). Thus, the predisposition to search for causes may not be limited to core domains—it may characterize knowledge acquisition in all domains.

How do children acquire the kind of causal knowledge that is viewed as theoretical understanding? That is, how do children's "theories" come to be, and how do they change? There have been many claims that such knowledge is produced by domain-specific learning mechanisms (e.g., Keil, 1989; Leslie, 1994;

Spelke et al., 1992; Wellman & Gelman, 1998); however, no such mechanisms have been described in any detail. It is certainly possible that learning proceeds differently in "core domains" than in other areas. In their first few years of life, children acquire a great deal of knowledge about inanimate objects, people, and plants and animals. This rapid learning suggests that children might use specialized mechanisms to learn about them. Then again, young children also have innumerable opportunities to observe and learn about inanimate objects, people, and plants and animals. Perhaps the number of learning opportunities, rather than the mechanisms themselves, is what distinguishes these domains from others where children acquire knowledge more slowly.

One promising approach to examining knowledge change in such domains focuses on the learning of "causal maps" (Gopnik & Glymour, 2002). Causal maps are well-organized mental structures that characterize the causal relations within a domain. Once established, causal maps allow individuals to reason about causal relations within a domain and to make predictions about the consequences of events and actions—even ones that have not been directly observed. According to Gopnik and Glymour, learning of such structures is based on patterns of variation and covariation experienced in the world. For example, a child might observe the pattern of covariation between animacy and self-generated motion—most animate objects move on their own, and most inanimate objects do not. Based on this consistent pattern, the relation between animacy and self-generated motion could become part of the child's causal map for the domain of biology. Once this causal map is established, the child can use it to predict that, if an object produces self-generated motion, that object is almost certainly animate.

Children as young as 2 years old have been shown to draw causal inferences based on patterns of variation and covariation. For example, in one study (Gopnik, Sobel, Schulz, & Glymour, 2001) children were presented with a machine called a "blicket detector," and they were told that some objects, called "blickets," made the machine light up and play music. Children were then presented with various patterns of covariation between two blocks and the activation of the machine. For example, some children saw the machine turn on when Block A was placed on it and when Blocks A and B were placed on it together, but not when Block B was placed on it alone. In this situation, children as young as age 2 inferred that Block A was a blicket, but Block B was not. In a second study, children used the causal knowledge that they had acquired in order to make the machine "stop" when requested to do so. Because they could use this causal knowledge in productive way (that is, in a way that they had not seen demonstrated), it was clear that they had learned a causal relation and not simply an association between the block and the machine's actions.

The tendency to posit causal relations based on patterns of covariation is a mechanism that could be used to generate theoretical understandings in a wide variety of domains, including both "core" domains and non-core domains such as baseball. Thus, the construction of causal maps appears to be a general learning mechanism that could give rise to domain-specific theoretical knowledge.

The construction of causal maps is a mechanism that seems especially apt for explaining the initial acquisition of theoretical knowledge. But once such knowledge is established, how does it change? As noted previously, one especially promising methodological tool for elucidating the process of change is the microgenetic approach. Until very recently, there had been no studies of theory change in children that used a microgenetic approach. However, recently some studies of this type have been conducted, and they are yielding promising results.

Amsterlaw and Wellman (2001) used a microgenetic approach to study the development of theory of mind, and in particular, the development of false belief understanding. In their study, some children received opportunities to learn about false belief understanding through stories about characters who experienced false beliefs. For example, children heard a story about Marcia, whose muffins were moved without her knowledge. Children predicted where Marcia would look for her muffins, and received feedback by seeing where she actually looked. Children were also asked to explain why she looked where she did ("Why is she looking in the drawer for her muffins?").

Amsterlaw and Wellman found that children were more likely to progress from a desire-based theory of mind to a belief-desire theory of mind when they had many opportunities to learn about false belief that were distributed over sessions. Furthermore, the results suggested that providing children with opportunities to *explain* false belief events led to improvements in their understanding of the events. These findings imply that, in naturalistic settings, children may learn about theory of mind through social interactions that focus on explaining events. Such social interactions presumably highlight the causal structure of the events (*why* Maxi looked for the chocolates in the cupboard), so they may compel children to restructure their causal maps for the domain.

The evidence to date suggests that multiple mechanisms are at play in the development of theoretical understandings. The construction of causal maps appears to rely on implicit learning processes that extract systematic patterns of covariation from observed events. Restructuring these causal maps may require explicit learning of causal relations that have not been learned implicitly. Such explicit learning may be especially likely to occur in social interactions that involve explanations. Future studies will be needed to elucidate how these change mechanisms work together over the course of development.

6. The development of intelligence reflects changes in brain structure and functioning as well as increasingly effective deployment of cognitive resources.

CURRENT KNOWLEDGE ABOUT THE DEVELOPMENT OF INTELLIGENCE

Intelligence develops through the interaction of brain maturation and experience. Changes in the size of the brain alone convey a sense of how much maturation occurs. The brain of an adult weighs four times as much as that of a newborn, with almost half of the increase occurring after age 5 (Lemire, Loeser, Leech, & Alvord, 1975). Parts of the cortex grow to 10 times their size at birth. Not all of the changes are from less to more, though. The density of synapses in many parts of the cortex reaches levels during early childhood greater than those in the adult brain (Huttenlocher & Dabholkar, 1997). This high density may allow superior learning of language and motor skills during this early period (Bjorklund, 1997).

The uneven maturation of different parts of the brain leads to a given cognitive function sometimes having different neural bases at different ages. In the first months after birth, subcortical areas, which already are relatively mature, play large roles in vision, hearing, and deployment of attention (Bronson, 1974; Johnson, 1998; Muir et al., 1979; Posner et al., 1998). By 4 to 10 months, cortical areas, which develop later, assume major roles in all of these functions. The early subcortical dominance leads to the cognitive system obtaining useful early input; the later cortical role provides more effective processing once the relevant areas are sufficiently mature (Johnson & Morton, 1991).

Brain development involves a mix of anatomical specificity and plasticity. For example, for almost all right-handed people and most left-handed people, language processing occurs predominantly in the middle of the left side of the brain. The specificity is sufficiently great that words whose main function is grammatical, such as "the," produce their largest activation in different areas of the left hemisphere than content words such as "dog" (Neville, 1995a). Remarkably, if the left side of the brain is damaged or surgically removed during the first year, language becomes localized on the right side of the brain and develops to near-normal levels (Stiles & Thal, 1993). If the damage occurs after the first year, language also is represented in the right hemisphere, but the later the damage, the less effective that language processing will be (Maratsos & Matheny, 1994).

These changes in the structure and functioning of the brain are only part of the story of the development of intelligence, though. Another large part involves experience leading to increasingly effective use of available cognitive resources. For example, even in the first few months, infants show some ability to deploy processing resources effectively. They orient to the most informative parts of the environment, track moving objects with their eyes, and form expectations of where interesting stimuli will appear (Aslin, 1993; Haith et al., 1993). It should not be surprising, however, that considerable growth occurs beyond these initial bases. With experience, children form representations that are increasingly complete, flexible, and robust.

Consider the trend toward representations becoming increasingly complete. When 1-month-olds examine objects, they only scan the contours; 2- and 3-month-olds scan the interiors as well (Salapatek, 1975). When 5-year-olds are presented conservation, class inclusion, and balance scale problems, they only represent a single important dimension; by age 8, children represent multiple relevant dimensions on these tasks (e.g., Case, 1992a; Halford, 1993). When

8-year-olds read stories, they focus on causal links within each episode; 14-year-olds also focus on causal links *across* episodes (van den Broek, 1989).

Examples of the trend toward children forming increasingly flexible representations also come from many areas and age groups. On false belief tasks, 4-year-olds shift more flexibly than 3-year-olds between what they know about a situation and what they know other people know about it (Wellman et al., 2001). Likewise, in classification tasks, 4-year-olds shift more flexibly than 3-year-olds between classifying an object along one dimension (such as color) and classifying it along another dimension (such as shape) (Zelazo et al., 1996). As they gain experience in arithmetic, school-age children choose strategies in ways that fit the demands of problems increasingly precisely (Lemaire & Siegler, 1995). Preadolescents and adolescents adjust their reading and writing strategies in response to instructions and time demands that have no effects on younger children's approaches (Kobasigawa et al., 1980; Zbrodoff, 1984).

The third sense in which adaptations to task environments become increasingly successful is robustness. Young children's understanding is often displayed only under ideal circumstances (Sophian, 1984). With age and experience, children come to use their competencies in demanding as well as facilitative situations. Thus, infants and toddlers, like older children, can find hidden objects in space after their own orientation relative to the objects has changed, but unlike the older children, they require nearby landmarks to do so (Acredolo, 1978; Huttenlocher & Newcombe, 1984). Two-year-olds can use a scale model to locate objects in rooms if the model is in a glass case, but not if they handle it, whereas 3-year-olds can use the model appropriately under either condition (DeLoache, 1995). Five-year-olds solve transitive inference, syllogistic reasoning, and analogical reasoning problems if misleading visual cues are not present or if facilitative wording is used. Not until years later, though, do children solve such problems under more challenging circumstances (Brown et al., 1986; Byrnes & Overton, 1986; Goswami, 1995a). Seventh graders interpret the equal sign accurately if it is presented by itself, but they interpret it as meaning "the total" if it is presented in an addition problem. By the college years, students interpret the equal sign accurately regardless of context (McNeil & Alibali, in press).

FUTURE ISSUES

Increasing understanding of brain maturation and deployment of cognitive resources raise the issue of how these factors interact to create individual differences in intelligence. Two views of individual differences in intelligence have already been discussed. One emphasizes differences along a single dimension—general intelligence. Differences in people's intelligence quotient (IQ) are viewed as reflecting differences in their general intelligence. A second view is Sternberg's (1985, 1999) triarchic theory. Here, individual differences in intelligence are viewed as deriving from differences in the efficiency of three classes of information-processing components: performance components, learning components, and metacomponents. Although these two approaches differ in many ways, they share the assumption that there is a common core to intelligence that manifests itself across domains.

One type of evidence for the existence of general intelligence is positive correlations in performance among items on different parts of intelligence tests. For example, children who perform successfully on items measuring vocabulary also tend to do well on items measuring spatial reasoning, arithmetic, and interpretation of proverbs. Another key piece of evidence is that IQ test scores are quite stable over long age periods. A third important piece of evidence is that scores on IQ tests predict grades in school quite accurately. Thus, knowing a first grader's score on an IQ test allows fairly accurate estimates of the child's future grades in high school. A fourth piece of evidence is that children with higher IQs tend to learn new material more quickly (Johnson & Mervis, 1994). These types of evidence have led many people to conclude that some children are higher in general intelligence than others and that intelligence is stable over long periods of time.

A number of critics have questioned these interpretations, however (e.g., Ceci, 1990; Gardner, Kornhaber, & Wake, 1996; Resnick, Levine, & Teasley, 1991). The positive correlations among the items on IQ tests may reflect the way in which items are chosen rather than the existence of a general intelligence. New IQ test items are chosen in part for correlating positively with existing IQ test items. Whole areas, such as art and music, in which performance does not tend to correlate with performance on existing IQ test items, are excluded.

With regard to the arguments concerning stability of IQ scores over long periods of time, the relations of early IQ scores to later school performance, and the relation between IQ and learning, one important issue is whether the stability involves intelligence, motivation, or both. Motivation to succeed in intellectual domains may influence performance on IQ test items, performance in school, and learning in laboratory situations alike. If so, and if such motivation is stable over time, it could lead to the observed relations among IQ test scores, learning of new material, and later intellectual performance.

More general criticisms of IQ tests also have been raised. One criticism focuses on the oversimplification inherent in characterizing individual differences in intelligence as ranks along a single dimension (the IQ score). Children's thinking differs along many dimensions, not just one. The tests also have been criticized for the inegalitarian implications of viewing some children as generally less intelligent than others and for confusing the products of intellectual activity with the processes that produced them. The fact that one child does better than another on an IQ test may reflect different amounts of prior relevant experience, or different skill in taking multiple-choice tests, or different maturation, rather than differences in any inborn quality.

These and other considerations led Gardner (1983; Gardner et al., 1996) to formulate the *multiple intelligences* approach. Gardner's basic idea is that what is usually called "intelligence" might better be thought of in terms of seven *intelligences*: linguistic, musical, logical-mathematical, spatial, bodily-kinesthetic, self-understanding, and social-understanding. He proposed that each intelligence applies to separate (though overlapping) domains, is based on a distinct symbol system, and includes separate change mechanisms.

Gardner specified several criteria for deciding whether a type of thinking is a separate intelligence. One involves localization within the brain. If a type of thinking is a separate intelligence, then damage to some specific area of the brain should have much more adverse affects on that type of thinking than on others. A second criterion is the existence of prodigies in the area—individuals whose excellence in the domain far exceeds what would be expected from other aspects of their intelligence. Thus, the existence of a Mozart—composing music at age 5, though not being especially smart in most other ways—is evidence for a separate musical intelligence. A third criterion is a distinct system for representing the domain, such as mathematical notation, oral language, or choreographers' representations of dance movements. A fourth is similar performance in different aspects of the domain; children good at one skill within a domain should be good at others as well.

Consider evidence that musical intelligence is a distinctive ability. Musical stimuli elicit activity primarily on the right side of the brain, unlike speech stimuli, which elicit activity primarily on the left side. Consistent with this analysis, Gardner (1983) noted that damage to the right temporal and frontal lobes usually interferes with music perception while leaving language perception relatively intact, whereas the reverse occurs when the damage is to the corresponding areas on the left side of the brain. Gardner also cited cases of severely retarded children who had had no formal instruction in music being able to play on the piano pieces that they had just heard for the first time. The same children exhibited only very limited learning abilities in other domains, suggesting that they learned music through different mechanisms than they used to learn other skills. Music clearly has its own notational system, and people who are musically gifted often are skilled at numerous instruments and modes of musical expression.

Gardner also saw evidence for the operation of distinct intelligences in the exceptionally strong motivation that some children have to exercise particular talents. When the great mathematician Pascal was a child, his father forbade him to talk about mathematics and severely discouraged him from reading about it. In spite of this harsh reaction, Pascal marked the walls of his room with charcoal, trying to find ways of constructing triangles with equal sides and angles (his father was not too happy with that either). He invented names for mathematical concepts, since he did not know the conventional words. He developed an axiomatic system for geometry and, in so doing, reinvented much of Euclid. He even dreamed of theorems and axioms—all of this in the face of a hostile environment.

The idea of separate intelligences has problematic aspects. Several of the abilities that Gardner classified as separate intelligences seem to be related.

Children's performance on tests of verbal, logical-mathematical, and spatial reasoning consistently correlate positively. This may be due to motivation to achieve in these areas being similar, but it could also be due to general intelligence influencing performance in all of these areas. Further, the existence of prodigies in an area may reflect the isolation of the area from other aspects of life rather than whether the ability is a separate intelligence. There are individuals who can quickly calculate what the day of the week will be on January 19, 6593, yet it would be hard to argue that calendar calculation is a separate intelligence.

Despite such problems, the idea of separate intelligences is intriguing. Children's performance often differs dramatically across domains, particularly when we include in the analysis types of intelligence not measured by IQ tests, such as artistic, athletic, and social intelligence. Viewing intellect as a set of distinct capacities could yield more precise descriptions of the ways that children's thinking differs than is possible in a single number. Thus, it may lead to a more nuanced understanding of the thinking of individual children.

> 7. Children's thinking develops within a social context. Parents, peers, teachers, and the overall society influence what children think about, as well as how and why they come to think in particular ways.

CURRENT KNOWLEDGE ABOUT SOCIAL INFLUENCES ON CHILDREN'S THINKING

People are profoundly social animals. Parents in every society, but not adults of any other species, teach their children the skills, attitudes, and values that they believe are important for succeeding in that culture. Children in every society, but not the young of any other species, constantly point out events of interest to anyone who will listen. These teaching and learning propensities are essential for cognitive development (Tomasello, 1999). A child who ignored other people, or who grew up in a world in which other people had no desire to communicate, could not develop normally. Fortunately, such situations almost never occur.

The prototypic example of social influences on children's thinking is parent-child interactions. When talking to infants, parents usually use the high-pitched, sing-song intonations known as infant-directed speech, a form of communication particularly effective in attracting and holding infants' attention (Fernald, 1992; Stern et al., 1982). When trying to help toddlers and preschoolers remember past events, parents ask questions in sequences that suggest scripts for organizing the activities into memorable forms (Hudson, 1990). When teaching problem-solving skills to school-age children, parents engage the children in the learning process by helping them identify the goals that need to be met, discussing strategies for meeting them, and helping them execute the strategies (Azmitia, 1996; Ellis & Rogoff, 1986).

Parents are not the only adults who influence the course of cognitive development. Girl Scout leaders who coordinate cookie drives help children acquire not only skills such as salesmanship and record keeping but also values such as politeness and promptness (Rogoff, 1995). Similarly, teachers who engage in reciprocal instruction teach a variety of important skills by providing scaffolding, in which they initially give children a great deal of support and gradually transfer responsibility to them (Palincsar & Brown, 1984).

Children are not passive recipients of these efforts; from day one they actively shape adults' interactions with them. Much of the reason that adults use infant-directed speech is that even newborns pay more attention when they do (Cooper & Aslin, 1990). By 4 months, infants verbalize more after adults talk to them; this leads to a simple form of turn taking, which encourages both adults and infants to "talk" to each other (Ginsburg & Kilbourne, 1988). The reciprocal influence extends well beyond language. Through expressions of interest and boredom, tugs on sleeves, dragging of feet, and demands of "Want it," children exercise considerable control over their elders. Older children and adolescents also tend to remember perfectly reasonable points that parents and teachers earlier made to them, and turn the points against their originators in totally unfair ways. In short, children and adults learn from one another.

Children also influence each other's development. One-year-olds imitate each other's behaviors well after the behaviors occur (Piaget, 1951). Four-year-olds adjust their language so that 2-year-olds can understand them (Shatz & Gelman, 1973). School-age children and adolescents collaborate effectively when they attend to and discuss each other's ideas (Azmitia & Montgomery, 1993; Berkowitz & Gibbs, 1985). Interactions with other children are beneficial for children in a variety of ways: they motivate children to try new tasks, they enable children to fine-tune their understanding by explaining what they know, and they provide opportunities to imitate and learn skills and to engage in discussions that increase their understanding (Azmitia, 1996).

In addition to these person-to-person interactions, the social world also influences cognitive development through providing a variety of tools for solving problems, including both physical tools and psychological ones. One-year-olds can use rakes to obtain toys (Brown, 1989; Chen & Siegler, 2000); 3-year-olds can use scale models to find hidden objects (DeLoache, 1995); and 7- to 11-year-olds can use maps to indicate how an ambulance should go to a destination (Karmiloff-Smith, 1979). And of course there are such omnipresent tools as spoken and written language and mathematical notation.

Finally, the culture as a whole communicates attitudes and values that influence cognitive development. East Asian languages facilitate learning of the base-10 system and fractions and thus enhance learning of early mathematics (Fuson & Kwon, 1992; Miller et al., 1995; Miura et al., 1999). Navajo society prizes thinking for oneself; probably not coincidentally, Navajo children both plan longer than Euro-American children before attempting to solve puzzles and allow less knowledgeable children more time to plan before showing them what to do

(Ellis & Schneiders, 1989). German society values organization; German teachers provide more instruction in organizational strategies than do teachers in the United States, and German children use such organizational strategies more often (Kurtz et al., 1990). In sum, parents, other adults, other children, and the broader culture all shape cognitive development.

FUTURE ISSUES

One key question for future sociocultural research centers on the nature of the support that other people provide for children's development: Do variations in support lead to variations in learning outcomes? Some evidence suggests that they do (e.g., Haden et al., 1997; Tomasello & Farrar, 1986). For example, Wood and Middleton (1975) asked mothers to help their 3- and 4-year-old children construct complex block pyramids. Children performed best on an independent posttest if their mothers' earlier instruction was sensitive to their skill level.

However, other recent research suggests that wide variations in the nature of adult support may lead to comparable learning outcomes. As described in Chapter 4, Göncü and Rogoff (1998) compared three types of adult support in a study of children's categorization. In one condition, adults articulated the category rationales for the children; in another condition, adults induced the children to articulate the category rationales using leading questions; and in a third condition, adults did both, first articulating the rationales themselves, and then prompting the children to do so. Despite these differences in the nature of adult support, children in all three conditions performed comparably on an independent posttest.

Why might variations in support matter in some cases, but not in others? More generally, what "counts" as appropriately sensitive support? One possibility is that the nature of sensitive support depends on characteristics of the learner. For some children, explicit, highly directive support (e.g., direct instruction or demonstrations) may be most beneficial, whereas for others, more implicit, indirect support (e.g., hints or leading questions) may be most effective. At present, little is known about how the nature of the support offered by adults interacts with individual differences in learners' personality characteristics and learning styles.

Another possibility is that the effectiveness of support depends on the relationship between the individuals involved in the interaction. If the relationship is a close one, and the adult is "tuned in" to the child's knowledge state, then minimal but appropriately targeted support may be quite effective. If the relationship is not a close one, more extensive and more direct support may be necessary in order to insure that the necessary information is successfully communicated to the child. Depending on the nature of the relationship, the child may also be more or less willing to accept highly directive support from a particular individual. For example, a child may be more willing to accept direct tuition from a teacher than from a parent or from an older sibling with whom there is a great deal of competition.

A third possibility is that the nature of sensitive support may differ across cultural contexts. As discussed in Chapter 4, cultures differ in the types of interactions between adults and children that are "usual" or expected. In some cultures, children tend to be segregated from adults' social and economic worlds, and many of their opportunities for learning take place in formal educational contexts. In other cultures, children are routinely integrated into adult activities, and many of their opportunities for learning occur by observing adults' activities in everyday situations. The nature and quantity of adult-child interactions differs in these cultural contexts, and this may lead to expectations on the part of both adults and children, about the nature of support that should be provided in specific situations.

A related issue is whether children learn different things depending on the nature of the social support that they receive. Some research suggests there may indeed be cognitive consequences to different patterns of social interaction. For example, as discussed in Chapter 4, cross-cultural differences in the nature of guided participation are linked with differences in patterns of attention management (Chavajay & Rogoff, 1999; Rogoff et al., 1993). Children in communities in which children are routinely integrated into adult activities are more likely to attend to multiple events simultaneously than are those in communities in which children are routinely segregated from adults' social and economic worlds. Whether these cultural differences in attention management are actually caused by the cultural differences in patterns of interaction is still open to question. However, the results are intriguing, and they suggest that this is an important area for continuing research.

To make progress on these issues will likely require a better understanding of the mechanisms involved in learning from social interactions. Precisely *how* does social interaction function to build individual knowledge? Several potential mechanisms have been identified, including internalization, guided participation, and collaborative learning; however, the operation of these mechanisms is not well specified. Theoretical progress on this issue will be necessary if we wish to be able to predict when or for whom learning will occur, or precisely what will be learned.

8. Increasing understanding of children's thinking is yielding practical benefits as well as theoretical insights.

CURRENT PRACTICAL CONTRIBUTIONS OF RESEARCH ON CHILDREN'S THINKING

Research on children's thinking is already yielding a variety of practical benefits. Many of the benefits with infants and toddlers have involved diagnosis and treatment of perceptual problems. Infants' preference for looking at stripes rather than gray surfaces provides a means to diagnose blindness in infancy (Dobson, 1983). Analyses of the timing of corrective surgery for crossed eyes has shown that the surgery should be conducted before age 4 months, if possible, and definitely before age 3 years (Banks, Aslin, & Letson, 1975).

Another large class of practical contributions involves conclusions about how to obtain valid testimony from children in court cases. These studies indicate that children as young as 4 years provide accurate, if incomplete, testimony when asked specific questions that do not indicate the questioner's preferred answer (Ceci & Bruck, 1998). However, the memories of children this young are especially vulnerable to the effects of leading questions, especially ones that are repeated frequently (Poole & Lamb, 1998). This vulnerability to leading questions extends to events involving their own bodies, including ones with sexual overtones (Bruck et al., 1995; Ornstein, Gordon, & Larus, 1992; Poole & Lindsay, 1995). Preschoolers' recollections are also especially susceptible to stereotypes about the people involved in the events (Leichtman & Ceci, 1995). Asking children to form visual images of a suspected crime that did not occur can lead to their saying and believing that the imagined events happened (Foley, Harris, & Herman, 1994; Parker, 1995). Similarly, asking children to draw an event that did not occur can lead to them reporting later that the event actually happened (Bruck, Melnyk, & Ceci, 2000). On the other hand, having them draw what they remember about an event, without specifying the particulars, adds to the validity of their verbal reports (Butler et al., 1995). These findings provide useful guidance concerning how the legal system should elicit testimony from children.

A final substantial class of practical contributions concerns schooling. Studies using the cutoff design have demonstrated that a one-year difference in age of entry into school does not influence how much first graders learn about math or reading (Bisanz et al., 1995; Morrison, Griffith, & Frazier, 1996). Studies of mathematical and scientific misconceptions have demonstrated that children often have systematic incorrect views that must be disconfirmed for learning to occur. This has been shown for areas as diverse as the shape of the earth (Vosniadou & Brewer, 1992), the speeds of moving objects (Levin et al., 1990), the reasons why objects balance (Pine & Messer, 1998), the magnitude of decimal fractions (Resnick et al., 1989), the meaning of the equal sign (McNeil & Alibali, in press), and the long subtraction algorithm (VanLehn, 1990). Promoting phonological awareness by teaching children to identify the separate phonemes within words has been found to enhance their later success in reading (Bradley & Bryant, 1983; Byrne & Fielding-Barnsley, 1995; National Reading Panel, 2000; Vellutino & Scanlon, 1987), as has teaching phonological recoding skills (Adams, 1990; Lovett et al., 1994) and comprehension monitoring (Palincsar et al., 1993; Rosenshine & Meister, 1994). Writing has been found to benefit from use of word processors (Bangert-Downs, 1993), and problem solving has been found to benefit from mediated instruction in which applications of computer programming concepts to other types of problems are emphasized (Klahr & Carver, 1988; Lehrer & Littlefield, 1993). In short, research on children's thinking is contributing to solutions of practical problems as well as to theoretical understanding of cognitive development.

FUTURE ISSUES

One important area in which knowledge about cognitive development is beginning to have practical benefits is in the design of curricula for use in educational settings. As the examples above suggest, knowledge about cognitive development has provided many insights about *why* some educational innovations work and others do not. However, one key issue for future research is determining how to translate findings about cognitive performance and learning in children into effective curricula for teaching academic skills, such as mathematical and scientific reasoning, reading, and writing.

Previous chapters have described some attempts to design curricula grounded in understanding of basic cognitive processes and theories of development. One example is the "reciprocal teaching" method for teaching reading comprehension skills (Palincsar & Brown, 1984) (Chapter 11), which relies heavily on the idea of scaffolding and other insights from sociocultural theories. A second example is a curriculum about rational numbers and mathematical functions, based on building up central conceptual structures (Kalchman et al., 2000; Moss & Case, 1999) (Chapter 3), which relies heavily on insights from information-processing theories.

An important challenge for work in this area involves how best to use technology to enhance students' learning. One type of technological tool that is beginning to be more widely used in educational settings is *intelligent tutoring systems,* which are computer-based tutors that are grounded in theories about learning and development. One example is the "Cognitive Tutor" for middle and high school mathematics developed by Koedinger and colleagues (Anderson, Corbett, Koedinger, & Pelletier, 1995; Koedinger, 2002; Koedinger & Anderson, 1998). Cognitive Tutors are designed to be used in an integrated fashion with a textbook and other course materials, so that the computerized tutors are used two days per week, with individual students working with tutors at stations in a computer lab, and the textbook and other materials are used three days per week in a traditional classroom setting.

Cognitive Tutors are designed based on a psychological model of the cognitive processes involved in mathematical problem solving. The model is central to the functioning of the tutor in two ways. First, the model is used to provide students with individualized support as they solve problems. For example, when students make typical errors, the cognitive model diagnoses them, provides appropriate feedback, and helps students find a solution strategy that works for them. Second, the cognitive model monitors students' performance across activities in order to diagnose students' strengths and weaknesses and to identify aspects of knowledge that students probably are missing. The tutor then adapts the selection of activities to enhance students' learning of important concepts and skills.

The cognitive model that underlies Koedinger and colleagues' mathematics tutors is a production system model, like the one described in Chapter 3. It represents the strategies that students might employ in solving problems, as well as their typical misconceptions, in terms of if–then statements (productions). Based on the model, the tutor may diagnose an individual student as lacking certain productions that are part of particular problem-solving strategies, or as having inaccurate productions that lead to errors. For example, a beginning algebra student might possess one or more of the following three productions:

(1) IF the goal is to solve $a(bx + c) = d$
      THEN rewrite as $bx + c = d/a$

(2) IF the goal is to solve $a(bx + c) = d$
      THEN rewrite as $abx + ac = d$

(3) IF the goal is to solve $a(bx + c) = d$
      THEN rewrite as $abx + c = d$ (misconception)

If a student were solving a problem and needed to solve the equation $3(4x + 2) = 66$, any one of these productions might be applied (with $a = 3$, $b = 4$, $c = 2$, and $d = 66$). If the student were to enter "$12x + 2 = 64$" as the next step in solving the equation, the Cognitive Tutor would diagnose this behavior as being the likely result of the student having the incorrect production (#3). It would then provide appropriate feedback to help the student correct the misconception.

Several studies have documented the success of Cognitive Tutors (Koedinger, 2002; Koedinger, Anderson, Hadley, & Mark, 1997). Both low- and middle-income students in Cognitive Tutor courses learned more than comparable students in comparison classrooms both on assessments of problem solving and on standardized assessments of basic mathematics skills. Thus, the individualized approach to assessment and instruction that is made possible by the tutors can have significant benefits for children's learning. Moreover, the tutors also have the potential to be used as a platform for research. The tutors can gather finely detailed information about the steps that students take in solving problems, and about the changes that occur as students learn. This information can then be used to refine and expand models of the processes involved in performance and learning. The potential of technological tools such as computer-based tutors, both for education and for research, is only beginning to be tapped, but the prospects are encouraging. In the 2003–2004 school year, Cognitive Tutor mathematics courses were in regular use in more than one thousand schools across the United States. The widespread dissemination of Cognitive Tutors is powerful evidence that cognitive theories of learning and development are beginning to make a real and important difference in educational practice.

Summary

The development of perception, language, memory, conceptual understanding, social cognition, problem solving, and academic skills have a great deal in common. Important unities exist in the issues, empirical findings, and mechanisms that produce changes in all aspects of children's thinking.

The largest issues in the study of children's thinking are "What develops?" and "How does development occur?" Four commonly advanced hypotheses about what develops are basic capacities, strategies, metacognition, and content knowledge. Each of these types of changes contributes to cognitive improvements in many areas and at many ages. An important goal for future research is to provide data that directly examine changes while they are occurring. Such data are critical for formulating better theories of cognitive development.

Four general classes of change processes that seem to be especially large contributors to cognitive development are automatization, encoding, generalization, and construction of new strategies. One challenge for future research is to determine whether there are specific change mechanisms that only operate in particular periods of life, or whether the same mechanisms produce change at all ages.

Infants and toddlers are far more competent thinkers than is immediately apparent. Impressive perceptual and conceptual competencies are apparent in the first year, as are general-purpose learning mechanisms. A key goal is to formulate models that demonstrate how the same child could generate both the impressive competence and the equally impressive incompetence that characterize early development.

Differences between the thinking of young children and adults no longer seem as huge as they once did. The narrowing has come from both directions. Young children have a variety of previously unsuspected capabilities. Adults think less rationally and scientifically than once was believed. In general, there is no single age at which children acquire a cognitive capability. Rather, understanding gradually increases over a prolonged period.

Existing knowledge about a topic exerts a pervasive influence on the acquisition of new knowledge. It increases the amount that children learn from particular experiences and also influences what they learn by leading them to focus on the material most likely to prove important. A major current challenge is to specify the role of high-level knowledge structures, such as theories of biology and mind, and to determine whether they differ in fundamental ways from narrower knowledge, such as understanding of baseball.

Development of intelligence involves changes both in the structure and functioning of the brain and in the efficiency with which cognitive resources are used. Neural development involves substantial increases in the size of the brain, shifts in the contributions of different parts of the brain to given behaviors, and decreasing plasticity to react to injuries to one part of the brain by relocating its typical functions to an undamaged area. Improvements in deployment of cognitive resources involve forming representations that are increasingly complete, flexible, and robust. Individual differences in intelligence appear to be much more complex than is reflected in the traditional index of intelligence, IQ. People seem to have multiple intelligences, and they may excel in one area while being unexceptional in others.

Children's thinking develops within a social context of parents, peers, teachers, and the broader culture. These social agents influence what children think about, the degree to which they acquire various skills, and their attitudes and values. The social world also influences motivation to think about some things rather than others. Cultural beliefs and values, as well as individual talents and interests, influence the content that children think about, and the way in which they think about it.

Knowledge about children's thinking has many practical applications. These include diagnoses and treatments of perceptual problems, means for eliciting accurate legal testimony, and instructional techniques and new curricula for academic subjects. Increasing understanding of child development is yielding practical benefits as well as deeper understanding of children.

Recommended Readings

Gardner, H., Kornhaber, M.L., & Wake, W.K. (1996). *Intelligence: Multiple perspectives.* Fort Worth, TX: Harcourt Brace College Publishers. A stimulating and well-written survey of alternative approaches to intelligence, with an emphasis on Gardner's multiple intelligences approach.

Gelman, S.A. (2003). *The essential child: Origins of essentialism in everyday thought.* New York: Oxford University Press. Essentialism is the idea that category members share important underlying properties, or "essences," that determine category membership and that cause other important characteristics of the category. This book presents a clear and compelling description of the role of essentialism in children's theories of biology.

Kuhn, D. (Ed.) (1995). Development and learning—Reconceptualizing the intersection. [Special issue.] *Human Development, 38,* 293–379. This special issue of the journal

Human Development presents the perspectives of 10 leading thinkers regarding the relation between learning and development. The differences in perspectives illustrate strikingly how much this issue is still "up for grabs."

Munakata, Y., McClelland, J.L., Johnson, M.H., & Siegler, R.S. (1997). Rethinking infant knowledge: Toward an adaptive process account of successes and failures in object permanence tasks. *Psychological Review, 104,* 686–713. Reconciling infants' competence and incompetence is one of the primary needs for advancing understanding of infant cognition. This article illustrates one way in which this goal can be achieved.

Poole, D.A., & Lamb, M.E. (1998). *Investigative interviews of children: A guide for helping professionals.* Washington, DC: American Psychological Association. An excellent translation of research findings into practical advice regarding children's eyewitness testing.

REFERENCES

ABOUD, F.E. (1988). *Children and prejudice.* Oxford, UK: Blackwell.

ACREDOLO, C. & HOROBIN, K. (1987). Development of relational reasoning and avoidance of premature closure. *Developmental Psychology, 23,* 13–21.

ACREDOLO, L.P. (1978). The development of spatial orientation in infancy. *Developmental Psychology, 14,* 224–234.

ACREDOLO, L.P., ADAMS, A., & GOODWYN, S.W. (1984). The role of self-produced movement and visual tracking in infant spatial orientation. *Journal of Experimental Child Psychology, 38,* 312–327.

ADAMS, M.J. (1990). *Beginning to read: Thinking and learning about print.* Cambridge, MA: MIT Press.

ADAMS, M.J., TREIMAN, R., & PRESSLEY, M. (1998). Reading, writing, and literacy. In I.E. Sigel & K.A. Renninger (Eds.), *Handbook of child psychology: Vol. 4. Child psychology in practice* (5th ed.). New York: Wiley.

ADAMS, R.J. (1987). An evaluation of color preference in early infancy. *Infant Behavior & Development, 10,* 143–150.

ADOLPH, K.E. (1995). A psychophysical assessment of toddlers' ability to cope with slopes. *Journal of Experimental Psychology: Human Perception & Performance, 21,* 734–750.

ADOLPH, K.E. (1997). Learning in the development of infant locomotion. *Monographs of the Society for Research in Child Development, 62*(3, Serial No. 251).

ADOLPH, K.E., & AVOLIO, A.M. (2000). Walking infants adapt locomotion to changing body dimensions. *Journal of Experimental Psychology: Human Perception & Performance, 26,* 1148–1166.

ADOLPH, K., VEREIJKEN, B., & DENNY, M.A. (1998). Learning to crawl. *Child Development, 69,* 1299–1312.

AGNOLI, F. (1991). Development of judgmental heuristics: Training counteracts the representativeness heuristic. *Cognitive Development, 6,* 195–217.

AHN, W.-K., GELMAN, S.A., AMSTERLAW, J.A., HOHENSTEIN, J., & KALISH, C.W. (2000). Causal status effect in children's categorization. *Cognition, 76,* B35–B43.

AHN, W.-K., KALISH, C.W., MEDIN, D.L., & GELMAN, S.A. (1995). The role of covariation versus mechanism information in causal attribution. *Cognition, 54,* 299–352.

ALIBALI, M.W. (1999). How children change their minds: Strategy change can be gradual or abrupt. *Developmental Psychology, 35,* 127–145.

ALIBALI, M.W., & DON, L.S. (2001). Children's gestures are meant to be seen. *Gesture, 1,* 113–127.

ALIBALI, M.W., & GOLDIN-MEADOW, S. (1993). Transitions in learning: What the hands reveal about a child's state of mind. *Cognitive Psychology, 25,* 468–523.

ALVAREZ, J.M., RUBLE, D.N., & BOLGER, N. (2001). Trait understanding or evaluative reasoning? An analysis of children's behavioral predictions. *Child Development, 72,* 1409–1425.

AMERICAN PSYCHIATRIC ASSOCIATION. (1994). *Diagnostic and statistical manual of mental disorders* (4th ed.). Washington, DC: Author.

AMES, G.J., & MURRAY, F.B. (1982). When two wrongs make a right: Promoting cognitive change by social conflict. *Developmental Psychology, 18,* 894–897.

AMSEL, E., GOODMAN, G., SAVOIE, D., & CLARK, M. (1996). The development of reasoning about causal and non-causal influences on levers. *Child Development, 67,* 1624–1646.

AMSTERDAM, B.K. (1972). Mirror self-image reactions before age 2. *Developmental Psychobiology, 5,* 297–305.

AMSTERLAW, J., & WELLMAN, H.M. (2001, October). *How do theories of mind grow? Insights gained from microgenetic research.* Poster presented at the meeting of the Cognitive Development Society, Virginia Beach, VA.

ANDERSON, J.R., CORBETT, A.T., KOEDINGER, K.R., & PELLETIER, R. (1995). Cognitive tutors: Lessons learned. *Journal of the Learning Sciences, 4,* 167–207.

ANDERSON, M. (1992). *Intelligence and development: A cognitive theory.* Oxford, UK: Blackwell.

ANDREWS, G., & HALFORD, G.S. (1998). Children's ability to make transitive inferences: The importance of premise integration and structural complexity. *Cognitive Development, 13,* 479–513.

ANDREWS, G., & HALFORD, G.S. (2002). A cognitive complexity metric applied to cognitive development. *Cognitive Psychology, 45,* 153–219.

ANGLIN, J.M. (1977). *Word, object, and conceptual development.* New York: W.W. Norton.

ANGLIN, J.M. (1986). Semantic and conceptual knowledge underlying the child's words. In S.A. Kuczaj & M.D. Barrett (Eds.), *The development of word meaning.* New York: Springer-Verlag.

ANGLIN, J.M. (1993). Vocabulary development: A morphological analysis. *Monographs of the Society for Research in Child Development, 58*(10, Serial No. 238).

ANISFELD, M. (1984). *Language development from birth to three.* Hillsdale, NJ: Erlbaum.

ANTELL, S.E., & KEATING, D.P. (1983). Perception of numerical invariance in neonates. *Child Development, 54,* 695–701.

ARTERBERRY, M.E., & BORNSTEIN, M.H. (2002). Infant perceptual and conceptual categorization: The roles of static and dynamic stimulus attributes. *Cognition, 86,* 1–24.

ARTERBERRY, M.E., CRATON, L.G., & YONAS, A. (1993). Infants' sensitivity to motion-carried information for depth and object properties. In C.E. Granrud (Ed.), *Visual perception and cognition in infancy*. Hillsdale, NJ: Erlbaum.

ASHMEAD, D.H., DAVIS, D.L., WHALEN, T., & ODOM, R.D. (1991). Sound localization and sensitivity to interaural time differences in human infants. *Child Development, 62*, 1211–1226.

ASLIN, R.N. (1981). Development of smooth pursuit in human infants. In D.F. Fischer, R.A. Monty & E.J. Senders (Eds.), *Eye movements: Cognition and vision perception*. Hillsdale, NJ: Erlbaum.

ASLIN, R.N. (1993). Perception of visual direction in human infants. In C.E. Granrud (Ed.), *Visual perception and cognition in infancy*. Hillsdale, NJ: Erlbaum.

ASLIN, R.N., & DUMAIS, S.T. (1980). Binocular vision in infants: A review and a theoretical framework. In L.P. Lipsitt & H.W. Reese (Eds.), *Advances in child development and behavior*. New York: Academic Press.

ASLIN, R.N., JUSCZYK, P.W., & PISONI, D.P. (1998). Speech and auditory processing during infancy: Constraints on and precursors to language. In D. Kuhn & R.S. Siegler (Eds.), *Handbook of child psychology: Vol. 2. Cognition, Perception & Language* (5th ed.). New York: Wiley.

ASTINGTON, J.W. (1991). Intention in the child's theory of mind. In D. Frye & C. Moore (Eds.), *Children's theories of mind*. Hillsdale, NJ: Erlbaum.

ASTINGTON, J.W. (1993). *The child's discovery of the mind*. Cambridge, MA: Harvard University Press.

ASTINGTON, J.W. (2000). Language and metalanguage in children's understanding of mind. In J.W. Astington (Ed.), *Minds in the making: Essays in honor of David R. Olson*. Oxford, UK: Blackwell.

ASTINGTON, J.W., & GOPNIK, A. (1988). Knowing you've changed your mind: Children's understanding of representational change. In J.W. Astington, P.L. Harris & D.R. Olson (Eds.), *Developing theories of mind*. New York: Cambridge University Press.

ASTINGTON, J.W., & GOPNIK, A. (1991). Theoretical explanations of children's understanding of the mind. *British Journal of Developmental Psychology, 9*, 7–32.

ASTINGTON, J.W., & JENKINS, J. (1999). A longitudinal study of the relation between language and theory-of-mind development. *Developmental Psychology, 35*, 1311–1320.

ATRAN, S. (1994). Core domains versus scientific theories. In L.A. Hirschfeld & S.A. Gelman (Eds.), *Mapping the mind*. New York: Cambridge University Press.

AU, T.K., SIDLE, A.L., & ROLLINS, K.B. (1993). Developing an intuitive understanding of conservation and contamination: Invisible particles as a plausible mechanism. *Developmental Psychology, 29*, 286–299.

AVIS, J., & HARRIS, P.L. (1991). Belief-desire reasoning among Baka children: Evidence for a universal conception of mind. *Child Development, 62*, 460–467.

AZMITIA, M. (1988). Peer interaction and problem solving: When are two heads better than one? *Child Development, 59*, 87–96.

AZMITIA, M. (1996). Peer interactive minds: Developmental, theoretical, and methodological issues. In P.B. Baltes & U.M. Staudinger (Eds.), *Interactive minds: Life-span perspectives on the social foundations of cognition*. New York: Cambridge University Press.

AZMITIA, M., & HESSER, J. (1993). Why siblings are important agents of cognitive development: A comparison of siblings and peers. *Child Development, 64*, 430–444.

AZMITIA, M., & MONTGOMERY, R. (1993). Friendship, transactive dialogues, and the development of scientific reasoning. *Social Development, 2*, 202–221.

BACKSCHEIDER, A.G., SHATZ, M., & GELMAN, S.A. (1993). Preschoolers' ability to distinguish living kinds as a function of regrowth. *Child Development, 64*, 1242–1257.

BADDELEY, A.D. (1986). *Working memory*. Oxford, UK: Oxford University Press.

BADDELEY, A.D. (2000). The episodic buffer: A new component of working memory? *Trends in Cognitive Sciences, 4*, 417–423.

BADDELEY, A.D., & HITCH, G.J. (1974). Working memory. In G. Bower (Ed.), *The psychology of learning and motivation: Advances in research and theory* (Vol. 8). New York: Academic Press.

BADIAN, N.A. (1983). Dyscalculia and nonverbal disorders of learning. In H.R. Myklebust (Ed.), *Progress in learning disabilities* (Vol. 5). New York: Stratton.

BAHRICK, H.P., BAHRICK, P.O., & WITTLINGER, R.P. (1975). Fifty years of memory for names and faces: A cross-sectional approach. *Journal of Experimental Psychology, 104*, 54–75.

BAHRICK, L.E. (1992). Infants' perceptual differentiation of amodal and modality specific audio-visual relations. *Journal of Experimental Child Psychology, 53*, 180–199.

BAHRICK, L.E., & LICKLITER, R. (2000). Intersensory redundancy guides attentional selectivity and perceptual learning in infancy. *Developmental Psychology, 36*, 190–201.

BAHRICK, L.E., MOSS, L., & FADIL, C. (1996). Development of visual self-recognition in infancy. *Ecological Psychology, 8*, 189–208.

BAI, D., & BERTENTHAL, B.I. (1992). Locomotor status and the development of spatial search skills. *Child Development, 63*, 215–226.

BAILEY, D.B., & BRUER, J.T. (Eds.). (2001). *Critical thinking about critical periods*. Baltimore: Paul H. Brookes.

BAILLARGEON, R. (1987). Object permanence in $3\frac{1}{2}$- and $4\frac{1}{2}$-month-old infants. *Developmental Psychology, 23*, 655–664.

BAILLARGEON, R. (1993). The object concept revisited: New directions in the investigation of infants' physical knowledge. In C.E. Granrud (Ed.), *Visual perception and cognition in infancy*. Hillsdale, NJ: Erlbaum.

BAILLARGEON, R. (1994). How do infants learn about the physical world? *Current Directions in Psychological Science, 3*, 133–140.

BAILLARGEON, R. (2002). The acquisition of physical knowledge in infancy: A summary in eight lessons. In U. Goswami (Ed.), *Blackwell handbook of childhood cognitive development*. Malden, MA: Blackwell.

BAKER, L. (1994). Fostering metacognitive development. In H. Reese (Ed.), *Advances in child development and behavior*, (Vol. 25). San Diego: Academic Press.

BAKER, L., & BROWN, A.L. (1984). Metacognitive skills and reading. In P.D. Pearson (Ed.), *Handbook of reading research, Part 2*. New York: Longman.

BAKER-SENNET, J., MATUSOV, E., & ROGOFF, B. (1992). Sociocultural processes of creative planning in children's play-crafting. In P. Light & G. Butterworth (Eds.), *Context and cognition: Ways of learning and knowing*. New York: Harvester Wheatsheaf.

BAKER-WARD, L., & ORNSTEIN, P.A. (1988). Age differences in visual-spatial memory performance: Do children really out-perform adults when playing Concentration? *Bulletin of the Psychonomic Society, 26*, 331–332.

BAKER-WARD, L., ORNSTEIN, P.A., & HOLDEN, D.J. (1984). The expression of memorization in early childhood. *Journal of Experimental Child Psychology, 37*, 555–575.

BALABAN, M.T., & WAXMAN, S.R. (1997). Do words facilitate object categorization in 9-month-old infants? *Journal of Experimental Child Psychology, 64*, 3–26.

BALDWIN, D.A. (1991). Infants' contribution to the achievement of joint reference. *Child Development, 55*, 1278–1289.

BALDWIN, D.A. (1992). Clarifying the role of shape in children's taxonomic assumption. *Journal of Experimental Child Psychology, 54*, 392–416.

BALDWIN, D.A. (1993a). Early referential understanding: Infants' ability to recognize referential acts for what they are. *Developmental Psychology, 29*, 832–843.

BALDWIN, D.A. (1993b). Infants' ability to consult the speaker for clues to word meaning. *Journal of Child Language, 20*, 395–418.

BALTES, P.B. (1997). On the incomplete architecture of human development: Selection, optimization, and compensation as foundation of developmental theory. *American Psychologist, 52*, 366–380.

BANGERT-DOWNS, R.L. (1993). The word processor as an instructional tool: A meta-analysis of word processing in writing instruction. *Review of Educational Research, 63*, 69–93.

BANIGAN, R.L., & MERVIS, C.B. (1988). Role of adult input in young children's category evolution: An experimental study. *Journal of Child Language, 15*, 493–504.

BANKS, M.S., ASLIN, R.N., & LETSON, R.D. (1975). Sensitive period for the development of human binocular vision. *Science, 190*, 675–677.

BARON-COHEN, S. (1987). Autism and symbolic play. *British Journal of Developmental Psychology, 5*, 139–148.

BARON-COHEN, S. (1991). The development of a theory of mind in autism: Deviance and delay? *Psychiatric Clinics of North America, 14*, 33–51.

BARON-COHEN, S. (2001). Theory of mind and autism: A review. *International Review of Research in Mental Retardation, 23*, 169–184.

BARON-COHEN, S., LESLIE, A.M., & FRITH, U. (1985). Does the autistic child have a theory of mind? *Cognition, 21*, 37–46.

BARRETT, M., & SHORT, J. (1992). Images of European people in a group of 5–10 year old English school children. *British Journal of Developmental Psychology, 10*, 339–363.

BARSALOU, L.W. (1985). Ideals, central tendency, and frequency of instantiation as determinants of graded structure in categories. *Journal of Experimental Psychology: Learning, Memory & Cognition, 11*, 629–654.

BARTLETT, E.J. (1982). Learning to revise: Some component processes. In M. Nystrand (Ed.), *What writers know: The language, process, and structure of written discourse.* New York: Academic Press.

BARTSCH, K., & WELLMAN, H.M. (1995). *Children talk about the mind.* New York: Oxford University Press.

BATESON, M. (1979). "The epigenesis of conversational interaction": A personal account of research development. In M. Bullowa (Ed.), *Before speech: The beginning of human communication* (pp. 63–77). New York: Cambridge University Press.

BAUER, P.J. (1995). Recalling past events: From infancy to early childhood. *Annals of Child Development, 11*, 25–71.

BAUER, P.J. (1996). What do infants recall of their lives? Memory for specific events by 1- to 2-year olds. *American Psychologist, 51*, 29–41.

BAUER, P.J., KROUPINA, M.G., SCHWADE, J.A., DROPIK, P.L., & WEWERKA, S.S. (1998). If memory serves, will language? Later verbal accessibility of early memories. *Development & Psychopathology, 10*, 655–679.

BAUER, P.J., & MANDLER, J.M. (1989a). Taxonomies and triads: Conceptual organization in 1- to 2-year-olds. *Cognitive Psychology, 21*, 156–184.

BAUER, P.J., & MANDLER, J.M. (1989b). One thing follows another: Effects of temporal structure on 1- to 2-year-olds' recall of events. *Developmental Psychology, 25*, 197–206.

BAUER, P.J., SCHWADE, J.A., WEWERKA, S.S., & DELANEY, K. (1999). Planning ahead: Goal-directed problem solving by 2-year-olds. *Developmental Psychology, 35*, 1321–1337.

BAUER, P.J., WENNER, J.A., DROPIK, P.L., & WEWERKA, S. (2000). Parameters of remembering and forgetting in the transition from infancy to early childhood. *Monographs of the Society for Research in Child Development, 65*(4, Serial No. 263).

BAYLEY, N. (1969). *Bayley scales of infant development.* New York: Psychological Corporation.

BEAL, C.R. (1990). The development of text evaluation and revision skills. *Child Development, 61*, 247–258.

BEAL, C.R. (1996). The role of comprehension monitoring in children's revision. *Educational Psychology Review, 8*, 219–238.

BEAL, C.R., & BELGRAD, S.L. (1990). The development of message evaluation skills in young children. *Child Development, 61*, 705–712.

BEAL, C.R., & FLEISIG, W.E. (1987, April). *Preschoolers' preparation for retrieval in object relocation tasks.* Paper presented at the biennial meeting of the Society for Research in Child Development, Baltimore, MD.

BECK, I.L., & MCKEOWN, M.G. (1984). Application of theories of reading to instruction. *American Journal of Education, 93*, 61–81.

BEHL-CHADHA, G. (1996). Basic-level and superordinate-like categorical representations in early infancy. *Cognition, 60*, 105–114.

BEILIN, H. (1977). Inducing conservation through training. In G. Steiner (Ed.), *Psychology of the 20th Century: Vol. 7, Piaget and beyond.* Zurich: Kindler.

BEILIN, H. (1983). The new functionalism and Piaget's program. In E.K. Scholnick (Ed.), *New trends in conceptual representation: Challenges to Piaget's theory?* Hillsdale, NJ: Erlbaum.

BELL, M.A., & FOX, N.A. (1992). The relations between frontal brain electrical activity and cognitive development during infancy. *Child Development, 63*, 1142–1163.

BELLUGI, U., LICHTENBERGER, L., JONES, W., LAI, Z., & ST. GEORGE, M. (2000). I. The neurocognitive profile of Williams syndrome: A complex pattern of strengths and weaknesses. *Journal of Cognitive Neuroscience, 12*(Suppl. 1), 7–29.

BEM, S.L. (1989). Genital knowledge and gender constancy in preschool children. *Child Development, 60*, 649–662.

BENEDICT, H. (1979). Early lexical development: Comprehension and production. *Journal of Child Language, 6*, 183–200.

BENSON, J.B., AREHART, D.M., JENNINGS, T., BOLEY, S., & KEARNS, L. (1989, April). *Infant crawling: Expectation, action plans, and goals.* Paper presented at the biennial meeting of the Society for Research in Child Development, Kansas City, MO.

BENTIN, S., HAMMER, R., & CAHAN, S. (1991). The effects of aging and first grade schooling on the development of phonological awareness. *Psychological Science, 2,* 271–274.

BEREITER, C., & SCARDAMALIA, M. (1982). From conversation to composition: The role of instruction in a developmental process. In R. Glaser (Ed.), *Advances in instructional psychology* (Vol. 2). Hillsdale, NJ: Erlbaum.

BEREITER, C., & SCARDAMALIA, M. (1987). *The psychology of written composition.* Hillsdale, NJ: Erlbaum.

BERG, C.A. (1989). Knowledge of strategies for dealing with everyday problems from childhood through adolescence. *Developmental Psychology, 25,* 607–618.

BERK, L.E. (1994). Why children talk to themselves. *Scientific American, 271,* 78–83.

BERKOWITZ, M.W., & GIBBS, J.C. (1985). The process of moral conflict resolution and moral development. In M.W. Berkowitz (Ed.), *New directions for child development: Peer conflict and psychological growth.* San Francisco: Jossey-Bass.

BERLIN, B., & KAYE, P. (1969). *Basic color terms: Their universality and evolution.* Berkeley: University of California Press.

BERMAN, K.F., OSTERM, J.L., RANDOULPH, C., GOLD, J., GOLDBERG, T.E., COPPOLA, R., CARSON, R.E., HERSCOVITCH, P., & WEINBERGER, D.R. (1995). Physiological activation of a cortical network during performance of the Wisconsin Card Sorting Test: A positron emission tomography study. *Neuropsychologia, 33,* 1027–1046.

BERMEJO, V. (1996). Cardinality development and counting. *Developmental Psychology, 32,* 263–268.

BERTENTHAL, B.I. (1993). Infants' perception of biomechanical motions: Intrinsic image and knowledge-based constraints. In C.E. Granrud (Ed.), *Visual perception and cognition in infancy.* Hillsdale, NJ: Erlbaum.

BERTENTHAL, B.I. (1996). Origins and early development of perception, action and representation. *Annual Review of Psychology, 47,* 431–459.

BERTENTHAL, B.I., & BAI, D.L. (1989). Infants' sensitivity to optical flow for controlling posture. *Developmental Psychology, 25,* 936–945.

BERTENTHAL, B.I., CAMPOS, J.J., & KERMOIAN, R. (1994). An epigenetic perspective on the development of self-produced locomotion and its consequences. *Current Directions in Psychological Science, 5,* 140–145.

BERTENTHAL, B.I., & CLIFTON, R.K. (1998). Perception and action. In D. Kuhn & R.S. Siegler (Eds.), *Handbook of child psychology: Vol. 2. Cognition, Perception & Language* (5th ed.). New York: Wiley.

BERTENTHAL, B.I., & PINTO, J. (1993). Complementary processes in the perception and production of human movements. In E. Thelen & L. Smith (Eds.), *Dynamic approaches to development: Vol 2. Applications.* Cambridge, MA: Bradford Books.

BERTENTHAL, B.I., ROSE, J.L., & BAI, D.L. (1997). Perception-action coupling in the development of visual control of posture. *Journal of Experimental Psychology: Human Perception & Performance, 23,* 1631–1643.

BERTONCINI, J., MORAIS, J., BIJELJAC-BABIC, R., & MCADAMS, S. (1989). Dichotic perception and laterality in neonates. *Brain and Language, 37,* 591–605.

BEST, C.T. (1995). Learning to perceive the sound pattern of English. In C. Rovee-Collier & L. Lipsitt (Eds.), *Advances in infancy research.* Norwood, NJ: Ablex.

BIALYSTOK, E., & HAKUTA, K. (1994). *In other words: The science and psychology of second-language acquisition.* New York: Basic Books.

BIGLER, R.S., SPEARS-BROWN, C., & MARKELL, M. (2001). When groups are not created equal: Effects of group status on the formation of inter-group attitudes in children. *Child Development, 72,* 1151–1162.

BILLMAN, D., & SHATZ, M. (1981). *A longitudinal study of the development of communication skills in twins and unrelated peers.* Unpublished manuscript, University of Michigan, Ann Arbor.

BISANZ, G.L., VESONDER, G.T., & VOSS, J.F. (1978). Knowledge of one's own responding and the relation of such knowledge to learning. *Journal of Experimental Child Psychology, 25,* 116–128.

BISANZ, J., & LEFEVRE, J. (1990). Mathematical cognition: Strategic processing as interactions among sources of knowledge. In D.P. Bjorklund (Ed.), *Children's strategies: Contemporary views of cognitive development.* Hillsdale, NJ: Erlbaum.

BISANZ, J., MORRISON, F.J., & DUNN, M. (1995). Effects of age and schooling on the acquisition of elementary quantitative skills. *Developmental Psychology, 31,* 221–236.

BIVENS, J.A., & BERK, L.E. (1990). A longitudinal study of the development of elementary school children's private speech. *Merrill-Palmer Quarterly, 36,* 443–463.

BJORKLUND, D.F. (1997). The role of immaturity in human development. *Psychological Bulletin, 122,* 153–169.

BJORKLUND, D.F., & COYLE, T.R. (1995). Utilization deficiencies in the development of memory strategies. In F.E. Weinert & W. Schneider (Eds.) *Memory performance and competencies: Issues in growth and development.* Hillsdale, NJ: Erlbaum.

BJORKLUND, D.F., MUIR-BROADDUS, J.E., & SCHNEIDER, W. (1990). The role of knowledge in the development of strategies. In D.F. Bjorklund (Ed.), *Children's strategies: Contemporary views of cognitive development.* Hillsdale, NJ: Erlbaum.

BJORKLUND, D.F., & ROSENBLUM, K.E. (2002). Context effects in children's selection and use of simple arithmetic strategies. *Journal of Cognition & Development, 3,* 225–242.

BLACK-GUTMAN, D., & HICKSON, F. (1996). The relationship between racial attitudes and social-cognitive development in children: An Australian study. *Developmental Psychology, 32,* 448–456.

BLADES, M., & SPENCER, C. (1994). The development of children's ability to use spatial representations. In H. Reese (Ed.), *Advances in child development and behavior* (Vol. 25). New York: Academic Press.

BLAYE, A., & BONTHOUX, F. (2001). Thematic and taxonomic relations in preschoolers: The development of flexibility in categorization choices. *British Journal of Developmental Psychology, 19,* 395–412.

BLAYE, A., LIGHT, P., JOINER, R., & SHELDON, S. (1991). Collaboration as a facilitator of planning and problem solving on a computer-based task. *British Journal of Developmental Psychology, 9,* 471–483.

BLEWITT, P. (1983). Dog vs. collie: Vocabulary in speech to young children. *Developmental Psychology, 19,* 601–609.

BLOOM, K. (1990). Selectivity and early infant vocalization. In J.T. Enns (Ed.), *The development of attention: Research and theory*. BV North-Holland: Elsevier Science Publishers.

BLOOM, K., RUSSELL, A., & WASSNBERG, K. (1987). Turn taking affects the quality of infant vocalizations. *Journal of Child Language, 14*, 211–227.

BLOOM, L. (1998). Learning language in and for conversations. In D. Kuhn & R.S. Siegler (Eds.), *Handbook of child psychology: Vol. 2. Cognition, perception & language* (5th ed.). New York: Wiley.

BLOOM, L., MARGULIS, C., TINKER, E., & FUJITA, N. (1996). Early conversations and word learning: Contributions from child and adult. *Child Development, 67*, 3154–3175.

BLOOM, L., TINKER, E., & MARGULIS, C. (1993). The words children learn: Evidence against a noun bias in early vocabularies. *Cognitive Development, 8*, 431–450.

BLOOM, P. (2000). *How children learn the meanings of words.* Cambridge, MA: MIT Press.

BOESCH, C. (1991). Teaching among wild chimpanzees. *Animal Behavior, 41*, 530–532.

BOESCH, C., MARCHESI, P., MARCHESI, N., FRUTH, B., & JOULIAN, F. (1994). Is nut cracking in wild chimpanzees a cultural behavior? *Journal of Human Evolution, 26*, 325–328.

BOHANNON, J.N. II., & STANOWICZ, L. (1988). The issue of negative evidence: Adult responses to children's language errors. *Developmental Psychology, 24*, 684–689.

BOMBA, P.C., & SIQUELAND, E.R. (1983). The nature and structure of infant form categories. *Journal of Experimental Child Psychology, 35*, 294–328.

BONVILLIAN, J.D., ORLANSKY, M.D., & NOVACK, L.L. (1983). Developmental milestones: Sign language acquisition and motor development. *Child Development, 54*, 1435–1445.

BONVILLIAN, J.D., & SIEDLECKI, T. (2000). Young children's acquisition of the formational aspects of American Sign. *Sign Language Studies, 1*, 45–64.

BOOTH, A.E., PINTO, J., & BERTENTHAL, B.I. (2002). Perception of the symmetrical patterning of human gait by infants. *Developmental Psychology, 38*, 554–563.

BORKOWSKI, J.G., CARR, M., & PRESSLEY, M. (1987). Spontaneous strategy use: Perspectives from metacognitive theory. *Intelligence, 11*, 61–75.

BORKOWSKI, J.G., JOHNSTON, N.B., & REID, N.K. (1987). Metacognition, motivation, and the transfer of control processes. In S.J. Ceci (Ed.), *Handbook of cognitive, social, and neuropsychological aspects of learning disabilities* (Vol. 2). Hillsdale, NJ: Erlbaum.

BORNSTEIN, M.H. (1989). Sensitive periods in development: Structural characteristics and causal interpretations. *Psychological Bulletin, 105*, 179–197.

BORNSTEIN, M.H., KESSEN, W., & WEISKOPF, S. (1976). The categories of hue in infancy. *Science, 191*, 201–202.

BORNSTEIN, M.H., & SIGMAN, M.D. (1986). Continuity in mental development from infancy. *Child Development, 57*, 251–274.

BOSCOLO, P. (1995). The cognitive approach to writing and writing instruction: A contribution to a critical appraisal. *CPC, 14*, 343–366.

BOUCHARD, D., & TETREAULT, S. (2000). The motor development of sighted children and children with moderate low vision aged 8–13. *Journal of Visual Impairment and Blindness, 94*, 564–573.

BOURGEOIS, J.-P. (2001). Synaptogenesis in the neocortex of the newborn: The ultimate frontier for individuation. In C.A. Nelson & M. Luciana (Eds.), *Handbook of developmental cognitive neuroscience*. Cambridge, MA: MIT Press.

BOWER, T.G.R., & WISHART, J.G. (1972). The effects of motor skill on object permanence. *Cognition, 1*, 165–172.

BOWERMAN, M. (1980). The structure and origin of semantic categories in the language-learning child. In M. Foster & S. Brandes (Eds.), *Symbol as sense: New approaches to the analysis of meaning*. New York: Academic Press.

BOWERMAN, M. (1982). Starting to talk worse: Clues to language acquisition from children's late speech errors. In S. Strauss (Ed.), *U-shaped behavioral growth*. New York: Academic Press.

BRADLEY, L., & BRYANT, P.E. (1983). Categorizing sounds and learning to read—A causal connection. *Nature, 301*, 419–421.

BRAINE, M.D.S. (1959). The ontogeny of certain logical operations: Piaget's formulation examined by nonverbal methods. *Psychological Monographs, 73*(Whole No. 475).

BRAINE, M.D.S. (1971). The acquisition of language in infant and child. In C.E. Reed (Ed.), *The learning of language*. New York: Appleton-Century-Crofts.

BRAINE, M.D.S. (1976). Children's first word combinations. *Monographs of the Society for Research in Child Development, 41*(1, Serial No. 164).

BRAINERD, C.J. (1978). The stage question in cognitive developmental theory. *Behavioral and Brain Sciences, 1*, 173–213.

BRAINERD, C.J, & ORNSTEIN, P.A. (1990). Children's memory for witnessed events: The developmental backdrop. In J. Doris (Ed.), *The suggestibility of children's recollections: Implications for eyewitness testimony*. Washington, DC: American Psychological Association.

BRAINERD, C.J., & REYNA, V.F. (1990). Gist is the grist: Fuzzy-trace theory and the new intuitionism. *Developmental Review, 10*, 3–47.

BRAINERD, C.J., & REYNA, V.F. (1995). Learning rate, learning opportunities, and the development of forgetting. *Developmental Psychology, 31*, 251–262.

BRAINERD, C.J., REYNA, V.F., HOWE, M.L., & KINGMA, J. (1990). The development of forgetting and reminiscence. *Monographs of the Society for Research in Child Development, 55*(3–4, Serial No. 222).

BRANCH, C., & NEWCOMBE, N. (1986). Race-related socialization, motivation, and academic achievement: A longitudinal and cross-sectional study. *Child Development, 57*, 712–721.

BRANNON, E.M. (2002). The development of ordinal numerical knowledge in infancy. *Cognition, 83*, 223–240.

BRANNON, E.M., & VAN DE WALLE, G.A. (2001). The development of ordinal numerical competence in young children. *Cognitive Psychology, 43*, 53–81.

BRANSFORD, P.W. (1979). *Human cognition: Learning, understanding and remembering*. Belmont, CA: Wadsworth.

BRENNAN, W.M., AMES, E.W., & MOORE, R.W. (1966). Age differences in infants' attention to patterns of different complexity. *Science, 151*, 354–356.

BRENNER, M.E., MAYER, R.E., MOSELEY, B., BRAR, T., DURAN, R., REED, B.S., & WEBB, D. (1997). Learning by understanding: The role of multiple representations in learning algebra. *American Educational Research Journal, 34*, 663–689.

BRETHERTON, I. (1984). Representing the social world in symbolic play: Reality and fantasy. In I. Bretherton (Ed.), *Symbolic play: The development of social understanding.* New York: Academic Press.

BRIARS, D., & SIEGLER, R.S. (1984). A featural analysis of preschoolers' counting knowledge. *Developmental Psychology, 20,* 607–618.

BRONFENBRENNER, U. (1979). *The ecology of human development: Experiments by nature and design.* Cambridge, MA: Harvard University Press.

BRONFENBRENNER, U. (1998). The ecology of developmental processes. In R.M. Lerner (Ed.), *Handbook of child psychology: Vol. 1. Theoretical models of human development.* (5th ed.). New York: Wiley.

BRONSON, G.W. (1974). The postnatal growth of visual capacity. *Child Development, 45,* 873–890.

BROOKES, H., SLATER, A., QUINN, P.C., LEWKOWICZ, D.J., HAYES, R., & BROWN, E. (2001). Three-month-old infants learn arbitrary auditory-visual pairings between voices and faces. *Infant and Child Development, 10,* 75–82.

BROWN, A.L. (1976). Semantic integration in children's reconstruction of narrative sequences. *Cognitive Psychology, 8,* 247–262.

BROWN, A.L. (1989). Analogical learning and transfer: What develops? In S. Vosniadou & A. Ortony (Eds.), *Similarity and analogical reasoning.* New York: Cambridge University Press.

BROWN, A.L. (1997). Transforming schools into communities of thinking and learning about serious matters. *American Psychologist, 52,* 399–413.

BROWN, A.L., BRANSFORD, J.D., FERRARA, R.A., & CAMPIONE, J.C. (1983). Learning, remembering, and understanding. In P.H. Mussen (Ed.), *Handbook of child psychology: Vol 3. Cognitive development.* New York: Wiley.

BROWN, A.L., & CAMPIONE, J.C. (1972). Recognition memory for perceptually similar pictures in preschool children. *Journal of Experimental Psychology, 95,* 55–62.

BROWN, A.L., & CAMPIONE, J.C. (1994). Guided discovery in a community of learners. In K. McGilly (Ed.), *Classroom lessons: Integrating cognitive theory and classroom practice.* Cambridge, MA: MIT Press.

BROWN, A.L., & CAMPIONE, J.C. (1996). Psychological learning theories and the design of innovative learning environments: On procedures, principles, and systems. In R. Glaser (Ed.), *Contributions of instructional innovation to understanding learning.* Hillsdale, NJ: Erlbaum.

BROWN, A.L., & DELOACHE, J.S. (1978). Skills, plans, and self-regulation. In R.S. Siegler (Ed.), *Children's thinking: What develops?* Hillsdale, NJ: Erlbaum.

BROWN, A.L., KANE, M.J., & ECHOLS, K. (1986). Young children's mental models determine analogical transfer across problems with a common goal structure. *Cognitive Development, 1,* 103–122.

BROWN, A.L., & SCOTT, M.S. (1971). Recognition memory for pictures in preschool children. *Journal of Experimental Child Psychology, 11,* 401–412.

BROWN, J.S., & BURTON, R.B. (1978). Diagnostic models for procedural bugs in basic mathematical skills. *Cognitive Science, 2,* 155–192.

BROWN, R., & MCNEILL, D. (1966). The "tip of the tongue" phenomenon. *Journal of Verbal Learning & Verbal Behavior, 5,* 325–337.

BROWN, R.W. (1957). Linguistic determinism and the parts of speech. *Journal of Abnormal and Social Psychology, 55,* 1–5.

BROWN, R.W., & HANLON, C. (1970). Derivational complexity and order of acquisition in child speech. In J.R. Hayes (Ed.), *Cognition and the development of language.* New York: Wiley.

BRUCE, D., DOLAN, A., & PHILLIPS-GRANT, K. (2000). On the transition from childhood amnesia to the recall of personal memories. *Psychological Science, 11,* 360–364.

BRUCHKOWSKY, M. (1992). The development of empathic cognition in middle and early childhood. In R. Case (Ed.), *The mind's staircase: Exploring the conceptual underpinnings of children's thought and knowledge.* Hillsdale, NJ: Erlbaum.

BRUCK, M. (1990). Word-recognition skills of adults with childhood diagnoses of dyslexia. *Developmental Psychology, 26,* 439–454.

BRUCK, M. (1992). Persistence of dyslexics' phonological awareness deficits. *Developmental Psychology, 28,* 874–886.

BRUCK, M., & CECI, S.J. (1999). The suggestibility of children's memory. *Annual Review of Psychology, 50,* 419–439.

BRUCK, M., CECI, S.J., FRANCOEUR, E., & RENICK, A. (1995). Anatomically detailed dolls do not facilitate preschoolers' reports of a pediatric examination involving genital touching. *Journal of Experimental Psychology: Applied, 1,* 95–109.

BRUCK, M., MELNYK, L., & CECI, S.J. (2000). Draw it again Sam: The effect of drawing on children's suggestibility and source monitoring ability. *Journal of Experimental Child Psychology, 77,* 169–196.

BRUER, J.T., & GREENOUGH, W.T. (2001). The subtle science of how experience affects the brain. In D.B. Bailey & J.T. Bruer (Eds.), *Critical thinking about critical periods.* Baltimore: Paul H. Brookes.

BRUNER, J.S. (1966). On cognitive growth. In J.S. Bruner, R.R. Olver, & P.M. Greenfield (Eds.), *Studies in cognitive growth.* New York, Wiley.

BRUNER, J.S. (1983). *Child's talk: Learning to use language.* New York: Norton.

BRUNER, J.S., GOODNOW, J.J., & AUSTIN, G.A. (1956). *A study of thinking.* New York: Wiley.

BRUNER, J.S., & KENNEY, H.J. (1966). On relational concepts. In J.S. Bruner, R.R. Olver, & P.M. Greenfield (Eds.), *Studies in cognitive growth.* New York: Wiley.

BUCKINGHAM, D., & SHULTZ, T.R. (2000). The developmental course of distance, time, and velocity concepts: A generative connectionist model. *Journal of Cognition & Development, 1,* 305–345.

BULL, R., JOHNSTON, R.S., & ROY, J.A. (1999). Exploring the roles of the visual-spatial sketch pad and central executive in children's arithmetical skills: Views from cognition and developmental neuropsychology. *Developmental Neuropsychology, 15,* 421–442.

BULLOCK, M., & GELMAN, R. (1979). Preschool children's assumptions about cause and effect: Temporal ordering. *Child Development, 50,* 89–96.

BULLOCK, M., & LUETKENHAUS, P. (1990). Who am I? The development of self-understanding in toddlers. *Merrill-Palmer Quarterly, 36,* 217–238.

BUSHNELL, E.W., & BOUDREAU, J.P. (1993). Motor development and the mind: The potential role of motor abilities as a determinant of aspects of perceptual development. *Child Development, 64,* 1005–1021.

BUSHNELL, I.W.R., SAI, F., & MULLIN, J.T. (1989). Neonatal recognition of the mother's face. *British Journal of Developmental Psychology, 7,* 3–15.

BUSSEY, K., & BANDURA, A. (1984). Influence of gender constancy and social power on sex-linked modeling. *Journal of Personality and Social Psychology, 47,* 1292–1302.

BUSSEY, K., & BANDURA, A. (1999). Social cognitive theory of gender development and differentiation. *Psychological Review, 106,* 676–713.

BUTLER, S., GROSS, J., & HAYNE, H. (1995). The effect of drawing on memory performance in young children. *Developmental Psychology, 31,* 597–608.

BUTTERWORTH, G. (2001). Joint visual attention in infancy. In A. Fogel (Ed.), *Blackwell handbook of infant development.* Oxford, UK: Blackwell.

BYRNE, B., & FIELDING-BARNSLEY, R. (1995). Evaluation of a program to teach phonemic awareness to young children: A 2- and 3-year follow-up and a new preschool trial. *Journal of Educational Psychology, 87,* 488–503.

BYRNE, B., FIELDING-BARNSLEY, R., & ASHLEY, L. (2000). Effects of preschool phoneme identity training after six years: Outcome level distinguished from rate of response. *Journal of Educational Psychology, 92,* 659–667.

BYRNES, J.P. (1988). Formal operations: A systematic reformulation. *Developmental Review, 8,* 66–87.

BYRNES, J.P., & OVERTON, W.F. (1986). Reasoning about certainty and uncertainty in concrete, causal, and propositional contexts. *Developmental Psychology, 22,* 793–799.

CALLANAN, M.A. (1990). Parents' descriptions of objects: Potential data for children's inferences about category principles. *Cognitive Development, 5,* 101–122.

CAMPIONE, J.C., & BROWN, A.L. (1984). Learning ability and transfer propensity as sources of individual differences in intelligence. In P.H. Brooks, R. Sperber, & C. McCauley (Eds.), *Learning and cognition in the mentally retarded.* Hillsdale, NJ: Erlbaum.

CAMPOS, J.J., ANDERSON, D.I., BARBU-ROTH, M.A., HUBBARD, E.M., HERTENSTEIN, M.J., & WITHERINGTON, D. (2000). Travel broadens the mind. *Infancy, 1,* 149–219.

CAMPOS, J.J., BERTENTHAL, B.I., & KERMOIAN, R. (1992). Early experience and emotional development: The emergence of fear of heights. *Psychological Science, 3,* 61–64.

CANFIELD, R.L., & HAITH, M.M. (1991). Young infants' visual expectations for symmetric and asymmetric stimulus sequences. *Developmental Psychology, 27,* 198–208.

CANFIELD, R.L., & SMITH, E.G. (1996). Number-based expectations and sequential enumeration by 5-month-old infants. *Developmental Psychology, 32,* 269–279.

CAPODILUPO, A.M. (1992). A neo-structural analysis of children's response to instruction in the sight-reading of musical notation. In R. Case (Ed.), *The mind's staircase: Exploring the conceptual underpinnings of children's thought and knowledge.* Hillsdale, NJ: Erlbaum.

CAREY, S. (1978). The child as word learner. In M. Halle, J. Bresnan, & A. Miller (Eds.), *Linguistic theory and psychological reality.* Cambridge, MA: MIT Press.

CAREY, S. (1985). *Conceptual change in childhood.* Cambridge, MA: MIT Press.

CAREY, S., & GELMAN, R. (Eds.) (1991). *The epigenesis of mind: Essays on biology and cognition.* Hillsdale, NJ: Erlbaum.

CARLSON, S.M., & MOSES, L.J. (2001). Individual differences in inhibitory control and children's theory of mind. *Child Development, 72,* 1032–1053.

CARLSON, S.M., MOSES, L.J., & HIX, H.R. (1998). The role of inhibitory control in young children's difficulties with deception and false belief. *Child Development, 69,* 672–691.

CARPENTER, M., AKHTAR, N., & TOMASELLO, M. (1998). Fourteen- through 18-month-old infants differentially imitate intentional and accidental actions. *Infant Behavior & Development, 21,* 315–330.

CARPENTER, T.P., CORBITT, M.K., KEPNER, H.S., LINDQUIST, M.M., & REYS, R.E. (1981). *Results from the second mathematics assessment of the National Assessment of Educational Progress.* Washington, DC: National Council of Teachers of Mathematics.

CARPENTER, T.P., FRANKE, M.L., & LEVI, L. (2003). *Thinking mathematically: Integrating arithmetic and algebra in elementary school.* Portsmouth, NH: Heinemann.

CARR, M., KURTZ, B.E., SCHNEIDER, W., TURNER, L.A., & BORKOWSKI, J.G. (1989). Strategy acquisition and transfer among American and German children: Environmental influences on metacognitive development. *Developmental Psychology, 25,* 765–771.

CARRAHER, T.N., CARRAHER, D.W., & SCHLIEMANN, A.D. (1985). Mathematics in the streets and in schools. *British Journal of Developmental Psychology, 3,* 21–29.

CARVER, S.M., & KLAHR, D. (1987). Assessing children's LOGO debugging skills with a formal model. *Journal of Educational Computing Research, 2,* 487–525.

CASE, R. (1978). Intellectual development from birth to adulthood: A neo-Piagetian approach. In R.S. Siegler (Ed.), *Children's thinking: What develops?* Hillsdale, NJ: Erlbaum.

CASE, R. (1985). *Intellectual development: A systematic reinterpretation.* New York: Academic Press.

CASE, R. (1992a). *The mind's staircase: Exploring the conceptual underpinnings of children's thought and knowledge.* Hillsdale, NJ: Erlbaum.

CASE, R. (1992b). The role of the frontal lobes in the regulation of cognitive development. *Brain and Cognition, 20,* 51–73.

CASE, R. (1998). The development of conceptual structures. In D. Kuhn & R.S. Siegler (Eds.), *Handbook of child psychology: Vol. 2. Cognition, perception, & language* (5th ed.). New York: Wiley.

CASE, R., & GRIFFIN, S. (1990). Child cognitive development: The role of central conceptual structures in the development of scientific and social thought. In C.A. Hauert (Ed.), *Developmental psychology: Cognitive, perceptuo-motor and neuropsychological perspectives.* Amsterdam: North Holland.

CASE, R., & MUELLER, M.P. (2001). Differentiation, integration, and covariance mapping as fundamental processes in cognitive and neurological growth. In J.L. McClelland & R.S. Siegler (Eds.), *Mechanisms of cognitive development: Behavioral and neural perspectives.* Mahwah, NJ: Erlbaum.

CASE, R., & OKAMOTO, Y. (1996). The role of central conceptual structures in the development of children's thought. *Monographs of the Society for Research in Child Development, 61*(1–2, Serial No. 246).

CASE, R., OKAMOTO, Y., HENDERSON, B., McKEOUGH, A., & BLEIKER, C. (1996). Exploring the macrostructure of children's central conceptual structures in the domains of number and narrative. In R. Case & Y. Okamoto (Eds.), *The role of central conceptual structures in the development of children's thought. Monographs of the Society for Research in Child Development, 61*(1–2, Serial No. 246).

CASE, R., SANDIESON, R., & DENNIS, S. (1987). Two cognitive developmental approaches to the design of remedial instruction. *Cognitive Development, 1,* 293–333.

CASE, R., STEPHENSON, K.M., BLEIKER, C., & HENDERSON, B. (1996). Central spatial structures and their development. In R. Case & Y. Okamoto (Eds.), *The role of central conceptual structures in the development of children's thought. Monographs of the Society for Research in Child Development, 61*(1–2, Serial No. 246).

CASELLI, M.C., BATES, E., CASADIO, P., FENSON, J., FENSON, L., SANDERL, L., & WEIR, J. (1995). A crosslinguistic study of early lexical development. *Cognitive Development, 10,* 159–199.

CASTLES, A., & COLTHEART, M. (1993). Varieties of developmental dyslexia. *Cognition, 47,* 149–180.

CAVANAUGH, J.C., & PERLMUTTER, M. (1982). Metamemory: A critical examination. *Child Development, 53,* 11–28.

CECI, S.J. (1989). On domain specificity . . . more or less general and specific constraints on cognitive development. *Merrill-Palmer Quarterly, 35,* 131–142.

CECI, S.J. (1990). *On intelligence . . . more or less: A bio-ecological treatise on intellectual development.* Englewood Cliffs, NJ: Prentice Hall.

CECI, S.J., & BRUCK, M. (1993). The suggestibility of the child witness: A historical review and synthesis. *Psychological Bulletin, 113,* 403–439.

CECI, S.J., & BRUCK, M. (1998). Child psychology in practice: Children's testimony. In I.E. Sigel & K.A. Renninger (Eds.), *Handbook of child psychology: Vol. 4. Clinical psychology in practice.* (5th ed.). New York: Wiley.

CECI, S.J., LOFTUS, E.W., LEICHTMAN, M., & BRUCK, M. (1994). The role of source misattributions in the creation of false beliefs among preschoolers. *International Journal of Clinical and Experimental Hypnosis, 62,* 304–320.

CHALL, J.S. (1979). The great debate: Ten years later, with a modest proposal for reading stages. In L.B. Resnick & P.A. Weaver (Eds.), *Theory and practice of early reading.* Hillsdale, NJ: Erlbaum.

CHANG, F.L., & GREENOUGH, W.T. (1984). Transient and enduring morphological correlates of synaptic activity and efficacy change in the rat hippocampal slice. *Brain Research, 309,* 35–46.

CHANGEUX, J.P. & DEHAENE, S. (1989). Neuronal models of cognitive functions. *Cognition, 33,* 63–109.

CHAVAJAY, P., & ROGOFF, B. (1999). Cultural variation in management of attention by children and their caregivers. *Developmental Psychology, 35,* 1079–1090.

CHAVAJAY, P., & ROGOFF, B. (2002). Schooling and traditional collaborative social organization of problem solving by Mayan mothers and children. *Developmental Psychology, 38,* 55–66.

CHEN, Z. (1996). Children's analogical problem solving: The effects of superficial, structural, and procedural similarity. *Journal of Experimental Child Psychology, 62,* 410–431.

CHEN, Z. (1999). Schema induction in children's analogical problem solving. *Journal of Educational Psychology, 91,* 703–715.

CHEN, Z. (2002). Analogical problem solving: A hierarchical analysis of procedural similarity. *Journal of Experimental Psychology: Learning, Memory & Cognition, 28,* 81–98.

CHEN, Z., & KLAHR, D. (1999). All other things being equal: Acquisition and transfer of the control of variables strategy. *Child Development, 70,* 1098–1120.

CHEN, Z., SANCHEZ, R.P., & CAMPBELL, T., (1997). From beyond to within their grasp: The rudiments of analogical problem solving in 10- and 13-month-olds. *Developmental Psychology, 33,* 790–801.

CHEN, Z., & SIEGLER, R.S. (2000). Across the great divide: Bridging the gap between understanding of toddlers and older children's thinking. *Monographs of the Society for Research in Child Development, 65*(2, Serial No. 261).

CHEN, Z., YANOWITZ, K.L., & DAEHLER, M.W. (1995). Constraints on accessing abstract source information: Instantiation of principles facilitates children's analogical transfer. *Journal of Educational Psychology, 87,* 445–454.

CHI, M.T.H. (1978). Knowledge structures and memory development. In R.S. Siegler (Ed.), *Children's thinking: What develops?* Hillsdale, NJ: Erlbaum.

CHI, M.T.H. (1981). Knowledge development and memory performance. In J.P. Das & N. O'Conner (Eds.), *Intelligence and learning.* New York: Plenum Press.

CHI, M.T.H., & KLAHR, D. (1975). Span and rate of apprehension in children and adults. *Journal of Experimental Child Psychology, 19,* 434–439.

CHOI, S. (2000). Caregiver input in English and Korean: Use of nouns and verbs in book-reading and toy-play contexts. *Journal of Child Language, 27,* 69–96.

CHOI, S., & GOPNIK, A. (1995). Early acquisition of verbs in Korean: A cross-linguistic study. *Journal of Child Language, 22,* 497–529.

CHOI, S., MCDONOUGH, L., BOWERMAN, M., & MANDLER, J.M. (1999). Early sensitivity to language-specific spatial categories in English and Korean. *Cognitive Development, 14,* 241–268.

CHOMSKY, N. (1972). *Language and mind.* New York: Harcourt Brace Jovanovich.

CHUGANI, H.T., & PHELPS, M.E. (1986). Maturational changes in cerebral function in infants determined by [18]FDG positron emission tomography. *Science, 231,* 840–843.

CHUGANI, H.T., PHELPS, M.E., & MAZZIOTTA, J.C. (1987). Positron emission tomography study of human brain functional development. *Annals of Neurology, 22,* 487–497.

CHURCH, R.B. (1999). Using gesture and speech to capture transitions in learning. *Cognitive Development, 14,* 313–342.

CHURCH, R.B., & GOLDIN-MEADOW, S. (1986). The mismatch between gesture and speech as an index of transitional knowledge. *Cognition, 23,* 43–71.

CLARK, E.V. (1973). What's in a word? On the child's acquisition of semantics in his first language. In T.E. Moore (Ed.), *Cognitive development and the acquisition of language.* New York: Academic Press.

CLARK, E.V. (1978). Strategies for communication. *Child Development, 49,* 953–959.

CLARK, E.V. (1993). *The lexicon in acquisition.* Cambridge, UK: Cambridge University Press.

CLARK, E.V. (1995). Later lexical development and word formation. In P. Fletcher & B. MacWhinney (Eds.), *The handbook of child language.* Cambridge, MA: Blackwell.

CLARKE-STEWART, A., THOMPSON, W., & LEPORE, S. (1989, May). *Manipulating children's interpretations through interrogation.* Paper presented at the biennial meeting of the Society for Research in Child Development, Kansas City, MO.

CLAVADETSCHER, J.E., BROWN, A.M., ANKRUM, C., & TELLER, D.Y. (1988). Spectral sensitivity and chromatic discriminations in 3- and 7-week-old human infants. *Journal of the Optical Society of America, 5,* 2093–2105.

CLEARFIELD, M.W., & MIX, K.S. (1999). Number versus contour length in infants' discrimination of small visual sets. *Psychological Science, 10,* 408–411.

CLEMENT, J. (1982). Algebra word problem solutions: Thought processes underlying a common misconception. *Journal for Research in Mathematics Education, 13,* 16–30.

CLIFTON, R.K., MUIR, D.W., ASHMEAD, D.H., & CLARKSON, M.G. (1993). Is visually guided reaching in early infancy a myth? *Child Development, 64,* 1099–1110.

CLIFTON, R.K., PERRIS, E.E., & BULLINGER, A. (1991). Infants' perception of auditory space. *Developmental Psychology, 27,* 187–197.

COHEN, L.B. (1972). Attention-getting and attention-holding processes of infant visual preference. *Child Development, 43,* 869–879.

COLE, M., & SCRIBNER, S. (1974). *Culture and thought.* New York: Wiley.

COLOMBO, J. (1993). *Infant cognition: Predicting childhood intellectual function.* Newbury Park, CA: Sage.

COLOMBO, J. (1995). On the neural mechanisms underlying developmental and individual differences in visual fixation in infancy: Two hypotheses. *Developmental Review, 15,* 97–135.

COLOMBO, J., O'BRIEN, M., MITCHELL, D.W., ROBERTS, K., & HOROWITZ, F.D. (1987). A lower boundary for category formation in preverbal infants. *Journal of Child Language, 14,* 383–385.

COLOMBO, J., & RICHMAN, W.A. (2002). Infant timekeeping: Attention and temporal estimation in 4-month-olds. *Psychological Science, 13,* 475–479.

COONEY, J.B., SWANSON, H.L., & LADD, S.F. (1988). Acquisition of mental multiplication skill: Evidence for the transition between counting and retrieval strategies. *Cognition & Instruction, 5,* 323–345.

COOPER, R.P., & ASLIN, R.N. (1990). Preference for infant-directed speech in the first month after birth. *Child Development, 61,* 1584–1595.

CORMAN, H.H., & ESCALONA, S.K. (1969). Stages of sensorimotor development: A replication study. *Merrill-Palmer Quarterly, 15,* 351–361.

CORRIGAN, R. (1975). A scalogram analysis of the development of the use and comprehension of "because" in children. *Child Development, 46,* 195–201.

CORRIGAN, R. (1988). Children's identification of actors and patients in prototypical and nonprototypical sentence types. *Cognitive Development, 3,* 285–297.

CORRIGAN, R., & ODYA-WEIS, C. (1985). The comprehension of semantic relations by two-year-olds: An exploratory study. *Journal of Child Language, 12,* 47–59.

COURAGE, M.L., & ADAMS, R.J. (1990). Visual acuity assessment from birth to three years using the acuity card procedures: Cross-sectional and longitudinal samples. *Optometry and Vision Science, 67,* 713–718.

COURTIN, C. (2000). The impact of sign language on the cognitive development of deaf children: The case of theories of mind. *Journal of Deaf Studies and Deaf Education, 5,* 266–276.

COWAN, N., NUGENT, L.D., ELLIOTT, E.M., PONOMAREV, I., & SAULTS, J. (1999). The role of attention in the development of short-term memory: Age differences in the verbal span of apprehension. *Child Development, 70,* 1082–1097.

COYLE, T.R., & BJORKLUND, D.F. (1996). The development of strategic memory: A modified microgenetic assessment of utilization deficiencies. *Cognitive Development, 11,* 295–314.

COYLE, T.R., & BJORKLUND, D.F. (1997). Age differences in, and consequences of multiple and variable strategy use on a multitrial sort-recall task. *Developmental Psychology, 33,* 372–380.

CRISAFI, M.A., & BROWN, A.L. (1986). Analogical transfer in very young children: Combining two separately learned solutions to reach a goal. *Child Development, 57,* 953–968.

CRONE, D., & WHITEHURST, G. (1999). Age and schooling effects on emergent literacy and early reading skills. *Journal of Educational Psychology, 91,* 604–614.

CROWDER, E.M. (1996). Gestures at work in sense-making science talk. *Journal of the Learning Sciences, 5,* 173–208.

CROWLEY, K., CALLANAN, M.A., JIPSON, J.L., GALCO, J., TOPPING, K., & SHRAGER, J. (2001). Shared scientific thinking in everyday parent-child activity. *Science Education, 85,* 712–732.

CROWLEY, K., CALLANAN, M.A., TENENBAUM, H.R., & ALLEN, E. (2001). Parents explain more often to boys than to girls during shared scientific thinking. *Psychological Science, 12,* 258–261.

CULTICE, J.C., SOMERVILLE, S.C., & WELLMAN, H.M. (1983). Preschooler's memory monitoring: Feeling-of-knowing judgments. *Child Development, 54,* 1480–1486.

CURTISS, S. (1977). *A psycholinguistic study of a modern-day "wild child."* New York: Academic Press.

CUSTANCE, D., WHITEN, A., & FREDMAN, T. (1999). Social learning of an artificial fruit task in capuchin monkeys *(Cebus apella). Journal of Comparative Psychology, 113,* 13–23.

CUSTER, W.L. (1996). A comparison of young children's understanding of contradictory mental representations in pretense, memory, and belief. *Child Development, 67,* 678–688.

CUTTING, A.L., & DUNN, J. (1999). Theory of mind, emotion understanding, language and family background: Individual differences and interrelations. *Child Development, 70,* 853–865.

DAMASIO, A.R., & DAMASIO, H. (1992). Brain and language. *Scientific American, 117,* 89–95.

DAMASIO, H., & DAMASIO, A.R. (1989). *Lesion analysis in neuropsychology.* London: Oxford University Press.

DAMON, W., & PHELPS, E. (1988). Strategic uses of peer learning in children's education. In T. Berndt & G. Ladd (Eds.), *Children's peer relations.* New York: Wiley.

DANEMAN, M., & TARDIF, T. (1987). Working memory and reading skills reexamined. In M. Coltheart (Ed.), *Attention and performance XII: The psychology of reading.* Hillsdale, NJ: Erlbaum.

DANNEMILLER, J.L. (2000). Competition in early exogenous orienting between 7 and 21 weeks. *Journal of Experimental Child Psychology, 76,* 253–274.

DANNEMILLER, J.L., & STEPHENS, B.R. (1988). A critical test of infant pattern preference models. *Child Development, 59,* 210–216.

DARWIN, C. (1877). A biographical sketch of an infant. *Mind, 2,* 286–294.

DASEN, P.R. (1973). Piagetian research in central Australia. In G.E. Kearney, P.R. deLacy, & G.R. Davidson (Eds.), *The psychology of aboriginal Australians.* Sydney, Australia: Wiley.

DAVIDSON, J.E., & STERNBERG, R.J. (1984). The role of insight in intellectual giftedness. *Gifted Child Quarterly, 28,* 58–64.

DAVIS, D.L., WOOLLEY, J.D., & BRUELL, M.J. (2002). Young children's understanding of the roles of knowledge and thinking in pretense. *British Journal of Developmental Psychology, 20,* 25–45.

DAY, J.D., & CORDON, L.A. (1993). Static and dynamic measures of ability: An experimental comparison. *Journal of Educational Psychology, 85,* 75–82.

DAY, J.D., ENGELHARDT, J.L., MAXWELL, S.E., & BOLIG, E.E. (1997). Comparison of static and dynamic assessment procedures and their relation to independent performance. *Journal of Educational Psychology, 89,* 358–368.

DAYTON, G.O., & JONES, M.H. (1964). Analysis of characteristics of fixation reflex in infants by use of direct current electro-oculography. *Neurology, 14,* 1152–1156.

DAYTON, G.O., JONES, M.H., AIU, P., RAWSON, R.A., STEELE, B., & ROSE, M. (1964). Developmental study of coordinated eye movements in the human infant. I. Visual acuity in the newborn human: A study based on induced optokinetic nystagmus recorded by electro-oculography. *Archives of Ophthalmology, 71,* 865–870.

DEAN, A.L., CHABAUD, S., & BRIDGES, E. (1981). Classes, collections, and distinctive features: Alternative strategies for solving inclusion problems. *Cognitive Psychology, 13,* 84–112.

DECASPER, A.J., & FIFER, W.P. (1980). Of human bonding: Newborns prefer their mothers' voices. *Science, 208,* 1174–1176.

DECASPER, A.J., & SPENCE, M.J. (1986). Prenatal maternal speech influences newborns' perception of speech sounds. *Infant Behavior & Development, 9,* 133–150.

DE LISI, R., & GALLAGHER, A.M. (1991). Understanding of gender stability and constancy in Argentinian children. *Merrill-Palmer Quarterly, 37,* 483–502.

DELOACHE, J.S. (1987). Rapid change in the symbolic functioning of young children. *Science, 238,* 1556–1557.

DELOACHE, J.S. (1989). The development of representation in young children. In H.W. Reese (Ed.), *Advances in child development and behavior* (Vol. 22). New York: Academic Press.

DELOACHE, J.S. (1991). Symbolic functioning in very young children: Understanding of pictures and models. *Child Development, 62,* 736–752.

DELOACHE, J.S. (1995). Early understanding and use of symbols: The model model. *Current Directions in Psychological Science, 4,* 109–113.

DELOACHE, J.S. (2000). Dual representation and young children's use of scale models. *Child Development, 71,* 329–338.

DELOACHE, J.S. (2002). The symbol-mindedness of young children. In W.W. Hartup & R.A. Weinberg (Eds.), *Minnesota Symposium on Child Psychology: Vol. 32. Child psychology in retrospect and prospect.* Mahwah, NJ: Erlbaum.

DELOACHE, J.S., & BURNS, N.M. (1994). Early understanding of the representational function of pictures. *Cognition, 52,* 83–110.

DELOACHE, J.S., CASSIDY, D.J., & BROWN, A.L. (1985). Precursors of mnemonic strategies in very young children's memory. *Child Development, 56,* 125–137.

DELOACHE, J.S., MILLER, K.F., & PIERROUTSAKOS, S.L. (1998). Reasoning and problem solving. In D. Kuhn & R.S. Siegler, *Handbook of child psychology: Vol. 2. Cognition, perception & language.* (5th ed.). New York: Wiley.

DELOACHE, J.S., MILLER, K.F., & ROSENGREN, K.S. (1997). The credible shrinking room: Very young children's performance with symbolic and nonsymbolic relations. *Psychological Science, 8,* 308–313.

DELOACHE, J.S., RISSMAN, M.D., & COHEN, L.B. (1978). An investigation of the attention-getting process in infants. *Infant Behavior & Development, 1,* 11–25.

DEMARIE-DREBLOW, D., & MILLER, P.H. (1988). The development of children's strategies for selective attention: Evidence for a transitional period. *Child Development, 59,* 1504–1513.

DEMETRIOU, A., CHRISTOU, C., SPANOUDIS, G., & PLATSIDOU, M. (2002). The development of mental processing: Efficiency, working memory, and thinking. *Monographs of the Society for Research in Child Development, 67*(1, Serial No. 268).

DEMETRIOU, A., EFKLIDES, A., & PLATSIDOU, M. (1993). The architecture and dynamics of developing mind. *Monographs of the Society for Research in Child Development, 58*(5–6, Serial No. 234).

DEMETRIOU, A., & RAFTOPOULOS, A. (1999). Modeling the developmental mind: From structure to change. *Developmental Review, 19,* 319–368.

DEMPSTER, F.N. (1981). Memory span: Sources of individual and developmental differences. *Psychological Bulletin, 89,* 63–100.

DEMPSTER, F.N. (1992). The rise and fall of the inhibitory mechanism: Toward a unified theory of cognitive development and aging. *Developmental Review, 12,* 45–75.

DEMPSTER, F.N. (1993). Resistance to interference: Developmental changes in a basic processing mechanism. In R. Pasnak & M.L. Howe (Eds.), *Emerging themes in cognitive development* (Vol. 1). New York: Springer.

DENNIS, S. (1992). Stage and structure in the development of children's spatial representations. In R. Case (Ed.), *The mind's staircase: Exploring the conceptual underpinnings of children's thought and knowledge.* Hillsdale, NJ: Erlbaum.

DEVALOIS, R.L., & DEVALOIS, K.K. (1975). Neural coding of color. In E.C. Carterette & M.P. Friedman (Eds.), *Handbook of perception,* (Vol. 5). New York: Academic Press.

DE VILLIERS, J. (1995). Empty categories and complex sentences: The case of wh-questions. In P. Fletcher & B. MacWhinney (Eds.), *The handbook of child language.* Cambridge, MA: Blackwell.

DE VILLIERS, J.G., & DE VILLIERS, P.A. (2000). Linguistic determinism and the understanding of false beliefs. In P. Mitchell & K.J. Riggs (Eds.), *Children's reasoning and the mind.* Hove, UK: Psychology Press.

DEVRIES, R. (1969). Constancy of generic identity in the years three to six. *Monographs of the Society for Research in Child Development, 34*(3, Whole No. 127).

DIAMOND, A. (1985). Development of the ability to use recall to guide action as indicated by infants' performance on AB. *Child Development, 56,* 868–883.

DIAMOND, A. (1990). Rate of maturation of the hippocampus and the developmental progression of children's performance on the delayed non-matching to sample and visual paired comparison tasks. *Annals of the New York Academy of Sciences, 608,* 394–433.

DIAMOND, A. (1991). Neuropsychological insights into the meaning of object concept development. In S. Carey & R. Gelman (Eds.), *The epigenesis of mind: Essays on biology and cognition.* Hillsdale, NJ: Erlbaum.

DIAMOND, A. (2000). Close interrelation of motor development and cognitive development and of the cerebellum and prefrontal cortex. *Child Development, 71,* 44–56.

DIMANT, R.J., & BEARISON, D.J. (1991). Development of formal reasoning during successive peer interactions. *Developmental Psychology, 27,* 277–284.

DIXON, J.A., & MOORE, C.F. (1996). The developmental role of intuitive principles in choosing mathematical strategies. *Developmental Psychology, 32,* 241–253.

DOBSON, V. (1983). Clinical applications of preferential looking measures of visual acuity. *Behavioral Brain Research, 10,* 25–38.

DODWELL, P.E. (1960). Children's understanding of number and related concepts. *Canadian Journal of Psychology, 14,* 191–205.

DOLGIN, K.G., & BEHREND, D.A. (1984). Children's knowledge about animates and inanimates. *Child Development, 55,* 1646–1650.

DOYLE, A.B. (1983). Friends, acquaintances, and strangers: The influence of familiarity and ethnolinguistic background on social interaction. In K. Rubin & H. Ross (Eds.), *Peer relationships and social skills in childhood.* New York: Springer-Verlag.

DOYLE, A.B., & ABOUD, F.E. (1995). A longitudinal study of white children's racial prejudice as a social-cognitive development. *Merrill-Palmer Quarterly, 41,* 209–228.

DOYLE, A.B., BEAUDET, J., & ABOUD, F.E. (1988). Developmental patterns in the flexibility of children's ethnic attitudes. *Journal of Cross-Cultural Psychology, 19,* 3–18.

DROMI, E. (1986). The one-word period as a stage in language development: Quantitative and qualitative accounts. In I. Levin (Ed.), *Stage and structure: Reopening the debate.* Norwood, NJ: Ablex.

DRUMMEY, A.B., & NEWCOMBE, N. (1995). Remembering versus knowing the past: Children's explicit and implicit memories for pictures. *Journal of Experimental Child Psychology, 59,* 549–565.

DUFRESNE, A. & KOBASIGAWA, A. (1989). Children's spontaneous allocation of study time: Differential and sufficient aspects. *Journal of Experimental Child Psychology, 47,* 274–296.

DUMMER, G.M., HAUBENSTRICKER, J.L., & STEWART, D.A. (1996). Motor skill performances of children who are deaf. *Adapted Physical Activity Quarterly, 13,* 400–414.

DUNBAR, K., & BLANCHETTE, I. (2001). The in vivo/in vitro approach to cognition: The case of analogy. *Trends in Cognitive Sciences, 5,* 334–339.

DUNBAR, K., & KLAHR, D. (1988). Developmental differences in scientific discovery strategies. In D. Klahr & K. Kotovsky (Eds.), *Complex information processing: The impact of Herbert A. Simon.* Proceedings of the 21st Carnegie-Mellon Symposium on Cognition. Hillsdale, NJ: Erlbaum.

DUNN, J. (1988). *The beginnings of social understanding.* Oxford, UK: Blackwell.

DUNN, J., BROWN, J., SLOMKOWSKI, C., TESLA, C., & YOUNGBLADE, L. (1991). Young children's understanding of other people's feelings and beliefs: Individual differences and their antecedents. *Child Development, 62,* 1352–1366.

DURKIN, D. (1966). *Children who read early.* New York: Teachers College Press.

DURKIN, D. (1974/75). A six-year study of children who learned to read in school at the age of four. *Reading Research Quarterly, 10,* 9–61.

EACOTT, M.J., & CRAWLEY, R.A. (1998). The offset of childhood amnesia: Memory for events that occurred before age 3. *Journal of Experimental Psychology: General, 127,* 1–15.

EACOTT, M.J., & CRAWLEY, R.A. (1999). Childhood amnesia: On answering questions about very early life events. *Memory, 7,* 279–292.

EATON, W.O., & RITCHOT, K.F.M. (1995). Physical maturation and information processing speed in middle childhood. *Developmental Psychology, 31,* 967–972.

ECHOLS, C. (1993). *Attentional predispositions and linguistic sensitivity in the acquisition of object words.* Paper presented at the biennial meeting of the Society for Research in Child Development, New Orleans, LA.

EDELMAN, G. (1987). *Neural Darwinism: The theory of neuronal group selection.* New York: Basic Books.

EDER, R.A. (1989). The emergent personologist: The structure and content of 3½, 5½, and 7½-year-olds' concepts of themselves and other persons. *Child Development, 60,* 1218–1228.

EDER, R.A. (1990). Uncovering young children's psychological selves: Individual and developmental differences. *Child Development, 611,* 849–863.

EFKLIDES, A., DEMETRIOU, A., & METALLIDOU, Y. (1994). The structure and development of propositional reasoning ability: Cognitive and metacognitive aspects. In A. Demetriou & A. Efklides (Eds.), *Intelligence, mind, and reasoning: Structure and development.* Amsterdam: North-Holland.

EHRI, L.C., NUNES, S.R., WILLOWS, D.M., SCHUSTER, B.V., YAGHOUB ZADEH, Z., & SHANAHAN, T. (2001). Phonemic awareness instruction helps children learn to read: Evidence from the National Reading Panel's meta-analysis. *Reading Research Quarterly, 36,* 250–287.

EIMAS, P.D., & QUINN, P.C. (1994). Studies on the formation of perceptually based basic-level categories in young infants. *Child Development, 65,* 903–917.

EIMAS, P.D., SIQUELAND, E.R., JUSCZYK, P.W., & VIGORITO, J. (1971). Speech perception in infants. *Science, 171,* 303–306.

ELBERT, T., HEIM, S., & ROCKSTROH, B. (2001). Neural plasticity and development. In C.A. Nelson & M. Luciana (Eds.), *Handbook of developmental cognitive neuroscience.* Cambridge, MA: MIT Press.

ELBERT, T., PANTEV, C., WIENBRUCH, C., ROCKSTROH, B., & TAUB, E. (1995). Increased use of the left hand in string players associated with increased cortical repesentations of the fingers. *Science, 220,* 21–23.

ELKIND, D. (1961a). Children's discovery of the conservation of mass, weight, and volume: Piaget replications Study II. *Journal of Genetic Psychology, 98,* 219–227.

ELKIND, D. (1961b). The development of quantitative thinking: A systematic replication of Piaget's studies. *Journal of Genetic Psychology, 98,* 37–46.

ELLIOTT-FAUST, D.J. (1984). The "delusion of comprehension" phenomenon in young children: An instructional approach to *promoting listening comprehension monitoring capabilities in grade three children.* Unpublished doctoral dissertation. London, Ontario: University of Western Ontario, Department of Psychology.

ELLIS, S., DOWDY, B., GRAHAM, P., & JONES, R. (1992, April). *Parental support of planning skills in the context of homework and family demands.* Paper presented at the annual meeting of the American Educational Research Association, San Francisco, CA.

ELLIS, S., KLAHR, D., & SIEGLER, R.S. (1993). *Effects of feedback and collaboration on changes in children's use of mathematical rules.* Paper presented at the Biennial Meeting of the Society for Research in Child Development.

ELLIS, S., & ROGOFF, B. (1982). The strategies and efficacy of child versus adult teachers. *Child Development, 53,* 730–735.

ELLIS, S., & ROGOFF, B. (1986). Problem solving in children's management of instruction. In C. Cooper (Ed.), *Process and outcome in peer relationships.* Orlando, FL: Academic Press.

ELLIS, S., & SCHNEIDERS, B. (1989). *Collaboration on children's instruction: A Navajo versus Anglo comparison.* Paper presented at the biennial meeting of the Society for Research in Child Development, Kansas City, MO.

ELLIS, S., & SIEGLER, R.S. (1997). Planning and strategy choice, or why don't children plan when they should? In S.L. Friedman & E.K. Scholnick (Eds.), *Why, how, and when do we plan: The developmental psychology of planning.* Hillsdale, NJ: Erlbaum.

ELLSWORTH, C.P., MUIR, D., & HAINS, S.M.J. (1993). Social competence and person-object differentiation: An analysis of the still-face effect. *Developmental Psychology, 29,* 63–73.

ELMAN, J.L. (1993). Learning and development in neural networks: The importance of starting small. *Cognition, 48,* 71–99.

ELY, R., & GLEASON, J.B. (1995). Socialization across contexts. In P. Fletcher & B. MacWhinney (Eds.) *The handbook of child language.* Cambridge, MA: Blackwell.

EMLER, N., & VALIANT, G.L. (1982). Social interaction and cognitive conflict in the development of spatial coordination skills. *British Journal of Psychology, 73,* 295–303.

ESBENSEN, B.M., TAYLOR, M., & STOESS, C. (1997). Children's behavioral understanding of knowledge acquisition. *Cognitive Development, 12,* 53–84.

ESKRITT, M., & LEE, K. (2002). "Remember where you last saw that card": Children's production of external symbols as a memory aid. *Developmental Psychology, 38,* 254–266.

ETCOFF, N.L., & MAGEE, J.J. (1992). Categorical perception of facial expressions. *Cognition, 44,* 227–240.

EVANS, J.L. (2002). Variability in comprehension strategy use in children with SLI: A dynamical systems account. *International Journal of Language and Communication Disorders, 37,* 95–116.

FABRICIUS, W.V. (1988). The development of forward search planning in preschoolers. *Child Development, 59,* 1473–1488.

FABRICIUS, W.V., & HAGEN, J.W. (1984). Use of causal attributions about recall performance to assess metamemory and predict strategic memory behavior in young children. *Developmental Psychology, 20,* 975–987.

FABRICIUS, W.V., & WELLMAN, H.M. (1993). Two roads diverged: Young children's ability to judge distance. *Child Development, 64,* 399–414.

FAGAN, J.F., & SINGER, L.T. (1983). Infant recognition memory as a measure of intelligence. In L.P. Lipsitt (Ed.), *Advances in infancy research* (Vol. 2). Norwood, NJ: Ablex.

FANTZ, R.L., FAGAN, J.F., & MIRANDA, S.B. (1975). Early perceptual development as shown by visual discrimination, selectivity, and memory with varying stimulus and population parameters. In L.B. Cohen & P. Salapatek (Eds.), *Infant perception: From sensation to cognition.* New York: Academic Press.

FARAH, M.J., MONHEIT, M.A., & WALLACE, M.A. (1991). Unconscious perception of "extinguished" visual stimuli: Reassessing the evidence. *Neuropsychologia, 29,* 949–958.

FARRAR, M.J., & GOODMAN, G.S. (1992). Developmental changes in event memory. *Child Development, 63,* 173–187.

FAY, A.L., & KLAHR, D. (1996). Knowing about guessing and guessing about knowing: Preschoolers' understanding of indeterminacy. *Child Development, 67,* 689–716.

FEIGENSON, L., CAREY, S., & HAUSER, M. (2002). The representations underlying infants' choice of more: Object files versus analog magnitudes. *Psychological Science, 13,* 150–156.

FEIGENSON, L., CAREY, S., & SPELKE, E.S. (2002). Infants' discrimination of number vs. continuous extent. *Cognitive Psychology, 44,* 33–66.

FELDMAN, D.H. (1995). Learning and development in nonuniversal theory. *Human Development, 38,* 315–321.

FELDMAN, N.S., & RUBLE, D.N. (1981). The development of person perception: Cognitive and social factors. In S.S. Brehm, S.M. Kassin & F.X. Gibbons (Eds.), *Developmental social psychology: Theory and research.* New York: Oxford University Press.

FERNALD, A. (1992). Meaningful melodies in mothers' speech. In H. Papousek, U. Jurgens, & M. Papousek (Eds.), *Origins and development of nonverbal vocal communication: Evolutionary, comparative, and methodological aspects.* Cambridge, UK: Cambridge University Press.

FERNALD, A., TAESCHNER, T., DUNN, J., PAPOUSEK, M., BOYSSON-BARDIES, B.D., & FUKUI, I. (1989). A cross-language study of prosodic modifications in mothers' and fathers' speech to preverbal infants. *Journal of Child Language, 16,* 477–501.

FERRARA, R.A., BROWN, A.L., & CAMPIONE, J.C. (1986). Children's learning and transfer of inductive reasoning rules: Studies of proximal development. *Child Development, 57,* 1087–1099.

FERRETTI, R.P., & BUTTERFIELD, E.C. (1986). Are children's rule-assessment classifications invariant across instances of problem types? *Child Development, 57,* 1419–1428.

FERRETTI, R.P., BUTTERFIELD, E.C., CAHN, A., & KERKMAN, D. (1985). The classification of children's knowledge: Development on the balance-scale and inclined-plane tasks. *Journal of Experimental Child Psychology, 39,* 131–160.

FIELD, D. (1987). A review of preschool conservation training: An analysis of analyses. *Developmental Review, 7,* 210–251.

FIGUERAS-COSTA, B., & HARRIS, P. (2001). Theory of mind development in deaf children: A nonverbal test of false-belief understanding. *Journal of Deaf Studies and Deaf Education, 6,* 92–102.

FIRTH, I. (1972). *Components of reading disability.* Unpublished doctoral dissertation, University of New South Wales, Kensington, N. S. W., Australia.

FISCHER, K.W. (1980). A theory of cognitive development: The control and construction of hierarchies of skills. *Psychological Review, 87,* 477–531.

FISCHER, K.W., & BIDELL, T.R. (1991). Constraining nativist inferences about cognitive capacities. In S. Carey & R. Gelman (Eds.), *The epigenesis of mind: Essays on biology and cognition*. Hillsdale, NJ: Erlbaum.

FISCHER, K.W., & BIDELL, T.R. (1998). Dynamic development of psychological structures in action and thought. In R.M. Lerner (Ed.), *Handbook of child psychology: Vol. 1. Theoretical models of human development* (5th ed.). New York: Wiley.

FISCHER, K.W., & FARRAR, M.J. (1988). Generalizations about generalization: How a theory of skill development explains both generality and specificity. In A. Demetriou (Ed.), *The neo-Piagetian theories of cognitive development: Toward an integration*. Amsterdam: North-Holland (Elsevier).

FISCHER, K.W., & GRANOTT, N. (1995). Beyond one-dimensional change: Parallel, concurrent, socially distributed processes in learning and development. *Human Development, 38*, 302–314.

FISHER, C., HALL, D.G., RAKOWITZ, S., & GLEITMAN, L.R. (1994). When it is better to receive than to give: Syntactic and conceptual constraints on vocabulary growth. *Lingua, 92*, 333–375.

FITZGERALD, J. (1987). Research on revision in writing. *Review of Educational Research, 57*, 481–506.

FIVUSH, R., & FROMHOFF, F.A. (1988). Style and structure in mother-child conversations about the past. *Discourse Processes, 11*, 337–355.

FIVUSH, R., & HAMMOND, N.R. (1990). Autobiographical memory across the preschool years: Toward reconceptualizing childhood amnesia. In R. Fivush & J.A. Hudson (Eds.), *Knowing and remembering in young children*. Cambridge, UK: Cambridge University Press.

FLAVELL, J.H. (1970). Developmental studies of mediated memory. In H.W. Reese & L.P. Lipsitt (Eds.), *Advances in child development and behavior* (Vol. 5). New York: Academic Press.

FLAVELL, J.H. (1971). Stage-related properties of cognitive development. *Cognitive Psychology, 2*, 421–453.

FLAVELL, J.H. (1982). On cognitive development. *Child Development, 53*, 1–10.

FLAVELL, J.H. (1984). Discussion. In R.J. Sternberg (Ed.), *Mechanisms of cognitive development*. New York: Freeman.

FLAVELL, J.H., BEACH, D.R., & CHINSKY, J.M. (1966). Spontaneous verbal rehearsal in a memory task as a function of age. *Child Development, 37*, 283–299.

FLAVELL, J.H., FLAVELL, E.R., & GREEN, F.L. (1983). Development of the appearance-reality distinction. *Cognitive Psychology, 15*, 95–120.

FLAVELL, J.H., FRIEDRICHS, A.G., & HOYT, J.D. (1970). Developmental changes in memorization processes. *Cognitive Psychology, 1*, 324–340.

FLAVELL, J.H., GREEN, F.L., & FLAVELL, E.R. (1993). Children's understanding of the stream of consciousness. *Child Development, 64*, 387–398.

FLAVELL, J.H., GREEN, F.L., & FLAVELL, E.R. (1995). Young children's knowledge about thinking. *Monographs of the Society for Research in Child Development, 60*(1, Serial No. 243).

FLAVELL, J.H., GREEN, F.L., & FLAVELL, E.R. (2000). Development of children's awareness of their own thoughts. *Journal of Cognition & Development, 1*, 97–112.

FLAVELL, J.H., & MILLER, P.H. (1998). Social cognition. In D. Kuhn & R.S. Siegler (Eds.), *Handbook of child psychology: Vol. 2. Cognition, perception & language* (5th ed.). New York: Wiley.

FLAVELL, J.H., ZHANG, X.-D., ZOU, H., DONG, Q., & QI, S. (1983). A comparison between the development of the appearance-reality distinction in the People's Republic of China and the United States. *Cognitive Psychology, 15*, 459–466.

FLEMING, V.M., & ALEXANDER, J.M. (2001). The benefits of peer collaboration: A replication with a delayed posttest. *Contemporary Educational Psychology, 26*, 588–601.

FODOR, J. (1992). A theory of the child's theory of mind. *Cognition, 44*, 283–296.

FOLEY, M.A., HARRIS, J., & HERMAN, S. (1994). Developmental comparisons of the ability to discriminate between memories for symbolic play enactments. *Developmental Psychology, 30*, 206–217.

FOORMAN, B.R., FRANCIS, D.J., FLETCHER, J.M., SCHATSCHNEIDER, C., & MEHTA, P. (1998). The role of instruction in learning to read: Preventing reading failure in at-risk children. *Journal of Educational Psychology, 90*, 37–55.

FRAISSE, P. (1982). The adaptation of the child to time. In W.J. Friedman (Ed.), *The developmental psychology of time*. New York: Academic Press.

FREUD, S. (1905/1953). Three essays on the theory of sexuality. In J. Strachey (Ed.), *The standard edition of the complete psychological works of Sigmund Freud* (Vol. 7). London: Hogarth.

FRIEDMAN, S.L., SCHOLNICK, E.K., & COCKING. R.R. (1987). Reflections on reflections: What planning is and how it develops. In S.L. Friedman, E.K. Scholnick & R.R. Cocking (Eds.), *Blueprints for thinking: The role of planning in cognitive development*. New York: Cambridge University Press.

FRIEDMAN, W.J. (1991). The development of children's memory for the time of past events. *Child Development, 62*, 139–155.

FRIEDMAN, W.J. (2000). The development of children's knowledge of the times of future events. *Child Development, 71*, 913–932.

FRIEDMAN, W.J. (2002). Arrows of time in infancy: The representation of temporal-causal invariances. *Cognitive Psychology, 44*, 252–296.

FRIEDMAN, W.J., GARDNER, A.G., & ZUBIN, N.R.E. (1995). Children's comparisons of the recency of two events from the past year. *Child Development, 66*, 970–983.

FRITH, U. (1989). *Autism: Explaining the enigma*. Oxford, UK: Blackwell.

FRYE, D. (2000). Theory of mind, domain specificity, and reasoning. In P. Mitchell & K.J. Riggs (Eds.), *Children's reasoning and the mind*. Hove, UK: Psychology Press.

FRYE, D., BRAISBY, N., LOWE, J., MAROUDAS, C., & NICHOLLS, J. (1989). Young children's understanding of counting and cardinality. *Child Development, 60*, 1158–1171.

FRYE, D., ZELAZO, P.D., BROOKS, P.J., & SAMUELS, M.C. (1996). Inference and action in early causal reasoning. *Developmental Psychology, 32*, 120–131.

FUSON, K.C., & KWON, Y. (1992). Korean children's understanding of multidigit addition and subtraction. *Child Development, 63*, 491–506.

GALOTTI, K.M., & KOMATSU, L.K. (1989). Correlates of syllogistic reasoning skills in middle childhood and early adolescence. *Journal of Youth and Adolescence, 18*, 85–96.

GALOTTI, K.M., KOMATSU, L.K., & VOELZ, S. (1997). Children's differential performance on deductive and inductive syllogisms. *Developmental Psychology, 33,* 70–78.

GARDNER, H. (1983). *Frames of mind: The theory of multiple intelligences.* New York: Basic Books.

GARDNER, H. (1993). *Multiple intelligences: The theory in practice.* New York: Basic Books.

GARDNER, H., KORNHABER, M.L., & WAKE, W.K. (1996). *Intelligence: Multiple perspectives.* Fort Worth, TX: Harcourt Brace College Publishers.

GARDNER, W., & ROGOFF, B. (1990). Children's deliberateness of planning according to task circumstances. *Developmental Psychology, 26,* 480–487.

GARNER, R., & REIS, R. (1981). Monitoring and resolving comprehension obstacles: An investigation of spontaneous text lookbacks among upper-grade good and poor comprehenders. *Reading Research Quarterly, 16,* 569–582.

GASKINS, S. (1999). Children's daily lives in a Mayan village: A case study of culturally constructed roles and activities. In A. Göncü (Ed.), *Children's engagement in the world: Sociocultural perspectives.* New York: Cambridge University Press.

GAUVAIN, M. (2001). *The social context of cognitive development.* New York: Guilford Press.

GAUVAIN, M., & ROGOFF, B. (1989). Collaborative problem solving and children's planning skills. *Developmental Psychology, 25,* 139–151.

GEARY, D.C. (1990). A componential analysis of an early learning deficit in mathematics. *Journal of Experimental Child Psychology, 49,* 363–383.

GEARY, D.C. (1994). *Children's mathematical development: Research and practical implications.* Washington, DC: American Psychological Association.

GEARY, D.C. (1996). The problem-size effect in mental addition: Developmental and cross-national trends. *Mathematical Cognition, 2,* 63–93.

GEARY, D.C., & BJORKLUND, D.F. (2000). Evolutionary developmental psychology. *Child Development, 71,* 57–65.

GEARY, D.C., BOW-THOMAS, C.C., FAN, L., & SIEGLER, R.S. (1993). Even before formal instruction, Chinese children outperform American children in mental addition. *Cognitive Development 8,* 517–529.

GEARY, D.C., BOW-THOMAS, C.C., & YAO, Y. (1992). Counting knowledge and skill in cognitive addition: A comparison of normal and mathematically disabled children. *Journal of Experimental Child Psychology, 54,* 372–391.

GEARY, D.C., & BROWN, S.C. (1991). Cognitive addition: Strategy choice and speed-of-processing differences in gifted, normal, and mathematically disabled children. *Developmental Psychology, 27,* 398–406.

GEARY, D.C., FAN, L., & BOW-THOMAS, C.C. (1992). Numerical cognition: Loci of ability differences comparing children from China and the United States. *Psychological Science, 3,* 180–185.

GEARY, D.C., HAMSON, C.O., & HOARD, M.K. (2000). Numerical and arithmetical cognition: A longitudinal study of process and concept deficits in children with learning disability. *Journal of Experimental Child Psychology, 77,* 236–263.

GELLATLY, A.R.H. (1987). The acquisition of a concept of logical necessity. *Human Development, 30,* 32–47.

GELMAN, R. (1982). Accessing one-to-one correspondence: Still another paper about conservation. *British Journal of Psychology, 73,* 209–220.

GELMAN, R. (1990). First principles organize attention to and learning about relevant data: Number and the animate-inanimate distinction. *Cognitive Science, 14,* 79–106.

GELMAN, R., & GALLISTEL, C.R. (1978). *The child's understanding of number.* Cambridge, MA: Harvard University Press.

GELMAN, R., & WILLIAMS, E. (1998). Constraints on thinking and learning. In D. Kuhn & R.S. Siegler, *Handbook of child psychology: Vol. 2. Cognition, perception & language.* (5th ed.). New York: Wiley.

GELMAN, S.A. (2003). *The essential child: Origins of essentialism in everyday thought.* New York: Oxford University Press.

GELMAN, S.A., COLEY, J.D., ROSENGREN, K.S., HARTMAN, E., & PAPPAS, A. (1998). Beyond labeling: The role of maternal input in the acquisition of richly structured categories. *Monographs of the Society for Research in Child Development, 63*(1, Serial No. 253).

GELMAN, S.A., & GOTTFRIED, G. (1996). Children's causal explanations of animate and inanimate motion. *Child Development, 67,* 1970–1987.

GELMAN, S.A., & OPFER, J.E. (2002). Development of the animate-inanimate distinction. In U. Goswami (Ed.), *Blackwell handbook of childhood cognitive development.* Malden, MA: Blackwell.

GELMAN, S.A., & TAYLOR, M. (1984). How two-year-old children interpret proper and common names for unfamiliar objects. *Child Development, 55,* 1535–1540.

GELMAN, S.A., & WELLMAN, H.M. (1991). Insides and essences: Early understandings of the non-obvious. *Cognition, 38,* 213–244.

GENTNER, D. (1982). Why nouns are learned before verbs: Linguistic relativity versus natural partitioning. In S.A. Kuczaj (Ed.), *Language development, Vol. 2: Language, thought and culture.* Hillsdale, NJ: Erlbaum.

GENTNER, D. (1988). Metaphor as structure mapping: The relational shift. *Child Development, 59,* 47–59.

GENTNER, D. (1989). The mechanisms of analogical transfer. In S. Vosniadou & A. Ortony (Eds.), *Similarity and analogical reasoning.* London: Cambridge University Press.

GENTNER, D., RATTERMAN, M.J., MARKMAN, A., & KOTOVSKY, L. (1995). Two forces in the development of relational similarity. In T.J. Simon & G.S. Halford (Eds.), *Developing cognitive competence: New approaches to process modeling.* Hillsdale, NJ: Erlbaum.

GENTNER, D., & STEVENS, A. (Eds.). (1983). *Mental models.* Hillsdale, NJ: Erlbaum.

GHOLSON, B., EMYARD, L.A., MORGAN, D., & KAMHI, A.G. (1987). Problem solving, recall, and isomorphic transfer among third grade and sixth grade children. *Journal of Experimental Child Psychology, 43,* 227–243.

GIBSON, E.J. (1969). *Principles of perceptual learning and development.* Englewood Cliffs, NJ: Prentice Hall.

GIBSON, E.J., & PICK, A.D. (2000). *An ecological approach to perceptual learning and development.* Oxford, UK: Oxford University Press.

GIBSON, E.J., & WALK, R.D. (1960). The "visual cliff." *Scientific American, 202,* 64–71.

GIBSON, J.J. (1966). *The senses considered as perceptual systems.* Boston: Houghton Mifflin.

GIBSON, J.J. (1979). *The ecological approach to visual perception.* Boston: Houghton Mifflin.

GINSBURG, A. (1983). *Contrast perception in the human infant.* Unpublished manuscript.

GINSBURG, G.P., & KILBOURNE, B.K. (1988). Emergence of vocal alternation in mother-infant interchanges. *Journal of Child Language, 15,* 221–235.

GLACHAN, M., & LIGHT, P. (1982). Peer interaction and learning: Can two wrongs make a right? In P. Light (Ed.), *Social cognition: Studies of the development of understanding.* Chicago: University of Chicago Press.

GLEASON, T.R., SEBANC, A.M., & HARTUP, W.W. (2000). Imaginary companions of preschool children. *Developmental Psychology, 36,* 419–428.

GOBBO, C., MEGA, C., & PIPE, M.E. (2002). Does the nature of the experience influence suggestibility? A study of children's event memory. *Journal of Experimental Child Psychology, 81,* 502–530.

GOLBECK, S.L. (1998). Peer collaboration and children's representation of the horizontal surface of liquid. *Journal of Applied Developmental Psychology, 19,* 571–592.

GOLDFIELD, B., & REZNICK, J.S. (1990). Early lexical acquisition: Rate, content, and the vocabulary spurt. *Journal of Child Language, 17,* 171–183.

GOLDIN-MEADOW, S. (2001). Giving the mind a hand: The role of gesture in cognitive change. In J.L. McClelland & R.S. Siegler (Eds.), *Mechanisms of cognitive development: Behavioral and neural perspectives.* Mahwah, NJ: Erlbaum.

GOLDIN-MEADOW, S. (2003). *The resilience of language: What gesture creation in deaf children can tell us about language learning in general.* New York: Psychology Press.

GOLDIN-MEADOW, S., & ALIBALI, M.W. (2002). Looking at the hands through time: A microgenetic perspective on learning and instruction. In N. Granott & J. Parziale (Eds.), *Microdevelopment: Transition processes in development and learning.* Cambridge, UK: Cambridge University Press.

GOLDIN-MEADOW, S., ALIBALI, M.W., & CHURCH, R.B. (1993). Transitions in concept acquisition: Using the hand to read the mind. *Psychological Review, 100,* 279–297.

GOLDIN-MEADOW, S., & FELDMAN, H. (1977). The development of language-like communication without a language model. *Science, 197,* 401–403.

GOLDIN-MEADOW, S., & MORFORD, M. (1985). Gesture in early child language: Studies of deaf and hearing children. *Merrill-Palmer Quarterly, 31,* 145–176.

GOLDIN-MEADOW, S., & MYLANDER, C. (1983). Gestural communication in deaf children: Noneffect of parental input on language development. *Science, 221,* 372–374.

GOLDIN-MEADOW, S., & MYLANDER, C. (1984). Gestural communication in deaf children: The effects and noneffects of parental input on early language development. *Monographs of the Society for Research in Child Development, 49*(3–4, Serial No. 207).

GOLDIN-MEADOW, S., & MYLANDER, C. (1998). Spontaneous sign systems created by deaf children in two cultures. *Nature, 391,* 279–281.

GOLDIN-MEADOW, S., MYLANDER, C., & BUTCHER, C. (1995). The resilience of combinatorial stucture at the word level: Morphology in self-styled gesture systems. *Cognition, 56,* 195–262.

GOLDIN–MEADOW, S., & SINGER, M.A. (2003). From children's hands to adults' ears: Gesture's role in the learning process. *Developmental Psychology, 39,* 509–520.

GOLDMAN, S.R., PELLEGRINO, J.W., & MERTZ, D.L. (1988). Extended practice of basic addition facts: Strategy changes in learning disabled students. *Cognition & Instruction, 5,* 223–265.

GOLDMAN-RAKIC, P.S. (1987). Development of cortical circuitry and cognitive function. *Child Development, 58,* 601–622.

GOLEMAN, D. (1993, April 6). Studying the secrets of childhood memory. *The New York Times,* pp. C1, C11.

GOLINKOFF, R.M., HIRSH-PASEK, K., LAVALLEE, A., & BADUINI, C. (1985). *What's in a word? The young child's predisposition to use lexical contrast.* Paper presented at the Boston University Conference on Child Language, Boston, MA.

GOLINKOFF, R.M., HIRSH-PASEK, K., MERVIS, C.B., FRAWLEY, W.B., & PARILLO, M. (1995). Lexical principles can be extended to the acquisition of verbs. In M. Tomasello & W.E. Merriman (Eds.), *Beyond names for things: Young children's acquisition of verbs.* Hillsdale, NJ: Erlbaum.

GOLINKOFF, R.M., SHUFF-BAILEY, M., OLGUIN, R., & RUAN, W. (1995). Young children extend novel words at the basic level: Evidence for the principle of categorical scope. *Developmental Psychology, 31,* 494–507.

GOMEZ, R.L., & GERKEN, L. (1999). Artificial grammar learning by 1-year-olds leads to specific and abstract knowledge. *Cognition, 70,* 109–135.

GÖNCÜ, A. (1993). Development of intersubjectivity in the dyadic play of preschoolers. *Early Childhood Research Quarterly, 8,* 99–116.

GÖNCÜ, A., & ROGOFF, B. (1998). Children's categorization with varying adult support. *American Educational Research Journal, 35,* 333–349.

GOODALE, M.A., & MILNER, A.D. (1992). Separate visual pathways for perception and action. *Trends in Neuroscience, 15,* 20–25.

GOODMAN, G.S., & CLARKE-STEWART, A. (1991). Suggestibility in children's testimony: Implications for child sexual abuse investigations. In J.L. Doris (Ed.), *The suggestibility of children's recollections.* Washington, DC: American Psychological Association.

GOODMAN, G.S., HIRSCHMAN, J.E., HEPPS, D., & RUDY, L. (1991). Children's memory for stressful events. *Merrill-Palmer Quarterly, 37,* 109–158.

GOODNOW, J.J. (1962). A test of milieu differences with some of Piaget's tasks. *Psychological Monographs, 76*(Whole No. 555).

GOPNIK, A., & ASTINGTON, J.W. (1988). Children's understanding of representational change and its relation to the understanding of false belief and the appearance-reality distinction. *Child Development, 59,* 26–37.

GOPNIK, A., & GLYMOUR, C. (2002). Causal maps and Bayes nets: A cognitive and computational account of theory-formation. In P. Carruthers, S. Stich & M. Siegal (Eds.), *The cognitive basis of science.* Cambridge, UK: Cambridge University Press.

GOPNIK, A., & GRAF, P. (1988). Knowing how you know: Young children's ability to identify and remember the sources of their beliefs. *Child Development, 59,* 1366–1371.

GOPNIK, A., & MELTZOFF, A.N. (1994). Minds, bodies, and persons. In S. Parker, M. Boccia & R. Mitchell (Eds.), *Self-awareness in animals and humans.* New York: Cambridge University Press.

GOPNIK, A., & SLAUGHTER, V. (1991). Young children's understanding of changes in their mental states. *Child Development, 62,* 98–110.

GOPNIK, A., SOBEL, D.M., SCHULZ, L., & GLYMOUR, C. (2001). Causal learning mechanisms in very young children: Two-, three-, and four-year-olds infer causal relations from patterns of variation and covariation. *Developmental Psychology, 37,* 620–629.

GORDON, B., ORNSTEIN, P.A., CLUBB, P.A., NIDA, R.E., & BAKER-WARD, L.E. (1991, October). *Visiting the pediatrician: Long term retention and forgetting.* Paper presented at the annual meeting of the Psychonomic Society, San Francisco, CA.

GOSWAMI, U. (1992). *Analogical reasoning in children.* Hillsdale, NJ: Erlbaum.

GOSWAMI, U. (1995a). Analogical reasoning and cognitive development. In H. Reese (Ed.), *Advances in child development and behavior, Vol. 26.* New York: Academic Press.

GOSWAMI, U. (1995b). Transitive relational mappings in 3- and 4-year-olds: The analogy of Goldilocks and the Three Bears. *Child Development, 66,* 877–892.

GOSWAMI, U. (2001). Analogical reasoning in children. In D. Gentner, K. Holyoak & B. Kokinov (Eds.), *Analogy: Interdisciplinary perspectives.* Cambridge, MA: MIT Press.

GOSWAMI, U., & BROWN, A. (1990). Higher-order structure and relational reasoning: Contrasting analogical and thematic relations. *Cognition, 36,* 207–226.

GOUBET, N., & CLIFTON, R.K. (1998). Object and event representation in 6 ½-month-old infants. *Developmental Psychology, 34,* 63–76.

GOUGH, P.B., & HILLINGER, M.L. (1980). Learning to read: An unnatural act. *Bulletin of the Orton Society, 30,* 171–196.

GRAHAM, F.K., LEAVITT, L.A., STROCK, B.D., & BROWN, J.W. (1978). Precocious cardiac orienting in human anencephalic infants. *Science, 199,* 322–324.

GRAHAM, T., & PERRY, M. (1993). Indexing transitional knowledge. *Developmental Psychology, 29,* 779–788.

GRANOTT, N. (2002). How microdevelopment creates macrodevelopment: Reiterated sequences, backward transitions, and the Zone of Current Development. In N. Granott & J. Parziale (Eds.), *Microdevelopment: Transition processes in development and learning.* Cambridge, UK: Cambridge University Press.

GRANOTT, N., & PARZIALE, J. (2002). *Microdevelopment: Transition processes in development and learning.* Cambridge, UK: Cambridge University Press.

GRANRUD, C.E. (1987). Size constancy in newborn human infants. *Investigative Ophthalmology and Visual Science, 28 (Supplement),* 5.

GRAY, E. (1993). *Unequal justice: The prosecution of child sexual abuse.* New York: MacMillan.

GREENBERG, D.J., & O'DONNELL, W.J. (1972). Infancy and the optimal level of stimulation. *Child Development, 43,* 639–645.

GREENFIELD, P.M. (1984). A theory of the teacher in the learning activities of everyday life. In J. Lave (Ed.), *Everyday cognition: Its development in social context.* Cambridge, MA: Harvard University Press.

GREENFIELD, P.M., & SMITH, J. (1976). *The structure of communication in early language development.* New York: Academic Press.

GREENHOOT, A.F. (2000). Remembering and understanding: The effects of changes in underlying knowledge on children's recollections. *Child Development, 71,* 1309–1328.

GREENOUGH, W.T., & BLACK, J.E. (1992). Induction of brain structure by experience: Substrates for cognitive development. In M. Gunnar & C.A. Nelson (Eds.), *Minnesota Symposium on Child Psychology: Vol. 24. Developmental Behavioral Neuroscience.* Hillsdale, NJ: Erlbaum.

GREENOUGH, W.T., BLACK, J.E., & WALLACE, C.S. (1987). Experience and brain development. *Child Development, 58,* 539–559.

GRIFFIN, S.A., CASE, R. & SANDIESON, R. (1992). Synchrony and asynchrony in the acquisition of children's everyday mathematical knowledge. In R. Case (Ed.), *The mind's staircase: Exploring the conceptual underpinnings of children's thought and knowledge.* Hillsdale, NJ: Erlbaum.

GRIFFIN, S.A., CASE, R., & SIEGLER, R.S. (1994). Rightstart: Providing the central conceptual prerequisites for first formal learning of arithmetic to students at risk for school failure. In K. McGilly (Ed.), *Classroom lessons: Integrating cognitive theory and classroom practice.* Cambridge, MA: MIT Press.

GRIGORENKO, E.L., JARVIN, L., & STERNBERG, R.J. (2002). School-based tests of the triarchic theory of intelligence: Three settings. *Contemporary Educational Psychology, 27,* 167–208.

GROSS–TSUR, V., MANOR, O. & SHALEV, R.S. (1996). Developmental dyscalculia: Prevalence and demographic features. *Developmental Medicine and Child Neurology, 38,* 25–33.

GRUBER, H.E., & VONECHE, J.J. (1977). *The essential Piaget: An interpretive reference and guide.* New York: Basic Books.

GUTTENTAG, R.E. (1984). The mental effort requirement of cumulative rehearsal: A developmental study. *Journal of Experimental Child Psychology, 37,* 92–106.

GUTTENTAG, R.E. (1985). Memory and aging: Implications for theories of memory development during childhood. *Developmental Review, 5,* 56–82.

HADEN, C.A., HAINE, R.A., & FIVUSH, R. (1997). Developing narrative structure in parent-child reminiscing across the preschool years. *Developmental Psychology, 33,* 295–307.

HAGEN, J.W., HARGROVE, S., & ROSS, W. (1973). Prompting and rehearsal in short-term memory. *Child Development, 44,* 201–204.

HAITH, M.M. (1980). *Rules that infants look by.* Hillsdale, NJ: Erlbaum.

HAITH, M.M. (1993). Future-oriented processes in infancy: The case of visual expectations. In C.E. Granrud (Ed.), *Visual perception and cognition in infancy.* Hillsdale, NJ: Erlbaum.

HAITH, M.M. (1994). Visual expectations as the first step toward the development of future-oriented processes. In M.M. Haith, J.B. Benson, R.J. Roberts, Jr., & B.F. Pennington (Eds.), *The development of future-oriented processes.* Chicago: University of Chicago Press.

HAITH, M.M., & BENSON, J.B. (1998). Infant cognition. In D. Kuhn & R.S. Siegler (Eds.), *Handbook of child psychology: Vol. 2. Cognition, perception, & language* (5th ed.). New York: Wiley.

HAITH, M.M., BERGMAN, T., & MOORE, M.J. (1977). Eye contact and face scanning in early infancy. *Science, 198,* 853–855.

HAITH, M.M., HAZAN, C., & GOODMAN, G.S. (1988). Expectation and anticipation of dynamic visual events by 3.5-month-old babies. *Child Development, 59,* 467–479.

HAITH, M.M., WENTWORTH, N., & CANFIELD, R.L. (1993). The formation of expectations in early infancy. In C. Rovee-Collier & L.P. Lipsitt (Eds.), *Advances in infancy research.* Norwood, NJ: Ablex.

HAKUTA, K., BIALYSTOK, E., & WILEY, E. (2003). Critical evidence: A test of the critical-period hypothesis for second-language acquisition. *Psychological Science, 14,* 31–38.

HALA, S., & CHANDLER, M. (1996). The role of strategic planning in accessing false-belief understanding. *Child Development, 67,* 2948–2966.

HALE, S. (1990). A global developmental trend in cognitive processing speed. *Child Development, 61,* 653–663.

HALE, S., BRONIK, M.D., & FRY, A.F. (1997). Verbal and spatial working memory in school-age children: Developmental differences in susceptibility to interference. *Developmental Psychology, 33,* 364–371.

HALFORD, G.S. (1982). *The development of thought.* Hillsdale, NJ: Erlbaum.

HALFORD, G.S. (1984). Can young children integrate premises in transitivity and serial order tasks? *Cognitive Psychology, 16,* 65–93.

HALFORD, G.S. (1993). *Children's understanding: The development of mental models.* Hillsdale, NJ: Erlbaum.

HALFORD, G.S. (1995). Learning processes in cognitive development: A reassessment with some unexpected implications. *Child Development, 38,* 295–301.

HALFORD, G.S., ANDREWS, G., DALTON, C., BOAG, C., & ZIELINSKI, T. (2002). Young children's performance on the balance scale: The influence of relational complexity. *Journal of Experimental Child Psychology, 81,* 417–445.

HALFORD, G.S., WILSON, W.H., & PHILLIPS, S. (1998). Processing capacity defined by relational complexity: Implications for comparative, developmental, and cognitive psychology. *Behavioral and Brain Sciences, 21,* 803–864.

HAMPSON, J., & NELSON, K. (1993). The relation of maternal language to variation in rate and style of language acquisition. *Journal of Child Language, 20,* 313–342.

HANICH, L.B., JORDAN, N.C., KAPLAN, D., & DICK, J. (2001). Performance across different areas of mathematical cognition in children with learning difficulties. *Journal of Educational Psychology, 93,* 615–626.

HAPPE, F.G.E. (1995). The role of age and verbal ability in the theory of mind task performance of subjects with autism. *Child Development, 66,* 843–855.

HARLEY, K., & REESE, E. (1999). Origins of autobiographical memory. *Developmental Psychology, 35,* 1338–1348.

HARM, M.W., & SEIDENBERG, M.S. (1999). Phonology, reading acquisition, and dyslexia: Insights from connectionist models. *Psychological Review, 106,* 491–528.

HARNISHFEGER, K.K., & BJORKLUND, D.F. (1994). Individual differences in inhibition: Implications for children's cognitive development. *Learning & Individual Differences, 6,* 331–355.

HARRIS, J.F., DURSO, F.T., MERGLER N.L., & JONES, S.K. (1990). Knowledge base influences on judgments of frequency of occurrence. *Cognitive Development, 5,* 223–233.

HARRIS, N.G.S., BELLUGI, U., BATES, F., JONES, W., & ROSSEN, M. (1995). Contrasting profiles of language development in children with Williams and Down Syndromes. *Developmental Neuropsychology, 13,* 345–370.

HARRIS, P.L. (1992). From simulation to folk psychology: The case for development. *Mind & Language, 7,* 120–144.

HARRIS, P.L. (2000). *The work of the imagination.* Oxford, UK: Blackwell.

HARRIS, P.L., BROWN, E., MARRIOT, C., WHITTALL, S., & HARMER, S. (1991). Monsters, ghosts, and witches: Testing the limits of the fantasy-reality distinction in young children. *British Journal of Developmental Psychology, 9,* 105–123.

HARTER, S. (1998). The development of self-representations. In N. Eisenberg (Ed.), *Handbook of child psychology: Vol. 3. Social, emotional, and personality development.* New York: Wiley.

HARTER, S. (1999). *The construction of self: A developmental perspective.* New York: Guilford Press.

HASHER, L., & ZACKS, R.T. (1984). Automatic processing of fundamental information: The case of frequency of occurrence. *American Psychologist, 39,* 1372–1388.

HATANO, G., & INAGAKI, K. (1994). Young children's naive theory of biology. *Cognition, 50,* 171–188.

HATANO, G., MIYAKE, Y., & BINKS, M. (1977). Performance of expert abacus operators. *Cognition, 9,* 47–55.

HATANO, G., SIEGLER, R.S., RICHARDS, D.D., INAGAKI, K., STAVY, R., & WAX, N. (1993). The development of biological knowledge: A multi-national study. *Cognitive Development, 8,* 47–62.

HEFFERNAN, N., & KOEDINGER, K.R. (1997). The composition effect in symbolizing: The role of symbol production versus text comprehension. In M.G. Shafto & P. Langley (Eds.), *Proceedings of the Nineteenth Annual Conference of the Cognitive Science Society.* Mahwah, NJ: Erlbaum.

HEIBECK, T.H., & MARKMAN, E.M. (1987). Word learning in children: An examination of fast mapping. *Child Development, 58,* 1021–1034.

HELD, R. (1993). What can rates of development tell us about underlying mechanisms? In C.E. Granrud (Ed.), *Visual perception and cognition in infancy.* Hillsdale, NJ: Erlbaum.

HERMER, L. & SPELKE, E.S. (1994). A geometric process for spatial reorientation in young children. *Nature, 370,* 57–59.

HERMER, L., & SPELKE, E.S. (1996). Modularity and development: A case of spatial reorientation. *Cognition, 61,* 195–232.

HERSCOVICS, N., & LINCHEVSKI, L. (1994). A cognitive gap between arithmetic and algebra. *Educational Studies in Mathematics, 27,* 59–78.

HESPOS, S.J., & BAILLARGEON, R. (2001). Reasoning about containment events in very young infants. *Cognition, 78,* 207–245.

HICKLING, A.K., & GELMAN, S.A. (1995). How does your garden grow? Early conceptualization of seeds and their place in the plant growth cycle. *Child Development, 66,* 856–876.

HIGGINS, C.I., CAMPOS, J.J., & KERMOIAN, R. (1996). Effects of self-produced locomotion on infant postural compensation to optic flow. *Developmental Psychology, 32,* 836–841.

HILL, E.L. (1998). A dyspraxic deficit in specific language impairment and developmental coordination disorder? Evidence from hand and arm movements. *Developmental Medicine and Child Neurology, 40,* 388–395.

HILL, E.L., BISHOP, D.V.M., & NIMMO-SMITH, I. (1998). Representational gestures in developmental coordination disorder and specific language impairment: Error types and the reliability of ratings. *Human Movement Science, 17,* 655–678.

HIRATA, S., & MORIMURA, N. (2000). Naive chimpanzees' *(Pan troglodytes)* observation of experienced conspecifics in a tool-using task. *Journal of Comparative Psychology, 114,* 291–296.

HIRSH-PASEK, K., & GOLINKOFF, R.M. (1996). *The origins of grammar: Evidence from early language comprehension.* Cambridge, MA: MIT Press.

HITCH, G.J., & MCAULEY, E. (1991). Working memory in children with specific arithmetical learning disabilities. *British Journal of Psychology, 82,* 375–386.

HITCH, G.J., & TOWSE, J.N. (1995). Working memory: What develops? In F.E. Weinert & W. Schneider (Eds.), *Memory performance and competencies: Issues in growth and development.* Mahwah, NJ: Erlbaum.

HOLOWKA, S., & PETITTO, L.A. (2002). Left hemisphere cerebral specialization for babies while babbling. *Science, 297,* 1515.

HOLYOAK, K.J., & THAGARD, P. (1995) *Mental leaps.* Cambridge, MA: MIT Press.

HOROBIN, K., & ACREDOLO, L. (1986). The role of attentiveness, mobility history, and separation of hiding sites on Stage IV search behavior. *Journal of Experimental Child Psychology, 41,* 114–127.

HOVING, K.L., SPENCER, T., ROBB, K.Y., & SCHULTE, D. (1978). Developmental changes in visual information processing. In P.A. Ornstein (Ed.), *Memory development in children.* Hillsdale, NJ: Erlbaum.

HUDSON, J.A. (1990). The emergence of autobiographical memory in mother-child conversation. In R. Fivush & J.A. Hudson (Eds.), *Knowing and remembering in young children.* Cambridge, UK: Cambridge University Press.

HUEY, E.B. (1908). *The psychology and pedagogy of reading.* Cambridge, MA: MIT Press.

HUGHES, C., & DUNN, J. (1998). Understanding mind and emotion: Longitudinal associations with mental-state talk between young friends. *Developmental Psychology, 34,* 1026–1037.

HUME, D. (1911). *A treatise on human nature.* (Original work published 1739–1740). London: Dent.

HUTTENLOCHER, J., & BURKE, D. (1976). Why does memory span increase with age? *Cognitive Psychology, 8,* 1–31.

HUTTENLOCHER, J., JORDAN, N.C., & LEVINE, S.C. (1994). A mental model for early arithmetic. *Journal of Experimental Psychology: General, 123,* 284–296.

HUTTENLOCHER, J., & NEWCOMBE, N. (1984). The child's representation of information about location. In C. Sophian (Ed.), *Origins of cognitive skills.* Hillsdale, NJ: Erlbaum.

HUTTENLOCHER, J., NEWCOMBE, N., & SANDBERG, E.H. (1994). The coding of spatial location in young children. *Cognitive Psychology, 27,* 115–147.

HUTTENLOCHER, P.R. (1990). Morphometric study of human cerebral cortex development. *Neuropsychologia, 28,* 517–527.

HUTTENLOCHER, P.R. (1994). Synaptogenesis, synapse elimination, and neural plasticity in human cerebral cortex. In C.A. Nelson (Ed.), *Minnesota Symposium on Child Psychology: Vol. 27. Threats to optimal development.* Hillsdale, NJ: Erlbaum.

HUTTENLOCHER, P.R., & DABHOLKAR, A.S. (1997). Regional differences in synaptogenesis in human cerebral cortex. *Journal of Comparative Neurology, 387,* 167–178.

ILG, F., & AMES, L.B. (1951). Developmental trends in arithmetic. *Journal of Genetic Psychology, 79,* 3–28.

IMAI, M., & GENTNER, D. (1993). *Linguistic relativity vs. universal ontology: Cross-linguistic studies of the object/substance distinction.* Paper presented at the annual meeting of the Chicago Linguistic Society, Chicago, IL.

IMAI, M., GENTNER, D., & UCHIDA, N. (1994). Children's theories of word meaning: The role of shape similarity in early acquisition. *Cognitive Development, 9,* 45–75.

INAGAKI, K. (1990). The effects of raising animals on children's biological knowledge. *British Journal of Developmental Psychology, 8,* 119–129.

INAGAKI, K., & HATANO, G. (1987). Young children's spontaneous personification as analogy. *Child Development, 58,* 1013–1020.

INAGAKI, K., & HATANO, G. (1996). Young children's recognition of commonalities between animals and plants. *Child Development, 67,* 2823–2840.

INAGAKI, K., & HATANO, G. (2002). *Young children's naïve thinking about the biological world.* New York: Psychology Press.

INHELDER, B., & PIAGET, J. (1958). *The growth of logical thinking from childhood to adolescence.* New York: Basic Books.

INHELDER, B., & PIAGET, J. (1964). *The early growth of logic in the child: Classification and seriation.* London: Routledge.

INHELDER, B., SINCLAIR, H. & BOVET, M. (1974). *Learning and the development of cognition.* Cambridge, MA: Harvard University Press.

JACKSON, A.L. (2001). Language facility and theory of mind development in deaf children. *Journal of Deaf Studies and Deaf Education, 6,* 161–176.

JACKSON, N.E. (1988). Precocious reading ability: What does it mean? *Gifted Child Quarterly, 32,* 200–204.

JACKSON, N.E., DONALDSON, G.W., & CLELAND, L.N. (1988). The structure of precocious reading ability. *Journal of Educational Psychology, 80,* 234–243.

JACKSON, N.E., DONALDSON, G.W., & MILLS, J.R. (1993). Components of reading skill in postkindergarten precocious readers and level-matched second graders. *Journal of Reading Behavior, 25,* 181–208.

JAKOBSON, R. (1981). Why "mama" and "papa"? *Selected writings: Phonological studies.* Paris: Mouton.

JAMES, W. (1890). *The principles of psychology.* New York: Holt, Rinehart, and Winston.

JANSEN, B.R.J., & VAN DER MAAS, H.L.J. (2001). Evidence for the phase transition from rule I to rule II on the balance scale task. *Developmental Review, 21,* 450–494.

JANSEN, B.R.J., & VAN DER MAAS, H.L.J. (2002). The development of children's rule use on the balance scale task. *Journal of Experimental Child Psychology, 81,* 383–416.

JENKINS, J.M., & ASTINGTON, J.W. (1996). Cognitive factors and family structure associated with theory of mind development in young children. *Developmental Psychology, 32,* 70–78.

JOHNSON, C.N. (1988). Theory of mind and the structure of conscious experience. In J.W. Astington, P.L. Harris & D.R. Olson (Eds.), *Developing theories of mind.* New York: Cambridge University Press.

JOHNSON, C.N., & WELLMAN, H.M. (1982). Children's developing conceptions of the mind and brain. *Child Development, 53,* 222–234.

JOHNSON, J.S., LEWIS, L.B., & HOGAN, J.C. (1995, March). *A production limitation in the syllable length of one child's early vocabulary: A longitudinal case study.* Paper presented at the biennial meeting of the Society for Research in Child Development, Indianapolis, IN.

JOHNSON, J.S., & NEWPORT, E.L. (1989). Critical period effects in second language learning: The influence of maturational state on the acquisition of English as a second language. *Cognitive Psychology, 21,* 60–99.

JOHNSON, K.E., & MERVIS, C.B. (1994). Microgenetic analysis of first steps in children's acquisition of expertise on shorebirds. *Developmental Psychology, 30,* 418–435.

JOHNSON, M.H. (1998). The neural basis of cognitive development. In D. Kuhn & R.S. Siegler (Eds.), *Handbook of child* psychology: Vol. 2. Cognition, perception & language (5th ed.). New York: Wiley.

JOHNSON, M.H., & GILMORE, R.D. (1996). Developmental cognitive neuroscience: A biological perspective on cognitive change. In R. Gelman & T. Au (Eds.), Handbook of perception and cognition: Perceptual and cognitive development (Vol. 13). Orlando, FL: Academic Press.

JOHNSON, M.H., & KARMILOFF-SMITH, A. (1992). Can neural selectionism be applied to cognitive development and its disorders? New Ideas in Psychology, 10, 35–46.

JOHNSON, M.H., MARESCHAL, D., & CSIBRA, G. (2001). The functional development and integration of the dorsal and ventral visual pathways: A neurocomputational approach. In C.A. Nelson & M. Luciana (Eds.), Handbook of developmental cognitive neuroscience. Cambridge, MA: MIT Press.

JOHNSON, M.H., & MORTON, J. (1991). Biology and cognitive development: The case of face recognition. Oxford, UK: Blackwell.

JOHNSON, M.H., POSNER, M.I., & ROTHBART, M.K. (1994). Facilitation of saccades toward a covertly attended location in early infancy. Psychological Science, 5, 90–93.

JOHNSON, S.C., SLAUGHTER, V., & CAREY, S. (1998). Whose gaze will infants follow? The elicitation of gaze-following in 12-month-olds. Developmental Science, 1, 233–238.

JOHNSON, S.C., & SOLOMON, G.E.A. (1996). Why dogs have puppies and cats have kittens: The role of birth in young children's understanding of biological origins. Child Development, 68, 404–419.

JOHNSON-GLENBERG, M.C. (2000). Training reading comprehension in adequate decoders/poor comprehenders: Verbal versus visual strategies. Journal of Educational Psychology, 92, 772–782.

JOHNSON-LAIRD, P.N. (1983). Mental models: Towards a cognitive science of language, inference, and consciousness. Cambridge, UK: Cambridge University Press.

JONES, G., RITTER, F.E., & WOOD, D.J. (2000). Using a cognitive architecture to examine what develops. Psychological Science, 11, 93–100.

JORDAN, N.C., LEVINE, S.C., & HUTTENLOCHER, J. (1995). Calculation abilities in young children with different patterns of cognitive functioning. Journal of Learning Disabilities, 28, 53–64.

JORM, A.F., & SHARE, D.L. (1983). Phonological recoding and reading acquisition. Applied Psycholinguistics, 4, 103–147.

JUEL, C. (1988). Learning to read and write: A longitudinal study of fifty-four children from first through fourth grade. Journal of Educational Psychology, 80, 437–447.

JUSCZYK, P.W., CUTLER, A., & REDANZ, N. (1993). Preference for the predominant stress pattern of English words. Child Development, 64, 675–687.

JUSCZYK, P.W., FRIEDERICI, A.D., WESSELS, J., SVENKERUD, V.Y., & JUSCZYK, A.M. (1993). Infants' sensitivity to the sound patterns of native language words. Journal of Memory & Language, 32, 402–420.

JUSCZYK, P.W., GOODMAN, M.B., & BAUMANN, A. (1999). Nine-month-olds' attention to sound similarities in syllables. Journal of Memory & Language, 40, 62–82.

JUSCZYK, P.W., HOUSTON, D.M., & NEWSOME, M. (1999). The beginnings of word segmentation in English-learning infants. Cognitive Psychology, 39, 159–207.

JUSCZYK, P.W., LUCE, P.A., & CHARLES-LUCE, J. (1994). Infants' sensitivity to phonotactic patterns in the native language. Journal of Memory & Language, 33, 630–645.

JUSCZYK, P.W., ROSNER, B.S., CUTTING, J.W., FOARD, F., & SMITH, L.B. (1977). Categorical perception of non-speech sounds by two-month-old infants. Perception & Psychophysics, 21, 50–54.

KADESJO, B., & GILLBERG, C. (1998). Attention deficits and clumsiness in Swedish 7-year-old children. Developmental Medicine & Child Neurology, 40, 796–804.

KAIL, R. (1984). The development of memory in children (2d ed.) New York: Freeman.

KAIL, R. (1986). Sources of age differences in speed of processing. Child Development, 57, 969–987.

KAIL, R. (1988). Developmental functions for speeds of cognitive processes. Journal of Experimental Child Psychology, 45, 339–364.

KAIL, R. (1991). Developmental changes in speed of processing during childhood and adolescence. Psychological Bulletin, 109, 490–501.

KAISER, M.K., McCLOSKEY, M., & PROFFITT, D.R. (1986). Development of intuitive theories of motion: Curvilinear motion in the absence of external forces. Developmental Psychology, 22, 67–71.

KALCHMAN, M., MOSS, J., & CASE, R. (2000). Psychological models for the development of mathematical understanding: Rational numbers and functions. In S. Carver & D. Klahr (Eds.), Cognition and instruction: Twenty-five years of progress. Mahwah, NJ: Erlbaum.

KALISH, C.W. (1996). Preschoolers' understanding of germs as invisible mechanism. Cognitive Development, 11, 83–106.

KALISH, C.W. (1997). Preschoolers' understanding of mental and bodily reactions to contamination: What you don't know can hurt you, but cannot sadden you. Developmental Psychology, 33, 79–91.

KALISH, C.W. (1998a). Reasons and causes: Children's understanding of conformity to social rules and physical laws. Child Development, 69, 706–720.

KALISH, C.W. (1998b). Young children's predictions of illness: Failure to recognize probabilistic causation. Developmental Psychology, 34, 1046–1058.

KALISH, C.W. (2002). Children's predictions of consistency in people's actions. Cognition, 84, 237–265.

KAPUT, J.J. (1989). Linking representations in the symbol systems of algebra. In S. Wagner & C. Kieran (Eds.), Research issues in the learning and teaching of algebra. Reston, VA: National Council of Teachers of Mathematics.

KARMILOFF-SMITH, A. (1979). Micro- and macro-developmental changes in language acquisition and other representational systems. Cognitive Science, 3, 91–118.

KARMILOFF-SMITH, A. (1986). Stage/structure versus phase/process in modeling linguistic and cognitive development. In I. Levin (Ed.), Stage and structure: Reopening the debate. Norwood, NJ: Ablex.

KARMILOFF-SMITH, A. (1992). Beyond modularity: A developmental perspective on cognitive science. Cambridge, MA: MIT Press.

KATZ, H., & BEILIN, H. (1976). A test of Bryant's claims concerning the young child's understanding of quantitative invariance. Child Development, 47, 877–880.

KAY, D.A., & ANGLIN, J. (1982). Overextension and underextension in the child's expressive and receptive speech. Journal of Child Language, 9, 83–98.

KEARINS, J.M. (1981). Visual spatial memory in Australian aboriginal children of desert regions. Cognitive Psychology, 13, 434–460.

KEE, D.W., & HOWELL, S. (1988, April). *Mental effort and memory development*. Paper presented at the annual meeting of the American Educational Research Association, New Orleans, LA.

KEELER, M.L., & SWANSON, H.L. (2001). Does strategy knowledge influence working memory in children with mathematical disabilities? *Journal of Learning Disabilities, 34*, 418–434.

KEENAN, E.O. (1977). Making it last: Uses of repetition in children's discourse. In S. Ervin-Tripp & C. Mitchell-Kernan (Eds.), *Child discourse*. New York: Academic Press.

KEGL, J.A., SENGHAS, A., & COPPOLA, M. (1999). Creation through contact: Sign language emergence and sign language change in Nicaragua. In M. DeGraff (Ed.), *Language creation and language change: Creolization, diachrony, and development*. Cambridge, MA: MIT Press.

KEIL, F.C. (1989). *Concepts, kinds, and cognitive development*. Cambridge, MA: MIT Press.

KEIL, F.C. (1992). The origins of an autonomous biology. In M. Gunnar & M.P. Maratsos (Eds.), *Minnesota Symposium on Child Psychology: Vol. 25. Modularity and constraints in language and cognition*. Hillsdale, NJ: Erlbaum.

KEIL, F.C. (1994). The birth and nurturance of concepts by domains: The origins of concepts of living things. In L.A. Hirschfeld & S.A. Gelman (Eds.), *Mapping the mind: Domain specificity in cognition and culture*. New York: Cambridge University Press.

KEIL, F.C., & BATTERMAN, N. (1984). A characteristic-to-defining shift in the development of word meaning. *Journal of Verbal Learning & Verbal Behavior, 23*, 221–236.

KEIL, F.C., SMITH, W.C., SIMONS, D.J., & LEVIN, D.T. (1998). Two dogmas of conceptual empiricism: Implications for hybrid models of the structure of knowledge. *Cognition, 65*, 103–135.

KELLER, A., FORD, L., & MEACHAM, J. (1978). Dimensions of self-concept in preschool children. *Developmental Psychology, 14*, 483–489.

KELLMAN, P.J. (1988). Theories of perception and research in perceptual development. In A. Yonas (Ed.), *Minnesota Symposium on Child Psychology: Vol. 20. Perceptual development in infancy*. Hillsdale, NJ: Erlbaum.

KELLMAN, P.J., & SHORT, K.R. (1987). The development of three-dimensional form perception. *Journal of Experimental Psychology: Human Perception & Performance, 13*, 545–557.

KELLMAN, P.J., & SPELKE, E.S. (1983). Perception of partially occluded objects in infancy. *Cognitive Psychology, 15*, 483–524.

KELLOGG, R.T. (1996). A model of working memory in writing. In C.M. Levy & S. Ransdell (Eds.), *The science of writing: Theories, methods, individual differences, and applications*. Hillsdale, NJ: Erlbaum.

KENT, R.D., & MIULO, G. (1995). Phonetic abilities in the first year of life. In P. Fletcher & B. MacWhinney (Eds.), *The handbook of child language*. Cambridge, MA: Blackwell.

KERKMAN, D.D., & SIEGLER, R.S. (1993). Individual differences and adaptive flexibility in lower-income children's strategy choices. *Learning & Individual Differences, 5*, 113–136.

KERMANI, H., & BRENNER, M.E. (2001). Maternal scaffolding in the child's zone of proximal development across tasks: Cross-cultural perspectives. *Journal of Research in Childhood Education, 15*, 30–52.

KERMOIAN, R., & CAMPOS, J.J. (1988). Locomotor experience: A facilitator of spatial-cognitive development. *Child Development, 59*, 908–917.

KIRKHAM, N.Z., SLEMMER, J.A., & JOHNSON, S.P. (2002). Visual statistical learning in infancy: Evidence for a domain general learning mechanism. *Cognition, 83*, B35–B42.

KISILEVSKY, B.S., HAINS, S.M.J, LEE, K., MUIR, D.W., XU, F., FU, G., ZHAO, Z.Y., & YANG, R.L. (1998). The still-face effect in Chinese and Canadian 3- to 6-month-old infants. *Developmental Psychology, 34*, 629–639.

KISILEVSKY, B.S., & LOW, J.A. (1998). Human fetal behavior: 100 years of study. *Developmental Review, 18*, 1–29.

KLAHR, D. (1978). Goal formation, planning, and learning by preschool problem solvers or: "My socks are in the dryer." In R.S. Siegler (Ed.), *Children's thinking: What develops?* Hillsdale, NJ: Erlbaum.

KLAHR, D. (1982). Nonmonotone assessment of monotone development: An information processing analysis. In S. Strauss (Ed.), *U-shaped behavioral growth*. New York: Academic Press.

KLAHR, D. (1985). Solving problems with ambiguous subgoal ordering: Preschoolers' performance. *Child Development, 56*, 940–952.

KLAHR, D. (1989). Information-processing approaches. In R. Vasta (Ed.), *Annals of child development: Vol. 6. Six theories of child development: Revised formulations and current issues*. Greenwich, CT: JAI Press.

KLAHR, D. (1992). Information processing approaches to cognitive development. In M.H. Bornstein & M.E. Lamb (Eds.), *Developmental psychology: An advanced textbook* (3rd ed.). Hillsdale, NJ: Erlbaum.

KLAHR, D. (2000). *Exploring science: The cognition and development of discovery processes*. Cambridge, MA: MIT Press.

KLAHR, D., & CARVER, S.M. (1988). Cognitive objectives in a LOGO debugging curriculum: Instruction, learning, and transfer. *Cognitive Psychology, 20*, 362–404.

KLAHR, D., CHASE, W.G., & LOVELACE, E.A. (1983). Structure and process in alphabetic retrieval. *Journal of Experimental Psychology: Learning, Memory & Cognition, 9*, 462–477.

KLAHR, D., FAY, A.L., & DUNBAR, K. (1993). Heuristics for scientific experimentation: A developmental study. *Cognitive Psychology, 25*, 111–146.

KLAHR, D., LANGLEY, P., & NECHES, R. (1987). *Production system models of learning and development*. Cambridge, MA: MIT Press.

KLAHR, D., & MACWHINNEY, B. (1998). Information processing. In D. Kuhn & R.S. Siegler (Eds.), *Handbook of child psychology: Vol. 2. Cognition, perception, & language* (5th ed.). New York: Wiley.

KLAHR, D., & ROBINSON, M. (1981). Formal assessment of problem solving and planning processes in children. *Cognitive Psychology, 13*, 113–148.

KLAHR, D., & WALLACE, J.G. (1976). *Cognitive development: An information processing view*. Hillsdale, NJ: Erlbaum.

KLEIN, J.S., & BISANZ, J. (2000). Preschoolers doing arithmetic: The concepts are willing but the working memory is weak. *Canadian Journal of Experimental Psychology, 54*, 105–116.

KLEMMER, E.T., & SNYDER, F.W. (1972). Measurement of time spent in communication. *Journal of Communication, 22*, 142–158.

KNUTH, E. (2000). Student understanding of the Cartesian connection: An exploratory study. *Journal for Research in Mathematics Education, 31*, 500–508.

KOBASIGAWA, A., RANSOM, C.C., & HOLLAND, C.J. (1980). Children's knowledge about skimming. *Alberta Journal of Educational Research, 26*, 169–182.

KOEDINGER, K.R. (2002). Toward evidence for instructional design principles: Examples from Cognitive Tutor Math 6. In D.S. Mewborn, P. Sztajn, D.Y. White, H.G. Wiegel, R.L. Bryant & K. Nooney (Eds.), *Proceedings of the Twenty-fourth annual meeting of the North American Chapter of the International Group for the Psychology of Mathematics Education, Vol. 1.* Columbus, OH: ERIC Clearinghouse for Science, Mathematics and Environmental Education.

KOEDINGER, K.R., & ANDERSON, J.R. (1998). Illustrating principled design: The early evolution of a cognitive tutor for algebra symbolization. *Interactive Learning Environments, 5*, 161–179.

KOEDINGER, K.R., ANDERSON, J.R., HADLEY, W.H., & MARK, M.A. (1997). Intelligent tutoring goes to school in the big city. *International Journal of Artificial Intelligence in Education, 8*, 30–43.

KOEDINGER, K.R., & NATHAN, M.J. (2004). The real story behind story problems: Effects of representations on quantitative reasoning. *Journal of the Learning Sciences*, 129–164.

KOHLBERG, L. (1966). A cognitive-developmental analysis of children's sex-role concepts and attitudes. In E.E. Maccoby (Ed.), *The development of sex differences.* Stanford, CA: Stanford University Press.

KOLB, B., & WHISHAW, I.Q. (2003). *Fundamentals of human neuropsychology* (5th ed.). New York: Worth.

KOONTZ, K.L., & BERCH, D.B. (1996). Identifying simple numerical stimuli: Processing inefficiencies exhibited by arithmetic learning disabled children. *Mathematical Cognition, 2*, 1–23.

KOSLOWSKI, B. (1996). *Theory and evidence: The development of scientific reasoning.* Cambridge, MA: MIT Press.

KOTOVSKY, L., & BAILLARGEON, R. (1994). Calibration-based reasoning about collision events in 11-month-old infants. *Cognition, 51*, 107–129.

KOWALSKI, K., & LO, Y.-F. (2001). The influence of perceptual features, ethnic labels and sociocultural information on the development of ethnic/racial bias in young children. *Journal of Cross-Cultural Psychology, 32*, 444–455.

KRAUSS, R.M., & GLUCKSBERG, S. (1969). The development of communication: Competence as a function of age. *Child Development, 40*, 255–266.

KRESS, G. (1982). *Learning to write.* Boston: Routledge & Kegan Paul.

KREUTZER, M.A., LEONARD, C., & FLAVELL, J.H. (1975). An interview study of children's knowledge about memory. *Monographs of the Society for Research in Child Development, 40*(1, Whole No. 159).

KRUGER, A.C. (1992). The effect of peer and adult-child transactive discussions on moral reasoning. *Merrill-Palmer Quarterly, 38*, 191–211.

KUCZAJ, S.A., (1978). Why do children fail to overregularize the progressive inflection? *Journal of Child Language, 5*, 167–171.

KUCZAJ, S.A., II. (1983). "I mell a kunk!" Evidence that children have more complex representations of word pronunciations which they simplify. *Journal of Psycholinguistic Research, 12*, 69–73.

KUCZAJ, S.A., II. (1986). General developmental patterns and individual differences in the acquisition of copula and auxiliary *be* forms. *First Language, 6*, 111–117.

KUHL, P.K. (1998). Effects of language experience on speech perception. *Journal of the Acoustical Society of America, 103*, 2931.

KUHN, D. (1989). Children and adults as intuitive scientists. *Psychological Review, 96*, 674–689.

KUHN, D. (1995). Microgenetic study of change: What has it told us? *Psychological Science, 6*, 133–139.

KUHN, D., AMSEL, E., & O'LOUGHLIN, M. (1988). *The development of scientific thinking skills.* Orlando, FL: Academic Press.

KUHN, D., GARCIA-MILA, M., ZOHAR, A., & ANDERSEN, C. (1995). Strategies of knowledge acquisition. *Monographs of the Society for Research in Child Development, 60*(4, Serial No. 245).

KUHN, D., & PHELPS, E. (1976). The development of children's comprehension of causal direction. *Child Development, 47*, 248–251.

KUHN, D., SCHAUBLE, L., & GARCIA-MILA, M. (1992). Cross-domain development of scientific reasoning. *Cognition & Instruction, 9*, 285–327.

KUN, A. (1978). Evidence for preschoolers' understanding of causal direction in extended causal sequences. *Child Development, 49*, 218–222.

KUNZINGER, E.L., & WITTRYOL, S.L. (1984). The effects of differential incentives on second-grade rehearsal and free recall. *The Journal of Genetic Psychology, 144*, 19–30.

KURTZ, B.E., SCHNEIDER, W., CARR, M., BORKOWSKI, J.G., & RELLINGER, E. (1990). Strategy instruction and attributional beliefs in West Germany and the United States: Do teachers foster metacognitive development? *Contemporary Educational Psychology, 15*, 268–283.

LANDAU, B., SMITH, L.B., & JONES, S. (1992). Syntactic context and the shape bias in children's and adults' lexical learning. *Journal of Memory & Language, 31*, 807–825.

LANGE, G., & PIERCE, S.H. (1992). Memory-strategy learning and maintenance in preschool children. *Developmental Psychology, 28*, 453–462.

LANGLOIS, J.H., RITTER, J.M., ROGGMAN, L.A., & VAUGHN, L.S. (1991). Facial diversity and infant preferences for attractive faces. *Developmental Psychology, 27*, 79–84.

LANGLOIS, J.H., ROGGMAN, L.A., & CASEY, R.J., RITTER, J.M., REISER-DANNER, L.A., & JENKINS, V.Y. (1987). Infant preferences for attractive faces: Rudiments of a stereotype? *Developmental Psychology, 23*, 363–369.

LANGLOIS, J.H., ROGGMAN, L.A., & MUSSELMAN, L. (1994). What is average and what is not average about attractive faces? *Psychological Science, 5*, 214–220.

LASKY, R.E., SYRDAL-LASKY, A., & KLEIN, R.E. (1975). VOT discrimination by four- to six-and-a-half-month-old infants from Spanish environments. *Journal of Experimental Child Psychology, 20*, 215–225.

LEAHY, R.L. (1983). The development of the conception of social class. In R.L. Leahy (Ed.), *The child's construction of social inequality.* New York: Academic Press.

LEARMONTH, A.E., NADEL, L., & NEWCOMBE, N.S. (2002). Children's use of landmarks: Implications for modularity theory. *Psychological Science, 13*, 337–341.

LEARMONTH, A.E., NEWCOMBE, N.S., & HUTTENLOCHER, J. (2001). Toddlers' use of metric information and landmarks to reorient. *Journal of Experimental Child Psychology, 80,* 225–244.

LEARY, M.R., & HILL, D.A. (1996). Moving on: Autism and movement disturbance. *Mental Retardation, 34,* 39–53.

LEBLANC, R.S., MUISE, J.G., & BLANCHARD, L. (1992). Backward masking in children and adolescents: Sensory transmission, accrual rate and asymptotic performance. *Journal of Experimental Child Psychology, 53,* 105–114.

LEE, D.N., & ARONSON, E. (1974). Visual proprioceptive control of standing in human infants. *Perception & Psychophysics, 15,* 529–532.

LEFEVRE, J., BISANZ, J., & MRKONJIC, J. (1988). Cognitive arithmetic: Evidence for obligatory activation of arithmetic facts. *Memory & Cognition, 16,* 45–53.

LEFEVRE, J., & KULAK, A.G. (1994). Individual differences in the obligatory activation of addition facts. *Memory & Cognition, 22,* 188–200.

LEFEVRE, J., KULAK, A.G., & BISANZ, J. (1991). Individual differences and developmental change in the associative relations among numbers. *Journal of Experimental Child Psychology, 52,* 256–274.

LEFEVRE, J.J., SADESKY, G.S., & BISANZ, J. (1996). Selection of procedures in mental addition: Reassessing the problem-size effect in adults. *Journal of Experimental Psychology: Learning, Memory, & Cognition, 22,* 216–230.

LEGERSTEE, M. (1991). The role of person and object in eliciting early imitation. *Journal of Experimental Child Psychology, 51,* 423–433.

LEGERSTEE, M., BARNA, J., & DIADAMO, C. (2000). Precursors to the development of intention at 6 months: Understanding people and their actions. *Developmental Psychology, 36,* 627–634.

LE GRAND, R., MONDLOCH, C.J., MAURER, D., & BRENT, H.P. (2001). Early visual experience and face processing. *Nature, 410,* 890.

LEHRER, R., & LITTLEFIELD, J. (1991). Misconceptions and errors in LOGO: The role of instruction. *Journal of Educational Psychology, 83,* 124–133.

LEHRER, R., & LITTLEFIELD, J. (1993). Relationships among cognitive components in LOGO learning and transfer. *Journal of Educational Psychology, 85,* 317–330.

LEHRER, R., & SCHAUBLE, L. (2002). Symbolic communication in mathematics and science: Co-constituting inscription and thought. In J.P. Byrnes (Ed.), *Language, literacy, and cognitive development: The development and consequences of symbolic communication.* Mahwah, NJ: Erlbaum.

LEICHTMAN, M.D., & CECI, S.J. (1995). The effects of stereotypes and suggestions on preschoolers' reports. *Developmental Psychology, 31,* 568–578.

LEICHTMAN, M.D., PILLEMER, D.B., WANG, Q., & KOREISHI, A. (2000). When Baby Maisy came to school: Mothers' interview styles and preschoolers' event memories. *Cognitive Development, 15,* 99–114.

LEMAIRE, P., BARRETT, S.E., FAYOL, M., & ABDI, H. (1994). Automatic activation of addition and multiplication facts in elementary school children. *Journal of Experimental Child Psychology, 57,* 224–258.

LEMAIRE, P., & SIEGLER, R.S. (1995). Four aspects of strategic change: Contributions to children's learning of multiplication. *Journal of Experimental Psychology: General,* 83–97.

LEMIRE, R.J., LOESER, J.D., LEECH, R.W., & ALVORD, E.C. (1975). *Normal and abnormal development of the human nervous system.* New York: Harper & Row.

LEMPERS, J.D., FLAVELL, E.R., & FLAVELL, J.H. (1977). The development in very young children of tacit knowledge concerning visual perception. *Genetic Psychology Monographs, 95,* 3–53.

LENNEBERG, E.H. (1967). *Biological foundations of language.* New York: Wiley.

LEONARD, L.B. (1995) Phonological impairment. In P. Fletcher & B. MacWhinney (Eds.) *The handbook of child language.* Cambridge, MA: Blackwell.

LESGOLD, A., IVILL-FRIEL, J., & BONAR, J. (1989). Toward intelligent systems for testing. In L.B. Resnick (Ed.), *Knowing, learning, and instruction: Essays in honor of Robert Glaser.* Hillsdale, NJ: Erlbaum.

LESGOLD, A., RESNICK, L.B., & HAMMOND, K. (1985). Learning to read: A longitudinal study of word skill development in two curricula. *Reading Research: Advances in Theory & Practice, 4,* 107–138.

LESLIE, A.M. (1982). The perception of causality in infants. *Perception, 11,* 173–186.

LESLIE, A.M. (1987). Pretense and representation: The origins of "theory of mind." *Psychological Review, 94,* 412–426.

LESLIE, A.M. (1991). The theory of mind impairment in autism: Evidence for a modular mechanism of development? In A. Whiten (Ed.), *Natural theories of mind: Evolution, development, and simulation of everyday mindreading.* Oxford, UK: Blackwell.

LESLIE, A.M. (1994). ToMM, ToBy, and agency: Core architecture and domain specificity. In L. Hirschfeld & S. Gelman (Eds.), *Mapping the mind: Domain specificity in cognition and culture.* Cambridge, UK: Cambridge University Press.

LEVIN, I. (1977). The development of time concepts in children: Reasoning about duration. *Child Development, 48,* 435–444.

LEVIN, I. (1982). The nature and development of time concepts in children: The effects of interfering cues. In W. J. Friedman (Ed.), *The developmental psychology of time.* New York: Academic Press.

LEVIN, I. (1989). Principles underlying time measurement: The development of children's constraints on counting time. In I. Levin & D. Zakay (Eds.), *Time and human cognition: A life-span perspective.* Amsterdam: Elsevier.

LEVIN, I., & DRUYAN, S. (1993). When sociocognitive transaction among peers fails: The case of misconceptions in science. *Child Development, 63,* 1571–1591.

LEVIN, I., & KORAT, O. (1993). Sensitivity to phonological, morphological, and semantic cues in early reading and writing in Hebrew. *Merrill-Palmer Quarterly, 39,* 213–232.

LEVIN, I., SIEGLER, R.S., & DRUYAN, S. (1990). Misconception about motion: Development and training effects. *Child Development, 61,* 1544–1557.

LEVIN, I., WILKENING, F., & DEMBO, Y. (1984). Development of time quantification: Integration and nonintegration of beginnings and endings in comparing durations. *Child Development, 55,* 2160–2172.

LEVINSON, S.C. (1997). Language and cognition: Cognitive consequences of spatial description in Guugu Yimithirr. *Journal of Linguistic Anthropology, 7,* 98–131.

LEVY, G.D., TAYLOR, M.G., & GELMAN, S.A. (1995). Traditional and evaluative aspects of flexibility in gender roles, social conventions, moral rules, and physical laws. *Child Development, 66,* 515–531.

LEWIS, C., FREEMAN, N.H., HAGESTADT, E., & DOUGLAS, H. (1994). Narrative access and production in preschoolers' false belief reasoning. *Cognitive Development, 9,* 397–424.

LEWIS, C., & OSBORNE, A. (1990). Three-year-olds' problems with false belief: Conceptual deficit or linguistic artifact? *Child Development, 61,* 1514–1519.

LEWIS, M., & BROOKS-GUNN, J. (1979). *Social cognition and the acquisition of self.* New York: Plenum.

LEWIS, M.D. (2000). The promise of dynamic systems approaches for an integrated account of human development. *Child Development, 71,* 36–43.

LEWKOWICZ, D.J., & TURKEWITZ, G. (1981). Intersensory interaction in newborns: Modification of visual preferences following exposure to sound. *Child Development, 52,* 827–832.

LIBEN, L.S. (1987). Information processing and Piagetian theory: Conflict or congruence? In L. S. Liben (Ed.), *Development and learning: Conflict or congruence?* Hillsdale, NJ: Erlbaum.

LIBERMAN, I.Y., SHANKWEILER, D., FISCHER, F.W., & CARTER, B. (1974). Explicit syllable and phoneme segmentation in the young child. *Journal of Experimental Child Psychology, 18,* 201–212.

LIE, E., & NEWCOMBE, N.S. (1999). Elementary school children's explicit and implicit memory for faces of preschool classmates. *Developmental Psychology, 35,* 102–112.

LIEVEN, E., PINE, J., & BALDWIN, G. (1997). Lexically-based learning and early grammatical development. *Journal of Child Language, 24,* 187–220.

LIITSCHWAGER, J.C., & MARKMAN, E.M. (1994). Sixteen- and 24-month-olds' use of mutual exclusivity as a default assumption in second label learning. *Developmental Psychology, 30,* 955–968.

LILLARD, A.S. (1993a). Pretend play skills and the child's theory of mind. *Child Development, 64,* 348–371.

LILLARD, A.S. (1993b). Young children's conceptualization of pretense: Action or mental representational state? *Child Development, 64,* 372–386.

LILLARD, A.S., & FLAVELL, J.H. (1990). Young children's preference for mental state versus behavioral descriptions of human action. *Child Development, 61,* 731–741.

LILLARD, A.S., & FLAVELL, J.H. (1992). Young children's understanding of different mental states. *Developmental Psychology, 28,* 626–634.

LILLARD, A.S., ZELJO, A., CURENTON, S., & KAUGARS, A.S. (2000). Children's understanding of the animacy constraint on pretense. *Merrill-Palmer Quarterly, 46,* 21–44.

LINDBERG, M.A. (1980). Is knowledge base development a necessary and sufficient condition for memory development? *Journal of Experimental Child Psychology, 30,* 401–410.

LINDBERG, M.A. (1991). A taxonomy of suggestibility and eyewitness memory: Age, memory process, and focus of analysis. In J.L. Doris (Ed.), *The suggestibility of children's recollections.* Washington, DC: American Psychological Association.

LITOVSKY, R.Y., & ASHMEAD, D.H. (1997). Development of binaural and spatial hearing in infants and children. In R.H. Gilkey & T.R. Anderson (Eds.), *Binaural and spatial hearing in real and virtual environments.* Mahwah, NJ: Erlbaum.

LITTLEFIELD, J., DELCLOS, V.R., BRANSFORD, J.D., CLAYTON, K.N., & FRANKS, J.J. (1989). Some prerequisites for teaching

thinking: Methodological issues in the study of LOGO programming. *Cognition & Instruction, 6,* 331–366.

LIVESLEY, W.J., & BROMLEY, D.B. (1973). *Person perception in childhood and adolescence.* London: Wiley.

LLOYD, P., MANN, S., & PEERS, I. (1998). The growth of speaker and listener skills from five to eleven years. *First Language, 18*(52, Pt 1), 81–103.

LOBEL, T.E., & MENASHRI, J. (1993). Relations of conceptions of gender-role transgressions and gender constancy to gender-typed toy preferences. *Developmental Psychology, 29,* 150–155.

LOCKE, J.L. (1983). *Phonological acquisition and change.* New York: Academic Press.

LOCKE, J.L. (1995). Development of the capacity for spoken language. In P. Fletcher & B. MacWhinney (Eds.), *The handbook of child language.* Cambridge, MA: Blackwell.

LOCKE, J.L., & PEARSON, D.M. (1990). Linguistic significance of babbling: Evidence from a tracheostomized infant. *Journal of Child Language, 17,* 1–16.

LOPEZ, A., ATRAN, S., COLEY, J.D., MEDIN, D.L., & SMITH, E.E. (1997). The tree of life: Universal and cultural features of folkbiological taxonomies and inductions. *Cognitive Psychology, 32,* 251–295.

LOVELL, K. (1961). A follow-up study of Inhelder and Piaget's *The growth of logical thinking. British Journal of Psychology, 52,* 143–153.

LOVETT, M.W., BORDEN, S.L., DELUCA, T., LACERENZA, L., BENSON, J.J., & BRACKSTONE, D. (1994). Treating the core deficits of developmental dyslexia: Evidence of transfer of learning after phonologically- and strategy-based reading training programs. *Developmental Psychology, 30,* 805–822.

LUCY, J. (1992). *Grammatical categories and cognition: A case study of the linguistic relativity hypothesis.* Cambridge, UK: Cambridge University Press.

LUCY, J., & GASKINS, S. (2001). Grammatical categories and the development of classification preferences: A comparative approach. In M. Bowerman & S.C. Levinson (Eds.), *Language acquisition and conceptual development.* New York: Cambridge University Press.

LUNDY, J.E.B. (2002). Age and language skills of deaf children in relation to theory of mind development. *Journal of Deaf Studies & Deaf Education, 7,* 41–56.

LURIA, A.R. (1973). *The working brain.* New York: Basic Books.

LYNCH, M.P., & EILERS, R.E. (1992). A study of perceptual development for musical tuning. *Perception & Psychophysics, 52,* 599–608.

LYNCH, M.P., EILERS, R.E., OLLER, D.K., & URBANO, R.C. (1990). Innateness, experience, and music perception. *Psychological Science, 1,* 272–276.

MACLEAN, M., BRYANT, P., & BRADLEY, L. (1987). Rhymes, nursery rhymes and reading in early childhood. *Merrill-Palmer Quarterly, 33,* 255–281.

MACNAMARA, J. (1982). *Names for things: A study of human learning.* Cambridge, MA: MIT Press.

MACWHINNEY, B. (1989). Competition and connectionism. In B. MacWhinney & E. Bates (Eds.), *The crosslinguistic study of sentence processing.* New York: Cambridge University Press.

MACWHINNEY, B. (1996). Lexical connectionism. In P. Broeder & J.M.J. Murre (Eds.) *Models of language acquisition: Inductive and deductive approaches.* Cambridge, MA: MIT Press.

MacWhinney, B. (1998). Models of the emergence of language. *Annual Review of Psychology, 49,* 199–227.

MacWhinney, B. (2002). The gradual evolution of language. In B. Malle & T. Givón (Eds.), *The evolution of language.* Philadelphia: Benjamins.

MacWhinney, B., & Chang, F. (1995). Connectionism and language learning. In C. Nelson (Ed.), *Minnesota Symposium on Child Psychology: Vol. 28. Basic and applied perspectives on learning, cognition, and development.* Mahwah, NJ: Erlbaum.

MacWhinney, B., & Leinbach, J., (1991). Implementations are not conceptualizations: Revising the verb learning model. *Cognition, 29,* 121–157.

MacWhinney, B., Leinbach, J., Taraban, R., & McDonald, J. (1989). Language learning: Cues or rules? *Journal of Memory & Language, 28,* 255–277.

Madole, K.L., & Cohen, L.B. (1995). The role of object parts in infants' attention to form-function correlations. *Developmental Psychology, 31,* 637–648.

Mandel, D.R., Jusczyk, P.W., & Pisoni, D.B. (1995). Infants' recognition of the sound patterns of their own names. *Psychological Science, 6,* 314–317.

Mandler, J.M. (2000). Perceptual and conceptual processes in infancy. *Journal of Cognition & Development, 1,* 3–36.

Mandler, J.M., & McDonough, L. (1993). Concept formation in infancy. *Cognitive Development, 8,* 291–318.

Mandler, J.M., & McDonough, L. (1996). Drinking and driving don't mix: Inductive generalization in infancy. *Cognition, 59,* 307–335.

Mandler, J.M., & McDonough, L. (1998a). On developing a knowledge base in infancy. *Developmental Psychology, 34,* 1274–1288.

Mandler, J.M., & McDonough, L. (1998b). Studies in inductive inference in infancy. *Cognitive Psychology, 37,* 60–96.

Manion, V., & Alexander, J.M. (1997). The benefits of peer collaboration on strategy use, metacognitive causal attribution, and recall. *Journal of Experimental Child Psychology, 67,* 268–289.

Manis, F.R., Custodio, R., & Szeszulski, P.A. (1993). Development of phonological and orthographic skill: A 2-year longitudinal study of dyslexic children. *Journal of Experimental Child Psychology, 56,* 64–86.

Manis, F.R., Seidenberg, M.S., Doi, L.M., McBride-Chang, C., & Peterson, A. (1996). On the bases of two subtypes of developmental dyslexia. *Cognition, 58,* 157–195.

Maratsos, M. (1998). Some problems in grammatical acquisition. In D. Kuhn & R.S. Siegler (Vol. Eds.), *Handbook of child psychology: Vol. 2. Cognition, perception & language.* (5th ed.). New York: Wiley.

Maratsos, M., & Matheny, L. (1994). Language specificity and elasticity: Brain and clinical syndrome studies. In L.W. Porter & M.R. Rosenzweig (Eds.), *Annual Review of Psychology:* (Vol. 45). Palo Alto, CA: Annual Reviews Inc.

Maratsos, M.P. (1973). Nonegocentric communication abilities in preschool children. *Child Development, 44,* 697–799.

Marchman, V. (1992). Constraints on plasticity in a connectionist model of the English past tense. *Journal of Cognitive Neuroscience, 5,* 215–234.

Marchman, V., & Bates, E. (1994). Continuity in lexical and morphological development: A test of the critical mass hypothesis. *Journal of Child Language, 21,* 339–366.

Marchman, V., Miller, R., & Bates, E.A. (1991). Babble and first words in children with focal brain injury. *Applied Psycholinguistics, 12,* 1–22.

Marcus, G.F. (1996). Why do children say "breaked"? *Current Directions in Psychological Science, 5,* 81–85.

Marcus, G.F. (2000). Pabiku and Ga Ti Ga: Two mechanisms infants use to learn about the world. *Current Directions in Psychological Science, 9,* 145–147.

Marcus, G.F., Pinker, S., Ullman, M., Hollander, M., Rosen, T.J., & Xu, F. (1992). Over-regularization in language acquisition. *Monographs of the Society for Research in Child Development, 57*(4, Serial No. 228).

Marcus, G.F., Vijayan, S., Bandi Rao, S., & Vishton, P.M. (1999). Rule learning in seven-month-old infants. *Science, 283,* 77–80.

Mareschal, D., French, R.M., & Quinn, P.C. (2000). A connectionist account of asymmetric category learning in early infancy. *Developmental Psychology, 36,* 635–645.

Mareschal, D., & Quinn, P.C. (2001). Categorization in infancy. *Trends in Cognitive Sciences, 5,* 443–450.

Marini, Z.A. (1992). Synchrony and asynchrony in the development of children's scientific reasoning. In R. Case (Ed.), *The mind's staircase: Exploring the conceptual underpinnings of children's thought and knowledge.* Hillsdale, NJ: Erlbaum.

Marini, Z.A., & Case, R. (1989). Parallels in the development of preschoolers' knowledge about their physical and social worlds. *Merrill-Palmer Quarterly, 35,* 63–88.

Marini, Z.A., & Case, R. (1994). The development of abstract reasoning about the physical and social world. *Child Development, 65,* 147–159.

Markman, E.M. (1979). Realizing that you don't understand: Elementary school children's awareness of inconsistencies. *Child Development, 50,* 643–655.

Markman, E.M. (1989). *Categorization and naming in children: Problems of induction.* Cambridge, MA: Cambridge University Press.

Markman, E.M. (1992). Constraints on word learning: Speculations about their nature, origins and domain specificity. In M.R. Gunnar & M.P. Maratsos (Eds.), *Minnesota Symposium on Child Psychology: Vol. 25. Modularity and constraints in language and cognition:* Hillsdale, NJ: Erlbaum.

Markman, E.M., & Wachtel, G.F. (1988). Children's use of mutual exclusivity to constrain the meaning of words. *Cognitive Psychology, 20,* 121–157.

Markovits, H. (1993). The development of conditional reasoning: A Piagetian reformulation of the mental models theory. *Merrill-Palmer Quarterly, 39,* 131–158.

Markovits, H., & Barrouillet, P. (2002). The development of conditioned reasoning: A mental model account. *Developmental Review, 22,* 5–36.

Markson, L., & Bloom, P. (1997). Evidence against a dedicated system for word learning in children. *Nature, 385,* 813–815.

Marschark, M., & West, S.H. (1985). Creative language abilities of deaf children. *Journal of Speech & Hearing Research, 28,* 73–78.

Marschark, M., West, S.A., Nall, L., & Everhart, V. (1986). Development of creative language devices in signed and oral production. *Journal of Experimental Child Psychology, 41,* 534–550.

MARTIN, C.L., EISENBUD, L., & ROSE, H. (1995). Children's gender-based reasoning about toys. *Child Development, 66,* 1453–1471.

MARTIN, C.L., & HALVERSON, C.F., JR. (1981). A schematic processing model of sex typing and stereotyping in children. *Child Development, 52,* 1119–1134.

MARTIN, C.L., & LITTLE, J.K. (1990). The relation of gender understanding to children's sex-typed preferences and gender stereotypes. *Child Development, 61,* 1427–1439.

MASATAKA, N. (1992). Pitch characteristics of Japanese maternal speech to infants. *Journal of Child Language, 19,* 213–224.

MASCOLO, M.F., & FISCHER, K.W. (1999). The development of representation as the coordination of component systems of action. In I.E. Sigel (Ed.), *Development of mental representation.* Mahwah, NJ: Erlbaum.

MASSEY, C., & GELMAN, R. (1988). Preschoolers decide whether pictured unfamiliar objects can move themselves. *Developmental Psychology, 24,* 307–317.

MASUR, E.F. (1982). Mothers' responses to infants' object-related gestures: Influences on lexical development. *Journal of Child Language, 9,* 23–30.

MASUR, E.F., MCINTYRE, C.W., & FLAVELL, J.H. (1973). Developmental changes in apportionment of study time among items in a multitrial free recall task. *Journal of Experimental Child Psychology, 15,* 237–246.

MATTYS, S.L., & JUSCZYK, P.W. (2001). Phonotactic cues for segmentation of fluent speech by infants. *Cognition, 78,* 91–121.

MATTYS, S.L., JUSCZYK, P.W., LUCE, P.A., & MORGAN, J.L. (1999). Phonotactic and prosodic effects on word segmentation in infants. *Cognitive Psychology, 38,* 465–494.

MATZ, M. (1982). Towards a process model for high school algebra errors. In D. Sleeman & J.S. Brown (Eds.), *Intelligent tutoring systems.* New York: Academic Press.

MAURER, D., & MAURER, C. (1988). *The world of the newborn.* New York: Basic Books.

MAURER, D., LEWIS, T.L., BRENT, H.P., & LEVIN, A.V. (1999). Rapid improvement in the acuity of infants after visual input. *Science, 286,* 108–110.

MAYBERRY, R.I. (1993). First-language acquisition after childhood differs from second-language acquisition: The case of American Sign Language. *Journal of Speech & Hearing Research, 36,* 1258–1270.

MAYBERRY, R.I., & EICHEN, E.B. (1991). The long-lasting advantage of learning sign language in childhood: Another look at the critical period for language acquisition. *Journal of Memory & Language, 30,* 486–512.

MAYBERRY, R.I., LOCK, E., & KAZMI, H. (2002). Linguistic ability and early language exposure. *Nature, 417,* 38.

MAYER, R.E., LEWIS, A.B., & HEGARTY, M. (1992). Mathematical misunderstandings: Qualitative reasoning about quantitative problems. In J.I.D. Campbell (Ed.), *The nature and origins of mathematical skills.* Amsterdam: North-Holland.

MCCALL, R.B., KENNEDY, C.B., & APPLEBAUM, M.I. (1977). Magnitude of discrepancy and the distribution of attention in infants. *Child Development, 48,* 772–786.

MCCARTHY, D. (1954). Language development in children. In L. Carmichael (Ed.), *Manual of child psychology.* New York: Wiley.

MCCLELLAND, J.L. (1995). A connectionist perspective on knowledge and development. In T.J. Simon & G.S. Halford (Eds.), *Developing cognitive competence: New approaches to process modeling.* Hillsdale, NJ: Erlbaum.

MCCLOSKEY, M., & KAISER, M. (1984). The impetus impulse: A medieval theory of motion lives on in the minds of children. *The Sciences.*

MCCUTCHEN, D. (1996). A capacity theory of writing: Working memory in composition. *Educational Psychology Review, 8,* 299–325.

MCCUTCHEN, D. (2000). Knowledge, processing, and working memory: Implications for a theory of writing. *Educational Psychologist, 35,* 13–23.

MCCUTCHEN, D., FRANCIS, M., & KERR, S. (1997). Revising for meaning: Effects of knowledge and strategy. *Journal of Educational Psychology, 89,* 667–676.

MCFADDEN, G.T., DUFRESNE, A., & KOBASIGAWA, A. (1986). Young children's knowledge of balance scale problems. *Journal of Genetic Psychology, 148,* 79–94.

MCGILLY, K., & SIEGLER, R.S. (1989). How children choose among serial recall strategies. *Child Development, 60,* 172–182.

MCGILLY, K., & SIEGLER, R.S. (1990). The influence of encoding and strategic knowledge on children's choices among serial recall strategies. *Developmental Psychology, 26,* 931–941.

MCLEAN, J.F., & HITCH, G.J. (1999). Working memory impairments in children with specific arithmetic learning difficulties. *Journal of Experimental Child Psychology, 74,* 240–260.

MCNEIL, N.M., & ALIBALI, M.W. (2002). A strong schema can interfere with learning: The case of children's typical addition schema. In C.D. Schunn & W. Gray (Eds.), *Proceedings of the twenty-fourth annual conference of the Cognitive Science Society.* Mahwah, NJ: Erlbaum.

MCNEIL, N.M., & ALIBALI, M.W. (2004). You'll see what you mean: Students encode equations based on their knowledge of mathematics. *Cognitive Science,* in press.

MCNEIL, N.M., & ALIBALI, M.W. (in press). Knowledge change as a function of mathematics experience: All contexts are not created equal. *Journal of Cognition & Development.*

MEHLER, J., JUSCZYK, P.W., LAMBERTZ, G., HALSTED, N., BERTONCINI, J., & AMIEL-TISON, C. (1988). A precursor of language acquisition in young infants. *Cognition, 29,* 144–178.

MELTZOFF, A.N. (1988). Infant imitation and memory: Nine-month-olds in immediate and deferred tests. *Child Development, 59,* 217–225.

MELTZOFF, A.N. (1995a). Understanding the intentions of others: Re-enactment of intended acts by 18-month-old children. *Developmental Psychology, 31,* 838–850.

MELTZOFF, A.N. (1995b). What infant memory tells us about infantile amnesia: Long-term recall and deferred imitation. *Journal of Experimental Child Psychology, 59,* 497–515.

MELTZOFF, A.N. (2002). Imitation as a mechanism of social cognition: Origins of empathy, theory of mind, and the representation of action. In U. Goswami (Ed.), *Blackwell handbook of childhood cognitive development.* Malden, MA: Blackwell.

MELTZOFF, A.N., & MOORE, M.K. (1977). Imitation of facial and manual gestures by human neonates. *Science, 198,* 75–78.

MELTZOFF, A.N., & MOORE, M.K. (1983). Newborn infants imitate adult facial gestures. *Child Development, 54,* 702–709.

MELTZOFF, A.N., & MOORE, M.K. (1989). Imitation in newborn infants: Exploring the range of gestures imitated and the underlying mechanisms. *Developmental Psychology, 25,* 954–962.

MELTZOFF, A.N., & MOORE, M.K. (1994). Imitation, memory, and the representation of persons. *Infant Behavior & Development, 17,* 83–99.

MENDELSON, M.J., & HAITH, M.M. (1976). The relation between audition and vision in the human newborn. *Monographs of the Society for Research in Child Development, 41*(4, Whole No. 167).

MENDELSON, R., & SHULTZ, T.R. (1976). Covariation and temporal contiguity as principles of causal inference in young children. *Journal of Experimental Child Psychology, 13,* 89–111.

MENN, L., & STOEL-GAMMON, C. (1995). Phonological development. In P. Fletcher & B. MacWhinney (Eds.) *The handbook of child language.* Cambridge, MA: Blackwell.

MERRIMAN, W.E., & BOWMAN, L.L. (1989). The mutual exclusivity bias in children's word learning. *Monographs of the Society for Research in Child Development, 54*(3–4, Serial No. 220).

MERRIMAN, W.E., MARAZITA, J., & JARVIS, L. (1993). Four-year-olds' disambiguation of action and object word reference. *Journal of Experimental Child Psychology, 56,* 412–430.

MERRIMAN, W.E., SCOTT, P., & MARAZITA, J. (1993). An appearance-function shift in children's object naming. *Journal of Child Language, 20,* 101–118.

MERVIS, C.B. (1987). Child-basic object categories and early lexical development. In U. Neisser (Ed.), *Concepts and conceptual development: Ecological and intellectual factors in categorization.* New York: Cambridge University Press.

METZ, K. (1985). The development of children's problem solving in a gears task: A problem space perspective. *Cognitive Science, 9,* 431–472.

MICHEL, G.F. (1998). A lateral bias in the neuropsychological functioning of human infants. *Developmental Neuropsychology, 14,* 445–469.

MILLER, G.A. (1956). The magical number seven, plus or minus two: Some limits on our capacity for processing information. *Psychological Review, 63,* 81–97.

MILLER, K. (1989). Measurement as a tool for thought: The role of measuring procedures in children's understanding of quantitative invariance. *Developmental Psychology, 25,* 589–600.

MILLER, K., & GELMAN, R. (1983). The child's representation of number: A multidimensional scaling analysis. *Child Development, 54,* 1470–1479.

MILLER, K.F., & BAILLARGEON, R. (1990). Length and distance: Do preschoolers think that occlusion brings things together? *Developmental Psychology, 26,* 103–114.

MILLER, K.F., & PAREDES, D.R. (1996). On the shoulders of giants: Cultural tools and mathematical development. In T. Ben-Zeev (Ed.), *The nature of mathematical thinking.* Hillsdale, NJ: Erlbaum.

MILLER, K.F., SMITH, C.M., ZHU, J., & ZHANG, H. (1995). Preschool origins of cross-national differences in mathematical competence. *Psychological Science, 6,* 56–60.

MILLER, L.T., & VERNON, P.A. (1997). Developmental changes in speed of processing in young children. *Developmental Psychology, 33,* 549–554.

MILLER, P.H. (1990). The development of strategies of selective attention. In D.F. Bjorklund (Ed.), *Children's strategies: Contemporary views of cognitive development.* Hillsdale, NJ: Erlbaum.

MILLER, P.H. (1993). *Theories of developmental psychology.* (3rd ed.). New York: W.H. Freeman and Company.

MILLER, P.H., & SEIER, W. (1994). Strategy utilization deficiencies in children: When, where, and why. In H. Reese (Ed.), *Advances in child development and behavior* (Vol. 25). New York: Academic Press.

MILLER, P.H., WOODY-RAMSEY, J., & ALOISE, P.A. (1991). The role of strategy effortfulness in strategy effectiveness. *Developmental Psychology, 27,* 738–745.

MILLER, S.A. (1976). Nonverbal assessment of conservation of number. *Child Development, 47,* 722–728.

MILNER, A.D., & GOODALE, M.A. (1995). *The visual brain in action.* Oxford, UK: Oxford University Press.

MIURA, I.T., OKAMOTO, Y., VLAHOVIC-STETIC, V., KIM, C.C., & HAN, J.H. (1999). Language supports for children's understanding of numerical fractions: Cross-national comparisons. *Journal of Experimental Child Psychology, 74,* 356–365.

MOHR, D. (1978). Development of attributes of personal identity. *Developmental Psychology, 14,* 427–428.

MONDLOCH, C.J., LEWIS, T.L., BUDREAU, D.R., MAURER, D., DANNEMILLER, J.L., STEPHENS, B.R., & KLEINER-GATHERCOAL, K.A. (1999). Face perception during early infancy. *Psychological Science, 10,* 419–422.

MONTGOMERY, D.E. (1992). Young children's theory of knowing: The development of a folk epistemology. *Developmental Review, 12,* 410–430.

MOON, C., COOPER, R.P., & FIFER, W.P. (1993). Two-day-old infants prefer their native language. *Infant Behavior & Development, 16,* 495–500.

MORFORD, J.P., & GOLDIN-MEADOW, S. (1997). From here and now to there and then: The development of displaced reference in homesign and English. *Child Development, 68,* 420–435.

MORFORD, J.P., & KEGL, J.A. (2000). Gestural precursors to linguistic concepts: How input shapes the form of language. In D. McNeill (Ed.), *Language and gesture.* Cambridge, UK: Cambridge University Press.

MORGAN, J.L. (1996). A rhythmic bias in preverbal speech segmentation. *Journal of Memory & Language, 35,* 666–688.

MORISSETTE, P., RICARD, M., & GOUIN-DECARIE, T. (1995). Joint visual attention and pointing in infancy: A longitudinal study of comprehension. *British Journal of Developmental Psychology, 13,* 163–177.

MORRIS, A.K., & SLOUTSKY, V.M. (1998). Understanding of logical necessity: Developmental antecedents and cognitive consequences. *Child Development, 69,* 721–741.

MORRISON, F.J., GRIFFITH, E., & ALBERTS, D. (1997). Nature-nurture in the classroom: Entrance age, school readiness and learning in children. *Developmental Psychology, 33,* 254–262.

MORRISON, F.J., GRIFFITH, E.M., & FRAZIER, J.A. (1996). Schooling and the 5–7 shift: A natural experiment. In A. Sameroff & M.M. Haith (Eds.), *Reason and responsibility: The passage through childhood.* Chicago: University of Chicago Press.

MORRISON, F.J., SMITH, L., & DOW-EHRENBERGER, M. (1995). Education and cognitive development: A natural experiment. *Developmental Psychology, 31,* 789–799.

MORRONGIELLO, B.A., FENWICK, K.D., HILLIER, L., & CHANCE, G. (1994). Sound localization in newborn human infants. *Developmental Psychobiology, 27,* 519–538.

MORRONGIELLO, B.A., HUMPHREY, G.K., TIMNEY, B., CHOI, J., & ROCCA, P.T. (1994). Tactual object exploration and recognition in blind and sighted children. *Perception & Psychophysics, 23,* 833–848.

MOSHMAN, D. (1998). Cognitive development beyond childhood. In D. Kuhn & R.S. Siegler (Eds.), *Handbook of child psychology, Vol. 2: Cognition, perception & language.* (5th ed.). New York: Wiley.

MOSIER, C.E., & ROGOFF, B. (1994). Infants' instrumental use of their mothers to achieve their goals. *Child Development, 65,* 70–79.

MOSS, J., & CASE, R. (1999). Developing children's understanding of the rational numbers: A new model and an experimental curriculum. *Journal for Research in Mathematics Education, 30,* 122–147.

MUGNY, G., & DOISE, W. (1978). Socio-cognitive conflict and structure of individual and collective performance. *European Journal of Social Psychology, 8,* 181–192.

MUIR, D., ABRAHAM, W., FORBES, B., & HARRIS, L. (1979). The ontogenesis of an auditory localization response from birth to four months of age. *Canadian Journal of Psychology, 33,* 320–333.

MULLER, E., HOLLIEN, H., & MURRAY, T. (1974). Perceptual responses to infant crying: Identification of cry. *Journal of Child Language, 1,* 89–95.

MUNAKATA, Y. (1998). Infant perseveration and implications for object permanence theories: A PDP model of the A-not-B task. *Developmental Science, 1,* 161–184.

MUNAKATA, Y., MCCLELLAND, J.A., JOHNSON, M.H., & SIEGLER, R.S. (1997). Rethinking infant knowledge: Toward an adaptive process account of successes and failures in object permanence tasks. *Psychological Review, 104,* 686–713.

MUNROE, R.H., SHIMMIN, H.S., & MUNROE, R.L. (1984). Gender understanding and sex role preference in four cultures. *Developmental Psychology, 20,* 673–682.

MURPHY, C.M., & MESSER, D.J. (1977). Mothers, infants, and pointing: A study of gesture. In H.R. Schaffer (Ed.), *Studies of mother-infant interaction.* London: Academic Press.

MURRAY, A.D., JOHNSON, J., & PETERS, J. (1990). Fine-tuning of utterance length to preverbal infants: Effects on later language development. *Journal of Child Language, 17,* 511–525.

MURRAY, F., & ARMSTRONG, S. (1976). Necessity in conservation and nonconservation. *Developmental Psychology, 12,* 483–484.

MURRAY, F.B. (1972). Acquisition of conservation through social interaction. *Developmental Psychology, 6,* 1–6.

MURRAY, F.B. (1987). Necessity: The developmental component in school mathematics. In L.S. Liben (Ed.), *Development and learning: Conflict or congruence?* Hillsdale, NJ: Erlbaum.

MUSSEN, P.H., CONGER, J.J., KAGAN, J., & GEIWITZ, J. (1979). *Psychological development: A life-span approach.* New York: Harper & Row.

MYERS, N.A., CLIFTON, R.K., & CLARKSON, M.G. (1987). When they were very young: Almost threes remember two years ago. *Infant Behavior & Development, 10,* 123–132.

NADEL, L., & ZOLA-MORGAN, S. (1984). Infantile amnesia: A neurobiological perspective. In M. Moscovitch (Ed.), *Infant memory: Its relation to normal and pathological memory in humans and other animals.* New York: Plenum.

NADIG, A.S., & SEDIVY, J.C. (2002). Evidence of perspective-taking constraints in children's on-line reference resolution. *Psychological Science, 13,* 329–336.

NAGELL, K., OLGUIN, K., & TOMASELLO, M. (1993). Processes of social learning in the tool use of chimpanzees (*Pan troglodytes*) and human children (*Homo sapiens*). *Journal of Comparative Psychology, 107,* 174–186.

NAIGLES, L.R. (1990). Children use syntax to learn verb meanings. *Journal of Child Language, 17,* 357–374.

NAIGLES, L.R., & HOFF-GINSBERG, E. (1995). Input to verb learning: Evidence for the plausibility of syntactic bootstrapping. *Developmental Psychology, 31,* 827–837.

NAITO, M., & MIURA, H. (2001). Japanese children's numerical competencies: Age- and schooling-related influences on the development of number concepts and addition skills. *Developmental Psychology, 37,* 217–230.

NARENS, L., GRAF, G., & NELSON, T.O. (1996). Metacognitive aspects of implicit/explicit memory. In L.M. Reder (Ed.), *Memory and metacognition.* Mahwah, NJ: Erlbaum.

NATHAN, M.J., STEPHENS, A.C., MASARIK, D.K., ALIBALI, M.W., & KOEDINGER, K.R. (2002). Representational fluency in middle school: A classroom study. In D.S. Mewborn, P. Sztajn, D.Y. White, H.G. Wiegel, R.L. Bryant & K. Nooney (Eds.), *Proceedings of the twenty-fourth annual meeting of the North American Chapter of the International Group for the Psychology of Mathematics Education, Vol. 1.* Columbus, OH: ERIC Clearinghouse for Science, Mathematics and Environmental Education.

NATIONAL COUNCIL OF TEACHERS OF MATHEMATICS. (2000). *Principles and standards for school mathematics.* Reston, VA: Author.

NATIONAL READING PANEL (2000). *Teaching children to read: An evidence-based assessment of the scientific research literature on reading and its implications for reading instruction.* Washington, DC: National Institute of Child Health and Human Development.

NAUS, M.J., & ORNSTEIN, P.A. (1983). Development of memory strategies: Analysis, questions, and issues. In M.T.H. Chi (Ed.), *Trends in memory development research.* New York: Karger.

NAZZI, T., BERTONCINI, J., & MEHLER, J. (1998). Language discrimination by newborns: Towards an understanding of the role of rhythm. *Journal of Experimental Psychology: Human Perception & Performance, 24,* 756–766.

NEEDHAM, A. (2000). Improvements in object exploration skills may facilitate the development of object segregation in early infancy. *Journal of Cognition & Development, 1,* 131–156.

NEEDHAM, A. (2001). Object recognition and object segregation in 4.5-month-old infants. *Journal of Experimental Child Psychology, 78,* 3–24.

NEEDHAM, A., & BAILLARGEON, R. (1997). Object segregation in 8-month-old infants. *Cognition, 62,* 121–149.

NEEDHAM, A., & BAILLARGEON, R. (1998). Effects of prior experience on 4.5-month-old infants' object segregation. *Infant Behavior & Development, 21,* 1–24.

NEEDHAM, A., BAILLARGEON, R., & KAUFMAN, L. (1997). Object segregation in infancy. In L.P. Lipsitt & C. Rovee-Collier

(Eds.), *Advances in infancy research* (Vol. 11). Norwood, NJ: Ablex.

NEISSER, U., & WEENE, P. (1962). Hierarchies in concept attainment. *Journal of Experimental Psychology, 64,* 640–645.

NELSON, C.A. (1995). The ontogeny of human memory: A cognitive neuroscience perspective. *Developmental Psychology, 31,* 723–738.

NELSON, K. (1973). Structure and strategy in learning to talk. *Monographs of the Society for Research in Child Development, 38*(1–2, Whole No. 149).

NELSON, K. (1978). How young children represent knowledge of their world in and out of language. In R.S. Siegler (Ed.), *Children's thinking: What develops?* Hillsdale, NJ: Erlbaum.

NELSON, K. (1993). The psychological and social origins of autobiographical memory. *Psychological Science, 4,* 1–8.

NELSON, K. (1996). *Language in cognitive development: The emergence of the mediated mind.* New York: Cambridge University Press.

NELSON, K. (1999). Levels and modes of representation: Issues for the theory of conceptual change and development. In P.H. Miller (Ed.), *Conceptual development: Piaget's legacy.* Mahwah, NJ: Erlbaum.

NELSON, K., & FIVUSH, R. (2000). Socialization of memory. In E. Tulving & F.I.M. Craik (Eds.), *The Oxford handbook of memory.* London: Oxford University Press.

NELSON, K., & HUDSON, J. (1988). Scripts and memory: Functional relationship in development. In F.E. Weinert & M. Perlmutter (Eds.), *Memory development: Universal changes and individual differences.* Hillsdale, NJ: Erlbaum.

NEVILLE, H.J. (1995a). Developmental specificity in neurocognitive development in humans. In M.S. Gazzaniga (Ed.), *The cognitive neurosciences.* Cambridge, MA: MIT Press.

NEVILLE, H.J. (1995b, June). *Brain plasticity and the acquisition of skill.* Paper presented at the Cognitive Neuroscience and Education Conference, Eugene, OR.

NEVILLE, H.J., & BAVELIER, D. (2002). Specificity and plasticity in neurocognitive development in humans. In M.H. Johnson, Y. Munakata & R.O. Gilmore (Eds.), *Brain development and cognition: A reader* (2nd ed.). Malden, MA: Blackwell.

NEVILLE, H.J., MILLS, D.L., & LAWSON, D.S. (1992). Fractionating language: Different neural subsystems with different sensitive periods. *Cerebral Cortex, 2,* 244–258.

NEWCOMBE, N. (1989). The development of spatial perspective taking. In H.W. Reese (Ed.), *Advances in child development and behavior* (Vol. 22). New York: Academic Press.

NEWCOMBE, N., & FOX, N.A. (1994). Infantile amnesia: Through a glass darkly. *Child Development, 65,* 31–40.

NEWCOMBE, N., & HUTTENLOCHER, J. (1992). Children's early ability to solve perspective-taking problems. *Developmental Psychology, 28,* 635–643.

NEWCOMBE, N., HUTTENLOCHER, J., & LEARMONTH, A. (1999). Infants' coding of location in continuous space. *Infant Behavior & Development, 22,* 483–510.

NEWCOMBE, N.S., DRUMMEY, A.B., FOX, N.A., LIE, E., & OTTINGER-ALBERTS, W. (2000). Remembering early childhood: How much, how and why (or why not). *Current Directions in Psychological Science, 9,* 55–58.

NEWCOMBE, N.S., & HUTTENLOCHER, J. (2000). *Making space: The development of spatial representation and reasoning.* Cambridge, MA: MIT Press.

NEWELL, A., & ROSENBLOOM, P.S. (1981). Mechanisms of skill acquisition and the law of practice. In J.R. Anderson (Ed.), *Cognitive skills and their acquisition.* Hillsdale, NJ: Erlbaum.

NEWPORT, E.L. (1990). Maturational constraints on language learning. *Cognitive Science, 14,* 11–28.

NGUYEN, S.P., & GELMAN, S.A. (2002). Four- and 6-year-olds' biological concept of death: The case of plants. *British Journal of Developmental Psychology, 20,* 495–513.

NICELY, P., TAMIS-LAMONDA, C.S., & BORNSTEIN, M.H. (1999). Mothers' attuned responses to infant affect expressivity promote earlier achievement of language milestones. *Infant Behavior & Development, 22,* 557–568.

NUCCI, L.P., & TURIEL, E. (1978). Social interactions and the development of social concepts in preschool children. *Child Development, 49,* 400–407.

OAKES, L.M. (1994). The development of infants' use of continuity cues in their perception of causality. *Developmental Psychology, 30,* 869–879.

OAKES, L.M., & COHEN, L.B. (1990). Infant perception of a causal event. *Cognitive Development, 5,* 193–207.

OAKES, L.M., & COHEN, L.B. (1995). Infant causal perception. In C. Rovee-Collier & L.P. Lipsitt (Eds.), *Advances in infancy research* (Vol. 9). Norwood, NJ: Ablex.

OAKHILL, J. (1988). The development of children's reasoning ability: Information-processing approaches. In K. Richardson & S. Sheldon (Eds.), *Cognitive development to adolescence.* Hillsdale, NJ: Erlbaum.

OAKSFORD, M., & CHATER, N. (1994). A rational analysis of the selection task as optimal data selection. *Psychological Review, 101,* 608–631.

OCHS, E., & SCHIEFFLEIN, B. (1995). The impact of language socialization on grammatical development. In P. Fletcher & B. MacWhinney (Eds.), *The handbook of child language.* Cambridge, MA: Blackwell.

OKAMOTO, Y., & CASE, R. (1996). Exploring the microstructure of children's central conceptual structures in the domain of number. In R. Case & Y. Okamoto (Eds.), *The role of central conceptual structures in the development of children's thought. Monographs of the Society for Research in Child Development, 61*(1–2, Serial No. 246).

OLLER, D.K., & EILERS, R.E. (1988). The role of audition in babbling. *Child Development, 59,* 441–449.

OLSON, D.R. (1988). On the origins of beliefs and other intentional states in children. In J.W. Astington, P.L. Harris & D.R. Olson (Eds.), *Developing theories of mind.* Cambridge, UK: Cambridge University Press.

OLSON, R.K., FORSBERG, H., & WISE, B. (1994). Genes, environment, and the development of orthographic skills. In V.W. Berninger (Ed.), *The varieties of orthographic knowledge I: Theoretical and developmental issues.* Dordrecht, The Netherlands: Kluwer Academic Publishers.

O'NEILL, D.K., ASTINGTON, J.W., & FLAVELL, J.H. (1992). Young children's understanding of the role that sensory experiences play in knowledge acquisition. *Child Development, 63,* 474–490.

OPFER, J.E., & GELMAN, S.A. (2001). Children's and adults' models for predicting teleological action: The development of a biology-based model. *Child Development, 72,* 1367–1381.

ORNSTEIN, P., GORDON, B.N., & LARUS, D. (1992). Children's memory for a personally experienced event: Implications for testimony. *Applied Cognitive Psychology, 6,* 49–60.

ORNSTEIN, P.A., MEDLIN, R.G., STONE, B.P., & NAUS, M.J. (1985). Retrieving for rehearsal: An analysis of active rehearsal in children's memory. *Developmental Psychology, 21*, 635–641.

ORNSTEIN, P.A., & NAUS, M.J. (1985). Effects of the knowledge base on children's memory strategies. In H.W. Reese (Ed.), *Advances in child development and behavior* (Vol. 19). New York: Academic Press.

OSHERSON, D., & MARKMAN, E. (1975). Language and the ability to evaluate contradictions and tautologies. *Cognition, 3*, 213–226.

OVERTON, W.F., WARD, S.L., NOVECK, I.A., BLACK, J., & O'BRIEN, D.P., (1987). Form and content in the development of deductive reasoning. *Developmental Psychology, 23*, 22–30.

PALINCSAR, A.S., & BROWN, A.L. (1984). Reciprocal teaching of comprehension-fostering and monitoring activities. *Cognition & Instruction, 1*, 117–175.

PALINCSAR, A.S., BROWN, A.L., & CAMPIONE, J.C. (1993). First-grade dialogues for knowledge acquisition and use. In E.A. Forman, N. Minick, & C.A. Stone (Eds.), *Contexts for learning: Sociocultural dynamics in children's development*. New York: Oxford University Press.

PANAGOS, J.M., & PRELOCK, P.A. (1982). Phonological constraints on the sentence productions of language-disordered children. *Journal of Speech & Hearing Research, 25*, 171–177.

PAPERT, S. (1980). *Mindstorms: Children, computers, and powerful ideas*. New York: Basic Books.

PARIS, S.G. (1975). Integration and inference in children's comprehension and memory. In F. Restle, R. Shriffrin, J. Castellan, H. Lindman, & D. Pisoni (Eds.), *Cognitive theory* (Vol. 1). Hillsdale, NJ: Erlbaum.

PARKER, J. (1995). Age differences in source monitoring of performed and imagined actions on immediate and delayed tests. *Journal of Experimental Child Psychology, 60*, 84–101.

PASCALIS, O., DE HAAN, M., & NELSON, C.A. (2002). Is face processing species specific during the first year of life? *Science, 296*, 1321–1323.

PASCUAL-LEONE, J.A. (1970). A mathematical model for transition in Piaget's developmental stages. *Acta Psychologica, 32*, 301–345.

PASCUAL-LEONE, J.A. (1989). Constructive problems for constructive theories: The current relevance of Piaget's work and a critique of information processing simulation psychology. In H. Spada & R. Kluwe (Eds.), *Developmental models of thinking*. New York: Academic Press.

PASSOLUNGHI, M.C., & SIEGEL, L.S. (2001). Short-term memory, working memory, and inhibitory control in children with difficulties in arithmetic problem solving. *Journal of Experimental Child Psychology, 80*, 44–57.

PAUEN, S. (2002). Evidence for knowledge-based category discrimination in infancy. *Child Development, 73*, 1016–1033.

PEÑA, E., IGLESIAS, A., & LIDZ, C.S. (2001). Reducing test bias through dynamic assessment of children's word learning ability. *American Journal of Speech Language Pathology, 10*, 138–154.

PERFETTI, C.A. (1984). *Reading ability*. New York: Oxford University Press.

PERLMUTTER, M., & LANGE, G.A. (1978). A developmental analysis of recall-recognition distinctions. In P.A. Ornstein (Ed.), *Memory development in children*. Hillsdale, NJ: Erlbaum.

PERNER, J. (1991). *Understanding the representational mind*. Cambridge, MA: MIT Press.

PERNER, J., RUFFMAN, T., & LEEKAM, S.R. (1994). Theory of mind is contagious: You catch it from your sibs. *Child Development, 65*, 1228–1238.

PERRET-CLERMONT, A.N., & SCHUBAUER-LEONI, M.L. (1981). Conflict and cooperation as opportunities for learning. In W.P. Robinson (Ed.), *European monographs in social psychology* (Vol. 24). New York: Academic Press.

PERRIS, E.E., & CLIFTON, R.K. (1988). Reaching in the dark toward sound as a measure of auditory localization in 7-month-old infants. *Infant Behavior & Development, 11*, 477–495.

PERRY, D.G., & BUSSEY, K. (1979). The social learning theory of sex differences: Imitation is alive and well. *Journal of Personality & Social Psychology, 37*, 1699–1712.

PERRY, M., CHURCH, R.B., & GOLDIN-MEADOW, S. (1988). Transitional knowledge in the acquisition of concepts. *Cognitive Development, 3*, 359–400.

PERRY, M., & LEWIS, J.L. (1999). Verbal imprecision as an index of knowledge in transition. *Developmental Psychology, 35*, 749–759.

PESKIN, J. (1992). Ruse and reprsentations: On children's ability to conceal information. *Developmental Psychology, 28*, 84–89.

PETERSON, C. (2002). Children's long-term memory for autobiographical events. *Developmental Review, 22*, 370–402.

PETERSON, C., & RIDEOUT, R. (1998). Memory for medical emergencies experienced by 1- and 2-year-olds. *Developmental Psychology, 34*, 1059–1072.

PETERSON, C.C., & SIEGAL, M. (1997). Domain specificity and everyday biological, physical, and psychological thinking in normal, autistic, and deaf children. In H.M. Wellman & K. Inagaki (Eds.), *The emergence of core domains of thought: Children's reasoning about physical, psychological and biological phenomena*. San Francisco: Jossey-Bass.

PETERSON, C.C., & SIEGAL, M. (1999). Representing inner worlds: Theory of mind in autistic, deaf, and normal hearing children. *Psychological Science, 10*, 126–129.

PETERSON, C.C., & SIEGAL, M. (2000). Insights into theory of mind from deafness and autism. *Mind & Language, 15*, 123–145.

PETITTO, L.A. (1992). Modularity and constraints in early lexical acquisition: Evidence from children's first words/signs and gestures. In M. Gunnar & M. Maratsos (Eds.), *Minnesota Symposium on Child Psychology: Vol. 25. Modularity and constraints in language and cognition*. Hillsdale, NJ: Erlbaum.

PETITTO, L.A. (1995). In the beginning: On the genetic and environmental factors that make early language acquisition possible. In M. Gopnik & S. Davis (Eds.). *The biological basis of language*. Oxford, UK: Oxford University Press.

PETITTO, L.A., HOLOWKA, S., SERGIO, L.E., & OSTRY, D. (2001). Language rhythms in baby hand movements. *Nature, 413*, 35–36.

PETITTO, L.A., & MARENTETTE, P. (1991). Babbling in the manual mode: Evidence for the ontogeny of language. *Science, 25*, 1483–1496.

PHELPS, K.E., & WOOLLEY, J.D. (1994). The form and function of young children's magical beliefs. *Developmental Psychology, 30*, 385–394.

PHILLIPS, A.T., WELLMAN, H.M., & SPELKE, E.S. (2002). Infants' ability to connect gaze and emotional expression to intentional action. *Cognition, 85,* 53–78.

PHILLIPS, S.B.V.D., GOLDIN-MEADOW, S., & MILLER, P.J. (2001). Enacting stories, seeing worlds: Similarities and differences in the cross-cultural narrative development of linguistically isolated deaf children. *Human Development, 44,* 311–336.

PIAGET, J. (1946a). *The development of children's concept of time.* Paris: Presses Universitaires de France.

PIAGET, J. (1946b). *Les notions de mouvement et de vitesse ches l'enfant.* Paris: Presses Universitaires de France.

PIAGET, J. (1951). *Plays, dreams, and imitation in childhood.* New York: Norton.

PIAGET, J. (1952). *The origins of intelligence in children.* New York: International Universities Press.

PIAGET, J. (1954). *The construction of reality in the child.* New York: Basic Books.

PIAGET, J. (1969). *The child's conception of time.* New York: Ballantine.

PIAGET, J. (1970). *Psychology and epistemology.* New York: Norton.

PIAGET, J. (1971). *The construction of reality in the child.* New York: Ballantine.

PIAGET, J., & INHELDER, B. (1969). *The psychology of the child* (H. Weaver, Trans.). London: Routledge & Kegan Paul.

PIAGET, J., INHELDER, B., & SZEMINSKA, A. (1960). *The child's conception of geometry.* London: Routledge & Kegan Paul.

PILLEMER, D.B., & WHITE, S.H. (1989). Childhood events recalled by children and adults. In H.W. Reese (Ed.), *Advances in child development and behavior* (Vol. 21). New York: Academic Press.

PILLOW, B. (1989). Early understanding of perception as a source of knowledge. *Journal of Experimental Child Psychology, 47,* 116–129.

PILLOW, B. (1993). Preschool children's understanding of the relationship between modality of perceptual access and knowledge of perceptual properties. *British Journal of Developmental Psychology, 11,* 371–389.

PILLOW, B.H., HILL, V., BOYCE, A., & STEIN, C. (2000). Understanding inference as a source of knowledge: Children's ability to evaluate the certainty of deduction, perception, and guessing. *Developmental Psychology, 36,* 169–179.

PINE, K.J., & MESSER, D.J. (1998). Group collaboration effects and the explicitness of children's knowledge. *Cognitive Development, 13,* 109–126.

PINKER, S. (1984). *Language learnability and language development.* Cambridge, MA: Harvard University Press.

PINKER, S., & PRINCE, A. (1988). On language and connectionism: Analysis of a parallel distributed processing model of language acquisition. *Cognition, 28,* 73–193.

PLAUT, D.C., MCCLELLAND, J.L., SEIDENBERG, M.S., & PATTERSON, K.E. (1996). Understanding normal and impaired word reading: Computational principles in quasi-regular domains. *Psychological Review, 103,* 56–115.

PLUNKETT, K. (1996). *Connectionism and development: Neural networks and the study of change.* New York: Oxford University Press.

PLUNKETT, K., & MARCHMAN, V. (1993). From rote learning to system building: Acquiring verb morphology in children and connectionist nets. *Cognition, 48,* 21–69.

PLUNKETT, K., & SINHA, C. (1992). Connectionism and developmental theory. *British Journal of Developmental Psychology, 10,* 209–254.

POLLAK, S.D., & KISTLER, D.J. (2002). Early experience is associated with the development of categorical representations for facial expressions of emotion. *Proceedings of the National Academy of Science, 99,* 9072–9076.

POOLE, D.A., & LAMB, M.E. (1998). *Investigative interviews of children: A guide for helping professionals.* Washington, DC: American Psychological Association.

POOLE, D.A., & LINDSAY, D.S. (1995). Interviewing preschoolers: Effects of nonsuggestive techniques, parental coaching and leading questions on reports of nonexperienced events. *Journal of Experimental Child Psychology, 60,* 129–154.

POOLE, D.A., & WHITE, L. (1991). Effects of question repetition on the eyewitness testimony of children and adults. *Developmental Psychology, 27,* 975–986.

POOLE, D.A., & WHITE, L. (1993). Two years later: Effects of question repetition and retention interval on the eyewitness testimony of children and adults. *Developmental Psychology, 29,* 844–853.

POSNER, M.I., ROTHBART, M.K., THOMAS-THRAPP, L., & GERARDI, G. (1998). Development of orienting to locations and objects. In R. Wright (Ed.), *Visual attention.* New York: Oxford University Press.

POULIN-DUBOIS, D., LEPAGE, A., & FERLAND, D. (1996). Infants' concept of animacy. *Cognitive Development, 11,* 19–36.

POULIN-DUBOIS, D., SERBIN, L.A., & DERBYSHIRE, A. (1998). Toddlers' intermodal and verbal knowledge about gender. *Merrill-Palmer Quarterly, 44,* 338–354.

POWLISHTA, K.K., SERBIN, L.A., DOYLE, A.B., & WHITE, D.R. (1994). Gender, ethnic, and body type biases: The generality of prejudice in childhood. *Developmental Psychology, 30,* 526–536.

PRATT, C., & BRYANT, P.E. (1990). Young children understand that looking leads to knowing (so long as they are looking through a single barrel). *Child Development, 61,* 973–982.

PRATT, M.W., KERIG, P., COWAN, P.A., & COWAN, C.P. (1988). Mothers and fathers teaching 3-year-olds: Authoritative parenting and adult scaffolding of young children's learning. *Developmental Psychology, 24,* 832–839.

PRECHTL, H.F.R., CIONI, G., EINSPIELER, C., BOS, A.F., & FERRARI, F. (2001). Role of vision in early motor development: Lessons from the blind. *Developmental Medicine & Child Neurology, 43,* 198–201.

PRESSLEY, M. (1995). What is intellectual development about in the 1990s? Good information processing. In F.E. Weinert & W. Schneider (Eds.), *Memory performance and competencies: Issues in growth and development.* Hillsdale, NJ: Erlbaum.

PRESSLEY, M., LEVIN, J.R., & GHATALA, E.S. (1984). Memory strategy monitoring in adults and children. *Journal of Verbal Learning & Verbal Behavior, 23,* 270–288.

PRESSON, C.G., & IHRIG, L.H. (1982). Using matter as a spatial landmark: Evidence against egocentric coding in infancy. *Developmental Psychology, 18,* 699–703.

PRIEL, B., & DESCHONEN, S. (1986). Self-recognition: A study of a population without mirrors. *Journal of Experimental Child Psychology, 41,* 237–250.

PYE, C. (1992). The acquisition of K'iche' Maya. In D. Slobin (Ed.), *The crosslinguistic study of language acquisition* (Vol. 3). Hillsdale, NJ: Erlbaum.

QUINE, W.V.O. (1960). *Word and object*. Cambridge, MA: MIT Press.

QUINN, P.C., & EIMAS, P.D. (1995). Peceptual organization and categorization in young infants. In C. Rovee-Collier & L.P. Lipsitt (Eds.), *Advances in infancy research* (Vol. 11). Norwood, NJ: Ablex.

QUINN, P.C., EIMAS, P.D., & ROSENKRANTZ, S.L. (1993). Evidence for representations of perceptually similar natural categories by 3-month-old and 4-month-old infants. *Perception, 22*, 463–475.

QUINN, P.C., & JOHNSON, M.H. (1997). The emergence of perceptual category representations in young infants: A connectionist analysis. *Journal of Experimental Child Psychology, 66*, 236–263.

QUINN, P.C., & JOHNSON, M.H. (2000). Global-before-basic object categorization in connectionist networks and 2-month-old infants. *Infancy, 1*, 31–46.

QUINTANA, S.M. (1994). A model of ethnic perspective-taking ability applied to Mexican-American children and youth. *International Journal of Intercultural Relations, 18*, 419–448.

QUINTANA, S.M. (1998). Children's developmental understanding of ethnicity and race. *Applied & Preventive Psychology, 7*, 27–45.

RABINOWITZ, M., & CHI, M.T.H. (1987). An interactive model of strategic processing. In S.J. Ceci (Ed.), *Handbook of cognitive, social and neuropsychological aspects of learning disabilities* (Vol. 2). Hillsdale, NJ: Erlbaum.

RABINOWITZ, M., & WOOLEY, K.E. (1995). Much ado about nothing: The relation among computational skill, arithmetic word problem comprehension, and limited attentional resources. *Cognition & Instruction, 13*, 51–71.

RACK, J.P., SNOWLING, M.J., & OLSON, R.K. (1992). The nonword reading deficit in developmental dyslexia: A review. *Reading Research Quarterly, 27*, 29–53.

RADZISZEWSKA, B., & ROGOFF, B. (1988). Influence of adult and peer collaborators on children's planning skills. *Developmental Psychology, 24*, 840–848.

RADZISZEWSKA, B., & ROGOFF, B. (1991). Children's guided participation in planning imaginary errands with skilled adult or peer partners. *Developmental Psychology, 27*, 381–389.

RAIJMAKERS, M.E.J., VAN KOTEN, S., & MOLENAAR, P.C.M., (1996). On the validity of simulating stagewise development by means of PDP networks: Application of catastrophe analysis and an experimental test of rule-like network performance. *Cognitive Science, 20*, 101–139.

RAKISON, D.H., & OAKES, L.M. (Eds.). (2003). *Early category and concept development: Making sense of the blooming, buzzing confusion*. London: Oxford University Press.

RAKISON, D.H., & POULIN-DUBOIS, D. (2001). The developmental origin of the animate-inanimate distinction. *Psychological Bulletin, 127*, 209–228.

RAMSEY, P.G. (1991). Young children's awareness and understanding of social class differences. *Journal of Genetic Psychology, 152*, 71–82.

RAYNER, K., FOORMAN, B.R., PERFETTI, C.A., PESETSKY, D., & SEIDENBERG, M.S. (2001). How psychological science informs the teaching of reading. *Psychological Science in the Public Interest, 2*, 31–74.

REDER, L.M., & SCHUNN, C.D. (1996). Metacognition does not imply awareness: Strategy choice is governed by implicit learning and memory. In L.M. Reder (Ed.), *Memory and metacognition*. Mahwah, NJ: Erlbaum.

REESE, H.W. (1962). Verbal mediation as a function of age level. *Psychological Bulletin, 59*, 502–509.

REICH, P.A. (1986). *Language development*. Englewood Cliffs, NJ: Prentice-Hall.

REPACHOLI, B.M., & GOPNIK, A. (1997). Early reasoning about desires: Evidence from 14- and 18-month-olds. *Developmental Psychology, 33*, 12–21.

RESNICK, L.B., CAUZINILLE-MARMECHE, E., & MATHIEU, J. (1987). Understanding algebra. In J.A. Sloboda & D. Rogers (Eds.), *Cognitive processes in mathematics*. Oxford, UK: Clarendon Press.

RESNICK, L.B., LEVINE, H.M., & TEASLEY, S.D. (1991). *Perspectives on socially shared cognition*. Washington, DC: American Psychological Association.

RESNICK, L.B., NESHER, P., LEONARD, F., MAGONE, M., OMANSON, S., & PELED, I. (1989). Conceptual bases of arithmetic errors: The case of decimal fractions. *Journal for Research in Mathematics Education, 20*, 8–27.

RHOLES, W.S., & RUBLE, D.N. (1984). Children's understanding of dispositional characteristics of others. *Child Development, 55*, 550–560.

RICE, C., KOINIS, D., SULLIVAN, K., TAGER-FLUSBERG, H., & WINNER, E. (1997). When 3-year-olds pass the appearance-reality test. *Developmental Psychology, 33*, 54–61.

RICHARDS, D.D., & SIEGLER, R.S. (1984). The effects of task requirements on children's life judgements. *Child Development, 55*, 1687–1696.

RICHARDS, J.E., & HOLLEY, F.B. (1999). Infant attention and the development of smooth pursuit tracking. *Developmental Psychology, 35*, 856–867.

RIESER, J. (1979). Spatial orientation of six-month-old infants. *Child Development, 50*, 1078–1087.

RIESER, J.J., GARING, A.E., & YOUNG, M.F. (1994). Imagery, action, and young children's spatial orientation: It's not being there that counts, it's what one has in mind. *Child Development, 65*, 1262–1278.

RIESER, J.J., HILL, E.W., TALOR, C.R., BRADFIELD, A., & ROSEN, S. (1992). Visual experience, visual field size, and the development of nonvisual sensitivity to the spatial structure of outdoor neighborhoods explored by walking. *Journal of Experimental Psychology: General, 121*, 210–221.

RITTER, K. (1978). The development of knowledge of an external retrieval cue strategy. *Child Development, 49*, 1227–1230.

RITTLE-JOHNSON, B., & ALIBALI, M.W. (1999). Conceptual and procedural knowledge of mathematics: Does one lead to the other? *Journal of Educational Psychology, 91*, 175–189.

RITTLE-JOHNSON, B., & SIEGLER, R.S. (1999). Learning to spell: Variability, choice, and change in children's strategy use. *Child Development, 70*, 332–348.

ROBERTS, K. (1988). Retrieval of a basic-level category in prelinguistic infants. *Developmental Psychology, 24*, 21–27.

ROBINSON, E.J., & ROBINSON, W.P. (1981). Egocentrism in verbal referential communication. In M. Cox (Ed.), *Is the young child egocentric?* London: Concord.

ROCHAT, P. (2001). Origins of self-concept. In G. Bremner & A. Fogel (Eds.), *Blackwell handbook of infant development*. Malden, MA: Blackwell.

ROCHAT, P., QUERIDO, J.G., & STRIANO, T. (1999). Emerging sensitivity to the timing and structure of proto-conversation in early infancy. *Developmental Psychology, 35,* 950–957.

ROEDELL, W.C., JACKSON, N.E., & ROBINSON, H.B. (1980). *Gifted young children.* New York: Teachers College Press.

ROESSLER, J., & DANNEMILLER, J.L. (1997). Changes in infants' sensitivity to slow displacements over the first six months. *Vision Research, 37,* 417–423.

ROGOFF, B. (1990). *Apprenticeship in thinking.* New York: Oxford University Press.

ROGOFF, B. (1995). Observing sociocultural activity on three planes: Participatory appropriation, guided participation, and apprenticeship. In A. Alvarez (Ed.), *Sociocultural studies of mind.* Cambridge, UK: Cambridge University Press.

ROGOFF, B. (1997). Evaluating development in the process of participation: Theory, methods and practice building on each other. In E. Amsel & K.A. Renninger (Eds.), *Change and development: Issues of theory, method, and application.* Mahwah, NJ: Erlbaum.

ROGOFF, B. (1998). Cognition as a collaborative process. In D. Kuhn & R.S. Siegler (Eds.), *Handbook of child psychology: Vol. 2. Cognition, perception, & language* (5th ed.). New York: Wiley.

ROGOFF, B., ELLIS, S., & GARDNER, W. (1984). Adjustment of adult-child instruction according to child's age and task. *Developmental Psychology, 20,* 193–199.

ROGOFF, B., MISTRY, J., GÖNCÜ, A., & MOSIER, C. (1993). Guided participation in cultural activity by toddlers and caregivers. *Monographs of the Society for Research in Child Development, 58*(8, Serial No. 236).

ROGOFF, B., TOPPING, K., BAKER-SENNETT, J., & LACASA, P. (2002). Mutual contributions of individuals, partners, and institutions: Planning to remember in Girl Scout cookie sales. *Social Development, 11,* 266–289.

ROSCH, E., & MERVIS, C.B. (1975). Family resemblances: Studies in the internal structure of categories. *Cognitive Psychology, 7,* 573–605.

ROSCH, E., MERVIS, C.B., GRAY, W.D., JOHNSON, D.M. & BOYES-BRAEM, P. (1976). Basic objects in natural categories. *Cognitive Psychology, 8,* 382–439.

ROSE, S.A., & FELDMAN, J.F. (1995). Prediction of IQ and specific cognitive abilities at 11 years from infancy measures. *Developmental Psychology, 31,* 685–696.

ROSE, S.A. & FELDMAN, J.F. (1997). Memory and speed: Their role in the relation of infant information processing to later IQ. *Child Development, 68,* 630–641.

ROSE, S.A., FELDMAN, J.F., & WALLACE, I.F. (1992). Infant information processing in relation to six-year cognitive outcome. *Child Development, 63,* 1126–1141.

ROSENGREN, K.S., GELMAN, S.A., KALISH, C.W., & McCORMICK, M. (1991). As time goes by: Children's early understanding of growth in animals. *Child Development, 62,* 1302–1320.

ROSENGREN, K.S., KALISH, C.W., HICKLING, A.K., & GELMAN, S. (1994). Exploring the relation between preschool children's magical beliefs and causal thinking. *British Journal of Developmental Psychology, 12,* 69–82.

ROSENSHINE, B., & MEISTER, C. (1994). Reciprocal teaching: A review of research. *Review of Educational Research, 64,* 479–530.

ROVEE, C.K., & FAGEN, J.W. (1976). Extended conditioning and 24-hour retention in infants. *Journal of Experimental Child Psychology, 21,* 1–11.

ROVEE-COLLIER, C. (1989). *The "memory system" of prelinguistic infants.* Paper presented at the Conference on the Development and Neural Bases of Higher Cognitive Functions, Chestnut Hill, PA.

ROVEE-COLLIER, C. (1995). Time windows in cognitive development. *Developmental Psychology, 31,* 147–169.

ROVEE-COLLIER, C. (1999). The development of infant memory. *Current Directions in Psychological Science, 8,* 80–85.

ROVEE-COLLIER, C., ADLER, S.A., & BORZA, M. (1994). Substituting new details for old? Effects of delaying postevent information on infant memory. *Memory & Cognition, 22,* 644–656.

ROVEE-COLLIER, C., EVANCIO, S., & EARLEY, L.A. (1995). The time window hypothesis: Spacing effects. *Infant Behavior & Development, 18,* 69–78.

RUBENSTEIN, A.J., KALKANIS, L., & LANGLOIS, J.H. (1999). Infant preferences for attractive faces: A cognitive explanation. *Developmental Psychology, 35,* 848–855.

RUBIN, D.C. (2000). The distribution of early childhood memories. *Memory, 8,* 265–269.

RUBLE, D.N., & DWECK, C.S. (1995). Self-perceptions, person conceptions, and their development. In N. Eisenberg (Ed.), *Social development.* Thousand Oaks, CA: Sage.

RUECKERT, L., LANGE, N., PARTIOT, A., APPOLLONIO, I., LITVAN, I., LE BIHAN, D., & GRAFMAN, J. (1996). Visualizing cortical activation during mental calculation with functional MRI. *Neuroimage, 3,* 97–103.

RUFFMAN, T., PERNER, J., NAITO, M., PARKIN, L., & CLEMENTS, W.A. (1998). Older (but not younger) siblings facilitate false belief understanding. *Developmental Psychology, 34,* 161–174.

RUFFMAN, T., SLADE, L., & CROWE, E. (2002). The relation between children's and mothers' mental state language and theory-of-mind understanding. *Child Development, 73,* 734–751.

RUSSELL, J. (1982). Cognitive conflict, transmission, and justification: Conservation attainment through dyadic interaction. *Journal of Genetic Psychology, 140,* 283–297.

RUSSELL, J., JARROLD, C., & POTEL, D. (1994). What makes strategic deception difficult for children—the deception or the strategy? *British Journal of Developmental Psychology, 12,* 301–314.

SACHS, J., & DEVIN, J. (1976). Young children's use of age-appropriate speech styles in social interaction and role playing. *Journal of Child Language, 3,* 81–98.

SAFFRAN, J.R. (2003a). Absolute pitch in infancy and adulthood: The role of tonal structure. *Developmental Science, 6,* 35–43.

SAFFRAN, J.R. (2003b). Statistical language learning: Mechanisms and constraints. *Current Directions in Psychological Science, 12,* 110–114.

SAFFRAN, J.R., ASLIN, R.N., & NEWPORT, E.L. (1996). Statistical learning by 8-month-old infants. *Science, 274,* 1926–1928.

SAFFRAN, J.R., & GRIEPENTROG, G.J. (2001). Absolute pitch in infant auditory learning: Evidence for developmental reorganization. *Developmental Psychology, 37,* 74–85.

SALAPATEK, P. (1975). Pattern perception in early infancy. In L.B. Cohen & P. Salapatek (Eds.), *Infant perception: From sensation to cognition.* New York: Academic Press.

SAMARAPUNGAVAN, A., VOSNIADOU, S., & BREWER, W.F. (1996). Mental models of the earth, sun, and moon: Indian children's cosmologies. *Cognitive Development, 11,* 491–521.

Samuelson, L.K., & Smith, L.B. (1998). Memory and attention make smart word learning: An alternative account of Akhtar, Carpenter and Tomasello. *Child Development, 69,* 94–104.

Samuelson, L.K., & Smith, L.B. (2000a). Children's attention to rigid and deformable shape in naming and non-naming tasks. *Child Development, 71,* 1555–1570.

Samuelson, L.K., & Smith, L.B. (2000b). Grounding development in cognitive processes. *Child Development, 71,* 98–106.

Saywitz, K., Goodman, G., Nichols, G., & Moan, S. (1991). Children's memory of a physical examination involving genital touch: Implications for reports of child sexual abuse. *Journal of Consulting & Clinical Psychology, 5,* 682–691.

Scardamalia, M., & Bereiter, C. (1984). Written composition. In M. Wittrock (Ed.), *Handbook of research on teaching,* 3rd edition. New York: Macmillan.

Schacter, D.L. (1987). Implicit memory: History and current status. *Journal of Experimental Psychology: Learning, Memory, & Cognition, 13,* 501–518.

Schauble, L. (1990). Belief revision in children: The role of prior knowledge and strategies for generating evidence. *Journal of Experimental Child Psychology, 49,* 31–57.

Schauble, L. (1996). The development of scientific reasoning in knowledge-rich contexts. *Developmental Psychology, 32,* 102–119.

Schellenberg, E.G., & Trehub, S.E. (1996). Natural musical intervals: Evidence from infant listeners. *Psychological Science, 7,* 272–277.

Schiefflein, B.B. (1990). *The give and take of everyday life: Language socialization of Kaluli children.* Cambridge, UK: Cambridge University Press.

Schlagmueller, M., & Schneider, W. (2002). The development of organizational strategies in children: Evidence from a microgenetic longitudinal study. *Journal of Experimental Child Psychology, 81,* 298–319.

Schlesinger, I.M. (1982). *Steps to language: Towards a theory of native language acquisition.* Hillsdale, NJ: Erlbaum.

Schlottman, A., Allen, D., Linderoth, C., & Hesketh, S. (2002). Perceptual causality in children. *Child Development, 73,* 1656–1677.

Schneider, B.A., Trehub, S.E., & Bull, D. (1979). The development of basic auditory processes in infants. *Canadian Journal of Psychology, 33,* 306–319.

Schneider, W. (1986). The role of conceptual knowledge and metamemory in the development of organizational processes in memory. *Journal of Experimental Child Psychology, 42,* 318–336.

Schneider, W., & Bjorklund, D.F. (1998). Memory. In D. Kuhn & R.S. Siegler (Eds.), *Handbook of child psychology: Vol. 2. Cognition, perception, & language* (5th ed.). New York: Wiley.

Schneider, W., Gruber, H., Gold, A., & Opwis, K. (1993). Chess expertise and memory for chess positions in children and adults. *Journal of Experimental Child Psychology, 56,* 328–349.

Schneider, W., Korkel, J., & Weinert, F.E. (1989). Domain-specific knowledge and memory performance: A comparison of high- and low-aptitude children. *Journal of Educational Psychology, 81,* 306–312.

Schneider, W., & Pressley, M. (1989). *Memory development between 2 and 20.* New York: Springer-Verlag.

Schneider, W., & Sodian, B. (1988). Metamemory-memory relationships in preschool children: Evidence from a memory-for-location task. *Journal of Experimental Child Psychology, 45,* 209–233.

Scholnick, E.K., & Wing, C.S. (1995). Logic in conversation: Comparative studies of deduction in children and adults. *Cognitive Development, 10,* 319–346.

Schwartz, D.L. (1995). The emergence of abstract representations in dyad problem solving. *Journal of the Learning Sciences, 4,* 321–354.

Schwebel, D.C., Rosen, C.S., & Singer, J.L. (1999). Preschoolers' pretend play and theory of mind: The role of jointly constructed pretence. *British Journal of Developmental Psychology, 17,* 333–348.

Seidenberg, M.S., & McClelland, J.L. (1989). A distributed, developmental model of word recognition and naming. *Psychological Review, 96,* 523–568.

Senghas, A., & Coppola, M. (2001). Children creating language: How Nicaraguan Sign Language acquired a spatial grammar. *Psychological Science, 12,* 323–328.

Serbin, L.A., Poulin-Dubois, D., Colburne, K.A., Sen, M.G., & Eichstedt, J.A. (2001). Gender stereotyping in infancy: Visual preferences for and knowledge of gender-stereotyped toys in the second year. *International Journal of Behavioral Development, 25,* 7–15.

Shaklee, H. (1979). Bounded rationality and cognitive development: Upper limits on growth? *Cognitive Psychology, 11,* 327–345.

Shaklee, H., & Elek, S. (1988). Cause and covariate: Development of two related concepts. *Cognitive Development, 3,* 1–13.

Shantz, C.U. (1983). Social cognition. In J.H. Flavell & E.M. Markman (Eds.), *Handbook of child psychology, Vol. 3: Cognitive development.* New York: Wiley.

Share, D.L., & Stanovich, K.E. (1995). Cognitive processes in early reading development: A model of acquisition and individual differences. *Issues in Education: Contributions from Educational Psychology, 1,* 1–57.

Shatz, M., & Gelman, R. (1973). The development of communication skills: Modifications in the speech of young children as a function of listener. *Monographs of the Society for Research in Child Development, 38*(5, Serial No. 152).

Shi, R., & Werker, J.F. (2001). Six-month-old infants' preference for lexical words. *Psychological Science, 12,* 70–75.

Shi, R., Werker, J.F., & Morgan, J.L. (1999). Newborn infants' sensitivity to perceptual cues to lexical and grammatical words. *Cognition, 72,* B11–B21.

Shimojo, S., Bauer, J.A., O'Connell, K.M., & Held, R. (1986). Prestereoptic binocular vision in infants. *Vision Research, 26,* 501–510.

Shrager, J., & Siegler, R.S. (1998). SCADS: A model of children's strategy choices and strategy discoveries. *Psychological Science, 9,* 405–410.

Shultz, T.R. (1980). Development of the concept of intention. In W.A. Collins (Ed.), *Minnesota Symposium on Child Psychology: Vol. 13. Development of cognition, affect, and social relations.* Hillsdale, NJ: Erlbaum.

Shultz, T.R. (1998). A computational analysis of conservation. *Developmental Science, 1,* 103–126.

Shultz, T.R. (2003). *Computational developmental psychology.* Cambridge, MA: MIT Press.

SHULTZ, T.R., ALTMANN, E., & ASSELIN, J. (1986). Judging causal priority. *British Journal of Developmental Psychology, 4*, 67–74.

SHULTZ, T.R., & BALE, A.C. (2001). Neural network simulation of infant familiarization to artificial sentences: Rule-like behavior without explicit rules and variables. *Infancy, 2,* 501–536.

SHULTZ, T.R., FISHER, G.W., PRATT, C.C., & RULF, S. (1986). Selection of causal rules. *Child Development, 57,* 143–152.

SHULTZ, T.R., SCHMIDT, W.C., BUCKINGHAM, D., & MARESCHAL, D. (1995). Modeling cognitive development with a generative connectionist algorithm. In T. Simon & G. Halford (Eds.), *Developing cognitive competence: New approaches to process modeling.* Hillsdale, NJ: Erlbaum.

SIEGAL, M., & PETERSON, C.C. (1994). Children's theory of mind and the conversational territory of cognitive development. In C. Lewis & P. Mitchell (Eds.), *Children's early understanding of mind: Origins and development.* Hillsdale, NJ: Erlbaum.

SIEGLER, R.S. (1976). Three aspects of cognitive development. *Cognitive Psychology, 8,* 481–520.

SIEGLER, R.S. (1978). The origins of scientific reasoning. In R.S. Siegler (Ed.), *Children's thinking: What develops?* Hillsdale, NJ: Erlbaum.

SIEGLER, R.S. (1981). Developmental sequences within and between concepts. *Monographs of the Society for Research in Child Development, 46*(2, Whole No. 189).

SIEGLER, R.S. (1986). Unities in strategy choices across domains. In M. Perlmutter (Ed.), *Minnesota Symposium on Child Psychology: Vol. 19. Perspectives on intellectual development.* Hillsdale, NJ: Erlbaum.

SIEGLER, R.S. (1987a). Strategy choices in subtraction. In J. Sloboda & D. Rogers (Eds.) *Cognitive processes in mathematics.* Oxford, UK: Clarendon.

SIEGLER, R.S. (1987b). The perils of averaging data over strategies: An example from children's addition. *Journal of Experimental Psychology: General, 116,* 250–264.

SIEGLER, R.S. (1988a). Individual differences in strategy choices: Good students, not-so-good students, and perfectionists. *Child Development, 59,* 833–851.

SIEGLER, R.S. (1988b). Strategy choice procedures and the development of multiplication skill. *Journal of Experimental Psychology: General, 117,* 258–275.

SIEGLER, R.S. (1994). Cognitive variability: A key to understanding cognitive development. *Current Directions in Psychological Science, 3,* 1–5.

SIEGLER, R.S. (1995). How does change occur: A microgenetic study of number conservation. *Cognitive Psychology, 28,* 225–273.

SIEGLER, R.S. (1996). *Emerging minds: The process of change in children's thinking.* New York: Oxford University Press.

SIEGLER, R.S. (2000). The rebirth of children's learning. *Child Development, 71,* 26–35.

SIEGLER, R.S. (2002). Microgenetic studies of self-explanation. In N. Granott & J. Parziale (Eds.), *Microdevelopment: Transition processes in development and learning.* Cambridge, UK: Cambridge University Press.

SIEGLER, R.S., & CROWLEY, K. (1991). The microgenetic method: A direct means for studying cognitive development. *American Psychologist, 46,* 606–620.

SIEGLER, R.S., & CROWLEY, K. (1994). Constraints on learning in non-privileged domains. *Cognitive Psychology, 27,* 194–227.

SIEGLER, R.S., & JENKINS, E.A. (1989). *How children discover new strategies.* Hillsdale, NJ: Erlbaum.

SIEGLER, R.S., & RICHARDS, D.D. (1979). The development of speed, time, and distance concepts. *Developmental Psychology, 15,* 288–298.

SIEGLER, R.S., & ROBINSON, M. (1982). The development of numerical understandings. In H.W. Reese & L.P. Lipsitt (Eds.), *Advances in child development and behavior* (Vol. 16). New York: Academic Press.

SIEGLER, R.S., & SHIPLEY, C. (1995). Variation, selection, and cognitive change. In T. Simon & G. Halford (Eds.), *Developing cognitive competence: New approaches to process modeling.* Hillsdale, NJ: Erlbaum.

SIEGLER, R.S., & SHRAGER, J. (1984). Strategy choices in addition and subtraction: How do children know what to do? In C. Sophian (Ed.), *The origins of cognitive skills.* Hillsdale, NJ: Erlbaum.

SIEGLER, R.S., & STERN, E. (1998). Conscious and unconscious strategy discoveries: A microgenetic analysis. *Journal of Experimental Psychology: General, 127,* 377–397.

SIEGLER, R.S., & SVETINA, M. (2002). A microgenetic/cross-sectional study of matrix completion: Comparing short-term and long-term change. *Child Development, 73,* 793–809.

SIGMAN, M., COHEN, S.E., & BECKWITH, L. (1997). Why does infant behavior predict adolescent intelligence? *Infant Behavior & Development, 20,* 133–140.

SILVER, E.A. (1983). Probing young adults' thinking about rational numbers. *Focus on Learning Problems in Mathematics, 5,* 105–117.

SIMON, T., & KLAHR, D. (1995). A theory of children's learning about number conservation. In T. Simon & G. Halford (Eds.), *Developing cognitive competence: New approaches to process modeling.* Hillsdale, NJ: Erlbaum.

SIMON, T.J., HESPOS, S.J., & ROCHAT, P. (1995). Do infants understand simple arithmetic? A replication of Wynn (1992). *Cognitive Development, 10,* 253–269.

SIMONS, D.J., & KEIL, F.C. (1995). An abstract to concrete shift in the development of biological thought. *Cognition, 56,* 129–163.

SIQUELAND, E.R., & LIPSITT, L.P. (1966). Conditioned head turning in human newborns. *Journal of Experimental Child Psychology, 3,* 356–376.

SLATER, A., MATTOCK, A., & BROWN, E. (1990). Size constancy at birth: Newborn infants' responses to retinal and real size. *Journal of Experimental Child Psychology, 49,* 314–322.

SLATER, A., & QUINN, P.C. (2001). Face recognition in the newborn infant. *Infant & Child Development, 10,* 21–24.

SLATER, A., VON DER SCHULENBURG, C., BROWN, E., BADENOCH, M., BUTTERWORTH, G., PARSONS, S., & SAMUELS, C. (1998). Newborn infants prefer attractive faces. *Infant Behavior & Development, 21,* 345–354.

SLEEMAN, D.H. (1985). Basic algebra revisited: A study with 14-year-olds. *International Journal of Man-Machine Studies, 22,* 127–149.

SLOBIN, D.I. (1986). Crosslinguistic evidence for the language-making capacity. In D.I. Slobin (Ed.), *The crosslinguistic study of language acquisition.* Hillsdale, NJ: Erlbaum.

SMETANA, J.G., & BRAEGES, J.L. (1990). The development of toddlers' moral and conventional judgements. *Merrill-Palmer Quarterly, 36,* 329–346.

SMETANA, J.G., & LETOURNEAU, K.S. (1984). Development of gender constancy and children's sex-typed free play behavior. *Developmental Psychology, 20,* 691–696.

SMILEY, P., & HUTTENLOCHER, J. (1989). Young children's acquisition of emotion concepts. In C. Saarni & P.L. Harris (Eds.), *Children's understanding of emotion.* Cambridge, UK: Cambridge University Press.

SMILEY, S.S. & BROWN, A.L. (1979). Conceptual preference for thematic or taxonomic relations: A nonmonotonic age trend from preschool to old age. *Journal of Experimental Child Psychology, 28,* 249–257.

SMITH, A. (1984). Early and long-term recovery from brain damage in children and adults: Evolution of concepts of localization, plasticity, and recovery. In C.R. Almli & S. Finger (Eds.), *Early brain damage* (Vol. 2). New York: Academic Press.

SMITH, L.B., JONES, S.S., & LANDAU, B. (1992). Count nouns, adjectives, and perceptual properties in children's novel word interpretations. *Developmental Psychology, 28,* 273–286.

SMITH, L.B., JONES, S.S., LANDAU, B., & GERSHKOFF-STOWE, L. (2002). Object name learning provides on-the-job training for attention. *Psychological Science, 13,* 13–19.

SMITH, M.E. (1926). An investigation of the development of the sentence and the extent of vocabulary in young children. *University of Iowa Studies in Child Welfare, 3*(Whole No. 5).

SMITH, N.V. (1973). *The acquisition of phonology: A case study.* Cambridge, UK: Cambridge University Press.

SMITH-HEFNER, B. (1988). The linguistic socialization of Javanese children. *Anthropological Linguistics, 30,* 166–198.

SNOW, C.E. (1986). Conversations with children. In P. Fletcher & M. Garman (Eds.), *Language acquisition: Studies in first language development.* Cambridge, UK: Cambridge University Press.

SNOW, C.E., & HOEFNAGEL-HOHLE, M. (1978). The critical period for language acquisition; Evidence from second language learning. *Child Development, 49,* 1114–1128.

SODIAN, B., ZAITCHIK, D., & CAREY, S. (1991). Young children's differentiation of hypothetical beliefs from evidence. *Child Development, 62,* 753–766.

SOJA, N.N., CAREY, S., & SPELKE, E.S. (1991). Ontological categories guide young children's inductions of word meaning: Object terms and substance terms. *Cognition, 38,* 179–211.

SOLOMON, G.E.A., & JOHNSON, S.C. (2000). Conceptual change in the classroom: Teaching young children to understand biological inheritance. *British Journal of Developmental Psychology, 18,* 81–96.

SOLOMON, G.E.A., JOHNSON, S.C., ZAITCHIK, D., & CAREY, S. (1996). Like father, like son: Young children's understanding of how and why offspring resemble their parents. *Child Development, 67,* 151–171.

SONNENSCHEIN, S. (1986). Development of referential communication skills: How familiarity with a listener affects speaker's production of redundant messages. *Developmental Psychology, 22,* 549–552.

SONNENSCHEIN, S. (1988). The development of referential communication: Speaking to different listeners. *Child Development, 59,* 694–702.

SOPHIAN, C. (1984). Developing search skills in infancy and early childhood. In C. Sophian (Ed.), *Origins of cognitive skills.* Hillsdale, NJ: Erlbaum.

SOPHIAN, C. (1987). Early developments in children's use of counting to solve quantitative problems. *Cognition & Instruction, 4,* 61–90.

SOPHIAN, C., & HUBER, A. (1984). Early developments in children's causal judgments. *Child Development, 55,* 512–526.

SOPHIAN, C., & STIGLER, J.W. (1981). Does recognition memory improve with age? *Journal of Experimental Child Psychology, 32,* 343–353.

SORCE, J.F., EMDE, R.N., CAMPOS, J.J., & KLINNERT, M.D. (1985). Maternal emotional signaling: Its effect on the visual cliff behavior of 1-year-olds. *Developmental Psychology, 21,* 195–200.

SPEAR, N.E. (1984). Ecologically determined dispositions control the ontogeny of learning and memory. In R. Kail & N.E. Spear (Eds.), *Comparative perspectives on the development of memory.* Hillsdale, NJ: Erlbaum.

SPEER, J.R., & FLAVELL, J.H. (1979). Young children's knowledge of the relative difficulty of recognition and recall memory tasks. *Developmental Psychology, 15,* 214–217.

SPELKE, E.S. (1976). Infants' intermodal perception of events. *Cognitive Psychology, 8,* 553–560.

SPELKE, E.S. (1994). Initial knowledge: Six suggestions. *Cognition, 50,* 431–445.

SPELKE, E.S. (2000). Core knowledge. *American Psychologist, 55,* 1233–1243.

SPELKE, E.S., BREINLINGER, K., MACOMBER, J., & JACOBSON, K. (1992). Origins of knowledge. *Psychological Review, 99,* 605–632.

SPELKE, E.S., & NEWPORT, E.L. (1998). Nativism, empiricism, and the development of knowledge. In R.M. Lerner (Ed.), *Handbook of child psychology: Vol. 1. Theoretical models of human development* (5th ed.). New York: Wiley.

SPELKE, E.S., PHILLIPS, A.T., & WOODWARD, A.L. (1995). Infants' knowledge of object motion and human action. In D. Sperber, D. Premack, & A.J. Premack (Eds.), *Causal cognition: A multidisciplinary debate.* Oxford, UK: Clarendon Press.

SPELKE, E.S., & VAN DE WALLE, G. (1993). Perceiving and reasoning about objects: Insights from infants. In N. Eilan, W. Brewer, & R. McCarthy (Eds.), *Spatial representation.* Oxford, UK: Blackwell.

SPENCER, J.P., SMITH, L.B., & THELEN, E. (2001). Tests of a dynamic systems account of the A-not-B error: The influence of prior experience on the spatial memory abilities of two-year-olds. *Child Development, 72,* 1327–1346.

SPERLING, G. (1960). The information available in brief visual presentation. *Psychological Monographs, 74*(Whole No. 176).

SPRINGER, K. (1995). Acquiring a naive theory of kinship through inference. *Child Development, 66,* 547–558.

SPRINGER, K. (1999). How a naive theory of biology is acquired. In M.E. Siegal & C.C.E. Petersen (Eds.), *Children's understanding of biology and health.* New York: Cambridge University Press.

SPRINGER, K., & KEIL, F.C. (1991). Early differentiation of causal mechanisms appropriate to biological and nonbiological kinds. *Child Development, 62,* 767–781.

SPRINGER, K., NGYUEN, T., & SAMANIEGO, R. (1996). Early understanding of age- and environment-related noxiousness in biological kinds: Evidence for a naive theory. *Cognitive Development, 11,* 65–82.

STANOVICH, K.E. (1986). Matthew effects in reading: Some consequences of individual differences in the acquisition of literacy. *Reading Research Quarterly, 21,* 360–406.

STANOVICH, K.E., SIEGEL, L.S., & GOTTARDO, A. (1997). Converging evidence for phonological and surface subtypes of reading disability. *Journal of Educational Psychology, 89,* 114–127.

STARKEY, P. (1992). The early development of numerical reasoning. *Cognition, 43,* 93–126.

STARKEY, P., & COOPER, R.S. (1980). Perception of numbers by human infants. *Science, 210,* 1033–1035.

STARKEY, P., SPELKE, E.S., & GELMAN, R. (1990). Numerical abstraction by human infants. *Cognition, 36,* 97–128.

STASZEWSKI, J.J. (1988). Skilled memory and expert mental calculation. In M.T.H. Chi, R. Glaser, & M.J. Farr (Eds.), *The nature of expertise.* Hillsdale, NJ: Erlbaum.

STERN, D.N., SPIEKER, S., & MACKAIN, C. (1982). Intonation contours as signals in maternal speech to prelinguistic infants. *Developmental Psychology, 18,* 727–735.

STERN, E. (1992). Spontaneous use of conceptual mathematical knowledge in elementary school children. *Contemporary Educational Psychology, 17,* 266–277.

STERN, E. (1993). What makes certain arithmetic word problems involving comparison of sets so difficult for children? *Journal of Educational Psychology, 85,* 7–23.

STERNBERG, R.J. (1984). Mechanisms of cognitive development: A componential approach. In R.J. Sternberg, (Ed.) *Mechanisms of cognitive development.* New York: Freeman.

STERNBERG, R.J. (1985). *Beyond IQ: A triarchic theory of human intelligence.* New York: Cambridge University Press.

STERNBERG, R.J. (1989). Domain-generality versus domain-specificity: The life and impending death of a false dichotomy. *Merrill-Palmer Quarterly, 35,* 115–130.

STERNBERG, R.J. (1997). *Successful intelligence.* New York: Plume.

STERNBERG, R.J. (1999). The theory of successful intelligence. *Review of General Psychology, 3,* 292–316.

STERNBERG, R.J., FERRARI, M., CLINKENBEARD, P., & GRIGORENKO, E.L. (1996). Identification, instruction, and assessment of gifted children: A construct validation of a triarchic model. *Gifted Child Quarterly, 40,* 129–137.

STERNBERG, R.J., TORFF, B., & GRIGORENKO, E.L. (1998). Teaching triarchically improves school achievement. *Journal of Educational Psychology, 90,* 374–384.

STEVENSON, H.W., & STIGLER, J.W. (1992). *The learning gap: Why our schools are failing and what we can learn from Japanese and Chinese education.* New York: Simon and Schuster.

STICHT, T.G., & JAMES, J.H. (1984). Listening and reading. In P.D. Pearson (Ed.), *Handbook of reading research, Part 2.* New York: Longman.

STIGLER, J.W. (1984). Mental abacus: The effect of abacus training on Chinese children's mental calculations. *Cognitive Psychology, 16,* 145–176.

STILES, J., BATES, E.A., THAL, D., TRAUNER, D.A., & REILLY, J. (2002). Linguistic and spatial cognitive development in children with pre- and peri-natal focal brain injury: A ten-year overview from the San Diego Longitudinal Project. In M.H. Johnson, Y. Munakata & R.O. Gilmore (Eds.), *Brain development and cognition: A reader* (2nd ed.). Oxford, UK: Blackwell.

STILES, J., & THAL, D. (1993). Linguistic and spatial cognitive development following early focal brain injury: Patterns of deficit and recovery. In M.H. Johnson (Ed.), *Brain development and cognition: A reader.* Oxford, UK: Blackwell.

STIPEK, D. (2002). At what age should children enter kindergarten? A question for policy makers and parents. *Social Policy Report of the Society for Research in Child Development, 16.*

STIPEK, D.J. (1984). Young children's performance expectations: Logical analysis or wishful thinking? In J.G. Nicholls (Ed.)., *Advances in motivation and achievement, Vol. 3: The development of achievement motivation.* Greenwich, CT: JAI Press.

STIPEK, D.J., GRALINSKI, J.H., & KOPP, C.B. (1990). Self-concept development in the toddler years. *Developmental Psychology, 26,* 972–977.

STOKOE, W.C., JR. (1960). Sign language structure: An outline of the visual communication system of the American deaf. *Studies in Linguistics, Occasional Papers, Vol. 8.*

STONE, C.A. (1998). The metaphor of scaffolding: Its utility for the field of learning disabilities. *Journal of Learning Disabilities, 31,* 344–364.

STRAUSS, M.S., & COHEN, L.P. (1978). *Infant immediate and delayed memory for perceptual dimensions.* Unpublished manuscript, University of Illinois at Urbana-Champaign.

STRAUSS, M.S., & CURTIS, L.E. (1984). Development of numerical concepts in infancy. In C. Sophian (Ed.), *The origins of cognitive skills.* Hillsdale, NJ: Erlbaum.

STRAUSS, S. (1972). Inducing cognitive development and learning: A review of short-term training experiments. I: The organismic-developmental approach. *Cognition, 1,* 329–357.

STRAUSS, S. (1982). *U-shaped behavioral growth.* New York: Academic Press.

STRERI, A., & SPELKE, E.S. (1988). Haptic perception of objects in infancy. *Cognitive Psychology, 20,* 1–23.

STROM, D., KEMENY, V., LEHRER, R., & FORMAN, E. (2001). Visualizing the emergent structure of children's mathematical argument. *Cognitive Science, 25,* 733–773.

STRYKER, M.P., & HARRIS, W. (1986). Binocular impulse blockade prevents the formation of ocular dominance columns in cat visual cortex. *Journal of Neuroscience, 6,* 2117–2133.

SUBBOTSKY, E.V. (1993). *Foundations of the mind.* Cambridge, MA: Harvard University Press.

SULLIVAN, K., & WINNER, E. (1993). Three-year-olds' understanding of mental states: The influence of trickery. *Journal of Experimental Child Psychology, 56,* 135–148.

SURBER, C.F., & GZESH, S.M. (1984). Reversible operations in the balance scale task. *Journal of Experimental Child Psychology, 38,* 254–274.

SWANSON, H.L. (1995). Effects of dynamic testing on the classification of learning disabilities: The predictive and discriminant validity of the Swanson Cognitive Processing Test. *Journal of Psychoeducational Assessment, 13,* 204–229.

SWANSON, H.L., & BERNINGER, V.W. (1996). Individual differences in children's working memory and writing skill. *Journal of Experimental Child Psychology, 63,* 358–385.

SWANSON, H.L., & LUSSIER, C.M. (2001). A selective synthesis of the experimental literature on dynamic assessment. *Review of Educational Research, 71,* 321–363.

TAGER-FLUSBERG, H. (1992). Autistic children's talk about psychological states: Deficits in the early acquisition of a theory of mind. *Child Development, 63,* 161–172.

TAGER-FLUSBERG, H. (2000). Language and understanding minds: Connections in autism. In S. Baron-Cohen, H. Tager-Flusberg, & D.J. Cohen (Eds.), *Understanding other minds: Perspectives from developmental cognitive neuroscience.* Oxford, UK: Oxford University Press.

TAMIS-LAMONDA, C.S., BORNSTEIN, M.H., & BAUMWELL, L. (2001). Maternal responsiveness and children's achievement of language milestones. *Child Development, 72,* 748–767.

TARDIF, T. (1996). Nouns are not always learned before verbs: Evidence from Mandarin speakers. *Developmental Psychology, 32,* 492–504.

TARDIF, T., GELMAN, S.A., & XU, F. (1999). Putting the "noun bias" in context: A comparison of English and Mandarin. *Child Development, 70,* 620–635.

TARDIF, T., SHATZ, M., & NAIGLES, L. (1997). Caregiver speech and children's use of nouns versus verbs: A comparison of English, Italian and Mandarin. *Journal of Child Language, 24,* 535–565.

TAYLOR, M. (1999). *Imaginary companions and the children who create them.* New York: Oxford University Press.

TAYLOR, M., & CARLSON, S.M. (1997). The relation between individual differences in fantasy and theory of mind. *Child Development, 68,* 436–455.

TAYLOR, M., ESBENSEN, B.M., & BENNETT, R.T. (1994). Children's understanding of knowledge acquisition: The tendency for children to report that they have always known what they have just learned. *Child Development, 65,* 1581–1604.

TEALE, W.H., & SULZBY, E. (1986). Emergent literacy: A perspective for examining how young children become writers and readers. In W.H. Teale & E. Sulzby (Eds.), *Emergent literacy: Writing and reading.* Norwood, NJ: Ablex.

TEASLEY, S.D. (1995). The role of talk in children's peer collaborations. *Developmental Psychology, 31,* 207–220.

THATCHER, R.W. (1992). Development as a dynamic system. *Current Directions in Psychological Science, 1,* 189–193.

THATCHER, R.W., LYON, G.R., RUMSEY, J., & KRASNEGOR, N. (Eds.). (1996). *Developmental neuroimaging: Mapping the development of brain and behavior.* San Diego, CA: Academic Press.

THELEN, E. (1989). Self-organization in developmental processes: Can systems approaches work? In M. Gunnar & E. Thelen (Eds.), *Minnesota Symposium on Child Psychology: Vol. 22. Systems and development.* Hillsdale, NJ: Erlbaum.

THELEN, E. (1992). Development as a dynamic system. *Current Directions in Psychological Science, 1,* 189–193.

THELEN, E. (1995). Motor development: A new synthesis. *American Psychologist, 50,* 79–95.

THELEN, E. (2001). Dynamic mechanisms of change in early perceptual-motor development. In J.L. McClelland & R.S. Siegler (Eds.), *Mechanisms of cognitive development: Behavioral and neural perspectives.* Mahwah, NJ: Erlbaum.

THELEN, E., & SMITH, L.B. (1994). *A dynamic systems approach to the development of cognition and action.* Cambridge, MA: MIT Press.

THOMPSON, R.F. (2000). *The brain: A neuroscience primer* (3rd ed.). New York: Worth.

TINCOFF, R., & JUSCZYK, P.W. (1999). Some beginnings of word comprehension in 6-month-olds. *Psychological Science, 10,* 172–175.

TODA, S., & FOGEL, A. (1993). Infant response to the still-face situation at 3 and 6 months. *Developmental Psychology, 29,* 532–538.

TOLMIE, A., HOWE, C., MACKENZIE, M., & GREER, K. (1993). Task design as an influence on dialogue and learning: Primary school work with object flotation. *Social Development, 2,* 183–201.

TOMASELLO, M. (1992). *First verbs: A case study in early grammatical development,* Cambridge, UK: Cambridge University Press.

TOMASELLO, M. (1995). Commentary. *Human Development, 38,* 46–52.

TOMASELLO, M. (1998). Uniquely primate, uniquely human. *Developmental Science, 1,* 1–30.

TOMASELLO, M. (1999). *The cultural origins of human cognition.* Cambridge, MA: Harvard University Press.

TOMASELLO, M. (2000). Do young children have adult syntactic competence? *Cognition, 74,* 209–253.

TOMASELLO, M. (2001). Cultural transmission: A view from chimpanzees and human infants. *Journal of Cross-Cultural Psychology, 32,* 135–146.

TOMASELLO, M., & BARTON, M. (1994). Learning words in nonostensive contexts. *Developmental Psychology, 30,* 639–650.

TOMASELLO, M., & BROOKS, P.J. (1999). Early syntactic development: A construction grammar approach. In M. Barrett (Ed.), *The development of language.* Philadelphia: Psychology Press.

TOMASELLO, M., & FARRAR, M.J. (1986). Joint attention and early language. *Child Development, 57,* 1454–1463.

TOMASELLO, M., KRUGER, A.C., & RATNER, H.H. (1993). Cultural learning. *Behavioral & Brain Sciences, 16,* 495–552.

TOMASELLO, M., & MANNLE, S. (1985). Pragmatics of sibling speech to one-year-olds. *Child Development, 56,* 911–917.

TRABASSO, T., ISEN, A.M., DOLECKI, P., McLANAHAN, A.G., RILEY, C.A., & TUCKER, T. (1978). How do children solve class-inclusion problems? In R.S. Siegler (Ed.), *Children's thinking: What develops?* Hillsdale, NJ: Erlbaum.

TRABASSO, T. & NICKELS, M. (1992). The development of goal plans of action in narration of a picture story. *Discourse Processes, 15,* 249–275.

TRABASSO, T., RILEY, C.A., & WILSON, E.G. (1975). The representation of linear order and spatial strategies in reasoning: A developmental study. In R.J. Falmagne (Ed.), *Reasoning: Representation and process.* Hillsdale, NJ: Erlbaum.

TRABASSO, T., & STEIN, N. (1995). Using goal-plan knowledge to merge the past with the present and the future in narrating events on line. In M.M. Haith (Ed.), *The development of future oriented processes.* Chicago: The University of Chicago Press.

TRABASSO, T., SUH, S., PAYTON, P., & JAIN, R. (1994). Explanatory inferences and other strategies during comprehension: Encoding effects on recall. In R. Lorch & E. O'Brian (Eds.) *Sources of coherence in reading.* Hillsdale, NJ: Erlbaum.

TRABASSO, T., VAN DEN BROEK, P., & SUH, S. (1989). Logical necessity and transitivity of causal relations in stories. *Discourse Processes, 12,* 1–25.

TRAINOR, L.J., & HEINMILLER, B.M. (1998). The development of evaluative responses to music: Infants prefer to listen to consonance over dissonance. *Infant Behavior & Development, 21,* 77–88.

TREVARTHEN, C. (1979). Communication and cooperation in early infancy: A description of primary intersubjectivity. In M. Bullowa (Ed.), *Before speech: The beginning of human communication.* Cambridge, UK: Cambridge University Press.

TRONICK, E., ALS, H., ADAMSON, L., WISE, S., & BRAZELTON, B. (1978). The infant's response to entrapment between contradictory messages in face-to-face interaction. *American Academy of Child Psychiatry, 1,* 1–13.

TROSETH, G.L., & DELOACHE, J.S. (1996, April). *The medium can obscure the message: Understanding the relation between video and reality.* Poster presented at the biennial meeting of the International Conference on Infant Studies, Providence, RI.

TUDGE, J. (1992). Processes and consequences of peer collaboration: A Vygotskian analysis. *Child Development, 63,* 1364–1379.

TUDGE, J., HOGAN, D., LEE, S., TAMMEVESKI, P., MELTAS, M., KULAKOVA, N., SNEZHKOVA, I., & PUTNAM, S. (1999). Cultural heterogeneity: Parental values and beliefs and their preschoolers' activities in the United States, South Korea, Russia, and Estonia. In A. Göncü (Ed.), *Children's engagement in the world: Sociocultural perspectives.* New York: Cambridge University Press.

TUDGE, J., & WINTERHOFF, P. (1993). Can young children benefit from collaborative problem solving? Tracing the effects of partner competence and feedback. *Social Development, 2,* 242–259.

TUNTELER, E., & RESING, W.C.M. (2002). Spontaneous analogical transfer in 4-year-olds: A microgenetic study. *Journal of Experimental Child Psychology, 83,* 149–166.

TURIEL, E. (1983). *The development of social knowledge: Morality and convention.* New York: Cambridge University Press.

TURIEL, E. (1994). The development of social-conventional and moral concepts. In B. Puka (Ed.), *Fundamental research in moral development.* New York: Garland Publishing.

TVERSKY, B. (1989). Parts, partonomies, and taxonomies. *Developmental Psychology, 25,* 983–995.

TVERSKY, B., & HEMENWAY, D. (1984). Objects, parts, and categories. *Journal of Experimental Psychology: General, 113,* 169–193.

ULLER, C., HUNTLEY-FENNER, G., CAREY, S., & KLATT, L. (1999). What representations might underlie infant numerical knowledge? *Cognitive Development, 14,* 1–36.

UZGIRIS, I.C. (1964). Situational generality of conservation. *Child Development, 35,* 831–841.

VALENZA, E., SIMON, F., & UMILTA, C. (1994). Inhibition of return in newborn infants. *Infant Behavior & Development, 17,* 293–302.

VAN DEN BROEK, P. (1989). Causal reasoning and inference making in judging the importance of story statements. *Child Development, 60,* 286–297.

VAN DER MAAS, H.L.J., & JANSEN, B.R.J. (2003). What response times tell of children's behavior on the balance scale task. *Journal of Experimental Child Psychology, 82,* 141–177.

VAN GEERT, P. (2000). The dynamics of general developmental mechanisms: From Piaget and Vygotsky to dynamic systems models. *Current Directions in Psychological Science, 9,* 64–68.

VANLEHN, K. (1990). *Mind bugs: The origins of procedural misconceptions.* Cambridge, MA: MIT Press.

VAN LOOSBROEK, E., & SMITSMAN, A.W. (1990). Visual perception of numerosity in infancy. *Developmental Psychology, 26,* 916–922.

VARNHAGEN, C.K., MORRISON, F.J., & EVERALL, R. (1994). Age and schooling effects in story recall and story production. *Developmental Psychology, 30,* 969–979.

VELLUTINO, F.R., & SCANLON, D.M. (1987). Phonological coding, phonological awareness, and reading ability: Evidence from a longitudinal and experimental study. *Merrill-Palmer Quarterly, 33,* 321–364.

VENEZKY, R. (1978). Reading acquisition: The occult and the obscure. In F. Murray, H. Sharp, & J. Pikulski (Eds.), *The acquisition of reading: Cognitive, linguistic, and perceptual prerequisites.* Baltimore: University Park Press.

VEREIJKEN, B., & THELEN, E. (1997). Training infant treadmill stepping: The role of individual pattern stability. *Developmental Psychobiology, 30,* 89–102.

VERSCHAFFEL, L., DE CORTE, E., & PAUWELS, A. (1992). Solving compare problems: An eye movement test of Lewis and Mayer's consistency hypothesis. *Journal of Educational Psychology, 84,* 85–95.

VICARI, S., CASELLI, M.C., GAGLIARDI, C., TONUCCI, F., & VOLTERRA, V. (2002). Langauge acquisition in special populations: A comparison between Down and Williams syndromes. *Neuropsychologia, 40,* 2461–2470.

VIHMAN, M.M. (1992). Early syllables and the construction of phonology. In C.A. Ferguson, L. Menn, & C. Stoel-Gammon (Eds.), *Phonological development: Models, research, implications.* Timonium, MD: York Press.

VILETTE, B. (2002). Do young children grasp the inverse relationship between addition and subtraction? Evidence against early arithmetic. *Cognitive Development, 17,* 1365–1383.

VOLKMANN, F.C., & DOBSON, F. (1976). Infant responses of ocular fixation to moving visual stimuli. *Journal of Experimental Child Psychology, 22,* 86–99.

VON HOFSTEN, C. (1982). Eye-hand coordination in newborns. *Developmental Psychology, 18,* 450–461.

VON HOFSTEN, C. (1993). Prospective control: A basic aspect of action development. *Human Development, 36,* 253–270.

VON HOFSTEN, C., & ROSANDER, K. (1996). The development of gaze control and predictive tracking in young infants. *Vision Research, 36,* 81–96.

VON HOFSTEN, C., & ROSANDER, K. (1997). Development of smooth pursuit tracking in young infants. *Vision Research, 37,* 1799–1810.

VOSNIADOU, S., & BREWER, W. (1992). Mental models of the earth: A study of conceptual change in childhood. *Cognitive Psychology, 24,* 535–585.

VURPILLOT, E. (1968). The development of scanning strategies and their relation to visual differentiation. *Journal of Experimental Child Psychology, 6,* 632–650.

VYGOTSKY, L. (1962). *Thought and language.* (E. Hanfmann & G. Vakar, Trans.) Cambridge, MA: MIT Press. (Original work published 1934)

VYGOTSKY, L.S. (1978). *Mind in society: The development of higher psychological processes* (M. Cole, V. John-Steiner, S. Scribner,

& E. Souberman, Trans.). Cambridge, MA: Harvard University Press.

WAGNER, R.K., & TORGESON, J.K. (1987). The nature of phonological processing and its causal role in the acquisition of reading skills. *Psychological Bulletin, 101*, 192–212.

WAKELEY, A., RIVERA, S., & LANGER, J. (2000). Can young infants add and subtract? *Child Development, 71*, 1525–1534.

WALDEN, T.A., & OGAN, T.A. (1988). The development of social referencing. *Child Development, 59*, 1230–1240.

WALKER, A.S. (1982). Intermodal perception of expressive behaviors by human infants. *Journal of Experimental Child Psychology, 33*, 514–535.

WALTON, G.E., BOWER, N.J.A., & BOWER, T.G.R. (1992). Recognition of familiar faces by newborns. *Infant Behavior & Development, 15*, 265–269.

WANG, X.L., BERNAS, R., & EBERHARD, P. (2001). Effects of teachers' verbal and non-verbal scaffolding on everyday classroom performance of students with Down syndrome. *International Journal of Early Years Education, 9*, 71–80.

WATERS, H.S. (1980). "Class news": A single-subject longitudinal study of prose production and schema formation during childhood. *Journal of Verbal Learning & Verbal Behavior, 19*, 152–167.

WATERS, H.S. (1989, April). *Problem-solving at two: A year-long naturalistic study of two children.* Paper presented at the biennial meeting of the Society for Research in Child Development, Kansas City, MO.

WATERS, H.S., & ANDREASSEN, C. (1983). Children's use of memory strategies under instruction. In M. Pressley & J.R. Levin (Eds.), *Cognitive strategies: Developmental, educational, and treatment-related issues.* New York: Springer-Verlag.

WATERS, H.S., & TINSLEY, V.S. (1985). Evaluating the discriminant and convergent validity of developmental constructs: Another look at the concept of egocentrism. *Psychological Bulletin, 97*, 483–496.

WAXMAN, S.R., & MARKOW, D.B. (1998). Object properties and object kind: Twenty-one-month-old infants' extension of novel adjectives. *Child Development, 69*, 1313–1329.

WAXMAN, S.R., & NAMY, L.L. (1997). Challenging the notion of a thematic preference in children. *Developmental Psychology, 33*, 555–567.

WEBER, R.M. (1970). *First graders' use of grammatical context in reading.* New York: Basic Books.

WEIGLE, T.W., & BAUER, P.J. (2000). Deaf and hearing adults' recollections of childhood. *Memory, 8*, 293–309.

WEINERT, F.E. (1986). Developmental variations of memory performance and memory related knowledge across the life-span. In A. Sorensen, F.E. Weinert, & L.R. Sherrod (Eds.), *Human development: Multidisciplinary perspectives.* Hillsdale, NJ: Erlbaum.

WEINSTEIN, B.D., & BEARISON, D.J. (1985). Social interaction, social observation, and cognitive development in young children. *European Journal of Social Psychology, 15*, 333–343.

WEIR, R.W. (1962). *Language in the crib.* The Hague, Netherlands: Mouton & Company.

WEISSMAN, M.D., & KALISH, C.W. (1999). The inheritance of desired characteristics: Children's view of the role of intention in parent-offspring resemblance. *Journal of Experimental Child Psychology, 73*, 245–265.

WELCH-ROSS, M.K., & SCHMIDT, C.R. (1996). Gender-schema development and children's constructive story memory:

Evidence for a developmental model. *Child Development, 67*, 820–835.

WELLMAN, H.M. (1990). *The child's theory of mind.* Cambridge, MA: MIT Press.

WELLMAN, H.M., CROSS, D., & WATSON, J. (2001). Meta-analysis of theory-of-mind development: The truth about false belief. *Child Development, 72*, 655–684.

WELLMAN, H.M., & GELMAN, S.A. (1992). Cognitive development: Foundational theories in core domains. *Annual Review of Psychology, 43*, 337–375.

WELLMAN, H.M., & GELMAN, S.A. (1998). Knowledge acquisition in foundational domains. In D. Kuhn & R.S. Siegler (Eds.), *Handbook of child psychology: Vol. 2. Cognition, perception, & language* (5th ed.). New York: Wiley.

WELLMAN, H.M., RITTER, R., & FLAVELL, J.H. (1975). Deliberate memory behavior in the delayed reactions of very young children. *Developmental Psychology, 11*, 70–87.

WELLMAN, H.M., & WOOLLEY, J.D. (1990). From simple desires to ordinary beliefs: The early development of everyday psychology. *Cognition, 35*, 245–275.

WELSH, M.C. (1991). Rule-guided behavior and self-monitoring on the Tower of Hanoi disk-transfer task. *Cognitive Development, 4*, 59–76.

WERKER, J.F., & DESJARDINS, R.N. (1995). Listening to speech in the 1st year of life: Experiential influences on phoneme perception. *Current Directions in Psychological Science, 4*, 76–81.

WERKER, J.F., GILBERT, J.H.V., HUMPHREY, K., & TEES, R.C. (1981). Developmental aspects of cross-language speech perception. *Child Development, 52*, 349–355.

WERKER, J.F., & TEES, R.C. (1984). Cross-language speech perception: Evidence for perceptual reorganization during the first year of life. *Infant Behavior & Development, 7*, 49–63.

WERNER, H., & KAPLAN, B. (1963). *Symbol formation: An organismic-developmental approach to language and the expression of thought.* New York: Wiley.

WERNER, J.S., & SIQUELAND, E.R. (1978). Visual recognition memory in the preterm infant. *Infant Behavior & Development, 1*, 79–94.

WERTHEIMER, M. (1961). Psychomotor coordination of auditory-visual space at birth. *Science, 134*, 1692.

WERTSCH, J.V., & HICKMANN, M. (1987). Problem solving in social interaction: A microgenetic analysis. In M. Hickmann (Ed.), *Social and functional approaches to language and thought.* Orlando, FL: Academic Press.

WHIMBEY, A. (1975). *Intelligence can be taught.* New York: Dutton.

WHITCOMB, D. (1992). *When the child is a victim.* (2nd ed.). Washington, DC: National Institute of Justice.

WHITE, L., & GENESEE, F. (1992, October). *How native is a near native speaker?* Paper presented at the Boston University Conference on Language Development, Boston, MA.

WHITEN, A., CUSTANCE, D.M., GOMEZ, J.C., TEIXIDOR, P., & BARD, K.A. (1996). Imitative learning of artifical fruit processing in children (*Homo sapiens*) and chimpanzees (*Pan troglodytes*). *Journal of Comparative Psychology, 110*, 3–14.

WHITNEY, P. (1986). Developmental trends in speed of semantic memory retrieval. *Developmental Review, 6*, 57–79.

WHORF, B.L. (1940). Science and linguistics. *Technology Review, 42*, 229–231, 247–248.

WIEGERSMA, P.H., & VAN DER VELDE, A. (1983). Motor development of deaf children. *Journal of Child Psychology and Psychiatry and Allied Disciplines, 24,* 103–111.

WILLATTS, P. (1990). Development of problem solving strategies in infancy. In D.F. Bjorklund (Ed.), *Children's strategies.* Hillsdale, NJ: Erlbaum.

WILLIAMS, K.G., & GOULET, L.R. (1975). The effects of cueing and constraint instructions on children's free recall performance. *Journal of Experimental Child Psychology, 19,* 464–475.

WIMMER, H., & PERNER, J. (1983). Beliefs about beliefs: Representation and constraining function of wrong beliefs in young children's understanding of deception. *Cognition, 13,* 103–128.

WINNER, E. (1988). *The point of words: Children's understanding of metaphor and irony.* Cambridge, MA: Harvard University Press.

WINNER, E., ROSENSTIEL, A.K., & GARDNER, H. (1976). The development of metaphoric understanding. *Developmental Psychology, 12,* 289–297.

WINSLER, A., CARLTON, M.P., & BARRY, M.J. (2000). Age-related changes in preschool children's systematic use of private speech in a natural setting. *Journal of Child Language, 27,* 665–687.

WINSLER, A., DIAZ, R.M., ATENCIO, D.J., McCARTHY, E.M., & CHABAY, L.A. (2000). Verbal self-regulation over time in preschool children at risk for attention and behavior problems. *Journal of Child Psychology and Psychiatry and Allied Disciplines, 41,* 875–886.

WINSLER, A., & NAGLIERI, J. (2003). Overt and covert verbal problem-solving strategies: Developmental trends in use, awareness and relations with task performance in children aged 5 to 17. *Child Development, 74,* 659–678.

WOOD, D. (1986). Aspects of teaching and learning. In M. Richards & P. Light (Eds.), *Children of social worlds.* Cambridge, UK: Polity Press.

WOOD, D., BRUNER, J.S., & ROSS, G. (1976). The role of tutoring in problem solving. *Journal of Child Psychology & Psychiatry, 17,* 89–100.

WOOD, D., & MIDDLETON, D. (1975). A study of assisted problem solving. *British Journal of Psychology, 66,* 181–191.

WOODWARD, A. (1995, March). *Infants' reasoning about the goals of a human actor.* Paper presented at the biennial meeting of the Society for Research in Child Development, Indianapolis, IN.

WOODWARD, A.L. (1998). Infants selectively encode the goal of an actor's reach. *Cognition, 69,* 1–34.

WOODWARD, A.L., MARKMAN, E.M., & FITZSIMMONS, C.M. (1994). Rapid word learning in 13- and 18-month-olds. *Developmental Psychology, 30,* 553–566.

WOOLFE, T., WANT, S.C., & SIEGAL, M. (2002). Signposts to development: Theory of mind in deaf children. *Child Development, 73,* 768–778.

WOOLLEY, J.D. (1997). Thinking about fantasy: Are children fundamentally different thinkers and believers from adults? *Child Development, 68,* 991–1011.

WYNN, K. (1992a). Addition and subtraction by human infants. *Nature, 358,* 749–750.

WYNN, K. (1992b). Children's acquisition of the number words and the counting system. *Cognitive Psychology, 24,* 220–251.

WYNN, K. (1995). Infants possess a system of numerical knowledge. *Current Directions in Psychological Science, 4,* 172–177.

WYNN, K., BLOOM, P., & CHIANG, W.-C. (2002). Enumeration of collective entitites by 5-month-old infants. *Cognition, 83,* B55–B62.

XU, F., & SPELKE, E.S. (2000). Large-number discrimination in 6-month-old infants. *Cognition, 74,* B1–B11.

YOUNG, R.M., & O'SHEA, T. (1981). Errors in children's subtraction. *Cognitive Science, 5,* 153–177.

YOUNGBLADE, L.M., & DUNN, J. (1995). Individual differences in children's pretend play with mother and siblings: Links to relationships and understanding of other people's feelings and beliefs. *Child Development, 66,* 1472–1492.

YOUNGER, B.A. (1990). Infant categorization: Memory for category-level and specific item information. *Journal of Experimental Child Psychology, 50,* 131–155.

YOUNGER, B.A. (1993). Understanding category members as "the same sort of thing": Explicit categorization in ten-month infants. *Child Development, 64,* 309–320.

ZABRUCKY, K., & RATNER, H.H. (1986). Children's comprehension monitoring and recall of inconsistent stories. *Child Development, 57,* 1401–1418.

ZAITCHIK, D. (1991). Is only seeing really believing? Sources of true belief in the false belief task. *Cognitive Development, 6,* 91–103.

ZAWAIZA, T.R., & GERBER, M. (1993). Effects of explicit instruction on math word-problem solving by community college students with learning disabilities. *Learning Disability Quarterly, 16,* 64–79.

ZBRODOFF, N.J. (1984). *Writing stories under time and length constraints.* Unpublished doctoral dissertation, University of Toronto, Toronto.

ZELAZO, P.D., FRYE, D., & RAPUS, T. (1996). An age-related dissociation between knowing rules and using them. *Cognitive Development, 11,* 37–63.

ZELAZO, P.D., & SHULTZ, T.R. (1989). Concepts of potency and resistance in causal prediction. *Child Development, 60,* 1307–1315.

ZEMBER, M.J., & NAUS, M.J. (1985, April). *The combined effects of knowledge base and mnemonic strategies on children's memory.* Paper presented at the biennial meeting of the Society for Research in Child Development, Toronto, Ontario.

ZENTALL, S.S., & FERKIS, M.A. (1993). Mathematical problem solving for youth with ADHD, with and without learning disabilities. *Learning Disability Quarterly, 16,* 6–18.

ZIMMERMAN, C. (2000). The development of scientific reasoning skills. *Developmental Review, 20,* 99–149.

ZINAR, S. (2000). The relative contributions of word identification skill and comprehension-monitoring behavior to reading comprehension ability. *Contemporary Educational Psychology, 25,* 363–377.

Author Index

Abdi, H., 73
Abraham, W., 171, 172
Aboud, F.E., 336, 337
Acredolo, C., 376
Acredolo, L.P., 287, 288, 427, 445
Adams, A., 288
Adams, M.J., 401, 402, 404, 408, 424, 452
Adams, R.J., 153, 156, 431
Adamson, L., 308, 432
Adler, S.A., 238
Adolph, K.E., 178, 348
Agnoli, F., 377
Ahn, W.-K., 57, 363
Akhtar, N., 316
Albert, D., 382
Alexander, J.M., 122, 124
Alibali, M.W., 103, 137, 219, 348, 392, 393, 398, 439, 440, 445, 452
Allen, D., 362
Allen, E., 121
Aloise, P.A., 252
Als, H., 308, 432
Altmann, E., 361
Alvarez, J.M., 310
Ames, E.W., 151
Ames, G.J., 124, 125
Ames, L.B., 384
Amsel, E., 352, 373
Amsterdam, B.K., 311
Amsterlaw, J., 57, 363
Andersen, C., 372
Anderson, J.R., 453, 454
Anderson, M., 82
Andreassen, C., 246
Andrews, G., 75, 353, 356
Anglin, J.M., 199, 201, 203
Anisfeld, M., 209, 210, 211
Ankrum, C., 156
Antell, S.E., 292
Applebaum, M.I., 151
Arehart, D.M., 360
Armstrong, S., 375
Aronson, E., 175
Arterberry, M.E., 57, 162
Ashley, L., 402
Ashmead, D.H., 171
Aslin, R.N., 5, 8, 9, 73, 155, 167, 191, 219, 307, 432, 444, 449, 452

Asselin, J., 361
Astington, J.W., 316, 317, 319, 323, 329, 330, 331, 424, 436
Atencio, D.J., 128
Au, T.K., 56, 436
Austin, G.A., 270
Avis, J., 318
Avolio, A.M., 178
Azmitia, M., 121, 122, 123, 124, 448, 449

Backscheider, A.G., 298
Baddeley, A.D., 70
Badian, N.A., 390
Baduini, C., 202
Bahrick, H.P., 72
Bahrick, L.E., 173, 174, 311
Bahrick, P.O., 72
Bai, D., 175, 287, 432
Bailey, D.B., 430
Baillargeon, R., 5, 55, 57, 159, 160, 161, 281, 289, 362
Baker, L., 256, 411, 437
Baker-Sennet, J., 358
Baker-Ward, L.E., 58, 228, 249
Balaban, M.T., 196
Baldwin, D.A., 202, 206, 308, 424, 436
Baldwin, G., 217
Bale, A.C., 97
Baltes, P., 18, 168
Bandi-Rao, 210
Bandura, A., 334, 335
Bangert-Downs, R.L., 418, 452
Banigan, R.L., 277
Banks, M.S., 452
Barna, J., 315
Baron-Cohen, S., 328, 329
Barrett, S.E., 73, 336
Barry, M.J., 128
Barsalou, L.W., 279
Bartlett, E.J., 418
Barton, M., 207, 316, 424
Bartsch, K., 314, 317
Bates, E., 187
Bates, E.A., 190, 197, 211
Batterman, N., 274
Bauer, J.A., 163

Bauer, P.J., 243, 244, 245, 273, 284, 358, 433
Baumann, J.F., 168
Baumwell, L., 119
Bavelier, D., 430
Bayley, N., 172
Beach, D.R., 248
Beal, C.R., 61, 247, 418, 419
Bearison, D.J., 123, 124
Beaudet, J., 337
Beck, I.L., 412
Beckwith, L., 12
Beilin, H., 58, 60, 92
Behl-Chadha, G., 277
Behrend, D.A., 322
Belgrad, S.L., 61
Bell, M.A., 239
Bellugi, U., 187
Bem, S.L., 334
Benedict, H., 196
Bennett, P.J., 323
Benson, J.B., 269, 294, 360
Bentin, S., 403
Berch, D.B., 391
Bereiter, C., 414, 415, 416, 417, 419, 429
Berg, C.A., 358
Bergman, T., 150
Berk, L.E., 128
Berkowitz, M.W., 449
Berlin, B., 156
Berman, K.F., 428
Bermejo, V., 295
Bernas, R., 119
Berninger, V.W., 417
Bertenthal, B.I., 143, 159, 172, 175, 179, 180, 187, 188, 197, 427, 432
Bertoncini, J., 166, 189
Best, C.T., 197
Bialystok, E., 214
Bidell, T., 437
Bigler, R.S., 337
Bijeljac-Babic, R., 189
Billman, D., 219
Binks, M.G., 113
Bisanz, G.L., 255
Bisanz, J., 73, 382, 384, 391, 452
Bishop, D.V.M., 428
Bivens, J.A., 128

497

SUBJECT INDEX